Wiley Series in Software Design Patterns

The WILEY SERIES IN SOFTWARE DESIGN PATTERNS is designed to meet the needs of today's software architects, developers, programmers and managers interested in design patterns. Frank Buschmann (Series Editor), as well as authors, shepherds and reviewers work collaboratively within the patterns community to strive for high-quality, highly researched, thoroughly validated, classic works, which document accepted and acknowledged design experience. Priority is given to those titles that catalog software patterns and pattern languages with a practical, applied approach in domains such as:

- Distributed systems
- Real time systems
- Databases
- Business information systems
- Telecommunications
- Organizations
- Concurrency
- Networking

Books in the series will also cover conceptual areas of how to apply patterns, pattern language developments and architectural/component-based approaches to pattern-led software development.

TITLES PUBLISHED

- PATTERN-ORIENTED SOFTWARE ARCHITECTURE, Volume 1
Frank Buschmann, Regine Meunier, Hans Rohnert, Peter Sommerlad and Michael Stal
978-0471-95869-7   476pp   1996   Hardback

- PATTERN-ORIENTED SOFTWARE ARCHITECTURE, Volume 2
Douglas Schmidt, Michael Stal, Hans Rohnert and Frank Buschmann
978-0471-60695-6   636pp   2000   Hardback

- A PATTERN APPROACH TO INTERACTION DESIGN
Jan Borchers
978-0471-49828-5   250pp   2001   Hardback

- SERVER COMPONENT PATTERNS
Markus Völter, Alexander Schmid, Eberhard Wolff
978-0470-84319-2   462pp   2002   Hardback

- ARCHITECTING ENTERPRISE SOLUTIONS
Paul Dyson, Andy Longshaw
978-0470-85612-3   384pp   2004   Hardback

- PATTERN-ORIENTED SOFTWARE ARCHITECTURE, Volume 3
Michael Kircher, Prashant Jain
978-0470-84525-7   312pp   2004   Hardback

- SECURITY PATTERNS
Markus Schumacher, Eduardo B. Fernandez, Duane Hybertson, Frank Buschmann, Peter Sommerlad
978-0-470-85884-4   600pp   2005   Hardback

Designing Distributed Control Systems

Designing Distributed Control Systems

A Pattern Language Approach

Veli-Pekka Eloranta
Johannes Koskinen
Marko Leppänen
Ville Reijonen

WILEY

This edition first published 2014

© 2014 John Wiley & Sons, Ltd.

Registered office

John Wiley & Sons Ltd, The Atrium, Southern Gate, Chichester, West Sussex, PO19 8SQ, United Kingdom

For details of our global editorial offices, for customer services and for information about how to apply for permission to reuse the copyright material in this book please see our website at www.wiley.com.

A catalogue record for this book is available from the British Library.

Cover image reproduced by permission of John Deere Forestry Oy.

ISBN 978-1-118-69415-2 (hardback)
ISBN 978-1-118-69413-8 (ebook)
ISBN 978-1-118-69414-5 (ebook)

Printed edition set in 10/12 point Sabon by WordMongers Ltd, Treen, Penzance, Cornwall
Printed in the UK

Dedicated to the memory of Ilkka Haikala (1952–2010)

Publisher's Acknowledgements

Some of the people who helped bring this book to market include the following:

Editorial and Production

Associate Director – Book Content Management: Martin Tribe

Associate Publisher: Chris Webb

Associate Commissioning Editor: Ellie Scott

Project Editor: Steve Rickaby

Shepherd: Janne Viitala

Editorial Manager: Rev Mengle

Senior Project Editor: Sara Shlaer

Editorial Assistant: Annie Sullivan

Marketing

Associate Director, Operations and Creative Marketing: Shaun Tavares

Marketing Manager: Lorna Mein

Assistant Marketing Manager: Dave Allan

Composition Services, Printed Edition

Steve Rickaby, WordMongers Ltd

About the Authors

Veli-Pekka Eloranta is a researcher at Tampere University of Technology who has worked with software architecture and agile software development methods for the past six years. He is an active member of the pattern community and a member of the program committees for PLoP and EuroPLoP. He has also chaired the VikingPLoP conference a couple of times.

Marko Leppänen is an active pattern enthusiast and researcher at Tampere University of Technology. His professional interests include software project management, agile methodologies, software architecture and patterns. He is also one of the organizers of the VikingPLoP conferences.

Johannes Koskinen is a post-doctoral research fellow at Tampere University of Technology, focusing on software architecture, web applications and cloud environments. As an experienced pattern writer he also gives lectures to several universities in Finland on the topic.

Ville Reijonen has experience as a pattern researcher, and has participated in the pattern collection effort. Currently he is leading an agile software development team in industry.

About the Shepherd

Janne Viitala has worked with software development for the machine control and control system domains since 1995, after receiving his MSc degree from Tampere University of Technology. He currently works for Sandvik Mining and Construction as a software architect, and lives in Pirkkala, Finland.

About the Foreword Author

Robert Hanmer is a director of The Hillside Group, an organization whose mission is to improve the quality of life for everyone who uses, builds, and encounters software systems. The Hillside Group also sponsors the Pattern Languages of Programming (PLoP) software pattern conferences. Bob is active in the software pattern community and has been programme chair at pattern conferences in the United States and overseas.

Bob is a consulting member of technical staff with Alcatel-Lucent near Chicago. Within Alcatel-Lucent, Lucent Technologies, and Bell Laboratories (same office, new company names), he is involved in the development and architecture of embedded systems, focusing especially on the areas of reliability and performance. Previously he designed interactive graphics systems used by medical researchers.

Bob is the author of *Patterns for Fault Tolerant Software* (Wiley) and *Pattern-Oriented Software Architecture For Dummies* (Wiley), and has written or cowritten 14 journal articles and several book chapters. He is a senior member of the Association for Computing Machinery, a member of the Alcatel-Lucent Technical Academy, and a member of the IEEE Computer Society. He received his BS and MS degrees in Computer Science from Northwestern University in Evanston, Illinois.

Contents

Foreword

The book you're reading captures the key architectural and design principles required to build work machines with distributed software control systems. The authors have studied the design of real machines for years to extract the most common, most useful principles, which they then explain for you in this book. It was worth the wait. I've been watching it develop as they brought patterns from it to many conferences to refine them and make the overall book more useful. I'm sure you'll find their analysis of the work machine control system environment and principles for building effective systems useful.

Machines are all around us. The machines of interest to the authors and readers of this book are both stationary and mobile machines. These machines work for us in industrial settings; the authors call them 'work machines'. They range from building-sized paper-making machines to small mobile loaders – other examples include fork lifts, mining drills, agricultural and forestry machines such as tractors or harvesters, trucks, excavators, elevators and more. Today's machines are more complicated than the machines of yesterday, which were controlled exclusively by mechanical means such as belts and pulleys. These complex modern machines benefit from computer control. The machines are also becoming ever larger and more capable, which makes a centralized control system infeasible and undesirable. The control system alternative is to distribute it across the components of the machine by putting controllers near the parts of the system being controlled.

These machines are expensive, long-lived, real-time systems that must operate continuously. They must operate when needed, to provide a return on their investment. These machines also have safety implications for the operator and the public. Veli-Pekka, Johannes, Marko and Ville examine the evolution from all-mechanical systems to systems controlled with distributed software from many different angles. The economics of maximizing the benefits of large investments in new machines and resulting maintenance is an example. This leads into the discussion of machines as a service and how the manufacturer can continue to profit from a machine once it has been sold. Essays by experts in key areas reinforce the author's analyses of the main themes. The practices needed to achieve satisfactory results are examined, both in terms of software engineering principles and industry-based quality standards. All of these themes are woven throughout the patterns in this book.

The main contribution of the book isn't the insightful discussion of distributed control systems and their current and future role in the world, but the eighty patterns. These patterns describe proven solutions to the problems inherent in distributed control system design. They will be useful to you whether you are designing a new system, maintaining an old one or just a student of successful software architecture.

Patterns describe proven solutions to specific problems with enough detail for you to reproduce the solutions in your successful design. The situation in which the problems exist – their context – is described, as well as the factors that make them hard problems to solve and that must be traded off against each other. This general 'pattern form' has been adapted for this book by including an explicit section of the consequences of applying each solution, which might point to additional patterns that should be applied. The individual patterns are structured to facilitate easy reading, with bold text used to indicate the key parts. Skimming the book by reading only the bold text gives you an overview of the entire language of distributed machine control patterns.

Patterns are 'mined' from existing systems – and the patterns in this book were mined by the authors from many different machines from many different machine manufacturers. During the pattern mining process the authors found many good ideas, but not every good idea is a real pattern. Each solution described as a pattern in this book was seen in at least three different machines, giving you confidence that the pattern's solution is a good one.

At least one of the known uses of each pattern is described for you at the end of each pattern in the text. These known uses provide an enlightening view of work machines and how the patterns can be realized. Patterns aren't meant to be applied blindly; the known uses give one example of a pattern's application. When you use the patterns to design your own system, you'll be adapting the patterns provided in this book to the precise circumstances of the system you are building.

The individual patterns will be useful by themselves, but their true power comes when the patterns are combined and used together. Together they enable the creation of systems that go further than is possible from applying only selected individual patterns.

The patterns in this book as a whole form a pattern language, and the chapters reflect specialized sublanguages such as configuration, data management, event management, fleet management, messaging, redundancy, start-up, updating and others. An especially large chapter covers patterns for the human-machine interface. This is an area that has been covered by other authors, mostly focused on computer systems or the web. The authors here look at the unique problems of how the operator interacts with a machine when the machine might be dangerous, or so large that not all its parts are visible.

The patterns in this book aren't the only ones that you'll use. The best way to use patterns as you start a new project is to create your own personal catalog. The patterns in this book provide the core for your distributed control system project catalog. Other published patterns, as well as other patterns that only you or your company know, will also be used. Throughout this book Veli-Pekka, Johannes, Marko and Ville make frequent reference to other pattern collections, such as my collection of software fault tolerance patterns, and also to relevant industry standards. Rather than rewrite and republish these other works, the authors point you to them as resources for your further study and inclusion in your pattern catalogs. This is also a sign that the authors realize that these eighty patterns aren't the only ones you'll need.

The patterns you'll find here are very insightful. I think you will find that they are all straightforward, and that many of them describe concepts you're familiar with. The authors do a great job of explaining how to apply them to the problem of designing machine control systems. I feel honored to have been asked to write this foreword and to contribute in a small way to the book. I have confidence that you'll find the book well-researched and useful as you study, design, build and maintain control systems for work machines.

Robert S. Hanmer
Author of 'Patterns for Fault Tolerant Software' and
'Pattern Oriented Software Architecture For Dummies'
Glenview, Illinois, USA

Acknowledgements

We embarked on this journey with the Sulake and Sulava projects in 2008–2011, funded by Tekes, the Finnish Funding Agency for Technology and Innovation, and led by Professor Kai Koskimies. We are very grateful for all the support, encouragement and feedback we received from Kai. The idea of writing a pattern book about machine control systems originated from Professor Ilkka Haikala (1952–2010), to whose memory this book is dedicated. Furthermore, we want to thank Professor Tommi Mikkonen for his support and feedback.

We want to acknowledge Vesa-Matti 'Härski' Hartikainen, who participated in the pattern collection effort in the early days of this work. We are grateful to Jari Rauhamäki and Pekka Alho for their feedback on our work and on contributions to this book.

We also want to express our gratitude to Janne Viitala, who tirelessly provided us rigorous feedback on the patterns, and provided his insights into the domain and the solutions presented in the book. In addition, we want to thank Mika Karaila for suggestions for improvement of the manuscript.

This book could not have been written without the openness and trust of Finnish machine manufacturing companies. Companies welcomed us to inspect their control systems and made it possible for us to interview experts in the domain. We would therefore like to thank all the companies that participated in this project: Acgo Power, Alstom Grid, Creanex, Epec, John Deere Forestry, Kone, Metso, Microteam, Remion, Rocla, Sandvik, Siemens, SKS Control, Space System Finland, Tana and Tidorum. We want especially to thank Kari Lehmusvaara for support, and John Deere Forestry for kindly providing the cover photo for the book. In addition, we would like to express our appreciation to the Forum of Intelligent Machines and Antti Siren for their collaboration.

We also want to thank many great people in the patterns community for inspiring discussions and feedback from writer's workshops. We want to express our gratitude especially to Jim Coplien for introducing us to patterns, Bob Hanmer for giving feedback on our work and George Platts for providing a known usage of the BEACON pattern. In addition, we want to thank the shepherds of our pattern papers for all PLoPs: Jorge L. Ortega Arjona, Bob Hanmer, Klaus Marquardt, Farah Lakhani, Dirk Schnelle-Walka and Michael Weiss. Thanks also to the great folks at Hillside and Hillside Europe.

We also want show our gratitude to Ellie Scott and rest of the Wiley team for their support during the writing of this book.

The authors would like to thank the Culture Fund of Pirkanmaa and the Kaute Foundation for grants to support the writing of this book. Marko and Veli-Pekka also want to express their gratitude to the Nokia Foundation for granting them a scholarship towards writing the book. In addition, Veli-Pekka would like to acknowledge the Emil Aaltonen Foundation for the award of a scholarship.

Pattern writing is highly collaborative work, and a peaceful and inspiring environment is required for successful pattern writing and workshops. We want to thank Kirsti and Kauko Reijonen for letting us use their cabin (Moosefabrik) for writing and workshopping the patterns.

Marko would like to thank all his colleagues, friends and family for their support and all the interesting discussions we have had – you know who you are. Huge thanks to Saana for all the patience during the most intensive months of writing, and for providing the chance to participate in this effort. Lastly, he wants to give a special credit to his WATCH-DOG pup Vihtori for trying to be a good boy.

Veli-Pekka would like to thank all coauthors, colleagues and friends for inspiring conversations and ideas – some of them have found their way into this book. He would also like to thank his Mom and Dad, and especially his big brother, Tero, for encouraging him to go forward with his academic career. Finally, he wants to thank his beloved wife Aija, for encouragement, support and for those moments of balance you need during the process of writing a book.

Johannes would especially like to thank his family: Anu, Kaisa and Helena. For them, this book meant lonely evenings, weeks and weekends. While his thoughts were somewhere else, working with this book, they were standing by him. He would also like to thank his coauthors Marko, Veli-Pekka and Ville (in alphabetical order), for providing the chance to write a book – and naturally for all those long discussions on the nature of science and software engineering.

Ville sends warm hugs to his family Ewa, Alvin and Sara, parents and sisters. It was intensive year with this book, apartment renovations and diapers – he couldn't have done all of this without you.

This book is really the result of many brains working at the same time, and many people have been involved along the journey from zero to patterns to a book. Big thanks go to all those people who have participated in any capacity in this effort. Finally, for long intensive discussions in and out of the sauna, Ville would like to thank his coauthors.

Lastly, we would like to thank you, the reader, for your interest in the subject.

CHAPTER 1

Setting the Landscape

*'Every thing must have a beginning ... and that beginning
must be linked to something that went before.'*

Mary Shelley, 'Frankenstein'

You are now reading a book about software architecture in a specific domain – machine control. The book is about both distributed and non-distributed systems, although focusing on the former. Furthermore, both stationery and mobile work machines are discussed in these pages.

As long as people have had machines at their command they have used them to make manual labor easier and more productive. After the invention of steam engines, machine development was fast. First, engines were used to power all kinds of automated equipment via belts and pulleys. When engines got smaller they were made portable. Then someone had the idea of mounting an engine on a frame so that the engine could move itself. These moving engines were the first tractors. After that, the evolution of moving machines really started. Engines have evolved into electrical, diesel and hybrid types. The frames are now more sophisticated and may include implements and booms to carry out special tasks, as the machines aren't just general purpose tractors any more, but highly specialized for specific work. The machine's tools and implements have also become more sophisticated and allow accurate and efficient execution of work tasks.

Figure 1.1: Old Lokomo forestry machines
Reproduced by permission of John Deere Forestry

For example, Figure 1.1 shows an old log crane loading a truck with logs. The primitive skidder in the photograph has towed the felled logs to the loading area from the stand. A modern forwarder would have a boom to transfer the logs to the cart and move them to the roadside. As the logs are not towed, the erosion of the ground is less and the logs can be cut to the correct length at the stand. Of course, a lumberjack could do that with a chainsaw as well, but a modern harvester makes cutting automated, so that just a couple of button presses are enough to transform a standing tree into precisely measured logs.

Most of this automation is done using software. Development of such software has followed similar paths as in other fields of work machines: a simple tractor has become a software-laden link in the production chain of food. Processes such as mills aren't run by skilled operators any more, but by millions of code instructions. Modern cars may have almost 200 controllers (Ebert & Jones, 2009), each running its own software. In a car, software can react faster and more precisely than an average human driver. Even if a skilled laborer could fare better than a computer-controlled machine in some environments, even people get exhausted. Software, on the other hand, does its work minutely and untiringly as long as required. In addition, the important differentiating innovations in machines on the hardware side have already been capitalized on, and commercial competition is down to software features: whoever can manufacture the machine with the best automation features and good usability is likely to increase their share of the market.

Software can take the machine to its limits: more efficiency and new features cannot be achieved without the support of control system software.

Figure 1.2 shows a modern mining machine that offers its operator many automated features that enhance its usability.

Figure 1.2: Modern work machines offer automated functionalities for the operator. Sandvik's DI-550 'down the hole' surface drill rig.
Reproduced by permission of Sandvik Mining and Construction

However, we feel that there is a chasm to be crossed. As software is a relative newcomer to machine control systems, and the basic machine control system software is developed in-house, the designers of control systems are rarely experts on software, as their background is in other fields such as automation engineering. Managers also seem to struggle with the business opportunities provided by software. To make things worse, software in the machine control domain is exceedingly difficult to design and implement, due to the complexity of the control systems and the special characteristics of the domain. To develop high-quality software systems that will improve the lives of customers a good knowledge of software engineering is required from all those involved. If the quality of the machine control system software cannot be trusted it can lead to life-threatening situations. For example, Toyota experienced well-known problems that were blamed on software (Murphy, 2013).

In our opinion the key property of software that determines the quality of the whole system is the software architecture. This book therefore approaches different facets of quality through the architecture and design of software systems.

The work machinery business has become service-oriented: selling a machine is only the start of long-lasting business cooperation and partnership between the manufacturer and the customer. This allows the manufacturer to gain revenue during the whole lifecycle of a machine, and provide a service that improves customer loyalty and willingness to invest further. Software can be a key enabler in customer service. However, it seems that manufacturers are starting to use processes that have proved dysfunctional in other fields, such as digital rights management to enable device lockdowns. One example of this is the battery rental process for the Renault Zoe (Hucko, 2013). We feel that software architecture should enable a degree of openness that will benefit all parties. In addition, machine control systems are increasingly networked, so 'systems of systems' are becoming more common. These systems of systems are a new area even in the software engineering field, and require the system architecture to have integration features designed in.

We discuss these themes briefly in this book. However, the book is meant to be a building block to help bridge the chasm between software systems and the domain of machine control. No extensive base of good software design solutions for machine control systems currently exists, but this book is intended to be a source of such knowledge. We feel that general principles should be correct before seeking 'God in the details', so the scope of the book is software architecture, not specific implementation aspects. We have chosen a systematic approach – patterns – as a medium for conveying knowledge.

1.1   Why Read this Book?

As you, dear reader, have picked up this book, something in its title or on the cover has kindled your interest. We expect that the book's audience will have widely varying backgrounds. You might already know something about the domain of control systems for work machines. At the very least, we expect that you share a common interest with us in these systems, whether you are a student or a seasoned veteran. The book should provide an easy introduction to the domain for a student or neophyte. In addition to the domain of work machinery, you may have some knowledge of software systems and their architectures. You might even have used your software skills in the machine control field. You could also be a fellow patterns enthusiast interested in seeing what sort of patterns are found in this field. Or you might be a manager whose responsibilities include communication with a software team developing such a system, and be mostly interested in business drivers of machine control systems. We hope this book will cover all these topics sufficiently to satisfy your interests.

If any of these fields are unfamiliar to you, don't worry. This book should be able to fill in the gaps and broaden your view of how distributed machine control system software is designed, and what constitutes state-of-the-art solutions. In addition, after reading the book, you should be able to share a common vocabulary with experts in the field.

The book relies heavily on the concept of patterns. For now, all you have to know is that patterns document good solutions to recurring design problems, and that they have become a popular way of presenting good design solutions systematically. As we have encountered the patterns documented here in practice, in actual designs within the industry, we can take it as read that such solutions are tried and tested. You can read more about how the patterns were obtained in *The Story of the Patterns in this Book* on page 86.

Even if you are an experienced designer of machine control systems, we hope that you will gain confidence in your own designs, and perhaps see some design rationales from a slightly new angle. In our opinion software architecture is especially important in the machine control domain, as the lifecycles of the systems are long. Furthermore, machine control software has perhaps become the key differentiating factor in the machine manufacturing business, having high value as a critical asset of the products. At the same time, the special characteristics of the systems in this domain (see *Characteristics of Distributed Control Systems* on page 12) make software architecture the solid base on which investment in software development can rest. If corners are cut in control system architecture design and the resulting architecture has flaws, it will most surely backfire sooner or later: technical debt is costly to repay in the machine control domain.

If you are interested in this book but are wondering whether you have the time for it, the following section describes a way to go through the book quickly to gain the 'big picture'.

1.2   How to Use this Book

This book is meant to be used in practice, read and re-read. This section describes how we think that the book could be most useful to you. If you are in a hurry, you should first know that it can be read in an hour just by reading the topics and *patlets* – the problem–solution pairs of the patterns. So we encourage you to browse the book in this way, to get an overall idea what the book is about, before diving into the details.

The main content of the book is the patterns it describes. A pattern's main content is its name, the problem it solves and the actual solution. We have highlighted these in the format used to describe the pattern: see *The Pattern Format Used in this Book* on page 90 for details. In addition, Appendix B contains a table that lists all patlets: the name, problem and solution triplets. Another common name for a patlet is *pattern thumbnail*.

We also have organized the patterns into a pattern language. The pattern language documents a logical order in which to apply the patterns. You can read about this in Chapter 4, which provides a detailed explanation of how to use the pattern language, and shows the pattern language in graph form. We have split the pattern language into sub-languages based on the main topics of the patterns: this division is also visible in the patterns chapters, Chapters 5–19.

The book also has a companion website, `www.wiley.com/go/controlsystemspatterns`, where you can read descriptions of those patterns that are not detailed in the book, and see a detailed graph of the pattern language. These were left out of the book due to space issues. We feel that these are best viewed on line, allowing you to browse the pattern language freely and see updated versions of all the patterns.

We suggest that you take a quick look at the pattern language graph on the companion website and examine the names of the patterns and their deployment in the various subtopics. Then you can move on to the patterns themselves and read through the problems and solutions. If a pattern awakes your interest, you can read it in more detail. If there are references to other patterns with which you are not yet familiar, the patlet table in Appendix B will help you. You should also check the position of patterns you aren't familiar with in the pattern language to get an idea of their context: the pattern language describes how the patterns fit together. As the domain is vast, though, there are missing parts, as some patterns are already described in other works. *Comparison with Previous Works* below provides pointers to further literature.

Appendix A provides a table listing quality attributes. We have arranged the patterns alongside a set of quality attributes, mostly taken from the ISO/IEC 9126 quality standard (ISO, 2001). We have listed our views on how these patterns affect the overall quality of system architecture. The quality attributes that are improved by using a pattern are marked with a plus sign, '+'. However, there is always a price to pay when a pattern is applied. Every pattern is a solution in the battlefield of opposing forces: quality attributes that are diminished by applying a pattern are marked with a minus sign, '−'. These signs don't mark any quantifiable properties: they only indicate that if you wish to gain the kind of quality improvements in your design that a specific pattern can provide, you should also beware of losing such properties. A software architect must decide if the trade-offs are worthwhile. For more information on quality, see Chapter 3, *Software Architecture and Quality*.

If you are hoping for quick recipes for successful design, you may be a bit disappointed. The patterns by their nature focus on the rationales and ideas behind a specific solution, not on technical details. A pattern describes the properties of a good solution, but may not give code examples or any actual class structures of the design. This book is not a programming manual or a cook book. We emphasize this by showing all the figures related to design as sketches instead of ready-made UML diagrams. While this book can give a student an overview of the topic and an introduction to the domain, it will not teach programming. We assume that you have earlier programming and design expertise.

The book can also be a valuable resource for managers working in the domain of work machines – it may give insight into what developers are talking about in design meetings.

1.3   Comparison with Previous Works

As you have now formed a picture of the contents of this book, you may still wonder how it stands compared to other works. The main idea of the book is to give you an idea of how to design distributed control system software architectures for work machines using patterns. If you are not familiar with the domain or with software engineering concepts, this book will definitely help you to acquire new insights. However, if you are already familiar with software patterns and machine control systems, you might wonder what you can gain by reading the book. There are, as you might know, other books that address topics similar to those introduced here.

Our vision was to create a book in which the patterns would constitute a specific whole – work machine software architecture. However, there are a number of books that we frequently reference. These other works have focused on specific aspects that also manifest themselves in our domain. For example, fault tolerance patterns (Hanmer, 2007) and patterns for memory conservation (Noble & Weir, 2001) are important aspects in all embedded software, and these are mentioned often in this book.

The patterns can provide some good solutions regardless of the exact domain. Hence there are some patterns that have been written before, such as WATCHDOG and HEARTBEAT. We nevertheless felt that these patterns have their own flavor in machine control systems: they deserve to get mentioned when the focus is on the peculiarities of this domain. The Software Engineering Institute (SEI) has collected *tactics*, which are, in a sense, generalized patterns (Bachmann et al, 2007). Tactics focus on a specific quality attribute, whereas patterns resolve many *forces*. There are tactics which are refined so that they are usable in the machine control domain, for example to improve availability (Scott & Kazman, 2009) or safety (Preschern et al, 2013).

Plenty of other books discuss the topics that are important in the domain. Many of these books are not related to the patterns approach. They usually focus more on a specific aspect that is related to machine control. For example, *Real-Time Systems* (Kopetz, 1997) and *Distributed Systems: Concepts and Design* (Coulouris et al, 2011). In these books solutions are given in free format and the focus is on the implementation of the solutions and their details, rather than on the architectural rationale of when and why to apply the solution presented. They are valuable companions after the design phase when you have to dive deeply into implementation of specific aspects of a control system.

Buschmann et al. have stated in the fifth book of their famous POSA series that the next big thing in patterns will be domain-specific pattern languages, and especially in the embedded domain (Buschmann et al, 2007a). We hope that we have answered this call on our behalf by collecting all this domain-specific design knowledge between these covers. We feel that the pattern language in this book makes a unique contribution, as so few pattern languages targeted towards building a whole system exist. Instead, many of the published pattern languages tackle specific aspects of various systems.

CHAPTER

2

The Domain of Distributed Control Systems

'The machine does not isolate man from the great problems
of nature but plunges him more deeply into them.'

Antoine de Saint Exupery, 'Wind, Sand and Stars', 1939

What is included in the domain of machine control systems is deliberately interpreted very widely in this book. The domain includes work machines, both mobile and stationary, and these machines include harvesters, fork lifts, trucks, tractors, loaders, lift cranes, elevators, water-cutting machines and many other types of machinery. These systems often are distributed for various reasons, but sometimes they are implemented in a centralized manner. This book discusses both kinds of systems: distributed and non-distributed, but focuses on distributed systems. In addition, many things related to machine control systems also hold for a wide range of process automation systems, such as paper manufacturing machines and electric power distribution systems. An example of such a system can be seen in Figure 2.1.

Although such automation systems look different than mobile work machines on the surface, their software applications do not differ so much. Some of the special characteristics of the software (see *Characteristics of Distributed Control Systems* on page 12) may be weighted differently in process control, but the main ideas are still the same. Often process automation systems might be more advanced than the control systems used in work machines, as resources, such as CPU power and memory available for the application, are usually more plentiful than on board a mobile machine. Most solutions presented in this book are useful for any machine control system.

Figure 2.1: Metso-supplied containerboard production line for
Liansheng Paper Industry (Longhai) Company Ltd
Reproduced by permission of Metso Automation Oy

Many of the running examples in the book are from mobile work machines, as they share the same basic structure. Almost everyone has seen an excavator moving large chunks of soil at a building site, or a tractor towing some implement across a field. Work machines usually have frames onto which all other parts are attached. This frame is propelled on a set of tires or continuous tracks – sometimes a combination of both. Figure 2.2 shows a John Deere 1910E forwarder with tires fitted with chains to give it more traction in soft ground. In some rare cases, the frame may be mounted on a set of legs. When a machine has to move, power is needed. If the machine has to move quite freely, an engine installed is installed, typically using diesel. Sometimes the engine is electric, or a hybrid system using a set of batteries. In some cases, when the area to move is limited, a machine can be powered from the grid via a cable, rails or contact wires. An electric motor then utilizes this power. The engines and motors are a part of the power train of the system. To complete the power train, some means for power transmission is also needed. The engine can rotate the tracks or tires via a transmission, or it may power a pump to generates hydraulic pressure for hydraulic drive motors. In some cases several electric motors drive the wheels directly.

In addition to moving around, a work machine must be able to manipulate its environment somehow. This is usually achieved by adding an implement or a boom to the machine. In some machines both may be present, and there might be several booms or implements. Figure 2.2 shows an example, in which a forestry machine has both an attached implement and a boom for picking up logs. A boom may have different types of heads, and the types of implements it takes may vary even on the same machine, depending on the current task.

Figure 2.2: A John Deere 1910E forwarder towing a scarifier. It is equipped with an 186 kw 9 liter engine, making it capable of operating in rough and sloping terrain.

Reproduced by permission of John Deere Forestry

If the machine has to be driven by a human operator, it needs a control station. The operator should be shielded from the hazards caused by the machine or the environment, and the operator should not be exposed to the weather, so a cabin is installed on the top of the frame to provide protection and comfort. Operator controls and indicators are located in the cabin; these are discussed in Chapter 16, *Human–Machine Interface Patterns*. The operator interface typically includes a PC for displaying data, joysticks for control and additional indicators, gauges, steering wheels, levers, pedals and so on. Figure 2.3 shows a typical operator cabin with some of these components. So a typical work machine consists of a frame, cabin, power train, boom and implements, all controlled by a machine control software system.

Figure 2.3: Typical cabin with operator controls and display

Reproduced by permission of John Deere Forestry

In this chapter we explore the kind of controllers that are used in these machines and the typical structure of the software running on them. We also describe the special characteristics of control systems that distinguish these systems from other software systems. Often these special characteristics cause problems in software development, and approaches to tackle these problems are discussed. As this book presents a pattern language that contains solutions proven in practice, some of the newest solutions and trends have not found their way into the patterns, so we describe new trends and emerging approaches in their own section, *New Trends in the Domain* on page 52.

2.1   Characteristics of Distributed Control Systems

Machine control systems are combinations of software and hardware designed to control and supervise machinery by means of various kinds of actuators and sensors. These actuators and sensors, along with controllers, are called *devices* in this book. A machine control system is essentially a piece of software that runs on embedded hardware units. These units are usually called electronic control units (ECUs), and can be either multi-purpose ECUs designed for generic machine control, or designed for a specific purpose.

In this book, we use term *node* to refer to units that are connected to each other via a network.

A multipurpose ECU (see Figure 2.4) can be used in various control applications, such as engine control or boom control. In a multipurpose ECU, the software application residing on the ECU defines the unit's purpose. The other option is to have specially designed ECUs whose hardware is customized for the unit's task. Such ECUs are not easily reprogrammed for a new application. Depending on the unit, ECUs can run applications written with the IEC 61131-3 programming environment, for example CoDeSys (3S-Smart Software, 2013), or in a generic programming environment, such as the C language for C16x derivative processors. C is the dominant programming language in such systems, covering up to 80 percent of the embedded devices manufacturing companies (Ebert & Jones, 2009). Qt is also widely used for user interfaces. One popular way to design programs for these systems is model-based design, for example using the Simulink environment by Mathworks (MathWorks, 2013) to model system behavior. From this model, the C code corresponding to the model can then be generated.

Figure 2.4: Multipurpose controllers by Epec – from front left to right, Epec 3724 Control Unit, Epec 5050 Control Unit and Epec 3606 Control Unit

Reproduced by permission of Epec Oy

The application on a control unit is basically a set of closed-loop control algorithms. Closed-loop control systems take a desired set point as an input and calculate a process variable corresponding to it as their output. For example, joystick x-axis values are read and the corresponding proportional hydraulic valve on a boom is opened relative to the position of the joystick. Ramps and other filtering may be needed to make the boom respond to the joystick movement smoothly. As the system is closed-loop, the error between the desired set point and the actual process variable is measured in a feedback loop, and the control algorithm tries to minimize this error. In the example above, the feedback loop of the process is acquired when the controller measures the current going through the coil of the valve and adjusts the valve's opening accordingly.

One controller usually takes care of a set of functionalities, such as multiple axes movement of a boom, so the unit will have several control loops running simultaneously. In its simplest form the architecture of such an application corresponds to SUPER LOOP[1] (Pont, 2001) – that is, an endless loop – in which all sensors are read in series and the actuators are controlled accordingly by their corresponding functions. Listing 2.1 shows a typical control loop structure.

```
while(true)
{
readSensors(sensorData[]);

 controlData[] = calculateControls(sensorData[]);

 controlActuators(controlData[]);
}
```

Listing 2.1: A basic control loop for a machine control system, in which sensors are read and actuators controlled in an infinite loop

Usually the machine control system is implemented as a distributed software system. There are many reasons for this, presented in detail in the ISOLATED FUNCTIONALITIES pattern (page 110). The first reason is that a divide-and-conquer approach makes software development easier. In addition, the sheer size of the machines is a driving factor in distribution. In a large machine the amount of wiring and latencies in control loops may cause limitations, which lead to a design in which functionalities are controlled by a dedicated unit located near the actuators and sensors. Figure 2.5 shows an example of such distribution. In the figure, the control system of a loader has been distributed across three units by applying the ISOLATED FUNCTIONALITIES and HUMAN–MACHINE INTERFACE (page 313) patterns. This results in a powerpack controller, loader controllers and a display for the machine operator. All these ECUs are connected using a controller area network bus and communicate in a ONE TO MANY (page 131) fashion.

In addition to basic control of the machine, the system has to transfer large amounts of information to and from control rooms, factory ERPs and other software systems. The reasons for transferring data to and from a machine are described in the REMOTE ACCESS pattern (page 361). The volume of information produced by machines has grown in recent years, and is now comparable to Big Data (Mike2.0, 2013). The chief limiting factor in utilizing all this information is the storage space on the machine and the limited transfer capacity of the remote connection.

Today high-end control system applications are larger than desktop applications (Ebert & Jones, 2009), and more complex due to their additional restrictions and characteristics. Developing such systems requires specific knowledge of the application domain, software practices to yield good quality, some mathematical modeling skills, formal design, expertise in the hardware, knowledge of the standard solutions of the domain and a broad view of security and safety issues. In addition, at least moderate skills in pro-

---

[1] Patterns are always referred to by placing the pattern name in SMALL CAPS.

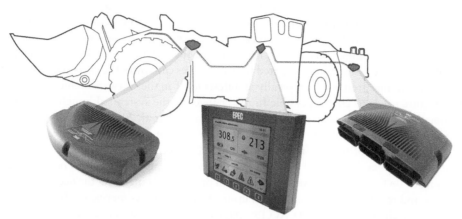

Figure 2.5: A loader in which the control system is distributed to two multipurpose controllers (Epec 5050 Control Units) and a display in the operator's cabin (Epec 2040 Color Display)
Reproduced by permission of Epec Oy

gramming and software development for a distributed environment are required. Developing distributed machine control systems is therefore a challenging task. The developer must also take into account any special characteristics of the control systems. These characteristics include the long lifecycle of the products, their distributed nature, real-time requirements for control and the need for fault tolerance. These properties emphasize the need for solid architecture in control systems. The long lifecycle will eventually show whether the software architecture of a control system can stand the test of time and maintain its quality.

In the following subsections we discuss each of these characteristics in more detail.

Long Lifecycle

Whereas a laptop computer or a smartphone is used only for 18 months on average (Xun et al, 2010) before being replaced by a newer model, a work machine can be in use for decades. For example, elevator systems are renewed only when absolutely necessary, and their lifecycle can be as long as 30 years. Similarly, a work machine model can be manufactured for ten years, and after the last machine has been manufactured, 15 years of support is expected at a minimum. The design might have started five years before the launch of the product, so at the end of the lifecycle the machine might use 30-year-old hardware.

From the software point of view a lifecycle of 30 years is an eternity. The hardware and software environment of the application is likely to change greatly during such a lifecycle. There are studies (Lientz & Swanson, 1980; Harrison, 1987; Glass, 2001) that indicate that 50 to 70 percent of the total lifecycle cost of a software system is incurred after the initial development, during the maintenance phase. Sixty percent of maintenance costs are generated by the development of new features and only 17 percent, for example, by error correction (Glass, 2001). There are also studies (Banker at al, 1993) claiming that software complexity significantly increases costs in the maintenance phase. Distributed control systems are complex in nature. They have hard real-time requirements and the systems are distributed. Complexity further increases when changes to the system are made during the maintenance period. Preparing for these changes may limit the increase in complexity. Preparing for anticipated future changes can lower the costs (Bengtsson et al, 2000), and this preparation typically manifests itself in the software architecture. The architecture needs to enable possible future changes to the system, although it may not automatically make maintenance itself cheaper (Lassing at al, 2002).

The maintenance problem is highlighted when work machine systems are interconnected with other software systems such as ERPs. Connectivity makes the system vulnerable to attacks via the network, and these security vulnerabilities needs to be addressed by using UPDATEABLE SOFTWARE (page 301). In practice this increases the need for maintenance and requires compatibility with up-to-date software components. For example, if a work machine has a REMOTE ACCESS (page 361) component, it needs to be up to date to protect the system from known exploits. The updated software for REMOTE ACCESS, however, may require higher performance from the hardware and can thus cause a need to also update the hardware. Alternatively, the selected REMOTE ACCESS software could be changed completely, implicating changes to the control system software and its software architecture. Keeping pace with security vulnerabilities, however, requires fast response times from developers, as vulnerabilities need to be fixed immediately.

Software maintenance as a term is a little misleading, as software, unlike hardware and other physical products, does not suffer wear and tear – it does not require maintenance as such. Ideally software could be used for decades and its perceived reliability just increase over the years. However, software is dependent on the hardware environment on which it runs, and this environment is likely to change during the lifecycle of a machine. For example, hardware parts may malfunction and be replaced. Even if the hardware does not malfunction, it suffers wear and tear, and thus its perceived reliability decreases over the years. Software might not be functional in a changed hardware environment, and thus changes to the software are required as well. If the same software is used for a long time, it becomes proven in use: no bugs have been observed during its use.

Figure 2.6 illustrates the perceived reliability of hardware and software during the lifecycle of a machine. In general, the hardware component's lifecycle might be shorter than the machine's lifecycle. This allows components to be slightly different to those used in the first version of the machine. The control system software needs to adapt to these changes. The need for adaptation can be diminished by using a HARDWARE ABSTRACTION LAYER (page 264), or almost removed by using a VIRTUAL RUNTIME ENVIRONMENT (page 272). By using the latter, the actual control system software can remain the same for decades. However, the VIRTUAL RUNTIME ENVIRONMENT still needs to be adapted to match the current environment.

Changes to hardware components can be triggered for various reasons. Either components available on the market change, or a component is changed by the machine manufacturer itself for some reason. When a hardware component is released it is typically

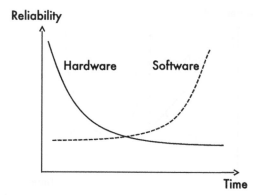

Figure 2.6: Simplified model of perceived reliability of software and hardware during the lifecycle of a machine. During the lifecycle the hardware suffers wear and tear, whereas software becomes proven in use.

expensive. After a while the unit price reduces as manufacturing volume increases. The hardware's design costs are divided across more and more units, so the unit price goes down. However, the hardware's manufacturing cost remains the same unless cheaper components are used. If cheaper components are used in the manufacturing of a hardware part, the component's firmware or driver may need to be updated. This may imply changes to the control system software as well. In addition, there might be variance in the quality of similar products over time. For example, a car manufacturer might experiment with different windshields, using thinner windshields for a batch of cars to see how they perform. If the windshields do not break in use, they continue using them. If however customers complain about broken windshields, and a lot of them need to be replaced, the manufacturer might revert to a thicker windshield. In the same way, manufacturers of controllers and other parts test where cost savings can be found.

Software has only a design cost, as the cost of copying software is negligible. If software is used in a number of machines, the cost of the design per sold machine goes down. Maintenance effort may also be calculated on unit price, but in many cases the maintenance cost is generated by the development of new features rather than bug fixes (Glass, 2001). Depending on the interpretation, development of new features might also include porting the software to an environment for which it wasn't originally developed.

Figure 2.7 illustrates the software and hardware price per unit during the lifecycle as more and more machines are manufactured. However, towards the end of the lifecycle of a hardware component, it is likely that the component will become more expensive as its availability decreases. Manufactured batches of components become smaller, and in the end the only way to obtain the component is to order it as a custom-made unit. In the case of hardware, therefore, the 'sweet spot' is somewhere in the middle of the lifecycle. Software can be copied again and again at near-zero cost once the software is designed. In the case of hardware, even though the design is the same, the cost of acquisition increases at

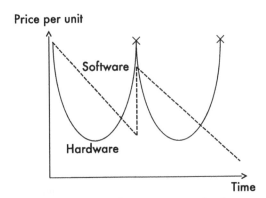

Figure 2.7: Simplified model of price per unit of software and hardware
during the lifecycle of a control system

some point, until the cost becomes untenable and the hardware needs to be changed. In this case, the software needs to be changed too.

Another option is to buy multiple components when they are cheap and store them to guarantee availability. However, warehousing components is not cheap either. During a product's lifecycle the software might need to adapt to multiple changes in the hardware. Eventually the software design can become so eroded by these changes that it needs to be redesigned from scratch. This gradual erosion of the design is caused by lack of architectural refactoring, and is often referred as *technical debt* (Cunningham, 1992). This means that the internal quality (see Chapter 3) of the software has decreased to a level at which it is no longer acceptable.

During the long lifecycle of a machine its design knowledge in the developers' and architects' heads is likely to evaporate, as noticed for example in (Kruchten, 2009). Furthermore, employees may leave the company during the years of development, so it is important to have good documentation of the design. This is discussed in more detail in *Documentation* on page 41. The focus of the expertise of employees is likely to change over time too. For example, in the seventies and eighties there were plenty of people capable of writing COBOL programs, but they are a rarity nowadays. Today, many companies are willing to pay high salaries for people capable of maintaining COBOL systems. As the lifecycle of a work machine can be three decades, human resources need to be taken into account when selecting technologies. It might not be wise to select niche or proprietary technologies, as experts even for mainstream technologies may not be available during the later years of the promised support period. Furthermore, if the software is subcontracted, expertise is more likely to disappear during the lifecycle of a product.

A long lifecycle comes with other issues. Many of the patterns in this book are related to tackling the challenges caused by a long lifecycle. During the lifecycle the machine might have multiple owners and their needs may vary. While the initial owner might not have needed some feature or other, its second owner might want it. The control system should therefore be adaptable to different needs during a machine's lifecycle. From the manufacturer's point of view, this might bring new revenue when the second owner purchases additional equipment for a machine. The control system software can support this by offering CONTROL SYSTEM OPTIONS (page 394). The lifecycle might be further extended by offering open interfaces for third-party developers: see *Openness for Third-Party Software* on page 60. This might make the machine a more intriguing choice, as after support has ended third-party developers could further extend its lifecycle by adding new features and updates through open interfaces.

The long lifecycle of machines necessarily means that there are machines from different generations in use in the field at the same time. If fleet management systems are used to increase cooperation between machines, high interoperability is required. Retrofit solutions for old machines can be used to attach them to the fleet. However, new generation machines could be prepared for future changes by opening up interfaces. Another option, not necessarily an alternative, is to make a machine highly updateable and prepare it for larger software changes, for example by offering a larger memory capacity than is currently required. However, in many cases the hardware is already outdated when the time for a software update comes. The sublanguage of software update patterns described in Chapter 15 provides some examples of how to solve update-related problems.

Long lifecycles also open new possibilities. A machine requires maintenance during use and a good portion of the total revenue can come from that. Manufacturers are therefore putting more effort into making maintenance easy, fast and correctly scheduled to avoid breaks in production. Control system software opens up possibilities for making maintenance even more efficient. When maintenance is uncomplicated and updates and support are offered for a machine, a customer is likely to be loyal and acquire the next machine from the same vendor. In other words, a machine's manufacturer is trying to build a long-lasting partnership with the customer that will benefit both parties.

Distribution

Machine control systems are usually distributed systems to some degree. In this section, we describe why this is the de facto approach to the domain, and the benefits and liabilities that follow. A distributed software system in this context is one that consists of several components that coordinate their actions as a whole by passing messages via an interconnecting medium. The control systems can be distributed just on board the machine, or the distribution can cross the physical boundaries of the machine by connecting to remote sites. Some systems exhibit both modes of distribution. On the machine, the interconnecting medium is usually some kind of *fieldbus* to which different devices are attached as nodes. Remote connections can be carried out with wireless links or with cable.

Distribution is a means to tackle challenges, not an end in itself. It is also quite common to have a non-distributed machine control system. Such a system might comprise a single computer with all sensors, actuators and operator controls directly connected to it. It is often the number of I/O ports on a single board that limits the control system size in a non-distributed approach.

As technologies evolve they tend to lead system architectures between two extremes: full-scale distribution, with dozens or hundreds of nodes with relatively low computational power, against single monolithic systems. Desktop computers have gone through the same kind of evolution. In the beginning, large mainframes were used with simple terminals. As computing power became cheaper, relatively fast computers running their own software were connected together via an office network. Nowadays it is common to use a thin client to connect to a server. Internet and cloud services make it possible to have dedicated services that aren't installed locally, but used in a distributed manner through a network. Usually network throughput and speed, rather than processing power, are the formative factors in distribution. When one takes connections to the outside world into consideration, machine control systems are definitely going to be distributed to some degree in the future.

Distribution is such a definitive and distinguishing characteristic of machine control systems that we felt it should even be part of the title of this book. Many of the problems that control system software needs to deal with are distribution-related. It is natural therefore that this book has a chapter dedicated to distribution patterns (Chapter 6).

There are many reasons why machine control systems design will become distributed. The machines are large and there are several physically separated points in the system where control is needed. Thus it is usually sensible to control functionality locally to cut down wiring cost and localize control. This approach also supports the well-known principle of *separation of concerns* (Hürsch & Videira-Lopes, 1995). Safety can be a driving factor too, as distributing functionality to several nodes eliminates the chance of a single fault unintentionally triggering the functionality. Distribution also increases fault tolerance. The decision of whether to make a system distributed or not is fundamental. The issues that need to be taken into account when making such a decision are explained in more detail in the ISOLATED FUNCTIONALITIES pattern (page 110).

For the machine control domain multiple technologies for building communication networks are readily available. Networks are discussed in the ONE TO MANY pattern (page 131). Several controller area network technologies are available. The CAN (ISO, 2003) bus is one of the most popular technologies, often accompanied with CANopen (CAN, 2013b). Other options include FLEXRAY (FlexRay, 2005), Local Interconnect Network (ISO, 2013) and EIA-485 (Global, 1998). These technologies are primarily designed for mobile machines and cars. There are also several competing technologies and protocols available for automation networking. They include but are not limited to Foundation fieldbus (IEC, 2003a), PROFIBUS (IEC, 2003b), EtherCAT (IEC, 2005a), HART (HART, 2013), SERCOS III (IEC, 2010b) and Modbus (Modbus, 2012). It seems that Ethernet-based technologies have a competitive edge, as their installation is quick and they integrate easily with a large base of devices. Because of their advantages, these bus technologies have also found their way into mobile machines.

The many competing technologies on the market has resulted in a 'fieldbus war', with different vendors trying to get their own bus accepted as the industry standard. The fieldbus wars and some comparison between different fieldbus technologies are presented in (Felser & Sauter, 2002). According to Felser and Sauter, the degrees of freedom for the manufacturers to implement their proprietary solutions have increased. By now it is clear that there are no clear winners in the fieldbus wars, as some bus technologies are more suited to certain purposes than others. For example, CAN and CANopen are good choices when high reliability is required, while PROFIBUS can handle large amounts of data at high speed. Perry Sink discusses the advantages and disadvantages of different fieldbus technologies in more detail in (Sink, 2013).

The selection of network technology is one of the most important design decisions, as different networks have their pros and cons. You must consider the physical environment, the availability of COTS components, reliability issues, the amount of wiring, the skills of the software developers, safety and security, price, interoperability with legacy systems, the need to communicate with office networks and so on. The technology is an integral part of the design, and it may be hard to change afterwards if another technology proves to be a better choice. As messaging is a large part of the functionality of a distributed machine control application, the selected technology affects the software. On the other hand, the communication technology also affects the hardware, as the controllers have to support the actual physical connection. In some automation applications it is not uncommon to encounter technologies that were selected thirty years ago. This emphasizes the importance of the communication technology – you may have to live with it for a long time. The architect should also consider the technology roadmap when planning the degree of distribution of a system.

Distribution also has its downsides. A famous quote attributed to Leslie Lamport was '*A distributed system is one in which the failure of a computer you didn't even know existed can render your own computer unusable*'. Messaging is not always reliable, so messaging protocols should have mechanisms to guard against lost and corrupted messages. Safety may be compromised if a message is corrupted such that the recipient thinks that the message is valid, but its information contents are interpreted wrongly. For example, a boom movement command message sent via the bus might have the desired displacement as a parameter, but the message is corrupted so that the interpreted direction of the movement is reversed. This may cause a serious danger to personnel and surroundings. Fault-tolerance is therefore an important issue in distribution. On the other hand, if correctness of delivery cannot be guaranteed, it is better not to try to communicate at all. There are some ready-made technologies such as DDS (OMG, 2007) that try to solve problems related to distribution. The majority of the patterns in this book also tackle these problems.

In distributed systems synchronization of operations may become hard due to 'clock skew'. If the various nodes try to synchronize via messaging, varying latency can cause problems. This book contains patterns to solve synchronization problems, for example GLOBAL TIME (page 124), and well-established protocols for clock synchronization exist.

Sometimes the system is distributed outside the physical borders of the machine. The key factor is then the connectivity with the outside world. Issues related to remote connections are discussed in REMOTE ACCESS (page 361). This allows the system to be a part of a fleet (see FLEET MANAGEMENT, page 372), communicate with other machines (see M2M COMMUNICATION, page 377), share information, be remotely controlled and so on. However, remote connections will also open the system up to remote attacks. Thus cyber security (see *Information Security* on page 65) has become an important issue as systems have been networked to the outside world.

Functional Safety

Safety is a topic that cannot be bypassed when talking about control systems. While software can take care of the automation of functionalities in the control system, it must not be done at the expense of safety. Implementing a safety system is more complex and expensive than a control system. There are many standards that have to be followed, and additional safety certifications may be required for the components related to such functionality. The SEPARATED SAFETY pattern (Rauhamäki at al, 2012a) is often used to isolate safety-related functionality from the rest of the system. Safety can therefore be a reason for choosing a distributed system. It must be borne in mind that designing a control system must be carried out such that a separate safety system can be added. Safety cannot be an afterthought, as it is often impossible to add a separate safety system if it is not thought out at the system design stage.

In one sense, in a system with a long lifecycle, safety also creates problems. New systems typically have innovations related to safety, as safety is an important marketing point and legislation has changed. Once users adopt such new safety systems, they adapt their behavior to the new experience of safety and change the way they behave when interacting with such systems. For example, anti-lock braking systems (ABS) were introduced to cars in 1970s and 1980s. Today, the majority of cars have ABS, as it is usually required by legislation. For example, ABS has been mandatory in the European Union since 2007. In a panic situation drivers used to ABS tend to just push the brake pedal fully, and not 'pump' it as was necessary to maintain control in older cars. If a driver used to ABS brakes drives an older car, it can therefore pose a safety risk. Similarly, new cars have a warning to indicate that a passenger has not fastened their seat belt; people might get used to receiving an alarm about the unfastened seat belt. An old car might not have such an alarm mechanism, so passengers might forget to fasten their seat belt in the absence of a familiar trigger. Similarly, older elevators may arrive at a floor a little off level: there might be a five centimeter step compared to the destination floor level. Once people have become accustomed to modern elevators always arriving exactly at the floor without such a threshold, they might not remember that older elevators might have this small step to the floor and might stumble and injure themselves. So the behavior of users also affects the safety of the system, and vice versa. A system considered to be safe today might not be so after couple of decades, once people have learned new habits and replaced old ones.

So functional safety is one of the most important things to consider when designing a control system. Poor safety can cost lives. We feel that safety is such as important aspect of these systems that we invited a safety systems researcher, Jari Rauhamäki, who is an expert in the field and has more experience on functional safety, to write the remainder of this section.

Safety-Related Aspects of Distributed Control Systems

Author: Jari Rauhamäki

Machinery is used to ease and speed up manufacturing, construction and processes beyond the possibilities of handwork and reliance on human labor. The tremendous capabilities of machines have been harnessed for an operator to process working substances, lift and transport heavy loads and people. These operations are executed using cutters, press benches, drills, fork lifts, elevators, harvesters, bulldozers and so on. Unfortunately, to make a machine effective in its intended task, hazardous elements are introduced into the system, as high forces and energies are required in the process. However, the operator and other personnel should not be exposed to the high forces and energies generated by the machinery.

The primary approach to achieving safety is to make the system inherently safe by design, meaning that any hazards introduced by the system are eliminated. Although this is the most effective approach, it is not always a suitable one in machinery applications. For example, in order to carry out its task, an elevator has to lift people, and a cutting machine has to use forces capable of injury to cut through metal or timber. In such case, the risk of injury can be mitigated by using passive and active measures. *Passive* safety measures include approaches that are not aware of the state of the system and environment. A typical passive measure is a physical barrier between people and the hazard source, for example a fence that prevents falls from a high ledge, or at least lowers the probability of such an event. Passive safety measures have their applications, but in machinery passive safety measures may prove to be too restrictive due to their fixed nature. Conversely, *active* safety measures are aware of the system state. They affect the system such that the realization of a hazard is wholly prevented, or the likelihood of its occurrence or the severity of its consequences are mitigated. These active safety measures are implemented by functional safety systems.

A functional safety system is a dedicated part of the system that is intended to ensure the safety of personnel. If machinery is operating normally and is operated correctly, it does not expose the operator or people around to risk. However, wear and tear, aging, heat and pollution, among other reasons – including user error, one of the main categories – may lead to a hazard causing injury or death. The purpose of a functional safety system is to detect hazardous states and transfer the system into a state that removes, or at least minimizes, the possibility of the realization of the hazard. For example, a pressing machine is stopped if movement is detected within the work area. Similarly, the heater element of a fluid container is shut down if the pressure or temperature becomes too high. Another example of a functional safety system is preventing a crane from lifting if it detects an overload. In practice, a machine may have several functional safety systems, each designed for a specific purpose. Functional safety systems usually consist of a closed-loop controller having inputs and outputs.

Development of a functional safety system into a controlled system begins with a hazard and risk analysis of the system. The analysis indicates the identified hazards introduced by the system and the risk related to these hazards. For example, in a pressing machine, the hazard of crushing a limb is identified and its risk is analyzed. In the following phases the hazards that introduce intolerable risk are mitigated. This is done by either decreasing the exposure or likelihood of the risk, or by decreasing the consequences of the hazard. Considering these aspects, a suitable mitigation mechanism is selected. In the context of a pressing machine, it could for example be determined that a functional safety system is employed to implement a safety function that stops the pressing machine if an object such as a human hand is observed in close proximity to the press element. This decreases the likelihood of the risk of crushing of a limb. When the safety function is developed, it must conform to relevant standards and/or regulations. This includes usage of recommended or required techniques and solution models, for example in the context of IEC 61508 (IEC, 2010a).

Development of active as well as passive safety is heavily guided by regulations and standards related to functional safety systems. According to Safebook 4, regulations in many countries are considered legally mandatory, whereas standards can be typically regarded as voluntary. However, there is a link between regulations and standards (Rockwell, 2011): the regulations often refer to standards for detailed technical requirements. As illustrated by Safebook 4, regulatory statements concerning safety in machinery systems include for example the European Machinery Directive (Machinery Directive, 2006) and Machinery and Machine Guarding of the General Occupational Safety and Health Rules (OR-OSHA, 2009). Significant standards in the domain of functional safety include IEC 61508 (IEC, 2010a), IEC 62061 (IEC, 2005b), EN ISO 13849-1 (ISO, 2006) and IEC 61511 (IEC, 2003c).

From a software developer's point of view these standards list requirements for the development process, techniques and methods to be used in development of software for a functional safety system. For example, IEC 61508 (IEC, 2010a) defines sets of recommended and non-recommended techniques and methods to be applied in the software development process. One has to either comply with the recommendations, or document why the recommendations were not applied. In the context of IEC 61508, a *safety integrity level* (SIL) is defined for the safety function depending on the severity and the likelihood of the hazard. The higher the SIL, the more techniques and methods are recommended by the standard to achieve the integrity level. Thus the higher the safety integrity level, the more burdensome is the development process, due to an increased amount of restrictive recommendations for the process. Moreover, the system will be more complex, as the higher integrity levels require specific technologies, such as voting and diverse redundancy.

The safety standards to be applied vary between countries and even between provinces within a country. For example, the standards applied in the European Union are different from those used in the United States. Fortunately there have been efforts to harmonize the standards, ISO and IEC being the most recognized organizations for producing international standards for the domain. However, regional and country specific standards still apply (IEC, 2010a). Safety aspects of machinery therefore need to be considered from the perspective of different standards. The variety of distinct standards increases a developer's headache, as the product and the development process have to comply with the requirements of different standards and regulations if a product is shipped to different regions of the world.

Regulations – as well as some of the standards – concerning the safety of machines are written at a high level of abstraction to cover all types of machines. Patterns can provide a way to narrow the gap between the practical design work and standards and regulations. For example, (Vuori at al, 2011) documents typical ways to conform to safety standards; by linking them with requirements and standards, design work can be potentially made more efficient.

Real-Time Behavior

Real-time performance issues are a central element of distributed control systems, as the systems need to react quickly to changes in the environment. Real-time software is basically just an application that has restrictions in its response times: the desired response must be available within a specific time from the actual event. It can also be seen as a function of the utility of specific information. In *hard real-time* environments the response must be available within a specific time frame; a piece of information has absolutely no use if it is produced before or after the desired time. In *soft real-time* environments, the utility of a computation result will only decrease if the response is late. Eventually, of course, its utility will become zero. In control systems, the systems are usually isochronous, meaning that events and responses should be synchronized. Thus, the time frame for a specific response to still be useful may also depend on other events. In everyday language, real-time requirements are often thought of as the control system exhibiting a quick response to an event. Normally this actually is the case; responses are needed within milliseconds, or sometimes even on a scale of microseconds. However, the definition only requires that the responses are guaranteed within some defined time span, otherwise the system has failed.

The reason for real-time requirements often lies within the controlled process itself. For example, if software controls the compensation of 50 Hz alternating voltage in a high voltage transmission grid, the control must react quickly enough to be able to follow the waveform of the voltage. The sine wave has a period of 20 milliseconds, and in order to sample it correctly, sampling must occur at at least twice the frequency of the voltage. Usually some oversampling is used to improve the accuracy of the measurement. In order to get ten sample points from the phase cycle of the voltage, a 2 millisecond sampling frequency is needed. If the sampling fails, the high voltage has enough power to physically destroy components in the system. Real-time requirements are therefore also related to safety.

Real-time aspects are closely knit with our *Patterns to Handle Scarce Resources* sublanguage (Chapter 11), as machine manufacturers usually implement real-time functionality with low-end hardware having limited processing power. If an event requires a fairly quick response, but the processor can execute only a small number of instructions within a time unit, the response will certainly be delayed. On the other hand, if the software architecture is well designed, consisting of several layers and interfaces, every additional function call will cause more instructions to be executed, aggravating the delay. Thus, within a tight budget for processing power, real-time constraints may cause the architectural rules to be violated. This may weaken other quality attributes, such as the maintainability of the system. Software optimizations are often implemented with software 'hacks', violating architectural rules. Typical tricks to make the software run faster include leaving out all dynamic allocations, or decreasing the control responsibility of the application by removing some operations.

Of course it is easy to think that the cure would be to increase processing power. Usually more efficient processors are available; as a corollary of Moore's Law (Moore, 1965), the processing power of microchips is increasing all the time. However, there are reasons why increasing processing power is not always a feasible option. First of all, the price of high-end components is usually a lot higher than low-end components. Mass-producers of controllers usually try to cut costs by selecting cheaper chips. It may also be that there are no sufficiently reliable processors available. In high-radiation environments, for example in space, only sufficiently robust processors can be used, and this may dictate the design. In many cases high-end hardware components are also more sensitive to vibration and dirt.

Other features may also be missing from processors that have more processing power. For example, a microcontroller might lack a suitable bus interface, or not have enough input or outputs ports. As real-time control has such specific requirements for a design, it is usually separated from the rest of the system, following the *separation of concerns* principle (Hürsch & Videira-Lopes, 1995). This is addressed in SEPARATE REAL-TIME (page 237), which divides a system into two levels, separating the real-time functionality from the rest of the system.

Even if there is enough processing power for the current requirements, performance optimization is still often driven to the limit. This may make optimization during the software lifecycle more challenging. However, often even the smallest optimization is worth considering, as the cumulative effect of optimizations is huge during the operational lifetime of a system. Consider a straddle carrier, used in harbors to stack and move containers around. If opening one valve in a such a system could be done even a fraction of a second faster, it could result in the saving of a second in the total handling process. The port of Shanghai currently handles 32 million containers per year (JOC, 2012). One second per handled container will result in a year's worth of saved time in total.

The basic architecture of a control system is an infinite loop, also known as a SUPER LOOP. As the SUPER LOOP is freewheeling in the sense that it just executes all instructions within it as fast as it can, it is poorly suited to sophisticated real-time control. It is easy to calculate the worst case execution time for a one cycle in a SUPER LOOP. It is then guaranteed that the control response will be always available to an event in that worst case execution time. Thus the upper limit for a response is bound. However, some of the actions in a loop may have varying real-time requirements, but would only be executed every nth cycle of the loop if the desired response time is a multiple of the loop time. It is easy to add some further conditions to the loop, such as adding a loop counter and an IF-clause that will evaluate true only on every nth loop execution. Listing 2.2 shows an example.

```
int a = 0;

while (true) // a loop with 10 ms execution time

{

  readInput1();
  readInput2();

  doOutput1(); // on every loop cycle (response time 10 ms)

  if (a%4==0){ //every fourth cycle (response time = 4 x 10ms = 40ms)
      doOutput2();
  }
a++;

}
```

Listing 2.2: An example of two functions within a SUPER LOOP
that have different response times

However, this adds variation to the loop execution time, and thus the response time for a single event may fluctuate greatly. It would be useful if the loop time could also be bound from the low end. This can be implemented by waiting for a clock interrupt at the end of the loop. First, the clock interrupt is initialized to cause an interrupt signal at the desired interval. At the beginning of the loop, the timer is set running. At the last instructions in the loop, the processor is commanded to wait for an interrupt before continuing, and the timer is reset. Waiting for an interrupt can be done in sleep mode on some processors, so some energy can also be saved. If the controller supports a real-time operating system (RTOS) such as VxWorks or RTLinux, it will provide all these features to make real-time control easier. In addition, using a proper RTOS makes applications more portable as long as the operating system itself has been ported to other platforms. The application developer's task is also easier, as many often-used services are provided by the operating system.

Fault Tolerance

Machine control systems usually have high fault tolerance requirements. These arise from the fact that availability is one of the most important quality attributes for a work machine. Downtime generates cost, as the machine is not producing or carrying out its tasks. In the worst case this cripples the whole production chain. In order to avoid downtime, the work process should not be affected by faults. Furthermore, faults should not escalate into failures, stopping the machine altogether. If this is not possible, usually some kind of functional degradation is better than a complete breakdown in the case of a fault. For example, the system should be functional to some extent even if a part of it is malfunctioning. This kind of fault tolerance sets some constraints for the design.

Any system may have design flaws that can cause faults. In the machine control domain these are quite rare compared to desktop applications and cheap consumer products. Work machines and control systems typically go through thorough testing and inspection before deployment. The designs of the systems are usually validated using a rigorous process, often required by legislation. All these are methods of *fault avoidance*. However, some latent faults may reside in a system, causing a failure when specific, usually untested, conditions are met. To mitigate these failures, fault tolerance is needed.

In addition to design flaws, faults may occur due to machines being subject to wear and tear. Machines are designed to be robust and *fault resistant,* but the environments in which they operate can be quite harsh. A drilling machines may be operated in hot and narrow tunnels, a forest harvester may encounter temperatures of 50 Celsius below zero, and an elevator may go through an earthquake. Work carried out by a machine is typically hazardous; rocks may crush a mining drill rig's parts, or logs may collide with a harvester's frame. Dust, splinters, mud, water, vibrations and impacts are involved. All this, and time itself, inflicts wear on the hardware, causing faults. The propensity of a system to encounter a fault is measured in *mean time between failures,* or MTBF. The control system software should detect faults and compensate for them if possible.

As faults cannot be avoided in any real-world setting, they have to be lived with. The need for fault tolerance stems from various causes. First, all stoppages cause losses, as an expensive machine can't produce value and return on its investment. A machine cannot produce what it was meant to, and maintenance personnel must be called in. If the machine is in a remote location, this is expensive and time-consuming. If stoppage is not allowed, a replacement machine is needed to continue the task the first machine was doing. The failed machine may be blocking a work site, such as a tunnel in a mine, stopping a replacement machine from being used. Even if the machine cannot continue working, it would be optimal if it could at least be driven to a place of service. If this is not possible, it should at least be able to move it from the work site. Furthermore, in autonomous systems, and systems that work in hazardous environments, a whole machine could easily be lost due to a single ill-timed fault. For example, if a satellite loses power because its thrusters fail to activate rotation of solar panels towards the Sun, the satellite could be lost forever.

The fault tolerance of a system should also prevent uncomfortable situations, such as those in which people get stuck. For example, passengers could be trapped in an elevator between floors if the control system fails. These situations do not usually cause hazards or create financial loss, but they give an unreliable image of the product. Usually these situations are solved with a LIMP HOME (page 185) approach, in which only the faulty subsystems are shut down and the rest of the machine can still operate. In some cases, faulty sensors producing unreliable values can be compensated for by estimation, allowing the process to be continued with foolproof values (see SENSOR BYPASS, page 189). This naturally disregards all optimizations, so the quality of service a machine is offering may not be the best possible. However, in some cases safety regulations may dictate that a machine must be put into a SAFE STATE (page 179) and not try to recover from a perceived fault. There are some cases, however, where fault tolerance is also a safety feature. For example a life support system should try to recover from all foreseeable faults.

Fault tolerance is also important in communication, as totally reliable communication channels are usually wishful thinking outside a laboratory environment. Most protocols used in machine control systems are designed such that packet loss, duplication, reordering and other faults are expected and do not prevent communication altogether. In high-error environments, loss of throughput, or other minor quality impacts such as growing latency, can occur. However, *Byzantine fault tolerance,* named after the Byzantine General's Problem (Lamport et al, 1982), in which the system is prepared for components to fail in arbitrary ways, has been expensive to achieve. Still, there are a few practical protocols that implement many of the required properties, such as UpRight (Upright, 2013).

In communications it is usually safer to stop communication altogether under high fault rates than risk a misunderstanding. Packet-based communication is therefore better than analog, as the quality of an analog signal usually merely degrades in fault conditions, leading to misinterpretation if the receiver does not know that the communication channel is not trustworthy. Packet-based protocols usually work such that the message either gets through completely or is not received at all.

There are several approaches that can be taken to provide fault tolerance. For example at the design level, *redundancy* is a common approach to fault tolerance (Avizienis, 1976). In *space redundancy,* redundant backup components are introduced to the design that are used only when a fault occurs. A backup component takes over the responsibilities of the main unit in the case of failure. Space redundancy can be applied in hardware, software and for information. For a discussion of hardware and software redundancy, see 1+1 RE-DUNDANCY (page 279). In some cases, redundant units can be *hot-swapped*, so that a faulty unit can be removed for repair or update without compromising system operation as a whole. The time used for maintenance should be short enough for the backup unit not to encounter a fault during that time. For information redundancy, the same information is computed in several places and a VOTING (page 282) mechanism is used to determine the correct result, whereas in time redundancy the same unit does the same calculations several times and the results are stored for later comparison. Sometimes an event may trigger a systematic fault in all redundant units. In order to be on the safe side, systems can be designed and implemented by different people or teams, preferably also using different hardware. This *diversity* will decrease the probability of a systematic failure.

If a system fails, it should fail well in contrast to failing badly (Mann, 2002). This means that a failure should not affect the whole system, but only a compartmentalized part of the system. In fault tolerance, it is important to notice all *single points of failure*, as they may cause the system to fail catastrophically. They also affect the design of redundancy: redundant units may read the same faulty sensor, which therefore acts as a single point of failure. If these single points of failure have low MTBF values, they will be the weakest links in the system and should be strengthened or duplicated. Also, no fault should propagate to systems that must not be affected by the fault, but the fault should be isolated in a single component of the system. For example, a single faulty node on a communication bus should not be able to stop all communications by repeatedly sending error frames. In addition, *checkpoints* can be saved, to enable the system to revert to a state before failure occurred. The consequences of any failure should be minimized as far as possible. For example, in a database server failure, only a portion of data should be lost, not the whole database. This idea is known as the *fail-soft* principle.

Fault tolerance also has disadvantages. Fault tolerance can mask problems, so that the operator might disregard a fault rather than reacting to it. If a subsequent fault occurs, it might have catastrophic consequences, as the system can no longer compensate for it. For example, a redundant unit may be lost but not replaced, as the process can still continue. If the backup unit also breaks, the whole system goes down. Sometimes the operator may not know that there is a fault in the system, if it is masked too well. Such situations should therefore be prevented by the control system by informing the operator clearly, and perhaps requiring additional measures to be taken if the system is to be used with an active but masked fault.

Redundancy also incurs costs, and may consume space and add weight to a system. The cost can be mitigated by lowering the quality of parts used, but this may result in more failure-prone systems than those without redundancy. In some cases, testing the system may be difficult if the system has too high a fault tolerance. A component with fault-tolerant software may also mask failures in other components it uses as inputs. If this component is later changed to a less fault-tolerant one, previously latent problems may cause havoc. In order to mitigate these, the subsystems should be designed to *fail-fast*, to make the failure clear. Processes are not then continued with faulty components, but the redundant unit may take over control as soon as possible. Fail-fast also aims to simplify fault tolerance, such that the design relies on the principle that very little needs to be done in the case of a failure – the redundant unit will carry on with the process. This helps to contain a fault in one component.

Redundancy with diversity also costs significantly more, as instead of simple replication, a redundant system is built using units that are designed and implemented separately using different technologies. Diversity is a good way to fight intrinsic faults, but there are *common cause failures* (Randell, 1987) that may depend on external events. For example, if a mining drill rig has redundant units placed side by side, a single ill-placed rock can crush both of them. Components should therefore be diversely located, have no common power supply and so on. This generates further cost.

Fault tolerance is closely related to *error tolerance*, in which the possibility of human error is removed, or its consequences significantly lowered. This is discussed in detail in MINIMIZE HUMAN INTERVENTION (Hanmer, 2007) and is an examples of the *poka-yoke principle* (Shingo, 1986). The easiest way in software systems is to ask for confirmation of important decisions from the operator. For example, if an operator tries to delete production data, the system should ask if they are sure. See TWO-STEP CONFIRMATION (page 321) for details.

Fault tolerance in our pattern language is more an aspect than a pattern sublanguage. Fault tolerance is built into the pattern sublanguages, and does not form a compact whole: the patterns tackling the aspect are spread throughout the pattern language. However, the patterns that are mainly aimed at fault tolerance can be divided into four different groups. The first group, WATCHDOG (page 101) and HEARTBEAT (page 120), discuss how malfunctions can be detected so that it is possible to start remedial actions. WATCH-DOGs are meant to monitor whether applications inside a single node are stalled, or have program cycles that take longer than designed. In HEARTBEATs, all nodes in a system send heartbeat messages periodically, and the health of the nodes, as well as the communication channels, are monitored.

The second group, LIMP HOME (page 185) and SENSOR BYPASS (page 189), describe how a machine can still be operable to some extent even when part of it is malfunctioning. This makes salvage operations possible and maintenance easier. Even if the machine cannot be used for productive work due to a malfunction, it may be possible to move it from the work site to a service area.

The third group, ERROR COUNTER (page 107) and DEVIL MAY CARE (page 190), shows how to distinguish substantial faults from false alarms or transient faults. These kinds of alarms are especially common when a system is starting up or when its operating mode is changing.

Finally, the last two patterns are about testing the health of the system. SELF-TESTS (page 106) describe how to test that all functionalities, including rarely used ones, are working normally. FORCED INPUT VALUE (page 106) in turn discuss how to find out whether a malfunction is in a control unit on the machine control level, or in the communication channel. For all readers interested in fault-tolerance patterns, there is a book on the subject written by Robert Hanmer (Hanmer, 2007).

2.2 Common Approaches and Challenges

The special characteristics of machine control systems impose many challenges for software development. Even so, the control system pattern language in this book focuses mainly on software architecture and design solutions. However, those solutions alone are not enough to provide a software system of high quality. A sophisticated software development process with good and pragmatic software engineering practices is needed. Although this book is mainly about software architecture, we cannot completely skip discussion of software engineering practices, as these two topic are interdependent. To illustrate this, Conway's Law states that 'organizations which design systems ... are constrained to produce designs which are copies of the communication structures of these organizations' (Conway, 1968). So we need to discuss software engineering practices as well. When Conway's Law is turned the other way around, you could say that it means that, while applying the solutions presented here, you also need to take the structure of your organization into consideration. For example, one of the key driving forces when deciding how to apply ISOLATED FUNCTIONALITIES (page 110) could be the communication structures of the organization building the software.

Agile software development has been adopted widely in the software industry since the publication of the Agile Manifesto (Agile Alliance, 2001). Sometimes Agile methods, for example Scrum (Schwaber, 1995), are said to poorly fit the development of embedded systems. However, this is not typically the case – rather vice versa: as more and more software features are developed for machine control systems, the need for shorter feedback loops increases. Legislation might require that safety-critical software is developed with traditional methods, but safety-critical parts can be isolated and the rest of the system developed with agile methods. Many machinery manufacturers have already adopted agile methods, as they allow faster response to changes in the business environment. Sadly, adoption and organizational transformation processes do not always take place painlessly in large organizations with fossilized habits. The challenges related to adopting agile methods, especially Scrum, are discussed in the next section, *Agile Development in the Control System Domain*.

Automated testing is a prerequisite for efficient high-quality software development. It also fits well with agile development. In the work machine domain, however, the testing might be challenging, as the hardware may be still non-existent when software development begins: it might not be built, or it might change during development. Furthermore, hardware components come with firmware, and firmware versions can change during the development cycle and cause problems in testing. There are ways to alleviate these problems, which are discussed in *Testing and Simulation* on page 37.

Machine manufacturers often produce a range of models to satisfy differing customer requirements. It is not beneficial to create separate control system software for each product model, so some means of product line engineering is often used. Nevertheless, product lines and product line engineering is a vast problem area. We present a short introduction to this topic in *Product Lines* (page 40): for a more thorough discussion you should refer to works such as (Pohl et al, 2005), or for a pattern-based approach, to Schütz (Schütz, 2006; Schütz, 2010; Schütz, 2011).

One of the defining characteristic of machine control systems is their long lifecycle. As a product must be supported for a long time, the personnel who build and maintain the software may change over time. Key people are likely to leave the project, for retirement or for another company. All architectural knowledge relating to a control system should therefore be made explicit – that is, documented. Documentation also helps developers to remember how the system was designed. Comprehensive software architecture documentation has substantial value in this domain. Unfortunately, the Agile Manifesto (Agile Alliance, 2001) is often misconstrued to indicate that while using agile methods there is no need for documentation. This is not the case. Agile methods do not suggest leaving tasks that have value undone – the opposite is true. We discuss this challenge in more detail in *Documentation* on page 41.

There are also some ready-made technologies that tackle the same problems as some of the patterns in our control system pattern language. In *Technologies* on page 43 we introduce some of these briefly. There are many approaches to choose from when developing software for machine control systems, but there are also pitfalls. The authors have witnessed some companies stumbling over these. *Common Pitfalls* on page 47 presents short-cuts that might seem like viable options, but will eventually cripple software development. *Tackling the Challenges* on page 51 presents a manifesto for control system development, which also explains how this philosophy can be put into practice to avoid the pitfalls described.

Agile Development in the Control System Domain

The Guru's Cat

Each time the guru sat for worship with his students the ashram cat would come in to distract them, so he ordered them to tie it up when the ashram was at prayer. After the guru died the cat continued to be tied up at worship time. And when the cat expired, another cat was brought into the ashram to make sure that the guru's orders were faithfully observed at worship time. Centuries passed and learned treatises were written by the guru's scholarly disciples on the liturgical significance of tying up a cat while worship is performed.

Anthony de Mello (de Mello, 1984)

As the story of the guru's cat allegorizes, it is easy to start following practices that become mere empty rituals if one has no idea of the rationale behind them. In software engineering organizations create processes that consist of practices. Usually, these practices have a solid rationale behind them. However, the value of a practice is usually context-dependent. If these practices are enforced by a process, there should be careful and repeated consideration of whether the process still really supports the main goal of producing a working software product. If people only see an empty ritual, it can be hard to say whether the real benefits of software practices are reaped. Following a process blindly can easily become the main goal, and the end result is forgotten.

In the machine control domain the close integration of software with hardware causes problems – it is common for the hardware to have long dictated how the software should be designed. The hardware is usually designed and developed in a rigid plan-driven way: hardware design is carried out by engineering teams that might include a hydraulics team, an electrical hardware team and teams that design the mechanical parts of the system. This approach is not necessarily a good one, merely a typical one. Both software and hardware have their own development cycles, and the hardware development cycle is usually the longer. If the software team has to wait for hardware to be manufactured, it results in features lagging behind market demand.

Most software teams would like to develop their products in a more agile way, as system requirements are not always clear when the development cycle begins. Some experimentation and prototyping is usually required to discover the limitations of the underlying hardware. In addition, modern software practices promote continuous integration, where any modifications made by developers are constantly – even several times a day – integrated with the mainline code and verified to ensure that the modification will work as a part of the software. Continuous or at least frequent integration is a key software development practice, to avoid integration problems in late stages of development. Integration problems at the end of a project often cause the project to miss its planned release date.

Unfortunately, misunderstandings of processes are commonplace. For example, the commonly known 'waterfall method' that was first described by Royce (Royce, 1970) has been passed on for decades as a solid process for software development. The model describes how an artifact neatly proceeds through different stages of development. However, even the original paper implied that the model should not be implemented directly, as the process will be risky and invite failure. To make matters worse, in their own interpretations of the model people have omitted the feedback loops between different stages of development. Feedback loops are present in Royce's model, as he recommends an iterative way of developing software. Nevertheless, the waterfall model still has its place, as it nicely describes the different stages in the software development cycle. It is natural that any artifact to be built will have stages, from idea to concrete usable product. Accordingly, the waterfall model says that a piece of software will have some 'system requirements' first, which evolve to 'software requirements'. From these requirements, an 'analysis' stage is carried out, then the process continues through 'program design' and 'coding'. The code will be subjected to 'testing' and eventually go into 'operation'.

Equivalent stages are also present in hardware design. In hardware design and development it may be reasonable to follow this model, so that there is a quality 'gate' before moving to each next stage, with a strict verification and validation process. Consequently, the hardware is designed and implemented almost without any iteration between stages. This happens because all changes to a hardware design in later stages would be costly, so good planning is essential. However, mimicking this approach does not work well for software: software is a more malleable and abstract concept. Forecasting emergent problems in software development would need a seasoned veteran, and still there would be need for iteration. In one sense, the waterfall model of stages has become a Guru's Cat, and transformed into a paragon for running a software project.

Consequently, people tend to believe that in software development things should be done right on the first try. Royce's article notices that postponing testing to a late stage of development leads to problems. If there are problems or misunderstandings in the previous stages, for example in requirements, it is expensive to correct them during testing. The only way to circumvent this is to have continuous and rapid feedback through all the stages, not just from one step to the preceding one.

Testing should be seen as a validation process to be run in parallel with development. Testing should be automated, to allow regression testing. Regression testing means that previously written code is tested with newly modified code to make sure that any modifications do not cause problems in code that has already been tested. Quick feedback loops for a software feature under development are the core of agile software development methods. Scrum (Schwaber, 1995) is one well-known agile method framework, and is one of the most popular approaches to software development in general (VersionOne, 2013). Scrum has close ties with patterns: the Scrum framework has been actively documented as patterns. There is a dedicated conference for Scrum patterns, ScrumPLoP (Scrum, 2013). The Scrum framework has several ways of obtaining feedback, both on products and the process itself. The main tool is *time framing* the development into fixed size time slots known as *sprints*. After each sprint, a demonstrable increment of the product should be ready to ship and feedback from the customer can be received.

Due to differing development models, an incompatible communication and delivery interface forms between hardware and software teams. Although agile practices are coming to control system software development, it has not happened without problems. Research has been done to identify the next challenges of agile methodologies, and they have been found to be the compatibility of agile teams with teams which are not working in an agile way (Baskerville et al, 2011). Agile methods suggest that a team should be cross-functional. As machine control software is closely knit with mechanics, hydraulics, automation and electrics, there should be some knowledge of those areas in the team. In any case, software teams have to communicate with hardware teams, so some common language is needed. In an agile approach, a work machine could be implemented such that one team takes care of implementation of a single functionality of the machine, from the basic mechanics to the software. For example, a team of four experts could develop a boom for a machine, including the mechanics, hydraulics, electronics and software, while another similar team could develop components for the drive train.

Agile methods can also be used to develop prototypes and pilot designs. For example, suppose that a team is developing new features, such as a bucket-levelling functionality for a loader. The design problem could be approached such that the pilot hardware is a generic controller, with all required sensors and actuators mounted on a traditional loader. The software team would then have a platform on which to develop their software in an agile way, to test ideas and produce a solid architecture. When the actual hardware is designed, it can take input from experience with the generic hardware and fully support the features needed by the software. The pilot software should then be easy to port to the production hardware. These pilots could also serve as the *minimum viable product* concept of Lean Start-Up development (Ries, 2011).

Agile also affects the architecture. As Conway's Law states (Conway, 1968), the organization of development goes hand in hand with the architecture. As the architecture of machine control systems is usually distributed, developers or development teams often focus on software running on a specific node. This architecture results from applying patterns such as ISOLATED FUNCTIONALITIES (page 110) and SEPARATE REAL-TIME (page 237). It also tends to be the case that a developer will have expertise in a specific type of software. A developer who has written mainly controller software for an IEC 61131-3 programming environment is not necessarily the best person to implement a HUMAN–MACHINE INTERFACE (page 313) with Qt. However, this kind of approach creates *silos* (Ensor, 1988) and lowers *the truck number* of the team (Coplien, 2011).

A silo is a mode of working in which information moves only up and down. In the case of software development, it means that people don't know what others are doing, how they are progressing and whether they have problems. If the dependencies between the different controller software applications are tight, this means that essential information is not communicated. Low truck number, on the other hand, means that people will become indispensable as they gain a lot of tacit knowledge in their own silo. If they 'get hit by a truck', leave the company, get seriously ill or even die, no one can step into their boots and carry on with development. Documentation will help here, but it is better to share information during the development process via, for example, daily scrums and promiscuous pair programming.

The silo problem is further emphasized if the software or software development is acquired from a subcontractor or, even worse, several subcontractors. Unfortunately, this is usually the case, as machine manufacturers typically are short of in-house software developers – they are traditionally hardware houses. Consequently, at least some parts of the software tend to be subcontracted. However, distributed teams and a distributed mode of working are challenging.

Scrum framework has the concept of a *product owner* (PO) role, who should know all the different views of all stakeholders for the software. From this information, the product owner should be able to make decisions about what the team should develop next to get the best possible return on investment. Machine control system software has many stakeholders, all the way from the operator to maintenance personnel, from assembly line workers to different software teams, hardware designers and of course business and marketing people. All these have their own viewpoint, and the product owner should then make decisions basing on the stakeholders' requirements.

In Scrum, the product owner constructs a product backlog of everything that must be done and organizes it in the best way to achieve the most out of the team's work investment. Of course, some of the stakeholders will have mandatory aspects to implement in the software, but the team has only a limited time to implement those and some prioritization has to be done. The product owner role is a challenging task even in traditional software development, let alone in machine control systems where there are even more stakeholders. Thus it is not surprising that the role is usually omitted in software projects (Eloranta et al, 2013a). This leads to problems, as no single person takes responsibility for the product backlog. Another common failure is that even if a product owner is nominally assigned, they are constantly overruled by managers higher in the organization. Responsibility and commitment is lost, as the product owner feels that they are not listened to and lack authority to drop items from the product backlog.

Safety is an important aspect when considering software development methods. Safety assessments for software require strict processes and thorough verification. In addition, some safety standards require that safety features are developed in a waterfall fashion, either in a forward engineering mode from requirements to code, or reverse engineering the required documents from developed code (Anderson & Romanski, 2011). This will hinder any agility in software development, as changes in assessed or thoroughly documented code would become too expensive, as certifications need to be redone. One can circumvent this problem by isolating safety-critical functions into their own component. This component can be certified in isolation. However, this requires that the safety component is also developed separately, but it still might need to cooperate with other parts of the system through its interfaces. Thus, an interface between two development teams emerges.

Agile methodologies rely heavily on the concept of 'done'. This means that a specific task will requires no further work. Developers should concentrate their efforts on a single task from beginning to end so that it quickly reaches the state of done. This principle is called *single piece continuous flow* in lean software development. However this is not possible if testing cannot be carried out immediately after code is deemed to be testable. Instant testing allows the developer to fix all bugs found immediately, while the structure of the code is still fresh in their mind. However, this hard to achieve in machine control systems, for reasons described in the next section.

Establishing a short feedback cycle from end users is also an essential part of agile philosophy. In machine control systems it is hard to have really fast deployment cycles, as machine operators would not welcome them, even if technology such as BUMPLESS UPDATE (page 310) allowed it. Even if an update would not stop a machine, it would be annoying and even dangerous if the controls changed slightly or an operation needed to be carried out in a new way. Safety features should never be updated without extensive verification. However, whether rapid feedback can be faked somehow remains as an interesting question. For example, simulators could help here.

Testing and Simulation

Testing of a machine control system can be done on several levels, varying from unit testing to usability testing. Because hardware development is not normally finished until near the end of a project, software teams do not have a proper platform to test their own products. In addition, testing the software on an actual machine could be cumbersome, dangerous or expensive, especially if the software is unfinished. Development teams therefore need simulators and simple *hardware-in-the-loop* (HIL) testing facilities to test software.

Machine control systems are tricky to test even in the best case. There are several reasons why it is markedly more difficult than testing, say, a desktop application. Machine control software is typically distributed. One important aspect in a distributed system is messaging. The functionality of the application on one controller therefore relies on messages from other controllers to work properly. For example, a harvester head module's feeding functionality needs messages from the cabin – a button-press to be activated and joystick position to be controlled. Timing and rate of change in the joystick movement may also be important. When the feeding is activated, it starts the feed rollers and simultaneously checks whether the measuring roll has moved. These input/output events must be somehow simulated for the application software and be in synchronization, so that the application will not deduce that feeding has stuck. Finally, the application sends measurement data as messages to the cabin, to be displayed to the operator on a graphical user interface. Thus, extensive stubbing of other functionalities is needed to carry out even the simplest tests in distributed systems.

Messaging between system nodes may also lead to hard-to-find timing problems. If bus timings are not taken into consideration, timing problems can arise after the whole system is integrated. Usually applications are run on hardware that has no diagnostic services, or even fault indicators, unless the developer or the real-time operating system provides them. Debugging message buses with an analyzer is therefore a common task for a machine control system developer. Common tools, such as CANalyzer (Vector Informatik, 2013), can be used in testing to simulate the rest of a system and to build test cases of a single node. Tools can also be used to record bus messages from a live system and use those as a stimulus for the software.

Agile methodologies usually rely on continuous integration and testing to promote delivery of working products in short intervals. Short and automated testing cycles are hard to attain in the domain of work machines. It may be impossible to arrange a location where the entire distributed system can be integrated continuously for automatic testing. It might be that only the most basic unit testing for a single control application can be arranged in a sprint. For example, performance tests can usually be run only when a considerable part of the system has been developed. Simple testing systems can be arranged for the development team to test their software. Usually this requires an emulation environment running on a desktop PC, so that control applications can be debugged without real controllers. Figure 2.8 shows a testing environment that can be run on a laptop.

Figure 2.8: A laptop simulator of a forestry machine.
The simulation can be controlled with authentic joysticks.
Reproduced by permission of John Deere Forestry Oy

Simulation is one approach to testing an application or system, as it provides a platform on which software features can be tested in a comfortable office setting. Simulators often employ the same hardware components as are used in the machine. This ensures that the control system is run in an authentic environment: the hardware-in-the-loop (HIL) approach. In addition, simulations of physical processes and the rest of the system can be provided with, for example, Matlab Simulink, or by a special simulation framework (Lahtinen & Leppänen, 2002). A typical simulator setup includes a PC running the simulator software, authentic hand panels, joysticks and pedals, the machine level controllers and buses. The simulator PC usually has a large screen, or several, to provide an immersive experience to the tester. An example of such a system is shown in Figure 2.9. These simulators can be also used to train the machine operators.

Simulations are usually custom-made for specific hardware and software setups. If extensive modifications are done to a machine's design the simulator software also needs to be updated. As simulator development is quite laborious and requires special skills, such as 3D modeling, and physics to simulate the behavior of physical parts of the machine, it is often acquired from simulator vendors. Machine manufacturers should bear in mind

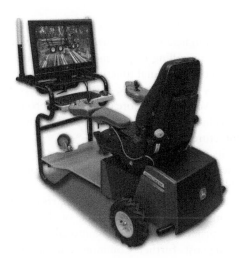

Figure 2.9: A simulator that can be used for various purposes,
from R&D to operator education

Reproduced by permission of John Deere Forestry Oy

that simulator development benefits if the machine control systems provide a degree of standardization and openness. In this way, the simulator software can be reused for several machine types from different vendors, lowering cost. *Openness for Third-Party Software* on page 60 provides more discussion of this topic.

Safety-related features are a further challenging aspect of testing. They may be hard to test, as they must be guaranteed always to work as intended. But it must be ensured that safety systems won't trigger needlessly, as availability would be lost. Some safety features cannot be tested in live systems – at least extensively – as their use may cause significant damage to the system and be expensive. For example, a safety feature might employ multiple airbags that are not reusable. On the other hand, in some test setups, either simulated or even live testing, it should be possible to shut down safety features, to see how the system would work in the case of malfunction of a safety system. Another scenario in which a safety system would need to be disabled is when the actual limits of the system are tested, for example to determine the critical capsizing angle of a machine by extending a boom or tool until the machine falls over. Safety testing is usually a well-controlled process, as safety standards require specific processes to be in place. Testing is an important part of safety conformance: for example, in *Part 6: Product development at the software level* of ISO 26262 (ISO, 2011b) for road vehicle safety there are several subsections that all fall into software testing. These subsections cover unit testing, system testing and safety requirements validation.

Product Lines

Customers need different types of products even though the products are meant for similar tasks. For example, a small field is more convenient to plow with a smaller tractor. In addition, some customers are willing to pay more to get more sophisticated features, while some are happy with only minimal functionality and no automation. As products usually share the same kinds of functionality, it would be unwise to produce and develop each product from scratch. Vendors therefore usually have product lines to support varying customer needs. A product line includes a number of related products that are developed by the same manufacturer.

There are many benefits to using product lines. Costs are reduced, as the products in the product line share the same hardware and software solutions; i.e., they share the same platform. This is possible as the products have common core functionality. This kind of similarity also makes logistics and inventory for spare parts easier, as a single part can be used in several different models, and as the lifecycle of the platform typically is longer than a lifecycle of a single product. Moreover, commonality of parts means larger manufacturing batches, reducing costs further. Common solutions allow the vendor to create tools that can be used for every machine in the product line. In addition, time-to-market for new products in the same product line is considerably decreased, as the existing design and parts can be used for them. This also means that similar products can be developed at the same time with a minimum effort.

In product lines products are typically based on the same control system components and control system software, to prevent maintenance effort growing too large. The control system software should therefore be adaptable to different kind of machines. To support scalability and reuse of control systems, a platform for the control system software is created that provides software functionality common to all products in the product line. The platform may also contain features that are used only for some products in the product line.

Product lines are closely related to the Geoffrey A. Moore's concepts of complex systems and volume markets (Moore, 2005). Complex system vendors produce a small number of high-value sophisticated custom solutions that are developed in active contact with the customer, while volume markets aim at low-cost, bulk one-size-fits-all products that need no direct sales. Moore argues that companies will have more efficient business models if they focus on either end of the scale. Product lines can support businesses where the platform is a volume market product, and the actual machines can be customized and integrated with existing solutions by means of variations.

The variance between products is achieved by augmenting the platform with variation points, where the platform's code is specialized with product-specific code. For more information on variance and variation points, see for example (Pohl et al, 2005), (Van Gurp et al, 2011), (Webber & Gomaa, 2004) or (Krueger, 2002). In practice variation points can be a set of interfaces that the products realize. Other mechanisms such as callbacks, and function pointers instead of direct function calls, are commonly used. The variations usually include control algorithms for various hardware components and support for optional accessories. The framework is typically configurable (COMPONENT-BASED CONFIGURATION, page 386), depending on the selected features and functionality of the machine, so the software for a specific product consists of only those parts of the platform that are really needed by the functionality and hardware of the product. This reduces hardware requirements for storage space, as the size of the software is decreased.

A platform for a product line usually dictates the main characteristics of the products in that product line. Making a platform is therefore a fundamental and usually also the most critical part of designing a product line. The platform may contain restrictions on the operations the product can carry out, and on what kind of functionality is supported. Usually this means that the operations supported by the platform are easy to implement for the product, but that others may require a lot more effort, or can even be impossible to implement. Changing the core solution of the platform later is usually cumbersome and costly, as all existing products are also affected. Careless changes to the platform may lead to version problems in which a product must use a specific version of the platform instead of the latest one, so that bug fixes in the latest version have to be back-ported to the older versions. On the other hand, if two or more different platforms are used inside the same product line, some of the benefits of having a product line are lost.

Product lines are therefore not a silver bullet for solving all problems. Each vendor must carefully consider whether they have so many similar products that the product line approach can be used, as product lines have drawbacks. Usually product lines are developed separately from the products themselves, even before the first product using the product line is implemented. This requires communication between different teams and increases the demand for software architecture documentation. A product line must be well documented to enable products to be built on top of it. In addition, product lines are inflexible when new features have to be added to products, or existing products need to be changed. It is necessary to decide whether a feature is so common among products that it should be in the shared platform, or whether the feature should be implemented for a single product and adapted to the platform later, if necessary. This may be cumbersome and restrictive if agile software development methods are used. As development of a platform takes time, increases costs and delays construction of the first products, it is considered that a product line should contain at least three products or models to be worthwhile. For example, according to software architect Janne Viitala (Viitala et al, 2013), if there is a need to change more than 20 percent of a system it is cheaper to build a new one from scratch.

Documentation

All complex systems have some documentation. Documentation can be considered to be done for two reasons (Coplien & Bjørnvig, 2010): to remember and to communicate. Documentation is especially important in the machine control system domain, as the lifecycle of a control system is typically very long. Eventually people will forget the structure of the software architecture and rationales of design decisions. Furthermore, when changes to an old system are required, the original participants in the design are no longer necessarily employed in the company. As machine manufacturers are rarely also software houses, they tend to subcontract and offshore software development. Documents are created to agree on the scope of subcontracting and to manage the parties involved in development. Although such documentation is not the best option to use in communication between stakeholders, it is often used to communicate the design to subcontractors. One should therefore always keep in mind that documentation is created mainly for remembering things, and preferably not for communicating.

The most typical question nowadays in software engineering is *how much is enough* for documentation. Documenting things in detail is expensive. Furthermore, extensive documentation is hard to keep up to date, and once documents get large enough nobody reads them. An unused document is waste in lean terms. The Agile Manifesto (Agile Alliance, 2001) emphasizes working software over comprehensive documentation. Sometimes this is misinterpreted to mean that nothing should be documented, and the source code of the application must work as the only documentation. Even though this could be enough for some domains, long lifecycles dash the hopes of developers and architects to survive without any additional documentation. The architect who designed the first implementation of a system may no longer be available, so any tacit knowledge they may have had of the system is lost without proper documentation. Naturally, the same applies to any stakeholder and to rationales behind their requirements.

If something more than just comments in the code is documented, at least one area should be covered, namely the *rationale* behind the architectural decisions made during the design of the system. Without this, the same questions and decisions must be gone through over and over again if a similar design choice is going to be made. In addition, there is no way to challenge the reasonability of decisions made long ago if the rationales behind them are not documented. The solution lives on in the design, as no one dares to question the solution – it is just the way it has always been done.

The following story from AT&T, told by Jim Coplien, illustrates the importance of understanding the rationale behind decisions. In 1982 a developer on AT&T's 3ESS electronic switching system wondered about a certain algorithm for trunk allocation. After a while the developer found out that the algorithm had been taken from the previous system, 2ESS. The developers of 2ESS, in turn, had followed the design of 1ESS. The developers of *that* system had followed the implementation of an old electromechanical switch, 5XB – they had simply adopted the algorithm from the previous system without ever questioning the rationale behind it. Later the 3ESS developer learned that the original developers of the old electromechanical 5XB system had chosen the algorithm in order to save a few relays and force down costs. This example demonstrates how solutions live on as folklore if their rationale is not documented.

Documenting a rationale is not an easy thing to do. Issues that feel important during development may not be interesting many years later. However, things that might have felt self-evident and thus not be documented might be the most important when making changes after a couple of decades. Often it is advisable to document rationales afresh, when the decision is made. Such a decision often is made in a meeting in which all its pros and cons are discussed. These discussions should be recorded to form the documentation, otherwise the information may vaporize.

Having up-to-date documentation for just one software version is not usually enough. As different versions of a product get shipped to customers they all need version-specific documentation, as changes during the lifecycle are likely. Thus some kind of document management is required. Document versioning still exposes developers to one common problem: how do you know which document version is the most recent? Often documentation lags behind development, and multiple versions of the same documents are in use. This might lead to misunderstanding when developers use outdated documentation as a basis for development. Effort therefore needs to be made to solve the versioning problem, such as using wikis, or architecture knowledge repositories such as TopDocs (Eloranta et al, 2012) to alleviate the problem.

One aspect that is typical of the machine control system domain is strong dependency between various versions of components: one version of a component depends on a specific version of another component, and will not work with other versions. Usually it can be guaranteed that a software component can be used only with a specific version of the hardware, its firmware and the components on which it is depending. It may therefore be necessary to back-port changes made to the current version to older versions of the software, which may be running on a different kind of hardware. The situation is even worse if there are customized versions for specific customers. This kind of combination of version dependency and long lifecycles requires well-documented code, good architecture documentation and information on which versions are compatible with each other. Fortunately, using configuration tools (see COMPONENT-BASED CONFIGURATION, page 386) can make managing different versions easier. Still, this does not decrease the need for proper documentation.

A long lifecycle also puts a great strain on documentation management systems. It is still too typical that after a call from a customer someone tries to find paper copies of blueprints from archives that are over 30 years old. Despite of this kind of manual archiving, documents are usually found sooner or later. But how about those produced today? Would it really be possible to manage the current documentation in, let's say, 2050? If files are stored in a digital format, will software still be available to read them?

Technologies

As an engineering field, machine control software development has plenty of technologies that are meant to solve problems encountered during the development process. Many of these technologies offer ready-made implementations of some of the problems presented in our patterns. However, designers sometimes still need to tackle problems for themselves, as the selected technology does not solve them. In addition, it is always good to understand the mechanisms working under the hood of selected technologies, and have a common vocabulary to document and communicate these solutions. For example, the problem described in ONE TO MANY (page 131) is often solved by adding ready-made bus cabling and components to the system, such as CAN. Furthermore, the problem described in HIGH-LEVEL PROTOCOL (page 137) could be solved by using CANopen. Real-time operating systems implement many of the patterns, such as HARDWARE ABSTRACTION LAYER (page 264). Corresponding technologies are listed in the patterns, so that you can decide whether to use an existing solution. There might still be a need to build solutions in-house, for example if you want to cherry-pick and a ready-made solution would be overkill. The forces in play while designing the solution will be helpful here.

There are a few technologies on the market that could be used in machine control systems. Often these technologies offer ready-made solutions to some of the problems described in our patterns, so often dictate what kind of architectural solutions need to be used. For example, AUTOSAR (AUTomotive Open System ARchitecture), which originated in the car industry, is an open and standardized automotive software architecture (AUTOSAR, 2013). While it may not be applicable as such to work machines, a lot can be learned from its architecture. AUTOSAR was developed by cooperating automotive manufacturers, suppliers and tool vendors. Its goal is to provide a basic infrastructure for developing software and user interfaces for cars. AUTOSAR describes a similar approach to system configuration management as is described in COMPONENT-BASED CONFIGURATION (page 386). To achieve decoupling between the software and hardware, AUTOSAR uses a layered architecture. The architecture consists of three layers: a basic software layer, the runtime environment and an application layer. In other words, AUTOSAR uses similar approaches to those described in HARDWARE ABSTRACTION LAYER and VIRTUAL RUNTIME ENVIRONMENT (page 272). In the future we may see similar open standards for the work machine domain. This would allow third-party developers to offer their services for multiple manufacturers, and shorten the development time from the machine manufacturer's side. *Openness for Third-Party Software* (page 60) gives more details.

Another well-known and promising solution is Data Distribution Service (DDS) (OMG, 2007). DDS is a machine-to-machine middleware standard based on publisher/subscriber architecture. To give a brief introduction to DDS, we have invited a researcher working on the topic to describe this approach in more detail.

Data-Centric Middleware:
Data Distribution Service (DDS) for Real-Time Systems

Author: Pekka Alho

One of the key requirements for distributed control systems is timely and reliable sharing of data to all interested nodes. Fortunately, most of the problems related to this subject have already been solved and implemented in standardized solutions as middleware.

Middleware is a key technology for enabling collaboration between control system nodes, abstracting the tedious and error-prone low-level infrastructure details for developers. By providing an abstracted communication layer for applications, middleware allows developers to focus on the actual application logic instead of platform-specific communication systems. Another goal of middleware is to simplify the task of building control systems from reusable components provided by multiple suppliers. Moreover, middleware can provide implementations for many of the communication patterns that are presented in this book.

One of the existing data-sharing middleware standards is the Data Distribution Service for Real-Time Systems (DDS), maintained by the Object Management Group (OMG, 2007). DDS is a decentralized (peer-to-peer) and data-centric middleware based on the PUBLISH/SUBSCRIBE model (Buschmann et al, 2007b). It is aimed at a wide range of systems that have strict performance and reliability requirements, including large-scale mission-critical systems and embedded systems. DDS has been successfully used in numerous research and industrial projects, including domains such as military, industrial control, unmanned vehicles and air traffic management.

For mobile work machines, potential applications of DDS include local communications between system nodes, collaboration between machines, fleet management and so on. The dynamic nature of DDS can also be used to support different machine configurations, add optional features, or implement fault resilience, since software modules are loosely coupled. Modules do not hold direct references to other modules, and they can be loaded or removed on-the-fly.

The key concepts of DDS are an information model of the system, global data space, topic-based publish/subscribe model and Quality of Service (QoS) policies. An information model captures the essential entities of the physical system and application logic; it represents the state of the system and the external or internal events that can affect it. Conceptually the model is similar to relational models in databases or class diagrams in object-oriented programming. Creating an information model consists of identifying entity types, which have data attributes assigned to them, and associations between the types. The difference to class diagrams is that the information model focuses only on data, not behavior. Both relational and object-oriented information models can be implemented fairly directly in DDS. Therefore the design effort also shifts from interfaces to creating an information model that is used as basis for communication, which will stay consistent for the intended lifetime of the system.

The data-centric approach of DDS is based on removing direct inter-module references. DDS nodes publish data to a distributed global data space asynchronously and anonymously, instead of using remote procedure calls or sending point-to-point messages to specific receivers. The middleware disseminates data to all participating nodes, acting as a single source of up-to-date system-wide state information. This increases the level of decoupling between communicating nodes and eases development of systems that are evolvable, scalable and robust. The DDS infrastructure does not have central brokers or servers that could act as a single point of failure or bottleneck – communication is peer-to-peer and device-to-device, which allows DDS to be run over ad hoc wireless networks (Alho & Mattila, 2013).

The publish/subscribe model enables DDS-based systems to scale effectively, since publishers do not specify recipients for data. Publishers register as data writers to a topic and interested subscribers can join the topic as data readers. A topic is essentially a user-defined extensible data type (defined in the information model) that has a set of QoS policies associated with it. The middleware automatically discovers new readers and writers, which means that new nodes can join the system on the fly, and that the system configuration can be changed dynamically. A single topic can have multiple readers and writers, as shown in Figure 2.10. One of the data elements in a topic can be chosen to be a key value, which can be used to further identify the incoming data.

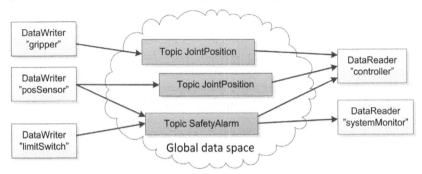

Figure 2.10: The concept of global data space and topics in DDS. In this example, deviceId is defined as the key for the topic JointPosition. SafetyAlarm has no key.

QoS policies provide the ability to specify various parameters such as deadlines, reliability, data lifespan, transport priority, resource limits and so on, to control local and end-to-end properties of DDS topics. The reliability policy, for example, can be defined to be either 'best effort' or 'reliable'. If a topic has its reliability policy set to 'reliable', the middleware guarantees that all data samples will eventually be delivered to data readers. This is desirable for commands or status updates, for example. With a 'best effort' policy, failed delivery of data will not be retried. This is useful if only the most recent data sample matters, for example a measurement for a control loop.

The middleware manages the data lifecycle according to the associated QoS policies, and enforces some policies on a requested versus offered basis. To read data from a topic, policies provided by publishers must match policies requested by the subscriber. QoS policies are also used to ensure real-time deadlines. Deadlines can be set for freshness of data, and a subscribing application is immediately notified if the expected data is late. However, the developer or system integrator must still decide what to do if they are exceeded, to avoid total system failure. End-to-end performance analysis for the system is also needed, to set reasonable policies that take into account affecting factors such as network structure.

DDS-based applications can be integrated with legacy and ERP systems, as protocol bridges are available for over 80 communication protocols. To enable interoperability between DDS implementations by different vendors, the standard includes a wire-protocol specification called Real-Time Publish-Subscribe protocol. The implementations themselves, however, are not directly interchangeable, since they have vendor-specific APIs and other implementation-specific features. This introduces the possibility of vendor lock-in, and therefore the choice of vendor should be carefully analyzed. Major vendors have implementations available on different licensing models, varying from open source to proprietary. Other differentiating factors include supporting tools, add-ons, ease of use and performance. Supported platforms typically include Linux, Windows, Solaris and Vx-Works.

On the whole, DDS seems to be a good match for the requirements of work machines, provided that the computing platform is capable of running a supported operating system. Concrete use cases for DDS in mobile machines can be found in (Prismtech, 2013) and include agricultural vehicle systems, where it is used to distribute data between the components inside a combine harvester, and for tethered control between a combine and a grain cart for unloading on the go. Middleware also has a crucial role in the implementation of various control system-related patterns, and the features of DDS can be utilized, for example, in fault tolerance patterns such as 1+1 REDUNDANCY (page 279) for redundant publishers, or HEARTBEAT (page 120) as a topic for node heartbeat signals.

A possible downside of DDS is that sending commands is not as straightforward as in client-server architectures. Since the standard does not support remote procedure calls, commands must be presented as data. Parsing of data complicates debugging, as it adds another potential source of faults. If data is parsed incorrectly, it may not be self-evident where the fault originated. Middleware also adds some overhead to message size, and consumes system resources. However, DDS implementations are targeted for systems that have strict performance and reliability requirements. Therefore, its implementations have typically been optimized and tested to suit the needs of these systems, and perform better than other publisher/subscriber implementations (Xiong, 2006). Finally, even though DDS is used in mission-critical applications, standard editions are not safety-certifiable, although some vendors also offer safety-critical editions with limited functionality.

Common Pitfalls

From previous sections it has become clear that machine control software development is far from an easy task. There are several ways in which things can go wrong, and in this section we discuss some of them. Some have already been discussed, but we wanted to present these pitfalls in one place to emphasize how important it is to avoid them. In a way, these are the common *anti-patterns* of the trade.

It is quite easy to start machine control system development in which each delivered machine type will be a separate project. In practice, this means that every customer has a customized machine with customized control system software. This will lead to serious problems if the production volume increases and the business model is not changed. Practices that suit a project-based approach well are incompatible with mass production. The software architecture of the system will be different too, as mass production requires different quality attributes than custom projects. Chapter 3, *Software Architecture and Quality*, offers a detailed explanation of how architecture affects software quality. For example, custom projects are usually maintained by the original R&D organization. In this case it is possible to use COTS components that require a vendor-specific tool to be parameterized and configured. However, as mass-produced machines are usually maintained by a separate organization, multiple vendor-specific tools will cause confusion. Maintenance personnel must have several tools to configure all the required modules that can be installed on machines. In addition, detailed knowledge is required to understand for example that some controllers and devices can be configured via a machine's graphical user interface, but there are a few components that require special care and their corresponding tools.

Vendor lock-in is a threat that lurks behind every design decision where the architect uses components that are not in-house products. Of course, it is sensible to use well-known, well-tested, mass-produced, relatively cheap and interoperable off-the-shelf components whenever it is possible. These decisions save resources, time and money, and usually results in higher quality when the component is well-suited for the environment. However, when a component is selected, one must pay careful attention to its technology roadmap and support lifecycle. If a COTS component is not perfectly suitable for the intended use, the rest of the system should accommodate to that, as COTS component vendors may be reluctant to make modifications to their product if the demand is low.

It may be lucrative to select a whole family of COTS components, as their interoperability is good and new products can be launched quickly. Furthermore, consultancy is easy to get from the vendor. However, if it is later discovered that the wrong technology has been used, it will be difficult to fix, as technologies are often a fundamental architecture decision that affects all other design decisions. Thus, even end-of-support for an operating system may require extensive modifications to applications if the system was not designed for this kind of change. Even if the change was anticipated and the system was designed with it in mind, preparations have their costs. Some of the architectural solutions that isolate applications from the underlying technologies cause latencies, may make the software more complex to develop, and may prevent optimizations that are platform-specific. Thus, a developer may, either intentionally or by accident, break the isolating architectural conventions and ruin portability.

Another common pitfall is internationalization (often abbreviated to 'i18n'). As machine manufacturers usually sell their products around the globe, localization is required. Even when selecting practices in the design phase, it must be ensured that the system conforms to the standards of a target country. Different standards and directives also affect the functionality of a machine. Thus, functionality may vary depending on the country or continent to which a machine will be shipped.

User interfaces must be such that they support different languages, even those which are read from right to left and so on. A single language package may cost tens of thousands of euros. In some market areas the operator-to-be may not even be able to read. In the user interface, cultural differences must also be taken into account when designing symbols and so on. For example, a symbol of a rabbit may not mean 'fast' in all countries. In addition, units, and time zones with different daylight saving time settings, can cause problems. For example, in Finland the change from daylight saving time to standard time occurs at 4 am. So a system used in Finland must be designed so that if something should happen every night at 3 am, it won't happen twice when the clocks change to standard time and the night has 3 o'clock twice. However, in other countries the time changes at a different hour, for example, 1 am in the UK. This needs to be taken into account in system design. Even the weather and other environmental conditions of the target market may affect the software. Of course, they will have the most impact on the electronic and mechanical design, but in some cases different algorithms may have to be developed to suit different environments. For example, measures meant for energy savings may cause problems in cold environments if dissipated heat cannot keep hardware de-iced. There are also options that are suitable for a specific geographical area, and it may be hard to convey these if the developers have no first-hand experience of the subject. For example, in forestry machines, eucalyptus trees have remarkably different handling characteristics compared to trees in the temperate zone.

Although subcontracting is common in the work machine domain, it also causes problems. These problems relate to the fact that distributed software development is always more challenging than with a local team (Herbsleb & Mockus, 2003). The organization will be dictated by the architecture, and vice versa, as Conway's Law indicates (Conway, 1968). Some of these problems were introduced in more detail in *Agile Development in the Control System Domain* on page 33. Subcontracting also creates a need for extensive documentation, as described in *Documentation* on page 41. Documentation has its own problems: it is hard to keep up to date, hard to make sure that the newest version is always in use, and it is always a less efficient way of communication than direct conversation.

Even if software development can be carried out with a collocated team, it will still have problems, as there are typically also interfaces to other teams: a software developer must interact with mechanical hardware, electronics and so on. Distributed development also leads to 'integration hell' if the whole system can only be tested as a whole at a late stage of development when all components are ready. This also applies to integration with hardware. Thus both hardware and all software teams should break out of their silos and cooperate.

If a hardware team and a software team have poor communication, the hardware team can be so separated from the everyday reality of the software developers that they choose cheaper components to cut down manufacturing costs. Sometimes this means omitting redundant hardware, choosing a processor with low computational capacity, choosing a smaller display or similar things. Unfortunately, if the action is not judged in the light of the whole development, a local optimization may look good. The hardware is a cost factor that affects every machine sold, so a few cents saved on a single machine results in more than a euro saved on a batch of hundred machines. However, a local minimum is rarely the minimum of the whole system. It may be lucrative to think that as hardware costs per unit but software is done only once, one should try to press the hardware costs down and try to compensate with software features and optimization. However, it may be that the software developers have to struggle with scarce hardware resources and spend lots of time designing and optimizing the applications. Furthermore, if they have to sacrifice good architectural practices or usability to the altar of cost effectiveness in hardware, both internal and external quality is lost (see *External Quality and Internal Quality* on page 77), causing loss of sales. In addition, resources are used in paying the technical debt: maintainability, bug fixes and development of new features will become expensive. Being a cheapskate may become expensive even in tools: compilers, debuggers, bus analyzers and other such tools are expensive, but may quickly pay for themselves in shortened development times.

Software architecture can also hold pitfalls. Architecture should support testing, good diagnostics and should be understandable, otherwise developers will face an eternal struggle and will never reach the set quality goals for the software. The system architecture should also support openness to other parties if specific features are desired to be outsourced to third parties.

Sometimes architects tend to invent quality attributes for a system (Buschmann et al, 2012), and over-generalization is one of the besetting sins of architects. This often leads to a situation in which developers use significant time in developing the architecture and improving the internal quality of the product, as described in *External Quality and Internal Quality* on page 77. This can be waste of resources if the investment does not return anything. As it is hard to predict the future, the intended reuse may not ever materialize. Some even argue that software reuse is a myth altogether (Schmidt, 1999; Tracz, 1988). Software that is too generalized becomes hard to grasp, as the design lacks sufficient concreteness – the mental model will be on too abstract a level. The architect's main duty is to keep the software architecture in balance between simplicity and complexity. Too simple an architecture is unusable if the world around it changes, and too complex an architecture can be too unintelligible to be used for its original purpose.

Product lines are an extension to the architecture, formed by the general parts shared by every product. They cause inertia in the development, as all changes to the product platform will affect multiple products. Product teams are not going to like it if the platform evolves too quickly and they have to aim for a moving target as a result. All changes should therefore be preplanned and communicated to the teams as a feature roadmap for the platform. It can also be hard for a product development team to make its wishes known in platform development, as all other teams also have to be taken into account. Thus it is usual that a product team develops features to suit their needs, and if the features are popular enough, they will be integrated into the platform.

Safety also affects the architecture and can be a pitfall. It would be expensive to spread safety features all through the software, as the safety assessments and conformance to safety standards would become burdensome. It is better to isolate safety systems into separated safety components. Safety standards may require extensive documentation and a rigidness from the development process that may be too constricting in normal feature development.

A standard may be a double-edged sword even on the technology side. On one hand, standards try to guarantee interoperability between components from different vendors and make it possible to use common tools in systems that conform to specific standards. On the other hand, vendors may have diverging interpretations of standards, and some features mandated by a standard may be optional to implement, so it may be hard to integrate components from different vendors. In addition, it is also common practice to implement company-specific features in the proprietary sections of technology standards. These features may be either improvements, which will work only with components from the same vendor, or attempts to hide commercial secrets and intellectual property. If proprietary features are used, only components from the same vendor can be used, and this may lead to vendor lock-in. Commercial secrets, on the other hand, may make it hard to provide common tools for a specific technology. Furthermore, standardization processes are usually slow, so standard approaches are mature and old compared to the state of the art.

Tackling the Challenges

To tackle these challenges, we introduce a manifesto for control system development. By following these four simple principles, we feel that many of the pitfalls listed in the previous section can be avoided. When you have your organizational values in place, you will obtain greatest benefit from the patterns in this book.

System thinking over local optimization. Any control system should be thought of as a whole and optimized as a whole, not locally on separate hardware or software levels. For example, saving three euros on a display component may add costs exponentially during software development. In addition, cheaper hardware may also be more error-prone and may require more work on the software side. So selecting a cheaper hardware component typically generates changes in software during the lifecycle of a machine. This will add significant cost. If you optimize the benefit for the customer, the customer is probably willing to pay the extra three euros for a fancier display if they get the machine they want.

Openness over proprietary solutions. In many cases, companies require substantial openness from component suppliers, but their own systems will be closed to third parties. However, a degree of openness could create innovation possibilities, support the creation of new features independently from the manufacturer, and enable their creation even after the initial product launch. For example, testing the system might become easier, as mass-produced simulators and test walls could be built against open interfaces. This would probably also lead to cheaper test and simulation environments.

Face-to-face communication over comprehensive documentation. Companies in the work machine domain employ subcontracting for many software features. However, outsourcing is hard even in traditional software development. The software team relies on several other teams, such as the hardware design team. Long lifecycles can cause systems to outlive a single person's career in a company. Transferring domain knowledge is challenging. Unfortunately, a document is generally an inefficient and one-way form of communication. If you have over 100 pages of architecture documentation, it will most likely be 'write-only' documentation – that is, never read by its intended audience. So, use face-to-face communication to transfer at least some of this knowledge to subcontractors, other teams and newcomers. Document only the things that absolutely need to be remembered.

Everybody, early on, altogether. Requirements for a machine should be gathered extensively in the early phase of its development. Software usually cannot be implemented separated from other stakeholders' wishes, such as hardware design or mechanics design. However, these stakeholders may not be using agile methods. Misunderstandings may be expensive: if software features are developed first and the planned hardware platform then changes, it is possible that the features cannot be run on the new hardware. In this case these features are rendered unusable, and a lot of development effort is wasted. So cross-disciplinary teams are required to work together towards a shared goal. Involve everybody, early on, altogether, as described in *Lean Architecture for Agile Software Development* (Coplien & Bjørnvig, 2010).

2.3   New Trends in the Domain

The patterns in this book are about the existing solutions in the field. However, while collecting the pattern language, we have seen many emerging trends in the domain. Some of them are purely business-related; machine manufacturers and machine owners are putting more and more emphasis on the management of the whole production chain and the management of already deployed machines. Work machines are used as a part of production chains where just-in-time delivery (Liker, 2003) is required: machines should produce output only when it is needed, so that it does not end up waiting in inventories.

Control system software has become an important differentiating factor in the market. Many manufacturers know how to make mechanically sound and efficient work machines, but the major differences between models are more and more based on the control system software. The software affects many aspects of the manufacturer's business and serves several stakeholders. Software features define the answers to many questions. What does the user interface look like? How easy is the machine is to operate? How good is the preventive maintenance's prediction rate? A machine manufacturer has to invest in software development to be successful in the market, both now and in the future.

As the number of services offered by the applications on work machine increases, more and more data is produced by them. As the volume of data collected from a machine increases, data analysis can no longer be carried out just by the hardware on the machine: it needs to be transferred to cloud services or other servers for analysis. This requires high throughput from communication channels on the machine. At the same time, as the machine has connections to the outside world and to open networks, it exposes the machine to attacks from the Internet. Information security therefore becomes a crucial aspect of the design. The emerging importance of information security is highlighted in a recent study (Eloranta et al, 2013a). To be able to patch vulnerabilities on a machine, it should be possible to update the control system easily. In practice, this often means that software updates can be delivered remotely, as it would be too laborious and expensive to have maintenance personnel visit each deployed machine.

The need for software in the control systems is growing. Manufacturers need to focus on their core competence, so they need to involve more stakeholders in control system software development. This requires a new level of openness from the system and manufacturer's side. While standardization of interfaces between parties might work as a solution, it is a slow and expensive way to solve the problem. Standardization takes time, and requires extensive participation from contributing parties. Versioning of standards might cause problems, as different vendors may adhere to different versions of a standard. A more open approach might be required in the future.

Another trend is towards stricter environmental standards to which a work machine must conform. Oil prices increase constantly, so we are likely to see new innovations for minimizing fuel consumption. Minimization of emissions and the environmental footprint of a machine throughout its lifecycle has become an important competitive advantage. Creating more environmentally friendly machines requires new approaches and technologies, for example new kinds of motors. These changes in work machine hardware are likely to affect the software, but how is yet to be seen.

On the process control side, networking of systems has gone so far that they are now closely following trends in traditional software engineering. Cloud services and virtualization of servers has become common practice in the domain. How these trends affect machine control is yet to be seen, but they definitely have applications there. Cloud servers can be used to process data from fleet management, and virtualization could be used for example to improve the security and portability of operator-level software.

As machines become more efficient and productive, a single customer probably won't need so many to run their business, so manufacturers must seek new business models. One of the most promising has been to offer extensive services to machines throughout their lifecycle. Eighty percent of manufacturer's revenue can nowadays originate from service business. Some manufacturers have even attempted to offer the machine itself as a service: a machine is no longer purchased, but rather the service the machine offers. This, and other new trends, are discussed in more detail in the subsections that follow.

Orchestrating Multiple Machines

Production management systems are becoming more widely used, in that various machines are part of a production chain and need to exchange information in order to produce additional value. This requires orchestration between different machines, interoperability between machines and other systems, and close integration with production management systems.

Consider an example from paper production. A paper mill uses wood pulp for making paper; to make the pulp, logs are needed as raw material. The demand for paper depends on economic cycles, and fluctuates over time: production must adjust to market demand. As the quality of the logs decreases when they are stacked, inventories must be kept as small as possible. A paper mill therefore must declare a need for raw material. This declaration is communicated to forest harvesters using a production management system. Such a management system typically consists of an enterprise resource planning application (ERP system), used to optimize workflow in the production chain. A request for raw material is sent to the operator by the ERP system as a work plan. The operator controls the harvester to cut the logs from the designated area, and sends the locations of log piles back to the ERP system, or directly to a forwarder. The forwarder receives the list of locations and fetches the logs in an optimal order, which might also be calculated by the ERP system. The forwarder brings the logs to the closest road, and informs a log truck that there is a load waiting, as shown in Figure 2.11. The log truck then transports the logs to the paper mill. Orchestrating operations in a production chain minimizes wait states in which a machine is waiting for work, and minimizes inventories of raw material.

Figure 2.11: Two forwarders working together to transport piles of logs
from the stand to a road for collection

Reproduced by permission of John Deere Forestry

Multiple machines in a production chain typically form a fleet. A fleet management system orchestrates the fleet to increase efficiency and productivity. Fleet management systems can also monitor the health of machines in the fleet, and compare their data to spot potential malfunctions before the event. However, an enormous volume of data is produced in a typical manufacturing system, as thousands of sensors record position, velocity, hydraulic oil flow, temperature and other variables hundreds of times a minute. This data needs to be stored and transferred from the machine to enable analysis. All this information collected from machines affects their orchestration, so fleet management often requires remote connections to machines. Naturally, this opens a threat, as machines are connected to the Internet. When speaking of modern embedded systems, one can hear the term *Internet of things*, as all kinds of machines and systems are interconnected via the Internet.

The most important function of a fleet management system is GPS, which allows tracking the location, direction and speed of a machine. This information is used, for example, to select the nearest available machine to carry out a task. It can also be used to create *geo-fencing* based alerts: for example, if a truck delivering goods is approaching the warehouse, fork lifts can be notified in advance that work is about to start. Using GPS tracking, machines can also be notified if they are approaching a traffic jam, for example allowing them to avoid the area and carry out their tasks more efficiently. Similarly, machines can avoid dangerous areas, for example accidents. Such changes in the environment can also affect global optimization of work. For example, if a road to a work area is blocked by roadworks, the machine may not reach the work area at all. In this case, the fleet management system could send another machine to the work site from another direction.

The functionality of a fleet management system typically includes diagnostic features, so that maintenance of the system can be planned and scheduled efficiently. This opens the possibility of comparing mileage, fuel consumption and CO_2 emissions of different machines. A fleet management application also allows over-the-air security, so that a vehicle cannot be started while it is marked as stopped or not in operation. Sometimes a machine can even be safely disabled by the fleet management system while in operation. For example, an authorized person could gradually decelerate a vehicle by downshifting, limiting the throttle capacity, or engaging the braking system via the management system. The system can also warn a machine operator that vehicle disabling is about to occur. After stopping a vehicle, the system can lock the brakes and prevent the engine from being restarted. This allows the fleet manager to recover stolen vehicles, while reducing the chance of lost or stolen cargo. Table 2.1 on the next page summarizes the most common usage scenarios and features of fleet management systems.

Control systems in work machines have limited processing power, and consequently detailed analysis of data cannot be executed on board, so data is gathered in a central repository. This gives the fleet management system a 'big picture' view. In addition, data can be compared to other machines to analyze how a specific machine is performing. However, machines in the fleet might come from different manufacturers, and creating a common means of communication is a challenge. Currently there are only a few standards for communications, one of the most popular being OPC/UA (Mahnke et al, 2009). Interface openness in fleet management is needed to allow interoperability of different kinds of machines. If the fleet management application uses common and open interfaces, it can be used to join the machine to the fleet while keeping the machine's interfaces accessible only to the developers of fleet management applications. For more details, see SYSTEM ADAPTER (page 378).

From the control system point of view, the machine is part of the fleet via REMOTE ACCESS (page 361) and FLEET MANAGEMENT (page 372) applications. The fleet management application gets up-to-date work plans from the server of the fleet management system, and, depending on the system, it shows them to the operator using an existing user interface, cabin PC or a tablet such as an iPad. A plethora of machines are in use already in the field. Many of these machines may already be quite old, manufactured by a variety of vendors, and usually do not have any kind of support for fleet management, so retrofit solutions are needed to orchestrate them. Typically, information from such machines is still collected manually, using an additional PC or tablet in the machine's cabin: the operator must input data such as production reports and work hours. A better approach would be

CAPABILITY	DESCRIPTION
GPS tracking	The location, speed and heading of a machine can be tracked and plotted on a map.
Diagnostic	Various information such as usage hours and fuel consumptions are gathered from machines. This also helps to manage the lifecycle of machines.
Geo-fencing	Alerts, notifications, functions and so on can be triggered when a machine enters or leaves a predetermined area.
Remote control features	A machine can be controlled remotely. For example, a machine can be activated or disabled using the fleet management application to prevent unauthorized use.
Driver profiling	The system monitors how efficiently the operator is working for comparison with other operators, helping to focus on specific aspects of operator training.
Trip profiling	Profiling can be used to create profiles of various trips for work planning, and to estimate how long a specific kind of trip will take.
Vehicle profiling	Profiling the vehicles can help to determine which machine is most suitable for a specific kind of work.
Vehicle efficiency	Monitoring helps to determine how efficiently a specific machine type is performing.
Work plans	Work plans can be delivered to the operator even during a shift, so that it is easier to respond to emerging production needs.
Production reports	A machine operator can send production reports to the ERP system directly from the machine's control system at the end of a shift.

Table 2.1   A short summary of possible capabilities of a fleet management system for orchestrating multiple machines

to add a module running the fleet management application separately from the old control system, and install the hardware, such as additional sensors, required by the fleet management system onto the machine, so that data can be collected automatically.

The possible capabilities of orchestrating multiple machines and ways to implement it vary greatly, so the topic is clearly worth its own pattern language. In this book we focus on how a single machine can be part of a fleet management system, and how communication between machines can be organized, as those are questions for which a single control system should provide answers.

Service as a Business

Services have been around as long as work machines. Maintenance services, if offered by a machine manufacturer or licensed subcontractors, are a way to generate revenue during the whole lifecycle of a product. Furthermore, well-conducted maintenance services promote customer loyalty, and give a feeling of good customer care and quality over the years of ownership. Service operations can be very lucrative; in some cases the average profitability of service operations has been more than 75 percent greater than overall business unit profitability (Glueck at al, 2007). Services are also a growing business area around the globe. In China during the past 25 years, for example, the service sector has grown by 191 percent (Paulson, 2006). Some of this growth is in traditional services, but manufacturing is also going through a paradigm shift from manufacturing to services. For example, in the automotive industry the average share of service and parts supply is more than 37 percent of the entire business (Deloitte, 2006).

It is also possible to sell not just work machines, but the core operation of the machine as a service. In this case the customer buys for example a drilling service, not the drill machine itself. The customer pays per drilled meter or some other basis of invoicing. In one sense, the machine is leased to the customer, and the machine manufacturer's responsibility is then to make sure that the service is available when the customer needs it. If a machine breaks down and the customer loses business due to this, there might be some need to compensate the customer. These compensations can quickly ruin any business that cannot guarantee availability. In any case, the customer will not be satisfied with the situation and may turn to other companies when they next need service. In addition, the time windows for service become smaller, so valuable time cannot be wasted on maintenance when a machine is needed. Thus preventive maintenance becomes a more important aspect of a machine's maintenance schedule, and the control system software should aid in planning these maintenance breaks.

As a machine has to be working whenever the customer needs its service, it demands high reliability, availability and fault tolerance from the machine control system. The software should therefore provide enough information for both repairs and preventive maintenance – see DIAGNOSTICS (page 350). Furthermore, fault tolerance should be maximized, even if it requires additional hardware investments, such as 1+1 REDUNDANCY (page 279). In general this focuses the business on monitoring deployed machines, optimizing their management and maintenance, and having more transparency in the organization to identify problem areas.

Moving to service business also offers an opportunity to move from mass production to customized products with a higher profit margin. As the production cost of a machine is only a fraction of its total price, its value comes from services and from how the machine can be used. A service-orientated business model clearly anticipates that all the information required to support a service business is available. In practice, this means that machines are no longer working individually, and it is essential for both the manufacturer's and the customer's business that data from several sources can be connected and analyzed.

Ecological trends emphasize the minimization of environmental footprint during the whole lifecycle of a product. One way to offer service to a customer is therefore to minimize manufacturing emissions by taking care of maintenance, so that a machine works optimally during its active years, and finally taking care of its decommission. For more information about environmental issues in the context of control systems, see *Energy Consumption and Eco-efficiency* on page 63. A machine control system can provide diagnostic data during its lifecycle, so that maintenance personnel can pinpoint problems remotely and prepare for repairs before they arrive at a customer site. Maintenance personnel's presence at a site is usually seen as a sign of good customer care (Figure 2.12).

The customer feels that they are getting value for money spent on service contracts, and the effect is maximized when maintenance breaks are short or non-existent, so proper preparation is crucial.

Figure 2.12: Metso service personnel on site in India

Reproduced by permission of Metso Automation Oy

One way to provide services is to offer additional applications during the lifetime of a machine. This usually requires some openness to third-party software; see *Openness for Third-Party Software* on page 60. Applications can give the end user more sophisticated and focused services than was possible with a basic control system. For example, a simple application could provide the operator with a means to contact the maintenance service if problems arise. This kind of application is easy to implement, and can create an atmosphere of good customer care, resulting in customer loyalty. In addition to single machine applications, fleet management can be seen as a service: FLEET MANAGEMENT (page 372) describes how to enable a machine to function as part of a fleet.

Autonomous and Intelligent Machines

There are working environments that are hostile or inconvenient for humans, such as inside a nuclear reactor, in mines or on the surface of Mars. In some working environments the work being carried out is so mechanical and repetitive that a human is unnecessary and would cost too much. Some of the tasks may have requirements for safety or response time that prevent human beings from carrying out the task. For such environments, where people would be at risk, automatically guided machines are used. Such machines can act autonomously without direct human intervention, and are most frequently used in industrial applications to move materials around a manufacturing facility or warehouse. In practice automatically guided machines are often mobile robots that follow markers or wires in the floor, or use vision or lasers. One recent example of autonomous machines is a driverless car developed by Google. The car drives at the speed limit stored in its map database, and maintains its distance from other vehicles using a system of sensors.

The problem with automatic guidance systems is that safety must be ensured. Autonomous machines must therefore usually be stopped at once if humans or unknown obstacles such as other machines enter the working area. On the other hand, there should be as few false alarms as possible to keep the system productive. A basic solution is to isolate the working area physically, so that entering the area stops moving machines automatically. As this is not always possible, safety vests or other clothes can be used to help a machine to notice a human being. However, it may be difficult to ensure that all personnel always wear the required clothing in the risk area. For example, a person might forget to wear a safety vest when entering such an area. This subject has been studied recently (Milos & Billar, 2013; Pradalier et al, 2005), as it may prevent the wide use of autonomous systems.

Intelligent autonomous machines are an evolutionary step from automated guided vehicles, and try to optimize their work based on previous experience. In practice this means that an intelligent machine has an artificial neural network that has some predefined configuration and is optimized via learning processes. Intelligent machines learn during their work, and with the help of artificial intelligence (AI) the machine learns the actions it should carry out as a reaction to a specific stimulus. For example, before office hours an intelligent elevator might automatically position itself on the ground floor, as people coming to work in the morning will need it there. Similarly, in the afternoon the elevator might relocate its home position to the upper floors of the building.

Such autonomous intelligence requires more information from the work environment and the machine's state. It is no longer enough to use preprogrammed work procedures, as the machine must be able to react autonomously to changes in its environment. For example, the Mars rover *Curiosity* is able to decide for itself how to drive safely on Mars (Webster, 2013). To do this, the rover must analyze images it takes during a drive to determine a safe route. Autonomous decision-making is beneficial in the case of *Curiosity*, especially when a route cannot be confirmed as safe by its ground control – communication delays caused by the distance between the Earth and Mars make this completely impractical.

If several machines share a work environment, autonomy requires extensive communication between them. They must exchange information about their decisions, and adapt their behavior accordingly to the current environment. One machine can propagate new information, such as changes in the work environment, to the rest. In this way the awareness of other machines about the environment can be extended. For example, a car can alert the next vehicle about ice on the road, so that it is ready to decrease speed to avoid an accident.

Autonomous and intelligent machines are relatively new in the domain of distributed machine control systems, and unmanned machines are often still operated remotely by humans. Only a few patterns, if any, have therefore emerged from existing designs. For this reason, the focus in this book is on the interfaces and data that one CONTROL SYS-TEM (page 96) provides to enable intelligence and autonomy. We also discuss the topic from a single work machine's point of view. The rest of the subject, such as artificial intelligence, communication networks for external servers, and ERP systems, may be discussed briefly, but their implementation is not the focus of this book, as these topics can easily form their own pattern language.

Openness for Third-Party Software

Traditionally business models have been vertical – that is, manufacturers have thought that acquiring an entire production chain, from raw materials to assembly, is beneficial for their businesses. This business model relies on advantages of economy of scale. A famous example of this is Ford's acquisition of rubber plantations to supply rubber for tires. However, long chains of production were prone to changes in the economic cycle. A single disturbance in the production chain could cause problems in the whole chain, where one stage did not have enough materials for production and later stages were lacking resources. Nowadays machine manufacturers are more focused on making specialty products. They focus on the design and assembly of machines. Some have also subcontracted the assembly and focused only on design. The business model of machine manufacturers is horizontal, meaning that their products are on the same level of refinement and share similar technologies – for example, manufacture of forest harvesters and forwarders. This enables manufacturers to get synergy from the technological expertise and the domain knowledge invested in their product platforms. Due to this more focused approach, the business remains viable even in bad economic situations as long as highly specialized products are needed.

To achieve a horizontal synergy the designs of machines typically are modular. For example, frames and booms are designed by the machine manufacturer, and a suitable engine is installed onto the frame. Modularity also reflects on the business via subcontracting. For example, as diesel engines are widely used in mobile machines, and manufacturers usually prefer similar engine designs, it is sensible to use engines that are developed by experts, so diesel engines are acquired from an engine subcontractor.

The same line of reasoning also holds for software, as a large proportion of software design has typically been subcontracted. This may be a result of machine manufacturers' belief that they are more orientated towards heavy industry than software development. However, there are software features whose development needs detailed experience in the domain. Subcontractors don't always have the expertise needed for the development of machine control system software for a specific domain, which may lead to problems. *Embedded Software: Facts, Figures and Future* (Ebert & Jones, 2009) states that after two to three years of learning curve, the cost savings for an outsourced software engineering project are just 10 to 15 percent.

It is often impossible or unfeasible for a machine manufacturer to produce all the software services, as they want to focus on their core business. The core functionality of a control system cannot therefore always fulfil all a customer's needs. In addition, there are several optional functionalities in modern mobile machine control system software that need specialized knowledge for their development. There are therefore niche business opportunities for machine control software that can be filled by third-party vendors, usually to extend the core functionality of the basic system. To make it possible for a third-party software provider to extend a system with missing services, even after a machine has already been deployed, there needs to be an extension mechanism. For example, a fleet management application from a third party could be integrated with a machine control system and could use GPS location information provided by the machine. In addition, a map software provider should be able to install their own maps on a work machine, to offer detailed geolocation information to the operator using topographical maps.

The extension mechanism of the control system software should make it a platform from the third-party software viewpoint. It should provide a runtime environment for third-party applications, and access to all required information and functions of the control system. To achieve real openness, a platform should be open for anyone to develop software for it. The platform interface should therefore be available and well documented.

In addition to third-party vendors, in-house development can be done on such a platform. This helps to focus development, as the interface between the application and the platform is known and well-defined. Using a platform interface for in-house projects also provides the platform developer with valuable feedback from the development team on the features of the platform. They can also test experimental features before they are launched to external developers. The platform should be also open for other product lines built on top of it. *Product Lines* on page 40 provides information about building product lines. Sharing a platform across product lines maximizes the device base for deployment of developed software. The ultimate goal is to transform the product into an *ecosystem* (Bosch, 2009).

An open interface has several advantages. It allows a third party to develop software on which the machine manufacturer is not willing to focus, and it grows the potential developer base. As was stated in Eric Raymond's famous essay, *The Cathedral and the Bazaar* (Raymond, 1999), 'many heads are inevitably better than one'. Innovations not thought of by the machine manufacturer may emerge as a significantly larger body of people develop their own software on top of the platform. This leads to more of a participatory business model than strictly controlled one. The machine manufacturer as platform provider should carefully consider giving third parties business opportunities and a solid ground on which to flourish. This creates a software ecosystem in which all parties benefit from each other. This can be seen in other domains, such as cellphones, in the form of application stores where third-party vendors can sell their own applications and generate revenue. The platform provider gets their share from licensing and provisions. The ultimate benefit will be a more satisfied customer. Furthermore, if a customer has invested a lot on software running on a specific platform, it creates 'stickiness': the customer is not willing to lose their investment by changing platforms. Of course, application stores are far from the current state of the art in machine manufacturing, but there have been some experiments, for example, with app stores for infotainment systems on cars (Eklund & Bosch, 2012).

An additional benefit of open interfaces is that third parties can take some responsibility for continuing support for a machine control system during its lifecycle. For example, adaptation to new hardware for retrofit to an older machine may be implemented as third-party software. In some cases, the customer can do their own modifications and additions to a system during its lifespan using an open interface. In the future a thriving open source community for specific machine control products could exist after official support has ended.

There are also downsides to open interfaces. Openness to third parties brings security and safety issues with it. Even though mechanical safety systems on a machine could prevent the most serious safety hazards, the availability of the system may be compromised if malfunctions occur in third-party software. For example, third-party software running on its own hardware is attached to the control system's bus can cause problems inadvertently even if it is not sending commands. If the third-party component sends error frames to the bus it can bring a whole bus segment to its knees. Information security is also an issue, as an attached module is already part of the control system, allowing it to gather information easily. This is addressed in THIRD-PARTY SANDBOX (page 355).

Liability is also often an issue. If something goes awry it is usually the machine manufacturer that is blamed. It is in the machine manufacturer's interests to make it really hard to cause harm using the machine control system and, equally importantly, to make it easy to prove whether third-party software has used the system in a dangerous way, or neglected safety rules. Some kind of an audit log is needed whenever a third-party application interacts with the base control system.

Machine manufactures must be aware that, after an interface is published, it should not be altered without good reason: third-party developers will lose business if their software stops working. It is an additional task for them to keep their software updated if the interface is changed, so they may consider abandoning the platform if there is no well-established plan on how its interface will evolve.

Standards are one way to establish known and safe interfaces between two different parties. However, any standardization process is relatively slow, and in rapidly evolving technologies lags behind the leading edge. A standardization committee should involve all relevant parties, or standards will only reflect the requirements of a subset of intended users. The same is true when a standard solution is adapted to new domains: the standard solution may be suboptimal in the new field. For example, CAN was originally developed to be used by the automotive industry, but has been widely adopted by neighboring domains such as machine control systems. Of course, it is possible to develop a new optimal standard for each domain, but the volume of hardware adhering to the existing standard, and the vast availability of existing COTS components, may outweigh the benefits of a new standard. Standardization opens ways for specific third parties to develop their own products without need for extensive customization. For example, if REMOTE ACCESS data (page 361) is standardized across all mobile work machines independently of the domain, DIAGNOSTICS (page 350) and maintenance will be easier to implement. OPC Unified Architecture (Mahnke et al, 2009) is an example of a standard for communication between machine control processes and third-party applications.

Energy Consumption and Eco-efficiency

One trend in control systems is eco-efficiency and minimization of energy consumption. This is often referred to as *cleantech*, meaning that the product or machine's efficiency is improved, while energy consumption, waste caused by the machine and so on is reduced. One particular area of improvement in energy saving is in the fuel consumption of work machines. For example, a loader truck might have a 48-liter diesel engine that has diesel consumption as high as 200 liters/hour under full load and uphill. Most of the energy consumed is transformed into the kinetic energy of the machine, but once the operator hits the brakes this kinetic energy is transformed into heat and lost.

Electricity can be used to level peaks in energy consumption. Diesel engines are no longer designed for maximum energy consumption peaks, but are smaller than is needed in a worst case. These smaller diesel engines are accompanied by electric motors that assist the diesel engine in a high consumption situation. The ideal machine for this kind of approach is one in which the need for energy varies greatly, where the average energy consumption is small compared to the peak.

In cars hybrids such as this have been used for years: the Toyota Prius was introduced in 1996. But hybrid passenger cars still remain marginal products, as customers still want power and performance from car engines. In the work machine domain, however, uptake might be faster in future, as energy can be conserved in more ways than in cars. Work machines such as lifts, fork lifts, harvesters and so on could store the potential energy of the mass being lowered in batteries or other energy storages. For example, the Kone EcoDisc Motor (Kone, 2013) uses gearless technology to reduce power consumption, and conserves energy by using a regenerative drive system to capture excess energy produced by the motor.

Hybrid motors in work machines often mean that electric motors work in parallel with the diesel engine. Another option is to put electric motors and a diesel engine in series, so that the electric motors generate all the power and the diesel engine is used to generate electricity for the motors. Using a series hybrid motor in a work machine makes it possible to save up to 60 percent of diesel consumption, according to Immonen (Immonen, 2013), and suggests that a diesel engine sized for the worst case wastes 70 percent of its energy on average. Often the peak performance required from the engine lasts only for 10 to 15 seconds, so electric motors could be used to help the engine momentarily. An additional benefit of hybrid technology is that a machine typically generates less noise due to the smaller diesel engine, increasing the comfort of the machine.

There are a few hybrid work machines currently on the market. For example, Prosilva has a hybrid-powered forest harvester, and Hitachi and Komatsu have hybrid models of their excavators. In the future we are likely to see more hybrids as emission laws become stricter. For example, the United States Environmental Protection Agency (EPA) and the European Union have set increasingly stringent emissions targets since 1996 to improve air quality (New Holland, 2013). Since 2011 machines have had to conform to the Tier 4 A standard, and from 2014 onwards will have to conform to the Tier 4 B standard. In the future emission standards are likely to get even stricter.

The immaturity of hybrid technology might hinder the adoption of hybrid engines. On the other hand, if oil prices rise significantly, hybrid motors might become a more tempting option. As less diesel fuel is required, the operating costs of a machine are lower. When the long lifecycle of the machine is taken into account, the savings from lower fuel consumption are significant. Eco-efficiency is no longer only about taking care of the environment, it also includes making a machine a more tempting option, as it can bring savings.

Another thing to consider is the weight of a machine. This is important, for example, in agricultural machines, where soil compaction is a problem. In the case of a forest harvester, a lighter machine would mean smaller tracks left behind in the stand (Figure 2.13). Hybrid engines do not necessarily lower the weight of a machine, but composite materials could be used instead of metal. Reducing weight also contributes to eco-efficiency, as the less the machine weighs, the less energy it needs to move, resulting in lower diesel consumption.

Figure 2.13: The heavier a tractor or harvester is, the deeper the tracks it leaves, causing soil compaction
Reproduced by permission of John Deere Forestry

From the control system software's viewpoint, eco-efficiency means that more decoupling from the mechanics is required. Control system product lines built today need to take into account that engines and transmissions might change radically in the future. More options for engines may be introduced, and changes to this variation point of product lines are likely. Interfaces to these subsystems should therefore be prepared for large changes. Hybrid motor solutions also increase the amount of control software required and make control algorithms more complex. Control algorithms may also need to keep valves in motion constantly, to avoid the need to use more energy to start movement because of friction. In an extreme case, energy saving might even require architectural changes, to allow shut-down of features that are not needed all the time.

The use of smaller diesel engines might lead to a shortage of electricity on board, so controllers should save energy whenever possible. In practice this might mean that parts of the system need to shut down to conserve energy, and be woken only when they are needed. For example, in the control loop of a controller the processor might be shut down to conserve energy during the idle time of the loop instead of running a housekeeping task. Energy-saving approaches used in the cellphone domain may also prove beneficial in the work machine domain.

Information Security

According to a recent study (Eloranta et al, 2013b) security is seen as the most important issue in work machines in the next five years, although currently it is in the bottom of the top ten important quality issues in machine control systems. These results are confirmed by further research in a more extensive but unpublished study from the same authors. However there has been lots of hype around security or cyber security in automation and process control systems since the Stuxnet worm became public (McMillan, 2010). Recent Finnish research (Tiilikainen & Manner, 2013) found that there are several systems in Finland whose fingerprint matching systems are directly accessible from the Internet, providing information about server applications and the operating system running the system. This knowledge allows an attacker to check whether there are any known vulnerabilities in the system. Such vulnerabilities can pose a serious threat, as these systems can still have factory default passwords and known security issues. Updating these can be a complex task for an inexperienced user, so people tend to leave them in the state they were at acquisition, leaving all vulnerabilities unfixed.

At the time of writing Stuxnet is the best known worm in automation systems (Kushner, 2013). It was probably tailored to attack the Iranian uranium enrichment infrastructure running Siemens' SCADA systems. It infected the control system even when it was separated from the Internet by an air gap (Shirey, 2007) – the worm entered via an infected memory stick. In addition to memory sticks, cellphones that can be charged via USB ports on control systems could possibly spread malware to secure systems behind firewalls, bastions and demilitarized zones.

Stuxnet proves that if an attacker is highly motivated and has enough resources, it is possible to attack industrial systems and to prevent missions being carried out, or to harm the system's owner financially. Motivations for an attack could vary from pure curiosity to financial, ideological or political ones. Any system can be a potential target for an attack, and even one exploitable hole in the system can be enough to enable an attacker to gain access. Systems must therefore be made secure enough to be uneconomical to attack. This is usually achieved by having several layers of barriers, both physical and computer-based, protecting the system like the layers of an onion. If an attacker gets through one layer of security in the 'onion' infrastructure, they must still work out how to penetrate subsequent layers. If the attack requires more resources than are justified by the potential benefit of the attack, they probably won't perpetrate an attack.

Information security is closely tied to safety. Safety emphasizes the prevention of accidental physical harm to the environment. However, data security is at least equally important, especially with increased automation and autonomous functionality. If a malicious attacker wants to wreak havoc, they can for example inject commands or control data into the system, causing it to work in an unexpected way. Safety is targeted against risk of accidents, but security, on the other hand, against deliberate attacks. Security becomes really important when the system has REMOTE ACCESS (page 361) capabilities and remote control of the system is possible.

A contemporary automation system is basically a networked information system (Figure 2.14). Machine control systems have long lifecycles, and updating them is often an operation that must be preplanned. For example, power plants cannot be shut down unless there is a reserve power plant to take care of the power supply. Similarly, if a mobile work machine is updated, it must be done while the system is not in use. If there is a known vulnerability in the system, it may be that it cannot be fixed because the system cannot be taken out of service for an update. Long lifecycles also mean that attackers have plenty of time to find vulnerabilities in systems and a considerable time to use them.

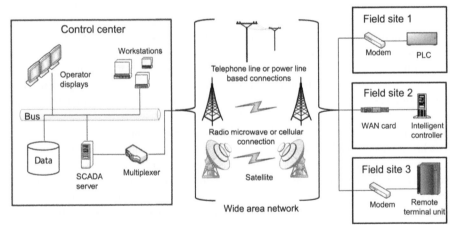

Figure 2.14: An example of several automation systems connected to a
control room via the Internet

Adapted from (Stouffer, 2005)

Information security must also be maintained over the whole lifecycle of a system. This includes the design and building/manufacturing phases of the system, right through to decommissioning. All sensitive data must be destroyed, and unused operator profiles and accounts must be closed. Access rights to any data should be up to date and all storage hardware should be destroyed safely. In the design phase, no sensitive information about the system architecture should be available to people who could attack before the system is fully secured.

Security can be preplanned in automation systems, as they are carefully designed and documented compared to the anarchistic nature of the Internet. It also helps that systems can often use at least some degree of physical security, such as locked doors protecting the control system hardware. Even if automation systems will only be updated on a cycle of several decades, the world surrounding them can change greatly. The servers collecting data remotely from machines, the office networks and so on have much shorter lifecycles. For example, Windows XP, still widely used in offices and control rooms, runs out of extended support in 2014. As XP was released in 2001, its lifetime was only 13 years.

Sometimes new technologies are retrofitted to control systems, such as remote diagnostics connections via cellular wireless, which can open up new attack vectors. As such peripheral systems can be acquired from multiple vendors, the software and hardware environment around the control system may move far from the one envisioned by the system designer. In CAN or other controller area networks, the critical point for access to the control system is the gateway component, if one is present in the system, which couples the Internet to the control system. This is the place that should be hardened against attacks.

Security in control systems differs from traditional Internet security: the objectives of information security are often contradictory to those of control systems. Control systems aim at availability first, then integrity, and finally security, whereas this order of priority is reversed for traditional IT systems. The Internet is also a best-effort based system, where message transfer times are not crucial, so security can be achieved at the application level. For example, a virus scanner may take a relatively long time to scan e-mails, as the transmit time is not important as long as the e-mail gets through. On the other hand, control systems can have strict real-time requirements, where catastrophe may result if a message is not delivered in time, so delays caused by conventional information security are not acceptable. Even with soft real-time requirements the usefulness of a message decreases as a function of time. In some cases real-time requirements are isochronous, and too early a delivery might cause trouble.

Control system design often relies heavily on subcontracting, third-party tools and COTS components. If these are provided by a third party that is not fully trustworthy it can pose a serious threat to cyber-security. Such systems, in order to carry out their function, usually have to be attached directly to the control system. If their provider wants to sniff information or cause disturbance in the systems, it would be very easy to do. Even if the original manufacturer is not malicious, such third-party components can have their own security vulnerabilities that cannot be fixed in the control system to which they are attached. The control system manufacturer therefore has to rely on the third party to provide security fixes. There are even commercial parties who provide tools that can be used to create security breaches in specific widespread systems: Agora SCADA+ by Gleg (GLEG, 2013) is one example.

Security is often breached by social engineering, sloppy processes and other human-related activities. For example, people can give away passwords on the phone to an assertive caller pretending to be a maintenance engineer trying to maintain a mobile machine. The world-famous hacker Kevin Mitnick used social engineering almost exclusively in his efforts to compromise computer systems. Ismail and Zainab (Ismail & Zainab, 2011) show that 94 percent of public libraries assessed in their research had high-level technological security measures, but over half of them were poorly prepared on the organizational side, so a lot of effort should be directed to these. As a primary principle of security, any system should be designed so that people can't inadvertently cause security risks – see the *poka-yoke* principle (Shingo, 1986). For example, systems should be designed so that no-one can insert a memory stick into the control system's USB port accidentally. This could be done by installing USB port locks, using non-standard USB ports, or even by gluing the ports shut if they are not required. If operators repeatedly install games on control room PCs, provide a games console for them to pass the time, and so on.

To minimize threat from the Internet, any system can be separated from it by an air gap, but as can be seen from the case of Stuxnet, this is not enough. Air gaps also prevent effective collection of data from the control system, remote control possibilities and other advantages of software automation. To gain most out of the software in an automation or machine control process, the system should be designed to be remotely accessible to specific parties. This can be done, for example, by clever use of demilitarized zones and VPN connections. A machine control system designer should consult network security specialists and IT personnel to make sure that information security is properly established. There is a large body of literature on security topics: for example, pattern-based approaches were described in (Schumacher et al, 2005) and (Fernandez, 2013). If a system is hard to access or operate by authorized personnel, there is always the risk that they will indulge in shortcuts and other measures that endanger the system's information security.

As tools for security threat countermeasures, the Industrial Automation and Control Systems Security ISA99 committee's work is being utilized by the International Electrotechnical Commission in producing the multi-standard IEC 62443 series. Threat models, such as STRIDE, can be used for classifying security threats (Howard & LeBlanc, 2003). Nowadays many Internet applications use the SSL protocol, which provides authentication and cryptography for messaging, but in many controller area networks the security situation is worse. Some analysis was given in, for example, (Wolf et al, 2004). However, there are mechanisms that can be used to mitigate the threats. For example, a CAN bus with flexible date rate (CAN FD) can be used to implement some security measures on the CAN bus. Some manufacturers have started to protect safety-relevant CAN messages with cryptographic algorithms: the whole message can be encoded, or modifications to the message data can be prevented, using a cipher-based message authentication code (CMAC) value – a kind of a secure checksum. As only the holder of the security key can produce the correct CMAC value, it identifies communication partners.

Security by obscurity, meaning that system security relies on the assumption that some information is only known by trusted parties, should not be trusted as the only countermeasure to attacks. However, there are several cases in which knowledge about systems should be restricted to trusted parties, making the effort for an attacker harder. For example, if the source code of a system is leaked, new vulnerabilities can easily be found. In the case of SCADA systems from several vendors, some security vulnerabilities have been published on Internet sites such as Bugtraq (SecurityFocus, 2010) without prior contact with their vendors. These 'zero-day' vulnerabilities give attackers a head start before vendors have time to fix problems and deliver updates to target systems.

Information security seems to be in its infancy in machine control systems, and it shows in this book. Not many patterns about information security are documented here, as not many security measures were encountered during the pattern mining process for the book. We do present a couple of patterns for improving information security, for example, VARIABLE GUARD (page 208) and THIRD-PARTY SANDBOX (page 355). Nevertheless, it seems that most work on more sophisticated information security is still on the drawing board in machine manufacturing companies. However, the situation is gradually improving, and the importance of the topic has been noted.

CHAPTER

3

Software Architecture and Quality

'To seek the timeless way we must first know the quality without a name. There is a central quality which is the root criterion of life and spirit in a man, a town, a building, or a wilderness. This quality is objective and precise, but it cannot be named.'

Christopher Alexander

Notions of quality may exist in software on many levels. They may refer to end user experience, the ability of the code to do what it is intended to do, different quality aspects of the software architecture, and to a system's capability to fulfil the quality requirements of the customer. In this book we focus mostly on the quality that is related to the software architecture.

In software engineering, architecture is often seen as the key element of the system, enabling high-quality design and implementation. Good software architecture helps the developer to maintain and further develop the code through the lifecycle of the system. When the designer outlines the architecture, they try to balance the trade-offs between different aspects of quality that might affect each other, such as extendability and performance. One of the greatest challenges in designing control system architectures is that the designer must pay attention to fundamentally different quality attributes than in other fields of software. The designer must therefore have a strong sense of quality in this domain in order to create system architectures that stand the test of time.

3.1   What is Quality?

Not many words, used so casually in everyday language, have raised such profound philosophical questions as the word 'quality'. We all prefer good-quality clothes and high-quality entertainment: every layman has an intrinsic sense of quality. Still, many philosophers have tried hard to define this word, and there are whole metaphysical systems defining the concept. Most people agree that quality can be perceived as subjective, and to some degree objective. In this book we define quality in machine control system design such that the design allows the operator to feel comfortable with the machine, the machine can be used to generate revenue, and has low production and maintenance costs. In addition, quality enables the customer to obtain only the features they need with the least possible investment and without unnecessary functionality. All this should be achieved while taking environmental and ethical values into account.

From the perspective of the machine manufacturer, quality manifests itself as a solid system that is easy to sell and to evolve to meet ever-changing customer requirements. These objectives are often achieved through software architecture. Architecture is usually seen as a means of taking the quality attributes of the software development process into account: the architecture is dictated by quality requirements rather than functional ones (Kazman & Bass, 1994). This book is mainly about describing architectural solutions that provide good quality design. In order to understand these patterns better, we should dig into quality more deeply.

Patterns as a concept have strong ties with the concept of quality. At the root of the whole patterns movement, in *The Timeless Way of Building*, Christopher Alexander presented the concept of the *quality without a name* (QWAN) (Alexander, 1979). Alexander says that the notion of subjectivity of quality arises because people can't describe any single, solid basis for the difference between good and bad buildings, implying that there is no objective difference between them, regardless of the fact that all people can experience the difference. He claims that this is because the single central quality that makes the difference cannot be named – it is too fundamental and difficult to describe, as any attempt to define it cannot capture its essence. So it's better to call it just the 'quality without a name'. It can be postulated that things that embody the quality without a name satisfy some deeply rooted psychological need within all human beings. For example, Alexander's LIGHT FROM TWO SIDES pattern states that people feel uneasy when they cannot see someone's face if the light is only coming from behind the other person. So it is sensible to have light sources, usually windows, on two sides of a room.

Obviously machine control software does not fulfil the same kind of basic human needs as houses do, but we feel that some kind of QWAN is achievable in such systems.

There are differences, however. In building architecture, people dwell inside the building and directly interact with the structure. The inhabitants should feel that the buildings support them and are comfortable. In software, however, the architecture is unseen by the end user, as their interaction is carried out via the user interface. The user should not feel frustrated when using the software. This is usually achieved when the software can accurately match the mental model of the user. For the developer, however, the architecture makes all the difference. The developer feels less cognitive stress if they do not have to push their limits in understanding the code when requested to implement new features or fix errors. Good structure and sensible modularization help the developer to focus and direct effort in the right place. Over-verbose code causes problems: people have limits to how much they can keep in their minds simultaneously. So short and structured code feels beautiful and has QWAN in it.

In Alexander's world, the liveliness comes from the organic growth and evolution of buildings. Every inhabitant can modify a building and the site to suit their needs. If the codebase is extended with new features and unplanned changes are made, this uninhibited organic growth leads to problems, as the software does not have any natural bounds. Uncontrolled changes to code tends to lead to 'spaghetti code' without a clear structure that will be hard to understand for a developer. Modifying this kind of code is stressful, as one cannot be sure what will work and whether new features will not break anything. However, a system can be evolved by making small changes gradually, thus building the system in organic way. This contrasts with heavy pre-planning and up-front design. But then the architecture needs to be thought out every time when making design decisions.

Robert M. Pirsig, in *Zen and The Art of Motorcycle Maintenance*, claims that quality cannot be defined, as it precedes any intellectual construction of itself (Pirsig, 1974). So quality is a very real property of all things, but is not subjective or objective, but rather something that lies outside of this duality. Pirsig proceeds to suggest that there are dynamic quality patterns and static quality patterns. Dynamic quality is perceived when something new and good is experienced, while static quality patterns exhibit the properties of quality that can be defined. Static quality patterns come to life when dynamic quality patterns are analyzed afterwards. When analyzing a new phenomena, it is possible to determine which of the static qualities contributed to its good quality. Patterns in this book fall into the category of static quality patterns; they are definitions of good solutions for distributed machine control design. In patterns, *forces* define the aspects of quality that the designer would like to improve, while *consequences* are the result – what happened when the pattern is applied. Thus, in a sense, a pattern is a function that transforms the design according to specific quality properties.

3.2   Quality Attributes

Good overall quality in machine control system design means that the system should be usable, extendable, have high performance and so on. So the quality itself has many facets, called *quality attributes*. Quality attributes have been discussed and researched in software engineering for decades. Many different taxonomies and categorizations have been published since. In this book, we focus on the ISO/IEC 9126-1 quality standard (ISO, 2001), which describes a well-known software quality model.

Figure 3.1: A harvester has to cut trees into logs reliably, accurately and efficiently according to operator commands, even in harsh environmental conditions
Reproduced by permission of John Deere Forestry

The model classifies quality as a tree-like structure having six main characteristics. Each of these main characteristics can be subdivided into further characteristics. The main quality characteristics for software are *functionality, reliability, usability, efficiency, maintainability* and *portability*. For example, sub-characteristics for portability are *adaptability, installability, coexistence, replaceability* and *portability compliance*. Each of these can be further divided into quality attributes that are verifiable and measurable in software products. As one can see from this list, many of the special properties of distributed machine control systems presented in *Characteristics of Distributed Control Systems* on page 12 are essentially quality attributes. Other attributes are needed, too. For example, a forest harvester similar to the one in Figure 3.1 has to have an efficient and well-performing system in order to cut trees quickly and accurately into logs of the desired length. This also requires good usability, as the operator has to spend a whole working day operating the machine. High reliability is also required, so that the system is operational whenever needed.

As quality attributes are abstract, a system cannot be described accurately in quality terms. For example, *modifiability* means that the system is designed to be malleable towards anticipated changes. A change that wasn't even dreamed of at the inception of the architecture will prove hard to implement, even if the system stakeholders had originally wished for high modifiability (Kazman & Bass, 1994). To really be quantifiable and verifiable, every quality attribute needs a context. A context defines how the quality attribute should be interpreted. For example, the context can be a development or a usage situation. The ISO standard therefore does not define actual quality attributes, but only gives characterizations of a specific attribute, and does not describe how to measure it in a specific context. Quality attributes vary between projects, and it is up to the people involved to come up with verifiable and measurable metrics of quality.

In real world systems any quality attribute cannot be achieved in isolation (Bass et al, 2003). Trade-offs exist between different quality attributes. For example, if one wishes to improve reliability by replicating parts of the system – see 1+1 REDUNDANCY (page 279) – modifiability may be lost. In addition, the cost of the system rises, and that is not acceptable, even though cost is not an ISO quality attribute per se. Safety is another important aspect of machine control systems that is not a quality attribute. Rather, it is the result of the combination of other quality attributes, such as reliability and efficiency, depending on the context. And of course the software architecture cannot alone provide safety; some functionality is also needed to support it. This also holds for true quality attributes. The system has to have some functionality as 'flesh' around the bones made from quality attributes such as performance and usability. There is also a runtime context for quality attributes in addition to the 'design time' architecture. Naturally, even attributes that exist mainly in the architecture can be ruined by poor implementation. For example, good structural modifiability can be greatly diminished by bad coding conventions.

Quality attributes can be essential to the marketing of a software product, as several of them are visible to end users. They can be used as marketing points, and so are of great interest to the business. For example, Apple phones are known for their good usability. Before Apple brought in their game-changing products, cellphone marketing was driven by the features provided by the phone. Apple invested in usability at the expense of an extensive feature set – this seemed to be the right decision. After the launch of the first iPhone, its usability seemed to attract customers and competitors were forced to catch up. While its competitors worked to improve the usability of their products, Apple had time to develop missing features to make their phone comparable. Thus it is not always easy to say which quality attribute is the most important.

Our patterns affect different facets of quality, described in the consequences part of each pattern. For quick reference we have collected the influences our patterns have on different quality attributes into a single table in Appendix A.

3.3   Measuring Quality

Quality has many different manifestations, and some of these can be very subjective. This often makes it hard to measure quality objectively. However, it is possible to devise metrics for some aspects of quality. One typical way to measure the quality of software is to count the detected defects in the product. Bugs are usually reported by the end user. This is an easily quantifiable variable, but it does not take into account the gravity of bugs. So it would be more useful to measure the effort spent on fixing bugs. The bug count is of course a critical issue in software development, as bugs can render functionalities unusable, cause safety and security problems and impair the overall usability of the software. However, a single ill-placed bug that causes system failure may cost millions, and can cause severe environmental damage. In extreme cases such bugs may even be fatal. So the severity of a bug has to be taken into account when measuring software quality in terms of defects. Serious bugs usually indicate that there are problems in the software development process, so root cause analysis for bugs should be carried out to weed out sloppy practices in the process.

There are other measurable aspects of quality than functionality. For example, *usability* is an important property that can be measured empirically by conducting usability studies (Nielsen, 1994a). These studies can provide concrete ideas to enhance usability and the user experience. Efficiency is usually relatively easy to measure, as in real-time systems it boils down to the question of whether the system can perform its tasks in a given time. However, tests to measure this must be carefully designed, to guarantee that the time limits can be accomplished under all circumstances the system may encounter. This comes back to the question of software bugs – does the system always function as intended?

Functional quality is closely allied with usability, but also implies measuring how many of the requirements are actually implemented in the product. Reliability can be measured as the system's availability, for example measured as *mission capable rate*, or the percentage of system downtime versus system uptime. Downtime can be further divided into planned and unplanned downtime. Planned downtime in the machine control domain includes pre-planned updates, machine maintenance and so on. Unplanned downtime includes machine malfunction and control system failures.

Some aspects of quality are more difficult to measure, for example maintainability and portability. Measuring them needs a thorough analysis of the source code, and still some prophecy is needed. McCabe's Cyclomatic Complexity (McCabe, 1976), Cohesion, Coupling (Stevens et al, 1974) and five different function point standards (ISO, 2011a; ISO, 2008; ISO, 2009; ISO, 2002; ISO, 2005) are usually used to measure maintainability. In addition, many scenario-based architecture evaluation methods, such as ATAM (Kazman et al, 2000) try to identify the relevant modifiability scenarios that the architecture might need to support in the future, to find out how maintainable and modifiable a system is.

Sometimes it may be possible to analyze modifiability reliably only after modifications are made to the source code. Some research results (Sjoberg et al, 2013) indicate that commonly used 'bad smells' and metrics of maintainability do not correlate with the actual maintenance effort. Sjoberg suggests that the only reliable metric for maintenance effort is lines of code. This reflects the fact that some aspects of quality are really elusive and hard to assess.

Quality is also one of the key factors in project management, the others being *resources*, *time* and *scope*. Resources here means the number of people working on the project.

Time defines the temporal dimension of the project – when the project should deliver something – while scope means the features the delivered product should have. Scope is closely knit with quality, which in this context means the perceived user experience – the external quality of the system. If project management fails to make the right decisions when the project is in crisis, people tend to sacrifice quality. This is mainly because thorough testing is easy to omit when under time pressure, and degraded quality is difficult to detect until a product is delivered. Early feedback from end users helps to detect the absence of critical quality properties. Compromising quality in favor of the project schedule can manifest in bugs or technical debt, and technical debt leads in the end to allocating more time to refactoring in the future.

3.4   External Quality and Internal Quality

In addition to quality attributes, the quality of a software product can be divided into external and internal quality. External quality represents the end user's view of the software, usually the functionality and the user interface, and internal quality the developer's view – the quality on the source code level. Both these sides of quality are important, and it is usually a business decision as to which should be emphasized. Internal and external qualities are mentioned in *Code Complete* by Steve McConnell (McConnell, 2004), where quality attributes are divided into two categories. Internal quality consists of *correctness*, *usability*, *efficiency*, *reliability*, *integrity*, *adaptability*, *accuracy* and *robustness*. External quality consists of *maintainability*, *flexibility*, *portability*, *reusability*, *readability*, *testability* and *understandability*. However, it is admitted that this division is not a clear-cut one, as many attributes affect both sides. For example, to achieve efficiency through optimizations, one often has to sacrifice portability.

External quality is in essence how the end user *feels* about the product. As a bare minimum, good external quality requires the system to function as the user expects and demonstrate no bugs that affect the user experience. Usability forms a large portion of external quality, as for the user the user interface *is* the software. The end user is not interested in the beautiful structure of the software or its architectural patterns – the design and inner workings of the system are invisible, or at least should be. In a sense, the external quality is embodied in what the system *does*.

To have correct functionality coupled with good usability, it is important to invest a reasonable amount of time in determining the end user's mental model of the tasks at hand. This implies that the system designer and developer should be able to think in the end user's terms. This may be hard if the developers have no domain experience. In business terms, if a product has good external quality, it will have users – that is, customers who are willing to buy the product. Investing in external quality therefore provides revenue for the company. In evolving software, external quality should be given greatest emphasis in the early stages of development. This will give customers a functional product early on, and their feedback can be used to guide evolution of the software.

There is also internal quality – the developer's and designer's feeling of product quality. Internal quality can be improved by coding conventions, good design and refinement of the system's architecture. It manifests itself in the system structure and all those things the system *is*. Development costs can be reduced in the long term by an architecture that is understandable and has well-designed extension mechanisms, but in the short term creating that architecture and improving internal quality generates costs. New features are easier to add and bugs are easier to find and fix when the software architecture is in good shape. Pre-planning is essential when designing a software architecture. However, even the best architecture cannot systematically support new features that weren't thought of at the planning stage. If the architecture supports all emergent requirements, it is usually more of a fluke than due to the designer's merit. Continuous refactoring of the architecture is therefore essentially investing in the well-being of the software development team. It has its price, however. Even if a suitable architecture can save cost by cutting down lead times for new features by making them easy to integrate into the system, planning and refactoring takes time and thus can be expensive.

Internal quality affects only the people who are directly involved with the development. This is usually small compared to the number of end users, so one would be tempted to emphasize external quality at the expense of internal quality. However, the importance of good internal quality grows when the lifecycle of the software is extended or the software is scaled. As work machines have long lifecycles, their software architecture should have good internal quality. It could be said that machine control systems are the last stand of traditional software architecture – many other kinds of software systems today focus more on external quality, as their short lifecycles allow it.

As far as we know there is only one architectural style that tries to combine internal and external quality as one. DCI (Data, Context, Interactions) architecture is based on capturing the user's mental model in the structures of the architecture. For more information on DCI, see (Coplien & Bjørnvig, 2010).

Omitting internal quality over time is referred to as *taking on technical debt* (Cunningham, 1992). If the system has too much technical debt, it will become almost impossible for the developers to implement new features or fix bugs. The longer the debt remains unpaid, the more complexity the system structure gains and the more challenging the implementation becomes. If the system architecture has deteriorated to this degree, the best option is usually to wipe the slate clean and make a fresh start. Due to the very long lifecycles of machine control software, architecture, as a vessel for conveying better internal quality, has an accentuated meaning. Architectural evaluations, such as ATAM (Kazman et al, 2000) or DCAR (Decision-Centric Architecture Reviews, van Heesch et al, 2014) can be a valuable tool for locating problems in architectural quality.

CHAPTER

4

About Patterns

'You look at where you're going and where you are and it never makes sense, but then you look back at where you've been and a pattern seems to emerge.'

Robert M. Pirsig, 'Zen and the Art of Motorcycle Maintenance'

As Robert M. Pirsig states in his famous book, *Zen and the Art of Motorcycle Maintenance* (Pirsig, 1974), it is hard to see patterns of behavior when you are involved with the activity at hand, but afterwards you can probably recognize patterns that emerged during the activity. The same idea is also identified by Snowden et al. in their Cynefin Framework for leaders' decision-making – in a complex environment causality can only been seen in retrospect. In such an environment, a leader should not impose a course of action, but patiently allow the right path to reveal itself (Snowden & Boone, 2007). This kind of environment is sometimes called a *domain of emergence*, as the environment is in constant change.

In a domain of emergence, patterns can be found when an activity is observed from the outside for long enough. Similarly, design patterns emerge in practice and are discovered – they are not invented. Christopher Alexander talks about 'patterns of events' – events that keep occurring in a specific place. Each building and each town is ultimately made out of these patterns (Alexander, 1979). Similarly, software architectures of control systems enable specific things to happen in the system. This book describes patterns for such software architectures. However, before diving into the patterns themselves, we need to take a deeper look at what patterns really are, how they work together, and how they are discovered and presented in this book.

4.1   Patterns – What are They?

To get the most out of the contents of this book, it is crucial to understand what patterns are. This section gives a short introduction to the basic concepts of patterns. If you want a more detailed description of the subject, a lot has been written about patterns. Well-known examples in the domain of software patterns include a beginner's introduction to patterns, *Pattern-Oriented Software Architecture For Dummies* by Robert Hanmer (Hanmer, 2013) and the long-running series of *Pattern-Oriented Software Architecture* (POSA) and *Pattern Languages of Program Design* (PLoPD) books.

Patterns, as a concept, have a history originating from the architecture of buildings and the works of Christopher Alexander. A pattern is in essence a design solution to a recurring problem in a specific context. The seminal works in patterns are Alexander's *A Pattern Language* (Alexander et al, 1977) and *The Timeless Way of Building* (Alexander, 1979). Christopher Alexander is an architect who is noted for his work on architectural theory. These include the idea of design patterns, which have been successfully adopted in other fields of expertise as well.

Patterns as a concept gained momentum in software engineering in the late 1980s when they were introduced at OOPSLA '87 (Kent & Cunningham, 1987) and have been actively pursued since. Pattern-oriented conferences have been organized on every continent except Antarctica. These conferences are the *Pattern Languages of Programs* (PLoP) series, and many of them are organized annually.

Every pattern is a solution to a specific design problem. To ensure the validity of a solution, it has to be found in practice several times. We have followed the original rule that three independent instances should be observed before declaring something as a recurring solution, a pattern. A problem and its solution alone are not enough to describe an effective design. Specific problems only arise in a specific context where the solution can be applied. Thus, every pattern includes its context – *where* the proposed solution is recommended.

A more elaborate definition of a pattern can be found from Alexander's *The Timeless Way of Building* (Alexander, 1979, p. 247), which states that '*Each pattern is a three-part rule, which expresses a relation between a certain context, a problem, and a solution. A pattern is at the same time a thing, which happens in the world, and the rule which tells us how to create that thing, and when we must create it. It is both a process and a thing; both a description of a thing which is alive, and a description of the process which will generate that thing.'*

This definition adds the notion that patterns contain their own rationale – *when* and *why* to apply a pattern. It also further defines patterns as a description of the form, the functionality of the form, and the process to build it. The rationale for a pattern includes *forces*. Forces are the issues that a designer must take into consideration when applying the pattern. They can be quality attributes the designer should improve, and they can also be trade-offs between several quality properties. There can be a conflict between different interests, and the designer has to balance these forces. The solution presented by a pattern should give the designer all the necessary information to make a decision about whether to apply a pattern. Thus, a pattern is not just a 'how-to' or a recipe, it should give the user a high-level solution and explain why to use the pattern; it should not meddle with details of implementation, but rather leave them open, as they typically vary depending on the situation.

A pattern describes a design in terms of a function that has a specific form that supports the function. For example, in building architecture, a library is a building that has a single purpose: to provide books, magazines, records and such material to the public to read, listen to and borrow. In the city of Tampere in Finland there is a famous library building, Metso ('wood grouse'), whose shape viewed from above is similar to the silhouette of a grouse. The building was designed by renowned architects Raili and Reima Pietilä. It has small intimate rooms for people to read books and magazines in a peaceful environment. It also has small partially enclosed spaces for people to listen to records via headphones. These spaces can be seen as an instance of the ALCOVE pattern from *A Pattern Language* (Alexander et al, 1977).

Figure 4.1: The main hall of the Metso library on the left and a reading space on the right

The main hall is a large open space filled with organized shelves of books ready to be loaned and returned – see Figure 4.1. The building's interior design and its form – its architecture – therefore closely follows its intended function – to be a library. The building would serve other purposes poorly, such as a living space, as it has so much space that it would be inconvenient to live in, and lacks facilities for basic human needs, such as cooking and bathing. In an analogous way, our patterns define functions characteristic of distributed machine control systems. These functions generate the form – the software architecture – of such a system. We therefore sometimes refer to our patterns as *generative* patterns. In turn, the form has to support the function. For example, ONE TO MANY (page 131) defines a messaging function whose implementation has the form of an interconnecting message bus. The form is of course important, and it is a part of what people call the software architecture, but actually its function is the key point here. The pattern captures both the function and the form, along with a rationale of why and when to apply it.

As can be seen from the analogy with buildings, patterns are a different concept than architectural *styles*. Architectural styles describe how things look, so they deal mostly with appearances. They are also strongly influenced by technology and time, and in addition their quality is more in the eye of the beholder. In buildings, the available set of construction techniques has an impact on how a building will look: for example, the invention of the pointed arch separates gothic designs from Romanesque buildings. In the same vein, a software architectural style is a method of construction with a set of notable features that characterize the style. For example, a microkernel is a well-known example of an architectural style geared to building operating systems. Operating systems could also be built, for example, by using a monolithic kernel design, but in practice most operating systems are hybrids of these two extremes, as both approaches have their own benefits and downsides.

Patterns focus more on function, not appearance or style. Arguably, patterns are more of a timeless concept, independent of the technology. Thus, patterns are the same regardless of the architectural style – a good gothic church design will still have the same idea of HOLY GROUND as a Romanesque church. The HOLY GROUND pattern described in *A Pattern Language* (Alexander et al, 1977) suggests separating the 'inner sanctum' from the commonplace ground by a series of precincts, each smaller and more sacred than the previous one. In a church people will enter from the churchyard into the nave and towards the altar. Only the priest is allowed to access the tabernacle, which is the most sacred place in a church.

It is also crucial to understand that patterns will work on the level of *form*, not in the details of structure. A pattern does not give exact details of implementation. For example, in the case of the Metso library, the outer walls of reading alcoves may be made of granite and the interior of concrete. On the other hand, the same idea of an ALCOVE may manifest itself in a old wooden house, where a wood-lined alcove is used for a private corner for the owner. In these cases, the material used in the walls – the structure – is completely different, but the form is the same. Similarly, our patterns do not provide code examples, as those are on the level of structure. There are however a few code examples in this book, but they are used to illustrate the form and the solution, not to provide code that can be used as such.

Of course there are also recurring solutions on the level of structure. The well-known practices of software structure are often called *idioms,* and provide hints and tips on how to achieve a specific result with the chosen programming language. For example, how the concept of a loop can be implemented varies between different programming languages. In C++ a loop can be done with `for` and `while` directives, different solutions suited to slightly different problems. However, a loop is pure structure, as it does not define the behavior that should be repeated in the loop. Such structures also can be used in various domains, whereas patterns work at the level of the domain itself. For example, SUPER LOOP (Pont, 2001) is a pattern that has the structure of a loop, but which also defines that, in a simple embedded control, this loop can be populated with tasks that the controller should carry out.

'Pattern' is relatively overloaded term, too. It has been used freely by different authors and the term has caused a lot of confusion. A remarkable portion of pattern literature may have the properties of patterns on the surface level: a pattern format has been used, has recurrence, and the solutions solve a specific problem in a context. Still, many of them deal with structure, not form. For example, the renowned book *Design Patterns: Elements of Reusable Object-Oriented Software* (Gamma et al, 1994) mainly provides detailed descriptions of structure to solve specific problems that arise in object-oriented design in the context of specific programming languages. Of course such descriptions of structure are also valuable, but they are not *generative* in nature – applying the patterns alone does not build a meaningful whole.

Patterns also provide a vocabulary of concepts that can be shared amongst people. For example, everyone who has the shared experience of reading this book, or of designing distributed machine control systems, can refer to a specific known solution with a common name, for example 1+1 REDUNDANCY (page 279). Now everyone who is familiar with this name can know at once what kind of structure and behavior someone is referring to without a lengthy explanation. This can also be seen in reverse: patterns form a language with whose grammar you have to be familiar in order to understand a specific design. Patterns organized as a *pattern language* help to solve problems when applied together in the design of large systems.

4.2   From Patterns to a Pattern Language

Design challenges are usually so large and complex that a pattern can be rarely used in isolation to solve them. A design challenge is best divided into smaller problems, and several patterns have to be used to successfully solve them. Therefore there must be some kind of structure to guide the designer in selecting patterns in a sensible order to tackle the design challenge at hand.

Patterns support this if they are organized into a *pattern language.* A pattern language is a concept that also originates from the works of Christopher Alexander (Alexander et al, 1977), guiding the designer in building a coherent whole using patterns as building blocks. Pattern languages have been published in other domains too, for example the organizational pattern language by Coplien and Harrison (Coplien & Harrison, 2004).

A pattern language is similar to a natural language: it has its own vocabulary, syntax and grammar. The vocabulary of a pattern language consists of a set of patterns. Analogously to a natural language, a set of words is not enough to communicate ideas – semantically meaningful sentences. Thus the pattern language needs a syntax – that is, a set of rules on how its patterns can be used as part of a greater whole. These rules are documented in the contexts of a pattern, explaining where a pattern can be used.

However, a set of words with a correct syntax is not enough to create meaningful sentences. A pattern enthusiast with no rationale behind their design decision would use patterns without any reasoning. The resulting design would be analogous to Noam Chomsky's famous example sentence in a natural language, '*Colorless green ideas sleep furiously.*' (Chomsky, 1957). The sentence is syntactically correct, but has no meaning semantically. Thus, patterns need a grammar, describing when to use a specific pattern. This is documented in the pattern's forces and its solution, explaining why and when to apply a pattern. If a pattern is not beneficial in the given design, or its trade-offs, for example with complexity and cost, would be too high, the pattern should not be used.

With all these properties, a pattern language manifests a generative grammar, in which there are specific rules if the sequence of words is to form a valid sentence. Pattern-wise, this means that a 'sentence' is a specific design that has been built by using 'words' – patterns in the language – in a specific order. This grammar separates pattern languages from mere pattern collections and pattern sets. In addition to the rationality of the design, the patterns should also support *piecemeal growth* of the architecture. According to (Alexander, 1975), 'piecemeal growth' means building a system gradually by applying the patterns one by one.

A software architecture grows by step-by-step utilization of patterns. Our pattern language starts from a single design decision, the most fundamental decision of them all: should a work machine have control system software at all? This problem is addressed in our CONTROL SYSTEM (page 96) pattern. If a designer chooses to have control system software, it opens a whole new can of worms: the control system architecture will have new problems that need to be solved. From this starting point, the designer should select patterns from the language in a consistent manner. The designer traverses the pattern language, shown as a graph in Figure 4.2, continuously battling new design problems. An arrow in the pattern graph can be read as *refines*. The pattern to which the arrow points refines the pattern from which the arrow originates. Thus, a design can be started from a single pattern, which is applied. This pattern will then form the design, and the designer can consider whether the design should be refined by applying further patterns. Thus many of the patterns are not present in every design, as the designer will apply only those patterns that are sensible in the context of the current design challenge.

For example, in Figure 4.2 the designer can choose to apply the CONTROL SYSTEM pattern, implementing it with a single node running a monolithic control application, then face the problem that the system operator needs to interact with the application, applying HUMAN–MACHINE INTERFACE (page 313). A screen and push buttons are introduced to

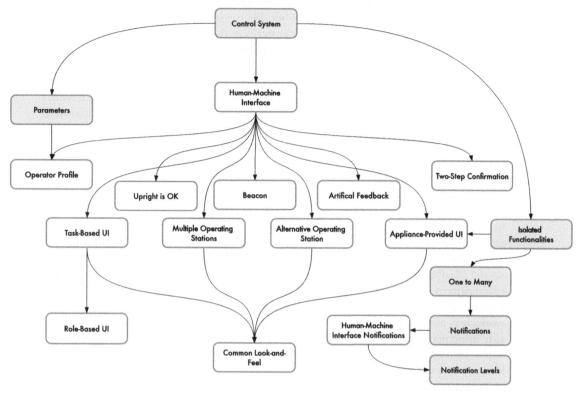

Figure 4.2: An excerpt from the pattern language presented in this book.
The full graph of the language can be seen on the companion website.

the system design. Now happy with the results, they decide that no further patterns need to be applied. However, when the system is used and new uses for it are introduced, ISO-LATED FUNCTIONALITIES (page 110) must be applied to tackle problems with long wiring between controller and sensors. Similarly, in *Organizational Patterns* (Coplien & Harrison, 2004), one has to have a COMMUNITY OF TRUST as a foundation of a functional organization. From this foundation, it is possible to apply further patterns to make a team more efficient. You can find examples of how our patterns are applied in Chapter 20, *Applying Patterns*.

In addition to refining other designs, some patterns can also be related to each other in other ways. Some are alternative solutions to similar problems that have different forces and perhaps different contexts. Thus they work like synonyms in a sentence. However, the related patterns aren't the same pattern, but they have slightly differing purposes. Similarly, changing a word to a similar word in a sentence can slightly change the overall meaning. One example of this in the patterns in this book is the relationship between

VECTOR CLOCK FOR MESSAGES (page 149) and GLOBAL TIME (page 124) – they both help with distributed system synchronization, but differ vastly in solution and forces.

Some of our patterns can utilize other patterns in their solution. Of course any other solution can be used if it provides the same function as the referenced pattern. In some cases a design problem is such that it can only be solved after a specific combination of patterns is applied; in this case the other patterns are mentioned in the context section of the pattern. One example of this could be HMI NOTIFICATIONS (page 340), which refines NOTIFICATIONS (page 156) by specifying that some NOTIFICATIONS should be shown to the user. However, the HUMAN–MACHINE INTERFACE (page 313) pattern must be applied to provide somewhere to display HMI notifications. Any sensible solution then needs both patterns to be applied, at least to some degree. This scheme is closely related to HMI NOTIFICATIONS using HUMAN–MACHINE INTERFACE in its solution, but the relationship is stronger.

The pattern language in this book is targeted at problems in distributed machine control systems. It is a vast domain, and the 80 patterns published in this language cannot tackle all the problems that can be encountered while designing such systems. We refer to many other works that cross to our domain, such as fault-tolerance (Hanmer, 2007) and several PLoP conference proceedings, where associated topics have been covered. Referenced patterns are part of our pattern language and should also be a part of the designer's toolbox, even though they are not shown in the pattern language graph. These other works may also include patterns that we haven't witnessed in our domain, so might provide more material than is needed in machine control system design. Each pattern describes other patterns that are related to the solution. You should check them, as they may lead you to a wider range of literature.

Our pattern language is organized into sublanguages to help you focus on the most interesting patterns. For example, if you are designing a system that does not have an operator, you can give the patterns in the HMI branch less attention. Similarly, if the platform used has ample computing resources, the 'scarce resources' sublanguage can be ignored altogether. It is important to bear in mind that we have documented only the most relevant patterns, so you may also have to explore other sources of information. For example, 1+1 REDUNDANCY (page 279) is the commonest redundancy solution in distributed machine control systems, but plenty of other redundancy solutions are documented elsewhere, such as TRIPLE MODULAR REDUNDANCY in (Douglass, 2002).

4.3   The Story of the Patterns in this Book

The patterns you will find here have come a long way from their first encounter to their description here. Each of the patterns was encountered independently in real world systems at least three times. All the patterns are deeply rooted in industrial practice. In other words, patterns are not invented – they emerge in practice and are discovered. In this section we will explain how the patterns were identified and refined. The process is also partially described by (Leppänen et al, 2009).

The pattern collection started in 2008 in a project called 'Sulake', which was funded by Tekes, the Finnish funding agency for technology and innovation. Between 2008 and 2010 the authors carried out approximately twenty software architecture evaluations, using a method similar to the *architecture trade-off analysis method*, ATAM (Kazman et al, 2000). The evaluations were carried out in companies manufacturing mobile work machines. In these software architecture evaluations we had an opportunity to examine the architectures of various machine control systems. The companies agreed to us collecting architecture solutions used in the systems during the evaluation sessions and documenting them as patterns. However, this meant that we had to promise not to publish solutions as such, as they could be trade secrets, so code examples from the actual products are not presented. The examples here are still similar to real-world systems, but they are not excerpts from the code of the actual systems, but rather written by the authors to demonstrate the design. Two and half year's work resulted in a report (Eloranta et al, 2010) that contained the first versions of the patterns and the pattern language.

Soon after the release of the report it became clear that the work was not finished, so it continued in another Tekes project called 'Sulava'. One of the authors worked in the domain for a while and spotted many solutions that had eluded our first attempt to create a pattern language. As the authors received feedback on the report from practitioners, colleagues, researchers and pattern enthusiasts, it seemed that radical changes were still needed, so we continued our pattern collection efforts until 2013. During this stage, for example, patterns for the HUMAN–MACHINE INTERFACE were added to the language. In the technical report (Eloranta et al, 2010) we used so-called *canonical form* (Portland, 2003) to document the patterns, but we were not happy with the format, as separate sections disrupted the flow of a story. We therefore decided to move to an adaptation of Alexandrian form (Portland, 2011) to make the text flow more smoothly – see *The Pattern Format Used in this Book* on page 90.

In the beginning we used *how to* style problems in Alexandrian form. However, we soon realized that problem statements in the patterns were like 'How to do the solution?', then the pattern explained the solution; the problem statement wasn't very informative if you didn't know the solution. So we removed the *how to* part from the problem statement. The result of this wasn't very satisfactory either, as now the problem statements sounded more like requirements: 'Because of X, there should be the solution', where X was the key driver for the solution. We noticed that it is surprisingly hard to come up with a good problem statement that really tackles the root cause for applying a pattern. Furthermore, the root cause should also be common to all instances in which the pattern was identified in industry. Currently the problem statement tries to describe the root cause for applying the solution, but we have sometimes failed to find the root cause. While the problem statements of some of the patterns deal with the root cause, there still are some patterns where it remains undiscovered. The 'star rating' of the patterns reflects this issue.

Our patterns are grounded in practice and industry. The initial set of patterns was collected during architecture evaluation sessions. In an architecture review, we identified and documented the most significant architecture decisions from the system. Harrison (Harrion et al, 2007) states that applying a pattern is essentially an architecture decision. The other way around, it means that each architecture decision identified from the design is potentially a pattern. The list of architecture decisions elicited during its evaluation therefore provided us with an initial set of pattern candidates. During the evaluation sessions all kind of solutions were discussed and new alternatives elicited, and sometimes recorded as pattern candidates. We did this by having one person whose only task was to write down pattern candidates on a wiki page. Once a pattern candidate had been identified three times, it was promoted to a pattern idea. At this stage an initial patlet was written and a dedicated wiki page created for the pattern: all notes relating to the pattern idea were moved to this wiki page.

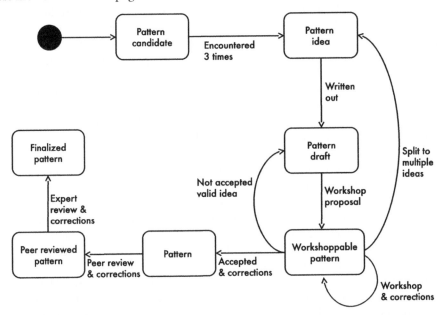

Figure 4.3: The pattern-writing process

Figure 4.3 illustrates the lifecycle of a pattern during the pattern mining process. The pattern writing process has evolved over the years, and was originally different than the one presented in the figure, which shows the process for writing the final versions of the patterns in this book. First the pattern candidate is identified. This can be done in three ways: in a software architecture evaluation, from literature, or by discussion with a domain expert. Once a candidate is identified from three independent sources, it is promoted to a pattern idea and the first version of the patlet – a problem–solution pair – is written. The first draft of the pattern is then written. Each of the pattern drafts has been workshopped at least once, either at one of the PLoP conferences (see Hillside Group, 2013) or in an internal workshop. See (Gabriel, 2002) for more information on writer's workshops.

After the first workshop four things can happen. If the quality of the pattern is high enough it might be accepted for peer review. For this, the author of the pattern must make minor corrections to the pattern based on feedback from the workshop. A pattern can also be rejected by the workshop if the idea was not elaborated correctly in its draft. In this case, the author writes a new draft for a subsequent workshop, probably from scratch. In the third case, the idea is captured correctly in the pattern, but the quality of the first draft is too low for the workshop to accept the pattern. In this case, the author makes corrections to the pattern and subsequent workshops are arranged. A fourth option is that the workshop discovers that the pattern idea was not focused enough, perhaps with multiple patterns written as one. In this case the pattern is split into multiple ideas and these are rewritten as separate pattern drafts. For example, ONE TO MANY (page 131) and HIGH-LEVEL PROTOCOL (page 137) were originally written as a single pattern called MESSAGE BUS (Leppänen, 2013). However, the pattern was long and confusing, so after a workshop at VikingPLoP 2013 it was split into two patterns.

After a pattern was accepted by the workshop and corrected, it was peer reviewed by another author, who could suggest improvements to the pattern. As the authors work in the academic world, we wanted to make sure that our patterns really have industrial relevance. Thus, after peer-review, patterns were sent to software architects working in industry for review, who made sure that the patterns were captured correctly. Sometimes the description of the implementation techniques were also refined based on the architect's comments. During this process our patterns were written in a way that prevented implementation details being traced back to any specific company and solution. For example, known usages come from the real systems, but may not be from the system mentioned in the example. Overall, the process by which our patterns were collected and refined resembles the grounded theory-based process described in (Hentrich et al, 2013).

The process of collecting and writing our pattern language took almost six years. During this period intermediate versions of some of the patterns were published in the proceedings of various PLoP conferences. The progress we have made is visible in those conference proceedings. Simultaneously with the pattern-writing process, we have been collecting more knowledge on the domain and on patterns. We have visited dozens of companies in Finland and Europe and interviewed experts in this domain. Software architects, developers, managers and so on gave invaluable feedback. These interviews have provided us with insights into many of the solutions presented in the patterns, and sometimes resulted in new patterns as more and more candidates were seen in practice. Based on the interviews, the names of some of the patterns were also changed, and aliases were identified.

Our approach, that a pattern needs to be identified three times in practice independently, of course means that all the newest solutions are ruled out, as they are not yet widespread. This might sound alarming, but it has at least one benefit: the newest solutions used in the domain may not yet have matured enough to be widely used, so the patterns really are solutions that are approved in practice. There are also patterns presented here that have been documented already. For example, HEARTBEAT (page 120) has been documented several times by several authors, for example (Hanmer, 2007). However, we wanted to document these patterns from the perspective of control systems, as they are central solutions in this domain. We also wanted to ensure that our pattern language contains most of the essential solutions for machine control systems.

To summarize, the patterns have come a long way to reach this book and you. We hope that you enjoy reading and using them as much as we enjoyed writing them. However, a pattern language is never complete – many open issues and undocumented patterns remain as new innovations emerge. We expect this work to continue and the pattern language to start living a life of its own. We hope that you will put these patterns to daily use and modify and update them. If you encounter new patterns, hopefully you will document them and share them with the community by submitting them to one of the PLoP conferences. In this way the pattern language can grow as new patterns complete it. We also hope that people will share their experiences with the patterns and their completions to the language in one way or another.

4.4   The Pattern Format Used in this Book

All the patterns in this book are presented using the same format for the sake of clarity and convenience. The pattern format used is a mixture of Alexandrian form (Portland, 2011) and canonical form (Portland, 2003). We have experimented with different pattern formats throughout the writing process, and ended up with this format as it seems to fit our patterns best. The pattern format used has the same parts as the canonical form: name, aliases, context, problem, forces, solution, related patterns, consequences and a known use. We have dropped the resulting context from canonical form as it breaks the flow of straight prose, and the next pattern in the language describes the resulting context in its context part anyway.

Patterns are always referred by placing the pattern name in SMALL CAPS. If the pattern is not from this book, the pattern name is also accompanied with a reference to the original source.

We have not used named sections in the patterns, as this would also break the flow. Instead we have used other ways to hint that a section changes. Each of the patterns has a unique name. These names have been introduced by practitioners during pattern interviews or architecture evaluations. However, some of the patterns we discovered did not have consistent names among practitioners, so we have had to name them. We have tried to select pattern names that make the patterns easy to remember. Sometimes practitioners had multiple names for a single pattern – the name given to a single pattern varied from company to company. For example, VARIABLE MANAGER (page 201) has been called a shared data repository, process image and so on depending on the company. In these cases we have selected the most common name and given other names as the 'also known as' part of the pattern description.

The essence of the problem and the heart of the solution are presented in **bold** typeface. This convention makes it possible to browse through the book to find a suitable pattern for the problem at hand just by reading the parts of the pattern that are presented in bold. The purpose of this formatting is to allow you to grasp and adopt the whole pattern language quickly. There are 80 patterns in the language, so reading the whole language would take hours. However, our format allows you to get the big picture before diving into the details of each pattern. Patlets of all patterns in the language are shown in Appendix B.

Every pattern in this book is accompanied by at least two pictures: an icon and a technical illustration. The icons might be related to the core of the solution or, in some cases, they might be more light-hearted and inspired by the name of the pattern. The icons are a visual aid to help you remember the patterns better, while the technical illustrations visualize and concretize the solution. These technical illustrations are hand-drawn on purpose. They are intentionally not ready-made UML diagrams that you should follow blindly, but merely visualize the basic idea of the solution so that it can be adapted to your design and to suit your needs.

The patterns begin by describing the context: the design situation in which the problem emerges. The context describes the patterns that might have already been applied to produce the current design situation. The icon related to the pattern is placed after the context. The next textual part of the pattern is the problem statement, which summarizes the essence of the problem described in the context and forces in a few sentences. The problem is presented in **bold**. Next, the forces elaborate the problem and discuss its different facets. After the forces, the core of the pattern's solution is described with a few sentences in **bold**. The solution is then elaborated further and described in more detail in the following paragraphs. The solution also contains the technical illustrations and optional code listings describing the pattern solution. Towards the end of the solution the problems emerging from the use of this solution are discussed. If related patterns exist to address these problems they are mentioned here. The following patterns in the pattern language are described towards the end of the solution part.

After the solution, three dingbats mark the beginning of the consequences part of the pattern. In this part, the benefits and liabilities of applying the pattern are explained. There then follow three more dingbats to separate the consequences section from known uses of the pattern. The known uses part describes the empirical background of the pattern, as evidence for its validity. Each of the patterns has been recognized at least three times in separate systems, although we give only one demonstration of a known use. To protect the material rights of the companies concerned, we have had to make some changes to the known uses. For example, the field of business might not reflect the actual business case where the pattern was recognized. However, this does not affect the fact that the actual solution has been identified in practice in a similar situation.

The relationship between problem and solution within an individual pattern is essential. We have invested many hours rephrasing the problem and solution parts to find the actual root problem in each pattern and to describe the essence of the solution. Each boldface solution tries to provide only the essentials required to solve the problem, but they are often general and abstract. More detail of the solution is presented in the following parts, but the core of the solution gives you the basic information you need to solve the problem in your own way. Your method should include adapting the core of the solution to your conditions and preferences.

The solution should however provide the invariant property that is common to all systems we have seen that have succeeded in solving the problem. Capturing the root problem and the solution is not an easy task, and we admittedly have not always fully succeeded, so the solutions presented in the patterns will vary in significance – some of the solutions presented are truer and more profound than others: we have more confidence in some of the solutions.

To make our confidence level clear, we have marked each pattern with asterisks: two, one or none. If a pattern is marked with two asterisks it means that we believe we have succeeded in capturing the root problem, and that the solution we have written captures an essential property common to all possible ways of solving the problem in the given context. In these patterns we believe that, to successfully solve the problem, one must apply the given solution at least to some extent. Our confidence in patterns with two asterisks is very high, and we think that the pattern addresses a property that a distributed control system's software architecture must have.

One asterisk means that we have made some progress in identifying the root problem for the solution, and that the solution itself is solid. However, other ways to solve the problem might also exist. You should treat the patterns with only one asterisk with a certain caution, and try to identify the alternative solutions in your design context. Additionally, the root problem in your context might be different than the one presented in the pattern.

Patterns with no asterisks indicate that we are certain that we have failed to capture the key property behind the solution, or that the solution is just one of many possible alternatives. We have still presented the solution, to give one possible way to solve the problem. However, the key property of the solution that is present in *all* possible solutions to the problem is almost certainly not captured in the pattern.

5

Pattern Language for Distributed Control Systems

'From the moment of my birth, to the instant of my death. There are patterns I must follow, just as I must breathe each breath.'

Simon and Garfunkel, from the song 'Patterns'

It is natural for a human being to categorize various objects that are encountered in nature or are purely abstract. Categorization helps us understand the relationships between objects and the relation of objects to the environment. For example, Plato introduced the idea of grouping objects based on their similar properties. Another example is the classification of all living things by Aristotle, which was in use until the time of Linnaeus. Categorization can be seen an essential process in cognitive science (Cohen & Lefebvre, 2005). Languages are build on the concepts of classification, and even infants categorize things (Goswam, 2010). One well-known classification scheme is the Dewey decimal system (Dewey, 1876).

One has to bear in mind that every classification is essentially an abstraction. The members of a class have several similar properties, commonalities, that is redundant information and thus suitable for abstraction. However, in all classifications some unique characteristics are also abstracted away. Almost any classification is used on concepts that escape the rules of the current classification method. These concepts will end up being anomalies, or classified under 'miscellaneous' or some similar umbrella term. In addition, people tend to have different ways of classification by conviction, which may even change over time. For example, the Dewey system now has deprecated sections, as the world has changed since 1876. Some people tend to classify things into categories, their subcategories and so on, while some collect things together as a single idea. This dilemma is handled by Berlin in his famous essay *The Hedgehog and the Fox*, in which people who tend to lump things together are affectionately known as 'hedgehogs', and their counterparts, people who focus on dissimilarities, are called 'foxes' (Berlin, 1953).

As the number of patterns in this book is so large, we need some kind of classification and grouping for them. We have therefore tried to find the middle ground, to satisfy both the foxes and the hedgehogs amongst our readers. As a basis we follow Plato's idea of categorization by similar properties, but follow only one classification rule. As the single defining property, we have organized the patterns according to the problem area to which the pattern can be applied. For example, we have classified patterns that are targeted at data management into a single category. These categories are called *sublanguages*.

SUBLANGUAGE	DESCRIPTION
Configuration	The sublanguage of configuration patterns about customization and adjustment problems.
Control System	CONTROL SYSTEM is the root pattern of our pattern language for distributed control systems. It provides control system software that controls the machine and has interfaces to communicate with other machines and systems.
Data Management	The sublanguage of data management patterns provides a means to share information between nodes efficiently and safely.
Distribution	The size of a control system is likely to grow during development and its lifecycle. Usually this can be handled by distributing the system as logically connected subsystems. The sublanguage of distribution patterns tackles the problems caused by distribution.
Event Handling	Events are quick changes in system state or hazardous situations that need to be handled as soon as possible. For this reason, event messages should be easily identifiable from other traffic and should not be lost because of a fault. This sublanguage describes how to communicate noteworthy or alarm events and state changes in a uniform way.
Fleet Management	The sublanguage of fleet management patterns describes problems that will arise when a machine is required to cooperate with other machines, with the work orchestrated by an external party such as enterprise resource planning systems.

Table 5.1 Descriptions of the pattern sublanguages

SUBLANGUAGE	DESCRIPTION
Hardware Abstraction	Software is always dependent on the selected hardware to some degree, but unfortunately it is seldom possible to use identical or even compatible hardware for decades. This sublanguage tackles the decoupling of hardware and software.
High-Level Services	Nowadays a work machine is part of a larger ecosystem. The high-level services sublanguage is a collection of patterns that adapt the control system to support various external systems.
Human–Machine Interface	A machine operator usually has some way to control a machine. Typically this is implemented with physical controls such as joysticks, pedals and displays. This sublanguage discusses how to implement a good interface for the operator.
Messaging	In a distributed control system, the nodes collaborate and every node has to be connected to all the nodes from which it needs information. The sublanguage of messaging patterns describes how information sharing should be organized so that the communication infrastructure will be scalable in terms of the number of nodes, and flexible in the locations where information is produced and consumed.
Operating Mode	A machine control system application is used in various operating contexts. These contexts dictate how the machine can and/or should be operated. The sublanguage of operating modes provides a way to handle different operating contexts at the application level.
Redundancy	Availability is a key property of many control systems, especially those controlling a continuous process. The sublanguage for redundancy discusses high availability and high correctness issues.
Scarce Resources	Embedded control systems usually have very limited resources available for applications. In practice this means that the software design must somehow compensate for missing resources. This sublanguage battles the challenges caused by a scarcity of resources.
System Start-Up	When a system is powered every device needs to go through various tests and initializations before the control application can start its own initialization routines. The system start-up sublanguage describes the procedures that are necessary after the system powers up.
Updating	As an increasing amount of functionality is implemented with software, the ability to update the system software is an important feature for work machines. This sublanguage describes the technologies for safely updating software on various scales of devices, from a single unit to the whole distributed system.

Table 5.1 Descriptions of the pattern sublanguages (continued)

As our pattern language for distributed control systems contains 80 patterns, we have categorized it into several sublanguages. Each sublanguage is described in Table 5.1 and has its own chapter. Each chapters begin with an introduction to the sublanguage and a sublanguage pattern graph. The pattern graph shows the relationships between the patterns in that particular sublanguage. Usually it is also necessary to show how those patterns are related to patterns in other sublanguages, which are shown in gray. The complete pattern language graph is too big to fit the pages of the book, so it is provided on the companion website at www.wiley.com/go/controlsystemspatterns.

Note that the boundaries of the sublanguages are vague. Some of the patterns deal with cross-cutting aspects, so it is not always clear to which sublanguage a pattern belongs. You can ignore the sublanguage boundaries if you wish – they are there just to help you grasp the big picture, and to show you what kinds of problems are solved with the patterns. You can always start at the root pattern, CONTROL SYSTEM (below), and follow the arcs of the graph to the next pattern. So, let's start with the root pattern, take the red pill, follow the white rabbit[1] and dive deeper into the rabbit hole.

5.1   Control System * *

You are designing a mobile machine system. The machine is expected to have high performance and to increase productivity compared to older models. This can be achieved by automating repetitive functionality. For example, a mining drill rig could automatically turn its boom to the correct angle and position for drilling. It might be hard or even impossible to implement this functionality using only mechanical and electronic parts. Furthermore, the machine control system should guide the operator: which tasks to do today, which tasks are already done, production reports, guidance for the operator on how to improve working habits and so on. The control system should also communicate with other machines and production systems to receive work orders and send production reports. Automation of functionalities to this extent is difficult and cumbersome to implement just with hardware.

The productivity of a work machine cannot be increased any further using traditional ways of building the machine – using hydraulics, electronics and mechanics. A new way to control the machine needs to be introduced to optimize the system functionality and to increase the number of automated functionalities. For the same reason, user experience needs to be enhanced, and the system needs to connect to external information systems to make the machine an integral part of the whole production chain.

The current hardware has already been taken to the limits of its performance, so new software-controlled hardware needs to be used to achieve more performance and productivity. Additionally, when using software, functionalities can be automated and the

---

[1] A reference to the movie *The Matrix*.

utilization rate of the hardware increased, as computer response times usually outperform a human operator. Another way to increase productivity would be to make larger machines or to use multiple machines. In the former case, the problem is that larger machines consume more fuel and are otherwise problematic in many environments. For example, a larger forest harvester will cause deeper tracks in the woods than a smaller harvester, or a large tractor will cause more soil compaction, making a field less suitable for growing grain. In the latter case, using more machines to increase productivity would mean using more machine operators. It might be hard to find well-trained operators, and they will also increase costs, so better productivity from the same hardware is required.

The mobile machine should assist the machine operator. It should inform the operator what to do next and how the functionalities of the machine can be activated, deactivated and controlled. Good usability of the machine should be maintained as the functionality of the machine increases. For example, the system should provide the machine operator with a view of system state, show status information and provide guidance to the operator for the task at hand, for example in text form. Only relevant information for the current operating context should be provided, so that the operator is not distracted from the current task.

When designing a mobile machine it is often necessary to provide different variations of the machine. For example, low-end machines may have only a subset of the features of high-end machines, and so the high-end versions will probably also have more software. These machine variations typically form a product family that shares common basic functionality. Additionally, some machine models may have options that are bought separately, and software for these options should also be provided. For example, a winch is an optional accessory that may be required if the machine is to be used on steep slopes. The system should support the addition of such accessories after sale.

Maintenance of the work machine should be made easy, to keep its utilization rate as high as possible. Maintenance personnel need to locate faults quickly, so the work machine should support this by offering diagnostics.

Preemptive maintenance should be supported. The work machine monitors its functions, and when the system notices an anomaly, such as an increase in fuel consumption, it should alert maintenance personnel that there might be a fault. Preemptive maintenance also makes it possible to plan maintenance. As the system 'knows' when it needs to be maintained, maintenance can be postponed until a suitable moment in production. This prevents maintenance from interfering with production.

Work machines operate in an adverse environment that can cause their electronics and mechanics to wear out. In many cases the hardware remains usable but needs adjustment to restore normal operation. This adjustment should be made easy, so that maintenance personnel or the machine operator do not need to physically adjust the machine.

Production chains have become quite complex. This complexity should be managed and the production chain optimized. For example, the paper processing industry uses a multi-stage process to bring logs from the forest into the factory. First the plant transmits the kind of raw material that is needed, then a forest harvester cuts and delimbs the required trees. The logs are then picked up by a forwarder and brought to the closest road, where a log truck picks them up and transports them to the factory. This production chain should be optimized to minimize the waiting time between the different stages and the time between order and delivery. In other words, goods are delivered 'just in time'. This requires interplay of the various work machines and production systems in the plants – a single machine needs to becomes a part of a larger production chain.

Sometimes a work machine requires constant supervision. For example, rock crushers may be damaged if not stopped immediately when a rock gets stuck. This requires the machine operator to supervise the situation even though they are not otherwise required to control the machine. If this kind of supervision can be automated, it frees human resources, perhaps to control multiple work units. For example, in a mining drill rig one operator could control multiple drilling processes simultaneously, as most of the process is automated. In some cases, it might even be possible to make the system completely automatic and not need an operator.

Even though experienced machine operators know how to control the machine, it might be hard to find such skills. Furthermore, human operators tend to become defocused during a long work shift, decreasing the accuracy of the work. For a machine operator to achieve high accuracy, for example driving near another machine with centimeters of precision, requires great concentration. A machine should therefore be able to help its operator to perform at this level of accuracy during long work shifts.

Once a machine is handed over to the customer, the hardware of the machine is more or less static. However, if new features are developed after the machine is delivered, the machine's owner has no way to use these new features. On the other hand, the machine's manufacturer has no opportunity to sell innovative features to the owner, although such features can be added to new machines. Therefore, there should be a way to add new features to a machine after delivery.

Faults in the system should be handled quickly. The machine operator's response times might be slower than the system's, so the system should automatically respond to those faults that it can handle. For example, it can stop when it notices a situation that might compromise safety.

Therefore:

Implement control system software that controls the machine and has interfaces to communicate with other machines and systems. The control system can automate many of the functionalities that were previously carried out manually by the machine operator. In addition, the control system can provide the operator with more fine-grained information about system state than could ever be provided without it. The control system also interacts with external information systems.

Design the system so that it has one or more controllers operating the machine. The controllers are connected to sensors, so that they get information from the surrounding world. Figure 5.1 illustrates the basic principle of a control system at a high level. Consider also adding a programmable automation controller (PAC) such as a PC or some other device with more power than programmable logic controllers (PLCs), to provide more processing capability and wider development options. Implement control system software that controls the machine and possibly uses sensor information in a feedback loop, to ensure that controlled actions are taking place and to check that no faults occur. The patterns in this language will help you to design the form of the system.

Figure 5.1: The basic principle of the control system at a high level

Once the work machine is controlled by software, the hardware can be utilized more efficiently and controlled in a way that conserves it. Software-controlled systems can perform many control operations far faster than a human operator. Furthermore, many control sequences can be automated, so less effort from the operator is required. For example, in a drilling machine, changing the drilling rod can be automated under software control.

The control system can supervise production automatically. When it notices a situation that might damage the machine or the environment, it can automatically shut down operation. In this way, continuous human monitoring is not necessary. This increases efficiency, as one operator can control multiple machines simultaneously. For example, in a mine a drilling process might take more than 30 minutes, depending on the depth of the drill hole. A machine operator can easily drive two or more machines, as the control system can shut down the drilling process if, for example, a drill bit gets stuck.

A control system can also make a work machine more cost-effective, as some features that were previously implemented with hardware can now be implemented with software. Some features may be easier to implement with software, so some of the hardware components may become obsolete. Software can be reused without extra cost, so when work machines are in mass production costs will decrease, as some hardware components can be omitted.

Once the system has CONTROL SYSTEM software all kinds of improvements can be considered. For example, HUMAN–MACHINE INTERFACE (page 313), THIRD-PARTY SANDBOX (page 355), UPDATEABLE SOFTWARE (page 301) and so on could be considered, depending on requirements. Figure 5.2 illustrates the pattern language graph and shows which patterns could be applied after CONTROL SYSTEM.

❖   ❖   ❖

As the work machine is now controlled by software, new features can be implemented that could not be implemented just with hydraulics and electronics. This increases system performance and productivity, as operation sequences can be automated. Furthermore, more advanced features such as a HUMAN–MACHINE INTERFACE (page 313), DIAGNOS-

TICS (page 350) and FLEET MANAGEMENT (page 372) can be implemented. The pattern graph in Figure 5.2 shows the options for the designer.

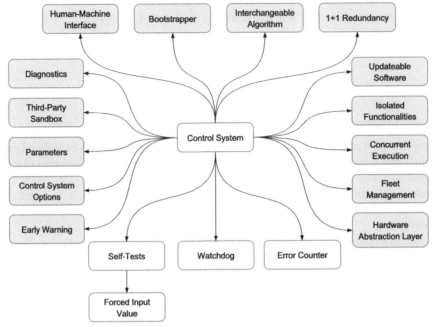

Figure 5.2: After the CONTROL SYSTEM pattern is applied there are many things that the architect can design next

The remainder of this chapter presents the patterns shown with a white background: the patterns with gray backgrounds are presented in the chapter dealing with the corresponding sublanguage.

New features can be added during the lifecycle of the machine by means of software updates. This is convenient for customers, as they don't need to buy new machines so frequently. It also produces revenue for the machine manufacturer, as the maintenance period of the machine is extended. In some cases, maintenance may bring over 75 percent of the manufacturer's revenue (Glueck at al, 2007). It also builds partnership between the manufacturer and the customer, as the customer can rely on the fact that the manufacturer will provide new features for the machine.

Implementing features that have traditionally been implemented with hardware can be cheaper with software. Although development costs with software might be higher than hardware, when the system is in production copying software costs nothing. Had a feature been implemented with hardware, the cost would depend on the number of machines produced.

When a control system is used, updating the system becomes possible, allowing new features to be added after the launch of the product. However, machine operators might be annoyed if updating is frequent.

The control system measures the environment via sensors. However, sensors might be inaccurate, or affected by the operating environment. For example, engine vibration can cause noise or transients on sensor signals. See DEVIL MAY CARE (page 190) or ERROR COUNTER (page 107) for ways to address these problems.

The control system can react to operating situations quicker than a human. This is beneficial, especially when designing safety mechanisms: if the system detects a fault, it can enter a SAFE STATE (page 179) automatically without consulting the machine operator.

Implementing the control system with one monolithic software component is a bad idea, as it would require extensive wiring, which is error-prone and costly. The control system should be distributed. For more details of this problem, see ISOLATED FUNCTIONALITIES (page 110).

If high availability is required from the system or from some of its service, 1+1 REDUNDANCY (page 279) is still needed, as the hardware on which the software runs may malfunction or be damaged.

A control system usually also requires an operating system to run. The lifecycle of the operating system might be much shorter than that of the work machine. At some point in the machine's lifecycle a need to change the operating system might arise. This is discussed further in OPERATING SYSTEM ABSTRACTION (page 269).

A modern straddle carrier moves containers in a harbor from a warehousing area to container lifts, and vice versa. A straddle carrier has control system software that is used to control the machine and to handle production information. The machine operator controls the machine using joysticks, dashboard buttons and so on, and sees machine status information via the screen in the cabin. Work orders are communicated from the harbor administration directly to the straddle carrier, so the operator knows which containers need to be moved next. Once the job is done, the machine can mark the location of containers and relay that information back to the harbor management system. The straddle carrier's operator can see new work orders from the user interface in the cabin. The straddle carrier also communicates with other carriers in the harbor area. Carriers negotiate with each other about the path that they should take to avoid collision or waiting time (for another carrier to get out of the way).

5.2   Watchdog * *

> *'In the field we had a code of honor, you watch my back, I watch yours.'*
>
> *John Rambo, in the movie 'First Blood', 1982*

…there is a distributed CONTROL SYSTEM in which the hardware may malfunction, or in which hardware failures can be caused by features of the operating environment, such as vibration, or electromagnetic compatibility (EMC) problems caused by a high power radio transmitter nearby. Some of these errors can be transient, in which case the system can recover from the error if the application is able to start remedial actions. However, hardware failure can prevent the application from being executed, or there may be bugs in applications, so that the application can become unresponsive. The error may cause the whole system to be in deadlock, so that it cannot recover by itself. If an autonomous control system hangs, it may become permanently disabled, as there is no operator to take care of remedial action. Thus it has to recover from faults without human intervention (see MINIMIZE HUMAN INTERVENTION, Hanmer, 2007).

To increase the safety of the whole system, malfunction of a node should be detected and recovery actions should be started automatically.

If the system is a *hard real-time* system, a node must guarantee a response within specific time constraints. The node is deemed to be malfunctioning if it fails to meet the response time requirements. Missing a deadline may be caused by hardware failure, such as a memory component in the system malfunctioning, or an error in an application, such as the execution of some calculation taking longer than expected. These kinds of missed deadlines are usually hard to detect, as the system seems to work normally, but missed deadlines can cause timing failures in another part of the system, as other nodes do not get required inputs on time.

A malfunction in a node should be noticed as soon as possible. When the malfunction is noticed early, the consequences are usually less harmful and propagation of the failure can be avoided (see ERROR CONTAINMENT BARRIER, Hanmer, 2007). In addition, the rest of the system should be informed about the malfunction – see FAULT OBSERVER (Hanmer, 2007) or NOTIFICATIONS (page 156).

In the case of a software malfunction, it should be easy for maintenance personnel to find the cause.

Mechanisms for monitoring the functionality of the node have to be robust and simple, so that they do not form a new potential source of failure. Monitoring should be independent of the operations of the node, and should not require a lot of resources such as CPU time or memory.

If the functionality is duplicated by applying 1+1 REDUNDANCY (page 279), the redundant node takes control if the primary node malfunctions. However, the original failure must still be detected. In addition, redundancy adds cost. If the functionality provided by the node is not critical to the whole system, the additional cost may not be justifiable. For such nodes it may be enough to minimize downtime by using available remedial action.

Therefore:

Add a watchdog component to put the node into a safe state if the application does not reset the watchdog within a given time limit.

Typically the watchdog component is a hardware circuit included in the node's processor, or an additional external hardware component. The watchdog's operation must be completely independent of the applications' operation. In its simplest form, the watchdog is a countdown timer that is initialized and started during system start-up. The timer is connected to the RESET line of the node's processor. When the timer reaches zero, it raises the RESET line and the processor is rebooted. Even though the application can usually change the time-out value, it cannot stop the watchdog timer once it is started, as this would stop the monitoring. The application must therefore reset the countdown timer periodically to prevent the watchdog from rebooting the processor. The application can reset the timer either by writing a new value to the watchdog's countdown register, or by signaling the watchdog's I/O line. Figure 5.3 illustrates the actions carried out by the application and the watchdog.

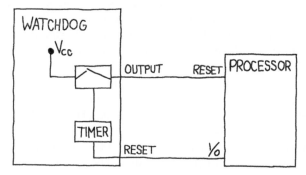

Figure 5.3: An external watchdog component connected to a processor's reset line

When designing the system the initial value of the watchdog timer is critical. The time-out interval is selected so that in normal operation the watchdog will never reset the node. The value used depends on how soon a malfunction should be noticed. The time usually varies from a few milliseconds to minutes, depending on the application. A greater value for the watchdog timer results in a longer interval for the application to reset the watchdog timer before the processor is rebooted. This reduces overhead caused by resetting the watchdog. On the other hand, too long an interval may make it impossible for the watchdog to prevent propagation of a failure to the rest of the system. Even though resetting the watchdog timer is a quick operation, it will still require some processor time. In addition, watchdog resets should be located in the right places in the program cycle, for example not inside long loops, if the execution time of the whole loop is critical and to be guarded by the watchdog. In other words, timer resets should occur such that application crashes or missed deadlines are really noticed. Listing 5.1 demonstrates the proper way to locate watchdog resets when using loops.

```
// The watchdog will reset the application after 100 ms
set_watchdog_timeout(100);

while (true) {
    // If the control took more than 100 ms, the system would be reset
    while (!control_ready) {
        read_sensors(inputs);
        calculate_control(inputs,outputs);
        set_controls(outputs);
        // As the physical components can be slow,
        // continue controlling as long as necessary.
        control_ready=is_controller_ready();
    }
    trigger_watchdog(); // Start the countdown again
    // other control actions...
}
```

Listing 5.1: Setting and resetting the watchdog

When a node is started, a BOOTSTRAPPER (page 288) can check whether the watchdog caused a reboot, and can start recovery actions if necessary. Usually such actions start by diagnosing the hardware (see SELF-TESTS (page 106) for further information). If the hardware appears to function without errors, the node is started normally, as the reboot was probably caused by an application error or transient hardware fault. It should be ensured that starting the system in normal operational mode instead of SAFE STATE (page 179) will not cause danger for the operator or the environment. In addition, reboots should be limited to a specific number of retries (see LIMIT RETRIES, Hanmer, 2007); and if the limit is reached, the hardware failure is deemed to be persistent. In that case, the system can be switched to a degraded mode (see LIMP HOME (page 185)), or the node shut down to prevent hardware damage. The rest of the system should be informed of the reboot, for example using NOTIFICATIONS (page 156).

Instead of directly rebooting the processor, the watchdog component can be connected to logic that shuts down the node's outputs and causes an interrupt, so that the application itself can try to recover from the failure. When the interrupt occurs, an interrupt handler is called and the application can, for example, enter a SAFE STATE (page 179), reboot the whole node, restart the malfunctioning application, or inform the other nodes of the situation. For example, when developing the system it is essential that the software state is preserved after a malfunction, so that the cause of the failure can be examined using debuggers. In fact, it is advisable to use this kind of watchdog action if automatic recovery actions are not needed.

By using watchdog interrupts, the watchdog can also be used to monitor the condition of the messaging channel or other nodes. The watchdog is reset just before sending a message, and once again after the message is received. If a reply has not been received within

a specified time, the watchdog interrupts the message wait and the node can start remedial actions, for example by entering a SAFE STATE, as communication is clearly not functioning properly.

The watchdog can also be implemented with its own monitoring application. A software implementation gives more flexibility in utilizing the watchdog. For example, the
system can have several watchdogs with different time-outs, and applications can register
functions that should be called by the watchdog in the case of a time-out. Monitored applications can reset the software watchdog by calling a defined resetting function, communicating via shared memory, or even by sending a special message using a HIGH-LEVEL
PROTOCOL (page 137). This mechanism can also be used to implement HEARTBEAT (page
120). However, software-based watchdogs are not reliable if the hardware of the node
malfunctions, as the failure could also affect the monitoring software. Software watchdogs should therefore be accompanied by hardware-based watchdogs.

If the node sends messages periodically, these can be also used to reset the watchdog's
countdown timer. In that case, a missed message may reveal an application malfunction.
With this approach, however, the correctness of the message content is not monitored.

If the availability of the node is critical, use 1+1 REDUNDANCY (page 279) to keep the
node's functionality running even if the node malfunctions. In such cases a watchdog can
be used to notice a malfunctioning node so that a redundant node can take over.

Similar watchdog patterns are described in (Douglass, 2002) and (Hanmer, 2007).
Webel and Fliege (Webel & Fliege, 2004) describe a WATCHDOG pattern for safety-critical systems defined with the formal specification language SDL (Specification and Description Language). For more details on SDL, see (ITU-T, 1999).

A watchdog checks that the application's execution is proceeding, as the watchdog is reset
periodically. It will notice only applications that are stalled or whose program cycle takes
longer than designed. It cannot tell whether the outputs or actions of the node are wrong.

With a watchdog, a stalled application is noticed and remedial actions can be started.
This minimizes downtime of the functionality provided by the node, and helps to prevent
failures from propagating to the rest of the system. Moreover, it decreases a need for human intervention, and in autonomous systems it may prevent the system from becoming
completely disabled. However, rebooting the node takes a while, and the system must be
designed so that the reboot interval will not jeopardize availability of the whole system.
The software state should be preserved, so that the root cause of a malfunction can be
found later by debugging. Thus rebooting the system is not always the best option.

If the watchdog resets the node repetitively, it implies either a software or hardware error in the node. For hardware errors, SELF-TESTS (page 106) can be used to reveal which
component is malfunctioning, and in some cases, especially with sensors, can bypass the
failing component with SENSOR BYPASS (page 189). A FORCED INPUT VALUE (page 106)
can be used to find out whether the malfunction lies in the communication channel or in
the node itself.

❖ ❖ ❖

A watchdog is used in work machines to ensure safety. Sometimes a watchdog is also used to recover from errors. For example, in a space probe, software is used to control various components, for example communication, radar and thrusters. As the operating environment is very hostile due to cosmic radiation, transient hardware failures can occur. The control application is also very complex, and no complex software is ever completely free from bugs. A watchdog component is therefore integrated into each subsystem to ensure that the system can recover from errors. The watchdogs have their own power supply to ensure independence from their monitored subsystem. One of these watchdogs is used for the communications subsystem. The output line of the watchdog is connected to the communication processor. The communication software resets the watchdog periodically by sending a pulse to one output port of the processor. The time-out of the communication watchdog is set to 10 seconds. If a bug in the communication software causes it to crash, the connection to ground control may be lost and no human operator can then reset the probe. However, as the communication software failed to reset the watchdog in time, it reboots the communication subsystem, restarting the crashed communication application. After connection is reestablished diagnostic data is sent to ground control. This enables the software team to find and fix the bug and upload a new version of the communication application to the probe.

5.3   Self-Tests *

Rarely used functionalities, such as safety functions, may fail silently, as they are not actively used. It may be hard to detect these latent malfunctions.

Therefore:

For each device, design a test sequence consisting of inputs and their corresponding outputs. Run the test sequence periodically or once in a while, for example during every third system start-up. If the test sequence fails, it triggers a failure notification.

For the complete pattern, please see www.wiley.com/go/controlsystemspatterns.

5.4   Forced Input Value

Functionality consists of a chain of units, their inputs and outputs. In a case of malfunction in specific functionality, it is hard to determine where the malfunction is by only monitoring the outputs of the chain. The malfunction can be in any of the control units or in the communication channel.

Therefore:

Create a mechanism that can be used to force the control unit's input to a specific value. This forcing mechanism is added to each control unit, but is separated from the communication channel. This make it possible to check whether the output of the control unit receiving the forced input corresponds to the expected output. If the output is not correct, the control unit is malfunctioning, otherwise the communication channel is broken.

For the complete pattern, please see www.wiley.com/go/controlsystemspatterns.

5.5   Error Counter *

Transient faults can occur in a system due to demanding conditions in the environment. These faults should not cause a machine to enter a SAFE STATE (page 179), as they clear themselves after a short while. Substantial faults should be distinguished from transient faults.

Therefore:

Create an error counter whose threshold can be set to specific value. The error counter is incremented every time a fault is reported. Once the threshold is met, an error is triggered. The counter is decremented or reset after a specific time has elapsed from the last fault report.

For the complete pattern, please see www.wiley.com/go/controlsystemspatterns.

CHAPTER

6

Patterns for Distribution

'Coming together is a beginning; keeping together is progress;
working together is success.'

Henry Ford

The size of a control system is likely to grow during its development and lifecycle. The amount of I/O on one device may become large, and a single processor unit might be under heavy load with I/O processing. In addition, developing and managing such monolithic software becomes hard when the number of features grows. Responsibilities and dependencies of different modules in the software become harder to understand as the number of modules increases. ISOLATED FUNCTIONALITIES (page 110) describes a 'divide and conquer' approach to distribute a system across logically connected subsystems. This makes the size of single subsystems more manageable. These subsystems implement their own part of the overall functionality of the machine.

Distributing and isolating functionalities comes at a price: new kinds of problems – and opportunities – emerge. For example, system start-up becomes more complex, and a

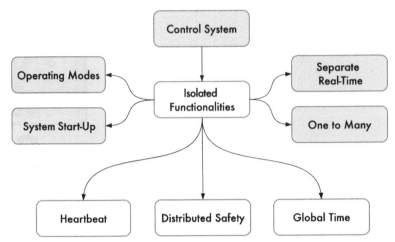

Figure 6.1: The sublanguage of distribution patterns and its main subsequent patterns

clear need for operating modes emerges. Communication between subsystems may become problematic. On the other hand, distribution opens possibilities for separating real-time from non-real-time functionality: all these topics are covered in their own chapters.

Figure 6.1 illustrates the sublanguage of distribution patterns, accompanied with subsequent patterns that tackle the problems caused by distribution and ISOLATED FUNCTIONALITIES.

Sometimes there might also be a need to distribute the system to ensure safe operation of the functionality, as explained in DISTRIBUTED SAFETY (page 116). This pattern describes a mechanism for dividing potentially harmful functionality into multiple nodes such that only cooperation between the nodes can trigger the whole functionality.

One important aspect of a distributed system is that its nodes share a common conception of time. Each node has own oscillator that can drift and thus cause clock skew. However, all the nodes need to share common time in order to collaborate properly. GLOBAL TIME (page 124) describes how this clock skew problem can be dealt with. HEARTBEAT (page 120) discusses how the health of a communication channel and the status of the connected nodes can be monitored by sending periodic heartbeat messages. Using HEARTBEAT makes it possible to detect malfunctions and start remedial action.

6.1   Isolated Functionalities * *

…there is CONTROL SYSTEM (page 96) software in a machine that has different capabilities, for example engine, drive, boom control and so on. Control system software is used to control all of these capabilities. As several functionalities are involved in implementing each capability, the software soon becomes large and unmanageable. For example, a driving capability needs functionalities from transmission and operator controls. Additionally, the amount of I/O required from a single device can become large, and a single processor unit might be under heavy load when all I/O needs to be processed. As new features are added, the code mass grows large and becomes hard to understand, as the same control system application needs to take care of all the functionalities and capabilities of the machine. This slows down development. In addition, the responsibilities and dependencies of different modules in monolithic control system software can be hard to understand, and make the system less maintainable.

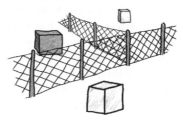

As the control system evolves and gains new features, it becomes hard to maintain and understand its structure. In addition, the processing power of a single device running the software may be exceeded.

Development and manageability of such monolithic software becomes hard as the number of features grows. Different developers or teams develop the features, so a single piece of software becomes hard to manage, as different teams need to build the software and other parts of the system are constantly changing. As the number of features grows, the code becomes hard to understand.

Developing different parts of the system may require specialist knowledge, for example developing algorithms for boom control. Furthermore, some parts of the system might be more safety-critical than others, and typically need to be certified. The certification process may take weeks or even months. Such parts should be developed separately, to support certification processes. In addition, safety-certified hardware is often expensive, and thus use of such hardware should be limited to safety-critical functionality only.

Testing a large entity at once is challenging, and it might be hard to pinpoint sources of errors. It should therefore be possible to compile and test different parts of the control system separately.

To minimize development time and save cost, one might want to use COTS – both for hardware and software components, or a mix of the two.

In many cases the machine manufacturers have a long tradition of building machines, but only limited experience of developing control systems. The manufacturer might therefore want to subcontract parts of the control system. Monolithic software is harder to subcontract, as there are no clearly decoupled logical entities – that is, modules that can be given to the subcontractor for implementation.

The implementation should be understandable. In many cases this means that there should be a single person who can fully understand the whole system or one of its components. If a component or the system is too large for one person to understand, the development becomes challenging.

During its lifecycle the control system is likely to grow, so it should be possible to add new features to the system easily. Monolithic software might be harder to manage, so adding new features might be hard.

A monolithic control system with a lot of features takes a lot of processing power to run. High-end controllers or PCs are relatively expensive to acquire: in many cases, the manufacturer would like to use low-end and therefore cheap hardware. This limits the size of a single application.

If the control system is implemented as a single monolithic application, it creates a *single point of failure* – if the control system software has a fault, it might disable the whole machine. However, it is advisable that malfunction of a single feature does not disable the whole system: only the malfunctioning features should be disabled.

A control device should be located close to the actuators and sensors (or I/O) it is using, otherwise the wiring to the actuators and sensors can become long, error-prone and fragile. Additionally, copper wire is relatively expensive and adds to the machine's weight, which in turn may require a larger engine, and so on.

Therefore:

Identify logically connected functionalities and compose these functionalities as manageable-sized entities. Implement each of these entities as their own subsystem in order to isolate functionalities.

Capabilities of the machine such as boom control or drive control typically form logical functional entities, so it is natural to divide the control system software into similar logical entities too. Each of these entities should be implemented as their own subsystem. In practice this means that each functional entity runs on its own hardware (typically a controller or PC) and has its own I/O. This approach means that required hardware and software for a specific functionality is bundled together and isolated from the rest of the system. Even though these functional entities implement their own part of the whole functionality of the machine, they may need to communicate with other entities. That's why there should be a way for these isolated functionalities to communicate with each other using separate wiring or a message bus (see ONE TO MANY, page 131).

In general there are three options when designing a control system. One is to create completely centralized systems. The second is to distribute the I/O and still have a centralized control component. The third way is to distribute the intelligence as well as the I/O. Each CONTROL SYSTEM (page 96) has elements from all of these three approaches, and balancing the three is the hard job an architect has to do. These design decisions are fundamental in nature and may have long-lasting consequences. For example, calculating boom kinematics could be implemented with three separate controllers. On the other hand, calculations could be carried out using one high-end controller. In the future, the high-end controller might become cheaper if it becomes popular and new more powerful technologies emerge. If this happens, using only one controller in the current system might be a viable option as the price comes down and the single unit is relatively easy to replace with newer technology, so maintainability is better than when using three processors. On the other hand, if the selected technology becomes a niche technology, its price may rise in the future, and three cheap controllers would be the better option. However, migrating from three controllers to one controller in the future might be a more costly option. In addition, if the software is reused in other machines, the architectural decision propagates beyond the machine's boundaries and limits the possibilities for reuse of the ready-made boom kinematics calculations. So the architect must consider these issues when deciding which functionalities should be grouped and how much of the system should be distributed.

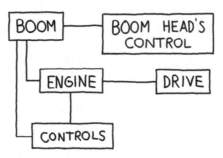

Figure 6.2: High-level isolation of functionalities in a typical control system. This kind of division is guided by the number of I/O ports required.

This division into smaller entities is guided by a couple of factors. Often cheap low-end hardware is preferred because of its cost, but such hardware has limited processing power and I/O ports. So, when the whole control system is divided into isolated functionalities, such as boom control, drive control, hull control and so on (see Figure 6.2), one might not want to stop there, but continue to isolate functionalities within an already-isolated functionality. In other words, if boom control is implemented with its own subsystem, but the hardware used does not have the required processing power for it, the functionality might need to be distributed further. For example, in the case of a forest harvester, one might want isolate the harvester head's functionality (sawing, feeding, marking etc.) from boom movement control. This also makes the control system's code more manageable, modular and understandable.

On the other hand, one limiting factor of distribution is the volume of communication between subsystems. Every time functionality is divided amongst separate controllers, the need for communication increases exponentially. Some structuring, as shown in Figure 6.2, might ease this problem, but at some stage the volume of communication required becomes the limiting factor in the distribution. Thus one should pay attention to the communication needs of controllers when designing the distribution, and try to design the system so that it supports those needs. If communication would increase considerably, one might not want to distribute such functionality.

Testing smaller code blocks is easier, and verifying that they behave correctly is also easier if the correct behavior of the functionality can be verified separately. However, some of the functionalities may behave differently when a specific set of other functionality is also present. So isolation of functionalities on one hand alleviates testing, as unit testing is easier, but on the other hand makes it more challenging, as the system may need to be tested again when new isolated functionalities are added to it. In other words, some dependencies between functionalities can be both invisible and surprising from the developer's point of view.

Reuse of functionalities may also guide the distribution process. The decision of whether kinematics should be developed on one controller, or its parts isolated to different controllers, depends on the situation. From the reuse point of view, a single isolated subsystem should be such that it can be reused and has value as a separate reusable part. These parts should be isolated from the rest of the machine's functionality to enable this reuse. On the other hand, one might want to use COTS components. If so, the division of functionalities should be designed in such a way that COTS components can be used to implement a part of the machine's functionality. However, component models in which the software and hardware form an isolated and non-separable package have their downsides. For example, when reusing the component the hardware may already be outdated. One can apply COMPONENT-BASED CONFIGURATION (page 386) to decide which hardware and software to use independently.

Sometimes the functionality itself creates the need for isolation. For example, safety-critical functionalities should be isolated from other functionalities by separate controllers. In this way, the safe operation of the functionality is more likely to be achieved. In addition, safety-critical functionality in many cases requires different development methods and complicated certification processes. If such functionality was not separated, the entire control system would need to comply with IEC 61508 (IEC, 2010a) or other such safety standards. For more details on tackling this problem, you can refer to SEPARATED SAFETY (Rauhamäki at al, 2012a).

Remember Conway's Law (Conway, 1968; Coplien & Harrison, 2004) when designing the distribution of the system. If multiple teams or subcontractors are implementing the control system software, the system probably needs to be divided into separate components so that different teams have natural interfaces with each other. If the system was monolithic, it would be difficult for different development teams to work on individual capabilities without creating ripple effects for each other. Once functionalities are isolated, you can localize the effect of changes to a single component. In practice, this often means that each team or subcontractor is working on a single isolated functionality. This is quite natural, as implementation of some functionalities, such as boom kinematics, requires special expertise. Experts should not need to focus on the whole system's design, but only be able to work on the specific part, for example a control algorithm. The system structure should therefore support this. In addition, a road map of the product may require division of the system into separate parts so that the implementation can be compartmentalized.

Sometimes potentially dangerous situations arise if the software controlling a functionality malfunctions. This kind of functionality may need to be distributed to two or more separate controllers – see DISTRIBUTED SAFETY (page 116) for more details. DOMAIN MODEL (Buschmann et al, 2007b) describes a way to create a model to guide the isolation of functionalities. ISOLATED FUNCTIONALITIES can be seen as a first step away from a BIG BALL OF MUD (Foote & Yoder, 1997) by creating structure for the program code using responsibilities and functionalities as a basis. This is often referred as *separation of concerns* (Hürsch & Videira-Lopes, 1995). The MODULAR ARCHITECTURE pattern (Weiss & Noori, 2013) describes a similar solution as a contribution enabler in the context of open source projects. SUBSYSTEM BY SKILL and several other patterns in *Organizational Patterns* (Coplien & Harrison, 2004) discuss the rationale behind decisions of whether to distribute a system.

As logically connected features are isolated to separate controllers, the control system software becomes more manageable, understandable and modular. This increases the maintainability of the system. Furthermore, some parts of the system can be subcontracted, given to separate teams for development, or bought as COTS components.

As the system is distributed to separate controllers, the malfunction of a single controller might not disable the whole machine. So even if some device is malfunctioning, the system remains usable to some extent.

Different parts of the system have different lifecycles. Some parts may last longer than others without change. For example, engine control is likely to remain untouched, whereas boom control might be changed many times over the lifecycle of the system design. Making such changes becomes easier if these parts are separated into their own subsystems. In addition, subsystems can easily be reused in other products.

Once the functionalities are isolated the system structure becomes much more complex. Separate subsystems need to exchange a lot of information, and this may not be easy to implement. Maintaining a distributed system is usually harder than maintaining a centralized system, as software components communicate with each other using signals and the application always needs to cope with the situation in which a signal is not received for some reason. Additionally, different kinds of services may need to be requested using asynchronous signals instead of local synchronized function calls, as it might be hard to fit all required services into a single node.

Even though the system is distributed, adding new devices may be challenging. Adding a device requires new wiring, and may require changes to other controllers' code. ONE TO MANY (page 131) describes situations in which there is a need to add, remove or change communicating parties during the lifecycle of the system.

When the number of isolated functionalities grows, the number of separate modules in the system also grows. This can make the system more error-prone, and make its integration and configuration laborious. Often the system's cost also increases. Furthermore, although the system has ISOLATED FUNCTIONALITIES, the component's software, hardware and firmware are still coupled. When the hardware or firmware version changes, modifications to the component's software are still required. HARDWARE ABSTRACTION LAYER (page 264), OPERATING SYSTEM ABSTRACTION (page 269) and COMPONENT-BASED CONFIGURATION (page 386) deal with these problems.

As the system is now distributed, system start-up becomes more complex. The nodes may have dependencies and must wait for another node to start up before they can start functioning. SYSTEM START-UP (page 293) tackles this problem.

Sometimes nodes may generate errors for a short period while the system is starting up and is not yet completely ready for normal operation. DEVIL MAY CARE (page 190) can be applied to solve these kinds of problems.

Often control systems have functionalities that have real-time requirements, and some of their functionalities are less critical. In some cases these functionalities are naturally part of the same logical entity. For example, a user interface has non real-time graphical applications, and controls such as pedals, joysticks and so on that do have real-time requirements. SEPARATE REAL-TIME (page 237) deals with this problem.

A forest harvester is a heavy vehicle employed in cut-to-length logging operations for felling, delimbing and *bucking* trees. A forest harvester is often used with a *forwarder*, which hauls the logs to a roadside landing so that the harvester does not have to. Harvesters move in the forest using wheels or tracks. A harvester is typically powered by a diesel engine or hybrid motor, and the harvesting functions are powered by the same motor via a hydraulic drive. Harvesting is carried out using a boom that carries the harvester head.

When designing control system software for a machine such as a harvester, the first logical entities can be detected easily – the different capabilities of the machine, such as wheels (or tracks), motor, boom and harvester head. These parts should be isolated from each other in the software. Additionally, one might want to have a dedicated controller for the hydraulic drive and the frame of the machine. After a while, it might be noticed that the harvester head controller becomes complex, as it has multiple devices to control: a chainsaw to cut the tree, delimbing knives, feed rollers to grasp the tree and feed it through the delimbing knives, diameter sensors and length sensors. So the architect makes a decision to isolate functionalities further within the harvester head, and makes the software modular based on the physical structure of the machine.

6.2 Distributed Safety *

...there is a CONTROL SYSTEM (page 96) that consists of ISOLATED FUNCTIONALITIES (page 110), so every node has clearly defined responsibilities. The nodes cooperate to fulfil the tasks the operator has initiated. However, some of these functionalities may present a high risk to health or cause damage if they do not function properly. As the hardware of a node can break down, or the application may have software bugs, a malfunction may cause the node to initiate actions that can cause an accident. In addition to such permanent malfunctions, transient malfunctions caused by the environment may initiate some functionality unintentionally. Communication in a distributed system cannot always be trusted, especially if it is possible for a message to be misinterpreted or corrupted during transmission.

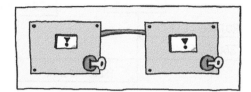

A single malfunction affecting the behavior of a node may result in a serious incident. The consequences of the malfunction are unacceptable, but it is hard to eliminate sources of malfunctions.

Every piece of hardware and any software component has a rate of failure. Even if both are low, the probability of a failure in a node is the product of these two factors.

Risk depends on the probability that a hazard occurs and the severity of the incident (Kinney, & Wiruth, 1976). Risks can be minimized in two ways: either by reducing their severity, or by reducing their probability. Some nodes control hazardous actions, where the severity cannot be lowered due to business and design restrictions; for example, a machine must move heavy loads to be productive. Thus to keep the risk minimized the possibility of a failure should be negligible.

In distributed systems, communication between nodes is essential, but should not resemble the game of 'Chinese whispers' – that is, the message should not change during its transmission. However, communication errors can occur due to environmental interference. As some messages may be corrupted in a working environment, there is a risk that a single message will occasionally be misinterpreted or lost. This should not trigger any hazardous functionality.

Therefore:

Divide potentially harmful functionality into multiple nodes that communicate with each other. For each of these nodes, implement only a part of the potentially hazardous functionality, so that only cooperation can trigger the whole functionality.

Consider functionality that can cause high-risk incidents and split it into independent actions. These actions should then be distributed across two or more nodes. In this way, none of the nodes can carry out the functionality alone without the cooperation of the other node(s). In the case of two nodes, for example, the division is usually designed so that the first node starts a process and other node carries out the rest of the functionality.

For example, in the case of boom movement (Figure 6.3) the operator moves a joystick, which sends a message that the boom should turn left. The message is received by the two nodes involved in the operation. One node controls the power pack that generates the hydraulic pressure (Figure 6.4). The other node uses the pressure to carry out the action – moving the boom. The probability that either of the nodes will encounter a malfunction is higher than in a single-node system, but neither of them can perform harmful actions

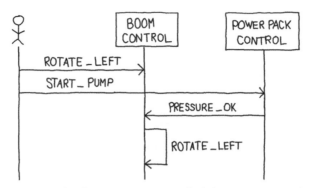

Figure 6.3: An example of communication in which boom movement functionality is distributed to ensure safety

Figure 6.4: The hydraulic pack of a forest machine

Reproduced by permission of John Deere Forestry Oy

alone. For example, in a system where there are three nodes each having mean error probability of 1 percent in ten years, the error probability for the whole system is 2.971 percent in ten years. If hydraulic pressure is built up but not used, nothing hazardous will happen, and if the other node tries to move the boom without hydraulic power, the boom will not move. Usually there is a wait time, in which the second action must be executed or the process will be reversed. For example, hydraulic pressure is kept available for only a short time, and if it is not used for boom movement the hydraulic pump stops and reports an error. In some cases, the system may enter a SAFE STATE (page 179) if it seems that it has malfunctioned. If the malfunction is transient the system can still continue working.

There is still the possibility of a common-mode failure, however, for example if the joystick sends erroneous messages that are interpreted as movement commands. To prevent that, the hydraulic power generation and the movement can be separated in the joystick. Separation is realized by using a limit switch that starts power generation when joystick movement closes the switch. The actual boom movement commands are generated from the messages sent by the joystick.

Note that it is not sufficient for a gatekeeper mechanism to ensure that a high risk functionality will not start unless another node sends a special message, a permission to start action. If the node malfunctions, nothing guarantees that it won't falsely decide that permission has been received and start the functionality unauthorized. Thus it is better to divide actions so that the nodes control physical processes that interlock with each other if not used in collaboration. In this way, distribution of hazardous action emerges more naturally, usually as a side-effect of the physical system design.

This pattern is a variation of US Air Force Instruction (AFI) 91-104, 'The Two Person Concept' (USAF, 2013), which is initiated to prevent accidental or malicious arming of nuclear weapons by a single person, and is similar to the SEPARATION OF DUTIES principle of accountancy (Szabo, 2004). VOTING (page 282) can be used to make decisions more reliable, but it requires duplication of functionality and thus may be expensive to implement. A hardware implementation of DISTRIBUTED SAFETY is usually referred to as *dual-channel safety switches*, where two series-connected separate switches must be active simultaneously for current to flow.

As one node cannot cause unwanted actions even if it malfunctions, overall system safety is improved. However, as two hardware components are involved, they are jointly more prone to malfunction. This means that the availability of the functionality can decrease. So DISTRIBUTED SAFETY should only be applied when the results of unwanted actions are catastrophic or the division of duties is natural. However, DISTRIBUTED SAFETY does not typically need any additional hardware, so it is an inexpensive way of improving system safety.

If the division of duties is not natural, dividing functions across two nodes makes the system harder to understand. It also makes development harder, as testing and debugging of the functionality must be done for a distributed system.

DISTRIBUTED SAFETY increases distribution, as functionality involves two or more nodes. This can increase communication and make response times longer.

In a satellite system, the satellite must part from the launch vehicle (LV) after reaching orbit. The connectors between the satellite and the launch vehicle are disconnected by means of small explosive charges. As this operation can be done only once, it is crucial that it happens only when it should. However, the launch procedure involves great forces caused by acceleration, and these forces may cause transient malfunctions in the satellite. Furthermore, orbital space is bombarded by cosmic rays, which may cause glitches in controller processors and communication. To make sure that the explosion will not occur until it should, the operation is divided between two controllers that are operated from the ground station. The ground station sends commands to the satellite, and both controllers must be active in order to remove the launch vehicle connectors. Firing the explosives requires two commands: the first command arms the explosives and the second command fires them. If the fire command is not received within five seconds of the arming command, the explosive charge is disarmed. If the explosion does not occur when it was meant to happen, the ground station can reposition the launch vehicle and try again, because is not problematic if the firing is delayed. However, an uninitiated explosion may render the satellite unusable.

6.3   Heartbeat * *

...there is a CONTROL SYSTEM (page 96) in which ISOLATED FUNCTIONALITIES (page 110) and ONE TO MANY (page 131) and/or HIGH-LEVEL PROTOCOL (page 137) have been applied, and nodes in the bus communicate to collaborate. Because of the collaboration, the functionality of a node can depend on another node. For example, to move a boom, the boom controller asks the hydraulic power controller to provide the necessary hydraulic pressure. However, all hardware is prone to malfunction. This means that a node cannot trust other nodes to be always able to take part in collaboration. For example, systems usually have messages that are sent only after a specific event has occurred. If a node has crashed or the bus has broken, event messages from the node are not sent. However, other nodes cannot detect this situation, as they do not know when event-based messages are supposed to be sent. Thus a node can fail silently, compromising the functionality of the whole system.

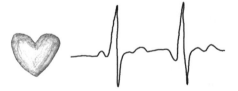

A node or a bus may malfunction silently. Any such malfunction should be detected in order to react to the situation.

To prevent dangerous situations, malfunction of a node should be detected before it causes the safety of the system to be compromised. If nodes collaborate in order to implement functionality, all nodes must be present to ensure safe operation.

When a malfunction is noticed early, the consequences are usually less harmful, and the propagation of the failure can be avoided (see ERROR CONTAINMENT BARRIER, Hanmer, 2007).

Communication channels may break down, so the health of a channel should be monitored continuously to ensure correct communication between nodes. If the communication channel is broken, remedial actions should take place as soon as possible to prevent dangerous situations.

Therefore:

Make a node send messages to another node at predetermined and regular intervals. The other node knows how long a message interval should be and waits for it. If the message does not arrive in time, remedial actions can be started.

To prevent the situation in which a node fails to detect failure in other node(s) or the communication bus, nodes should send a message, called a *heartbeat*, at predetermined and regular intervals. There are nodes in the system that expect these heartbeat messages, and act as monitoring nodes. In this way, the messages act as a proof that the communication channel *and* the message-sending node are functional. If no heartbeat message is received from a node within the predefined interval, the system can assume that the node is malfunctioning. If heartbeat messages aren't received from any of the other nodes, it indicates that the bus (or all the other nodes) are malfunctioning. For example, in the case shown in Figure 6.5, node A can assume that the bus is broken, as it will not receive a heartbeat from any of the other nodes. On the other hand, from node C's point of view, only node A is malfunctioning, as it can receive heartbeats from nodes B and D. However, the error situation is still detected and remedial actions can be started. To find out of the source of the malfunction, you can use FORCED INPUT VALUE (page 106).

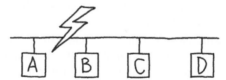

Figure 6.5: In the case of a wire break, the bus might be divided into two individual buses

There are two variants of the heartbeat mechanism: the monitoring node may request the heartbeat (*pull*), or a node may autonomously send a notification (*push*). In the case of a push-type heartbeat, the nodes monitor each other so that they know the status of nodes with which they are collaborating. There may be a centralized master node, a FAULT OBSERVER (Hanmer, 2007), which monitors the health of the system by sending heartbeat requests to all other nodes. In this case, UNIQUE CONFIRMATION (page 154) can be used to identify the individual heartbeat messages between the master node and the other nodes. Independently of the mechanism used, the node waiting for a heartbeat message can start remedial action if a heartbeat message fails to arrive within a predefined time. Usually this means that the node enters a SAFE STATE (page 179). To prevent false alarms, you can use an ERROR COUNTER (page 107), so that a single missed message will not start recovery actions. This is recommended, as for example in the case of a CAN bus messages can easily get lost. In addition, a node should send heartbeat messages only if it is functioning normally, so it might not be a good idea to send heartbeat messages automatically from the messaging driver without the intervention of the control application. This prevents a situation in which the driver sends the heartbeat even though the control application is not functioning properly.

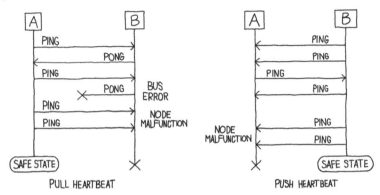

PULL HEARTBEAT   PUSH HEARTBEAT

Figure 6.6: Pull and push types of heartbeat mechanism

Figure 6.6 illustrates the different mechanisms for a heartbeat. A pull mechanism is shown on the left side of the figure. Node A acts as a monitoring node and monitors node B. In the case of a bus malfunction, the heartbeat message is lost. Later in the example node B crashes. As the monitoring node has not received heartbeat replies from node B, it enters a SAFE STATE (page 179). A push-type mechanism is shown on the right-hand side of the figure. The cooperating nodes A and B send heartbeat messages to the bus. In this example, node A crashes and B enters a SAFE STATE.

Bus technologies typically include a means of checking the health of the messaging channel. For example, an EtherCAT bus can detect that a communication wire has broken. In addition, commonly used communication protocols have dedicated heartbeat message types. For example, CANopen (CAN, 2013a) has a HEARTBEAT protocol that is used to monitor its nodes and verify that they are alive. A node periodically sends a special heartbeat message with the node's status information. The period for the heartbeat is defined in the object dictionary of the device. CANopen also specifies a pull-type heartbeat mechanism: a network management (NMT) master is a specific network node that requests the other nodes in the network (NMT slaves) to transmit a message with their current communication state. If a node does not respond to the request within a specific time, the master node can broadcast the failure of the node to the rest of the system. NMT slaves also monitor whether they have received a request from the NMT master.

If the nodes' message exchange is based on time-triggered communication, messages are automatically sent periodically. Using these messages as a heartbeat allows the additional traffic caused by heartbeats to be reduced: instead of waiting for a dedicated heartbeat message, a missing periodic message indicates a problem in a node or the communication channel.

A node normally starts to send heartbeat messages immediately after SYSTEM START-UP (page 293). A monitoring node can deduce the current configuration of the system based on the heartbeat messages. This makes it possible to have optional nodes on the bus and adjust the operation of the machine based on the installed CONTROL SYSTEM OPTIONS (page 394). For more advanced start-up processes, you can consider SYSTEM START-UP or START-UP NEGOTIATION (page 297).

Hanmer describe a similar pattern, HEARTBEAT, in (Hanmer, 2007). Saridakis has a version of HEARTBEAT, called I AM ALIVE, in (Saridakis, 2002).WATCHDOG (page 101) can be used to monitor the health of a single node without a separate monitoring node. HEARTBEAT is usually used in 1+1 REDUNDANCY (page 279) to monitor the functionality of the master node.

As nodes send heartbeat messages periodically, the health of the nodes and that of the communication channels are monitored. A malfunction is detected from a missing heartbeat message and remedial actions can be started.

Although the communication of nodes is monitored, their operations are not. It could happen that a node can send a response to a heartbeat query even if its applications are not working properly. This might be the case especially with COTS components, so HEARTBEAT should be used in combination with other fault-tolerance mechanisms.

Dedicated heartbeat messages add extra traffic to the bus. However, in some cases periodically sent messages can take the place of dedicated heartbeat messages. In this case no additional bus load is caused by the HEARTBEAT.

It is not always known whether a node, or the communication channel between nodes, is malfunctioning. Other measures need to be taken to find out which part of the system is malfunctioning.

In a log truck, a node connected to a CAN bus monitors the weight of the load. To protect axles and wheels, it is important not to overload the truck. The monitoring node measures the weight of the cargo and will send an overload notification only if the limit value is exceeded. A potential overload is reported to the operator using the HUMAN–MACHINE INTERFACE (page 313) of the cabin PC. The limit value of the overload warning can be configured from the PC, as PARAMETERS (page 380) has been applied. As the node sends notifications only in the case of overload, it must be ensured that the load-monitoring node is working during loading, so HEARTBEAT is used. The monitoring node sends CANopen heartbeat message once a second to the cabin PC. If the cabin PC does not receive a heartbeat message for five seconds, the HMI informs the operator that overload monitoring has failed.

6.4   Global Time *

ALSO KNOWN AS CLOCK SYNCHRONIZATION

…there is a distributed CONTROL SYSTEM (page 96) with ISOLATED FUNCTIONALITIES (page 110). The nodes cooperate to orchestrate the functions of the machine. Cooperation may require high-precision synchronization of the nodes so that they execute operations at the correct moment. The system clocks of the nodes are likely to drift and cause clock skew. Sometimes a system might have strict real-time requirements and the precision of operations might be less than 1 millisecond. To reach this level of precision, synchronization pulses are used in scheduling. In addition, 1+1 REDUNDANCY (page 279) might have been used to duplicate the implementation of a functionality. In this case, the active unit and the passive unit need to be synchronized to enable quick switch-over in the case of failure of the active unit.

Different nodes in the system have their own internal clocks that can be set to the wrong time or which can drift and result in clock skew. However, all the nodes need to share common time in order to collaborate properly.

The nodes are collaboratively carrying out operations that need to be executed at exactly the right moment. However, the nodes' clocks are inaccurate and may drift, resulting in clock skew and in actions that are executed out of sync. This offset between clocks is due to the fact that the clocks are not running at exactly the same rate, as their oscillator frequencies might have small differences, causing the clocks to run at slightly differing rates. Furthermore, the actual frequency of oscillators is not always constant, but may depend on the ambient temperature, for example. Sometimes also clock skew alone can cause problems, such as the case of a Patriot missile failure during the Gulf War (Arnold, 2000). A Patriot missile system's clock drifted because of inaccuracies in calculations, causing failure after 100 hours of runtime. The result was that the Patriot was unable to intercept an incoming missile, its designed role.

Sometimes there might be a need to start operations at exactly the same time. This cannot be carried out by sending messages, as messages on a bus have non-deterministic traversal times. Therefore there should be another way to synchronize the start of an operation.

If a system needs to use system time to log all the data and events in the system, the nodes need to share the same system time. Otherwise, as different nodes might have the wrong system time set for them, or because of clock skew, logged events will be in the wrong order when their log files are merged, for example for DIAGNOSTICS (page 350). The correct order of log events is needed for reliable fault analysis and debugging of the system. VECTOR CLOCK FOR MESSAGES (page 149) could be used to find out the correct order of log events, but might require too much storage space to store vector clocks on each node. Additionally, VECTOR CLOCK FOR MESSAGES increases the message payload, which is not acceptable in all cases. Furthermore, in some cases system time is still required to timestamp log entries, as a vector clock does not provide human-readable time.

If STATIC SCHEDULING (page 234) has been applied and separate units need to collaborate and function synchronously, the real-time tasks on all nodes must be started at exactly the same moment. Thus units need to have synchronization pulses that fire at the same time. In addition, time-triggered ONE TO MANY (page 131) traffic requires synchronization pulses or a similar mechanism to manage the bus traffic.

If 1+1 REDUNDANCY (page 279) has been applied, both units (active and passive) run the same process. These units might be physically distributed to prevent failure of both units in cases of failure caused by the environment, for example fire or flood. If this is the case, they need to be able to share the same common time, as otherwise, during a unit's switchover from hot spare to active, the clock skew could manifest itself as a glitch in operation or in the logs. The system clock of the unit may drift independently of other units and thus cannot be used to solve the problem. If VOTING (page 282) has been applied, voters need to share the same system time to know how much time they have to produce voting results.

Shared common system time might also be required in some environments to facilitate the management and scheduling of global resources such as a shared network. Each node might have its own time window to send messages to the messages bus in a ONE TO MANY fashion. These windows need to be synchronized, otherwise collisions might occur.

Therefore:

Use a single node's clock, for example a master unit's clock or external time source, such as a GPS or an atomic clock time signal, to provide global time and to synchronize clocks on all nodes. The external clock can also offer synchronization pulses to pace the collaboration of multiple nodes.

In the simplest case a single node acts as master unit, and its time is used to synchronize the clocks or actions in the system. For example, to synchronize the message bus traffic, a node sends synchronization messages containing one-byte timestamps, indicating the time in the system. Other nodes synchronize their clocks to this time. CANopen synchronization protocol's SYNC message (CAN, 2013a), for example, can be seen as such a synchronization message.

If global time is needed between different units or systems, more advanced mechanisms are required. In this case, a GPS clock or other external time source, such as the Network Identity and Time Zone (NITZ) of the GSM network (3GPP, 2013), is added to the sys-

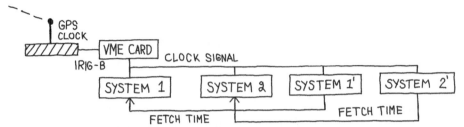

Figure 6.7: An example system in which global time is used to synchronize the clocks of redundant units

tem. Additionally, a dedicated unit that has an accurate oscillator frequency is also added. The oscillator frequency is then altered using an IRIG time-code (RCC, 2004) signal that is received from the GPS clock. Typical commercial GPS clock units are capable of producing synchronization intervals of 1 microsecond using IRIG B time-codes. When the time-code signal is lost, the oscillator keeps the system's global time correct with good accuracy. Figure 6.7 illustrates the structure of such a system. In this example, a COTS GPS clock is connected to a VersaModule Eurocard (VME card) whose oscillator frequency is adjusted using the IRIG B signal produced by the GPS clock. There are two subsystems (System 1 and System 2). Both of these have redundant backup units (System 1' and System 2'), which are slaves to the primary unit. A master unit synchronizes its time by reading a time value from the VME card.

The unit(s) requiring the time (System 1' and System 2' in Figure 6.7) read it from the unit providing the time (System 1 and System 2). In this way, the acquired time is off only by the duration of a read operation. The read operation takes around 10 microseconds maximum in practice, and the clock skew caused by this is normally negligible, as the resolution used in the system time is not that accurate. Naturally, if the read takes place over a bus, this might add delays and thus cause clock skew. In Figure 6.7 the clock signal is also provided for System 1' and System 2' for the case where the master malfunctions. If the system clock is directly altered by using time from an external source and not by adjusting oscillator frequency, you need to take care that all operations are executed correctly despite the changed system time. For example, if the system time is moved forward, some scheduled operations may not get executed. Thus changing the system time directly is usually not recommended.

Normally only the master unit reads the time from the unit providing it, then the master synchronizes the time with its slave (redundant) units. In this case, the rest of the nodes can be synchronized with the master unit's time using, for example, Cristian's algorithm (Cristian, 1989), which describes a probabilistic way for synchronizing clocks in an unreliable network with unbounded message delays.

If a GPS clock is used to deliver synchronization pulses for STATIC SCHEDULING (page 234), you should have a dedicated signal wire from the oscillator unit to synchronized units. A more straightforward option is to synchronize the clocks of the statically scheduled nodes and use the local system time to deliver the synchronization pulses.

If REMOTE ACCESS (page 361) has been applied, the system can synchronize the clocks of different nodes with an external server using the Network Time Protocol (NTP) (Mills, 1989; Mills, 1991). This might be a viable option when a GPS clock cannot be used because the work environment of the machine is problematic, for example indoors or in mines. To synchronize a node's clock with a remote server while using NTP, the node must compute the round-trip delay and offset, which are then used to synchronize the node's clock. There are ways to use time servers other than NTP. In a simple case, the local time server provides a reference time that can be queried by other nodes. These nodes then update their clocks accordingly. Alternatively, the server can poll a set of nodes for their time and then calculate a new common time for the system, which is sent back to the client nodes. In this case, the time server also adjusts its own time. For more details, see the algorithms proposed by Kopetz and Ochsenreiter (Kopetz & Ochsenreiter, 1987), or the synchronization algorithm of Berkeley Unix (Gusella & Zatti, 1987). When working with EtherCAT systems, you might want to look at distributed clocks for ready-made implementations (Beckhoff, 2013).

The clocks of the nodes in the system can be synchronized using an external time source, so timestamps can be used reliably to track events. For example, log entries in a centralized log can be trusted to be in the right order, as all nodes share the same time. Furthermore, actions requiring the participation of multiple nodes can be started at exactly the same time. If the nodes share a common global time, it might even reduce the need for communication, as communication for coordination of execution is not required.

New hardware may be required to communicate with or use the external clock, increasing costs. The system also becomes dependent on this external source, and it acts as an additional external error source. The external clock also creates a single point of failure.

If time servers are used locally on the machine, the approach makes the system more complex and causes additional bus loading.

As clocks of redundant nodes (see 1+1 REDUNDANCY, page 279) are synchronized with GLOBAL TIME, the synchronization pulses used in STATIC SCHEDULING (page 234) will fire at exactly the same moment on different units.

A reactive power compensation unit is used to filter the reactive power in the power grid caused by electrical appliances. In this kind of system 1+1 REDUNDANCY is used to increase the availability of the unit that carries out the compensation operations on the electrical power. There are two reasons for duplication of units: firstly, in three-phase systems each phase has its own identical compensation unit. Secondly, each of these units has a hot spare that can take over if the active unit malfunctions. The redundant units are physically distributed around the reactive power compensation unit's site to prevent the failure of all units in case of fire. If one unit is damaged because of fire, another will still be functional and able to cut off the power.

All redundant units use STATIC SCHEDULING to run their process synchronously with the rest of the system. Synchronization is required to ensure that operations are applied to the electrical power in equal phase, so the system uses dedicated trigger signals that control the application's execution. GLOBAL TIME is used to add a GPS clock and oscillator unit to the system. The oscillator unit is used to synchronize the clock of the master unit. Hot spare units then synchronize their time with the time of the master unit. In the event of a malfunction of the active unit, the passive unit must continue execution from exactly the same code block, otherwise the system would be considered to have failed. This won't be a problem, as all the clocks of the individual units are synchronized, and thus will deliver a synchronization pulse at exactly the same moment.

CHAPTER

7

Messaging Patterns

'Communication usually fails, except by accident.'

Wiio's Law

In a distributed control system the nodes collaborate, and each node has to be connected to all those nodes from which it needs information. However, the physical wiring required for this dictates the communication structure. This means that redesign of the wiring or software on several nodes is needed if the communication requirements change. The sublanguage of messaging patterns shown in Figure 7.1 describes how information sharing should be organized so that the communication infrastructure will be scalable (in terms of the number of nodes) and flexible (in terms of the locations where information is produced and consumed). It also provides the means to decouple control applications from low-level messaging.

ONE TO MANY (page 131) is the root pattern of this sublanguage. It builds a network called a *bus*, on which all nodes share the same communications medium. This makes it easier to design the system wiring, as all communication is carried out over just a few wires. After applying ONE TO MANY, there are several ways to improve the system. HIGH-LEVEL PROTOCOL (page 137) adds an additional level of abstraction, decoupling the actual applications from basic communication services, and provides a basis for more sophisticated services, such as VARIABLE MANAGER (page 201). MESSAGING INTERFACE (page 143) describes how to change the selected bus technology or protocol without having to change the application code. MESSAGE GATEWAY (page 148) describes how to connect different kinds of message channels. MESSAGE CHANNEL MULTIPLEXING (page 148) in turn separates the communication channel from the actual physical bus by creating virtual channels.

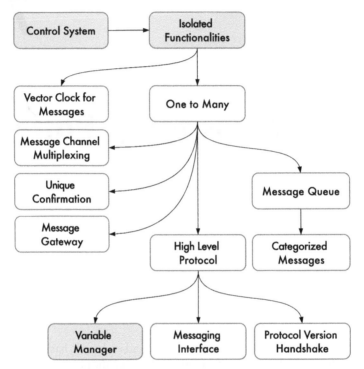

Figure 7.1: The sublanguage of messaging patterns

A distributed control system might have nodes that use different protocol versions for communication. With PROTOCOL VERSION HANDSHAKE (page 143) you can determine the most expressive version of the messaging protocol that can be used in the system. Communication can be further improved with UNIQUE CONFIRMATION (page 154), which provides a means to handle situations in which similar messages need confirmation responses and these responses may be received in the wrong order.

MESSAGE QUEUE (page 143) and CATEGORIZED MESSAGES (page 148) make messaging asynchronous, allowing individual nodes to have different messaging rates and cycle times. Messages can be categorized according to their importance, based on type, sender or receiver, size and so on. The last pattern in this sublanguage, VECTOR CLOCK FOR MESSAGES (page 149), shows how to determine the order of messages sent over the bus, which helps in debugging.

7.1   One to Many   * *

ALSO KNOWN AS BROADCAST, PUBLISHER-SUBSCRIBE

'The wonderful thing about modern technology is the amount of communication and information-sharing it facilitates. And the awful thing about modern technology is the amount of communication and information-sharing it facilitates.'

Mark McGuinness, 'Time Management For Creative People'

...there is a CONTROL SYSTEM (page 96) with ISOLATED FUNCTIONALITIES (page 110), so the system is divided into several nodes. As the nodes have to collaborate, every node has to be connected to all those nodes from which it needs information. Similarly, a node has connections to all other nodes that use the information it provides. Usually these connections are dedicated wires over which communication is carried out. Two-way communication requires at least one wire, creating a mesh (Figure 7.2) in which the communication requirements of each node form a connection to other nodes. The nodes are coupled to each other by this extensive wiring. If the system design evolves during its lifetime and communication requirements change, it can propagate change to the wiring. Alternatively, the nodes can have routing capabilities in their software that allows a sending node to reach a recipient via intermediating nodes.

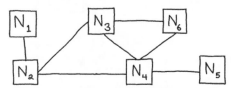

Figure 7.2: A communication mesh with extensive wiring between nodes

Every node has to know how to reach the recipients for information it produces, and this forms tight coupling between nodes. If communication requirements change, redesign of wiring or software on several nodes is necessary.

Physical wiring for communication dictates the communication structure. However, a work machine's design may change over time, as new hardware with different capabilities is added, or the software evolves to have more optimized algorithms. The communication needs of devices may therefore change, as information is produced and consumed in new parts of the system. In such evolving designs, fixed wiring is too rigid a solution. Adding wiring afterwards is laborious, and sometimes even impossible, as the cable raceways may already be full. It may also be difficult or impossible to add new devices after the design phase because the wiring harness only has connectors in predefined places.

In some cases the same CONTROL SYSTEM (page 96) application should be executable on products that have slightly different hardware but still belong to same product family. To allow software reuse, the communication infrastructure should be flexible.

The communication infrastructure should also be scalable, so that new participants can join the information exchange. Communication should allow both an increase in the number of communicating parties and in the amount of information sent by participants. However, the amount of wiring required should be minimized. Wiring is relatively expensive, adds weight and takes up space. The more wiring there is, the harder it is to make it immune to electromagnetic interference or breakage. Assembly of the machine should also be fast. Extensive wiring is slow and error-prone to install, as assembly-line personnel need to install multiple connections: wiring for communication between nodes should consist only of a minimal number of cables, to allow easy installation. Figure 7.3 shows an assembly line for forest harvesters.

Figure 7.3: Assembly of machines should be fast and easy, to optimize the assembly line
Reproduced by permission of John Deere Forestry

There should be a uniform way to communicate with different nodes in the system, so that the developer does not have to be involved in communication details when designing applications. Furthermore, it is crucial that the communication method does not depend on which nodes are message recipients, to avoid errors in development.

Therefore:

Build a network in which all nodes share the same communication medium. A bus network topology is normally used to connect nodes. Nodes send information as messages over this medium. All nodes can receive all messages from the network, and can see if there is anything relevant to them on the bus.

Communication between nodes should be carried over a shared medium to which all nodes are connected. This usually consists of a single cable connected in a bus network topology. In rarer cases communication can be wireless. In these cases, a sender node transmits a message using radio waves and all other nodes receive all messages sent.

Typically however a bus topology is used: the communication medium physically connects the communicating devices and allows information to be sent between nodes (Figure 7.4). The connecting cabling creates the physical layer that is the foundation for data exchange. Information is presented as voltage/current changes that are interpreted as binary data. The data forms messages that all nodes should be able to understand. The physical layer and messages are usually implemented using a commercial solution, such as a CAN bus (CAN, 2013b; ISO, 2003), as these have solved many problems that can arise in the design of such systems. Other physical topologies exist, such as star configurations. A star topology may be used if all branches of the star get all messages, but in the case of CAN, for example, this requires the system to include a central active component such as a hub or a switch.

Figure 7.4: An example of a bus topology network typical of work machines

Every node can now listen to the communication medium and pick up relevant messages. A message is a *frame* consisting of bits. The frame has several predefined parts, which can be single bits or longer sequences of bits. Typically the frame has header and payload fields. The header consists of an optional sender address field, message identifiers and a separate data payload field. Additional fields include a flag indicating whether the message is an acknowledgement, the start of a frame sequence, the end of a frame, intermission bits, message identifiers and so on. The message sender does not have to know which nodes are interested in its messages, only what information is supposed to be published. This information is encapsulated in messages that are *broadcast* to all nodes. Broadcasting means that all nodes can receive all messages sent, and no recipient addressing is used. For example, as in Figure 7.4, an operator uses controls, such as a joystick, which send control messages to the message bus. The boom controller can read this broadcast message and move the boom accordingly. The receiving node usually does not need to know the actual sender, it just reads every message from the bus, and discards the message if it does not contain information it needs. This abstracts the physical location of devices from control applications. As the only interface between the nodes is the messages, it is quite easy to move functionality from one node to other, or even nodes from one location to another.

When designing wired connections, the same considerations apply as when installing any other cabling. For example, you should consider external forces that can break the wiring. However, the situation is usually eased by the fact that communication cabling consists of only a few wires, and machine joints can be negotiated using sliding ring connections.

If two or more nodes try to communicate at the same time, a collision occurs and the bit stream on the bus can become garbled. When messaging is carried out in a point-to-point fashion, collisions happen only when both parties of a channel send their messages simultaneously. Collisions can happen frequently in shared communication channels, as any message sent to the bus requires the communication channel for a specific time span. The probability of a collision increases when the number of nodes on the bus grows. In a shared channel the probability of collision can be diminished if nodes simultaneously listen to the bus when sending messages. If there is message traffic on the bus, the node must refrain from sending its own messages. However, if one node starts transmitting messages too often, the other nodes will have difficulty getting their messages through, as they must wait for a silent period. This is commonly called the *babbling idiot's problem* (Kopetz, 1997) and can be addressed by BUS GUARDIAN (Herzner et al, 2004).

Waiting for a silent moment does not solve the collision problem completely – several nodes may still start sending their message simultaneously when they detect that the message channel is silent. Such messages will collide and the information will not get through. In some bus technologies, bus collision causes both senders to wait for a random interval before trying again. If another collision occurs because sender nodes happen to wait for the same interval, or a third node wants to send its messages, the waiting nodes double their maximum wait period. This mechanism is called *binary exponential backoff* (IEEE, 2008a). It is not well-suited to real-time applications, as it can cause a sender to encounter a long and nondeterministic wait time.

Collision can be detected by comparing any sent data bit to the actual bit on the bus. If the bit on the bus is high when the node is sending a low bit, the node should stop sending immediately, as it means that another node is sending a message at the same time. This prevents the message from being garbled and allows the other node to get its message through. The CAN bus uses this mechanism: at the beginning of the message is a sender id, which also defines the priority of the node: see CATEGORIZED MESSAGES (page 148). A high priority node's identification will get through, as its identification bit pattern will have a dominant bit earlier in the message. The dominant bit is a bit that retains its value on the bus in the case of collision regardless of the bits other nodes send. As sharing of the communication channel is the root cause of collisions, the only way to be sure that they won't happen is to remove sharing by using MESSAGE CHANNEL MULTIPLEXING (page 148). MESSAGE CHANNEL MULTIPLEXING can also be done temporally, so that every message or node has a guaranteed time slot in which it can communicate. Such solutions are known as *time-triggered protocols*, and are used for example in aerospace and aeronautical applications such as FADEC (full authority digital engine control; Riley, 1986).

As messaging channels are rarely totally reliable, there should be some basic capability for error detection. For example, if the message frame has predefined bits that should be always on or off, framing errors can be detected if these bits do not conform to the message definition. In addition, a checksum can be calculated for parts of the message; for example, a CAN bus performs a CRC (cyclic redundancy check) over the data parts of the message. Furthermore, any node should detect whether there are messages on the communication channel that seem to originate from it. This indicates an error situation, which may stem from misconfiguration of the nodes (two nodes having same address) or bit errors in node addresses. This event should be broadcast to all other nodes on the system and to the machine operator.

Selecting a bus standard that is widely used gives the benefits of mass production. Such standard solutions have solved problems related to messaging methods suitable for specific domains. Some examples in machine control include the CAN bus, FLEXRAY (FlexRay, 2005), Local Interconnect Network (ISO, 2013) and PROFIBUS (for example Weigmann & Kilian, 2004) using multi-drop EIA-485 as the physical connection standard. As several vendors adhere to the same standards, ready-made devices such as sensors are available that support standard communications. This makes the system designers' job easier, avoiding the need for proprietary solutions. However, using commercial solutions may cause unwanted dependencies.

Selecting a commercial communication protocol affects the choice of hardware, and vice versa. Vendor lock-in can easily occur when all components must be acquired from a single vendor. A long product lifecycle may further amplify these problems if support for a specific communication solution ends. Proprietary components may also have limited availability in some parts of the world, making it difficult to acquire spare parts for off-the-shelf solutions. In some cases commercial standards have many stakeholders, and the development of the communication solution may be led by companies from other domains. This leads to development being driven by other industrial requirements than your own, and these requirements might bias quality attributes of the system design more than is desirable. For example, the CAN bus is heavily driven by the automotive industry, and its applications have different requirements than those of the work machine industry – cars need quick response times, but the volume of information is smaller. In a work machine more data might need to be transferred, but slower response time may be adequate.

This pattern is an example of PUBLISHER/SUBSCRIBER (Buschmann at al, 1996). It is also documented in the context of DDS middleware as ONE TO MANY (Real Time Inn., 2011). MESSAGE CHANNEL (Buschmann et al, 2007b) and MESSAGE BUS (Hohpe & Woolf, 2003) describe similar mechanisms for building communication channels between nodes, but in different domains.

❖   ❖   ❖

Nodes on a bus may communicate with each other, and the communication infrastructure will be scalable in terms of the number of nodes, and flexible in terms of the locations where information is produced and consumed. For example, if the physical location of a sensor or an actuator changes in the design, it is easy to accommodate the changed messaging requirements for these nodes. In addition, a message recipient is not usually interested in the actual location of a sending node. Location transparency allows additional flexibility in connecting the hardware devices to the connectors. However, the physical properties of the bus and the number of message collisions may set a maximum for the number of nodes on a single bus segment.

As every node listens to all messages on the bus, they can also act as monitoring points for inspecting the condition of the message channel. Thus, the more nodes there are on a bus, the smaller the chance of residual communication errors, making the system safer.

It is easier to design the wiring of the system, as all communication is carried out over just a few wires. Production costs are cut, as fewer wires need to be installed on a machine, and each device does not have to be wired to all other devices. However, the message bus acts as a single point of failure, but as the communication protocol can provide a HEARTBEAT (page 120) service, communication failures are usually easy to detect. For safety reasons it is usually better not to try to communicate at all when the reliability of the message channel is compromised.

As nodes do not subscribe per se to specific messages, but it is their responsibility to read relevant messages from the bus, a sending node cannot know whether its message has been delivered to interested parties if the message channel is not reliable. Some mechanism to acknowledge delivery is therefore needed. For example, in the case of a CAN bus (ISO, 2003), messages are sent with a recessive ACK bit. Other nodes acknowledge messages they are able to receive by setting the ACK bit as dominant on the bus. Nevertheless, a sender does not know if any nodes used its message, and a more elaborate acknowledgement mechanism may be needed.

The selected communication protocol and the physical bus may set constraints for the communication infrastructure. For example, the transfer rate or the length of the bus may be limited. In some cases, the maximum length of dropdown lines – the wiring connecting the device to the bus – and the minimum and minimum distance between nodes to avoid signal reflections may become an obstacle to cable design. Even if wiring consists of only a few cables that are easy to extend, physical connectors are still needed near the location of a new node or device.

In some cases the physical layout of the system makes it hard to use a bus topology. For example, if the system consists of two clearly separated locations where nodes reside, it may be difficult to connect these isolated groups with a cable. It would then be sensible to segment the bus into two separate zones and connect them with a MESSAGE GATEWAY (page 148).

A truck has multiple controllers, as the system design dictates that subsystem controllers should be located as close as possible to the subsystem hardware, to minimize the amount of wiring needed for actuators and sensors. For example, the engine controller is mounted in the engine compartment, on the engine itself.

The controllers should work in cooperation, so the units must communicate with each other. The nodes are connected with a CAN cable that consists of three signal wires, CAN HI, CAN LOW and ground wires, terminated at both ends. This cabling allows the nodes to send SAE J1939 messages to other nodes (SAE, 2013; formerly the Society of Automotive Engineers). The SAE J1939 protocol is designed so that all messages are broadcast to other nodes, making it easy to accommodate additional nodes on the bus. For example, if a trailer is attached to a truck, the nodes on the truck and the trailer can communicate with each other. If the sending node needs to specify a receiving node, the protocol allows addition of the destination node's address to the message.

The messages also have a 29-bit PGN (parameter group number) field that tells the receiving node the purpose of the message and allows its recipient(s) to quickly determine what kind of data the message contains. The PGN field defines whether the message is for a specific recipient or is a broadcast message. It also contains the source address of the message and, in a specific part of the header, the rate of transmission and the message's priority. This part of the header also includes the information indicating the type of payload. For example, the header could contain information that the payload indicates oil temperature. The parameter part contains the actual payload of the message. Each specific parameter group has the same data length in bytes, data type, resolution, offset, range and a reference label or tag. The SAE J1939 standard also allows multipart messages and definition of new parameters. Sending messages longer than the maximum length of a frame (8 bytes) is possible using higher-level services. It also has an address claiming mechanism and built in diagnostics.

7.2   High-Level Protocol * *

...there is a CONTROL SYSTEM (page 96) with ISOLATED FUNCTIONALITIES (page 110). The individual nodes communicate in a ONE TO MANY (page 131) fashion using messages that have simple metadata information and a data payload. However, there are several different communication requirements, such as real-time machine control, video streaming, REMOTE ACCESS (page 361) connections and so on. These contexts have different requirements for communication, which may even be contradictory. For example, there can be a trade-off between high data throughput and deterministic real-time response, as it is usually hard to have both properties on the same communication channel simultaneously. The minimal generic set of communication services that would suit all these requirements is not enough alone to serve all of them, so much development effort on more sophisticated services is needed. On the other hand, if all possible communication services were implemented as one all-round service, it would be too cumbersome to use, and the requirements of extreme cases would never be met because of communication trade-offs. For example, high security of communication often reduces the throughput of the communication channel, so it is hard to design a protocol where these would coexist. In addition, no matter what approach is made to implementing communication services, the messaging protocol used will still be coupled with the selected bus technology. This means that changing the bus technology used would also require changes to the control applications.

It is difficult to match a single messaging solution to all the communication requirements that can arise in a specific domain without tightly coupling communication with the selected technology.

Messaging is an important part of applications in any distributed system, and a great deal of functionality is built upon assumptions about messaging infrastructure. However, messaging should be flexible enough that applications do not have to be changed if the messaging infrastructure changes.

Future messaging needs can be hard to predict, as the control system may have an extremely long lifecycle. Devices in the system should be interoperable, regardless of their vendor. Thus any messaging should be interpretable by selected third-party devices and components from the same product family, to increase the possibility of software reuse. In addition to third-party software, standardization in messaging helps in adopting COTS components to the system. Testing and analysis is easier if messaging adheres to a known standard solution with a ready-made tool set. Adequate spare parts need to be kept in stock: standard solutions can also help with this.

As the various communication needs have such fundamentally differing communication requirements, it is difficult to use a general-purpose messaging scheme. For example, if messaging requires hard real-time responses, it is hard to achieve high data throughput. Thus, it must be possible to optimize messaging for a specific requirement and domain.

Therefore:

Add a high-level protocol to decouple applications from low-level messaging. The payload of low-level messages should hold information that can be interpreted by a higher-level protocol. The high-level protocol forms a basis for additional services, such as acknowledgements, addressed messages and so on.

Organize the communication architecture in layers based on the chosen messaging scheme (see ONE TO MANY, page 131). The cabling is the foundation for data exchange, the *physical layer*. On this layer information is exchanged by means of voltage/current changes that are interpreted as binary data. When you have this infrastructure in place, create a common language called a *message protocol*. The message protocol defines the means of transferring data over the physical layer by creating a *data link* layer. Now there are two layers of protocols, the data link layer and the physical layer, already implemented by ONE TO MANY if it is applied. These two layers are the two lowest levels of the Open Systems Interconnection (OSI) model (ISO, 1994). The OSI model describes a seven-layer protocol stack, and defines which services should reside on which layer.

All protocols transfer information as data fields embedded in messages. The information contained in the payload can be interpreted as a higher-level protocol message, which in turn is capable of carrying its own data payload. Multiple levels of protocols can be stacked by using lower-level protocols to carry a higher-level protocol as data: the OSI model is based on this. The lower level does not know anything about the semantics of the data it carries, so it can transfer any higher-level protocol without customization. If higher-level messages are too larger to fit into one lower-level data field, they can be split over several lower-level messages. In addition, a mechanism on the higher level is needed to construct high-level messages from small chunks carried by the low-level protocol. Making this kind of construction easier usually requires sophisticated services from the low-level messages, such as retaining the order of messages, notification of lost messages, resend requests and so on. See Figure 7.5 for an example, in which the L1 layer protocol message carries one L2 layer protocol message in its payload. Every message has a payload, as well as metadata such as headers, error correction information, trailing bits for padding and so on. The L3 level message is too large to fit in one L2 level message, and so needs to be divided into two L2 level messages.

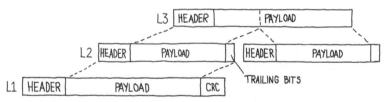

Figure 7.5: An example of nesting of higher-level protocol messages in lower-level messages

The protocol architecture consists of a stack of several layers which add progressively more sophisticated services to the physical layer's raw bits. If a lower-level protocol only conveys the data and does not provide sophisticated services, a higher-level messaging protocol should provide them. A protocol can provide common control concepts for addressing, handshaking, information sharing, data flow control, sophisticated error detection, some basic concepts about connections, and data streaming, transportation and network layers are usually built on top of the physical and the data-link layers, which may include the concepts of connection, data flow control and host addressing. Finally, the topmost layer of the stack is the application itself, which understands the semantics of the transported data.

In most protocols there are a couple of layers that add addressing to messages. Addressing can use several layers: there can be separate physical and logical addressing schemes for devices. Each layer may have its own address, and even if the lower level reads a message from the communication channel, the higher levels can perform finer-grained filtering based on the addresses and message identifications, rather than passing it upwards through the protocol stack. There are several addressing strategies. Messages can be broadcast to all nodes (see ONE TO MANY, page 131) or sent to a specific node in *unicast* fashion using an addressing scheme. On the bus, a sender node is only interested in the logical recipient of the message, and even this is not important when a message is broadcast. The same goes for the recipient: it usually does not need to know the actual sender, and just reads all messages from the bus. If a message is not addressed to the node, or does not contain information the node needs, it simply discards the message. If messages are meant for a subset of nodes, a *multicast* addressing scheme is needed.

In the *fieldbus* technology CANopen (CAN, 2013b), the physical and data link layers are usually implemented by CAN (ISO, 2003). The layers above that, including the transportation and application layers, are in the scope of CANopen.

Figure 7.6 shows an example of a layered protocol stack in which a sensor application process measures hydraulic pressure. This information is encapsulated in the application layer data. Under the application layer, the transportation layer is configured such that the measurements are sent periodically, and will not need any kind of acknowledgement from data consumers. The data link layer adds information about the sender's logical address identification. The lowest level physical layer sends the data in ONE TO MANY fashion as a simple bit stream. Other nodes read this bit stream and interpret it a message, passing it on to the data link level, where it is identified as interesting (or not) based on the sender's address. The data is passed to the transport layer, where it is interpreted as periodic information that does not require acknowledgement. If the message is a request, the transport layer automatically acknowledges the sender. On the application layer, the application on the node can read the pressure information and use it in its own operations. All dependencies between protocols are now between adjacent protocols in the stack, and the application only uses the application protocol interface.

In many cases it is not sensible to devise an in-house messaging protocol, as many available solutions are available from third-party vendors, for example CANopen, J1939 (SAE, 2013), PROFIBUS (Weigmann & Kilian, 2004) and FLEXRAY (FlexRay, 2005). Most of these implement several layers of protocol architecture, and have a selection of devices that directly support the whole protocol stack, making it easier to integrate them into the system design. These ready-made solutions are therefore often called *integration platforms* instead of protocols. The protocol messages act as an integration interface, and the nodes' hardware, firmware and software can be thought of as a single component. However, problems arise when different vendors implement different sets of features that are defined as optional in the standards, have different interpretations of the standards,

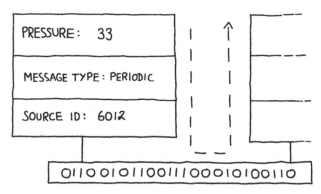

Figure 7.6: An example of several protocol layers stacked upon each other

have bugs and performance issues and so on. See COMPONENT-BASED CONFIGURATION (page 386) and MESSAGING INTERFACE (page 143) for details.

You should use discretion when selecting a commercial protocol, as there is a risk of vendor lock-in. The selection of protocol is a fundamental design decision, and might have long-lasting consequences, as the communication infrastructure needs huge investments in devices and software. In addition, tools, diagnostics equipment and so on usually depend heavily on the protocol. Acquiring these tools can be costly for machine manufacturers, so tools should be selected to have as long a lifespan as possible. The lifespan of the selected messaging scheme is likely to last at least as long as that of one product family. However, any protocol may evolve during the lifespan of a product, and there might be nodes on the same bus that use newer versions of the chosen protocol, for example if a node needs to be replaced with one with a newer hardware version. This problem is addressed by PROTOCOL VERSION HANDSHAKE (page 143).

When implementing your own applications using a protocol stack, it is useful to 'wrap' protocol handling in a library, which will abstract the actual messaging mechanism used. This library is called a MESSAGING INTERFACE (page 143). VARIABLE MANAGER (page 201) can be seen as one way to abstract the actual communication. If the bus capacity is limited and some messages need to get through regardless of bus load, using CATEGORIZED MESSAGES (page 148) will help. Usually commercial protocols implement simple prioritization mechanisms to avoid collisions. If the messaging parties need asynchronous communication, this can be solved by applying MESSAGE QUEUE (page 143), which can be implemented on several protocol layers. To provide the most suitable communication solution for different parts of the machine, a designer may have to select several bus technologies, for example to integrate a J1939-based engine bus to a CANopen-based vehicle bus. When a system design uses several bus technologies, MESSAGE GATEWAY (page 148) can be applied to connect different buses together.

MESSAGE CHANNEL (Buschmann et al, 2007b) and MESSAGE BUS (Hohpe & Woolf, 2003) describe similar mechanisms for building communication channels between nodes, but in different domains. HIGH-LEVEL PROTOCOL (page 137) allows straightforward implementations of client-server patterns such as those presented in (Aarsten et al, 1996). For more information about building protocol layers, see for example PROTOCOL LAYER (EventHelix, 2013a) and LAYERS (Buschmann et al, 2007b). Patterns related to protocol system architecture can be found in (Pärssinen & Turunen, 2000).

A high-level protocol adds an additional level of abstraction, decoupling the actual applications from basic communication services. Changes in communication are now only visible to the application on the highest-level protocol interface. However, some bus capacity is sacrificed by sending several nested protocols: every protocol adds its own metadata, consuming space in the data payload.

Most problems associated with messaging have already been solved with COTS protocols. The effort of designing an efficient messaging method can therefore be reduced to selecting a suitable ready-made protocol implementation such as CANopen. In addition to reducing the design effort, standard solutions allow the use of third-party devices and tools. It also helps to have solutions to communication problems that are proven in practice.

Protocols can provide more sophisticated services on top of basic messaging, for example protocols that are optimized for a single purpose, such as HEARTBEAT (page 120) or time synchronization between nodes.

Selecting a suitable protocol stack allows the designer to tailor services to the system. The only dependencies are on the lower-level protocols, so if a lower-level protocol has to be changed due to outdated technology, new messaging requirements or similar reasons, only the interface to that protocol changes. As a higher-level protocol does not care about the protocols below the next lower layer, it does not matter if the whole stack underneath changes as long as the same level of service is guaranteed at the protocol interface as is provided for the upper level. On the other hand, if no replacement is available for the protocol with the same level of service, the design is stuck with the original choice.

A bulldozer uses the CANopen protocol to connect its CAN-based devices. The bulldozer's application protocol conforms to the CiA 415 profile for road construction machinery (CAN, 2005). The physical layer is a high speed CAN bus carrying the CAN 2.0 protocol. These CAN messages carry CANopen version 4.3 events, for example closed-loop control messages to the leveling mechanism of the bulldozer. When the main computer sends a command to the controller that implements leveling, it maps the event to a PDO message and passes this to its CAN driver. The CAN message data field includes a CANopen event, which is transferred to the leveling controller. The controller reads the message and identifies that the message is relevant from the message description. It then maps the event to the command and adjusts the leveling mechanism as required.

7.3   Messaging Interface *

A high-level protocol may change over time, or the same control system software may be used in different communication setups. This should not require changes to the implementation of applications.

Therefore:

To make the application independent of the system bus technology and messaging protocol, construct a common application programming interface (API) to provide uniform messaging functionality. The API provides methods, for example for sending and receiving messages. Messages consist of data presented in the form of programming language structures.

For the complete pattern, please see `www.wiley.com/go/controlsystemspatterns`.

7.4   Protocol Version Handshake

Nodes should use the latest version of a communication protocol, as it is probably the most efficient. However, a system may also have nodes that use older protocol versions, and there must be a way to communicate with them. The most efficient protocol common to all nodes should be determined.

Therefore:

Design a handshake sequence common to all protocol versions. In the handshake, all nodes announce the highest protocol version they support during system start-up. Once nodes have announced their highest version, each node selects the highest common version for communication.

For the complete pattern, please see `www.wiley.com/go/controlsystemspatterns`.

7.5   Message Queue * *

ALSO KNOWN AS MESSAGE BUFFER

…there is a distributed CONTROL SYSTEM (page 96) in which several nodes communicate in ONE TO MANY (page 131) fashion via a message bus. The main responsibility of each node is to control a specific functionality. These functionalities have real-time requirements that set a working cycle time for the node. However, as parts of the whole system, nodes have to collaborate by communicating, and thus they are dependent on messaging, as sending messages requires other nodes to be silent, and receiving a message usually requires that some action be taken. A node cannot risk its main function by sacrificing too much time to messaging. Designing the system so that all nodes have to be synchronized for messaging wastes resources, or is impossible. In other words, MESSAGE CHANNEL MULTIPLEXING (page 148) has not been used to multiplex messages.

Individual nodes have different messaging rates and cycle times, so a message cannot be processed immediately at the receiving end. On the other hand, sending a message might not be possible at a given moment, as some other communication might be taking place on the bus.

Message exchange with other nodes should not interfere with a node's own functionality, even though messaging rates might differ due to different control responsibilities. All nodes should be able to send and receive messages regardless of other nodes and the current load on the bus. A sender should not have to wait for a suitable moment when the bus is free before sending a message. In addition, the receiving node should always have enough spare time to receive the message before a new message is sent to the bus. Nodes should be able to send and read messages when their processing load allows. In addition, the nodes' communication capacity may vary greatly depending on their function. Some real-time nodes have busy control loops and only some time for vital messaging, while other nodes might have ample time.

In an unsynchronized system, the volume of messages sent at a specific moment cannot usually be predicted, as it depends on the environment and operator stimulus. The number of messages sent can vary, as some nodes produce a high volume of message traffic, while other nodes do not. The same goes for receiving messages – some nodes get a lot of information from the bus, while others may not need any information for their function. This typically makes it impossible to predict bus load. Even if the messaging protocol dictates that messages should be sent periodically, the processing time for a message may still vary and cause unexpected delays.

The order of messages is usually important, as message data represents the state of the machine at the moment the message was sent. If this is the case, it is crucial to read messages in the order in which they were sent.

Therefore:

Spread message rate differences by making messaging asynchronous. Add queues to each node for receipt and transmission of messages. Implement mechanisms for putting messages in the queue and sending messages from the queue. The same mechanism can read messages from the bus, add them to the received messages queue, and notify the application about new messages.

First, for all nodes requiring asynchronous messaging, add separate message queues for sending and receiving messages. If a node has multiple messaging channels, each of them needs a pair of queues. The actual queues are typically in memory, holding the messages in the order they are to be or sent or were received. Usually messages are stored in an area of memory that applications and the message queuing component can read and write. The actual implementation of queues may vary, but arrays or linked lists are common solutions. An array might have fixed length, or dynamically grow and shrink. A dynamic queue never runs out of space as long it fits in the node's memory. However, as messaging should be as fast as possible, take into account that dynamic memory management consumes resources: this might make it impossible to make message processing time-deterministic. The same holds for linked lists, but they have the additional weakness that updating list links requires time. You can combine both static and dynamic allocation by placing shorter queues in a reserved pool from which additional space can be taken if the active queue runs out of space.

A good way to implement a message queue is by means of a *ring buffer,* where the data array is connected end-to-end. This means that the next element after the last element of the buffer is the first element. In addition to the buffer itself, two pointers indicate the first and last elements of the queue. In this way moving the elements in the array is never necessary. When a new message is received, it is inserted after the last element in the queue, and the pointer to the last element is updated to point to the new message. When the first element in the queue is processed, it is not removed, but the pointer to the first element is updated to point to the next element in the queue. CIRCULAR BUFFER in the Portland Pattern Repository gives further details (Portland, 2007).

In the simplest cases the application can handle message queuing by itself. Typically, the application polls the queue whenever it has time to do so, to see if there is anything to process. This approach is not always feasible, as an application developer is not usually interested in details of message processing, and the application must reserve time to process the queue. To have a full-blown message queuing service, a mechanism to process the message buffer must be designed in addition to the buffers themselves. This is usually implemented as a separate thread or process, so that it can work concurrently with the application. A message service's foremost duty is to handle the queuing of the messages. In addition, it must support a way to notify the application that there are messages ready to be read. In the simplest cases a notification flag can be used, but usually a more sophisticated mechanism is needed, as the application must block its normal function while processing the queue. This mechanism is typically an interrupt, or in more advanced designs the queue processing service may use a registered callback mechanism. When a message is processed into the receive queue, the callback function is called and the application can access the message for further inspection. The message queue works in 'first in, first out' (FIFO) fashion, so that the oldest message in the queue gets processed first, preventing the order of received messages being changed.

The processing mechanism's work is two-fold per buffer. As shown in Figure 7.7, at the sending end it fills the buffer with the messages application A is delivering to the message channel. Whenever possible, the message queue processing component takes the oldest message in the queue and outputs it to the bus. The output rate might be restricted, due to limited time slots on the bus or collision avoidance. At the receiving end, the compo-

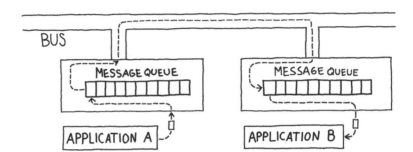

Figure 7.7: Message queues at the sending and receiving end of the communication channel

nent reads the messages from the bus in the order they were received, puts them into the buffer as soon as they are received and notifies application B. The application at the receiving node reads received messages from the buffer as soon as it has time. The message is removed after being read from the queue, which can mean either actual deletion of a list element or just updating the pointer from the first element to the next queued element.

If the message queue service is encapsulated with an interface, the basic operations required consist of the following methods: *read message, send message, get queue size*. In more complex cases you might consider more advanced methods, such as *remove specific message, clear queue*, and *register callback function* for specific types of messages. Callbacks are also useful if there are multiple applications on a node that are each only interested in their own types of message. If callbacks are not available, message processing can use a filter mechanism to check whether there are new messages for the application.

A message queue is usually implemented so that there is a small buffer at the hardware level and a bigger one at the messaging hardware driver level. In this way the application does not need to care about the basic queuing of messages unless the application developer wants to implement more sophisticated features for the queue.

It may be helpful to add an override system to the queue for use if an emergency situation requires immediate response. This could allow emergency messages to circumvent the queue completely and be processed as soon as they are received. The contents of a message queue usually have no use in an emergency situation. However, this can cause problems, as message order is lost, and might be problematic if the system returns to normal operation after the emergency situation.

Buffer size depends on many variables and is an important design issue. If too small, there might be buffer overflows, possibly causing unpredictable behavior or security issues. Even if overflow is prohibited, messages will be lost. EARLY WARNING (page 169) can be used to decrease the chance of possible buffer overflows, or to determine a suitable buffer size.

If the order of received messages is not important, you can consider using FRESH WORK BEFORE STALE (Hanmer, 2007) to determine the processing order of messages. This pattern provides a solution to the problem that, as messages are queued, they can become obsolete while waiting for processing. The pattern treats queues in these situations as 'last in, first out' (LIFO). In this way, the newest and probably more urgent messages get processed first. However, queuing messages gives the application the opportunity to decide which messages should be sent or read first; see CATEGORIZED MESSAGES (page 148) for details.

A similar mechanism for message queuing was described in (Douglass, 2002), but it focuses mainly on communication between threads, not nodes on a bus.

Message queues result in a system that has the ability to communicate asynchronously without messaging being constrained by the bus rate. Resource utilization of the nodes and the bus itself is improved, as congestion peaks can be leveled during quieter periods. Messages are not lost, and their order is preserved even during traffic peaks. This makes the system more scalable, as adding new nodes typically does not require redesigning messaging schemes.

Message queuing does require some resources, as messages must have a storage space while queued, and queue processing takes additional time. If the storage buffer space is fixed length, it must accommodate the worst case number of messages, thus wasting space in other situations. If the space is too small, messages may be lost or the application might crash.

The message queuing service helps application development, as it hides the technical details of the bus. An application can just send and read messages using the queues, and does not have to be concerned with timing issues. On the other hand, if nodes have to synchronize their operation precisely, this is more difficult, as a sender cannot be sure when the receiver actually reads a message.

A full-blown message queueing service is used in a forest harvester in which nodes communicate via a CAN message bus. The harvester head's node listens to the cabin PC for commands, and in return sends state information and measurements (for example saw blade position, feed rollers status, tree diameter and fed length). In the harvester head's controller unit, the CAN hardware has a buffer that queues messages that are to be sent or received from the bus. When the application code needs to send a message, it passes it to the CAN driver software component, which inserts the message into the queue. The application code does not have to worry about the details of message transmission. It can rely on the message queue to send the message to the bus whenever there is a suitable free slot, and thus does not have to block its own execution. At the receiving end, when the message is read from the bus, the CAN driver notifies the control application that there are new messages in the queue by means of an interrupt, and that action should be taken to process the messages before the queue overruns.

7.6   Categorized Messages * *

As a message channel has limited throughput, not all messages will be delivered immediately. However, some messages relate to events, which may require immediate attention.

Therefore:

Add a category to messages according to their importance. Importance can be based on type, sender or receiver, size and so on. Separate MESSAGE QUEUE (page 143)) are implemented for each category.

For the complete pattern, please see www.wiley.com/go/controlsystemspatterns.

7.7   Message Channel Multiplexing *

To allow deterministic operation of a machine, it needs to be ensured that messages get delivered. A node may 'babble' to the bus and prevent other nodes from communicating.

Therefore:

Separate the communication channel from the physical bus by creating virtual channels. Virtual channels can be multiplexed onto one physical channel by dividing the channel into time slots. A virtual channel can also be divided over several physical buses.

For the complete pattern, please see www.wiley.com/go/controlsystemspatterns.

7.8   Message Gateway * *

ALSO KNOWN AS MESSAGE CHANNEL GATEWAY, CONVERTING MESSAGE FILTER

Parts of a machine may have different communication needs, so various messaging channels are required. The parts need to cooperate as a whole, so the messaging channels should be connected.

Therefore:

Add a message gateway component to the system which routes message traffic between message channels. If needed, the component can filter messages according to specific criteria defined in the system configuration. In addition, the component translates messages from one protocol to another.

For the complete pattern, please see www.wiley.com/go/controlsystemspatterns.

7.9   Vector Clock for Messages *

...in a distributed CONTROL SYSTEM (page 96) (page 96) with a message bus (see ONE TO MANY, page 131) there are multiple nodes that communicate with each other. Before sending a message, the node timestamps message with the current time so that, if something goes wrong, the order of messages sent throughout the whole system can be determined. This is required, for example for DIAGNOSTICS (page 350), to find the root cause of failures. Unfortunately, the internal clocks of the nodes are not accurate, and clocks drift over time because of oscillator inaccuracy. This clock drift can make the perceived and recorded orders of the messages unreliable. GLOBAL TIME (page 124) cannot be used to synchronize the clocks if the nodes do not have a way to deliver synchronization pulses, or if it would cost too much to use the required hardware. In extreme cases, where very strict real-time response times are required, and even if clock synchronization could be used, the resolution used in timestamping might not be accurate enough. So normal timestamping is not sufficient to determine the order of messages reliably.

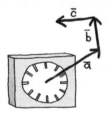

In the case of failure the order of messages sent over the bus needs to be determined reliably to find out what caused the failure. However, the exact moment when a message was sent is not important.

For DIAGNOSTICS it is useful to determine the order of sent and received messages in the whole system. Additionally, it should be possible to be sure whether a message triggered the sending of other messages by other nodes, or whether those messages were sent independently of the initial message.

Development testing of the system and analysis of the causes of faults become easier if the order of sent and received messages is known. For example, if the system encounters a fault or a bug is detected, the situation can be reconstructed by sending the same messages in simulator. This requires that the exact order of messages is known and recorded.

The system clocks of the nodes in a distributed system are not accurate and may drift, resulting in a clock skew. If events occurring in the system were logged using timestamps from drifting clocks, different nodes would have a different perception of the order of events. In the case of centralized logging, the logged order of events will differ from the real order of messages. If these logs are gathered and analyzed to trace a fault or other interesting event, it may be impossible to determine the order of events because of clock skew. The order of events is more important for diagnostics than the actual time when an event occurred.

In a distributed system where nodes communicate over a bus, message traversal always involves some delay which is probably unknown. System clock values on the nodes increment independently during this traversal time, and therefore it is hard to assert anything about the temporal relationship of two messages when using normal timestamps. For example, suppose node A sends a message to node B and timestamps the message with its current time. Node B's clock has drifted and its clock is behind than of node A. Node B simultaneously sends a message to node A and timestamps it with B's timestamp value (smaller than A's). However, as A's message takes some time to be delivered to B, node B might perceive that node A has sent the message after node B's message was sent. Of course this was not the situation. So other mechanisms are needed to determine whether one event occurred before the other, or whether nothing can be said about their relationship.

In asynchronous and sporadic communication, the sending times of messages is not known beforehand, so the order of messages cannot be deduced later. When communication is synchronous, the moment of message sending *is* known. However, the moment when a periodically sent value changes cannot be known beforehand, and so needs to be recorded to allow later diagnosis of faults.

Therefore:

Add a message counter to each node. This counter is increased whenever the node sends a message. Also add a vector clock to each node, which is used to timestamp all messages sent in the system. This vector clock consists of separate message counter values for all nodes, including the sending node's own counter. A node's vector clock is updated when a message containing a vector clock timestamp larger than receiving node's clock is received, or when the node's own message counter is increased.

Each node in the system has its own message (or event) counter, which is an integer value indicating how many messages the node has sent, or how many local events have occurred. In a system with N nodes, a vector clock is an array of N integers. A vector clock provides *logical time*, which consists of the node's own message counter value and other nodes' message counter values. When a node sends a message, it timestamps the message by attaching the current vector clock value to the message. This is called a *vector clock timestamp*. For example, in a system with four nodes, a node's vector clock could have the values [4,3,5,1], and when the node sends a message it attaches this vector clock value to the message. This means that node A (the first value in the array) has sent four messages, its local message counter value is 4, and the node's perception of other nodes' message counters are 3, 5 and 1. The vector clock on a node is updated according to the following simple rules:

1 Initially all values of each vector clock on each node are zero.

2 Just before a node timestamps an event using its vector clock, it increases its own message counter by one and updates this to the vector clock.

3 A node adds a vector clock timestamp to every message it sends.

4   When a node receives a vector timestamp in a message, it compares it with its own vector clock value and takes the greatest value message counter node-wise. In other words, it merges the changes. For example, in a three-node system, a node's vector clock could have values [1,1,1]. The node receives a message containing a vector clock timestamp having values [0,1,2]. The resulting vector clock value on the node after merging these two timestamps would then be [1,1,2].

This approach makes it possible to determine the causality between two messages by comparing their vector timestamps. A message was sent after another message only if all message counter values in the vector clock timestamps are the same or greater than in the other message. For example, a message having a vector clock timestamp of [1,1,1] was sent earlier than a message having one of [1,1,2], as all its vector clock values are the same, or less, than the other message's. If there is no causality between the messages, nothing can be said about the order of the two messages, but only that they occurred independently of each other. For example, it cannot be determined which of the messages having timestamps [1,1,1] and [0,2,1] was sent first, as neither of the vector clock timestamps have all message counter values the same or greater than the other.

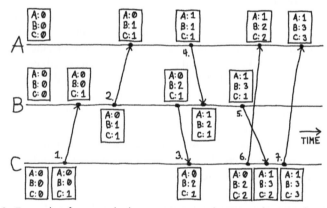

Figure 7.8: Example of vector clocks in messaging between three nodes A, B and C

Figure 7.8 illustrates an example of vector clocks in a system with three independent nodes. Initially each node's vector clock is [0,0,0], meaning that nodes A, B and C have not sent any messages. Now node C needs to send a message and increases its own message counter to 1. C updates its message counter value to its vector clock and attaches its vector clock timestamp to the message that is sent to node B (message 1). When B receives the message, it compares all the values in the received vector clock timestamp to its own vector clock. It sees that node C's perception about node A is zero, which is the same value that node B has, so it doesn't update this part of its own vector clock. The same applies for node B's own vector clock timestamp value. Then node B notices that the vector clock timestamp received with the message has a larger value for node C's message counter, so B updates its own vector clock, as this had a smaller value. Then B creates an event and sends a message to node A (message 2). Now B's message counter is increased to 1, so it updates its value for its own vector clock. This vector clock is used to create the vector clock timestamp for the message. Now node A receives the message and updates its own vector clock in the same way as node B did earlier.

As the example shows (messages 3 and 4 in Figure 7.8), nodes can also send messages independently of each other: nodes A and B send messages simultaneously. It cannot be said later which event took place first: was it node A that sent a message to node B (message 4), or node B that sent a message to node C (message 3)? The same applies for messages 5 and 6. However, it can be seen from the vector clock that neither of these messages could cause another message to be sent. Normally, in a system using ONE TO MANY (page 131), this is not a big problem, as all nodes receive the messages. In the example illustrated in Figure 7.8 only unicast messages are used, which makes the vector clock update frequency slower. In a system using a message bus the update frequency is inherently higher – in general messages are always sent consecutively. However, the order of messages can change because of the timings of message sending, MESSAGE QUEUE(s) (page 143), or if messages are prioritized using CATEGORIZED MESSAGES (page 148). It may also be useful to track changes in the values sent over the bus using vector clocks, rather than using a sent message count.

Sometimes it might be necessary also to count local, internal, events that do not need to be communicated to other nodes. These internal events can be virtually anything that happens locally on the node, such as mode changes, counter resets, etc. This gives better resolution for the vector clock, as external events (messages received) can be aligned with local events with better accuracy. If local events are used, the node's event counter (and vector clock) is increased by one with every event that takes place, regardless of whether it was an external or an internal event. In this case, it might be the case that when node B receives the first message from node C, the vector clock in the message might contain values [0,0,6], for example, and node B's own vector clock could have values [0,11,0]. So the time when the message was received would be equivalent to [0,11,6]. In addition, the receipt of a message might also increase the event counter in the receiving node. If this was the case, the time when the message was received would be [0,12,6].

In a system with a periodic messaging scheme, a data value is sent periodically regardless of its value. For example, a temperature reading might be sent every tenth of a second. In a system like this it is not very useful to increase vector clock values every time a message is sent. It is better to count value changes – the node increases its message counter only when a periodically sent value such as a temperature reading changes, not when each message is sent.

While timestamps generated with vector clocks are useful in logs, to analyze the order of occurred events, it is still a good idea to add system clock time to the log entries as well, as it makes analyzing the logs easier. For example, if a machine operator remembers that a fault or anomaly occurred around 4 pm, a maintenance engineer can browse the log entries from that time. Vector clock timestamps are not visible to the operator, so they do not help in this case.

If the system has the capability to record all the messages and their corresponding vector clocks, the vector clock mechanism can be used to synchronize data between nodes.

For example, if a node is offline for some reason, for example because of a cable break, the vector clock mechanism can be used determine which messages the node has missed. These messages can then be delivered to the node to synchronize its state. However, this kind of approach is not suitable for real-time use, so it is advisable to do such synchronizations during SYSTEM START-UP (page 293) or as EARLY WORK (page 259).

Sometimes it is useful for a node to maintain an estimate of the other nodes' vector clocks. This approach is referred to as a *matrix clock*. For more details, see (Raynal & Singhal, 1996). FAULT OBSERVER (Hanmer, 2007) or BLACK BOX (page 355) can be used to create an entity in the system that can log the order of events. In addition, DIAGNOSTICS (page 350) can use vector clocks to analyze the root cause of a fault: sent messages can be repeated in the same order in a simulator. As the message sequence can be repeated in the simulator, the code is easier to debug to analyze the cause of a fault.

Causality of events can be determined reliably. This helps in implementing system DIAGNOSTICS and finding the root cause of a fault. Using vector clocks, nothing can be said about events that have occurred simultaneously. However, this is not normally important when locating a fault.

If a malfunction is noticed in a machine and its vector clocks are used to record the order of messages, the situation leading to the malfunction can be repeated in a testing or simulation environment. This makes debugging easier, as it does not need to be carried out on real hardware. This presumes that the vector clocks and corresponding messages are stored somewhere, which requires storage space.

The volume of storage needed to store vector clocks and the volume of extra message payload is proportional of the number of nodes in the system. If there are a large number of nodes, the storage space requirement may become huge. However, there are ways to minimize the payload increase of messages. For example, (Raynal & Singhal, 1996) present techniques where only the changes to the vector clock are transferred over the bus.

A mining drill rig's control system uses vector clocks to timestamp all messages sent to the message bus in ONE TO MANY (page 131) fashion. BLACK BOX is used to record all the messages and their vector clock timestamps. A hydraulic hose in the boom breaks, causing a failure in the control system. Both boom controller and drill controller fail, the hydraulic pump reports a failure, and the system enters a SAFE STATE (page 179). The machine operator is informed that there are multiple failures in the system via the HUMAN–MACHINE INTERFACE (page 313). The operator starts a system DIAGNOSTICS application, which uses vector clock information to determine the order of the error messages received. The diagnostics show that the hydraulic pump was first to send a message about low hydraulic pressure, and when the boom controller and the drill controller received this message, they also sent error messages to the bus. Now the diagnostic application can instruct the machine operator to check the hydraulic pump and hydraulic hosing. In this way, the problem can be located by the operator.

7.10   Unique Confirmation

Messages in a distributed system may be delivered out of sequence. If all acknowledge messages are identical, the receiver has no means to determine which request was acknowledged.

Therefore:

For each request message, assign a unique identifier, which is represented in its own field. When the message is acknowledged, the response message contains the same unique identifier as the request. The requester keeps track of messages that are not yet acknowledged. In this way, the receiver of an acknowledgement always knows to which request the response applies, and can resend the request if necessary.

For the complete pattern, please see www.wiley.com/go/controlsystemspatterns.

CHAPTER

8

Event-Handling Patterns

'You may not control all the events that happen to you,
but you can decide not to be reduced by them.'

Maya Angelou, 'Letter to My Daughter'

In a distributed control system the nodes cooperate with each other. In order to collaborate, a node exchanges information on the current state of the system, and sends results from its computations to other nodes. In addition to state information, other events may arise that need to be dealt with. These events may be rapid changes in system state, or hazardous situations that must be handled as soon as possible. For this reason, event messages should be easily identifiable from other traffic, and should not be lost because of a fault. On the other hand, periodic sending of a status may not be viable option, as it would congest the bus.

NOTIFICATIONS (page 156) describes how to communicate noteworthy or alarm events and state changes in a uniform way. NOTIFICATION LEVELS (page 162) adds level information to notifications, so that the severity of an event can be distinguished, and makes it easy to remedy the situation in a severity level-specific way. For example, events that need urgent attention can be handled before other events. NOTIFICATION LOGGING (page 166) introduces a way to store notifications, so that you can determine which notifications have occurred even if the machine has already stopped. In many cases this helps to find the root cause of a fault.

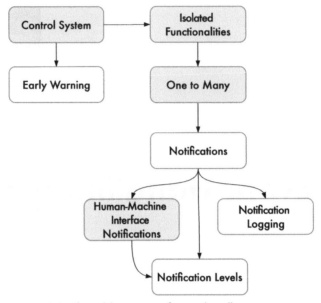

Figure 8.1: The sublanguage of event handling patterns

The last pattern in the sublanguage of event handling patterns (Figure 8.1) describes how to add an EARLY WARNING (page 169) mechanism to indicate when a resource, such as a message buffer, permanent storage space or CPU time, is about to run out, so that the control system can detect the situation and remedial actions be started. This is important, as insufficient resources may crash the whole system or cause a hazardous situation.

8.1   Notifications *

ALSO KNOWN AS ALARMS, EVENTS

...there is a distributed CONTROL SYSTEM (page 96) with ISOLATED FUNCTIONALITIES (page 110). The nodes communicate in a ONE TO MANY (page 131) fashion using a communication channel such as a CAN bus. Many messages are sent through the bus. As the system is distributed in nature, nodes need to know the status of other nodes: that they are functioning correctly and in which state or OPERATING MODES (page 175) they are. Nodes need to react to changes in system status quickly, or hazardous situations can arise. For example, when a bus fault occurs the situation needs to be recognized immediately so that remedial action, such as entering a SAFE STATE (page 179), can be taken. However, the communication channel cannot be trusted, as the work machine environment exposes the bus to vibration and dirt. The bus may sometimes malfunction momentarily, losing some messages. However, it is of great importance that all messages related to state changes and faults are delivered to the nodes interested in such messages.

The nodes have many kinds of status changes, for example a change of an operating mode, or a malfunction. Other nodes in the system need to react to or be aware of these status changes. However, it cannot be assumed that a single status message will get through.

Reaction to changes in the system's status must be rapid. When a malfunction occurs, there may only be a fraction of a second to prevent catastrophe. When a node malfunctions, therefore, the other nodes should react to the situation immediately to start remedial actions, such as entering a SAFE STATE.

Events in the system should be delivered in a rapid and deterministic way. If a node sends a message to a bus each time a state changes, there will probably be a flood of messages to the bus in the case of a malfunction as all nodes report it. Furthermore, if a malfunction is transient, it can be hard to detect when the malfunction has cleared, so that other nodes may not be aware of the current status.

When bus loading is high, other traffic on the bus should not delay the delivery of event information. To make the system safe and robust, event handling must be supported. At the same time, the event system should be easy to understand for developers. Event handling should therefore be consistent throughout the system.

If SEPARATE REAL-TIME (page 237) has been applied, the system will be divided into at least two levels: machine control and operator. On the operator level there might be a cabin PC running a HUMAN–MACHINE INTERFACE (page 313). A PC is typically slow to boot up compared to the controllers in the system. If an error or malfunction occurs during boot up of the cabin PC it might go unnoticed, as there is no means to inform the operator.

Although modern bus technologies are highly fault-tolerant, a single message on the bus might be lost due to a transient communications fault. Such faults might be caused for example by a faulty connector, or due to vibration of the cable. Status messages should therefore be communicated in a periodic manner to ensure their delivery. However, as there are multiple nodes in the system, the bus load might increase unacceptably if every node sends periodic status messages.

It should be relatively easy to add new events, modify events, or remove support for events. For example, if CONTROL SYSTEM OPTIONS (page 394) is used to create support for accessory devices, new events are likely to be added when accessory devices are installed.

Events occurring in the system should be traceable; that is, it should be easy to detect where an event has originated. If the source of the event can be traced, it should be possible to find the root cause of the event easily, such as a malfunctioning component.

Therefore:

Store event-related data in a ring buffer on the node producing the information. When an item is inserted into the ring buffer an event counter is incremented. Communicate this event counter value to the bus, so that other nodes interested in the status of the node can detect when new data is available in the ring buffer. They can then read the ring buffer contents using asynchronous communication.

Add a ring buffer (see CIRCULAR BUFFER, Portland, 2007) and an event counter to each node. The ring buffer stores all data relating to events. Every time the state of the ring buffer changes – that is, when a new item is added or removed – an event counter is incremented by one. The node should send the event counter value to the bus periodically. For example PDOs can be used in the case of CANopen (CAN, 2013b). Another option is to send a notification event until it is acknowledged. However, this might require defining responsibilities for who should acknowledge the notification.

Other nodes that are interested in the status of the node sending its counter value can detect changes in its state by reading the counter value. If the event counter value on the bus has changed, it means that there is a change in the node's state. In this case, the node interested in status information reads the actual event data from the ring buffer by requesting this data from the node where the event occurred. The node sends the contents of its ring buffer to the requesting node. The event data is not removed from the ring buffer, as other nodes may need to read it too. For example SDOs can also be used in the case of CANopen. Whatever mechanism is used for reading the status, it should employ a protocol that has a handshake for the data transfer, otherwise the data might not get transferred, causing problems.

If VARIABLE MANAGER (page 201) has been applied, the easiest way for a node to detect changes in the status of other nodes is to provide each node's event counter as a variable in the VARIABLE MANAGER so that other nodes can access it. As the ring buffer is a data buffer rather than a numerical variable in the VARIABLE MANAGER, it cannot be directly accessed as a VARIABLE MANAGER variable. However, the VARIABLE MANAGER could offer an interface for reading its status buffer data using SDOs. This avoids the developer having to implement a request for status information.

What an event is might depend on the system, but typically changes in operating mode or detection of a fault are recognized as events. When an event occurs, information relating to it is stored in a ring buffer. Data in the ring buffer typically consists of an id field, state information, notification data, an event description and a timestamp, as shown in

Figure 8.2. Each event data message has its own type identifier (ID) with which the notification can be identified. In addition, the id could have some semantics. For example, the first two or three values may pinpoint the origin of the notification: which sensor or actuator caused the notification. For example, ID 501 could mean that the oil pressure is low, and ID 502 could mean that the oil pressure has reached a critical level.

| ID | STATE INFORMATION | NOTIFICATION DATA | TIMESTAMP | DESCRIPTION (OPTIONAL) |

Figure 8.2: Typical structure of a notification: ID, state information, notification data, timestamp and optional description

The node that detects an event timestamps the moment the event was noticed. Problems might emerge if the node reading the notification data and the node producing it have clock skew: GLOBAL TIME (page 124) can be applied to remedy this.

Sometimes event notifications also have states. Typically these states are 'normal' (notification off), 'active' (notification on) and 'inactive' (notification on). When the system is started, the notification's state is 'normal', but when a notification is triggered, its state changes to active. When the node orchestrating the operation of the system (typically a cabin PC on the operator level; see SEPARATE REAL-TIME, page 237) acknowledges the notification, its state is changed to inactive. The acknowledgement process can take place as follows: when a malfunction is detected, the cabin PC node reads the status of a malfunctioning node from its ring buffer. The graphical user interface on the cabin PC shows HMI NOTIFICATIONS (page 340) to the machine operator, who acknowledges it by pressing a button in the user interface. If the malfunction is such that the machine can continue operating, the notification is then cancelled by setting the status of the event to 'inactive'. This means that the actual malfunction is still present in the system, but it is currently inactive. When the malfunctioning functionality is next used, the state of the notification (see Figure 8.3) may change back to 'active'. Inactive faults may reset themselves after time, or when the system is rebooted. The status is changed back to 'normal' when the malfunction is reset. Different policies might be in use; for example, changing only some notifications back to 'normal'. Some inactive faults may be triggered back to 'active' after a specific period, for example, if oil pressure was too low and a notification was activated. The operator acknowledges the notification and sets it to inactive. Such a notification should become active again after a specific time if the oil pressure remains too low.

The state diagram shown in Figure 8.3 illustrates the state changes of notifications. As Figure 8.3 shows, there might be also a separate counter to record how many times the notification has been active. This might be useful for proper handling of transient faults, allowing the system to ignore an event until it has occurred several times. See ERROR COUNTER (page 107) for more details.

Notifications can have additional information describing events attached to the notification by the originating node. Once the notification data is retrieved, for example by a cabin PC, it can show this information to the operator, for example using HMI NOTIFI-

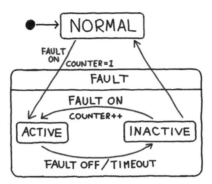

Figure 8.3: States of a notification: normal, active and inactive

CATIONS (page 340). This information can be used for further analysis and logging; see NOTIFICATION LOGGING (page 166) for more details.

A text description of the event is typically not included in the message, as it would have to be transferred over the bus, increasing the bus load. Text descriptions are therefore mapped to notification IDs by the node reading the notification on receipt. This description can then be written to a log file or used in an appropriate way.

The solution described here is based on a scheme in which the node that produces a notification buffers the events. Sometimes a simpler approach might be for the receiving node to buffer events. In this approach, the producer just sends 'fault on' and 'fault off' messages to the bus for each fault event. These events are timestamped and processed at the receiving end. If this approach is used, notifications sent to the bus can be bundled. For example, a 32-bit bus signal – that is, a variable in a VARIABLE MANAGER (page 201) – can represent 32 different states of devices ('fault on' or 'fault off'). This is a simpler solution and therefore suitable for systems with limited resources. However, the problem with this approach is that if the receiving node has not booted up, or is otherwise malfunctioning, the state information might be lost, as no nodes are recording the events for the non-functional receiving node.

The various fields in notifications, such as id and descriptions, can be configured using a system-wide configuration file, such as an XML file that is used to generate the notifications used in the system. The configuration file can contain notification IDs for each event, and a list of nodes that are interested in each notification. Every node should take care of triggering the notifications and incrementing the event counter. For more information on system configuration, see COMPONENT-BASED CONFIGURATION (page 386).

If several kinds of notifications of varying importance exist, you should consider applying the solution described in NOTIFICATION LEVELS (page 162). NOTIFICATION LOGGING (page 166) can be used to record the history of which notifications have occurred in the system. CATEGORIZED MESSAGES (page 148) can be used to define priorities between notification messages and other messages. There are also times when a notification can be ignored, for example during start-up, as described in DEVIL MAY CARE (page 190). You should also take care that notifications are given at the proper moment, not too late when nothing can be done to remedy the situation. EARLY WARNING (page 169) gives further details on this issue. In addition, EARLY WARNING can be applied to the ring buffer where the data is stored, to avoid data loss in event handling. The ring buffer size is selected during development based on the estimated volume of events. In a normal system 50 elements in a ring buffer should be sufficient. When multiple simultaneous notifications are active, the system should probably enters a SAFE STATE (page 179), as it is likely that there is a malfunction, so 50 elements should be enough to store all the events during normal operation.

Exceptional and noteworthy events or state changes can be broadcast system-wide in a unified way. It is easy to add, modify or remove events using a configuration file read by the notification service.

Timestamping of events is accurate, as the same node that detects the event also generates a timestamp for it. In addition, none of the notifications are lost: a ring buffer has a finite size, and in a flood of events some of the event data might be lost. However, even in this case a receiving node knows that it has not received all events. EARLY WARNING can be applied to remedy this problem.

Notifications can be used to deliver information to the notification receiver (cause, origin, etc.) without causing excessive bus load, as the actual data is requested only when needed. Furthermore, a periodically sent event counter can be used as a HEARTBEAT (page 120) signal.

Notification states allow notifications to be active or inactive. This makes it possible to deliver the same notification again if the cause of the problem has not been removed. This can make a machine more reliable, as inactive faults can re-emerge periodically.

Notification messages can be recognized among other traffic on the bus relatively easily. This makes debugging or recording DIAGNOSTICS (page 350) data easier.

Notifications in a distributed system may cause additional bus traffic, as the event counter is sent periodically. Notifications can therefore decrease system performance if bus throughput is a problem. However, the mechanism lowers the worst case bus load, as the number of events does not necessarily increase when a malfunction occurs.

Configuration of notifications can often be automated, especially if COMPONENT-BASED CONFIGURATION (page 386) is in use. However, configuring notifications might sometimes require some additional manual work. Even when no extra work is required, the notification IDs and descriptions need to be documented.

In a forest harvester, the harvester head uses notifications to inform the rest of the system about anomalous or noteworthy events taking place in its domain. Suppose that the marker (used to mark cut trees) runs out. The harvester head control application generates a fault and increases its event counter. The event counter is passed to other nodes using VARIABLE MANAGER (page 201). The cabin PC notices the change in the harvester head's event counter. It requests data from the harvester head about the event, and receives notification data containing the notification id that corresponds to the event that occurred (no marker). The notification data contains information on the marker container's current fill level, and the information that the notification state has been set to 'active'. Once the application on the cabin PC receives this data, it can display a notification to the machine operator using HMI NOTIFICATIONS (page 340). The operator acknowledges the notification and its status is changed to 'inactive'. The operator can continue working normally without any marker. If the operator tries to mark trees, however, the state of the notification is again changed to 'active' and the operator gets a new error message on the cabin PC's screen. Once the marker container is refilled and the marker functionality has been used successfully once, its notification status is changed to 'normal'. This reset also happens if the system is rebooted.

8.2 Notification Levels * *

….there is a distributed CONTROL SYSTEM (page 96) in which NOTIFICATIONS (page 156) are used to communicate noteworthy events. However, different kinds of events can occur, such as operating mode changes, faults, errors and system state changes. More granularity in notifications could be useful, as different events have different consequences. Sometimes you need to inform the operator that a process they have started is completed, for example an automated sequence of boom placement. Some of the events might have state, while others are stateless, such as notification of the completion of a function. Faults, however, often have states. For example, if a node detects a fault in a sensor reading, it activates the notification process. Once the system or the machine operator has acknowledged this notification, the state of the fault will be 'inactive' (if the malfunction does not prevent the system from functioning). In general, different events have consequences of different severities.

Different kinds of notifications should be grouped according to their severity in order to be able to determine their consequences in a deterministic way.

Different kinds of events may have different consequences. To allow rapid development and avoid programming errors, it should be easy to distinguish between different event types and to handle the consequences of a specific event type. Furthermore, some event types may need faster response than others, to prevent an error from propagating or to start remedial actions to avoid a hazardous situation.

Some events, such as faults, might stop some operations. On the other hand, some events might be an essential part of normal functionality. Events that can make the system stop functioning should be handled first. Generally, events should be processed in the order of severity of their consequences.

An event *not* occurring in the system might indicate a fault or failure. For example, if an automatic control sequence is initiated, but the node does not respond with a message signalling the completion of a function within a predefined time, it might be malfunctioning. The system should be able to detect those situations in which an event is absent for too long.

Therefore:

Add notification level information to notification data. Typical notification levels are notices, warnings and faults. The notification receiver has its own way of remedying the situation for each level. In addition, notification data is processed by dealing with the most urgent notifications first, to ensure short response times.

Typically there are three levels of notifications in the system. Additional levels can be used whenever necessary. The level affects how a node receiving the notification reacts to it. If multiple events are active simultaneously, the node should process them in their order of severity. The node first processes events whose level is 'fault', then warnings, and finally all notices. Figure 8.4 shows the structure of a notification message when using notification levels.

ID	STATE INFORMATION	NOTIFICATION LEVEL	NOTIFICATION DATA	TIMESTAMP	DESCRIPTION (OPTIONAL)

Figure 8.4: Typical structure of a notification message including a notification level

The *faults* level is used to indicate that some part of the system is malfunctioning. For example, if a boom positioning sensor has failed, the boom controller detects this and creates a fault notification in its notification ring buffer (see NOTIFICATIONS, page 156). When the other nodes on the bus notice this, they may enter a SAFE STATE (page 179) automatically, and propagate the fault by changing their state, adding state information to their event buffers and sending incremented event counters to the bus. If SAFE STATE has not been applied the fault still needs to be propagated somehow. If HMI NOTIFICATIONS (page 340) is used, fault level notifications typically cause automatic actions from the system even if the notification is not yet visible to the operator, to ensure fast response.

Warning level notifications are used to indicate that an event that needs operator attention has occurred. For example, if the oil pressure of the engine becomes low, a warning is given. Operation can still be continued, but there is an anomaly in the system that should be dealt with soon or a fault will occur. Typically, warning level notifications are also shown to the operator, but they do not require automatic actions from the control system.

The *notice* notification level consists of events that are *supposed* to happen in the system. For example, when the machine operator starts the system's SELF-TESTS (page 106), the process will run on its own. When this process has finished, a notice level notification should be triggered to indicate completion. If HMI NOTIFICATIONS are applied, the user interface can show this notice level notification to the operator. Some of the notice level notifications, however, are not intended for the operator, but are merely used to indicate some other event, such as an operating mode change (see OPERATING MODES, page 175). For example, when an operator or maintenance engineer activates a calibration mode, notice level notification can be used to propagate state change in the system.

Notification levels are added to the notification data as a new field. Sometimes the first (or some other) digit of the notification id can be used to express the notification level, for example 1 for notices, 2 for warnings and so on. The node reading a notification can use this level information to determine the priority of messages. Typically faults are most urgent, then warnings, and lastly notifications. However, you can also use different granularity for notifications, for example operating event, info event, warning and fault. In this case the priority may be different.

In principle, all notifications have states, as described in NOTIFICATIONS (page 156), but when notifications are enhanced with levels, all notification states may not be necessary. For example, notice level notifications rarely need states – they just indicate that an event has occurred. Thus the status field of a notice level notification might not be in use. One option is to use normal status for all notice level notifications, and just never change the state. Another option is to have a different data structure for different levels. However, this might make uniform processing of all notifications more challenging.

When multiple notifications are active simultaneously, they should be processed in their order of importance, for example faults first, then warnings, etc. Within a single notification level, such as a fault, it might be necessary to prioritize notifications. If this is the case, you should consider adding new notification levels. When using notification levels it might be necessary to use CATEGORIZED MESSAGES (page 148) to ensure that high priority notifications are processed first at the receiving end.

Different kinds of events can be distinguished easily using separate notification levels. This makes implementation of HMI NOTIFICATIONS (page 340) easier, for example, as each level can have its own method of display in the user interface. Handling events also becomes more systematic, as the control system can react automatically to notifications on a specific level, but wait for the operator's response for other notifications. Similarly, NOTIFICATION LOGGING (page 166) and user interface views can also easily deduce which notifications to log and display.

Notification levels enable the system to remedy a specific kind of events in the required way. For example, when a fault occurs, a machine can always enter a SAFE STATE (page 179) automatically without human intervention (see MINIMIZE HUMAN INTERVENTION, Hanmer, 2007).

When using notification levels it is easy to create a priority order for notifications. This is especially useful if multiple notifications are active simultaneously. However, within a notification level, a finer-grained approach might be needed, or new levels added. Notification levels are relatively easy to add, modify and remove, but implementing the processing of different levels in all nodes may require a lot of work, as all nodes should be able to identify different levels.

Deducing notification states becomes more complex, as all states are not necessarily used in some notification levels. In addition, notification levels increase message size slightly, although this is usually not a problem.

The operator of a forest harvester activates tree cutting by pressing a button on the control panel. Once the machine has finished cutting the tree, the harvester head creates a notification informing the system that the cutting operation has finished. The level of this notification is 'notice', as this event does not require human intervention. The event counter is increased and also updated in the VARIABLE MANAGER (page 201). The event counter value is sent to the bus and the cabin PC running the user interface receives this message. Once received, the notification triggers a state change in the system, as the system is now ready for the next operation. Additionally, the cabin computer lights up an LED on the dashboard informing the operator that they can start feeding the log through the delimbing knives.

In another example, an operator is driving a forwarder to the stand to pick up logs. On the way the engine controller detects that the oil pressure is low. The engine controller generates a warning level notification. This notification is read by the cabin PC. Once the notification is received by the cabin PC, it illuminates a warning light using BEACON (page 336) and sounds a warning, alerting the operator to the situation. As the notification is just a warning, the warning text disappears from the screen after a couple of seconds, but the dashboard light is still lit, as the fault still exists, but its state is changed to inactive. If the engine controller notices that the oil pressure reaches a critical level, it can generate a fault level notification.

In a third example, an operator has started the sawing process for a log and the saw chain breaks. The harvester head generates a fault notification and sends it to the bus. All nodes go to a SAFE STATE (page 179) on receiving this notification, which means that they stop the current operation. A fault is displayed to the operator on the user interface after the system has entered the SAFE STATE. Now the operator needs to change the saw's chain. Once they have done that, they must restart the system to disable the fault notification. At start-up the machine runs diagnostics that determine whether the saw is OK, and as it detects that this is the case, resets the notification state to 'normal'.

8.3 Notification Logging *

…there is a distributed CONTROL SYSTEM (page 96) in which noteworthy or alarm events are communicated using NOTIFICATIONS (page 156). Nodes fetch the notifications from their producers. The real-time environment makes it hard to detect the source of a fault or error while the machine is operating. Furthermore, some situations that generate a notification are transient, for example a notification indicating high oil temperature. The oil might have already cooled by the time the notification is delivered to the operator, so the temporary fault situation might go unnoticed. However, the machine's manufacturer wants to gather information on typical faults for their own analysis, so that faults typical for the model can be avoided in future.

To find out which transient faults have occurred and to analyze the root cause of a fault, there should be a way to find out which notifications have occurred in the system. It should be possible to view the notifications that occurred after the machine has been stopped.

In many cases, when a fault or error occurs, the root cause of the fault cannot be deduced at the time as the environment is too fast-paced. It might seem that a controller is faulty, but the fault might be caused by another controller or broken sensor. Sometimes the whole event might go unnoticed because the situation normalized soon after the notification was triggered. For these reasons, it should be possible to find out later exactly what happened.

The order in which events occurred may be important in solving the root cause of a fault. It should be possible to know reliably the order in which events occurred. Sometimes it is also necessary to know the exact time and the state or operating mode of the machine when an event occurred (see OPERATING MODES, page 175). For example, if the machine malfunctions momentarily, the machine operator can report the approximate time of malfunction to maintenance personnel. To track the problem, the control system should offer a means of analyzing information related to malfunctions that occurred in a specific time period.

Diagnostics during routine maintenance of the machine should be able to tell what kind of errors have occurred. There should be a way to produce a report of severe events.

It is valuable, for research and development, to know the typical faults and errors occurring in the machine, so it should be possible to collect statistics about error events occurring in the system. In this way, the next version of the system (software or hardware) can be developed so that these faults can be avoided.

Therefore:

Create a logging mechanism that logs notifications that occur in the system. Add timestamps, if necessary, and notification source to all logged notifications, allowing the order of notifications to be deduced.

There are two strategies for logging notifications: you can implement a centralized logging mechanism on one of the nodes, or create separate logs on each node. In a distributed solution, a node creates a log entry when it creates a notification in its event buffer. When the logs are accessed, either using a separate tool or via a HUMAN–MACHINE IN-TERFACE (page 313) using a cabin PC graphical user interface, they are gathered from the nodes, merged and displayed.

Another option is to create a single log file on the master node, which is usually the cabin PC. In practice, this means that the cabin PC needs to listen to all system events and query their event information during operation. The nodes themselves keep the event information in RAM, so it will be lost in the event of power failure. The benefit of a centralized approach is that a cabin PC can typically store even large log files. A dedicated node can be used to store logs.

A log entry should contain at least a notification id, notification data, state information and timestamp. Additional fields can be used whenever necessary. For example, notification levels might also be important. A log entry's timestamp should contain the time when the event occurred. Depending on the approach to logging, the timestamp of receipt of the event can be included. Figure 8.5 illustrates the typical design of notification logging.

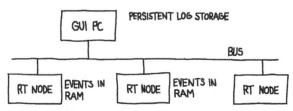

Figure 8.5: The typical structure of notification logging

Log entries can be kept in memory, but entries should be written into a file eventually. However, if log entries are written to a file as soon as they are created it can decrease system performance. It is therefore advisable to keep log entries in memory and write them to a file periodically, to balance RAM usage and system performance. If no file system is available, logs must be kept in memory or sent to another node for storage. Balancing between RAM usage and system performance depends on the volume of notifications typical of the system. If there are normally only a few, they can probably be written to a file as they occur, but if there are hundreds of messages a second you might consider a different approach. You should also take into account the case of power failure, when log entries stored only in memory will be lost. Storing log entries in memory is therefore a trade-off between reliability and traceability. The interval at which log entries are written to file depends on how critical the log data is: the most critical information should probably be written to a separate log file immediately.

Using timestamps for log entries can be troublesome: nodes system may not share a common time due to clock drift. If this is the case, keeping the notifications originating from various nodes in sequence might be impossible. In that case you can use VECTOR CLOCK FOR MESSAGES (page 149) or GLOBAL TIME (page 124) to resolve this. If VECTOR CLOCK FOR MESSAGES is applied, log entries should still contain a human-readable time value, as it makes debugging easier. If clock time local to the node is used to determine the order of log entries, despite its problems, the timestamp should use the most accurate resolution of time common to all nodes.

Logging is typically implemented in a centralized manner, as shown in Figure 8.5. A HUMAN–MACHINE INTERFACE (page 313) is often used to access the logs. NOTIFICATION LEVELS (page 162) can affect the way events are shown on a graphical user interface: often only faults and warnings are shown to the operator. Other NOTIFICATIONS (page 156) can also be logged for use by maintenance personnel. However, the machine operator is rarely interested in seeing all NOTIFICATIONS, as this will make important ones harder to spot.

In time log files can become large, requiring excessive disk space, so should be cleared periodically, for example when the system is updated, or during routine maintenance, as opportunity allows. Sometimes it might be acceptable to clear log files during a reboot. Another option for disk space management is to use log rotation. This means that there are for example five log files, each of which contain 5,000 entries. Once the first log file is full, the second file is used to store subsequent entries, and so on. Once the fifth log file reaches its maximum size, the first file is deleted and used again. This allows over 20,000 log entries to be stored. Alternatively, you might consider using a lightweight database system such as SQLite (SQLite, 2013) for logging instead of plain log files.

If necessary, you can also filter notifications to be logged: not all notifications may be relevant from the logging point of view. Filtering log entries should be defined based on the context. If NOTIFICATION LEVELS (page 162) is used it should be easy to determine which levels should be logged and which not. It might also be a good idea for each notification level to have its own log file, so that a single file won't grow too large, or just a dedicated log file for the most critical notifications. It might also be advisable to be able to disable filtering when necessary, for example for debugging or maintenance purposes. NOTIFICATION LOGGING can be used as a basis for implementing DIAGNOSTICS (page 350) or BLACK BOX (page 355).

Notifications can be recorded in log files for later examination, for example to determine the root cause of a fault, or for tracking down transient faults. This also helps to implement a DIAGNOSTICS service or BLACK BOX.

The order in which notifications occurred can be determined later by gathering all log files. This makes locating a fault easier, as it shows the order of events.

Notification logging can decrease system performance, as a log entry must be created for each notification. If notifications are stored in RAM and have not yet been transferred from the originating node to a central store, they can be lost in the event of power failure.

In a mining drill rig notification logging is used at the operator level. The machine control nodes store events in RAM, and nodes interested in NOTIFICATIONS data request it from the originating node(s). The drill rotation sensor detects that the drill has stuck, and creates a notification for this event. The cabin PC notices the increase in the rotation sensor's event counter, so it requests the notification data from the sensor using CANopen's SDO protocol. Once the cabin PC has received this data, it timestamps it and adds to the log file. As the notification is of a 'fault' level – see NOTIFICATION LEVELS (page 162) – the system enters a SAFE STATE (page 179). HMI NOTIFICATIONS (page 340) of the fault is displayed to the operator, who acknowledges it. The machine cannot continue operation as the fault is still active, so the operator calls a maintenance engineer. Using a separate tool, the maintenance engineer accesses all log entries, giving more information on the problem and allowing analysis of any potential malfunction.

8.4 Early Warning * *

> *Computer Voice: (alarm sound) Warning: Out of dark matter fuel.*
> *Leela: That's not a warning! A warning's supposed to come*
> *before something bad happens.*
> *Computer Voice: (alarm sound) Warning: Engines will shut down in one second.*
> *Leela: That's more like it.*
>
> *Excerpt from conversation in 'Futurama: Bender's Game' animation film (2008)*

…there is a distributed embedded CONTROL SYSTEM (page 96). Only limited resources for memory, CPU time or slots in the MESSAGE QUEUE (page 143) are available. Resources must be available for machine control tasks to be run safely, otherwise hazardous situations may occur. Similarly, no messages should be lost due to MESSAGE QUEUE overflow, as lost messages result in an inconsistent system state. However, all resources are not statically reserved, and might therefore become exhausted at runtime. This situation must be detected by the control system so that it can start remedial action.

In a control system, resources (for example CPU time, memory, oil and so on) can run out. The control system needs to start remedial actions to avoid hazardous consequences before resource availability reaches a critical level. A situation in which a resource is about to run out should be detected, as insufficient resources may crash the whole system or cause a hazard. For example, message buffer overflow could crash the system: it is too late to react to the situation once the resource has already become depleted.

Resource usage cannot always be known during development, and can be discovered only at runtime. There should be a way to test that runtime resources are sufficient for the system. Often testing needs to be carried out using the actual machine hardware. In this case, the testing process should not cause danger to the testers.

To make the machine cost-effective, available resources should be sufficient for machine operation, but use of excessive resources should be avoided. Often the resources required can only be determined when testing the system in field tests. There should be a safe way to determine the resources needed.

Usually resources cannot be increased dynamically. For example, message buffer sizes are statically allocated, or only a certain amount of memory may be available for an application. Sometimes dynamic allocation of resources is not used, to avoid the programming errors that are more likely when allocating resources dynamically. Furthermore, poorly designed dynamic memory allocation may lead to memory fragmentation, which will lead to unpredictable response times and system behavior (Nilsen & Gao, 1995, p. 151; Masmano et al, 2008). Dynamic resource allocation is also slower than static allocation, so is often not an option.

Some resources, for example oil in the engine or flash memory rewrite cycles, are consumed over time. The machine operator should be informed when such a resource is about to run out to, so that they have time to react to the situation, for example by booking maintenance.

Therefore:

Add an early warning mechanism that monitors the available level of a resource. Before the resource runs out, the mechanism warns concerned parties, such as the machine operator, so that remedial action can be taken.

An early warning mechanism can be added to monitor the consumption of different resources in the system. It warns the control system or the machine operator when a resource is about to be exhausted. Implementation details depend on the resource monitored. Basically this means that a trigger is added at a specific consumption level of a resource. When this level is reached, a predefined remedial action is triggered. Typically the remedial action is to notify the machine operator, for example by using BEACON (page 336)) or HMI NOTIFICATIONS (page 340), or by notifying other nodes using NOTIFICA-TIONS (page 156).

In the case of a message buffer (see MESSAGE QUEUE, page 143), early warning would be triggered when a specific usage level of buffer or queue is reached. Suppose a message buffer contains slots for 100 messages. Once the message buffer holds 70 messages an early warning would be triggered. This allows the system to react to the situation and, for example, start processing message of higher priority while the buffer still has room for new messages. For example, in a system that stores messages in a ring buffer, the first message in the buffer will be overwritten and lost when the buffer is full unless the system checks whether the buffer is full before adding a message to it. However, even if the system checks whether the buffer is full, the mostly recently received message will be lost, as it cannot fit in the buffer. If NOTIFICATION LEVELS (page 162) has been applied, notifications of different severity levels can still be sent when early warning limits have been reached. For example, a warning could be sent when the buffer has reached 70 percent capacity, and fault notification triggered once its maximum capacity is reached and the system has entered a SAFE STATE (page 179). Figure 8.6 illustrates the early warning mechanism when using a message queue.

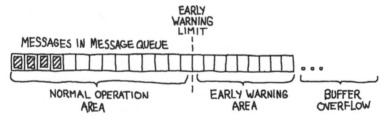

Figure 8.6: An example of an early warning mechanism when used with MESSAGE QUEUE

Determining early warning limits is not always straightforward. You at least need to consider the following factors when choosing an early warning limit. First, how rapidly remaining resources are consumed, and second, how much time the system needs to react to the situation. However, early warning limits should be as close as possible to the level at which reaction would be too late, otherwise the early warning mechanism will generate false alarms that might be distracting for the operator. You can estimate when the early warning should be given from these factors. In practice situations vary, so the final early warning limit can only be found during system testing.

An early warning mechanism can also be used to monitor other resources. For example CPU load can be monitored; once it reaches a critical level an early warning is given so that all nonessential processes can be terminated. Similarly, memory consumption can be monitored, and early warning given to the application when the application is running short of free memory. The application can then free allocated memory that is not mission-critical.

An early warning mechanism makes testing on the target hardware safer, as the system can, for example, be stopped once an early warning limit is reached. This makes it possible to test whether system resources are adequate for the application. If early warning is constantly triggered by excessive use of resources, the resource should be increased. Alternatively, an early warning limit might be too low and should be adjusted. PARAMETERS (page 380) can be applied to make warning limits easily adjustable. You can apply NOTIFICATION LOGGING (page 166) to record notifications and analyze resource consumption.

An early warning mechanism can be seen as an instantiation of *Kanban* (Ohno, 1988). A Kanban card is a message that signals a depletion of product, parts or inventory that needs to be replenished. When an inventory part's producer receives the Kanban card, it triggers replenishment of that product. Similarly, EARLY WARNING informs the consumer of a resource that it is about to run out. An identical mechanism is used in monitoring physical quantities such as a car's fuel: in addition to a fuel gauge, there is a light indicating that fuel is about to run out.

The control system can detect a situation in which resources are about to run out. Remedial actions can be started before resources run out, and problematic situations handled gracefully. This makes the system more operable and fault tolerant.

The real resource consumption can be found during system testing, as the system can be tested safely on real hardware. This saves cost, as no extraneous resources have to be installed to ensure that resources won't run out.

Early warning makes it possible to test the system on actual hardware, since buffer overflows or other resource shortages can be detected. In this way, hazardous situations caused by unavailability of resources are prevented when testing with actual hardware.

The warning mechanism may decrease system performance slightly, as limit values have to be checked. For example, if an early warning system is applied to a message buffer, every time a new message is received the application must check whether the early warning limit for buffer occupancy has been reached.

An X-ray machine uses an early warning mechanism for system temperature monitoring. The temperature can be lowered by activating a ventilation unit. Unfortunately, the ventilation system is quite noisy, and its use should be avoided while a patient is being treated. Thus the temperature might rise while the system is in use. The system uses three levels of early warning. When the temperature reaches 80 degrees Celsius the system sends an early warning notification and activates the ventilation system. If the temperature continues to rise, the system sends a second warning at 90 degrees Celsius and turns off some non-critical functionalities. If the temperature continues to rise for some reason, the system will enter a SAFE STATE (page 179) at 110 degrees Celsius.

CHAPTER

9

Patterns for Control System Modes

'My life has two modes. One is sitting around writing and contemplating or building things. The other is execution mode. It takes a while to switch from one to the other.'

Trent Reznor

A machine control system is used in various operating contexts. These contexts dictate how a machine can and/or should be operated. For example, during a software update, controllers should not initiate any movement and actuators should be turned off for safety reasons. However, the controllers and bus should be active. Similarly, if a parking brake is engaged, the control system can block movement.

Some situations occur so rarely that it is not viable for them to have their own controls, such as dedicated buttons or joysticks in the user interface. This means that the operating context also affects the machine's user interface and the kind of information that is displayed to the operator. In addition, operation of the machine by maintenance and assembly personnel can be seen as a different context from the machine control system software's point of view.

173

The easiest way to handle different operating contexts at the application level is to have modes that correspond to specific operating contexts. This allows the application developer to write simpler code, as it is possible to separate the functionality of each mode. OPERATING MODES (page 175) describes how to design a system such that it can support multiple operating contexts. The next pattern, SAFE STATE (page 179), adds a dedicated 'safe' mode that can be entered if the control system encounters a malfunction that it cannot handle autonomously. LIMP HOME (page 185) and SENSOR BYPASS (page 189) describe how a machine can still remain in limited operation even when part of it is malfunctioning. This makes salvage operations possible, and maintenance easier. Safetywise it is a step backwards from having only a SAFE STATE in the system: even if the system cannot be used for productive work due to a malfunction, it may still be possible to move the machine from the work site to a service area. DEVIL MAY CARE (page 190) shows how to distinguish substantial faults from false alarms or transient faults. False alarms are especially common when a system is starting up, or when the operating mode is changing and operation has not yet stabilized.

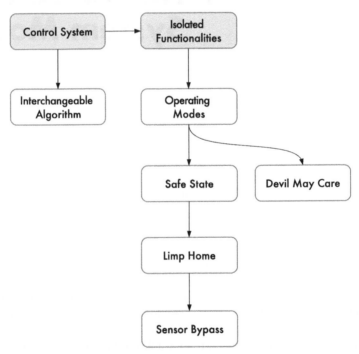

Figure 9.1: The sublanguage for control system modes. These patterns describe how to tackle the problems introduced by multiple operating contexts.

Various operating contexts also affect how the control application should control the machine, as different operating contexts have different requirements for control algorithms. It is hard to handle all usage situations with only a single control algorithm. IN-

TERCHANGEABLE ALGORITHM (page 193) shows how to implement variants of a control algorithm as independent reusable components and use an algorithm selector component to determine which variant of the control algorithm should be used in a specific context.

Figure 9.1 illustrates the sublanguage of patterns concerned with operating modes. It provides a solid foundation on which patterns in other sublanguages can base their own solutions when adding a new operating mode to a design.

9.1   Operating Modes * *

...there is a distributed CONTROL SYSTEM (page 96) that is used in multiple operating situations. For example, a forestry forwarder can be used both for picking up timber with its grappler and for driving and hauling logs to the nearest road. There are also situations in which the system is not used by the operator, for example when it needs maintenance or has encountered a fault. These operating contexts are different than the normal operating context, and some of the machine's functionalities might need to be limited or disabled. For example, during a software update the forwarder cannot be used for driving or loading timber, as all actuators should be turned off for safety reasons, leaving only the bus and nodes active and the user interface showing only information about the update's progress.

Different operating contexts create different requirements for the control system. These requirements are contradictory or not valid in all operating contexts. However, the control system is normally used in only one operating context at a time. During design time it is sufficient to focus on the subset of requirements that apply in a specific operating context.

The control system usually has multiple operating contexts and can have many user roles: in addition to control by an operator, the machine can also be used by maintenance and assembly personnel. As the system must support many functionalities, the user interface can easily become cluttered if dedicated screens, buttons and other controls are required for each operating context's functionality. Some of the operating contexts are used rarely, so it is not viable for them to have their own controls if existing user interface components could be used. In addition, new operating contexts not though of during design can arise.

It should be possible to use the machine in all operating contexts without dangerous consequences. Operating contexts have different safety mechanisms and regulations. For example, while a harvester is cutting trees and its boom is operational, it is not possible to feed a tree towards the harvester's cabin. However, other people must still stay outside the 50-meter danger zone around the boom. Suppose the harvester's head malfunctions and a maintenance engineer is called to diagnose the problem. In this situation, it should be possible to inspect the machine and move around it without danger: for example, the maintenance engineer should be able to disconnect the harvester head module without causing unwanted movement. If the engineer needs to run self-diagnostic tests on the system, this should not cause danger to the operator or the environment.

As a distributed control system consists of multiple nodes, it is crucial that all nodes are aware of the operating context. On the other hand, it is cumbersome for an application developer to build functions that depend on many different situation flags or are conditional on other applications. For example, if every application must ask the cabin controller whether the parking brake is engaged, the bus load will be high and real-time requirements more difficult to fulfil. In addition, programming errors are more likely, as a developer must remember to check the status of the brake if it affects the functionality of the application being designed.

Therefore:

Design the system so that it has multiple modes that correspond to specific operating contexts. While the system is in a mode, it only allows use of those functionalities that are relevant for the current operating context.

Identify the machine's operating contexts and design the software so that they are implemented as separate system modes. For example, there may be a mode for normal operation, a maintenance mode, a fault-handling mode, a software update mode and so on. Each mode should have only the functionalities available that are needed to carry out the use cases of the current context. After the main modes have been identified, they may be nested hierarchically. For example, normal operation might have submodes for driving and for parking. A submode may itself have submodes, but it is important to keep the hierarchy simple – a good rule of thumb is to use only three levels of mode nesting. The user interface for functionalities may be shared between several modes. For example, if a system has separate driving and loading modes, one joystick can be used for controlling both the movement of the boom and for driving, as these modes aren't enabled simultaneously. The user interface can show only information relevant to the current mode, and can be updated automatically – see TASK-BASED UI (page 326) for details.

Typically one of the high-level modes is the default mode, which is entered when the system starts up, and other modes a need specific action for their activation. Such actions can be the operator changing the mode via the user interface, or events triggered by the control system itself, either from external stimuli or other nodes. Figure 9.2 shows an example system in which the normal operating mode is the initial mode, and a specific action has to be taken to enter the software update mode. For example, mounting update media on the cabin PC can trigger a mode change (arrow 1 in Figure 9.2).

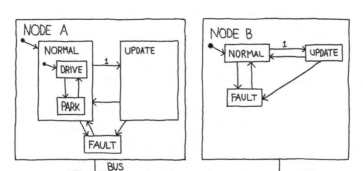

Figure 9.2: An example of a mode-based system's modes

As with all other modes, fault handling must be thought out in the early stages of system design. Early consideration is crucial, as it is very hard to add fault handling after the business logic has been designed and implemented: it is laborious to refactor code to add modes that were not thought of earlier. This can be remedied using a separate fault-handling mode that is entered when a fault occurs, halting normal operation until the fault is cleared. Both normal and update modes might encounter a fault, both of which are handled by a special mode. When the fault is cleared, the system returns to its previous state.

All nodes in a distributed system must keep track of the current system mode. This requires that nodes coordinate mode changes. When a mode-changing action is taken, information about the mode change must be propagated throughout the whole system. This requires a communication mechanism, so that all parts of the system always share the same concept of the current mode. VARIABLE MANAGER (page 201) is a good way to implement this, as it is designed for sharing information such as mode variables. Nodes keep track of the current mode using a variable; whenever an event occurs that causes the mode to change, it is communicated to other nodes. NOTIFICATIONS (page 156) can also be used as mode-changing events. One way to implement this is to define a specific node as the one responsible for the main modes, usually the cabin PC on the operator level (see SEPARATE REAL-TIME, page 237), which can command its slave nodes to execute their (simpler) state machines. This approach makes implementation easier, but it requires the communication channel to be robust and trustworthy, so that slave nodes can act under any circumstances. It also introduces a single point of failure.

Using modes allows application developers to write simpler code, as it is possible to merely poll the state variable once per application cycle to keep functionality within a single mode. In the case of SUPER LOOP (Pont, 2001) this might mean a simple switch-case construction whose cases correspond to different operating modes. It is also easier to add new modes afterwards, as this only requires the implementation of the mode and a triggering event to enter it. It is easier to test the system, as modes are kept separate, and only specific events can cause the application to enter a mode. Modes have a strong connection to state machines, so for example the system designer can use UML state diagrams when documenting and designing system modality (OMG, 2011). There are even pragmatic approaches that rely fully on the state paradigm when designing and implementing software systems. For example, Samek's Quantum Leaps (Samek, 2008) and Boost state chart libraries (Dawes et al, 2013) can be used as frameworks for developing modes. These approaches are well-suited to systems that have strong modality, which distributed machine control systems often exhibit.

As nodes have ISOLATED FUNCTIONALITIES (page 110) and strictly limited responsibilities, all modes are not relevant to all nodes. Usually all nodes will obey the higher-level modes (normal mode, fault mode etc.), but submodes are only relevant to a subset of nodes. For example, a parking mode is relevant only to engine, transmission and cabin controllers, but a boom is not affected by it, so the boom controller's normal mode is not divided into submodes. Typically only one node is responsible for informing the others when a specific mode-changing event occurs. This avoids conflict between nodes caused by them having different perceptions of the global mode. However, some modes, such as the fault mode, can be initiated by any node; when a node receives an event triggering the fault mode it enters the corresponding mode and propagates this information to other nodes. This ensures that the whole system is driven into fault mode whenever any node encounters a fault it cannot resolve by itself.

The operator must be informed of all mode changes that affect user operation, to avoid their trying to perform an action that is denied in the current mode but possible in another. In the field of usability engineering this is called a *mode error* (Foraker, 2013). An example of this would be for the operator to try to drive while the parking mode is activated – they must not be lead into thinking that something is broken because the machine won't move. To avoid this, the operator must be informed that the parking brake is on via the user interface. BEACON (page 336) can be applied to catch the operator's attention.

The European Machinery Directive mandates that an emergency stop function must be available and operational at all times regardless of the operating mode (Machinery Directive, 2006). The directive also requires that a mode selector overrides other modes and must be lockable in each position.

This pattern can be refined by adding special modes for driving the system into a SAFE STATE (page 179) in which risk of harm to personnel or the environment is minimized. If the system encounters a fault but is still operable to a limited extent, implementing a LIMP HOME (page 185) mode is advisable, to avoid a situation in which a single fault incapacitates the whole control system. One situation in which modes are really helpful is when implementing an ALTERNATIVE OPERATING STATION (page 330), where there should be a mode that enables only the currently used operating station and disables all others.

When a system employs a mode-based design its main functionality becomes easier to understand, as the modes isolate the different operating contexts in a compact way, and it is relatively easy to validate support for all use cases. Modes also encourage piecemeal growth of system architecture, as the main functionality can be implemented separately from more elaborate use cases. However, some functionalities may need to be implemented in multiple modes. This may clutter the design, as a module may have to check which mode it is in. Modes may also help to vary products within a product family, as they can provide an easy way to enable or limit the functionality of the control system.

As the current mode in a distributed system is not usually stored centrally, it must be communicated to all nodes that comprise the system. If mode-change messages are lost, the nodes may have varying perceptions of system state, and can thus can make contradictory judgments based on this misperception.

Modality is a good approach for fault detection and isolation. If an error is encountered in an operating mode, the system may enter a special fault-handling mode. During development it may be possible to find and correct bugs faster, as they are probably confined to a single mode. Modes also make the implementation simpler, as developers can have confidence that, when the system is in a specific mode, preconditions are taken into account during a mode change. This avoids the need to keep checking things that are certain while the system is in the mode. For example, the parking brake is always on while in the parking mode, and the transmission has the parking lock on, so the developer does not need to check these once the system has entered that mode.

It is relatively easy to use third-party frameworks to implement modes and to develop tools to generate code from models. For example, IEC 61131-3 has a *sequential function chart* (SFC) graphical programming language that describes modes as charts with steps, transitions and links (IEC, 2010a). Tools may also be used to validate the conformity of the software to the requirements if some uniform way to show modes as states and events as state transformations has been applied.

A train control system has several modes for different use cases. For example, there are separate modes for the situation in which the train is being used in the public transportation network, and for that when it is in the workshop for assembly or maintenance. The control system has stricter safety regulations when in use on the railway network, but workshop personnel may use it more freely. The workshop mode also collects more diagnostics data than the normal mode, which can be used to diagnose problems. The train also has separate modes for use when with and without passengers. For example, the upper speed limit is higher while transporting empty carriages. In addition to these modes, it has an uncalibrated sensor mode in which the top speed is limited and the train calibrates its sensors over a five kilometer distance. If this succeeds, the train can switch to calibrated sensor mode and run at full speed.

9.2   Safe State * *

...there is a machine CONTROL SYSTEM (page 96) that consists of several hardware components. These components may for example be sensors and actuators, and if the system has ISOLATED FUNCTIONALITIES (page 110) connected by a message bus, there can be several controllers and computers communicating in a ONE TO MANY (page 131) fashion.

These hardware components may break down, and the control applications may contain bugs that cause the system to malfunction. The system has OPERATING MODES (page 175) to enable state-based behavior, and consequently controllers have a fault-handling mode that is entered whenever a malfunction is detected. The control system cannot always resolve the root cause of these breakdowns or bugs, and the system may react in an unexpected way if it is controlled normally while the malfunction is active. This could cause hazardous situations and harm to the machine itself, the environment, the operator or others.

When the control system tries to control a part of the machine that is malfunctioning, the machine may respond in an unpredictable way. Consequently, the machine may harm the operator, machine or surroundings. These kinds of situations should not take place.

The system should never cause harm to people or the environment, even during a malfunction. This is one of the general principles of the European Machinery Directive (Section 1.1.2, Machinery Directive, 2006). This might be difficult to ensure, as malfunctions can cause unpredictable behavior. A malfunction may occur suddenly and at any moment, so countermeasures to ensure safety should be as rapid and autonomous as possible, as the operator's reaction time might be too long to prevent a hazard.

The hardware is usually designed so that all actuators will enter a passive safety mode and cannot move when the system loses power, as described in DE-ENERGIZED SAFETY (Rauhamäki & Kuikka, 2013). For example, rotating parts have brakes that need power to keep them off; if power is lost, the brake engages and stops rotation. In an another example, if a hydraulic pump fails, valves keep the hydraulic cylinder pressurized, stopping the piston from moving and preventing hydraulic fluid from flowing back to the reservoir. However, it is not always sensible to turn subsystems off if they don't present a hazard: some parts of the system may provide essential life-support services and should be kept running as long as possible. Furthermore, some subsystems may be safer if not switched off.

Usually the system cannot resolve the root cause of a malfunction automatically. For example, in a distributed system a node can't autonomously deduce whether a lost HEARTBEAT (page 120) is due to failure of another node, the message bus, or the node's own hardware. In addition, the node cannot rely on other nodes providing it with any useful information during a malfunction, so it must be able to do all hazard-prevention actions autonomously. Even if communication remains possible and reliable, collaboration usually takes too much time to be a safe way to react to a malfunction.

Therefore:

Design a safe state that can be entered if the control system encounters a malfunction that cannot be handled autonomously. The safe state is such that it prevents the machine from causing harm. The safe state is device and functionality dependent and is not necessarily the same as the unpowered state.

As the system has OPERATING MODES (page 175), the control application usually enters a fault-handling mode whenever it detects a malfunction. In this mode the application checks whether it can do something to correct the malfunction. If the application cannot handle the fault, it should enter a safe state and propagate the information about the malfunction to other nodes as well. The safe state is a high-level system mode, separate from the normal operational mode. There is only one safe state, which is defined according to the system's requirements in its operating environment. Usually this means that all nodes stop normal control operations.

When a failure occurs, the system enters a safe state and may perform safety operations, for example triggering mechanical safety mechanisms. The system will not re-enter the normal operating mode until the failure is corrected and a reset action is carried out. The reset action might be initiated by the operator or maintenance personnel from the user interface, or it might just be rebooting the system. If the system reboots and the malfunction is still active, it enters the safe state directly. One typical way to drive a node to a safe state is by means of a WATCHDOG (page 101) mechanism. When the WATCHDOG triggers and boots the node, it can automatically enter a safe state during the reboot. When the node has rebooted, it can run SELF-TESTS (page 106) to see if the fault has cleared. If the fault is no longer active the node can continue normal operation, otherwise it must wait for human intervention. Usually the safe state is a safety function required by IEC 61508 certification (IEC, 2010a). A separate safety function makes system design simpler, as only safety-critical parts require certificated hardware and software. For further details of this separation, see SEPARATED SAFETY (Rauhamäki et al, 2012b).

The safe state is usually reserved for the most severe failures, as once entered the system cannot give further value and cannot be used for productive work. Typically the node that detects a malfunction will propagate information of the failure to other nodes. For example, in the case of CANopen, the node can send a periodic status message to other nodes which contains state information. An EMCY message can be used as 'single shot' information. When nodes receive this message they enter their own safe state, eventually bringing the entire system into a safe state. Active propagation of safe state using messages provides rapid response to failure but may be unreliable, as the fault may prevent a node from sending messages, or the message bus itself may be faulty. This has to be taken into account when designing the safe state propagation mechanism.

In some cases, propagation may be initiated as a side-effect of the safe state. For example, if a node enters its safe state it will no longer generate its HEARTBEAT (page 120) so that other nodes can deduce that there was a failure. This passive propagation of fault information is reliable but may be slow, as response time is directly proportional to the

HEARTBEAT rate: other nodes have to wait at least one HEARTBEAT cycle to be sure that the faulty node has failed.

In a complex multi-node system with clearly separated subsystems, it is usually possible for just some of the nodes to enter a safe state. Remaining subsystems can then still function regardless of the fault. For example, if SEPARATE REAL-TIME (page 237) has been applied, the control system is divided into two levels: operator level and machine control level. If a machine control level subsystem fails, the operator level monitoring subsystems may still function and give additional information about the failure.

If the system is autonomous, it is advisable to design it such that remote communication is available even in a safe state. This will allow personnel to remotely connect to it, use DIAGNOSTICS (page 350) data to analyze and solve the problem, and even upload new control system software if needed. For example in a satellite, if an internal control communication channel between the nodes is lost, the system enters a safe state. However, the satellite must still keep its solar panels directed towards the sun, to keep the system powered and the communication antenna directed at the Earth. This allows ground control to examine the collected diagnostics data and determine why the system entered its safe state. Ground control can use also a diagnostics channel for control messages, instead of the failed control channel, to keep the satellite operational. The ground team may devise new control software and upload it to the satellite before it is lost due to depleted battery power.

Normal safety regulations might also apply in the safe state. This means that normal operator safety areas, and requirements for safety gear etc., will also hold in the event of failure. If this is the case, the operator must be informed whether the system still has activity, for example by using BEACON (page 336), even if it appears to be unpowered. This is especially important if a maintenance engineer tries to repair the system while it is in a safe state. In Figure 9.3, for example, the harvester head has to be fully disabled in order to change the saw chain safely. A good rule of thumb is to design the safe state so that the system automatically becomes more safe if some parts are incapacitated. This is achieved by designing the hardware so that it does not need control or power to enter the safe state. A safe state should also be passive, in the sense that it can be maintained for an indefinite period. In a modern nuclear reactor, for example, the magnetically attached control rods that inhibit the nuclear reaction when inserted into the reactor core will be automatically dropped into the core when the control system fails to provide power to hold them up. This passively stops fission if the control system is not functioning properly.

For a discussion of system design that prevents mistakes from being made, or makes them obvious at a glance, see the *poka-yoke* principle (Shingo, 1986). A well-known example of this is a car welding robot that attaches nuts to a sheet metal panel that is later welded to the car. The nuts are fed automatically from a container and are welded to the metal panel in predefined positions. If the feed process jams or misfeeds, the machine will passively stop the operation, because electrical power for the welding electrode is fed through the nut. The machine therefore remains idle if a nut is not present, and there is zero possibility of a sheet metal panel having none or only some of its nuts attached. This kind of defect would only be noticed later, perhaps even after the sheet metal has been

Figure 9.3: After a harvester saw chain has become too worn to be used safely, installation of a replacement chain must be a safe operation

Reproduced by permission of John Deere Forestry Oy

welded to a car body and some other part is about to be attached, but there are no nuts for the bolts on the part to fit into. For more information, see (Ricard, 1987).

LIMP HOME (page 185) is an approach to failures that are not so severe. LIMP HOME is a mode that allows simple functionality to be preserved regardless of a failure. LIMP HOME can only be used in situations in which a clearly separate and well-defined part of the system is malfunctioning. In this case, it is possible to continue use of the rest of the system without presenting a safety threat. Usually the system will enter the safe state in the case of failure and then inspect to determine whether it is safe to perform limited actions. It may then enter a LIMP HOME mode automatically in order to still provide some service. Figure 9.4 shows the general idea of limiting functionality by using modes: SAFE STATE usually does not provide anything other than crucial life-support functionality, if any, while a LIMP HOME mode has some functionality, while the normal mode has all the functionality required to carry out the tasks for which the system was designed.

Safe failure fraction (SFF) is the probability of safe failures compared to unsafe failures; Figure 9.5 illustrates the probabilities of failures in an example system. The IEC 61508 standard (IEC, 2010a) has guidelines for calculating SFF. A safe state increases a system's tendency to fail towards safety, and hence minimizes the number of dangerous failures. In other words, entering a safe state can be seen as a safe failure. Each *safety integrity level* (SIL) has a specified level for required SFF, so higher SIL levels require the system to fail to a safe state more often. Applying SAFE STATE transforms most dangerous detected failures into safe detected failures.

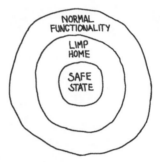

Figure 9.4: Limiting the system functionality by modes

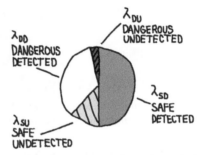

Figure 9.5: The division into safe and unsafe failures
(dangerous but detected failures are considered safe)

The system enters a predetermined safe state in the case of a malfunction. This safe state usually prevents further harm to the environment, the operator or the system itself. It is a fast and automatic way to stop all risky actions without the operator reaction time being an issue. However, the safe state might not be easy to determine, as the machine may face unforeseen situations. In some situations, the safe state may cause more harm if an unexpected fault or a combination of errors happens – for example, if the safe state has no override mechanism to allow moving the machine away from a fire that has triggered the safe state. LIMP HOME (page 185) can be used to remedy this.

It is easier for the application developer to make the system enter a safe state if an unexpected error is encountered. This prevents the system from crashing, which would cause additional hazards.

Recovering from the safe state usually requires human intervention, and thus might cause additional unavailability of the system. However, the situations in which a safe state is entered are usually so grave that this is permissible.

An industrial process has cooling and heating phases. A fieldbus connects process monitoring and controlling I/O cards, which are programmable logic controllers (PLC), together with higher-level services that are located in a control room. The control room PC polls the cards at a fixed interval and the I/O cards keep track if when they are read by a higher-level device. Reading the cards therefore acts as a HEARTBEAT (page 120). If polling ceases for a specific time, the I/O cards decide that the higher control level has crashed. As a card can no longer make any reliable decisions without control room guidance, it enters a safe state to prevent further harm. This safe state is device-dependent and may also affect other parts of the system. For example, for the card that controls the pumps that move cooling fluids, the safest action is to stop the process that needs cooling. Stopping only the cooling pump would cause overheating and further damage. On the other hand, for the air flow controller that regulates the volume of cooling air in the process, the safest action is to open the air intake and leave it open until the safe state is reset. Any excess air does not cause any safety hazards, as the only consequence will be to cool the substance being processed.

9.3   Limp Home *

…there is a CONTROL SYSTEM (page 96) that consists of several hardware parts, such as sensors and actuators. If the system is distributed, it consists of ISOLATED FUNCTIONALITIES (page 110) and uses ONE TO MANY (page 131) communication. Some parts are purely hardware and some parts include software applications. The complete functionality of the machine depends on the functionalities provided by all these separate parts. However, some are only used in specialized functionalities and specific OPERATING MODES (page 175). All hardware can malfunction, but it is useful if the whole machine is not incapacitated when something breaks. The machine would be totally unusable if it entered a SAFE STATE (page 179) in the event of any failure.

Even when part of the machine is malfunctioning, the machine should still be operable at least some to extent in order to make salvage operations possible and maintenance easier.

It is not always sensible to incapacitate the whole system if a non-critical subsystem malfunctions. If part of the system exists only to make the working environment more pleasant, or to automate control sequences, the operator might want to keep working even if this functionality is lost. Maintenance of such parts of a system can be postponed until a scheduled maintenance break, or until the machine leaves the work site.

Even if the system can no longer be used for productive work due to a malfunction, it is useful if a self-propelled machine can move from a work site to a service area. In addition, a machine may malfunction in such a way that it blocks the work site and must be removed to leave the site available to other machines. It helps if the system can do this removal by itself. This holds even if moving could cause additional damage, if the cost of retrieving the machine is greater than the cost of repairing additional damage or unavailability of the work site.

Moving parts of a machine can block maintenance personnel's access to a faulty part, or cause a serious hazard, for example if some heavy moving part of the machine is overhanging the best maintenance position. Such parts should remain movable even if the rest of the machine has stopped working.

There are usually functions that profoundly affect the overall safety of a system. These functions should be kept working as long as possible in any situation. Even if the system has a SAFE STATE (page 179) to prevent hazards, there are situations in which the system should still function even if it risks further machine damage. For example, suppose a forest harvester has lost engine oil pressure due to damage to its sump and has entered a SAFE STATE and stopped to prevent further damage. If there is a risk that the machine can later be engulfed in a forest fire, it is far better to be able to drive it away from the fire, even if starting the engine could cause it excessive wear.

Even safety functions that are related to preventing risks to people may be disabled if the person operating the machine, such as a maintenance engineer, knows how to limit the risk of hazard. For example, if the cabin door sensor has broken, it causes the system to be immobile due to safety regulations forbidding driving with a door ajar. However, a maintenance engineer may be qualified to drive the machine if they can check that the door is properly closed.

Therefore:

Divide sensors and actuators into groups according to their functionalities, such as drive train, boom operations and so on. Groups may overlap. A malfunctioning device only disables the groups it belongs to, and other groups remain operable.

Identify functionalities that can be performed in most situations. As OPERATING MODES (page 175) has been applied, this is usually the default mode that the system enters after SYSTEM START-UP (page 293). The default mode can contain, for example, driving. All sensors and actuators that are mission-critical for driving are required for the basic safe operation of the machine, so these devices form the mandatory device group enabling the basic functionality. When the basic functionality is identified, it is extended with more sophisticated functions, called *services*. Additional hardware that is needed for implementing these services is optional, so will be a part of an optional devices group. If some hardware part in a group then malfunctions, only the affected group and its functionalities will be disabled. The service requiring hardware in this group will no longer be available, but the rest of the system is unaffected and the operator can continue with degraded functionality. As the system is complex and hardware may be shared between several functionalities to save cost, the group of devices that are required for a specific service may overlap with another service's group. If such an overlapping device malfunctions, both services will be incapacitated, so the designer should try to include a device in only one group if possible, so that its malfunction will only incapacitate one service.

If a malfunctioning device affects some high-level functionality, the operator must usually use their expertise to compensate for the situation. For example, if an automatic boom positioning service is lost the operator can still position the boom manually. In this case system productivity may be diminished, but operations can otherwise continue normally. It is crucial for the system designer to identify devices that enable only automated control sequences and ensure that a manual operation mode is possible. Another example of the LIMP HOME principle is SEPARATE REAL-TIME (page 237). If the machine control level malfunctions, it is isolated from the operator level and will not stop high-level services from working. DIAGNOSTICS (page 350) and REMOTE ACCESS (page 361) will still be available for locating the root cause of the malfunction. Conversely, if the operator level malfunctions, the system should be designed so that the machine control level can still be used to operate the machine.

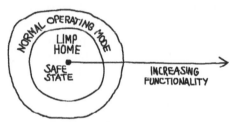

Figure 9.6: Limp home mode only has a subset of the functionalities of normal mode

Usually limp home mode is entered from SAFE STATE (page 179), which is an approach for severe failures. When a machine detects a malfunction it goes to a safe state to prevent the failure from propagating or causing further harm. The system then has more time to inspect the situation, for example, by using SELF-TESTS (page 106). If the failure can be isolated to a subsystem, only that subsystem stays in the SAFE STATE, and the rest of the system can be used normally. Figure 9.6 shows these modes in an 'onion model', and their scope in terms of functionality. The system must be designed so that a faulty node entering limp home mode will not propagate the SAFE STATE to other nodes as it would normally do. This is done to allow nodes that are part of an isolated subsystem to work independently of the fault.

If the system encounters a malfunction in the machine control functionality, it should be possible to switch to a degraded operating mode within the current mode. If a sensor is lost, machine control can no longer operate optimally, but may still be able to keep the system running by making suboptimal but safe decisions. For example, if the air mass sensor in a car's fuel injection system fails, the engine control module (ECM) cannot calculate the correct stoichiometric ratio for the air/fuel mixture. If the air/fuel mixture is too lean it burns too hot and can damage the engine. So the ECM enters limp home mode, in which it injects enough fuel to keep the mixture rich in all situations, to avoid engine damage. However, too much unburned fuel may eventually damage the catalytic converter, so limp home mode is only a temporary solution, to keep the car running just long enough to drive it to a repair shop. Usually the engine fault light (see BEACON, page 336) is lit to remind the driver of the situation. As the rich fuel mixture cannot generate the full power from the engine, the car's maximum speed is limited to prevent the driver from driving for an extended period in limp home mode and to minimize the damage caused by the unburned fuel.

The system should become fully inoperable only if its operation will compromise the safety of people or harm the machine. Usually this means that some electrical, electronic or programmable electronic safety systems have failed and the system relies on mechanical safety. Even then, an override mode that gives full manual operating control should be permitted for use in unforeseen situations, such as salvaging the machine from a hazardous situation. This can be implemented by applying SENSOR BYPASS (page 189), which allows circumvention of faulty sensors. For example, if a tractor is under maintenance and has been disassembled to the extent that its safety systems prevent it being driven out of the machine shop, maintenance engineers can still bypass the safety systems to prevent the tractor from, for example, being burned by welding sparks. The safety bypass may be a 'dead man's switch', which an engineer must push continuously to make the system work. Safety integrity levels (SIL) are usually more easily achieved if the dead man's switch is implemented only in hardware. The hardware designer should try to make sure that, if a subsystem breaks down, it will not lock the rest of the system up. For example, a failed boom that is grasping an object should be able to release the object to ensure that the machine can be driven from the work site.

If limp home mode can invalidate the manufacturer's warranty or cause hazardous situations, an authentication method to prevent its inadvertent activation is essential. Only some operator roles (see ROLE-BASED UI, page 327) should be allowed to activate limp home mode. BLACK BOX (page 355) can be used to document the fact that the system has been in limp home mode, so that it can be proved whether the system warranty is invalidated. Limp home mode is usually exited when maintenance personnel have repaired the incapacitated subsystem and rebooted the control system. Some additional actions, such as resetting the mode via the user interface or a separate software tool might be also required.

If START-UP NEGOTIATION (page 297) has been applied, the system can detect whether the nodes required for limp home mode are available. This makes limp home safer, as the system can prevent all operations automatically if limping home is not safe with the existing hardware configuration.

After devices are grouped according their criticality, the operator can decide to use the system even if some non-critical part of it has failed. This allows the machine to still produce value even when some of its parts are incapacitated. This increased fault tolerance prevents the machine from becoming stuck in middle of a work process.

Limp home mode may also prevent a machine's operator from getting into inconvenient or risky situations. For example, if an elevator encounters a fault, it may diagnose the problem and decide that it is still safe to move to the next floor and let passengers out. However in some cases breakdown of a subsystem may incapacitate the whole system.

Sometimes one device might be used by several functions, which can make it difficult to design device groupings. However, such devices are good targets for applying 1+1 RE-DUNDANCY (page 279) if high availability is needed.

A machine in limp home mode cannot usually produce the same value compared to a fully working machine. For example, engine power might be limited compared to normal operation.

Using limp home for an extended period might cause damage to a machine, so this mode should be used only for salvage operations. Usually a BEACON (page 336) is activated while the system is in limp home mode, to ensure that the operator knows that they are using the system in a mode that might cause harm in the long term.

A fire truck has a boom with an attached cage by which firefighters can be lifted to height if rescue missions require it. If the boom malfunctions while the firefighters are in the elevated cage, they will be stuck there. As the cage is usually used in rescue situations, it can be near a fire or similar hazard. Therefore it is crucial to get the firefighters down even if there is no way to operate the boom with its normal controls. Evacuation with ladders, or climbing down the boom, would be too dangerous. So the system is equipped with a 'bleed down' device that can be operated from the cage, and turntable control panels on the side of the truck. These allow the boom to be lowered and the working cage brought to the ground safely even if no hydraulic pressure is available.

9.4   Sensor Bypass *

Some sensors are used in a system design merely to give small advantages in productivity or in the operator experience. When this kind of sensor malfunctions, it can cause sub-optimal operation or stop the whole machine.

Therefore:

For each sensor of minor importance, implement a mechanism to replace the sensor's output value with a substitute value. The value can be a default, a user-defined value, a simulated value or the last known good value. In the event of a malfunction in the sensor, the substitute value can be used temporarily.

For the complete pattern, please see www.wiley.com/go/controlsystemspatterns.

9.5   Devil May Care *

ALSO KNOWN AS STEADY STATE

…there is a CONTROL SYSTEM (page 96) having OPERATING MODES (page 175). SYSTEM START-UP (page 293) and changing the operating mode usually means that the system has to go through larger state transitions than during normal operation. Thus, sensors may momentarily measure values that are different than normal operating levels and processes may require some time to stabilize. For example, engine oil pressure has to be raised from zero to its operating level, and moving parts have to overcome their static friction if immobile, requiring more power and time than during normal use. If the system has ISOLATED FUNCTIONALITIES (page 110), different parts of the system may exhibit varying response times to changes in the operating mode. Thus there are situations in which not all nodes are ready for an operation, or have a different concept of the current operating mode. A node's error detection mechanism may consider all these transient situations as faults and start error recovery actions in vain. The node may even send additional state change messages as it goes into fault-handling mode. These messages propagate the error to the rest of the system, generating more unnecessary state changes.

As the system is not yet ready to work normally due to start-up or mode changes, all kind of transient errors and faults can occur. However, these clear themselves after the system has stabilized, so any error recovery actions caused by transient errors would compromise system performance.

Usually mode change, start-up or shut down operations take time, as the system is driven into the desired state. During this sensor values may be off-limit, as the physical world resists the change with friction, inertia, viscosity or hysteresis, depending on the application. This is normal and should not be interpreted as errors by the control system.

If the system has multiple controllers, these usually have different start-up times. If the system has been powered up, some controllers are already on line, while others are still in their start-up phase. Thus, when a controller is programmed to listen to other nodes, to deduce the structure of the system or their HEARTBEAT (page 120), it may consider the system faulty and initiate error recovery actions, such as entering a SAFE STATE (page 179). This should be avoided. The same might also apply for operating mode changes.

As nodes have limited storage space, the system usually has a very small amount of persistent data. The current device configuration and the position of the machine's various parts therefore have to be deduced during SYSTEM START-UP (page 293). If VARIABLE MANAGER (page 201) has been used, for example, all variables are uninitialized and the nodes request updated information. If all nodes do this when the system is starting up it may cause excessive bus loading.

In a start-up phase, the system usually has more time than during normal operations, as it does not yet need to respond to strict real-time requirements. The length of the start-up phase is not usually crucial, as starting is a relatively infrequent event. For example, a machine might be started only once per work shift.

The operator may be confused if the system sends HMI NOTIFICATIONS (page 340) about transient errors. For example, the operator might get a message about a clogged oil filter while the system is still warming up because the oil is cold and too viscous to flow normally. This might cause them to initiate unnecessary repair actions or think that the notification system is not working properly. This can lead to mistrust of the control system and cause the operator to ignore notifications that are valid.

Therefore:

For transient phases, define a time interval in which the system may ignore predefined error situations. The system must reach a steady state before this period has elapsed. A steady state means that the system is ready for normal operation.

Whenever the system is undergoing a state transition or a mode change, there should be a period during which the system ignores sensor values that would otherwise be erroneous. For example, if an engine is started, the engine control module (ECM) should ignore the oil pressure for a while, as the oil pump takes time to raise it to normal levels. In the simplest cases this interval is a predefined period. The ECM will wait for, say, 30 seconds while the oil pressure rises. Sometimes the period may be a parameter adjustable by the operator via a HUMAN–MACHINE INTERFACE (page 313), or a value that is deduced from some other value (see PARAMETERS, page 380). In the case of oil pressure, for example, if the outside temperature is very cold the oil will be more viscous and it will take longer to prime the oil pump and raise the oil pressure to an acceptable level. The system may then adjust the wait period to 45 seconds to compensate for this. Another approach would be to wait until a measured value has reached the desired level and stayed there for some period. The system can then decide that a steady state has been reached, after which all deviations from sensor limits can be considered as errors. A DEVIL MAY CARE approach should also be used when considering when to send HMI NOTIFICATIONS (page 340) about anomalous situations to the operator.

It is important to remember that in a distributed system having ISOLATED FUNCTIONALITIES (page 110) it is not sufficient for a node to wait for itself to attain steady state: temporary errors may still occur while the rest of the system is under transition. Even if other nodes send messages to confirm that they are in a steady state, you need to ensure that the node has not missed this confirmation message because it was still under transition itself. Usually this can be resolved by sending a periodic status message that nodes can use to indicate that they have reached steady state. For example, CANopen has a

HEARTBEAT (page 120) mechanism in which the HEARTBEAT message contains the originating node's status. This status is a byte whose value defines whether the node is in a boot-up, stopped, operational or pre-operational state. In any case, nodes should wait at least for the start-up time of the slowest node to be sure that the system is fully operational. However, if all nodes wait for the same period, problems may arise if all nodes then start communicating simultaneously. For example, if VARIABLE MANAGER (page 201) has been applied to the system, many variables will be uninitialized when the execution of the application on a node begins. Naturally, if the system uses periodic messaging in which all variables have a fixed update frequency, this is not a problem. However, if the nodes try to acquire initial values for variables using query-and-response messaging, the bus load will be high. To prevent this, each node can use a unique wait period after the minimum wait time, or they may have a random delay in their start-up sequence. In some cases a node may listen to the bus to determine when bus traffic has stabilized before trying to communicate. However, it may be difficult to prevent the case in which two nodes both decide that the system is stable and start communicating simultaneously.

It is also crucial to define what kind of errors can take place before the system has reached steady state. For example, it is normal for oil pressure to be low during the first few seconds after engine start-up, but other abnormal sensor readings, such as over-temperature engine coolant, are indications of real problems and should never be ignored. However, sensor readings may exhibit a lot of noise during start-up due to electromagnetic interference and other environmental noise. EARLY WORK (page 259) can be an additional source of sensor noise, as the system may work in a different way while it is priming itself during start-up. Figure 9.7 shows spikes in a signal with a different error threshold for start-up. The signal reaches operational level quickly, but still exhibits spikes that exceed the normal operating threshold. These spikes should not count as errors, as the system is not yet in normal operating mode.

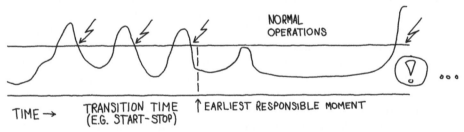

Figure 9.7: Over-threshold sensor readings during start-up are ignored for a wait period. After that time a signal out of bounds is considered an error.

ERROR COUNTER (page 107) can be used to solve problems caused by start-up spikes. Usually ERROR COUNTERs have more relaxed values for the start-up phase. ERROR COUNTER values and the threshold values for faulty signals can be stored as PARAMETERS (page 380). If OPERATING MODES (page 175) are applied to create a separate start-up mode, this may use a different parameter group for monitoring if specific signals have abnormal values, while the parameter group for normal operations is enabled when the situation has stabilized. If PARAMETERS are used to adjust thresholds and wait times, you need to ensure that replaced controllers acquire the correct values when installed.

This pattern is similar to RIDING OVER TRANSIENTS (Hanmer, 2007).

After DEVIL MAY CARE is applied the system is not held up trying to recover from errors that are normal to a transient situation. Resources are not wasted in error recovery initiated by situations that will clear themselves over time. The operator is not confused by error messages that are unjustified.

There are times, however, when error detection could have noticed a malfunction earlier, but is delayed due to waiting for the DEVIL MAY CARE period before reporting the error. The DEVIL MAY CARE period is always a trade-off between quick error recovery and the risk of judging a normal transient situation as erroneous.

It may be difficult for the system designer to know what errors can be ignored, especially if a combination of two or more errors that would individually have been ignored could indicate a real problem.

In a V8 engine an engine control module (ECM) uses a lambda sensor to balance the air-fuel (A/F) mixture that is injected into the cylinder. The lambda sensor is essentially an oxygen sensor that is usually attached to the exhaust manifold, with its zirconium dioxide tip located in the exhaust gases. The lambda sensor burns the residual oxygen in the exhaust gases and produces a voltage that is proportional to the amount of excess oxygen. The output voltage is 0.54 volts for the optimal A/F ratio of 14.35:1, which is called 'lambda value 1'. Correspondingly, a 5 percent rich mixture has lambda value of 0.95. Under normal operation, the ECM uses the sensor information to adjust the ratio of intake air to injected fuel in order to have a stochiometrically correct mixture. The engine is controlled to run at lambda value 1 so that the fuel burn process is optimized. However, a typical lambda sensor needs reach at least 250 degrees Celsius to work properly. So when the car is started the ECM must operate in open-loop mode, as it cannot trust the readings from the lambda sensor. If the sensor is heated only by the exhaust gases, it takes several tens of seconds to warm up. In some applications the lambda sensor has an internal heating element to reduce the warm-up time to less than ten seconds. The ECM must take this time in account when adjusting the air/fuel mixture.

9.6   Interchangeable Algorithm *

ALSO KNOWN AS ISOLATED CONTROL ALGORITHM, STRATEGY

…there is a CONTROL SYSTEM (page 96) that enables a machine operator to control different kind of functionalities. The CONTROL SYSTEM can automate some maneuvers, or assist the operator to carry out their tasks in some other way. Depending on the situation, the functionality may need more precise control, or even a completely different control method. For example, when controlling the boom of a truck crane, the load might sway differently depending how far the boom is extended. The automated control may therefore need to act differently, or the operator may need to compensate for sway manually. The CONTROL SYSTEM is designed to automate as many operations as possible, to increase productivity, and so there is typically a control algorithm to control automated functionality. Usually one control algorithm is not optimal in all situations. Although the algorithm can be parameterized to some extent, this may not be sufficient to make it optimal in all situations.

Different usage situations have different requirements for the control algorithm. It is hard to handle all situations just by parameterizing a single control algorithm.

Different situations or OPERATING MODES (page 175) place different requirements on the control system, so a single algorithm cannot handle all situations.

When developing the system different control algorithms are developed for the same purpose. It should be possible to test which of them suits the system best. It makes testing easier if the control algorithm can be tested on the target hardware, or run on a PC using an application such as Matlab while the rest of the system is running on the target hardware. This allows the developer to make quick changes to the algorithm and test their effect. A control algorithm might be developed by a someone other than the rest of the control application, as algorithm development may require special skills. If the developer of the control application can stub the algorithm, separate development of the application and the algorithm becomes easier.

Different products have different hardware setups which may require different control algorithms. For example, heavier and lighter booms can be used in machines within a product family. The control system software is similar in all machines within the product family, but the control algorithms for booms are different. When adapting the control system from one machine to another, changes to the software should be minimized.

Control algorithm development can be expensive, so the same algorithm might be used in different machines. However, changes to the rest of the control system should be minimized.

Therefore:

Implement variants of the control algorithm as independent components. Add an algorithm selector component that provides the application with access to the control algo-

rithm. When the control algorithm is called, the selector component determines which variation of the control algorithm should be used in the context of the call, and calls the selected implementation of the algorithm. The application uses the selector component instead of the actual algorithm.

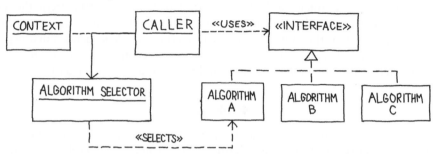

Figure 9.8: Algorithms A, B and C all realize the same interface requested by the algorithm selector. The control application calls the algorithm selector, not the algorithm itself.

Implementing an algorithm selector using an object-oriented programming language is straightforward. First, design the control algorithms for different usage situations as objects, and design an interface that suits them all. Particular care needs to be taken to design an interface that does not need to be changed often. Parameters for the control algorithm can be delivered in a struct, for example, so that the number of parameters can be changed easily later. Create a class or module that takes care of algorithm selection. The control application can then use this selector module. The control application calls the selector module with appropriate parameters and the selector module forwards this call for the control algorithm. Figure 9.8 illustrates the connections of the algorithm selector and the algorithm modules. The control algorithm selected depends on the current context. The selector component determines the context using information provided by the control application as a parameter, or by using extra input from other modules. If OP-ERATING MODES (page 175) is applied, for example, the algorithm selector can receive mode changes and select the correct algorithm based on the current mode.

If object-oriented programming languages are not used, the interface is replaced with a function pointer. In this case the algorithm selector is not necessarily a module, but can be a function pointer that points to the correct control algorithm. The logic for determining the correct control algorithm can be encapsulated in its own module. Sometimes function pointers cannot be used. For example, the Misra C standard forbids the use of non-constant function pointers (Rule 104, required, Mira, 2013). Function pointers are not available in some languages, such as Occam (INMOS, 1988). In this case simple switch-case structures can be used instead.

In more sophisticated cases, fragments of the control algorithm may need to be changed depending on the context. In this case, the algorithm selector module contains the body of the algorithm, and fragments of the algorithm can be changed using the methods described earlier. Another option is to implement the selection of different sub-algorithms in the control application. In this case, the function pointers to the correct subalgorithm are given to the algorithm as parameter(s). The downside of this approach is that the complete algorithm is no longer encapsulated in a single module, so reusing the algorithm as such becomes harder.

To be able to take advantage of the INTERCHANGEABLE ALGORITHM pattern, the control algorithm must have a clearly defined interface in terms of its inputs and outputs. Interaction with the algorithm must use only that interface: no dependencies that bypass the abstraction should be created by bypassing the interface, otherwise the control application becomes dependent on the algorithm and the algorithm is no longer interchangeable.

A control algorithm or part(s) of it can be changed easily, even at runtime. This makes evaluating different control algorithms during development possible, perhaps to find out which are the most efficient. The control system can change the control algorithm automatically, depending on OPERATING MODES (page 175) or operating context. This makes automation of functionalities on a machine easier.

Control algorithms are usually tested in a simulation environment, to see how efficient they are. As the control system has a clearly defined interface for the algorithm, it should be relatively easy to export the algorithm from a simulation environment such as Matlab and integrate it with the control system. In this case, some mechanism to handle communication with the simulation environment is required between the interface and the algorithm class. So a new parent class is added to the solution to handle communications with the simulator environment. This helps in prototyping the algorithms.

Isolating the algorithm guides the design, so that the control algorithm is located in a single module and not scattered throughout the code. This makes the algorithm more understandable and easier to modify. The algorithm itself is isolated from the application logic, and the application programmer does not have to be concerned with the details of the algorithm.

It can be challenging to find a minimal but adequate interface for a control algorithm. Future changes in the algorithm can also propagate changes to the interface.

A high level of correctness is required for context selection. If the control system changes the control algorithm automatically, it can be annoying for the operator if the algorithm is changed when it is not supposed to be. It could even cause a hazard if the operator expects the machine to be in specific context but it is not.

Abstraction can slightly increase response times, as algorithm calls need to pass through an extra layer.

The automatic boom positioning application of a pile driver uses GPS location to position the boom to the correct location and angle for pile placement. However, GPS location may not always be accurate, and subsequent readings from the GPS module may contain significantly different locations. Some sort of filtering is therefore required for the

GPS location information. Filtering needs to be carried out differently when the machine is moving than when stationary. INTERCHANGEABLE ALGORITHM is used to isolate the filtering algorithm so that various variants can be used easily. The automatic boom positioning application calls an algorithm selector component to get the filtered position information. The algorithm selector reads velocity information for the machine from a VARIABLE MANAGER (page 201). Based on this information, the algorithm selector uses a suitable filter algorithm. The algorithm selector component chooses which algorithm to use to get the filtered location information. This allows the correct algorithm to be chosen at runtime without the boom positioning application needing to know any details of the GPS location filtering.

CHAPTER

10

Patterns for Data Management

'It is a capital mistake to theorize before one has data. Insensibly one begins to twist facts to suit theories, instead of theories to suit facts.'

Arthur Conan Doyle, 'The Adventures of Sherlock Holmes'

A typical control system consists of several independent nodes with their own areas of responsibility. In order to carry out their tasks and collaborate with other nodes, the nodes need to share the current system-wide state and gather information on their environment and from other nodes. However, if information sharing is implemented by a synchronous query-and-answer based scheme, data queries interrupt a node while it waits for the requested data. In addition, information exchange for collaboration should not be the responsibility of the control application itself.

The sublanguage of data management patterns shown in Figure 10.1 provides a means of sharing information between nodes efficiently and safely. The cornerstone of the sublanguage is VARIABLE MANAGER (page 201), which stores system-wide state information as variables, and also provides interfaces for reading and writing them. Using VARIABLE

199

MANAGER, the system can share all information in a unified way throughout the system. In addition, developers can use a single consistent interface and variable-naming scheme to access data regardless of its origin – that is, whether produced locally or by another node. Some of the information consists of countable quantities; COUNTERS (page 221) describes how to deal with these.

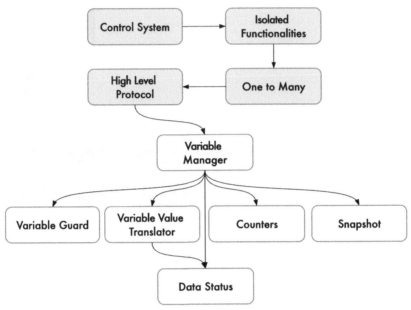

Figure 10.1: The sublanguage of data management patterns for solving problems of data sharing in distributed control systems

It is usually essential to know whether data is trustworthy, up-to-date and not originating for example from a faulty sensor, but a data consumer cannot deduce this from the variable's value. To tackle this problem, DATA STATUS (page 217) shows how to add status information and other metadata fields to each variable in a system. With third-party applications it might be necessary to restrict the information each application can produce and consume. VARIABLE GUARD (page 208) describes how third-party software can be prevented from accessing sensitive information controlled by a VARIABLE MANAGER.

In addition to providing a means to store information, this chapter's sublanguage also contains a couple of patterns for higher-level services. VARIABLE VALUE TRANSLATOR (page 211) describes how all variables in a system can be converted to any predefined units that a data consumer may require. SNAPSHOT (page 221) shows how to capture system-wide state information from a VARIABLE MANAGER so that it can be used later, for example for debugging or further analysis.

10.1   Variable Manager * *

...there is a distributed machine CONTROL SYSTEM (page 96) that consists of several independent nodes having their own areas of responsibilities (see ISOLATED FUNCTIONALITIES, page 110). The nodes must collaborate efficiently to carry out their tasks, so they connect to a message bus, allowing them to communicate in ONE TO MANY (page 131) fashion. To carry out these tasks, the nodes gather information from their environment using sensors and perform computations using this sensor information as input. In addition to this information, the actions they perform alter the system state, and this state information must also be preserved. There is information for high-level operations, such as an oil temperature limit to trigger an emergency stop. Some of this information is purely for local use in the nodes themselves, but some is needed by other nodes, for cooperation.

Information exchange for collaboration is not within the responsibility of a local application, as the main purpose of the application on a specific node is to control some part of the machine. To facilitate efficient collaboration between nodes, however, the nodes need to share information.

As a machine responds to stimuli from the environment or operator commands, normally only information about the current situation is relevant. This means that there is no need for long-term storage of information, as persistent information is only needed for more specific services. It also means that the information itself may have real-time requirements: a node should have quick access to all required information. However, as the bus has a limited data transfer speed and communication initialization overhead, all communication between nodes will have some inherent latency. Because of this latency, it is not sufficient to use a simple query-and-answer based communication scheme to share information, as this is too slow for a real-time environment. The communication channel also has limited bandwidth, so information cannot be accessed remotely whenever demanded, as constant queries from other nodes for updates load the bus in a non-deterministic way. As bus usage and consequently its maximum latency are hard to predict, the bus can become overloaded.

If information sharing is implemented by a synchronous query-and-answer-based scheme, queries interrupt a requesting node's tasks, as it has to wait for an answer. An information-producing node also has to react to a received query. These both deflect nodes from more urgent activities. The more nodes that are present in a system, the more bus capacity they consume, and the more interruptions will occur as the number of communicating nodes grows. An asynchronous query-and-answer method does not remedy the situation much, as an application has to add polling or callback mechanisms to check for an answer, and also some book-keeping mechanism to keep track of whether messages have been answered.

It should be easy to add new consumers and producers of information to the system. The core system may be extended by optional features that have to cooperate with the rest of the system. Some of these options may be developed long after the core system is released. This kind of system evolution can cause changes in the need for processing and sharing information over time. This means that an application developer may not know which other applications will use the information it produces. In addition, as the system evolves, some of the previously local information sources may become nodes on the bus; for example, a sensor that was previously connected to an I/O channel on a node might be replaced with one attached directly to the bus. Thus information producers and consumers must be decoupled from each other. This must be done in such a manner that an information producer does not need to know which other nodes use the information it provides. Equally, an information consumer should not need to know where the information it acquires originated. In addition to vendor-made features, some new features could be made by a third party. These third-party components or applications should have a way to access some of the information that is produced by the system if they need it in order to carry out their function.

All this, combined with the fact that lots of information might have to be managed in a distributed control system, means that an application developer may have to be concerned with implementation details of the messaging protocol. In the optimal situation, a developer should be able to use all information in a uniform way, regardless of its source or type. However, different nuggets of information can have different real-time requirements and updating needs. The situation might be made worse if some nodes host multiple applications, all of which can consume and update information. A poorly designed system could result in such a node requesting a specific data item several times if multiple applications need to access the same information source. The application developer should be able to use all information in a uniform way regardless of its source and other usages.

Therefore:

For each node, add a component, VARIABLE MANAGER, that stores the system information as variables and provides interfaces for reading and writing them. To make the information global, it is also sent to the bus whenever a variable is locally updated through the interface. Similarly, the VARIABLE MANAGER updates the corresponding variables when it reads updated information from the bus.

All relevant information that a distributed system uses should be presented as variables. A variable in this context is a uniquely named piece of information that is necessary for the operation of the machine, such as engine temperature or hydraulic pressure. A variable can also represent production information, such as the number of holes drilled or the species of tree that is currently being sawn. Some variables might be compositions of information that is tightly coupled. In the simplest case, variables are just global source code variables that can be accessed directly. In more elaborate solutions, the name of a variable can be some kind of enumeration, an address or an index. For example, CANopen presents variables as index/sub-index number pairs (CAN, 2013b). A symbolic name such as a text string can be mapped to these numbers, but are not usually used in processing due to efficiency issues. Some kind of macro expansion is normally possible, such as placing a `#define` clause in the code to give an integer a human-readable name. Some information is fundamentally analog and continuous in nature, usually those variables that represent measurements of physical phenomena such as engine cooling liquid temperature or the position of a joystick, despite the fact that they are presented as discrete samples having a specific sample rate. On the other hand, some information is discrete, countable items such as the number of trees felled, or system states such as parking brake status or tree species classifications.

To manage these variables conveniently, a VARIABLE MANAGER component should be added on every node. This stores all relevant variables and provides access to them through interfaces. Every node has its own set of relevant variables – relevant because the node itself produces this information, either by measuring it from sensors or by processing it from several information sources. Information relevancy can also result from the fact that the node needs the information for further processing, or to control actuators connected to it. The VARIABLE MANAGER interface provides a set of methods to atomically write and read the variables by referencing them with their unique names. Interface methods guarantee that any information that is currently accessed is mutually excluded – that is, not used by any parallel processes. Whenever a node processes information, receives a new sensor reading or otherwise produces new information that is relevant to system operation, it must update the values of the variables that correspond to this new information.

To propagate changes in local variables to other interested parties, a node's VARIABLE MANAGER communicates with other VARIABLE MANAGERs on other nodes using a ONE TO MANY (page 131) mechanism. Every VARIABLE MANAGER listens to the communication bus in order to update all variables that are relevant to it. To achieve this, the variables should be mapped to messages on the communication channel, so that every shared variable has a message with which it can be transferred via the bus. The mapped variable on a message is usually referred to as a *signal*. If the mapping from variables to messages and vice versa is done manually, it is laborious and error-prone, as it must be done separately for each node. The mapping can be automated using an XML file, spreadsheet or similar configuration tool that allows a developer to design the variable space, so that the unique symbolic name of a variable can be used in an application without having to be concerned about the actual messaging scheme or identification numbers on the bus.

For example, Figure 10.2 shows two nodes that share a common signal, JoyX, that represents a joystick's X-axis position. Process A samples the actual value and stores it as a variable, where Process B can access it. Whenever the variable is updated, the local node's VARIABLE MANAGER propagates the change to the other node, where Process C can also

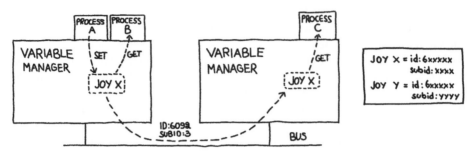

Figure 10.2: Sharing joystick data between two different units
with their own VARIABLE MANAGERs

access the data. The change in the variable is propagated to the node running Process C via the bus using a CANopen object dictionary entry with index 6092 and subindex 3. At the other node, the object dictionary entry is automatically mapped to the correct variable.

The communication between VARIABLE MANAGERs is carried out on the bus by broadcasting messages that carry the values of the local variables of the source node. Depending on the message size and available space for data, these messages can include either one or several variable values. As these messages are broadcast, all the other VARIABLE MANAGERs can listen to the bus and receive all messages. A recipient node can decide whether the information in a message is relevant to its function, and information producers do not need to know about the information's consumers. Information sharing becomes transparent to applications, as a VARIABLE MANAGER just updates the corresponding variable values whenever its node receives a relevant message. Conversely, if an application updates information that is used elsewhere, the VARIABLE MANAGER sends the corresponding message automatically.

In addition to sharing variables globally, a VARIABLE MANAGER can be used locally to a node for inter-process communication. Such variables are configured to be local and so have no messages mapped to them. This means that they are not sent to the bus at any time, but applications on the same node may access them and exchange information with other applications using them. This eases development, as applications can use the same method for storing their local and global data, and there is no fundamental difference in using local or remote values. However, if an application on another node needs these variables later, the VARIABLE MANAGER must be reconfigured to map them to messages so that the VARIABLE MANAGER on the remote node can update its local copies. Automation can help with this: a configuration tool can map formerly local variables to messages if a new information consumer is introduced to the system. Usually recompilation of the whole system is needed.

The sending of update messages can be triggered on variable change or periodically. If a measured value is naturally analog and continuous, it is advisable to sample the measurement at a fixed rate and send change messages periodically. A recipient can decide if the change in value is significant, and noise-induced changes can be ignored using an application-specific threshold. For example, suppose a boom's extension is controlled by a joystick's Y-axis position, sampled by an A/D converter with a 5 millisecond sample rate. The boom position is then stored in the VARIABLE MANAGER's storage as a variable, and mapped to a message that is sent to other nodes periodically every fifth millisecond. This allows the boom controller to determine whether the operator is keeping the joystick steady, or has changed its position, and act accordingly. If information is naturally discrete and represents some sort of state change, for example park brake status, it is not always advisable to send it periodically.

It is the designer's responsibility to decide whether a variable should be updated at fixed intervals or whenever its value changes. However, in some cases the message channel can be unreliable. For example, if a CAN bus is used a bad CAN driver might cause messages to be lost. So in practice messages might need to be repeated or sent periodically even when their value is discrete. For periodic messages the bus usage can be forecast at compile time. With event-triggered messages, however, a fault can generate so much traffic that the bus load can become excessive; this is hard to predict at compile time.

Thus bus configuration requires detailed knowledge of the nature of variables and their assumed refresh rates. For example, a measurement with 50 millisecond sample rate could be sent on a bus with an even higher rate to ensure that the message gets through. On the other hand, if the measured variable is a slowly changing one, such as outside temperature, it might be reasonable to update this variable only when it changes by more than a predefined threshold value. Still, many variables need to be broadcast once, when they are updated. For example, in the case of a CANopen bus a designer must make a choice, mapping variables either to a timer-driven and periodically sent PDO frame, or to an event-based PDO frame.

If a node must react immediately to a system state change, it may be better not to use a VARIABLE MANAGER to store data. If an urgent message is received, the node then just interrupts its current task and carries out the actions mandated by the message. This ensures that information that is used as the basis for the action is always up to date, and the node need not allocate storage space for variables. If a communication need is more event-based and requires immediate action, NOTIFICATIONS (page 156) is a better option.

When a system starts up there can be many uninitialized variables in a VARIABLE MANAGER, as the system has not yet produced or measured any information. These uninitialized variables must be prevented from use by adding metadata. Usually a single bit to indicate that the data is not yet initialized is sufficient; see DATA STATUS (page 217) for details. The start-up phase can also cause variables that are sent on a per-change basis to trigger their corresponding messages. To prevent the bus being overloaded by such messages, consider using some sort of time interval before triggering a change message, and implement a mechanism such as DEVIL MAY CARE (page 190) in the VARIABLE MANAGER. A VARIABLE MANAGER can also store a timestamp with each variable, with other metadata provided by DATA STATUS. This is to prevent the use of outdated values, or to detect bus failure if messages take a long time to arrive.

A variable manager is not suitable for storing all information, as the mutual exclusion and interface overhead causes latency. For example, purely local and big blobs of information are typically not stored in a VARIABLE MANAGER. If information is updated frequently in a VARIABLE MANAGER, it may also trigger an excessive volume of messages. If information is such that it needs fast access or its update rate is high, it might be better to store the information only in an application's local memory space. If such information needs to be shared with other processes, consider using LOCKER KEY (page 250) instead, when the VARIABLE MANAGER can be used to store the locker key itself. If the information is a counter that it is usually incremented or decremented by a fixed amount, COUNTERS (page 221) can be used. Using COUNTERS removes the need to read a variable from the VARIABLE MANAGER, incrementing or decrementing it and writing it back to the VARIABLE MANAGER, by offering a service that does all this with one method call.

If SEPARATE REAL-TIME (page 237) is used, it may be advisable to have a special VARIABLE MANAGER on the node at the operator level that stores all system information. This enables addition of new services, as high-end nodes tend to have more processing power and disk storage space. Such services might include collection of information for DIAGNOSTICS (page 350) to monitor the health of the system, a SNAPSHOT (page 221) of all information to allow restoration of system state in a test environment, REMOTE ACCESS (page 361) for exchanging information with off-board applications and a VARIABLE VALUE TRANSLATOR (page 211) to offer information in different unit systems. It also makes system debugging and testing easier, as one node maintains a comprehensive set of all system variables.

Similar patterns have been widely documented, as VARIABLE MANAGER is a variant of the widely-known PUBLISHER-SUBSCRIBE pattern (EventHelix, 2013b). VARIABLE MANAGER is essentially a special version of CACHING (Kircher & Jain, 2004), and can be seen as a version of REPOSITORIES (Garlan & Shaw, 1994), as it stores all shared data in a common storage location. CANopen's Object Dictionary can also be used to implement a simple version of VARIABLE MANAGER (CAN, 2013b), and PLC programming uses 'tags' as names assigned to devices. This pattern is similar to OBSERVER (Gamma et al, 1994), where all registered observers are notified automatically when a single datum entity changes. In VARIABLE MANAGER these changes are propagated globally. Data Distribution Service for Real-Time Systems (DDS) (OMG, 2007) is an example of an implementation of VARIABLE MANAGER in the machine control systems domain.

Using a variable manager component allows a system to share all information in a unified way. All shared information can be rendered location-transparent, as an information consumer does not have to know the source of the information. Location transparency makes it easy to change data location and to add new sources of information, as information consumers are not interested in its producers, only in the information. This decoupling of nodes is recommended in the IEC 61508-3 safety standard (IEC, 2010a).

As variables can be updated periodically, information may be old when it is needed. Detection of outdated information and requests for new values take time, so reaction times may be longer. Prolonged reaction times may make this solution unsuitable for event-based systems.

As variables are stored locally to a node, they consume node storage space. Nodes are usually low-end devices, so these resources may already be scarce: such nodes rarely have any mass storage. This might lead to problems if the system is scaled and the volume of stored information grows. This is particularly true if history information is needed, for example for DIAGNOSTICS (page 350): data volume might grow to inconvenient proportions. This suggests moving these services to the operator level and having a node with mass storage that is able to dump history data to a database periodically.

A VARIABLE MANAGER allows a developer to access information using a single consistent interface and variable naming scheme regardless of whether the data is produced locally or remotely. It is also possible to implement tools that can aid in DIAGNOSTICS, for example for data visualization and debugging, when all important data is presented using variables. However, the variable namespace may become cluttered during the long lifecycle of a control system, especially if the system has many shared variables. When a new variable is introduced, the designer must ensure that the name assigned to it is not already used. When a variable is removed, it must be ensured that no node is using it. An automatic tool can be used to detect these situations based on the VARIABLE MANAGER configurations. Versioning of the configurations can be alleviated by using CONFIGURATION PARAMETER VERSIONS (page 385).

It may be hard to design a suitable updating and invalidating strategy for a variable. If it is updated too often, it causes excessive bus load. On the other hand, if remote nodes get an update too infrequently, their calculations may be imprecise and important events may pass unnoticed. Not all information is suitable for storage in a VARIABLE MANAGER: suitability depends on the need for sharing and requirements for the variable's access rate. Also, a VARIABLE MANAGER's data is usually not preserved across power cycles, so this scheme is not suitable for saving persistent data. If persistent storage is needed, for example for PARAMETERS (page 380), there should at least be non-volatile memory for them. If the volume of data that must be stored is large, a mass storage database solution at the operator level is advisable.

As all information is shared, any node might update a variable and other nodes use it in their operations. Thus an erroneous or malicious update of shared information will propagate to the whole system. If this is seen as a risk, a mechanism such as VARIABLE GUARD (page 208) is advisable.

A forest harvester control system consists of multiple nodes, some of which are on the machine control level, while one is a high-end control PC at the operator level. All these nodes are connected by a CAN bus and have their own VARIABLE MANAGERs with relevant variables. When the machine is felling a tree, the harvester head module (HHM) node is used to command the feeding of the tree. During the feeding process, the HHM measures the length of the log using a measuring wheel and stores this information as a variable in its VARIABLE MANAGER. The HHM uses this variable in its own operations, as feeding must be stopped within the desired cutting window, which is a variable set by the operator before cutting has started. Cutting itself is a fully local operation, as the round trip latency for communicating this information to another node and getting a 'stop' command as a reply would be too long. However, the cabin PC uses the same variable (feed length) from its VARIABLE MANAGER to display information to the operator on how the feed process is progressing.

10.2   Variable Guard *

> *(Wagstaff is at the speakeasy's door and is asked for a password)*
> *Baravelli: Hey, what's-a matter, you no understand English? You can't come in here unless you say 'Swordfish'. Now I'll give you one more guess.*
> *Professor Wagstaff: ...swordfish, swordfish... I think I got it. Is it 'swordfish'?*
> *Baravelli: Hah. That's-a it. You guess it.*
>
> *From 'Horse Feathers', 1932*

...there is a distributed machine CONTROL SYSTEM (page 96) using VARIABLE MANAGER (page 201). In addition, the system has third-party components that are executed in a THIRD-PARTY SANDBOX (page 355). Operations of these applications rely on the data produced by the rest of the control system. The THIRD-PARTY SANDBOX runs applications from several vendors; some vendors might be trusted subcontractors, some open source communities, or anything in between. Consequently, the amount of trust varies between different vendor types, and affects what data a third-party application may access. For example, the navigation software on the machine is made by a third-party vendor due to map data licensing issues, but GPS location information is produced within the machine itself. Because this location data is also used by the core system and fleet management, the navigation software should not be able to alter location data or cause any other problems by accidentally altering other system state variables. To summarize, no sensitive data should be accessed by the third-party software, to ensure system safety and data security.

To allow third-party applications from untrusted parties to access the data produce by the control system, it must have control over what information each application can produce and consume.

The machine manufacturer is promoting system openness (open interfaces/open data) in the hope of getting better software developed for their platform by third parties. So third-party applications must have access to system data. It is inflexible and error-prone to hard-code all information sources as methods in the THIRD-PARTY SANDBOX interface. As the VARIABLE MANAGER acts as the normal interface to the system's data, third-party software should also be able to use it.

Control system testing is carried out in a simulator, where the actual hardware is used in the loop (HIL testing). Developing this testing and simulation environment is easier if the team developing the test platform can access the system data via the VARIABLE MANAGER.

REMOTE ACCESS (page 361) opens the control system to outside parties, which may need to access on-board data. This creates an attack vector and creates a risk to the safety and security of the system. REMOTE ACCESS applications are usually developed as separate projects from the control system, as they need a different skill set to that of the development team for the core system. However, remote applications need well-defined access to control system variables, so resemble trusted third-party applications.

Third-party software cannot be allowed to access any sensitive information (the operator's personal information, business-critical data and so on) and may not alter control information in the core system, as this could compromise overall system safety. Even if the third-party software is trusted, it is easier to prove the core system's safety conformance to guarantee that the third-party software cannot even accidentally alter any safety-related state variables. In some cases, even trusted applications need additional safeguarding, as programming errors, hacking and physical malfunctions can cause applications to inadvertently change variables that they should not touch.

Therefore:

Design a mechanism to guard the variables that checks whether an application is allowed to read variable values or submit their own changes to system state information. The mechanism is the only component that can directly access the VARIABLE MANAGER.

As THIRD-PARTY SANDBOX (page 355) and VARIABLE MANAGER (page 201) have been applied, the system has a VARIABLE MANAGER at the operator level (see SEPARATE REAL-TIME, page 237) that collects and stores all global system information in a single location. Third-party software usually provides only operator-level applications, as real-time applications are safety-critical and must be provided only by trusted parties, for liability reasons. If a third-party application in the THIRD-PARTY SANDBOX has to read variables from the VARIABLE MANAGER, its developers are given a special interface called a VARIABLE GUARD, along with the documentation on how to use it.

The interface includes a configuration where access rights for all variables have been defined. The interface should provide read-only access to the core system variables, and may also hide the existence of some variables completely. The interface itself can be implemented using a dynamic library file and an interface description, for example, so that the inner workings of the VARIABLE MANAGER need not to be exposed to third-party developers. In this way malicious changes to the machine's data is impossible. The third-party software may be assigned a unique user identification (UUID) string that it must

provide to the interface functions to gain access to specific variables. In this way the VARI-
ABLE GUARD provides read-only access to information that is configured to be immutable
by third-party software, and ensures that no sensitive information can be read.

If third-party developers wish to store their own data in the VARIABLE MANAGER, they
should be able to create their own variables. This can be implemented by using the VARI-
ABLE GUARD's interface method for reserving third-party variables, or by using an additional configuration file to reserve new variables for the applications. These variables will
have unlimited read and write rights for the third-party software, but the VARIABLE MAN-
AGER will not propagate their changes to low-end nodes. Having their own variables
makes application development easier, as developers have a uniform way to access data
regardless of its origin. In Figure 10.3 the third-party software has read-only access to system variables and full access to its own variables, but can manipulate both via the same
interface. However, if third-party software developers can allocate new variables freely,
they can excessively tax storage space on the high-end node, and access times may become longer because the VARIABLE MANAGER must handle a large volume of variables.
Some kind of limit to the number of third-party variables or their size should therefore be
enforced in the VARIABLE GUARD interface.

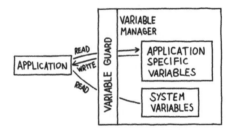

Figure 10.3: A third party with access to a specific set of variables via a VARIABLE GUARD

Access to all variables can be configured during development using a file or some other
tool. This gives the system designer control over which variables other parties can read.
Usually by default there is no access to any variables, and the designer can customize an
interface with exclusive access to specific variables. The configuration can be implemented as an XML file or a similar description of the variables and their access rights. Naturally this configuration must be such that it is internal to the interface, and third-party
developers should not be able to change any access rights using the configuration file. In
a more advanced solution, authorization for variable access may be session-based, so that
a third party needs to authenticate only once when the VARIABLE GUARD is first invoked.
In some cases a VARIABLE GUARD may include an option to dynamically revoke all access
rights for specific third-parties, for example if abuse is reported. The revocation may be
executed by some means such as a 'blacklist' file on a memory stick, or uploaded via a
REMOTE ACCESS (page 361) interface.

In some cases it is possible to use OPC Unified Architecture for third-party security
(Mahnke et al, 2009). It is possible to have an OPC UA server that allows access to only
that data that is separately configured to be readable. Extensive literature is available on

data security, for example (Denning, 1982). PROTECTION PROXY (Buschmann at al, 1996) is a similar solution to the pattern presented here. It creates a proxy that acts as the access point to sensitive data.

After implementing the VARIABLE GUARD, third-party software can have controlled access to relevant control system information, which is presented as variables in the VARIABLE MANAGER. The variables that the third-party software needs can be shared without fear of malicious or erroneous changes to system information, and all sensitive data is hidden from third-party software developers.

Testing and REMOTE ACCESS (page 361) systems can have access to control system data. However, special care should be taken when designing the interface to ensure that all sensitive data is really protected. It is usually better to grant access on a variable-by-variable basis than to offer inclusive access. Feelings of false security can rise when a guard is applied, as a badly-designed interface may leak information.

A mining drill rig has to communicate with a FLEET MANAGEMENT (page 372) application. The fleet management system has a server that is located in the mine's control room. Communication is carried out using a GPRS modem. The fleet management application is developed by a separate team and only needs production and location information from the drill rig, not minute details about sensor values and so on. Therefore it is sensible to add an interface for the fleet management application to the drill rig's data, a VARIABLE GUARD, which only allows limited access to the machine's control parameters. The fleet management-specific data is stored in separate variables on the drill rig. These variables are reserved using a VARIABLE GUARD method, and are not communicated over the bus. This prevents the mining drill rig sending any sensitive data to the fleet management application accidentally. On the other hand, the rig's operator has access to the fleet management data in the fleet management server via the fleet management application.

10.3 Variable Value Translator

…there is a distributed machine CONTROL SYSTEM (page 96) that consists of several independent nodes that represent ISOLATED FUNCTIONALITIES (page 110). The nodes gather data from the environment using sensors and perform computations from this data. To facilitate collaboration through information sharing with other nodes, the data is presented as variables in a VARIABLE MANAGER (page 201). Many of the variables represent measurements of physical quantities, at various resolutions. The units used for these measurements can vary from one node to other. For example, the length of a tree may be measured by the harvester head node as rotations of a metering wheel, but an algorithm in the boom control unit that calculates the required force to support the tree from its center of mass uses centimeters in its internal algorithms. To handle these differences, the nodes should be aware of the units in which a value is measured or calculated, and a common system of units should be used in the system to make it easier to understand and maintain.

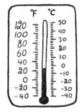

Different devices may use various measuring units internally, but they should also be able to use each other's information about the surrounding environment. Hard-coding of unit translations is not scalable, and the same translations may be needed throughout a system.

The control system uses sensors to measure physical quantities in order to have information about the environment. The value of a physical quantity is a product of a numerical value and a unit, for example 2.7 meters. Measurement results therefore usually have two parts: magnitude and dimension, conveyed as units. However, some quantities do not have units and are dimensionless, such as planar angles, or strain, which is defined as the ratio of deformed length to initial length, this division cancelling out the units of length. In software measured values are often compared with other measurements or predefined invariant values. One example of this could be comparing engine coolant temperature to predefined safety limits to ensure that the coolant will not boil. Comparisons of magnitude can only be done if the units are the same.

Controllers use sensors to measure physical quantities. The real world causes some change in the sensor that can be interpreted as an analog signal, which is sampled at a known rate and converted to a fixed resolution digital value, called the *raw* value. Low-end devices usually only use these raw values from analog-to-digital conversion as the basis for their operation. Raw values from different devices are usually not directly comparable with each other. To make system-wide data compatible, raw values can be scaled, for example to metric units, although some vendors may use different measurement standards, for example metric versus Imperial.

If measurement values are communicated between different controllers, both ends of the communication must have the same concept of their values. Variance in measurement units makes adding new devices to the system challenging, as measurements made by devices and their calculations may be incomprehensible to each other when communicated via the message bus.

Mixing units, such as adding inches and centimeters together when calculating distances, may cause extremely dangerous situations and even loss of life, so a system should be designed so that the possibility of this kind of error is minimized. The Mars Climate Orbiter is a well-known example of mixing units, as its thrusters, made by Lockheed Martin, provided navigation commands in pound seconds instead of the NASA-approved metric system (Stephenson et al, 1999). Usually it is not possible to alter the measurement units of a data-producing device, due to lack of a suitable configuration feature or just the vendor's decision. If various consumers of the data require the measured value in different formats, it is the system developer's responsibility to use the correct units and resolutions. In some high-end products measured data can contain additional information, such as the same data in other units, or a metadata field containing the units in which the data is represented.

Nodes and devices may be acquired from multiple vendors; either from subcontractors or as common off the shelf (COTS) components. Their manufacturers may be located in different countries and use varying standards of measurements, so devices may use differing units for their measurements. This is more likely with COTS components, as manufacturers of mass-produced devices do not usually customize their interfaces to meet individual customers' needs. In addition, if the manufacturer of a specific component goes out of business, or the component has to be changed during the lifecycle of the system, it is vital to ensure that replacement devices support the same units as the rest of the system.

In addition to development difficulties caused by differing units, the machine operator must be taken into account if any of the measured values are to be displayed on the HU-MAN–MACHINE INTERFACE (page 313). The operator might only be familiar with their own native measuring system, and may not be familiar with units used by the developers of parts of the system. To ensure that an operator can operate the machine efficiently, the user interface should display only familiar units. For example, if the operator is familiar with speed as kilometers per hour, it may be dangerous if the speedometer displays miles per hour.

Therefore:

Add a converter service to the VARIABLE MANAGER. The service includes interfaces to store and retrieve variables in suitable units regardless of the units the VARIABLE MANAGER uses internally.

As low-end nodes often have limited resources, their measurements of physical quantities are not normally presented in standard units in their internal operations, but rather use raw digital sensor data. Raw data is usually the direct output from the A/D conversion of sensor data, presented as an integer. This avoids the need for any special conversion services for data that is only for local use. This makes sending, receiving and processing the data quicker. However, when the node has to communicate with other nodes, it should use some previously agreed units instead of raw values. In addition, some high-end applications may need different units than the core system's raw data, so a translation service interface is needed.

If both SEPARATE REAL-TIME (page 237) and VARIABLE MANAGER (page 201) have been applied, the VARIABLE MANAGER on the high-end node is likely to store all system-wide variable data. In this case, the most natural place to implement the translation ser-

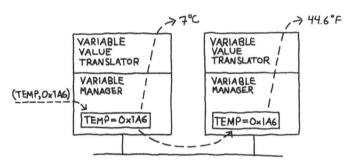

Figure 10.4: A system with VARIABLE VALUE TRANSLATORs on each node

vice interface is the VARIABLE MANAGER on the high-end node. The high-end node has enough processing power to execute all required translations. The VARIABLE MANAGER (VM) itself can use any suitable units for storing data internally. The interface is used to get the value of any variable stored in the VM in the units requested. In Figure 10.4 a node fetches the raw value from a temperature sensor and stores it in the VM. The VARIABLE VALUE TRANSLATOR interface is then used to retrieve the temperature in Celsius or Fahrenheit. In simple cases, the application may just call a method with some name like getTempInCelcius(). The VARIABLE VALUE TRANSLATOR service can be used several times for a specific value. For example, if a raw value of 0x1A6 is read from the A/D converter, representing a temperature of 7.0 degrees Celsius, it can be scaled to 70 for calculations made within a machine control level node and displayed on the cabin PC as 44.6 degrees Fahrenheit.

In more sophisticated versions, the interface method usually implements parameters for the name of the accessed variable, the value of the variable and its units. If writing a new variable, the VARIABLE MANAGER can translate the value to its internal storage units, or store the value as it is and change the units as requested. When reading variables, the variable name and units are passed. The interface then returns the value in the correct units. For example, in Figure 10.4 a method getVar(TEMP,CELSIUS) could be used. If the requested units are not valid for the variable the interface will return an error code, an exception, or use some other mechanism.

There are several ways to define the required unit conversions for a specific variable. A simple strategy is to use a configuration file that maps every variable to a specific unit and defines translation formulas for other units. As the system evolves and new units are introduced, however, someone has to maintain the configuration files, creating a risk of failure if a variable is incorrectly configured or uses the wrong units. This kind of misconfiguration may have catastrophic consequences. A large system might have thousands of variables, so maintaining the configuration data can be a gargantuan task. In CANopen, for example, input/output objects can be assigned an SI unit object. CAN-Cia 303-2 provides a standard way to implement the presentation of units and prefixes for analog signals (CAN, 2000).

Another way of having variables with units is to add a metadata field to data that defines the unit of the measurement – see DATA STATUS (page 217). Dedicated functions for converting units to other systems can then be used. If the data is communicated over a bus, the metadata field makes the message larger, but may make the data payload smaller. However, this requires less reconfiguration if a data-producing node is replaced with another that uses different units.

When designing the conversion interface and translation functions, you need to take several issues into consideration, especially if values are compared as ratios, or mathematical operations are performed to them. First, when comparing physical quantities, the rule of thumb is to ensure that they use the same units. However, some units are defined as derivations of others. Such units can be regarded as specially named mnemonics: for example, in the SI system one liter is defined as one cubic decimeter, and one Newton is a shorthand for the force required to accelerate 1 kilogram of mass at the rate of 1 metre per second squared. Special units such as these can in most cases be treated as and compared as their equivalents, but this is not true in all cases. For example, fuel consumption may be defined as liters per 100 kilometers. As liters are cubic decimeters, liters per kilometer reduces the unit to square meters, which is a unit of area, but it does not make sense to compare these two.

There are many different classes of measurements whose values cannot easily be compared. In the simplest cases, comparisons are done between ordinal measurements, for example rankings, which have no units. Although ordinal measurements have no units, there is naturally no sense in comparing two ordinals of different types, such as the number of read errors on a bus to the number of holes drilled. However, some ordinal values may be composites of each other, so their units can be converted and become comparable. For example, if three work shifts always sum to one work day, work shift and work day values can be compared easily. COUNTERS (page 221) gives more information about ordinal measurements.

Most measurements that are of interest in engineering algorithms are described in Stevens' measurement theory (Stevens, 1946), and Nicholas R. Chrisman's article (Chrisman, 1998) further extends the levels of measurements. Conversions between classes require more care than just changing the unit of measurement within a class.

Units are only one aspect of a larger problem, *localization*, also known as *internationalization*, and colloquially referred to as 'i18n' for short. Other aspects of localization, such as time zones and languages, can be addressed by using PARAMETERS (page 380) to configure a machine for a specific locale. For example, Qt uses a comprehensive tool set for multi-language applications and is thus one possible way to solve localization problems in machine control systems (Digia, 2013b).

Variables in a system can be presented using predefined units that the operator or software modules may require. Development is simplified, as a developer does not need to care which units are in use in other parts of the system and can choose freely from any convenient system of units. Testing is also simplified, as hardware-dependent raw values are only used locally to nodes, while more sophisticated applications can use human-readable units. However, this pattern does not guarantee that a developer will remember to convert units, so special care must be taken if a system does not use the same units uniformly throughout.

In a strict real-time environment it may be impossible to implement variable translation due to time constraints. This pattern is therefore normally used only for non-real-time system functions.

Conversion uses processing power on nodes at the machine control level. Sending values to a high-end node for conversion is not a viable option due to the resulting processing delays. It also uses bus capacity, which may already be a scarce resource.

VARIABLE VALUE TRANSLATOR makes it easier to internationalize the system, as the control system already supports several unit systems. Testing, debugging and logging may be easier if the system can provide human-readable units. Applications in a THIRD-PARTY SANDBOX (page 355) can also use suitable units more easily.

A hardware designer is not limited to using components that use the same units as the system, as translation can be used to convert data to the units the rest of the system uses.

An autonomous fork lift truck carries loads from shelf to shelf or to a loading area in a warehouse. The system has one controller and some intelligent actuators and sensors. The control application uses several sensors to guide the fork lift to the correct loading spot. These include velocity sensors, limit switches and so on. Its hydraulic valves and electric motors are controlled by sending them messages defining the movement they have to carry out. These sensors and actuators have been acquired from different subcontractors, and some of them use different units than the main system. The scaling of raw values also vary from device to device. The fork lift establishes its initial position in the warehouse by closing switches on the floor of the loading area.

In the warehouse the fork lift calculates its position by reading acceleration information from its sensors. This information is given in raw values: each sensor keeps track of one axis, and the resulting number ranges from −65335 to 65535, corresponding to the acceleration along that axis.

The fork lift truck has a long lifespan, so broken sensors and actuators must be replaceable easily, perhaps with those from a different vendor. New sensors might provide acceleration data in m/s^2. However, these can be used, as a conversion service is implemented by the VARIABLE MANAGER on the main node. This converts messages containing measured values into SI units, and the main node consistently uses SI units in all calculations. All control values in messages are translated into the correct units for the actuators. Sensors and actuators can therefore use any units they wish as long as the converter is properly configured.

10.4   Data Status *

'If I give you a hint and tell you it's a hint, it will be information.'

Diana Wynne Jones, 'Howl's Moving Castle'

...there is a CONTROL SYSTEM (page 96) in which a VARIABLE MANAGER (page 201) is applied to share system state information. However, the data in the VARIABLE MANAGER might originate from a faulty sensor, or be outdated. Consumers should not blindly trust the data, as they cannot know if it is produced by a properly functioning sensor or node. A data consumer also cannot deduce the status of the data producer from the data, as it may still seem valid. Carrying out calculations using values from faulty sensors can lead to incorrect results and is not acceptable. It is vital to know whether data can be trusted.

10 11 1000
DATA ???

A data consumer cannot deduce its correctness based only on its contents. However, to function safely, the consumer must know whether the data is trustworthy and up to date, and does not originate from an inaccurate sensor.

Sensors can malfunction in many ways and produce faulty or inaccurate data. Inaccurate data might be still usable for some purposes, but cannot be used in calculations that could compromise safety. A data consumer needs to know whether the data can be trusted. Which data is valid and which faulty must be known.

'Safe' values – values that cause no movement – should not be used to indicate that a sensor has failed. For example, if a zero value is used to indicate failure of a joystick, a receiving node cannot determine whether the joystick is broken or is just centered. The receiver of the joystick signal therefore cannot inform other nodes about the fault, or take remedial action.

A VARIABLE MANAGER is used to transfer state information from its originating to its receiving node(s), decoupling them from each other. A receiver cannot know if the data originates from a faulty sensor. The sensor's status signal could be stored as a variable in the VARIABLE MANAGER and a receiver could monitor it. However, it is cumbersome to read two values instead of one, and the receiver becomes dependent on the status signal. This is problematic, especially if a node uses values derived from the original measurement: consumers of such data would need to monitor the status of all nodes that participated in its creation. If the data originates from a time before the sensor failed it could still be valid, even though the sensor's status signal indicates that the sensor has failed, and vice versa. Additionally, if the faulty sensor's data is used for calculations, any consumer of the calculated results must keep a record of status signals, to know what the status of the sensor/data originating node was at the moment the data was produced.

Data may become outdated as the machine's environment changes. It becomes invalid in the current context and should not be used, as conclusions based on it are no longer valid.

Therefore:

Add status to each variable in the system as meta-information. Status information indicates the age and/or the state of the information (OK, 'INVALID', DERIVED_FAIL etc.). This allows a data consumer to see whether the data is fit to use for its purposes.

Add one or more metadata status variables to each variable. Metadata status variables can for example contain information on the status of the data's producer, a timestamp to indicate when the data was produced, the units of measurement and so on. Adding metadata information to a variable naturally means that a structured data type needs to be used. Listing 10.1 illustrates an example struct containing data status.

```
// Enumeration for data status
enum Status {OK, FAIL, DERIVED_FAIL};
enum Unit {METER, FOOT};

// Variable type when Data Status pattern has been applied
Struct integerVariable{
    int value;
    Status status;
    long int timestamp;
    Unit unit;
};
```

Listing 10.1: An example struct demonstrating how metadata is added to a variable

In addition to adding data status to variables, you must define the semantics of what happens to metadata when arithmetical operations are applied to the data. When two variables are added, for example, the resulting metadata fields need to be derived from the metadata of both source variables. You need to define rules for other operations on metadata when necessary. Consider the metadata fields `Status`, `Unit` and `timestamp` in Listing 10.1. If variables containing status values of `OK` and `FAIL` are added, the result would be `DERIVED_FAIL`, because one of the variables originated from a faulty sensor and the other from a correctly working sensor. A consumer of the resulting variable now knows that one of the start values was unreliable. Similarly, operations for adding two `FAIL` statuses, `DERIVED_FAIL` and `FAIL`, and `DERIVED_FAIL` and `OK`, need to be defined: these operations should always result in a `DERIVED_FAIL` status.

Often data status is manually propagated by assigning the correct status to the metadata field (see Listing 10.2). However, in this case a programmer might make mistakes, forgetting to update the status or assigning an incorrect value to the status variable. If automatic propagation of status is required, special properties from the runtime environment are required. For example, a virtual machine running an application as bytecode might be required to implement automatic status propagation. While using virtual machines, however, automatic propagation of statuses might be challenging. For example, if a value is updated within an `if` statement, it might be hard for the developer to understand what happens (see Listing 10.3). In this case, the situation could be corrected by always checking a signal's status before assigning its value to a variable. This is quite easy to check at runtime. Another option is to update the status manually when a result is calculated (see Listing 10.2). However, in this case a programmer might still make mistakes.

```
otherSignalValue.value = signal.value + 1;
otherSignalValue.status = signal.status;
```

Listing 10.2: Updating the status of a variable manually when performing an operation

```
// Problematic variable update. Runtime environment might not be able to
// propagate the status change automatically
if( signal.value == 42 ){
    otherSignal.value = 8;
}

// Possible solution for the above problem situation
if( isValid(signal) && signal.value == 42){
    otherSignal.value = 8;
}
```

Listing 10.3: Automatic status propagation might be hard to understand in some situations

A metadata field defines the units of measurement of the value. To calculate using two variables, they must have the same units. If they have different units, they cannot for example be summed without first converting their value to the same units – see VARIABLE VALUE TRANSLATOR (page 211). When summing two variables their timestamps also need to be considered. Sometimes the resulting variable should have the older timestamp of the two start values, as the derived value describes the environment when the older value was measured. Sometimes the newer timestamp might be the better option. A data consumer should have its own application-specific 'time-to-live' value for data, so that it can compare it with the data's timestamp to check whether it is still fit to use. Using a timestamp metadata field requires that nodes have a common concept of time – see GLOBAL TIME (page 124) for more details.

The main limitation of a DATA STATUS approach is that COTS components are not likely to support it. So not all data will contain metadata, and calculations involving data containing metadata and data without it must be defined. For example, in Listing 10.1 a new status value UNKNOWN could be added to indicate that the data value has no metadata. If COTS usage is extensive it may even completely prevent use of DATA STATUS. In some cases it might be possible to add simple OK/FAIL information to the data when received by in-house applications, but this would make the application dependent on the COTS component and the topology of the network. It might be possible to add information about the units of measurement during system configuration, especially if COMPONENT-BASED CONFIGURATION (page 386) is used.

DATA STATUS can be used when implementing LIMP HOME (page 185), for example by adding a fail bit to the metadata; when the fail bit is on, the system automatically enters a SAFE STATE (page 179). If an operator or maintenance engineer activates the LIMP HOME mode, it might mean that the control system uses simpler control algorithms. The simpler algorithm might not be as efficient as the normal algorithm, but does not require the failed part, such as a sensor. INTERCHANGEABLE ALGORITHM (page 193) can be used for algorithm selection.

DATA STATUS can be seen as an instance of the *Caveat Lector* principle, in which the reader is responsible for deciding whether the text should be trusted. (Saha, 2012) discusses the use of metadata of signals and local parameters such as name, minimum, maximum and default values in the context of CANopen based systems. (Saha, 2013) discusses SI unit scaling and management for CANopen systems. DDS (OMG, 2007) offers ready-made solutions for setting different quality of service policies for publisher/subscriber topics, for example limiting the durability and lifespan of a topic and providing status information from the publisher of data using a deadline policy.

When data contains metadata describing its trustworthiness and freshness, a data consumer can determine whether to use it. Separately monitoring status signals for sensors is not required, as the metadata will indicate whether the data originates from a faulty source. Derived values will also contain similar status information.

With proper metadata a data consumer can know the accuracy of a signal, and can use this information to make decisions if the data is accurate enough.

COTS components may not support this approach. If COTS use is extensive, the benefits from this approach might be too small compared to its implementation effort. It might also be that metadata is not available at all for some information.

DATA STATUS increases bus loading, as metadata also needs to be transferred over the bus. If throughput is already critical, the load caused by metadata might be excessive and another bus technology should be considered.

In a tree nursery saplings are planted in pots. As they grow, they need to be moved further apart. This is a laborious task, so a robot is used to automate it. This robot is autonomous and has a CONTROL SYSTEM (page 96) with a VARIABLE MANAGER (page 201) to share system state information. When making autonomous decisions, the control system needs to know the age of measurement data and whether it can be trusted, so DATA STATUS is applied.

Metadata fields defining data status are added. Sensors send information over the bus in their native message format, and metadata is added to it when it is received by the central node. The central node contains all system state information, so it is easy to add the metadata defining the sensor's state to the data. Different status values are used:

```
OK                        abnormal_update_rate
abnormal_rate_of_change   unidentified_failure
valid_above_normal        valid_below_normal
```

…and so on. In addition, the time when the data was received is added to the metadata as a timestamp. When route calculation algorithms and other automated functionalities use this data, they can use the metadata information in decision-making. If the sensor data is outdated, the robot can initiate a rotation sequence in which the robot turns through 360 degrees to probe the environment and update its measurement data. DATA STATUS makes it easier for the algorithm developer to check whether data is outdated. Furthermore, the algorithm is not dependent on separate status signals provided by the VARIABLE MANAGER (page 201).

10.5   Counters *

A system has events whose frequency of occurrence is interesting. These occurrences are countable quantities that may need to be stored persistently. One event may affect several countable quantities, some of which are global and some used only by a limited set of nodes. It is not always clear which node is responsible for storing the quantity.

Therefore:

Create a service that provides counting functionality for different purposes. The service should offer different kind of counters, for example non-resetting usage counters, maintenance counters and resettable counters. The counters can count up or down, or can be driven by a timer.

For the complete pattern, please see www.wiley.com/go/controlsystemspatterns.

10.6   Snapshot *

…there is a CONTROL SYSTEM (page 96) in which a VARIABLE MANAGER (page 201) stores system-wide state information as variables. The state of the system is in continuous change, and the values of the state variables are updated frequently. As many variables are usually involved in representing the information, their previous values are usually overwritten to save storage space. Testing and debugging, however, may require historical values, as the current state of the system does not contain enough information about past events. It is useful to examine the system-wide status at a specific moment. For example, if the control system software crashes, the system state variables at the moment when the crash occurred could help to reproduce the crash when debugging the software in the development environment.

The system-wide state is complex and changes all the time. Because of this, the operator or developer is usually not interested in system state as long as the machine functions normally. However, it is useful to examine the system-wide state at a specific moment later, to analyze and test the system after something of interest has occurred.

State variables change frequently, so storing all historical data changes may require huge amounts of storage. Storing just the history of one variable will not record the whole system-wide state. As changes in variable values do not take place synchronously and may depend on each other, to recover the system-wide state at a specific moment may require going through all variable changes since initialization.

A system may function normally for hours but, because of a transient error, may suddenly malfunction. Malfunctions like this can be triggered by software errors that cause the system to enter an undefined or erroneous state. Such errors are difficult to debug, as reproducing the malfunction in the development environment may require deep knowledge of the state of the system at the moment of the crash.

During development it is sometimes possible to use software simulation in place of real hardware parts. This is useful if the control software needs to be tested without the hardware. For example, the hardware might not yet exist, or be impossible to use for safety or cost reasons. When a test is initialized, physical parts need manual adjustment to be in the correct initial state and position. With simulated parts, however, there is no need to adjust them to correspond to an assumed physical state, so a simulated part can represent any desired physical state as long as the state variables of the simulated part are initialized accordingly.

Testing a system in real time may be impossible, as the number of variables that define the system-wide state is usually high and their changes rapid and continuous. It is hard to follow all changes, so some transients may pass unnoticed. After a crash the system usually continues changing its state variables for some time, as it is not possible to freeze the system immediately after a malfunction.

Therefore:

Implement a mechanism to save all state variables, along with the timestamp from the VARIABLE MANAGER (page 201), as a snapshot. Create a toolset in the development environment to analyze and restore system-wide state from the snapshot, for further use.

The simplest way to implement a snapshot mechanism is to have a dedicated VARIABLE MANAGER that can make a copy – a snapshot – of its internal data structures. During copy creation the VARIABLE MANAGER is locked for further variable updates and changes are buffered. After the copying process is complete, the lock is released and the buffered variable changes are applied. Finally, the copy is stored to persistent storage as a snapshot file. This allows variables in the VARIABLE MANAGER to be changed even while a snapshot file is being stored. If SEPARATE REAL-TIME (page 237) has been applied the system will be divided into machine control and operator levels. More processing power and storage space is usually available at the operator level, so it is a natural place to locate the VARIABLE MANAGER that supports the SNAPSHOT functionality.

If it is not possible to modify the functionality of the VARIABLE MANAGER, you can use a dedicated node with a snapshot application that queries all variables from its own VARIABLE MANAGER and stores the values in the snapshot file. To acquire system-wide state information, the dedicated node should receive all variable changes from the bus. Using this approach strongly decouples the node's VARIABLE MANAGER from the snapshot mechanism. However, this decoupling has serious drawbacks: for example, snapshots can no longer be taken atomically, as the regular VARIABLE MANAGER does not have buffering functionality. Variables can change during the snapshot process, so even if the snapshot takes only a fraction of a second, it no longer represents the system-wide information at a specific moment. Moreover, extensive usage of VARIABLE MANAGERs will increase system load and decrease performance.

The snapshot file can be created either after a crash is detected, or periodically. It is usually worth taking a snapshot of system state if a predefined event, such as an operating mode change (see OPERATING MODES, page 175), has occurred. The operator could also take a snapshot of system state manually if it is needed for testing or analysis purposes.

An XML file is typically used to save snapshot data. The file usually has a timestamp indicating its creation time, plus variable names and their values. DATA STATUS (page 217) values can also be stored if necessary, along with other metadata for variables. Listing 10.4 shows an example of a snapshot file. The fragment contains information about two variables: oil temperature in Celsius, and a pressure value from sensor 1231 whose units are defined as bars (unit = 0x4e) with a prefix (0xfd, meaning 10^3) scaling the pressure value to millibars.

The obvious way to use a snapshot is for testing. When a system crashes, a snapshot of the current system state is created and stored automatically. The system's developers can analyze the problem with debuggers, analyzers and simulators by importing the system state information from the snapshot file. The tool reads the state variable information from the snapshot and initializes the corresponding internal variables to those of the file's contents. The initial system state of the test environment is now the same as the system that crashed. Using the system state information data generated by the system crash allows programming errors to be found.

```
<snapshot version="1.0">
  <timestamp="1365587580"/>
    <variable name="TEMPERATURE_OIL">
      <value>23.243</value>
      <unit>0x2D</unit>
    </variable>
    <variable name="PRESSURE_SENSOR_1231">
      <value>1432</value>
      <unit>0x4e</unit>
      <prefix>0xfd</prefix>
    </variable>
    ...
</snapshot>
```

Listing 10.4: An example fragment of a snapshot file

Another use for SNAPSHOT is *regression testing*, in which a system is tested by rerunning previously-completed tests. Regression testing checks whether system behavior has changed or whether fixed faults have reemerged, and helps in automated system testing. Regression tests require a specific initial system state, so that tests can be systematically selected. To be efficient, it should be possible to have an initial state for the tests. This state differs from the inherent state of the system after start-up. Using a snapshot file allows you to restore a preferred initial state for the tests.

In some cases it is not possible to take a snapshot after a system has crashed. For example, the system may have a WATCHDOG (page 101) that resets the system in the event of failure, or a crash may render the VARIABLE MANAGER (page 201) inaccessible. However, you might want to analyze the root cause of a failure afterwards, even when the system is malfunctioning. Consider applying BLACK BOX (page 355) to record selected events.

A similar SNAPSHOT pattern is described in (Loyall et al, 2002), where it is used to get a consistent view of a system's state to support runtime decisions about quality of service (QoS) parameters in embedded systems. CHECKPOINT (Hanmer, 2007) is used to avoid loss of results by saving global state information. SNAPSHOT (Carlson et al, 1998) describes a mechanism for preserving the value of a variable at a specific point in time in an environment where the properties of the variable change over time. For example, if a price variable has a discount applied at some point and a calculation needs to be carried out to get the current price, SNAPSHOT can be used to take a copy of current prices. The MEMENTO software design pattern (Gamma et al, 1994) describes a mechanism to save and restore an object's state.

System-wide state information can be stored for later analysis. This is useful in testing, as the situation at the moment of a crash can be reproduced in a simulator or test envi-

ronment. This makes it possible to test the application without using the actual hardware.

The system state captured from a real machine can be used as a starting point in a
training simulator. For example, machine operators can be trained to handle a new machine by providing them with real-life situations.

When developing a system, regression testing using a simulator may be essential to improve the quality of the application. Regression testing can be enabled by restoring the
state of the simulator to a defined point using the snapshot file.

SNAPSHOTs make it possible to repeat a scenario in a test environment to find the root
cause of a failure. This is useful if there is no clear assumption about the error that caused
the failure. Properties of the system, such as performance, can be analyzed to identify
bottlenecks.

Taking a snapshot can jeopardize real-time behavior of a system if a modified VARI-
ABLE MANAGER (page 201) is not available at the operator level. A snapshot mechanism
may be difficult to implement, and the system state information can consist of large quantities of variables, so it may be cumbersome to save and upload the entire state information in bulk. Sometimes it might be better to have a snapshot mechanism on each node,
so that the bus load to a centralized VARIABLE MANAGER is reduced.

All value changes may not be present in a centralized VARIABLE MANAGER at the moment of a crash, as there is always some latency in transfer. The failure causing the crash
can be analyzed using snapshot information from the failed node, although the overall
system state at the moment of failure may be unclear.

Taking snapshots decreases the performance of the system, and consumes resources
such as CPU time and persistent storage. It might also be difficult to select the right time
for the snapshot. If the snapshot is taken just after an error has occurred, it will not reveal
the whole path leading to the erroneous situation, so the root cause of the error may not
be so easily deduced.

A harvester has REMOTE ACCESS (page 361) so that DIAGNOSTICS (page 350) data can be
sent to the service center. To increase accuracy, an oil pressure variable value is corrected
in the engine controller by adding a calibration value, which is calculated by dividing the
predefined scaling value with the oil temperature value minus an offset. The calibration
value depends on the oil temperature, and the offset is used to adjust the calibration value
for different environments. The offset is set slightly higher than the opening temperature
of the oil cooler thermostat (90 degrees Celsius). However, the divisor of the calibration
equation will be zero if the oil temperate is exactly 93.5 degrees Celsius. The system may
function normally as long as the value of the oil temperature variable is within its normal
operating range. If the machine is used a hot environment, however, the oil temperature
may rise too high, causing a division by zero error in the calibration process and crashing
the whole system.

When the machine is serviced the oil temperature remains in its normal range and the
situation leading the control system to crash cannot be reproduced, making it tedious to

find the root problem. In this case the root problem was a missing test for division by zero before calculating the calibration value.

SNAPSHOT is applied to find the cause for this mysterious malfunction. When notification of the division by zero error is sent, a snapshot file is created. When the REMOTE ACCESS connection is next used to retrieve DIAGNOSTICS data, the snapshot files are sent along with DIAGNOSTICS data. The SNAPSHOT files are analyzed by the manufacturer using a simulator. Maintenance personnel now notice the high oil temperature value. This information leads the tester to the root cause of the malfunction. A new software version is prepared to fix the calibration calculation problem. When the harvester is next serviced the engine controller software is updated and the problem is removed.

CHAPTER

11

Patterns to Handle Scarce Resources

'Where words are scarce they are seldom spent in vain.'

William Shakespeare

Embedded control systems differ from normal desktop computers, as they usually have very limited resources for applications. This is mostly due to cost effectiveness, although also other restrictions, such as the space available for a CPU unit, might dictate the selection of hardware. In any case, if a manufacturer can save a couple of euros by selecting an older or cheaper low-end technology, this scales up rapidly if sales of a machine are in the thousands or hundreds of thousands.

SEPARATE REAL-TIME (page 237) is the root pattern for this sublanguage. It divides a control system into separate levels based on its real-time requirements. As non-real-time operations are on their own level, they do not interfere with critical real-time operations. Similarly, real-time operations are located on the machine control level. On this level, real-time requirements are in most conflict with the processing power of limited hardware resources. A control system typically needs to react to a stimulus in microseconds. This

227

requirement is often tackled on the machine control level using a CPU whose processing power was common for desktop computers ten years ago. This means that the software design must compensate for missing resources. This chapter describes patterns for tackling these challenges: Figure 11.1 shows the sublanguage of patterns to cope with challenges caused by scarce resources.

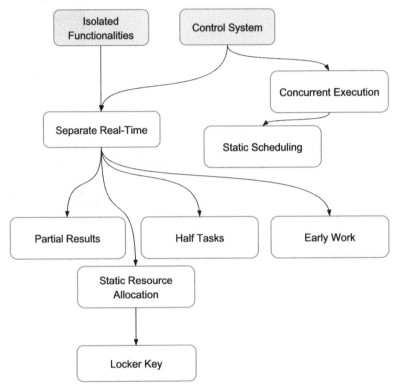

Figure 11.1: The sublanguage of patterns for handling scarce resources

When trying to meet real-time requirements, the most critical part of a control application is its main control loop. There are several ways to ease the critical task of the control loop. One is to try to carry out as many support tasks as possible before the application enters its control loop. This is described in EARLY WORK (page 259). Another is to divide tasks into smaller parts so that their work is spread over a longer period. This usually means that resource consumption and the response times of the application are reduced. HALF TASKS (page 254) and PARTIAL RESULTS (page 243) give more information on task division. Finally, real-time applications should be predictable and their response times guaranteed. This can be achieved by reducing the number of dynamic decisions made in the control loop and making them at the design, compile or development stages instead. This approach to static resource use is covered in STATIC RESOURCE ALLOCA-TION (page 247) and STATIC SCHEDULING (page 234). The latter pattern refines CONCUR-

RENT EXECUTION (page 229), which discusses sharing CPU resources so that several tasks can be executed at the same time. LOCKER KEY (page 250) also discusses how processes can utilize shared resources.

11.1 Concurrent Execution * *

...there is a CONTROL SYSTEM (page 96) in which SEPARATE REAL-TIME (page 237) is used to divide functionality into machine control and machine operator levels. The machine control level applications may contain a SUPER LOOP (Pont, 2001), which executes operations cyclically, such as reading a sensor value and controlling actuators, so that the same operation repeats every nth millisecond. Usually the operations are implemented as functions, so SUPER LOOP contains function calls in a predefined order. There are also counters for those operations that are not executed on each loop cycle. Listing 11.1 illustrates a typical application with the SUPER LOOP architecture.

```
int counter=0;
do_initializations();
// main control loop cycle

while(true)
{
  counter++;
  read_sensors();
  calculate_values();
  update_signals();
  if (counter%5==0)
  {
    // this is called every 5th loop cycle
    send_values_as_messages();
  }
}
```

Listing 11.1: A typical application using a SUPER LOOP architecture

When the number of operations in a system increases, a SUPER LOOP architecture does not scale.

Some operations are triggered by an event, so not all operations are run periodically in the control loop. It is cumbersome to handle events with the SUPER LOOP architecture. For example, while a system is reading a temperature sensor value it must still be able to react to alarms from other nodes. With a SUPER LOOP architecture all operations are statically defined and the current operation can only be interrupted for a short time.

Following the principle of *separation of concerns* (Hürsch & Videira-Lopes, 1995) increases understandability and eases programming. Unfortunately, a SUPER LOOP architecture does not support separation of concerns very well.

When timing of cyclic operations become more complex, it may be difficult to construct a suitable control loop cycle. For example, it is hard to find a common loop cycle time if some operations must be executed every 10 milliseconds, one every 22.5 milliseconds and one every 49 milliseconds. In addition, a loop's cycle time varies depending on the operations executed. This may cause problems if the operations have strict real-time requirements.

The number of real-time operations can vary during the lifecycle of a product. For example, a system update might include new hardware, control of which requires new software operations. CONTROL SYSTEM OPTIONS (page 394) may also cause operations to be disabled or enabled, depending on the options selected for the product, changing the number of operations required in the system.

To keep costs low in embedded systems, the processor usually contains a single core, so only one operation can be executed at a time.

Therefore:

Collect operations that depend on each other into entities called *tasks*. Implement a ready queue for tasks that are ready to be executed. Implement a scheduler that takes the first task from the queue for execution. When the task has finished, it is returned to the queue if it needs to be executed again later. Alternating the execution of tasks creates a sense of concurrency.

A task is a function block whose code is executed, and the task is finished when execution of the function ends. The control application now contains tasks, a runtime environment with the scheduler to run the tasks, and optional utility functions. The runtime environment provides a method for putting a task into a ready queue. When the system starts up, the tasks are started by the runtime environment or by the application. Some of the tasks may be dynamically started when an event occurs, to handle operations required by the event, such as giving a response to a request.

The elements in the ready queue are addresses to *task control blocks* (also known as *process control blocks*, or PCBs). The PCB contains information on the tasks: the memory address of the task's code and other information needed by the scheduler. For example, a task usually has its own stack space, so the address of the stack needs to be stored somewhere. When the task is selected for execution, the stack pointer is updated accordingly. Figure 11.2 shows the structure of the ready queue.

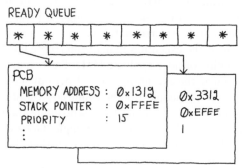

Figure 11.2: A ready queue contains pointers to process control blocks
that contain a task's meta-information

Some tasks may have a long execution time without strict response time requirements. Maintenance and self-diagnostic tasks such as checking memory for errors, for example, are usually called 'housekeeping' tasks and are executed only when execution time is available. To avoid housekeeping tasks blocking the whole system, they must give up their CPU time to higher-priority tasks. This can be done by the task itself, either by calling a method to tell the scheduler to select the next task from the ready queue, or by a timed interrupt. The latter is called *round-robin scheduling*, in which a time slice is assigned to each task and, after the time slice has elapsed, the scheduler selects a new task to be executed. A task is resumed the next time a time slot is assigned to it. This prevents any one task stealing all the CPU time.

In advanced scheduling systems tasks can have priorities. Here specific tasks are executed before others, for example because they have real-time requirements. To support this, the ready queue is replaced with a priority queue, so that the most important task (the task with highest priority) is always selected first. Priority information is stored in the tasks' PCBs. It is also possible to have more than one ready queue: scheduling will take less time if each priority level has its own queue. The highest priority queue is always checked first in the scheduling process.

Even though a ready queue makes an application easier to understand, it does not itself solve periodic task problems, as the scheduler just runs tasks in a specific order. To solve periodic task problems, a system usually contains a second queue (called a *waiting queue*) and a timer. The timer causes an interrupt after a predefined interval. The interrupt handler for the timer checks timing information from the meta-information of the tasks in the waiting queue. All tasks that need to be executed now are moved from the waiting queue to the ready queue. The developer can schedule tasks to be executed periodically by adding a scheduling command at the end of the task. In some environments a developer can configure the task to be rescheduled automatically when it has completed.

The tasks in the waiting queue can also wait on other events, such as incoming messages or signals from other tasks. Information on an event for which a task is waiting is stored in the PCB. If priorities are used, the scheduling process is started if any of the tasks moved from the waiting queue have a higher priority than the task currently being executed. The scheduler selects the task with the highest priority for execution, after which it resumes execution of the interrupted task.

Switching tasks lengthens the execution time of interrupted tasks. To reduce jitter in execution times, you should consider applying HALF TASKS (page 254) or PARTIAL RESULTS (page 243) to minimize the execution times of periodic tasks. Jitter in tasks with strict real-time requirements can jeopardize their time constraints. To prevent this, such tasks should have high priority. In addition, special scheduling algorithms should be used instead of a basic round-robin scheme – see for example (Goossens, 1999; Burns, 1991; Davis & Burns, 2011). The scheduler should also detect when deadlines are missed and notify the rest of the system.

Listing 11.2 demonstrates a periodically executed task. Assume that the timer interrupt interval is set to 10 milliseconds. A task `MEASURE_WEIGHT` needs to be executed every 50 milliseconds. To handle this, the task is moved from the waiting list after five timer interrupts. Once the task is executed, it reschedules itself to be executed after 50 milliseconds.

```
task MEASURE_WEIGHT
{
// Read the weight sensor value
  weight=read_sensor(WEIGHT_SENSOR);
  // Update the signal according the sensor value reading
  update_weight_signal(weight);
  // Reschedule the task to be executed after 50 ms
  // Put the task back to the waiting list
  schedule(MEASURE_WEIGHT, 50ms);
  // The task MEASURE_WEIGHT will be executed again later
}
```

Listing 11.2: A periodic task that reads a sensor and updates a signal periodically

When tasks are executed concurrently, you must take care that shared resources are mutually excluded – that is, simultaneous access to a shared resource is not allowed. When one task needs access to a resource it must lock other tasks out of the resource. Operating systems usually provide common mechanisms for locking, such as semaphores (Stalling, 2008). If semaphores are not available, you can use spin locks and disabling interrupts (Stalling, 2008). However, to allow interrupt handlers to operate correctly, interrupts should only be disabled for a few instructions. Mutual exclusion can cause issues such as deadlock, starvation and priority inversion (Dijkstra, 1965; Lampson & Redell, 1980). The problems encountered in the Mars Pathfinder are a well-known example of such issues (Reeves, 1997).

If a controller has an operating system, this usually provides a ready-made scheduler. It is also possible to separate scheduling from that provided by the operating system (Mollison & Anderson, 2011). Separation allows you to use scheduling algorithms that a real-time operating system (RTOS) platform does not support natively. If the number of tasks is known beforehand and does not change during execution, you can consider applying STATIC SCHEDULING (page 234) to schedule tasks at compile time. With STATIC SCHEDULING real-time requirements are already met, and potential problems can be detected during development. For example, (Pont, 2001) provides patterns to implement different types of scheduling algorithms. Extensive literature is available on parallelism, for example (Stalling, 2008; Mattson et al, 2004; OPL, 2010). (Ortega-Arjona, 2010) presents architectural patterns for concurrent and distributed programming. A conference for parallel programming patterns, ParaPLoP, has been arranged a couple of times.

As operations are isolated as tasks, the software is easier to modify as it evolves or new options are selected. Side-effects of changing the timings of periodic operations are limited to the relevant task, as operations are called by the scheduler, not from the main loop with hard-coded timings.

If tasks have strict real-time requirements it might be impossible for the scheduler to guarantee that their deadlines are met. This can be remedied using high priorities for real-time tasks, and keeping their execution time and those of interrupt handlers as short as possible.

Shared resources must be reserved for one task at a time, using a locking mechanism such as semaphores. Programming in a concurrent environment is difficult and therefore error-prone, and usually requires programmers with special skills. In addition, using a locking mechanism slows down execution of an application.

If one task needs results from another task, synchronization of the tasks is needed. This may require additional communication between tasks. Even though operating systems usually provide a mechanism for inter-task communication, synchronization of tasks can lead to concurrency issues such as deadlocks.

With limited processor power in an embedded systems, the scheduling operation should be fast and have a small runtime overhead.

In a welding robot, a node handles welding arm positioning and quality control of the weld. The node communicates with a process controller via a CAN bus, to exchange process information such as parameters and quality statistics. To make programming less error-prone, arm positioning and quality control are separate tasks. Messaging is also handled in its own task. As these tasks should be executed simultaneously, CONCURRENT EXECUTION has been applied. The tasks are started during the boot process of the node. The arm positioning task is scheduled to be executed periodically on a 30 millisecond interval, and the messaging task wakes up whenever there is a new message in the receiving or sending buffer (see MESSAGE QUEUE, page 143). The quality control task is a continuous task with lowest priority, as it does not have strict real-time requirements. It can therefore be interrupted by other tasks.

11.2   Static Scheduling * *

...there is a CONTROL SYSTEM (page 96) in which SEPARATE REAL-TIME (page 237) is used to divide functionality into machine control and machine operator levels. CONCURRENT EXECUTION (page 229) has been applied to execute operations on the machine control level as concurrent tasks. The tasks have strict real-time constraints with hard deadlines. The most important requirement of a hard real-time system is predictability, and task deadlines must be met regardless of system load, otherwise the execution of the task is considered to have failed. Failing to meet a deadline usually causes propagation of the failure, leading the whole system to fail.

	MON	TUE	WED	THU	FRI
8-9		FRA			
9-10		FRA	PHY	BIO	SPA
10-11	MAT	GEO	BIO	MAT	SPA
11-12	BIO	MAT	GEO	PHY	LAT
12-13	GEO	PHY	SPA		LAT
13-14			SPA		

In a real-time environment, tasks should always be executed at a defined moment, to prevent system failure. However, scheduling can cause variance in the response times of applications, jeopardizing predictability.

Fast response times are required in real-time environments. A scheduling operation should therefore be lightweight, with very little runtime overhead. Additionally, only limited processor power is available in embedded systems.

Real-time applications should be predictable and response times should be guaranteed. For example, an action might have to be completed in 1 millisecond.

It can be difficult to analyze the behavior of an application with concurrent tasks, as it is not always known a priori which task is executed at a specific moment. Changes in the environment may change response times, thus changing the scheduling of tasks.

Therefore:

Design scheduling with time slots of fixed length and divide the application into executable blocks. These may for example be functions or code blocks. The executable blocks are assigned to time slots at compile time.

In order to schedule tasks, processor time is divided into time slots called *minor cycles*. Application code is also divided into executable blocks, with a dedicated execution period (for example, every 10 milliseconds). The period defines how often the block is executed, and must be a multiple of the minor cycle time. Minor cycles constitute the complete schedule, called the *main cycle*. The maximum execution period is the length of the main cycle. In each minor cycle, code from one or more execution blocks is executed. Scheduling is synchronized using a synchronization pulse (like an external clock interrupt), which starts each minor cycle.

In its simplest form each minor cycle consists of a sequence of function calls. Scheduling can be carried out by defining each function call as an execution block and specifying a period for it. Based on this information, the compiler maps the code into minor cycles. The total execution time of a code block cannot be longer than the minor cycle time.

Dividing code into blocks can be automated. If the time consumption of all operations is known a priori, the schedule of tasks can be built during compile time based on knowledge of execution times, the required order of tasks, and deadlines. The worst-case execution times of operations are used for scheduling so that scheduling cannot fail at runtime. In a distributed system interaction between nodes can also affect scheduling. For example, if node A sends a message to node B, these two operations (sending a message and receiving a message) should have a dependency such that reading the message buffer in B should be scheduled to happen immediately after A has sent the message.

```
Block A Period 40 {
  temp=getTempSensorReading();
  FilterAndStoreReading(temp);
}
Block B Period 80 {
  ntemp=getFilteredReading();
  setHeatingControl(ntemp);
}
Block C Period 160 {
  updateLCD();
  sendTemperature();
}
```

Listing 11.3: An example of the execution blocks of a temperature controller application

As an example, consider a control application that adjusts the heating system of a room based on a temperature sensor, to maintain the desired temperature. The application is divided into execution blocks A, B, and C (see Listing 11.3). Block A, with a period of 40 milliseconds, reads temperature from the sensor, filters it and stores the filtered value. Block B controls the heating system based on the filtered temperature value, running once every 80 milliseconds. Finally, Block C updates the user interface every 160 milliseconds. The main cycle time of 160 milliseconds is divided into four 40 milliseconds minor cycles. The first minor cycle will therefore have code from all the blocks, and the rest of the minor cycles contain code from blocks depending on their period. As Block A has a period of 40 milliseconds, its code is executed in each minor cycle. Block B has code executed every second minor cycle, and Block C's code only in the first cycle. Figure 11.3 illustrates the scheduling of the system.

If all CPU time is reserved for execution blocks, no other external interrupts except the synchronization pulse can be handled, as the CPU load can be very high. If the system must have interrupts, the worst-case execution time for interrupt handling should be known beforehand, and a corresponding time should be reserved for the interrupt handlers for each minor cycle. Usually the interrupt handler just sets a flag, and the actual

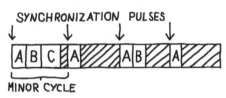

Figure 11.3: Static scheduling of three execution blocks

interrupt processing is done periodically in its own task – see HALF TASKS (page 254) for more information.

As well as time-critical statically scheduled tasks, a system may also have non-time-critical longer-running tasks, perhaps housekeeping tasks such as self-diagnostics or maintenance. One way to execute these is to 'slice' them by applying PARTIAL RESULTS (page 243). The non-time-critical tasks are then divided into blocks that are scheduled to run in minor cycles along with time-critical tasks. An easier way to handle housekeeping tasks is to use priorities and a dynamic scheduler – a scheduler that selects the task to be executed at runtime. This allows the static scheduler to be implemented as a single high-priority task that interrupts any lower-priority dynamic tasks. If execution time is available from static tasks, the housekeeping tasks are executed. Thanks to priorities, static real-time tasks are not delayed by lower-priority housekeeping tasks.

You can use GLOBAL TIME (page 124) to synchronize execution between multiple nodes for increased cooperation accuracy. If system communication takes place in a ONE TO MANY (page 131) fashion, you can statically schedule messaging by applying STATIC RESOURCE ALLOCATION (page 247) to allocate time slots for time-triggered communication.

When processes are scheduled statically, runtime overhead is minimized, as all scheduling decisions are made beforehand. On the other hand, pure static scheduling prevents dynamic processes being created at runtime: once a schedule is defined, it cannot be changed during execution. As operations are divided into execution blocks, one operation is always complete before another is started, and there is no need for interlocking mechanisms such as semaphores.

If worst-case estimations of execution times are known beforehand, processes can never overrun. In addition, there is no need to support unsuccessful scheduling, as enough CPU time is always available.

The compiler can give an error message if the defined scheduling is not possible. Scheduling is predictable, as time slots are fixed and the number of tasks is always the same. However, it might be impossible to calculate execution times in all cases. Usually worst-case estimations are used, which will lead to lower CPU utilization. Unlike dynamic scheduling, static scheduling cannot make use of any free time in time slots.

Static scheduling makes a system more predictable. However, its average response time depends on the cycle times, and it is usually longer than with event-based, dynamically scheduled systems.

A task needs to be split into a number of fixed-sized blocks. This may be error-prone if carried out manually. In addition, changing the code in execution blocks may be time-consuming, as cycle times set upper limits on the execution time of a single block. In addition, period times must be multiples of cycle times. If the execution time of a changed block exceeds its limits, it must be divided into two blocks.

Debugging a system is easier, as its tasks are always scheduled for execution in the same order. You can therefore execute the application in a debugger knowing that operations are in the same order as before. This also makes remote debugging easier.

This pattern can also help in documenting the system. The scheduling scheme can be visualized as a graph to show when each operation is executed. It is also possible to discover specific metrics about the application, such as the actual number of operations per second, or the execution time of an operation.

A medical imaging system requires precise documentation for its safety certification. The documentation must contain exact timing information. To achieve this, a static scheduling scheme is used to achieve precise timing of operations. The operation's response times must be constant, and the number of operations per minute that can be executed with the chosen hardware must be documented. In addition to metrics, the scheduling graph is included as a part of the documentation. The system development environment also contains tools for debugging and analyzing the system. For example, when the system has entered a SAFE STATE (page 179), the debugger is attached via REMOTE ACCESS (page 361) and the current state of the application is read. For debugging purposes, the synchronization pulse given to the scheduler by a hardware timer is disconnected (that is, scheduling is paused) and scheduling is then controlled by the debugger. This allows the minor cycles to be executed step by step. When normal operation is required, the synchronization pulse is reconnected.

11.3   Separate Real-Time * *

...there is a distributed CONTROL SYSTEM (page 96) to which ISOLATED FUNCTIONALITIES (page 110) has been applied. There are therefore multiple nodes in the system. A single node's functionality can be implemented by one or more applications. Some functionalities are related to controlling the machine, while high-level functionalities offer the operator a graphical user interface and communicate with remote systems via REMOTE ACCESS (page 361). These high-level functionalities might need a lot of resources, and their execution times are unpredictable. On the other hand, the machine control functionalities typically have strict real-time requirements, and their response times should be deterministic. The high-level functionalities require data from the machine control level to implement their operations. For example, DIAGNOSTICS (page 350) requires data from nodes. The high-level functionalities therefore need to exchange information with the machine control level. If high-level functionality is implemented on the same node as machine control functionality, the fulfilment of real-time requirements needs to be guaranteed.

There are always machine control functionalities in a system. To increase the productivity and operability of the machine, the system needs to offer high-level functionality such as a graphical user interface, DIAGNOSTICS and so on. The high-level functionalities' behavior may compromise the real-time requirements of machine control functionalities.

Real-time applications must meet their timing requirements, otherwise they are considered to be malfunctioning. Thus real-time functionality must not be interfered with by other functionalities of the system. Response times of real-time applications typically range from a few milliseconds to couple of hundred milliseconds, although they can sometimes be only a few hundred microseconds or less. On the other hand, high-level functionalities do not have strict real-time requirements, and response times in seconds is often sufficient. However, high-level functionalities may consume resources such as CPU time from real-time functionalities and cause them to malfunction – to fail to meet their real-time requirements – if both run in parallel on the same hardware. This could lead to hazardous situations.

It should be possible to use separate teams to develop the real-time functionality and high-level functionality. Different developers and teams have different skill sets, and may specialize in specific kinds of applications. Thus incremental development of the software should be supported by the architecture. Different programming languages are normally used for real-time applications than for high-level functionalities. If different teams work on different parts of the system, each team only needs development tools for the specific part they are working on.

In many cases high-end services are resource-heavy and need more processing power than real-time functionality. It should be possible to use common low-end hardware to save cost for machine control, but there is also a need for high-level functionalities, and these services require more sophisticated hardware. This kind of hardware is vulnerable under the harsh conditions where the machine is used, so it might not be suitable for machine control applications.

High-end services are not mission-critical from the machine's point of view. They provide additional value but are not required to control the machine. Malfunction of a high-level functionality should not affect the availability of the machine, and under no circumstances should malfunction of a high-level functionality prevent the operator from using the machine.

Section 1.2.4.3 of the European Machinery Directive (Machinery Directive, 2006) mandates that the system's emergency stop must halt any hazardous process as quickly as possible. This requires rapid response times and must override any operations currently being executed. This mechanism therefore needs to be separated from normal machine control and high-level functionality, as it needs to be available even when other parts of the system are malfunctioning.

Therefore:

Divide the system into separate levels according to real-time requirements, for example into machine control and machine operator levels. Real-time functionalities are located on the machine control level, and non-real-time functionalities on the machine operator level. The levels cannot interfere with each other, as they use a message bus or other medium to communicate with each other.

This real-time separation means that all applications having real-time requirements are logically placed on the same level – the machine control level. Despite this logical division, the applications can still reside on different nodes, taking care of ISOLATED FUNCTIONALITIES (page 110). Multiple applications might run on the same node, but all such applications are either real-time or non-real-time. All non-real-time applications are placed on the operator level, and real-time applications on the machine control level. Operator-level applications should not be able to control any actuators directly and cause movement. Operator-level applications are typically run on a PC in the machine's cabin, while machine-control applications run on their own dedicated controller, for example a programmable logic controller (PLC).

Emergency stop can be implemented as its own level. Usually it is implemented purely with hardware, and is used to remove power from the machine control level and inform other levels that emergency stop has been activated. The rest of the system can then make any required state changes (see OPERATING MODES, page 175) and inform the operator. If emergency stop is implemented as its own level, other safety certified functionalities can be placed on the same level. On the other hand, if emergency stop is implemented on the machine control level, it usually means that the whole machine control level needs to be safety certified. Safety certification of the whole machine control level would be an expensive and rigid process.

Figure 11.4 illustrates a system with three separate levels. The operator level hosts a graphical user interface (GUI) for the operator, a DIAGNOSTICS (page 350) application and REMOTE ACCESS (page 361) for communication with other systems. All machine-control-related controllers, such as engine, drive, frame and boom controllers, reside on the machine control level. The emergency stop level functionality is used to power off these controllers. The operator level exchanges information with the machine control level using a message bus (see ONE TO MANY, page 131), in this case a CAN bus. The operator level can be operational when the machine control level is unpowered, for example due to a fault. This allows the operator level to be used to diagnose any fault that causes the machine control level to malfunction and become unpowered by the emergency stop

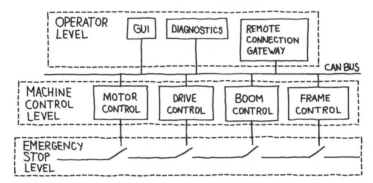

Figure 11.4: Example architecture of a system where SEPARATE REAL-TIME has been applied

function. On the other hand, if the cabin PC malfunctions and operator-level functionality is lost, the machine can still be operated using only the machine control level, at least to some extent. HUMAN–MACHINE INTERFACE (page 313) describes how an HMI can be implemented to allow the operator to use the machine while the operator level is malfunctioning.

When machine-control and operator levels are able to use the same kind of hardware, it might be possible to separate real-time functionality from non-real-time functionality using only a single node. For example, if Linux is used with a real-time kernel such as Xenomai (Xenomai, 2012) or Red Hat Enterprise MRG Linux (Red Hat, 2013), a system can run both real-time tasks and non-real-time tasks on the same core. In such real-time operating systems (RTOS) task priorities are used to implement real-time functionality. The highest-priority task wanting CPU time always gets it within a fixed time after the event that woke the task. The latency of a task therefore only depends on the tasks running at equal or higher priorities, and all other tasks can be ignored. Often real-time tasks in an RTOS are run with the highest priority, so that they get the resources they need from non-real-time tasks run at lower priority. Sometimes there might be separate scheduler for real-time tasks. RTOSs often provide a way to exchange information between real-time tasks and non-real-time tasks.

Real-time operating systems also help to make real-time applications more portable, as the applications are developed using the operating system's services. If the operating system has been ported to other platforms, it may just be a matter of recompilation to move the application to a new platform. For this reason, it is advisable to use RTOSs, such as FreeRTOS (Real Time Eng., 2013) or μC from Micrium (Micrium, 2013), even if real-time tasks separated to their own node. Usually a SUPER LOOP (Pont, 2001) based solution makes the application dependent on the hardware.

Nowadays multi-core CPUs are quite common and their popularity is growing. These can be used to run real-time tasks on one or more core(s) and non-real-time tasks on the rest of the available cores, so separate hardware is not necessarily needed. Although this might provide an easy way to solve the real-time separation problem, the approach is not common because of the relatively high price of multicore processors. This approach may introduce errors that are hard to detect, as parts of the hardware are shared between different cores. Thus the safety of the system might be harder to verify.

Separating real-time tasks from non-real-time tasks also gives flexibility to software development, as non-real-time tasks can be implemented using desktop application programming languages and libraries. For example, the Qt cross-platform library (Digia, 2013a) is used often in GUI development. On the other hand, machine-control application development on low-end controllers such as PLCs may require their own development, testing and simulation environment, which might not be so common. In many cases machine-control applications need to be implemented using the limited feature set of C, or some domain-specific language.

Normally operator, machine-control and emergency-stop levels are sufficient. Sometimes only the first two are used. However, in a complex system with a number of hierarchical subsystems, it might be necessary have more levels to separate functionalities with differing requirements. In a train, for example, there might be more than one high level: a high-level control system in a coach and a high-level control system for the whole train that interacts with the railway traffic control system. The division into different levels should be carried out so that using intermediate levels to deliver information between producer and consumer levels is avoided, as it may make levels interdependent and cause problems if some levels become unavailable.

If you need to run third-party software on a machine, the logical place to implement a THIRD-PARTY SANDBOX (page 355) is on the operator level, as it usually has sufficient processing power. If the third-party software is located on the non-real-time level it cannot interfere with real-time control of the machine. This implies that third-party applications cannot have real-time requirements. Generally this is still a viable option, as third-party application suppliers should rarely be responsible for implementing basic machine-control functionality. When the third-party applications' functionality is limited to the operator level, it cannot interfere with machine control and cannot compromise system safety.

Resources are typically scarce on the machine control level, and measures need to be taken to address this problem. You might run maintenance tasks that do not have strict real-time requirements as a housekeeping task on this level, and respond to new tasks by using HALF TASKS (page 254). On the machine control level it might be necessary to ensure that scheduling or resource allocation always succeeds at runtime, and that execution times of machine-control application do not exceed the limits set for them. STATIC SCHEDULING (page 234) and STATIC RESOURCE ALLOCATION (page 247) address this problem. Additionally, some calculations might need to be carried out during start-up if time or resources are insufficient during the application's normal operation. EARLY WORK (page 259) discusses this in more detail. Sometimes real-time applications on the same node need to send data to each other. Copying large memory blocks might be time-consuming, so you might want to consider using LOCKER KEY (page 250) instead. The SEPARATE REAL-TIME pattern can be seen as a special case of LAYERS (Buschmann et al, 2007b) or LAYERED ARCHITECTURE (Rubel, 1995).

Isolating real-time functionality and non-real-time functionality on separate levels that communicate in ONE TO MANY (page 131) fashion over a bus prevents non-real-time functionality from interfering with real-time functionality. This makes a system more robust and fault-tolerant. The development of different levels can be given to separate software development teams, and functionalities can be implemented in parallel. The real-time functionality can be tested alone, to guarantee that it fulfils its timing requirements, and that non-real-time functionality cannot interfere with real-time functionality.

The operator-level hardware typically has more processing power, so higher abstraction level programming languages and libraries can be used. This increases productivity.

If a fault occurs, a system needs to react quickly, for example by entering a SAFE STATE (page 179). A SAFE STATE usually requires that machine control is stopped and safety measures put in place. To implement this, it should be easy to determine which parts of the system need to be stopped and which can be still be active. Separation into machine-control and operator levels makes it possible to take the machine control level to a SAFE STATE and still diagnose the problem using services provided by the operator level. Conversely, if there is a fault on the operator level, the machine control level is still operable and can be used to control the machine, at least to some extent.

Separating high-level functionality from machine control makes lifecycle management of the hardware easier. On the operator level, a PC can be upgraded without worrying about issues such as pulse-width modulation outputs' dither frequencies, A/D converter bit rates and other issues that are not typical in a PC environment. Such issues can be tackled on the machine control level by selecting suitable hardware, while the PC can be upgraded independently of these properties, even after a machine is deployed.

Creating interfaces between different levels may sometimes be challenging. If there are more than two levels information may need to be passed through some of the levels en route to its target level. It might also be hard to decide the right number of levels. Too few levels may not separate different concerns of the system sufficiently, while too many levels can make it too complex.

A reactive power compensation unit has a control system that has strict real-time requirements on the machine control level. However, there is also a remote user interface (UI) and operator level, used to transfer information from the machine control level to the remote UI. The remote UI and operator-level applications are non-real-time. Figure 11.5 shows this division into separate levels. The control system has two user interfaces: local and remote. The local user interface provides a HUMAN–MACHINE INTERFACE (page 313) for the operator, while controls are implemented on the machine control level. The controllers on the machine control level measure the process, read sensor data and present it on the local UI, which can be used to manipulate the compensation process. The machine control level also delivers sensor data to the operator level as status information via a fieldbus. The operator level uses this data for DIAGNOSTICS (page 350) and passes the status information to a remote UI using REMOTE ACCESS (page 361). This makes it possible to control the process remotely when the local UI is switched off. Control commands can be sent from the remote location; these are received by the operator level and forwarded to the machine control level, which controls the process according to the commands.

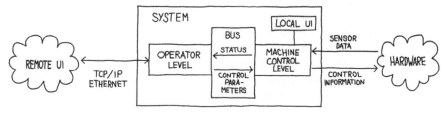

Figure 11.5: Illustration of a reactive power compensation unit's control system architecture at a high level

11.4   Partial Results

...there is a CONTROL SYSTEM (page 96) in which SEPARATE REAL-TIME (page 237) has been used to decouple real-time tasks from non-real-time tasks by creating at least two levels: a machine control level and an operator level. All the machine's control functionality, such as controlling a boom or engine, is implemented on the machine control level. Control applications on this level can usually be characterized as simple endless loops – see SUPER LOOP (Pont, 2001) for details. PLCs typically have scan cycles that are instances of this SUPER LOOP design principle. SUPER LOOP means that STATIC SCHEDULING (page 234) is used to schedule tasks at design time and there is no need for the operating system to take care of scheduling. Listing 11.4 shows an example of a typical control application using this approach.

```
while( true){ // One cycle must not exceed 50 ms to meet real-time requirements

/* Control actions */
read(sensor_1_value);  // takes 1-2 ms
read(sensor_2_value);  // takes 1 ms
do_control_action_1(); // takes 1-5 ms
read(sensor_3_value);  // takes 1-2 ms
do_control_action_2(matrix); // may take up to 35 ms, but sometimes returns
immediately

/* Complex calculations */
var matrix = calculate_new_matrix_values(necessary_inputs[]); // takes 20 ms
}
```

Listing 11.4: Typical structure of an application on the machine control level

As the example shows, the execution time for each loop may be completely taken up with reading sensor values and performing those machine control actions that need to be done within one loop cycle. If additional tasks arise, such as the calculation of boom kinematics, which requires matrix calculations (`calculate_new_matrix_values`), the required loop execution cycle (50 milliseconds in the example) may be exceeded. This means that the real-time requirements for the control application may sometimes not be met, as the control actions and sensors reading can no longer be carried out within a single cycle. On the other hand, these requirements might sometimes be met. In the example, if the `do_control_action_2` function returns immediately, timing requirements are met. So, the hardware is sufficient to run all operations, but on some loop cycles there are too many tasks to be executed to meet the timing requirements. The results of complex calculations, however, are not needed on every loop cycle, perhaps every *n*th cycle. Relaxing the loop's cycle time is not an option, as the response times for machine control would not be met.

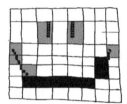

Some real-time tasks need more time than the control loop's cycle time allows. However, the results of long real-time tasks are typically needed only every *n*th loop cycle.

The control application is implemented with a loop that performs all machine control. In many cases the loop's cycle time is dictated by the response time requirements for machine control. So the loop's cycle time cannot be relaxed, otherwise these requirements will not be met. A system might have hard real-time tasks such that, if the required loop's cycle time is not met, the system is considered to have failed. Normally, there is a WATCHDOG (page 101) or similar mechanism that ensures that the real-time requirements are met. If a loop cycle takes too long, the WATCHDOG will interrupt operation and reboot the system.

The hardware on which the control application is running does not have the required processing power, memory or other resources to do all control *and* perform complex calculations within one loop cycle, as some calculations could take too long. However, there is enough time to compute part of the complex calculation. The hardware cannot be upgraded with more processing power, as this would increase production costs, consume more power, or wouldn't physically fit in the controller's installation bay. Furthermore, new hardware might be overkill, as it might have much more processing power or memory than the existing hardware. This could suffice if timing requirements were no longer a problem, whereas new hardware could have extraneous or unused resources.

Interrupt-based scheduling for task execution might be a simple way to solve the problem, but interrupts are not always available. Either there is no interrupt mechanism on the selected hardware, tasks are too large to be carried out in interrupts, or interrupts are disabled. SUPER LOOP (Pont, 2001) is a simple and understandable way to implement a control application, whereas interrupts would make the application more complex.

There may be no operating system available for the selected hardware, or the operating system cannot be used for scheduling for some reason.

In real-time systems, the system's response should be deterministic and control must take place at specific intervals. Large tasks endanger the response time requirements and the determinism of the system, even if they are executed only every nth loop cycle.

Therefore:

Implement longer tasks so that an nth part of the task is executed in each loop cycle and the partial result is stored to memory. This allows new results from longer tasks to be ready every nth loop cycle.

Instead of carrying out the whole of a longer task during one loop cycle, compute part of it. For example, if one tenth of the whole calculation is performed every loop cycle, its result is ready every tenth loop cycle. This requires storing state information between loop cycles. How much of the whole operation should be performed during each cycle depends on three factors: first, what is the required cycle time and how long will execution of the whole task take? Second, how frequently are its result needed? Finally, how many parts can the long operation be divided into? These factors should allow you to determine what proportion of the whole operation can be carried out within one cycle. Sometimes parts of a long task might differ in length between loop cycles. For example, on the first cycle a long table may need to be split into parts, which are processed on subsequent cycles. So the time required by parts of a large task may vary between loop cycles.

In many cases carrying out only part of an operation requires storage of intermediate results. For example, if matrix multiplication is performed in steps, its intermediate results need to be kept in memory, as well as variables that record where to resume calculation on subsequent cycles. Sometimes initial data such as sensor values need to be stored, as they must remain the same during the whole calculation. Once the whole operation is completed, the result can be used in control processes and a new calculation can be initiated. Listing 11.5 demonstrates this.

Some calculations allow an estimate of their result to be computed quickly, while an accurate result takes more time. PARTIAL RESULTS can be applied slightly differently for such calculations. Typically, the time until the result needs to be ready affects how many cycles are used for the calculations. If you can generate an estimated result on the first cycle, but further cycles will make it more accurate, the limiting factor becomes the time by which the result must be ready. A more accurate result could lead to better control, but possibly a less accurate result could also be used. In this case, each round of calculation can produce a result, but the more cycles and the more CPU time are available, the more accurate the result will be.

```
static int index = 0;
bool calculation_completed = false;
var partial_result_matrix;

while( true){

/* Control actions */
read(sensor_1_value);
read(sensor_2_value);
do_control_action_1();
read(sensor_3_value);
do_control_action_2(matrix);

/* Complex calculations */
partial_result_matrix =
calculate_fragment_of_matrix_values(necessary_inputs[], index,
calculation_completed); // takes max. 5 ms

if( calculation_completed){
  matrix = partial_result_matrix;
}
```

Listing 11.5: Application structure when using PARTIAL RESULTS

By applying this pattern, complex operations or calculations can be carried out on relatively slow and low-end hardware without upgrading it. This decreases the cost of the system. Control response times can be met while complex operations are calculated on the same node.

New results are available only every nth cycle, n depending on the chosen fraction of the calculation performed during each cycle. This may make control less accurate. In some cases, an estimate of the result can be made during the first cycle and refined on following cycles.

The solution may require more memory, as intermediate results need to be stored between loop cycles.

The application becomes more complex and harder to understand, so incautious changes to the code are more likely to cause bugs.

Some tasks cannot be divided into parts small enough to be calculated within a loop cycle. If this is the case, this pattern cannot be used.

An autonomous warehouse fork lift truck employs multiple PLCs to read digital and analog inputs from various sensors, execute logic applications and pass digital and analog outputs to hydraulic and pneumatic actuators. For example, the motor controller might have a cycle time of around 50 milliseconds. To save cost, the motor controller PLC is also used to calculate the optimal route of the truck through the warehouse. It needs to control the actuators with a 50 millisecond interval or the system goes to a SAFE STATE (page 179). However, this cycle time is too short for route calculation, as this can take up to 100 milliseconds and there are only 25 milliseconds of free time in each loop cycle. The route calculation algorithm is implemented so that it is executed in five parts, each taking around 20 milliseconds of CPU time. On each loop cycle, one of the five parts is executed; after the fifth cycle a new route calculation is ready for use. The response time of the route calculation becomes 250 milliseconds, but this still meets the requirements, as responding to a changed route does not have any strict timing constraints.

11.5   Static Resource Allocation * *

...there is a CONTROL SYSTEM (page 96) to which SEPARATE REAL-TIME (page 237) has been applied. The machine control level usually has limited memory, bus bandwidth and processing power. Resources required by real-time applications must be available immediately, as there is no time to wait for other processes to free them. For example, boom control uses a closed-loop control system in which boom movement is computed from sensor measurements over a hundred times a second, and each movement has to be made at the correct moment.

Real-time applications have to perform their operations within a given time to avoid severe failure, so the required resources must always be available.

Allocating resources dynamically may lead to hard-to-detect programming errors such as memory leaks. Even though this could be addressed using a garbage collector, it requires processor time and other resources. In addition, deallocating memory using garbage collectors is nondeterministic, and deallocation timing is not always known beforehand.

With real-time applications there is little or no time for resource allocation. Nondeterministic timing of dynamic resource allocation makes it hard or impossible for a service to meet strict real-time requirements, as resource allocation can take up more than the time available for the service.

Allocating and deallocating memory leads to fragmentation. As larger memory blocks are split into smaller ones during memory allocation, there may eventually not be a memory block large enough to fulfil an allocation request.

As controllers have limited memory, a system can run out of memory if its applications try to allocate more memory than is available. This usually crashes the system.

Resource requirements for control applications are usually known beforehand. For example, a PID controller requires memory for history data, but the amount required does not change dynamically.

Therefore:

Assign all the resources required for real-time applications at design time. When an application starts the actual resources, for example memory blocks, are reserved for it. This prevents execution time being affected by the nondeterministic timing of resource allocation.

Static resource allocation is easy to implement – just avoid dynamic resource allocation. The worst-case resource usage of a service is determined at design time, and system resources shared based on this usage. The actual method used for resource determination depends on the circumstances – if the required resources are not easy to calculate, you can use EARLY WARNING (page 169) to ensure that there are sufficient. For example, if you know that a service uses two kilobytes of memory for message buffers, you can reserve this in the controller's memory space. In this way all memory requirements can be checked and the corresponding memory area reserved for them. Figure 11.6 shows memory allocation between the operating system (OS) and two applications (App1, App2).

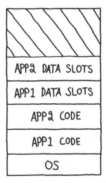

Figure 11.6: Static resource allocation for two applications and an operating system

When a service is executed it does not allocate additional resources, but uses only the resources preallocated for it, for example predefined memory space for message buffers. There is no need to allocate memory, as the runtime environment takes care of this. Programming languages such as C even provide a means to statically allocate memory space for variables. Note that this kind of static allocation may reserve memory from a different memory area. Controllers may have more than one memory area or bank for applications, but, for example in C, some of the variables are allocated from the stack, which is limited in size.

It is also possible to pre-allocate all resources when an application starts, using regular allocation methods such as `malloc` in C, instead of assigning them at design time. This allows you to implement static resource allocation using the dynamic memory routines available in operating systems. However, this increases an application's start-up delay, as all allocations are carried out during the start-up and initialization phase, before normal operation of the application. Note that if the underlying memory management supports paging or virtual memory, the allocated memory must be mapped to the physical memory, for example with `mlockall()` in the case of Linux. If not, only the corresponding virtual memory area is reserved for the application, and allocation is done at runtime via page faults, as the application actually uses the reserved memory area. This is usually unacceptable with real-time applications, as paging causes nondeterministic response times. Allocating all resources at start-up can be seen as an instance of EARLY WORK (page 259).

In some environments it is possible to combine all applications, their initialized memory areas and other resources into a single memory image, which is stored in the controller's permanent memory and loaded into working memory by a BOOTSTRAPPER (page 288). After the image is loaded, execution starts from a predefined memory address and no allocation or memory initialization is required. The memory image can be regarded as a SNAPSHOT (page 221) of the node's initial state. The memory image can reside in the controller's permanent memory and be executed from it, so does not need to be copied into the controller's RAM.

Static resource allocation allows you to know if the controller contains less resources than are needed to execute the applications. If there aren't enough resources, the application can be relocated to another node, the node's hardware can be upgraded, or the resource requirements cut down. For example, if periodic messages require more capacity than the bus can provide, the interval between messages can be adjusted to reduce bus traffic.

If ONE TO MANY (page 131) is applied to a system, STATIC RESOURCE ALLOCATION can be used to allocate time slots for time-triggered communication – see for example ISO 11898-4 (ISO, 2004). To statically allocate CPU time for critical services, you can use STATIC SCHEDULING (page 234) to share processor time for each service. To allocate memory statically, FIXED ALLOCATION (Noble & Weir, 2001) or STATIC ALLOCATION (Douglass, 2002) can be used.

When all required resources are reserved for a real-time service, it can never run out of resources. However, it may sometimes be hard to predict the resources needed at design time.

As resources allocated to real-time services are not available for other services, static resource allocation usually means increased resource requirements and more efficient hardware. With dynamic resource allocation, the resource requirements can usually be calculated based on average resource usage, as all resources are seldom in use at the same time.

Allocating resources statically also increases the efficiency of real-time services, as allocation is done beforehand. Predictability of execution also increases, as there is no nondeterministic timing of resource allocation. Response times are therefore faster and deterministic, as the service need not wait for resources to be deallocated by other processes.

As there are no additional memory allocations or deallocations, memory does not get fragmented and there are no memory leaks.

As all allocations are carried out statically, it is difficult to support dynamic resource allocation. Applications may therefore have to have their own routines to handle dynamic resource allocations. For example, dynamic memory allocation can be supported by reserving a static memory area and sharing it dynamically.

In a tram, the electric motor control applications share the resources of a single node. The design divides memory space into various slots, with each slot assigned to applications. There are no memory management routines, as each application uses only its own slots. Instead the starting point of the slot – a memory address – is stored in the corresponding application variables. For example, the address of the slot reserved as a message buffer for received messages is stored in a variable defined by the designer. Applications for the node and their initialized variables are stored as a memory image. This image is copied from flash memory to the node's RAM memory when the system starts up. After start-up, the node starts the initialization routine of the runtime environment, which in turn starts the applications.

11.6 Locker Key *

…there is a CONTROL SYSTEM (page 96) to which CONCURRENT EXECUTION (page 229) has been applied to schedule several tasks. These tasks cooperate to realize the functionality of the machine. For cooperation, tasks must communicate with each other. To prevent concurrency problems, such as a need for semaphores, the tasks do not call each other's methods directly. Instead, they use a message-passing mechanism (for example Snir at al, 1995), which decouples the tasks. A task can send a message to another task to exchange information or start an operation. A task may also listen for messages to receive them. Typically a message consists of a message identifier and optional message data. The message identifier defines the semantics of the message data, such as temperature, the status of the system or image. The data in the message itself may contain additional metadata, such as the length of the data. As tasks are isolated from each other, communication requires copying the message from an allocated memory block in the sender's address space to a block in the receiver's address space. Communication between tasks can be frequent and messages can be large, so copying data can take a lot of processor time. Because both sender and receiver have their own message buffers, a message exists at two different memory addresses at the same time, increasing overall memory consumption.

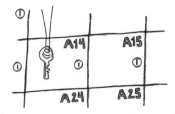

Copying large amounts of message data from one task to another takes time and requires resources. This may jeopardize the performance of the system.

With large messages, copying message data between memory areas takes time and may require dynamic memory allocation, which leads to fragmentation of memory, as various sized memory blocks are allocated and freed all the time. Copying can make message sending a time-consuming operation. The situation is especially problematic if messages are delivered to more than one receiver.

When a message is received the receiver uses its own memory to store the message data. As the controllers have limited memory, receiving a large message can cause memory overrun. In addition, sacrificing processor time for copying makes it hard for a task to meet strict real-time constraints.

Therefore:

Allocate shared memory for communicating tasks. Divide the memory into slots called *lockers*, which are identified with a key, such as a memory address. Store message data from a sending task to a locker and send a message containing only the locker key. The message receiver then uses the key to access the message data from the locker.

Typically a controller has a memory area that can be shared among the controller's tasks. All the tasks can access this shared memory space. A memory area large enough for all the communication needs of the controller is allocated from this shared space, for example by applying STATIC RESOURCE ALLOCATION (page 247). This memory area is divided into message lockers. A locker is a predefined memory area that can be used to store message content. The locker size is usually determined from the largest message size. It is also possible to have lockers with varying sizes.

Each locker has a key that is used to identify it. The key can be a number, a universally unique id (UUID), a memory address and so on. If there are no security reasons to limit access to the locker, the memory address should be used by interface methods to allow direct access to the message. Performance is increased, as the key can be used to store or access message data directly in the locker's memory space without first copying it. With direct addresses a message sender and receiver can store the locker memory address and use it to read further messages from the locker even if they are addressed to other tasks. This kind of key is therefore not suitable for untrusted environments – see THIRD-PARTY SANDBOX (page 355) and VARIABLE GUARD (page 208).

Lockers are used via an interface. The interface should contain methods to request a locker for message data, access the data inside the locker, duplicate keys for sharing the same information with multiple receivers, and free the locker so that it can be used for other messages. The methods keep a record of free lockers and keys. If the same locker is used by more than one receiver, LOCKER KEY can use a counter to determine when the locker should be freed. The counter is increased when a sender duplicates the key for each receiver, and each method call to free the locker decreases this counter by one. When the counter reaches zero, the locker is freed. However, a message sender must know the number of locker users beforehand, otherwise the locker cannot be freed properly. Lockers can also have a defined lifetime, and a housekeeping task to frees lockers automatically that have been reserved for too long. This is useful if a task has crashed without freeing the locker keys.

Listing 11.6 and Figure 11.7 illustrate the use of a LOCKER KEY. A message sender requests a locker and receives a locker key (node A in Figure 11.7). Using the key, the sender inserts the message data in the acquired locker. The locker key is then sent to the receiver (node B in the figure), which uses the key to access the message from the shared space. Finally, node B frees the locker after it has accessed the message data.

```
task MessageSender
{
    // Request a new locker key
    Locker_Key key=requestLockerKey();
    // Get address to shared memory
    StatusMessage* address=(StatusMessage*)getLockerWriteAccess(key);
    // Fill in the message data. This is a local function
    prepareStatusMessage(address);
    // Send message identifier and the key to the receiver
    sendMessage(MessageReceiver, STATUS_MESSAGE, key);
    // The locker will be freed by the receiver
}

task MessageReceiver
{
    // Receive a message
    Message* msg=receiveMessage();
    // Handle status messages
    if (msg->type==STATUS_MESSAGE)
    {
        // Message data will contain a locker key
        Locker_Key key=msg->data;
        StatusMessage* address=(StatusMessage*)getLockerReadAccess(key);
        handleStatusMessage(address);
        freeLockerKey(key);
    }
    else{ // other messages
        ...
    }
}
```

Listing 11.6: Interprocess communication using LOCKER KEY

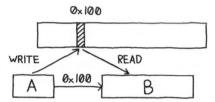

Figure 11.7: Using a locker and sending a key – a memory address – to the recipient

This pattern can also be applied for communication between nodes if shared storage is possible. In this case, the locker key is sent via a communication medium such as CAN, and the actual message data is located in the shared storage space. Typically, this kind of shared memory can be only accessed by copying data from a node's memory to the shared storage and back. A faster communication channel with larger bandwidth, for example Ethernet, can be used for copying the data, but it cannot be used for communicating between nodes. In this case, the LOCKER KEY method will still be faster than sending the same message data using the normal communication medium that interconnects the nodes, such as a CAN bus.

No dynamic memory allocation is required for messages. This is especially useful if a system has strict real-time requirements, as there is little or no time for resource allocation.

If direct memory addresses can be used as keys for lockers, no memory copying is needed. This increases performance, as messages can be read straight from the locker.

LOCKER KEY allows asynchronous communication, as the receiver can fetch the message data from the locker when there is time for message processing. However, the locker should be freed as soon as possible, because a lack of lockers may prevent sending further messages.

Only the message identifier and locker key are transferred when a message is sent. This increases performance, as the message data is not delivered by the message-passing mechanism.

Message multicasting, that is, ONE TO MANY (page 131) communication, is complex to implement, as the number of receivers must be known beforehand.

LOCKER KEY is not suitable for untrusted applications, as typically no memory protection is available in a shared memory area. As there are no physical memory limits, a task may also overwrite or corrupt other messages due to programming errors.

In a space probe images taken by a camera are further analyzed to reject those that have failed. This analysis process saves communication bandwidth with the ground station. However, the analysis process takes a long time, so images are moved from the camera task to a dedicated analysis task for processing. As an average image size is five megabytes, LOCKER KEY is applied to allocate lockers that can be accessed by the tasks. The camera task requests a locker, copies image data from a local buffer to the locker, and sends an 'image ready' message that includes the locker key to the analysis task, which in turn puts the key into a queue. If the results of image analysis show that the image is good enough to be sent to Earth, the task sends the same key to the communication task, which transmits the image to the ground station and frees the locker. If the image is rejected, the locker is freed directly by the image analysis task. In both cases, a new analysis process can be started with a new image from the queue.

11.7   Half Tasks *

ALSO KNOWN AS TOP AND BOTTOM HALVES

'In any moment of decision, the best thing you can do is the right thing, the next best thing is the wrong thing, and the worst thing you can do is nothing.'

Theodore Roosevelt

…there is a CONTROL SYSTEM (page 96) in which SEPARATE REAL-TIME (page 237) creates a machine control level that holds real-time functionality. This kind of functionality must be able to guarantee that scheduled tasks are executed on time. The system has predefined tasks that form the control loop. It is possible to achieve proper timing of tasks in the control loop as their execution times are known beforehand. However, intermittent tasks such as device interrupts must also be handled. If an intermittent task takes a long time to complete, significant delay may occur before the code in the main control loop is executed again. This causes jitter – variation in the control loop's execution times. To maintain deterministic response times, jitter should be as small as possible. However, an intermittent task may also contain actions with strict real-time requirements, and so need to be executed quickly. Interrupts, for example, must be acknowledged as soon as possible, to permit subsequent interrupts to occur.

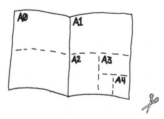

To maintain determinism in response times, real-time tasks must be executed within a specific time window. However, intermittent tasks can occur that require immediate attention, such as device interrupts. These can interfere with the real-time requirements of an interrupted task.

Not all tasks are run periodically in the control loop. Some tasks are triggered by an event such as a device interrupt. The source of the interrupt may require acknowledgement that the task has started. The task should therefore be started immediately, so that the source of the interrupt does not need to wait for an acknowledgement. However, the interrupt-driven task may involve non-real-time processing that could be carried out later.

It is possible to disable interrupts when the control loop is executed. However, device interrupts should be acknowledge quickly, as further interrupts cannot occur before the previous one is acknowledged. Interrupts should not be disabled for long, as this may cause unpredictable operations in devices or missed data. For example, CAN devices may have small buffers, perhaps 4 to 16 messages long; if messages are not read promptly, they are lost. If interrupts are enabled and an interrupt requires time-consuming handling, this can cause tasks that were executing when the interrupt occurred to fail to meet their real-time requirements.

Such intermittent tasks may contain demanding data processing that requires resources, such as CPU time or memory, that are not available when the task is triggered. However, the resources may be freed when another task completes.

Therefore:

Divide intermittent tasks into two parts. The first part acknowledges that the task is received and marks the fact that there is more work to do. The second part does the actual work while real-time tasks are not being executed.

The first part usually handles only work that must be done immediately. To prevent jitter in control loop execution times, the first part should take as little time as possible. After any time-critical actions are carried out, it is usually possible to postpone the rest of the task until a more suitable time. To support this, a queue is needed where an intermittent task can register itself for later execution. The queue can for example contain function pointers, flags or other data to identify registered tasks. A handler task is added to the control loop to manage the queue. When the handler is scheduled to be executed, typically after all the other tasks are executed in the control loop, the handler iterates the queue and executes the suspended tasks. If more than one task is waiting, the handler can execute either one or all of them in one loop cycle. If the execution times of the suspended tasks are known and the time available can be estimated, the handler can continue executing the queued tasks as long as time is available. You can use EARLY WARNING (page 169) to detect whether there are more queued tasks than were expected at design time.

When a task is divided into parts, the first part is usually related to device- and platform-dependent operations, such as handling an interrupt. For example, a device might trigger an interrupt when new values are ready in its registers. The first part of the task needs to read the registers and save the values before acknowledging the interrupt, as the register values will be overwritten by subsequent values. The second part of the task consists of platform-independent actions, such as processing the values stored by the first part of the task, notifying other tasks, or storing the processed values to a VARIABLE MANAGER (page 201).

Figure 11.8 demonstrates the effect of applying this pattern. Tasks A and B are scheduled so that A gets executed every 13 milliseconds and B 5 milliseconds after task A has started. The solid arrows in the figure show the beginning of the cycles, while dashed arrows mark the start point of task B. Task A takes 4 milliseconds and B 5 milliseconds. The rest of the scheduling cycle (4 milliseconds) is reserved for further intermittent tasks and interrupts. If an interrupt occurs during execution of task A, the interrupt handler (i) starts and task A is suspended until the interrupt handler has completed. If the execution time of the interrupt handler is more than 1 millisecond, task B cannot begin on time. This scenario is demonstrated in the second cycle in Figure 11.8. The interrupt handler took 3 milliseconds and task B was delayed by 2 milliseconds. If HALF TASKS is applied (on the right of the figure), the interrupt handler is divided into two parts and the first part of the interrupt handler takes only a short time. The second part of the handler (I) is executed in a reserved time slot after tasks A and B, so task B's deadlines are met.

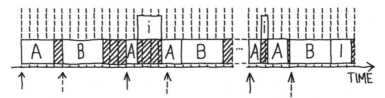

Figure 11.8: Scheduling interrupts without (left) and with HALF TASKS (right)

```
GPS_IRQ_Handler() {
    // The device provides values that we need in part 2.
    // So save them.
    retrieve_device_values(GPS_DEVICE,GPS_COORDINATES,coordinates);
    // Add the second part to queue
    add_to_task_queue(GPS_IRQ_HalfTask);
    // Acknowledge the GPS device so the further interrupts can occur
    ack_IRQ_port(GPS_DEVICE);
}

// This code is executed after control loop tasks
GPS_IRQ_HalfTask() {
    extrapolate_route_from_current_location(coordinates, route);
    update_state_variables(VAR_ROUTE, route);
}
```

Listing 11.7: GPS example with HALF TASKS

Listing 11.7 shows an example of how interrupt handling of a device can be divided into two parts. The example involves a GPS module that causes an interrupt when new coordinates are available. The interrupt handler reads the current position value from registers in the module and extrapolates route information based on the location. If the GPS signal is weak, new location data packets are received infrequently. Extrapolation is a time-consuming operation, so is done only when a new position is received, using an interrupt handler instead of the main control loop. The first part (GPS_IRQ_Handler) contains all the device and platform-dependent parts of the task. The coordinates are saved by the first part of the handler, as they may no longer be available after the interrupt is acknowledged. The first part of the handler also registers the second part (GPS_IRQ_HalfTask) for later execution. This is done by adding the task to the queue (add_to_task_queue). After the first part of the interrupt handler completes, interrupts are re-enabled and subsequent interrupts can occur. The second part of the handler contains the processing of coordinates to update route information.

In some cases it is possible to integrate the second part of the HALF TASKS into the main control loop, so that the actual work is carried out by real-time tasks. It may be sufficient to set a flag to indicate that the interrupt has occurred. This allows you to apply PARTIAL RESULTS (page 243) if the time required for handling the interrupting task is longer than is available in one cycle of the main loop. For example, suppose a device triggers an interrupt when a new sensor value is ready to be read via its I/O port. The interrupt handler does not read the value directly, but sets a flag to inform the control loop about the interrupt, then acknowledges the interrupt. A task in the control loop then tests the flag and if necessary reads the new sensor value from the device. Reading values in the control loop is useful if communication with the device is time-consuming. Timing issues are easier to manage at a predefined point in the control loop than in the interrupt handler. Race conditions can also be avoided; the task where the sensor reading can change is known beforehand, as the value cannot be changed by the interrupt handler in the middle of the task, avoiding the need for critical sections with guards. Listing 11.8 demonstrates this issue. If data is updated by the interrupt handler, the value of WEIGHT_SIGNAL may change while the code is executed. Using HALF TASKS, the value is updated only after the task's code has completed.

```
if (signalValue(WEIGHT_SIGNAL) != 0) {
    // It should be ensured that the signal value is still greater than zero
    // With the pattern, the values are never updated during the execution
    // of task's code
    pressure = pressure_constant / signalValue(WEIGHT_SIGNAL)
}
```

Listing 11.8: Avoiding critical sections with HALF TASKS

Most operating systems use an instance of HALF TASKS to split their interrupt handler into two halves. For example, Linux refers to the first part as the *top half* and the second part as the *bottom half* interrupt handler. The bottom half is implemented as a tasklet (Corbet at al, 2005), a function that is scheduled to run once at a suitable later time chosen by the system.

This pattern can be used only with those intermittent tasks that do not have to run to completion within a specific time window, as the second part of the task may be executed after an undefined interval. If this pattern is used with STATIC SCHEDULING (page 234), a dedicated time slot should be reserved beforehand to handle the second parts of the intermittent tasks, otherwise there may not be enough time to execute all the tasks.

The response time of the system becomes more deterministic and real-time requirements are met, as long-running intermittent tasks do not cause unpredictable delays in the execution of real-time tasks. The intermittent tasks are executed when no other tasks are running. However, this delays the completion time of the intermittent tasks.

If HALF TASKS is used to buffer bus messages so that messages are handled after the main control loop, response times may get significantly longer from a requester's point of view. If a request is received just after the control loop has started, the response is sent after the whole loop's execution time. The average delay is half of the whole loop execution time. However, handling messages during the control loop may cause serious jitter to control loop execution times, especially if there are many requests. One way to handle this issue is to use a separate coprocessor to handle messaging. On the other hand, as a new request cannot be sent before a response, using HALF TASKS may prevent a (non real-time) requester from jeopardizing the response times of the real-time part of the system.

The execution times of interrupt handlers are kept short, as the first part of the handler executes only the platform-dependent, time-critical parts of the handler. Thus it is easier to avoid missed interrupts and missed data, because interrupts are only disabled for a short time.

It may be hard to split the code into two parts such that the second part contains most of the task. The completion of the task is asynchronous from the source of the event, for example the device that caused the interrupt. The source therefore cannot know when a triggered task has completed.

If an intermittent task take longer than is available in one control loop cycle, scheduling will still fail even if HALF TASKS has been applied. However, it may be possible to apply other patterns like PARTIAL RESULTS (page 243) to address this problem.

A CAN bus is used to connect different nodes in a truck. MESSAGE QUEUE (page 143) is applied for the transmission controller, as it has very limited processing power. The CAN bus is connected to the controller by using a CAN module. The hardware of the CAN module is abstracted using a device driver. The device driver controls the module and provides an interface to the application on the transmission controller. The interface contains methods for sending and reading CAN messages and registering a callback function, so that the application can be notified if new messages are received and read them via the interface.

When the CAN module hardware reports the arrival of a new message, an interrupt handler in the CAN module's device driver is called. The interrupt handler is divided into two parts by applying HALF TASKS. The first part retrieves the message, stores it to a statically allocated ring buffer, and acknowledges the interrupt by reading and resetting the status register of the CAN module, leaving it ready for further messages. As the CAN hardware contains a buffer only for one message, it is important to read the buffer as soon as possible. Later the second part of the handler is executed. It has a lower priority than the transmission controller's control tasks, and therefore gets executed only when there is idle time. The second part calls the application's registered callback function to notify the application about the received message. The application uses the device driver's interface to read the message from the ring buffer. If other messages have been received before the application is notified, the application can read all the messages from the buffer at once.

11.8 Early Work *

…there is a CONTROL SYSTEM (page 96) to which SEPARATE REAL-TIME (page 237) has been applied to meet the strict real-time requirements of machine control tasks. Usually task operations consist of reading an input, calculating and setting the outputs for actuators based on the inputs, and storing or sending the output value for use by other controllers. These operations are executed periodically in a control loop. Other operations exist, such as initialization operations, or reading parameters for a control algorithm. These operations are not part of the actual control even though their results may be required by the control loop. Usually such operations do not have strict real-time requirements, but they may consume more processor time or other resources than simple control loop operations. Executing these operations in the control loop can jeopardize real-time requirements.

Because the system has strict real-time requirements, its response times must be predictable and fast. However, some operations may take a long time, or consume too much resources, for immediate response.

There are usually no strict real-time requirements for a system when it is booting up and not yet in the normal operating mode – see OPERATING MODES (page 175). Start up can take longer, as long as the times are predictable after the start-up phase.

Tasks have preparatory operations that can be executed to help them execute their main operations.

The functionality of a machine may need complex and/or extensive calculations. For example, a boom control algorithm may need floating-point multiplications, matrix calculations and trigonometric functions. However, only a limited amount of processing power is available at the machine control level, shared by all applications, and the processor usually has only basic calculation capabilities. This means that response times can be long. Shorter response times would need a CPU with better performance, but changing the hardware increases costs. Applying PARTIAL RESULTS (page 243) is not an option if the results are needed in every control loop cycle.

When the system is in normal operating mode (see OPERATING MODES, page 175), all the tasks share all resources. The resources are shared either in a predefined way using STATIC RESOURCE ALLOCATION (page 247), or dynamically, so that each task can allocate resources based on their current need. In either case, the resource needs of the tasks should be as small as possible, so that expensive hardware components can be avoided.

Some operations are executed only once and can free resources after completion. For example, memory for temporary results is needed when calculating a matrix for boom kinematics, but it can be freed after the calculation is completed.

Therefore:

Prepare the task's execution beforehand by doing some of the task's work in advance. The preparations can be done at compile time or runtime, but before the main task is executed. Once the task has finished its preparations, it must free unnecessary resources so that they are available for the preparations of other tasks.

The task's work is divided into two steps: the first step is used to initialize and prepare for the second step, which is the task's execution in the control loop. The second part uses the results from the first part. It is also possible to save a task's initialization results to permanent storage for further use, and just load them when the task is next started. If the task notices changes in the working environment that invalidates the saved results, it can start re-initialization. In some cases, the re-initialization can be started manually by the operator.

The preparations can be carried out at development time, compile time or runtime. The initialization part of a task can include calculating values for runtime variables based on current configuration parameter values. Some complex calculations can also be partly pre-calculated at compile or initialization time. This is illustrated in Listing 11.9. A typical initialization phase task is to adjust the control algorithm parameters based on the current working environment. For example, when an automatic combine harvester is started, the navigation control fetches the latest weather forecast from a remote server. The weather information is used later to optimize the working process of the harvester.

Some features that require queries to other nodes can be done during the task's start-up, and the queried values cached for future use. For example, a harvester has applied START-UP NEGOTIATION (page 297) and needs to adjust its functionality based on its attached components. The cabin PC is a master node and queries the current hardware set-up, including software versions and types of components. This information is cached so that it is quickly available at runtime without further queries being required. Based on these values, the machine can select the correct algorithms to be used for the current hardware.

Initialization tasks can be executed sequentially, so that each task can have the maximum resources available. After initialization of one task, any unnecessary resources are freed for the next task. After all tasks are prepared for execution, the controller can enter

```
// This task prepares MovementControl
task initMovementControl
{
   // Pre-calculate movement variables
   for (i=0;i<360;++i) {
      angles[i]=1.132*sin(i)*cos(i)**2;
   }
}


// This is the main operation
task MovementControl
{
   // These are fixed at compile time
   const int mov_vec[]={CONST_X*PART_ID_123_X, CONST_Y*PART_ID_123_Y...};

   int partid=queryMotorId();

   // Initialize the movement
   initMovementControl();

// Start the control
   while(1) {
      // read the current angle
      current_angle=readAngleSensor();
      setMotorPosition(angles[current_angle]*mov_vec[partid]);
   }
}
```

Listing 11.9: Using pre-calculated values to increase performance of the control loop

its normal operating mode and start executing its control loop. Consequently, as any re-source-heavy steps are already complete, more resources are available for the tasks that run in normal operating mode. This helps to meet the real-time requirements set for tasks. In addition, as tasks that are prepared beforehand seldom require extra resources in normal operation, applying STATIC SCHEDULING (page 234) and STATIC RESOURCE ALLOCATION (page 247) is easier.

You can also use EARLY WORK in normal operating mode. Using a new feature usually starts a new task. When a task is started, it initializes itself and starts its main operation after its initialization step. However, as the controller is already in its normal operating mode, resources to initialize the new task may no longer be available. You can therefore apply PARTIAL RESULTS (page 243) to initialize the task in smaller steps. This makes the initialization and response time to start a feature longer. On the other hand, further re-quests for the same feature are immediate, as initialization of its control task has already been done. If CONCURRENT EXECUTION (page 229) has been applied and the system has priorities for its tasks, the initialization phase can be executed at a lower priority, thus not interfering with real-time tasks. After its initialization phase is complete, the task's pri-ority is returned to normal and the task starts its main operation. In a similar way, chang-es in parameters may require re-initialization, and recalculating control variables can be handled as a background process. After the calculations are ready, the variables in the control algorithm are updated accordingly.

EARLY WORK can be seen as one operating mode that is executed before the normal operational mode (see OPERATING MODES, page 175). Pre-calculations usually cause system start-up time to be longer, and may require more resources than can be used in normal operating mode. You should consider applying DEVIL MAY CARE (page 190) to minimize the effect of transient errors during the initialization phase.

Resource requirements are smaller in normal operating mode, as resource-heavy task initializations are carried out during the start-up phase. In addition, response times are usually shorter, as time-consuming calculations can be pre-calculated.

The time used in system start-up is increased. However, this is usually not critical for the operator. From the usability point of view, it is better to have a longer wait period once at system initialization than multiple short waits that can impair usability. EARLY WORK can be carried out, for example, while the machine's engine is starting.

Storing the results of pre-calculations may require additional memory. When applying this pattern, you might need to make a trade-off between CPU time and memory usage.

A forest harvester needs trigonometric functions to control its boom movements. As the processor does not have instructions for sines or cosines, these calculations must be carried out using an approximation formula, which will take more time than the processor's native operations. As these values are used extensively, EARLY WORK is applied to pre-calculate sine and cosine values for a set of angles. These are stored in a table that is indexed with the rounded integer value of the angle. This avoids the need for complex calculations, which are reduced to just fetching values from the table during a control task.

CHAPTER

12

Patterns for Decoupling Software and Hardware

'Adapting old programs to fit new machines usually means adapting new machines to behave like old ones.'

Alan J. Perlis

One of the key properties of mobile work machines is their very long lifecycle. The lifecycle of the control system software is therefore also usually long, and is independent of the lifecycle of the hardware on which it runs. A hardware component from a specific vendor may only be part of the hardware design for a relatively short time compared to the software's control algorithms. It is also common for hardware components to come from various hardware vendors, and for several generations of hardware components to be used together.

The software is always dependent on the selected hardware to some degree, but unfortunately it is seldom possible to use identical or even compatible hardware over decades. Moreover, the same control system software and applications may be used with totally different hardware designs. Thus hardware changes should not make the software design

263

obsolete. In practice this means that the software may have to adapt to hardware changes. To minimize the need for adaptation, dependencies between software and hardware parts should be minimized. In the optimal case the software and hardware are totally decoupled from each other. This allows either the hardware or software to be changed or updated independently.

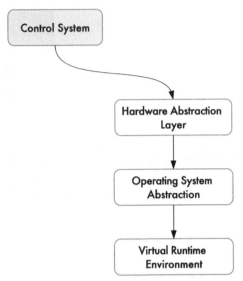

Figure 12.1: The sublanguage for decoupling hardware and software

The following sections present a sublanguage of three patterns to tackle decoupling of hardware and software, as shown in Figure 12.1. These three patterns can be used either separately or together, as the patterns operate at different abstraction levels. HARDWARE ABSTRACTION LAYER (page 264) decouples software from individual hardware components, so that similar hardware components can be accessed in a uniform way regardless of manufacturer and model. OPERATING SYSTEM ABSTRACTION (page 269) allows you to implement applications that can be used with various operating systems. Finally, VIRTUAL RUNTIME ENVIRONMENT (page 272) provides full decoupling using a virtualized environment, so that applications no longer depend on the actual hardware used in a machine.

12.1 Hardware Abstraction Layer * *

...there is a CONTROL SYSTEM (page 96) in which applications must access two types of device to control the machine: sensors and actuators. Sensors provide input data for the applications, and applications use actuators, such as valves and motors, to manipulate the environment. It is usually possible to identify different types of device. For example, all temperature sensors have common characteristics: they output an analog or digital value according the current temperature. In addition, the possible actions for all devices in the same category are the same: reading a value corresponding a sensor's measurement, or giving control signals to the actuators. However, even though devices are used for the same purpose, their outputs and control signals might vary between models and devices from different vendors.

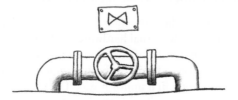

Each vendor may have its own way of controlling hardware devices. If all the devices are controlled in a vendor-specific way, it makes the application code dependent on the selected hardware. To make applications portable, the hardware should be decoupled from the applications.

The lifecycle of a control system is usually long and is independent of the lifecycle of its devices. In many cases, the devices' lifecycle is shorter. During the lifecycle of the product, there may be a need to change device manufacturer, for example if a current device is no longer available. Standardized ways for different vendors' devices to interpret control signals seldom exist. Thus a change of device vendor may usually require changes to the way the hardware is controlled. For example, each vendor may have a different method for reading the measurement of a temperature sensor. One vendor could prefer a 4-20 mA current loop that corresponds to a specific – usually vendor-specific – temperature range, while others output their reading digitally. A change of device may therefore require changes in the application code. It may be error-prone and expensive to modify code.

The system may have CONTROL SYSTEM OPTIONS (page 394) and a need for new options might arise, making it difficult to predict future changes in hardware. New devices may be required or existing ones discarded as needs change. A need for different sensor types may even emerge. The application should be unaffected by the implementation details of devices. For example, changing the vendor of a sensor should not cause changes in multiple places in the application.

A product platform can support multiple machines with different hardware within the same product family. To save cost, the same control applications may be used in various products regardless of their physical devices. Thus the application should be easily portable.

Devices often have vendor-specific features. Using such features may make application development faster, but it will also make the application dependent on vendor-specific hardware if the features are not available on other vendors' products. To avoid vendor lock-in, it should be possible to have a common feature set that is used for all products.

Therefore:

Create a *hardware abstraction layer* (HAL) between the application software and the hardware implementation of the control mechanisms of devices. In this layer, provide generic interfaces to access devices of a specific type in a uniform way. A HAL abstracts implementation details of the hardware behind these interfaces.

Classify devices into groups by their functionality. For example, temperature sensors form a single group regardless of the actual hardware used for temperature measurement. Similarly, all bus interface cards are classified into the same group. For each classification group, create a generic interface to a HAL, called an *application interface*, with methods to control the devices in the group in a uniform way. The implementation details of the hardware are hidden by the interface. The control application then uses the application interface to command a device instead of accessing it directly. In practice, this means that programmers don't need to know the details of individual devices, and the applications will be compatible with any device in the group. This makes applications portable as long as the interfaces to the HAL remain the same.

The HAL translates the method calls from the applications to device-dependent control signals. The application can read measurement data from the sensors in a format common to the device type by using methods provided by the HAL. Such formats can be simple binary (on/off), or a sample of a continuous signal. In the latter case, the data can for example be expressed as a percentage of the device's maximum value, an absolute angle in degrees, or using predefined types such as degrees Celsius. As measured data can be in various formats, you can use a VARIABLE VALUE TRANSLATOR (page 211) to translate data from one format to the other. To increase portability, the HAL can provide generic data types for applications. For example, if an application needs to read a temperature sensor's value, it uses the read method offered by the application interface to get the value from the sensor. There are several types of sensors that have differing word lengths for their return value. These can be abstracted to a generic data type that is processor architecture independent. The HAL can also contain generic methods common to all devices, such as self-check, initialization and device configuration.

Device vendors can usually provide device configuration files – electronic data sheets (EDS) – that are used to configure the specific device or device types. The file can also be used to configure the application interface methods of the HAL. The format of an EDS file may depend on the vendor, development tools and environment used, and sometimes configuration must be done manually. A HAL can sometimes provide a common interface for developers to implement devices compatible with the HAL. Some device types may already have a generic, standardized interface, so that all devices implementing the interface can be accessed in the same way.

As there are usually variations in the capabilities of devices in a device group (such as the resolution of different sensors), a HAL interface design is usually based on the least common denominator. However, the interfaces can overcome this limitation by containing support for reflection, such as querying the type and capabilities of the device. The application can use the information to adapt its PARAMETERS (page 380) to suit the hardware available. However, this kind of reflection reveals information about the hardware details to the application and can thus cause abstraction leaks. An abstraction leak makes porting the software to other hardware platforms more difficult (Kiczales, 1992). Using vendor-specific device properties usually leads to vendor lock-in, as it might be difficult to find a replacement part with the same properties. Thus it is usually best to use only the capabilities common to all the devices. Figure 12.2 illustrates a HAL layer between the application and the hardware, as well as the use of drivers.

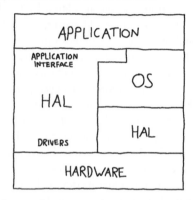

Figure 12.2: Illustration of an architecture with two HALs, one for applications and one within the operating system (OS).

As a HAL adds an extra layer between hardware and applications, it increases latencies and may jeopardize the determinism of the system. This may make it difficult to develop real-time applications with strict timing requirements. In addition, as it abstracts the actual actions needed to access the device, the time required for access is usually unknown to the application developer. For example, reading a value from a sensor may be shown as a single method call for the developer, but in practice it might be a time-consuming operation requiring a lot of communication between the controller and the sensor.

If a controller contains an operating system, the operating system uses its own HAL. The point of a HAL in operating systems is to abstract actual hardware from the kernel of the operating system, thus making the operating system more portable (see Figure 12.2). In addition, an application can still use its own HAL to access the hardware. You can use OPERATING SYSTEM ABSTRACTION (page 269) to abstract the operating system from applications.

If a VARIABLE MANAGER (page 201) has been used, it provides variables that abstract details of devices in a similar way as a HAL. A VARIABLE MANAGER can use a HAL to update its variables, to avoid device dependency. ONE TO MANY (page 131) decouples different hardware devices that are connected directly to a CAN bus, such as nodes and CANopen sensors. The bus provides common messages and a standardized interface to access devices, so there is no need to use a HAL for such devices. Sometimes, for example with FLEET MANAGEMENT (page 372), there is a need to abstract the whole machine. You can use a SYSTEM ADAPTER (page 378) to tackle this problem.

Peng and Dömer introduced unified hardware abstraction layer architecture for embedded systems (Peng & Dömer, 2012). (McCollum, 1996) describes how TYPE LAUNDERING can be used to abstract hardware interfaces from application layer code. The HAL pattern can be seen as a layer introduced by LAYERS (Buschmann et al, 2007b) or LAYERED ARCHITECTURE (Rubel, 1995).

As all device-dependent operations are encapsulated by the HAL, a device can be replaced without any changes to applications. However, it may be difficult to design an interface that is generic enough but which still takes into account the differences between devices of the same group. In addition, as device interfaces are designed based on the least common denominator, some advanced device functions may be unavailable to the application developer. However, this helps to force the developer to use only commonly available features, decreasing the possibility of vendor lock-in.

Similar hardware devices, or hardware devices of the same type, can be used through a uniform interface. This makes application porting easier. Developers don't have to care about implementation details of individual devices. However, implementing the interface and device drivers may require more effort than accessing the devices directly. In addition, without proper support in the HAL or existing device drivers, a device cannot be used by applications. Developers may also try to circumvent the abstraction layer.

It may be difficult to develop applications using a HAL if they have strict real-time requirements. A HAL abstracts the actual actions needed to access the device, so the time required for device actions is usually unknown to a developer. In addition, a HAL adds an extra layer between applications and devices, so using it may increase latencies and require more processing power.

In a harvester a sensor is used to read oil temperature for the engine control application. Several vendors provide the temperature sensors, but the properties of the sensors differ slightly between vendors. The sensors are directly connected to the engine controller's I/O ports with a 4-20 mA current loop connection, so there is no bus to decouple the device from the controller. The measurement range may differ between sensors, so that in one sensor 4mA could mean minus 20 degrees Celsius, while another sensor has zero Celsius as the lowest possible measured value. The harvester manufacturer does not want to commit to one sensor vendor for financial reasons; the manufacturer invites vendors to tender for sensor supply annually. As modifications to application code are expensive and error-prone, a HAL is used to hide differences between sensor models. When the application needs a temperature value, the HAL is used to scale and linearize the sensor's raw temperature value to a range of 0...100 Celsius, according to the characteristics of the actual sensor used. This also allows code reuse, since the same control algorithm can be used with various work machine hardware if the same HAL is available.

12.2   Operating System Abstraction *

...there is a CONTROL SYSTEM (page 96) in which the hardware of the controller is abstracted by applying HARDWARE ABSTRACTION LAYER (page 264). This provides a hardware-independent layer so that applications can access various hardware components in the same way. An operating system is used to provide common services, such as device management, scheduling and memory management for the platform. In some cases, the applications may have a different lifecycle to the operating system used for the platform. For example, support for an operating system may end, and it must be updated in the middle of the product's lifecycle. If the operating system is changed, applications need to be ported to a new operating system.

The lifecycles of applications and the underlying operating system may differ. It should be possible to change the operating system with only minimal modifications to the application code.

Operating systems provide useful services for applications and abstract the hardware from the applications. The operating system provides an API which the application uses to access hardware. Usually these APIs are unique for the operating system, and porting an application from one operating system to another may be challenging. It should not affect the control logic of the application for different platforms.

The operating system may be a freely available one such as Linux, a commercial off-the-self product (COTS) or an in-house product. Usually the same operating system is selected for all products in a product family.

In some cases a customer may require a specific operating system to be used in a machine, to ensure compatibility with the customer's other information systems. In addition, the customer may want to be able to use specific third-party applications that requiring a particular operating system. To support these requirements, the control system applications need to be compatible with various operating systems.

As the operating system abstracts the hardware, the control applications can be used in various products. However, the applications depend on the operating system used; when the operating system changes, applications need to be adapted for the new operating system. However, the same applications are used for various product platforms. In addition, the number of different versions of the control applications should be minimized, as supporting and updating multiple versions is error-prone and requires extra effort.

An operating system version may need to be changed when support for the current version ends. In some cases, the application interface of the operating system changes as the version changes. This may require modifications to the applications' code.

There may be legacy applications that run on top of an obsolete operating system. It should be possible to port these applications to a new operating system with little effort, as developing a new version of the application may be costly.

An application cannot be easily changed or replaced with new one, as a new application with only a few hours of use may contain bugs. In addition, the maturity of applications is an important aspect, especially in safety-critical environments. Safety standards, such as IEC61508 (IEC, 2010a), require revalidation of an application after modifications, so it is desirable to change software as little as possible.

Therefore:

Create an abstraction layer that implements all OS-dependent services. Use only this abstraction layer for OS services in application code.

Identify all OS-dependent services needed by the application, such as memory management and graphical UI support. Create a new operating system-dependent layer, an *operating system abstraction* (OSA), to interface with these services, and use its interface instead of those provided by the operating system. This provides a stable interface for applications even though the operating system interfaces change. This is shown in Figure 12.3. The abstraction layer should contain the services that the operating system would normally offer to the applications. The application calls the abstraction layer, which in turn translates a call to one or more corresponding operating system calls. Usually an OSA includes various operating system-independent data types for the applications.

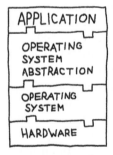

Figure 12.3: An OPERATING SYSTEM ABSTRACTION layer decouples the application from operating system-dependent functions

Operating systems differ in the set of services they provide for applications. In some cases it might be difficult or impossible to provide a service in an OSA layer if the underlying operating system has no support for it. For example, a memory management system for dynamic memory allocation can be implemented by an OSA layer regardless of the support for it from the operating system. However, if the operating system does not support memory protection, it may be impossible to provide this kind of support via an abstraction layer.

Some operating systems may require additional steps, like registering an application or calling an initialization method before an application can be executed. To ensure that methods are executed when necessary, an application should always call the initialization method of the OSA when starting, even if it is not required by the current operating system.

Operating systems may already have a common standard interface that can be used instead of an OSA. For example, POSIX (IEEE, 2008b) is a specification defined by the IEEE for maintaining compatibility between operating systems. Using the APIs defined by POSIX, it is possible to change from one operating system to another as long as both systems support POSIX interfaces. It is usually possible to port an application to a new system just by recompiling it.

Some operating systems have existing cross-platform application frameworks, such as Qt (Digia, 2013a) or SDL (Simple DirectMedia Layer) (SDL, 2013), which can be used to abstract the underlying operating system. With such frameworks an application can be ported to another operating system just by selecting the corresponding library implementation for the target operating system and recompiling the application.

Emulator libraries are available for some operating systems. These libraries provides a compatibility layer that acts like an abstraction layer, so that an application can be designed for one operating system but also compiled for another. The compatibility layer translates the operating system calls like an OSA. Unlike an OSA, the compatibility layer is not linked with the application if the application is compiled for the 'native' operating system. With a similar technique, the whole operating system can be emulated with an external emulator, so that the same application can be executed on various operating systems. The emulator consists of a compatibility layer and a method to start the application. The emulator starts the application so that it will use the compatibility layer for operating system method calls. The application itself does not know whether it is running on the native or an emulated operating system.

If the hardware is likely to change and recompilation of an application is not possible, you could apply VIRTUAL RUNTIME ENVIRONMENT (page 272) to virtualize the whole runtime environment, including the hardware and the operating system. The application then needs no recompilation even if it is used on various platforms.

An OSA encapsulates all the OS-dependent parts, and a single team can develop an OSA layer for various platforms. The common API makes application development easier, as developers need not to know the characteristics of various operating systems. However, developing an OSA requires a lot of expertise.

Using generic data types instead of those provided by the programming language eases porting an application from one hardware platform to another, as the compiler can do at least some part of the required adaptations. For example, integer types with a well-defined bit size may prevent compatibility problems when the processor used by a control system changes.

The application can be executed with various operating systems, as it does not depend on the operating system used. If the operating system changes, the application code does not need to be changed. However, the OSA layer needs to be updated when the operating system underlying it changes. In addition, the OSA layer and the application need thorough testing after changes in the operating system.

Usually cross-platform application frameworks focus only on specific area such as a graphical user interface, so might not have all the functionality required by an application. In that case, some of the functionality must be provided by other means, such as using other frameworks, or writing your own library for the functionality. However, it may be impossible to support some required functionality if it requires support from the underlying operating system. As the services provided by the OSA layer are common to all operating systems, supporting multiple operating systems may prevent use of the more advanced features of some operating systems. Those features might be more efficient or provide extra functionality.

Using an extra layer between applications and the operating system usually decreases system performance. This could be critical in applications with strict real-time requirements.

If cross-platform application frameworks are used, the application becomes dependent on the libraries and their changes. Using some proprietary libraries can lead to vendor lock-in.

A harvester's cabin has a PC that provides a graphical user interface for the operator. The PC's hardware may vary in different harvester products. The harvester vendor has previously selected Windows for the harvester product family, but now the customer wants to use Linux. As the application supporting the user interface is designed to be used with various operating systems, it uses Qt to implement various UI elements. This makes it easier to develop the application so that it can be executed on different harvester products, just by using the corresponding Qt library and recompiling the application.

12.3 Virtual Runtime Environment * *

ALSO KNOWN AS VIRTUAL MACHINE

...there is a CONTROL SYSTEM (page 96) with one or more controllers that execute one or more applications each. These control applications provide services and functionalities for the control system. Usually the lifecycle of the control applications is longer than that of desktop applications, as the machine is used for at least ten years. Because of this long lifecycle, some hardware controller components are likely to break down and need to be replaced. Having a large spare parts inventory is expensive, and the size of an inventory is hard to determine. Having too many parts in the inventory causes extraneous costs, as unused spare parts become obsolete when support for them ends. If the inventory is too small and runs out of spare parts during the support period, components have to be replaced with updated versions. The newer versions are likely to be cheaper and have better availability. Thus the same applications will probably be run using different kinds of hardware. OPERATING SYSTEM ABSTRACTION (page 269) abstracts only the operating system used, and thus applications may still need recompilation or even modifications when ported from one hardware platform to other. Applications might even be impossible to port because no compiler is available for the programming language in the target system.

Hardware is likely to change during a long product lifecycle, so applications need to be ported to run on new hardware. However, porting by recompiling the application is not always possible or desirable.

The applications in a control system typically have a long lifecycle. The functionality they provide usually does not change between different products or product generations, but it can be tuned with a set of PARAMETERS (page 380). Thus the actual application code does not need to be changed even if the hardware changes. For example, a harvester head controller application can be used with various harvester head hardware models just by adjusting its parameters. As technology evolves and more advanced designs come into mass production, some components can be replaced with new, compatible and cheaper ones. However, the same application is used to provide the same functionality as in earlier hardware versions of the product.

Applications are executed in a specific environment. This environment consists of processor(s), memory, various input/output ports, and optionally an operating system. The operating system abstracts some parts of the hardware, but there still are some details, such as a processor's instruction set, that cannot be abstracted. As the runtime environment depends on the hardware, applications must be adapted when the hardware changes. This adaptation can be almost anything from recompilation to rewriting a whole application from scratch. The adaptation process may be costly, and is usually error-prone. In addition, the modifications lead to new revisions or branches of the software, which makes configuration management harder and increases costs.

To support application portability, it is usually possible to provide limited backward compatibility within the same hardware product family. Backward compatibility is often achieved through hardware-supported emulation. For example, a newer processor can run the instruction set of an older processor in emulation, or a new 16-bit A/D converter can be run in 8-bit compatibility mode. However, emulation of old hardware is not always implemented on available hardware that is compatible with the work machine.

In many cases third-party hardware components are used in a system. With such components it is usually not possible to select the desired development tools. The development tools for the third-party hardware may not be compatible with the control application. It should however be possible to use existing control applications while using third-party components.

Therefore:

Virtualize the runtime environment by creating a hardware-independent execution platform for applications. The applications are compiled for the environment and executed in it. The runtime environment is ported to all the desired platforms.

The *virtual runtime environment* (VRE) is an application that is executed on the controller (called the *host system*). The main idea of virtual runtime environments is to hide the real runtime environment of the system and provide an abstracted, virtual version of the hardware to applications (see Figure 12.4).

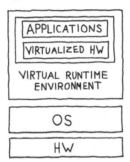

Figure 12.4: A VIRTUAL RUNTIME ENVIRONMENT separates applications from the actual operating system and hardware

A VRE translates an application's virtual device access to corresponding real device access. This isolation ensures that changes in the hardware are not visible to the application, as the application's runtime environment remains unchanged. In some cases, some virtual devices may not have a counterpart in the real system. In this case, the functionality is provided by the VRE alone. For example, a virtual runtime environment could contain floating-point operations even though the host CPU can only use integers. The floating-point operations are handled by the interpreter (see below) of the VRE. However, emulated floating-point operations take significantly more time than those performed in hardware.

Development of control applications for a virtual runtime environment does not differ from that for the real runtime environment. Applications are written in the selected programming language and compiled to assembly language or bytecode for the virtual runtime environment. When developing for a VRE the properties of the runtime environment, such as the endianness of the CPU, are always known beforehand and independent of the actual target hardware. Developed applications need not to be recompiled, as they can be executed in various host systems as long as the virtual runtime environment remains the same.

A VIRTUAL RUNTIME ENVIRONMENT can also be used to support a legacy platform's hardware that is no longer available. In this case, the whole hardware of the platform is emulated by the VRE, or a suitable runtime environment is provided to execute legacy applications. For example, an embedded computer with an ARM-based CPU and real-time operating system can be used to provide a virtual runtime environment for a legacy control system running a programmable logic controller (PLC) application. The VRE emulates the input and output ports of the PLC and reflects their state changes to the system state variables. There are now two different ways to execute the actual PLC application. One is to provide an emulated environment only for the application itself. In this case, the VRE functions as an interpreter, which provides the same functionality for the program as the emulated PLC device by using the host computer's capabilities. The other way is to emulate the legacy PLC device with the VRE. In the latter case, all the necessary components of the PLC device have their virtual counterparts, and the control logic or operating system of the PLC device is executed on the emulated hardware. In this way the PLC program itself is executed by the emulated PLC system in the same way as it was executed with the real hardware. This allows you to have all the properties of the emulated device, but the VRE required for the virtual environment is harder to implement. In contrast, the former method does not allow you to have an operating system, as only the application is executed by the required VRE.

Several commonly used commercial or open source VREs exist, so it may be a good idea to use them instead of writing an in-house VRE from scratch. For example, Codesys from 3S-Smart Software Solutions GmbH (3S-Smart Software, 2013) is used in a wide range of devices. For consumer devices, the Java Runtime Environment has many commercial and open source implementations for various platforms. If you decide to implement a virtual runtime environment, various publications are available on this topic (for example Smith & Nair, 2005; Craig, 2006). Virtual runtime environments are also addressed by VIRTUAL MACHINE (Douglass, 2002).

VIRTUAL RUNTIME ENVIRONMENT provides a stable environment even when the hardware varies between products. A VRE enables you to use the same software independent of the actual platform used. This independence simplifies configuration management, as the application does not need to be modified or recompiled for new hardware. In addition, it is easier to update the hardware components, because the changes do not reflect on the application level – only the VRE needs to be changed. On the other hand, a VRE itself must be updated, maintained and ported to new platforms.

Legacy software can be executed even if the required legacy hardware is no longer available. The software is executed in the virtual runtime environment, which provides the functionality that the software requires.

It is possible to emulate functionality not provided by the hardware used. For example, floating-point emulation makes processor design simpler and reduces costs. However, emulated functionalities are usually less efficient compared to hardware-based ones.

With a virtual runtime environment the properties of the runtime environment are always known beforehand and independent of the actual target hardware. This eases development and makes it more robust.

The ability to emulate functionalities of existing devices can also be used to provide an environment for developing and testing in which the whole system can be executed without the target device.

Because a VRE-emulated processor has fixed instruction execution times, the cycle rate of the application is always the same and independent of the physical processor speed. In other words, the application runs at the same rate regardless of the hardware.

Because a VRE is an additional layer between the real hardware and the application and requires additional execution time, it may be difficult or impossible to use virtual runtime environments in systems with strict real-time requirements. This can be compensated for to some degree by having more efficient hardware, but this costs more.

When using a VRE the application is isolated from physical devices. This eases implementation of THIRD-PARTY SANDBOX (page 355) and access control. As the application uses virtual devices, access rights can be checked and an operation continued only if the application has permission to use the device. Moreover, if DATA STATUS (page 217) has been applied, the status of data can be forced to a desired value by the VRE even if the application itself doesn't support data status. For example, an invalid input status could always imply invalid output status, and the result does not need to come from the application inside the VRE.

As a VRE is complex and costly to implement, it is not feasible to use one if there are only a few products in the product family, the lifecycle of the products is short, or the hardware is not likely to change.

An in-house development environment is used in a power plant control system. The development environment and the programming language are designed for controlling the outputs of the varistors for compensation of reactive power. The applications are executed in a virtual runtime environment, as the actual execution hardware may vary. When the application is compiled, the result is a bytecode file understood by the virtual runtime environment. The runtime environment contains an interpreter that executes the code line by line. If the application changes an output value, the change is reflected to the output of the device by the virtual runtime environment.

CHAPTER

13

Redundancy Patterns

"This parrot is no more. It has ceased to be. It's expired and gone to meet its maker. This is a late parrot. It's a stiff. Bereft of life, it rests in peace. If you hadn't nailed it to the perch, it would be pushing up the daisies. It's rung down the curtain and joined the choir invisible. This is an ex-parrot."

Mr Praline redundantly explaining that his parrot is dead in the 'Dead Parrot' sketch, Monty Python's Flying Circus, 1969

Availability is a key property of many control systems, especially ones controlling a continuous process. The controlled process may not easily be stopped, and there should be only minimal breaks in production. In addition, high availability is a mandatory property of a system if the functionality provided by the system is safety-critical. High availability usually means that the system must be able to recover from faulty situations. Redundancy is usually the easiest way to ensure system availability in the event of failure. If a part malfunctions, there is still a spare part to take over. This topic is covered by 1+1 REDUNDANCY (page 279), a solution to provide simple redundancy through duplication. The pattern also discusses common causes of failure, and how to protect against them by using different versions of software and hardware.

Sometimes high correctness of functionality is important as well as high availability. Such systems typically make autonomous decisions. It is not acceptable for hazardous situations to arise due to faulty decisions that are based on incorrect information caused by software or hardware failure. Even though 1+1 REDUNDANCY provides high availability, systematic errors such as bugs that are present in all redundant units are very hard to spot, as comparing the outputs of redundant nodes does not reveal the error. You can apply VOTING (page 282) with diverse hardware to achieve this.

If a single output is determined from those of several units that provide independent data, the correctness of decisions can be very high, and can be improved further with additional redundant units.

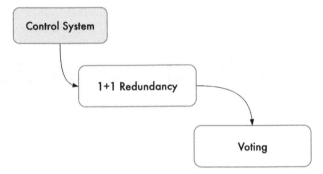

Figure 13.1: The sublanguage for redundancy

Even though the sublanguage for redundancy (Figure 13.1) contains only these two patterns, it covers the most common uses of redundancy in the mobile work machine domain. There are several other ways to implement and use redundant systems, such as using multiple tests, checkpoints or recovery blocks before a final output is decided (see for example Nelson, 1990). Because of the complexity of these redundancy mechanisms, they are seldom used in work machines. It is usually easier and more cost-effective to use physical safety systems to power down the system in the event of a critical malfunction that could harm the machine or the environment. However, the situation may change in the future as unmanned autonomous systems become more common.

13.1   1+1 Redundancy * *

'Thanks to the redundancy of language, yxx cxn xndxrstxnd whxt x xm wrxtxng xvxn xf x rxplxcx xll thx vxwxls wxth xn "x" (t gts lttl hrdr f y dn't vn kn whr th vwls r)'

Steven Pinker

...there is a CONTROL SYSTEM (page 96) with high availability requirements. High availability is needed if its functionality is safety-critical and so should be in operation at all times. For example, controllers for the quality of electrical power in a transmission grid must always be available, to ensure continuous delivery of electrical power. Some systems need to be continuously available throughout their planned lifecycle. For example, a satellite must function for at least three years to accomplish its mission and cover its cost. However, even the most sophisticated hardware is likely to be less reliable than is required to meet such extreme availability requirements.

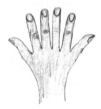

Some of a system's functionalities are mission-critical and so need be available at all times. However, it is possible for the hardware or software providing the functionality to fail or crash.

Losing some critical functionality that is a part of a larger process may block the whole process. For example, if a controller for the drying section of a paper-making machine breaks down, the whole machine cannot produce any output. To keep the process running, any mission-critical functionality should be available at all times.

In some cases it is not possible to replace broken hardware, as the system might be located in an environment that is either hard to reach or hostile to human beings, such as a nuclear waste repository, or space.

Safety standards usually set requirements for safety-critical systems. For example, an ISO standard (ISO, 2006) mandates that a safety-critical system in Category 3 must not fail in the event of a single fault.

It may be possible to recover from a system malfunction caused by transient errors by rebooting. However, sometimes restarting a unit is too slow and does not meet availability requirements. There may also be no guarantee that a restart will recover the system from the fault situation.

If a safety-critical functionality becomes unavailable, its failure may cause great cost or even loss of life. For example, a unit measuring radiation exposure should have high availability and should never silently fail, as human lives depend on it.

Therefore:

Duplicate any unit that controls a critical functionality. Assign one of the duplicates to active control of the functionality, and the other to be in *hot standby* mode. If the active unit fails, the hot standby unit takes over control of the functionality.

Both active and hot standby units run the same operation in their own copy of the same application using similar hardware, but the functionality is controlled only by the output of the active unit. If the active unit fails, the hot standby unit becomes the active unit, allowing control to be maintained.

After switch-over the failed unit can be restarted, repaired or replaced, and it becomes the new standby unit. To achieve the same state as the active unit, the new standby unit may also need to synchronize its state information and other data from the active unit. To run the application without glitches during switch-over, the two units share inputs and PARAMETERS (page 380), and can use GLOBAL TIME (page 124) to ensure synchronous operation.

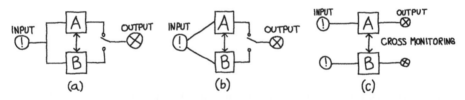

Figure 13.2: Different implementation options for redundancy: a) only units are duplicated, b) units have their own channels, and c) sensors and actuators are also duplicated

Selecting the active unit can be done manually using a hardware switch, or via REMOTE ACCESS (page 361). Any malfunction should be noticed as soon as possible, and switchover should take place immediately to minimize downtime, or to prevent harmful situations. Typically, switch-over is implemented by having both units' outputs connected to the same channel and just changing the unit whose output signal is used to control the functionality. Figure 13.2 (a) illustrates this configuration. To increase availability and avoid a single point of failure, both units can have their own dedicated input and output channels (Figure 13.2 (b)). When very high availability is needed, sensors and actuators should also be redundant (Figure 13.2 (c)).

Redundant units must cross-monitor each other to determine whether switch-over is necessary. HEARTBEAT (page 120) is a commonly used technique, which sends messages between nodes at regular intervals. If the hot standby unit notices that the active unit is not sending a heartbeat signal, it can take over control immediately and reboot or shut down the other unit. Conversely, the active unit can monitor the hot standby unit. Heartbeat messages can also be used to synchronize data and state information between active and hot standby units. WATCHDOG (page 101) should be used for self-monitoring. If the watchdog is triggered, the unit detecting this alerts the other unit that a failure has occurred.

You should take common-mode failures (Randell, 1987) into account when cloning functionality. It is wise not to use the same software and hardware for redundant units, to prevent a programming error common to both units causing them to malfunction at the same time. Redundant units should also be physically separated from each other, to reduce the risk that both fail due to environmental conditions. They should also have their own power supplies, so that they are not vulnerable to the same power supply issues. The Ariane 5 launch vehicle is a well-known case of common-mode failure (Gleick, 1996). It had two inertial reference systems (IRSs) with identical hardware and software. The active IRS declared a failure due to a software exception, and control was moved to its back-up unit. The backup IRS then failed for the same reason, causing the rocket to start its self-destruction procedure.

There are also other ways to implement redundancy. For example, if switch-over time is not critical, the standby unit can be powered off to save power. Before switch-over, the unit is powered up and booted. In this case the backup unit is also called a *cold standby* unit. It is also possible to have more than one standby unit and use an additional device to decide which output should be used for controlling the system. These methods are usually referred as '1ooN' (one out of N). For example, if there are three redundant units and only one is active, it is said that the system has '1oo3' redundancy.

Douglass describes several patterns for redundancy, such as HOMOGENEOUS REDUNDANCY to protect against random failures by using multiple identical processing channels, and HETEROGENEOUS REDUNDANCY, which applies diverse processing channels to protect against both random and systematic failures (Douglass, 2002). If high correctness is required of a system, you can use VOTING (page 282) to determine the correct output of redundant units. Hanmer describes a collection of error-detection patterns that can be used to detect failure of redundant units (Hanmer, 2007). FAILOVER (Hanmer, 2007) is a similar pattern to 1+1 REDUNDANCY, as it describes how error-free execution can continue when the active unit of a redundant pair fails. REDUNDANCY (Hanmer, 2007) describes a similar solution to increased availability as is described here.

When mission-critical units are duplicated, the availability of a system is protected in the case of failure of a single unit. The system can continue operation even though one of the units has failed.

The maintenance of a unit does not cause breaks in operation, as the backup unit can function normally while the active unit is repaired. For example, it is possible to update the software in a backup unit while the active unit is still operating. After updating is complete, switch-over takes place and the second unit is then updated.

Redundant units may take more space, consume more power and need more maintenance. This increases costs and may sometimes make it impossible to create redundancy, for example if there is no room for a backup unit. In addition, communication between the units increases the complexity of the system.

A system compensating for deviations in the quality of power in an electrical transmission grid must be available 99.9999 percent of the time. This means that the system can only be unavailable for less than 31.5 seconds per year. The system is duplicated to ensure high availability. The active unit controls the compensation process. Both units are connected to a redundancy control unit (RCU). An RCU is an intelligent optical switch that selects an active controller according to the operating status of the control system. If one unit fails, it causes a WATCHDOG (page 101) to drive the unit into a SAFE STATE (page 179). The standby unit notices the malfunction, as the RCU sends an error signal to the standby unit. After receiving the error signal, the standby unit becomes the active unit and takes over control immediately. The failed unit had synchronized the control parameters with the standby unit once a minute, so that it is ready to take over without any break in service.

13.2   Voting *

> *King Arthur: I am your King.*
> *Woman: Well I didn't vote for you.*
> *King Arthur: You don't vote for Kings.*
> *Woman: Well how'd you become King then?*
>
> *Excerpt from a discussion between King Arthur and a woman*
> *in the film 'Monty Python and Holy Grail' (1975)*

…there is a CONTROL SYSTEM (page 96) whose requirements for high availability are addressed by applying 1+1 REDUNDANCY (page 279). Because of this redundancy, the system consists of several subsystems, one acting as an active subsystem and providing the output for the whole system, while the others are backup subsystems. The system makes decisions automatically, such as which action to take next, based on the output (see MINIMIZE HUMAN INTERVENTION, Hanmer, 2007). The operating environment may contain many sources of errors, such as hardware or software errors, or inaccuracies in measurements, which can make autonomous decisions unreliable. However, the system must make autonomous decisions, so the consequences of errors should be minimized.

A high level of correctness is required in a system with autonomous functions. Even though 1+1 REDUNDANCY offers high availability, it does not ensure correctness of a single decision, as the master unit can give erroneous results.

Autonomous decisions made by a system should always be based on reliable information. Potentially dangerous situations may occur if information is not correct due to a failure in a unit or sensor. It is not always possible for operators to recognize and handle faults, as their reaction time might be too slow, or some errors pass unnoticed. Sometimes just providing an operator may be too costly to be feasible. A hazardous operating environment may also make a human presence impossible, for example for a satellite or a nuclear waste repository.

Fault tolerance in a control system is usually achieved through redundancy in hardware. The greater the number of redundant units used in a system, the smaller the possibility that all of them fail at the same time. With simple redundancy, a *master* unit provides the output and the others remain on standby, taking control if the master unit fails. Because the outputs of the units are not compared, systematic errors in sensors are hard to notice. Similarly, software bugs are hard to detect if the same software versions are used in all units. The master unit can therefore give incorrect output values even if it appears to be functioning correctly.

Autonomous systems that cannot rely on human intervention seldom offer the possibility of interactive fault diagnosis and recovery action. The only way to ensure continuous operation is for the system to detect a fault in one unit and stop using it.

Because of limited space in a work machine and/or to reduce cost, redundancy may lead to the use of cheaper and thus less reliable components. The system should be scalable in terms of redundant components without compromising correctness.

Therefore:

Use redundant units to compute the control output independently, and add an additional unit, called a *voter*, to collect their output as votes. The voter determines the correct output based on the votes.

Each of the independent redundant units (Unit1...UnitN in Figure 13.3) provides their own separate concept of the output – these are the votes. The voter receives these as inputs and determines the correct, final output. 'Correctness' is based on the chosen voting technique, which depends on the system; majority voting is the simplest and most commonly used. With three units, for example, if at least two units vote for taking some action, the voter will send the action command as its result. Other techniques can include consideration of other parameters, such as the reliability of the units, or dynamically changing weighting factors. For example, factors can be based on history data for the units. Sometimes voting can be a simple hardware solution in which a majority of redundant physical components, such as valves or relays, must have the same value to start an operation.

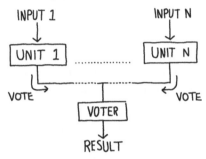

Figure 13.3: A voting mechanism consists of three or more units, two or more to cast votes and a further unit to calculate the results

In the case of analog signals voting can be continuous – that is, the voter's output follows the outputs of the redundant units without any interruption. With digital signals, votes are produced periodically and the overall output is updated accordingly. In such periodic voting the units must be synchronized by a common time signal. The voting process can also be triggered by the environment, so that the voter samples its inputs and updates its output after a specific trigger. This may also require connections between the voter and the redundant units to tell them to update their votes; this adds complexity and jeopardizes the independence of the units.

With majority voting, the more units are used for voting, the greater the number of failing units can be masked. For example, to mask simultaneous failure in two units, five units are needed altogether. If a faulty unit can be identified, you can use NOTIFICATIONS (page 156) or DATA STATUS (page 217) to inform the rest of the system about the failure. If a reliable output cannot be decided by voting, the system typically goes to a SAFE STATE (page 179). However, sometimes it might be better to continue operation and use an invalid, predefined value as output to signal an error. For example, if the system normally produces positive integers, an invalid value could be −1. By applying DATA STATUS this kind of invalid output can be marked as NaN (not a number).

A significant problem with voting is that the output values of the redundant units must be comparable. With switches this is easy, as a switch is either open or closed. With continuous signals, a vote can be regarded as correct if the vote is within some error margin of other votes. The output of the voter is then determined based on its inputs, for example by using the median of the correct votes.

If the input of a redundant unit is incorrect, its output will be also incorrect even if the unit is fully functional. Sensors should therefore also be replicated, to ensure correct inputs for the redundant units. Different software implementations in each unit are also worthwhile, to avoid common-mode faults in software or design. This technique is called

N-version programming (see for example Avizienis, 1985). The voter can also take the reliability of each redundant unit into consideration and determine the unit that is most likely to be giving the correct answer. However, this will require knowledge of each unit and/or additional acceptance or self-checking tests. You can use ERROR COUNTER (page 107) to keep track of individual units' reliability.

VOTING is mainly used in safety-critical systems in which extreme correctness is required. International standards for safety-critical systems such as IEC 61508 (IEC, 2010a) and IEC 61511 (IEC, 2003c) may require the use of VOTING to obtain the necessary safety integrity level (SIL). For example, an airplane might use a voter component to calculate the course for the autopilot. The voter uses five separate voting units that are implemented using three different techniques. Up to two of the units can fail or malfunction without compromising system safety.

Even though a voter unit is usually a simple unit that can be designed to be robust, it still creates a single point of failure. To remedy this, you can use WATCHDOG (page 101) to monitor the voter. You can also use LIMP HOME (page 185) to select an output value from one of the redundant units if the voter fails.

Several voting patterns with different voting techniques are described by Ashraf Armoush (Armoush, 2010). RELIABLE HYBRID (Daniels, 1997) presents a framework for fault-tolerant application development. A similar pattern to VOTING is also documented by Hanmer (Hanmer, 2007).

Decisions must be based on correct premises and a control system should refuse to operate if a reliable decision cannot be made. By using voting, failure in a minority of units will not cause an erroneous result and thus an incorrect decision. Multiple units generate output signals, and the voter masks any failures by deducing a correct result from those of the redundant units. If even one of the redundant units does not agree on an output value, the voter can inform the rest of the system, for example by applying DATA STATUS (page 217).

Redundant units can 'fail fast' without trying to recover from their failure: with a voter, a single unit failure is detected, an operator can be informed and the failed unit replaced. The voting process can even notice invalid but correct-looking outputs of voting units regardless of the cause of their failure.

There should be no dependencies between redundant units, to decouple them so that they do not influence each other's outputs or propagate failures when crashing. VOTING cannot protect against common-mode failures in which multiple units malfunction simultaneously because of a common fault. For example, a cable break will cause the whole subsystem to fail if the redundant units or the voter share the same power supply. This requirement for independence can make design more difficult. For more information on common-mode failures, see for example (Smith & Simpson, 2004).

To mask failures in software, each redundant unit should have its own software implementation. So, if N units are used for redundancy, there need to be N disparate implementations of their functionality, independently implemented by *N* separate development teams. The cost of this approach is usually too high.

The voter typically does not communicate directly with the redundant units, and does not affect their operation. However, the voter creates a single point of failure. Fortunately, a voter component is usually robust and simple.

The control system of a sweeping machine has its own vehicle identification number (VIM), 184. All seven nodes in the system are aware of the VIM, as it is stored in the nodes' persistent memory. A node breaks down and is replaced by maintenance personnel. The replacement part originates from another machine having a VIM of 244. When the node is plugged in to the system, it still contains the number 244. To maintain the identity of the system, the voting procedure is used to identify the machine's current VIM during system start-up. Each node reports its understanding of the machine's VIM, and the VIM that gets the majority of votes (in this case 184) is chosen. This identification number is updated on all nodes.

14

Patterns for System Start-Up

> '*The secret of getting ahead is getting started. The secret of getting started is breaking your complex overwhelming tasks into small manageable tasks, and starting on the first one.*'
>
> Mark Twain

Starting up a large distributed system is not a trivial task. A control application requires a stable runtime environment to carry out its functions. When the system is powered up, every device needs to go through various tests and initializations before the control application can start its own initialization routines. In the context of the whole system, the order of starting up devices becomes important. A node may need to wait for other nodes to start up before it can start its own booting process. Sometimes the order in which nodes start up may depend on the devices that are attached to the machine. In this case the only way to ensure proper start-up of the system is to decide the node start-up order dynamically, by negotiation, after the system is powered up.

The system start-up sublanguage shown in Figure 14.1 describes the necessary procedures after a system powers up. BOOTSTRAPPER describes how to ensure that the environment is in a defined state after every start-up sequence. It also tackles situations in which only a limited amount of memory and persistent storage is available when the system powers up.

Using BOOTSTRAPPER, an application developer does not need to worry about the hardware: the hardware is initialized and verified before the application starts. SYSTEM START-UP (page 293) is applicable to systems in which the start-up order is meaningful. It also checks that each node is fully functional before the whole system starts its control functionality. START-UP NEGOTIATION (page 297) refines SYSTEM START-UP by adding a negotiation procedure to support dynamic configuration of machines. This makes it unnecessary to know beforehand which devices a system has, only those it must have. Each node announces its existence and requirements, so that the proper start-up order can be deduced dynamically based on this information.

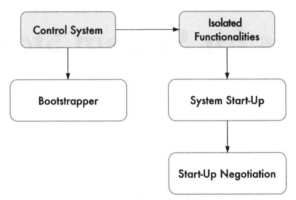

Figure 14.1: The system start-up sublanguage describes how to boot up a system correctly

14.1 Bootstrapper * *

...there is a CONTROL SYSTEM (page 96) that consists of hardware parts and application(s). Hardware has to be prepared before the application can be given control. For example, memory must be activated by making it visible in processors' memory address space, and initialized by writing zeroes to it. Additionally, no hardware is immune to errors, faults or wear. Unexpected issues may emerge if a control application is run on faulty hardware. For the application developer, it would be preferable if the whole environment is in a defined state after every start-up sequence, so that the application does not need to initialize the environment itself.

Before an application can be started the hardware should be in a defined state. Uninitialized hardware may cause unexpected behavior in the application.

After power up, the basic functionality of the hardware has to be activated with the correct parameters. For example, memory and internal buses need to be activated. If these are not initialized, or are initialized incorrectly, it is unlikely that the system will work.

Usually there is only a limited amount of memory and persistent storage available when a system powers up. The program code required for activating all the hardware may not fit in the memory or persistent storage that is available during power-up. Additional memory and persistent storage might only be available after they have been activated and set up.

Diagnostics and self-tests, such as memory error checking and bus connection checks, should be done before commencing a node's task. A self-test operates at the lowest level possible with the hardware. Creating such tests usually requires deep knowledge of the hardware, so it should not be an application programmer's task to develop them.

A node's application might be stored on a variety of different media. It cannot always be known beforehand on which connected media the application resides: some way to discover it might be required. There could also be multiple alternative applications in the system, or even alternative versions of the same application. In this case some way to select the correct application to be loaded is needed.

A system might be created by bundling together COTS hardware from multiple vendors and adding in-house hardware on the top of it. The COTS hardware cannot initialize all hardware and hardware combinations in the system. It is the responsibility of the system manufacturer to integrate them and create an initialization process for the whole system.

Therefore:

Initialize the hardware during start-up so that the system is always in a consistent state. Where necessary, divide start-up into sequential stages, to overcome any resource limits and to implement *separation of concerns* (Hürsch & Videira-Lopes, 1995). Add a bootloader component with its own responsibilities for each stage.

Each bootloading stage adds flexibility to the boot process. This kind of flexibility is usually needed on more sophisticated units such as a PC. For example, the persistent memory available during start-up is often limited, and therefore the first stage bootloader can only contain essential initializations. The foundations for the second stage are created in the first stage by setting up a storage device, initializing memory and loading the second stage into memory. As an example of separation of concerns, a motherboard manufacturer does not know where their board is going to be used, so the motherboard only takes care of its own set-up. Additional stages are required to handle the system beyond the motherboard.

The first stage after power-up is referred to as *bootstrap loading* or *boot loading*. This initializes the basic functionality of the hardware. The bootstrap code is usually stored in limited persistent memory such as ROM or EEPROM, to be available immediately during start-up (Figure 14.2). A CPU wakes up and executes program code from a defined memory address in persistent memory. One of the bootstrapper's first tasks is to activate the various system buses, such as the memory, data and control buses. Proper bus timings have to be used to ensure correct behavior, otherwise data loss and undefined errors will occur. When the buses have been activated, the volatile memory, RAM, can be activated. Additionally, a storage device may be activated, along with peripheral devices such as serial ports. This is the minimum that a bootstrapper must do to enable loading later stages or running an application.

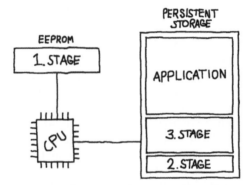

Figure 14.2: Boot loading is the first stage after power-up. Subsequent stages residing in persistent storage are used to initialize other parts of the system.

The bootstrapper's first stage should also contain power on self-tests (POST) for processor, memory, controllers, system buses and other basic hardware. POST helps to detect hardware errors, both during software development and in use. During development hardware bugs are often time-consuming to diagnose and fix, so the hardware should be as stable as possible. The thoroughness of testing depends on the requirements for the system. For example, an undetected hardware error in a satellite might lead to it becoming unrecoverable. After the POST phase, an additional bootloader stage may be loaded to memory and executed. Later stages may contain their own set of POST tests for those parts of the hardware that they have enabled. Hardware manufacturers often provide the first-stage bootloader, as it usually requires extensive knowledge of the hardware's internals that only they possess.

The location of the second-stage bootloader is often fixed – that is, it is expected to reside at a specific location in activated persistent storage. This makes the task of loading the second stage easier, as it requires fewer resources from the first-stage bootloader. As the second-stage code resides on media with more space, and as more volatile memory is available, it can do much more than the first stage. Typically the second-stage bootloader enables additional devices. Such devices could be, for example, mass storage and additional memory, networking and wireless interfaces, and peripheral devices such as keyboards and displays. Sometimes the second stage functions as a stepping-stone to a third stage. For example, the second stage could search all storage media such as SD cards, memory sticks or hard drives for the third stage code. In such designs the second stage is more like an extension of the first stage.

In some embedded systems later stages are not required, or are undesirable due to timing issues. For example, safety systems in a power plant have high-availability requirements. Loading the main application as soon as possible requires that the hardware is tightly coupled with the software, so that additional set-up or testing is not required. Device initialization is usually a fast process, but more time might be spent on self-tests, such as an extensive memory test. Consequently, tests are sometimes divided into two groups: quick power-on self-tests, and more extensive DIAGNOSTICS (page 350). Even when timing is not crucial users should not be kept waiting, so it is not always feasible to run time-consuming tests on each boot-up.

A more advanced bootloader may contain further functionality, such as a user interface, logic for selecting and booting alternative applications, a backup service, rescue mechanisms such as rescue mode, software update functionality such as is described by UPDATEABLE SOFTWARE (page 301), and so on. If the bootloader can execute more than one application, there should be some way to select which one to use. There can be many reasons for having multiple applications, such as providing a way to use different versions of the software, having a separate rescue mode application, bundling extensive diagnostic test, or ensuring higher availability by applying 1+1 REDUNDANCY (page 279). A selection mechanism can be implemented with software or with a hardware switch.

Boot loop detection is a typical rescue mechanism. In a boot loop system, failure is detected by a WATCHDOG (page 101), which reboots the system. The WATCHDOG detects the failure again, and reboots the system again – and again: a *boot loop*. One way to implement boot loop detection is to have a counter that increases at each start-up attempt and resets on successful shut-down. If the counter value is larger than zero during start-up, it implies that the system was not shut down properly. When the value is larger than one, it implies that it has crashed multiple times and may be in a boot loop. In this case the operator is alerted, an alternative version of the application could be started, or the system might be halted at start-up.

Sometimes third parties should not be allowed to tamper with the system's software. SECURE BOOT (Löhr et al, 2010) describes a solution for securing a bootloader and system from modification and external tampering by using checksums or cryptographically signed bootloaders and applications. Only software with a valid checksum or signature can be loaded and executed. Part of the verification process is done in hardware. This makes a bootloader more secure, as hardware is next to impossible to modify. This type of solution is used for example in SIM cards, electronic cash cards, game consoles and some cellphones.

BOOT LOADER (Schütz, 2006) describes this problem area and solutions from an x86 PC and hardware perspective. Many of the ideas presented in this pattern also apply to other hardware or CPU set-ups even if the hardware details differ. Several existing boot loaders are available. For example, Das U-Boot (DENX, 2013) is targeted at embedded systems, and RedBoot (eCos, 2013) also allows execution of applications via Ethernet.

Bootloading and POST tests verify that the system is in a predefined state and that the required components are functional. This creates a stable base that can be relied on. Application developers do not need to check whether the hardware is working. However, as not everything can be tested, testing just ensures that common errors are detected. Additional availability can be achieved with 1+1 REDUNDANCY (page 279) on hardware. Availability can also be increased by having a rescue mode by which one can roll back to an old software version.

When a bootloader is divided into stages, each stage provides a higher level of service than the previous stage. Typically the hardware vendor concentrates on hardware details in the first stage bootloader, while the company using the hardware adds functionality of their own in later-stage bootloader(s).

The first stage bootloader is usually highly hardware-dependent; creating it requires deep knowledge of the hardware and how to program it. Typically hardware registers are manipulated, and a low-level language such as assembler is used in some parts of the bootloader. This requires detailed knowledge and a skill set that an application developer rarely possesses.

If system initialization is implemented using multiple bootloaders, start-up may be slowed. In many cases a delayed start-up sequence is an acceptable trade-off for the ability to select from different boot-up configurations. When a system should start its role immediately after powering up a wait period is not acceptable. Too long a start-up period is also a usability issue from the operator's perspective.

When an ARM CPU is powered on, its registers are set to predefined values. The processor then starts to execute code from address 0x00000000. This memory address is located in the CPU's internal on-chip ROM. The first stage bootloader is preloaded in ROM by the hardware manufacturer. The bootloader initializes the system by setting busses, clocks, stacks, interrupts and so on. After this, the bootloader identifies the boot media by looking for a bootloader signature, first on external flash memory, then from USB memory.

If it does not detect a second stage bootloader, the first stage bootloader halts the system. If the bootloader is found in flash or USB memory, the first stage loads it into internal RAM and sets the CPU's program counter to the second stage bootloader's start address. The second-stage bootloader is responsible for loading the operating system into memory. For this, the memory first has to be initialized by setting up the controller, memory re-fresh rate and so on. The second-stage bootloader is configured to launch operating systems from specific locations. After memory is initialized, it tries the first such location. If it does not find an operating system there, it tries the next address, and so on. If it can-not find any operating system, it halts the system. When it finds a suitable signature, it loads the operating system into memory and transfers execution to the operating system.

14.2 System Start-Up * *

...there is a CONTROL SYSTEM (page 96) to which ISOLATED FUNCTIONALITIES (page 110) has been applied. When the system is powered on, different nodes start their BOOTSTRAP-PER (page 288) process, which may take varying times before the nodes are ready for op-eration. Each node's own BOOTSTRAPPER prepares the runtime environment only for the node itself, and no node is responsible for the whole system. As the nodes have to coop-erate, they may need functionality or input values from other nodes – that is, there are usually functional dependencies between devices. For example, a satellite's camera may require preheating before it can start operating, so the heater controller must be started before the camera can be used. In a similar way, an application may require information from other application(s) in order to start its own operation.

The nodes in a system have varied start-up times and their functionality may depend on other nodes. If one node depends on another node, it must not start its functionality be-fore the other node is ready to allow correct operation.

When a node is powered up, the BOOTSTRAPPER tests the node. If there is a malfunction in a node, this is detected during the tests and the node usually fails to start. This means that some system functionalities are missing. As a failed node cannot inform other nodes about its own malfunction, another node should be able to detect the failure.

A control system usually consists of subsystems. However, starting up a complex sub-system may take considerable time. Its start-up time usually depends on the functionality of a node, and physical and mechanical operations may be involved that can take time. For example, it may take several minutes to heat a device to a defined temperature, or to boot up a high-end node such as a cabin PC.

The nodes are not operating in isolation. They require inputs from other nodes and provide results used by other nodes. This forms a chain of dependencies between nodes.

A node may need specific inputs to be available before starting its operations, to ensure that it can operate correctly and safely.

There usually aren't any strict real-time requirements for a system when it is booting up and not yet in normal operating mode (see OPERATING MODES, page 175). In practice this means that more resources are available for EARLY WORK (page 259) during start-up, and the start-up process can take longer, as the system does not necessarily need to respond quickly.

Hardware mechanisms can be used to power up specific devices before others. For example, time-delay relays and simple logic boards are commonly used to delay the start-up of some devices when a system is powered up. Such hardware solutions can only provide a rigid start-up sequence with fixed delays, so they have very limited possibilities for configuring a start-up sequence based on the system's set-up.

Therefore:

Design the start-up order of devices based on their dependencies, boot-up times and resources requirements. Based on this order, divide nodes into *master* and *slave* nodes. A master nodes wait for its slave nodes before they start operating. When a slave node has started, it signals its master node. When all the slave nodes of a master node have started, the master node enters its normal operating mode.

The start-up order is defined by the dependencies between the nodes. If node A requires some functionality or information from node B, B must be operational first and A can start its operation only after B has started successfully. The correct start-up order is designed during development. This order is used to form a list of slave nodes for which a master node has to wait. This list is stored in the master node, which waits for a signal from its slave nodes. When a slave node has started successfully, it sends a predefined boot signal to all fellow slave nodes and to its master node indicating successful start-up, or starts sending a HEARTBEAT (page 120) signal. When the master node receives this signal, it knows that the corresponding slave is operating. After all slave nodes have started up, the master node can start its own operation. As the master node cannot start its own application before the slaves are ready, start-up is usually implemented as one stage of a BOOTSTRAPPER (page 288), or as the first operation the master node's application performs before starting its main functionality.

After a master node has entered normal operating mode, it is therefore guaranteed that all the slave nodes are powered up and in normal operating mode. A master node's application may still need some additional means to ensure that the required services are functioning correctly. The first tasks of the master node's application are therefore to ensure that its operation can be continued safely, and to request its slave nodes to start their own functionality by sending them a message.

Usually there is some predefined time-out value by which the slave nodes need to respond, to prevent the master from waiting for the slaves forever. If a signal is not received from a slave within a specific time period, the master enters a SAFE STATE (page 179). In a similar way, the slaves may monitor HEARTBEAT (page 120) signals from the master node and enter their own SAFE STATE if the master node cannot start up. Depending on the functionality provided by a missing node, the system may still be able to LIMP HOME (page 185). If a separate boot signal is used instead of a HEARTBEAT, there should be some kind of acknowledgement mechanism, so that a missed boot signal does not affect the start-up procedure. On the other hand, a boot signal received during normal operation indicates that a node has restarted, for example because of a WATCHDOG (page 101), and thus may be malfunctioning. Remedial actions can then be started.

A whole system is started up by applying SYSTEM START-UP recursively. In a system there is least one slave-only node that reaches its normal operating mode first, and one master-only node that is started when all other nodes are functioning. Other nodes can act as masters, waiting for their slaves to wake up, and/or as slaves if another node depends on them. First those nodes that do not depend on other nodes boot and enter normal operating mode. Second, the nodes with slaves – master/slave nodes – start operation after all slave nodes on which they depend have started. Finally, the final master node, which is not a slave for any other node, can enter normal operating mode, and the system is then ready to function.

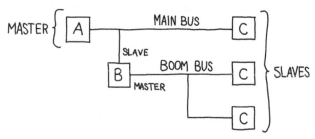

Figure 14.3: An example starting order for a system. Node A is master-only node, node B acts as master and slave, and C nodes are slave-only.

Figure 14.3 illustrates an example of system start-up. As C nodes do not depend on the functionality of any other nodes, they are slaves for node A on the main bus and for B on boom bus, and can be started without waiting. Once the C nodes have booted up, they start sending HEARTBEAT signals to the bus. Node B notices that there are two slave nodes in the subsystem bus sending HEARTBEATs, starts its own application, and also starts sending HEARTBEATs to both buses. This informs the slaves that their master node has also started up. Finally, node A detects HEARTBEATs from nodes C and B, so starts. Node A then sends a predefined command to all nodes to tell them that the system is ready and that all nodes are operating normally.

You can apply HIGH-LEVEL PROTOCOL (page 137) to provide a protocol to manage system start-up. For example, CANopen (CAN, 2013a) defines a way to start communication after a system has powered up. CANopen defines nodes to be in *pre-operational mode* after power-up. When the system's network management (NMT) master starts, it resets all client nodes' CANopen communication stacks. This reset causes the nodes to send a special 'I am booting' message (BOOT), allowing the master to detect all the nodes on the bus. The NMT master executes several conformance tests for each node, such as version number checking and updating the nodes' software or parameters if required. If a client node passes the tests it is allowed to enter operational mode. After all the nodes have started, the application on the NMT master node can decide whether to enter operational mode, indicating a successful start-up. In the case of failure, the corresponding nodes enter the stopped mode.

A machine can also use other start-up methods in addition to the messaging-based start-up sequences described above. It can have a dedicated monitoring node that wakes up first. This monitoring node can perform system tests of the core functionality before starting up other nodes. It coordinates the correct start-up sequence by starting devices up one by one according to a predefined schedule. This keeps resource consumption, for example electrical power or hydraulic pressure, lower, as only one node is started at a time. The monitoring component can easily adapt to changes in system configuration, as the start-up list is only stored in one place.

In addition to starting up a system, there are similar functional dependencies between nodes when shutting it down. When the operator turns the power off, the control system typically remains powered for a couple of minutes, often implemented with timed relays. This is useful when nodes require additional shut-down procedures. For example, the power-pack controller must remain in operation until it has ensured that the hydraulic pressure has reduced to a safe level. An additional time window after power-off is also usually required to allow the cabin PC to shut itself down in a controlled way. You can handle such shut-down dependencies in a similar way to that described in this pattern.

The system start-up phase can be interpreted as an operating mode (see OPERATING MODES, page 175) which the system enters before starting normal operations. If COMPONENT-BASED CONFIGURATION (page 386) has been applied, the start-up order of the nodes – that is, which nodes are masters and which are slaves – can be generated automatically based on the current system configuration. You can use CONTROL SYSTEM OPTIONS (page 394) to support optional functionality. This means that some of the slave nodes on the master node's list are optional, and PARAMETERS (page 380) are used to select which of the nodes are mandatory for the master to start normal operation. If the configuration of the system changes dynamically, a fixed node start-up order may be too restrictive. For example, a machine can have optional functionality that depends on the nodes that are attached to the bus. You can use START-UP NEGOTIATION (page 297) to negotiate the correct start-up order and available functionality dynamically.

MULTI-PHASE STARTUP (Kenji, 2001) describes a similar mechanism for starting up a system with subsystems that are dependent on one another. Process Control Daemon (PCD) for embedded Linux (PCD, 2013) can be used to ensure a controlled start-up sequence inside a single node. This provides a means to configure the sequence using start and end conditions. A process A is started only after some start condition has been satisfied. Similarly, the process depending on A will not be started until the end condition for A is satisfied.

System start-up can be defined so that nodes start after power-on in their dependency order, to allow graceful system-wide start-up. Each node ensures that its information or functionality dependencies are working correctly. If a node fails to start up, dependent nodes can decline to start their own operations, thus preventing other nodes from starting. This allows control applications to assume a working environment when they start.

Starting up the system may take longer, as nodes must wait for other nodes to start up before they can begin their own start-up procedures. On the other hand, the *fail-fast* principle (Shore, 2004) is followed and system start-up is stopped when a node cannot itself start up.

A strict start-up order could make system configuration changes, such as adding or removing nodes, harder to apply. If a new node is added it might affect the start-up order, and in the worst case new lists would have to be constructed for every master node in the system.

Communication topology may dictate the start-up order, so that the optimal order may not be achieved. Because signaling of successful start-up is required, slave nodes must typically be in the same subsystem as their master node. Alternatively, additional communication channels are required to signal successful start-up.

When a satellite is powered on for the first time after its launch, its systems are cold. It is the responsibility of the start-up routine to wake the system in a way that ensures that nothing breaks. Initially essential subsystems are self-tested by BOOTSTRAPPER (page 288) and started up. Energy must be conserved until energy resources are checked and passed as safe for use, so a satellite must open its solar panels before power-consuming systems can be used. After the system is in a minimal and stable working state, and electrical power is secured, different devices are woken up in the correct order. In some cases a device must not be used immediately: for example, a camera at −270 Celsius will break if operated cold. It therefore has to be warmed up before any other device or application is allowed to use it. Such an accident is prevented by keeping the camera disabled until it is heated to a predefined temperature. If something unexpected happens, for example the heating system does not start, the master node notices and the satellite enters a LIMP HOME (page 185) mode in which it just keeps itself alive so that its ground station personnel can decide what to do.

14.3   Start-Up Negotiation

A system's configuration may change between start-ups. Some devices are mandatory to ensure safe operation. In addition, optional devices might provide additional functionality. The available functionality is hard to determine from the current set of devices.

Therefore:

Create a mechanism in which all nodes announce themselves by sending a message to the bus after starting up. In the message, a node declares its existence and announces its capabilities. Design a central node, a *negotiator*, that gathers this information and builds a list of the nodes that are present. Using this list, the negotiator determines the available functionality. A node is ignored if it does not declare its presence within a specific time.

For the complete pattern, please see www.wiley.com/go/controlsystemspatterns.

CHAPTER

15

Software Update Patterns

'It is only the modern that ever becomes old-fashioned.'

Oscar Wilde

As an increasing amount of functionality is implemented with software, the ability to update system software is an important feature in work machines. Software alone does not require maintenance or updating. However, the hardware can wear out or break and need to be replaced; this might also necessitate changes to the software. Spare parts might be different, or have different firmware versions, requiring changes to the control system. In many cases, changes to a hardware part or its firmware may require bringing it in from the field for maintenance, for example if special equipment is required for updating its firmware. It is therefore easier in many cases to allow software update to be carried out in the field.

Modern work machines are highly networked and often support REMOTE ACCESS (page 361). While remote monitoring and diagnostics open up new possibilities, they also pose risks in the form of vulnerabilities. If a new vulnerability is discovered in a COTS component, it needs to be patched to prevent unauthorized access to the machine. Sometimes vulnerabilities can also compromise safety, if an attacker can affect machine functionality through a vulnerability. The importance of rapid and effortless update will increase in future.

Software update also has liabilities. For example, failed update of a single node may prevent the whole machine from booting up. In this case the only way to recover might be to replace the unit. So there are issues that one should keep in mind when considering software updates. This is extremely important if updates are carried out remotely, for example via REMOTE ACCESS, as a machine might become unrecoverable after a failed software update. If the machine is located in a hostile environment that makes human intervention impossible, a failed update might mean that the machine is lost.

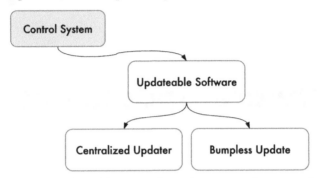

Figure 15.1: The sublanguage for updating control system software

The sublanguage shown in Figure 15.1 covers software updating. UPDATEABLE SOFTWARE (page 301) describes how the software of a single unit can be updated safely over a wire by using a separate update application. This makes it possible to retry the update after a failure, even automatically, as external help is not always available. In a distributed system such as is created by applying ISOLATED FUNCTIONALITIES (page 110), updating a single node may lead to version incompatibilities between the new software version and the rest of the system. This kind of software version discrepancy between subsystems is a problem, as subsystems need to cooperate. This can be solved by applying CENTRALIZED UPDATER (page 305), which provides an easy way to update a whole system with compatible software versions. A dedicated updater component distributes software to the nodes that require new software versions, ensuring version compatibility. This can even be carried out dynamically during system start-up if START-UP NEGOTIATION (page 297) has been applied.

The final pattern in this sublanguage, BUMPLESS UPDATE (page 310), discusses the situation in which software update must be carried out without jeopardizing system availability. This is common in systems that must operate continuously, such as paper manufacturing machines: software update must take place while the machine continues normal operation.

15.1 Updateable Software * *

…there is a CONTROL SYSTEM (page 96) whose start-up sequence is handled by BOOT-STRAPPER (page 288). OPERATING MODES (page 175) has been applied, so the system has several different modes. The system might be in use for decades. During such a long life-cycle a machine's operating requirements change; unless the machine can adapt, it becomes obsolete. For example, if its software cannot be modified to meet changes in legislation, the system can no longer be used.

During a long lifecycle a system's requirements are likely to change for various reasons. The system should be adaptable to these changes to maintain its efficiency.

It is difficult to predict all future software requirements, as such requirements may not yet have arisen. The only way to enable future flexibility is to be able to change software after deployment. New requirements might involve, for example faster operation, better accuracy, better energy efficiency, use of different hardware, compliance with new legislation and so on. Change is a certainty in systems with lifecycles of decades. If software renewal is not an option, the system's value will be diminished by each new requirement it cannot fulfil.

Cost is an important issue when a system is designed. Tight budgeting might result in a system that is sufficient only for its initial deployment. Future needs should nevertheless be considered, so that changes in the software do not always require changes in the hardware, and vice versa. If a replacement part is no longer readily available, producing a replacement might be costly and have a long lead time.

Changing software should be easy and quick, to minimize maintenance time. If software and hardware are coupled, changing software also requires changing hardware. In work machines all fragile components such as electronics have protective covering. Components might be in a hard-to-reach location. Replacing components might require manpower or expertise that is not always available.

Systems that implement REMOTE ACCESS (page 361) might be exposed to security attacks from the Internet if their applications have vulnerabilities. Such vulnerabilities may give an attacker access to sensitive information, and in the worst case jeopardize safety. Software with vulnerabilities should be updated as soon as possible, to prevent harmful consequences.

Therefore:

Place software on rewriteable persistent storage that is large enough for future needs. Use hardware that has enough capacity to accommodate additional future functionality. Implement an update mode to handle system update. Deliver new software over a wire and implement a separate updater application that updates the control application.

The usual way for an update to commence is to put the system into a separate update mode (see OPERATING MODES, page 175). This is usually done either by the operator or maintenance personnel, by pressing a button on the machine's user interface. A separate updater application is implemented, stored on separate ROM or rewriteable persistent storage such as flash memory or a memory stick. In some cases, the updater application can also be loaded to memory as the first step of the update process over the wire. Figure 15.2 illustrates a typical situation in which an updater application is located on the same flash memory as the control application.

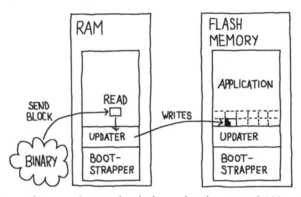

Figure 15.2: An updater application loads the update binary to RAM and from there writes the updated application to flash memory block by block

Depending on how much RAM the system has, the update package can be either loaded partially or completely to memory. The application being updated, located on persistent storage such as flash, can then be updated either in one operation or block by block. During the update process persistent memory is rewritten with data from the update package.

During update the (sub)system being updated is flagged as such, so that its control application cannot be started, and other applications can see that the subsystem is not available, to prevent undefined behavior. If updating is aborted, the application written to persistent storage will be incomplete and in an inconsistent state. When all data from the update binary is written, the update is verified and the update flag removed. The system can then be rebooted to put the new application into use. Update flags are usually stored in a separate rewriteable persistent memory area, such as NVRAM reserved for status flags, system options, settings and so on.

If a system boots while an 'under-update 'flag is set, the BOOTSTRAPPER (page 288) loads the updater application instead of its default application. This provides a simple way of entering the update mode, and ensures that none of the system's normal function-alities are active while an update is in progress. An alternative method is to change the operating mode while the main application is active by loading and running the updater application. Because the main application has to ensure that all the activities are termi-nated – that is, no threads are running – this is more complex than booting into an update mode.

An update can always fail due to power loss, memory errors, malfunctioning hardware and so on, so should be verified. This can be done, for example, by doing a byte-by-byte comparison or by calculating a checksum. Only when the update is written successfully can the 'under-update' flag be removed. If the update process fails, it can be retried. Some-times failure is caused by some external recoverable issue, such as power failure, so a sec-ond attempt might be successful. If an error is detected multiple times during update or verification, the operator should be notified and the system halted, as the problem is probably unrecoverable by normal means. 1+1 REDUNDANCY (page 279) makes it possi-ble retain a copy of the previous software version as backup. If update or booting up the system fails even after several retries, the backup software version can be automatically used to boot the unit (see LIMIT RETRIES, Hanmer, 2007).

Usually a unit's software is divided into several levels that are updated separately. Its control application is updated in-place over a wire (for example a CAN bus or Ethernet). The next level is the runtime environment; updating this may need the unit to be detached from the machine and the update carried out with a software tool. The lowest level, the bootloader, is seldom updated, as this would need vendor-specific updating tools. This kind of division is a trade-off between the need to change software and the risk that a mal-function during update may make the system unrecoverable.

Updating the updater application itself is risky, as there might no way to restart the process if it fails. Updater applications should therefore be as small and simple as possible to reduce the need for their own update. Applying 1+1 REDUNDANCY to duplicate mem-ory provides a way to recover from updater failures. With this approach the updater ap-plication is first updated in secondary storage; if that update is successful, the updater application in primary storage is also updated. If the update of the updater application in secondary storage fails, the updater in primary storage can still be used to retry the up-date process. This approach ensures that there is always a copy of the updater application that is functioning properly.

More storage space should be available than is required by the first version of the soft-ware. As new versions may contain new features, they are likely to require more memory. There should initially therefore be extra memory space to allow larger software versions in future. How much more space depends on the system's purpose and development path. If systems are to be produced in large quantities it might be reasonable to probe future requirements to find a suitable storage size. If only a few systems are shipped, researching this is probably not cost-effective. However, if a system does not have enough storage for future functionalities, squeezing its software into less memory will make programming more complex and costly.

If system architecture is distributed by applying ISOLATED FUNCTIONALITIES (page 110) more than one subsystem may need to be updated. Software version discrepancies between subsystems might be a problem, as subsystems need to cooperate. There may therefore be a need for safeguards that prevent updates if a new subsystem software version is not compatible with software in other subsystems. This usually means that the compatibility of various software versions must be tested. To avoid version discrepancies, the system is typically updated as a whole. Often CENTRALIZED UPDATER (page 305) is used to ensure compatibility of software versions on all nodes. In a system with multiple nodes, a node being updated should inform all other nodes that it is in update mode (see OPERATING MODES, page 175).

Updating software may require additional safeguards. It should not be possible to run updates by mistake, and updating should be protected from unintentional or malicious use. ROLE-BASED UI (page 327) describes how to allow only specific users to access the update functionality. A mechanism to allow only cryptographically signed updates may be needed to protect a machine from updates originating from suspicious sources.

The pattern described here is similar to SOFTWARE UPDATE (Hanmer, 2007).

The system maintains its value longer, as it can be updated when new features, bug fixes and other enhancements become available. A machine's service contract might cover some updates, while others might be treated as enhancements and used to generate more revenue. The ability to update control software should not be used as a way to release unfinished software versions and get end users to act as software testers.

UPDATEABLE SOFTWARE makes the system more secure, as security vulnerabilities can be fixed by updates.

Updating the software makes software more complex compared to non-updateable systems. In addition, the update process can fail for various reasons. Update processes should therefore be as robust as possible, to avoid machine unavailability, and it should be possible to retry an update after a failure. It is preferable if update retries are commenced automatically, as external intervention is not always available. Sometimes a failure might be caused by hardware, so retrying the update will not help. A failure might be due to an error that is unrecoverable without spare parts, for example exhausted memory. If the system is costly, spare part delivery times could be long, or it might be impossible to change parts due to the environment in which the machine is used, so more safeguards should be available for update recovery, such as 1+1 REDUNDANCY of hardware. This adds cost, but may significantly extend the machine's lifecycle.

Extra rewriteable persistent storage adds the flexibility to support future requirements. This adds cost, but the same design can be reused in a machine that consists of many updateable nodes. Rewriteable storage is not as cheap as ROM, but the flexibility gained should be adequate to offset such costs, even in the short term.

The update process should not be accessible maliciously or be able to be activated unintentionally. Suitable safeguards should be put in place. Designing and implementing these safeguard and access controls will increase cost.

A bug has been detected in a harvester's grappler controller. Its manufacturer delivers the update to the customer by e-mail, who saves it on a memory stick. A maintenance engineer halts the machine and connects the memory stick containing the update to the cabin PC's USB port. The update tool requests the grappler controller to enter its update mode. After the controller reboots and activates its update mode, the update application on the controller sends a notification that it is in update mode. The update tool sends the new software to the grappler controller's updater application over the bus, block by block. After writing the new code to persistent memory, the updater verifies it by calculating a cyclic redundancy checksum (CRC) and comparing it to the CRC delivered with the new software. After the update is verified as correct, the update tool requests the controller to return to its normal operating mode. The controller reboots into the updated grappler application and propagates its change to normal operating mode to other nodes.

15.2   Centralized Updater *

…there is a CONTROL SYSTEM (page 96) that has been distributed by applying ISOLATED FUNCTIONALITIES (page 110) and whose nodes communicate in ONE TO MANY (page 131) fashion. Nodes communicate with each other to cooperate. The operator is able to interact with the system using a HUMAN–MACHINE INTERFACE (page 313). UPDATEABLE SOFTWARE (page 301) allows each node to be updated individually. Node updates are transferred over some communication channel, such as a bus. Updating all nodes one by one is a tedious manual task. It is also potentially error-prone, as a maintenance engineer may forget to update a node, leaving the system with incompatible software versions.

Updating each node individually in a distributed system may cause a node's software to be incompatible with the rest of the system. This may result in an inoperable machine.

Each node should have a software version that is designed to co-function with other nodes. Specific versions of distributed software are developed and tested together so that their compatibility can be guaranteed. Nodes with untested combinations of software versions might cause compatibility issues and the machine might not function properly.

Updating a system manually node by node is time-consuming and cumbersome, increasing maintenance costs. A human lapse may cause problems when an incorrect software version is used, the wrong node is updated, or updating some node is forgotten. The update task should therefore not be handled by a person. MINIMIZE HUMAN INTERVENTION (Hanmer, 2007) gives more details.

If a new node is added, it might have a software version that is incompatible with the rest of the system. It should be possible to update the whole control system to compatible software versions, so that the new node can function properly.

In the case of an update failure, it should be possible to retry the update process automatically. If updating fails, a maintenance engineer should be informed and alternative ways to solve the problem offered if possible. It should not be the maintenance engineer's task to try to figure out what went wrong.

Therefore:

Deliver compatible software for all nodes bundled in a single package. Create a centralized updater component that distributes the software to nodes from the bundle. This updater component supervises the update process.

When the centralized updater is activated and the system placed into update mode, it orders each node to enter its own update mode (see OPERATING MODES, page 175). The update is carried out using a single update bundle. This bundle is basically a compatibility tested snapshot of all existing software for all the nodes in the system, including optional nodes. For each node, the centralized updater takes the node-specific part from the bundle and transmits it to the relevant node if the updater detects that the node has a different software version. The node may receive the whole update before commencing update, or it may start updating by rewriting its persistent memory as soon as it receives the first part of the update. In either case, each node's update application should keep the centralized updater informed of its current status. When a node's update has finished, it notifies the centralized updater. After all nodes have been updated, the centralized updater requests the nodes to enter their normal operating modes.

The CENTRALIZED UPDATER should be accompanied by a user interface view, so that the maintenance engineer can operate the update functionality. System status can be queried via the user interface, to check the software versions of the nodes, and to check that they are consistent with the bundle version. A new bundle can be delivered on removable media, or by a wireless extension to REMOTE ACCESS (page 361). The new bundle is verified as valid and then copied to the centralized updater component. Multiple bundles can be stored, and the maintenance engineer can update the system to any chosen bundle version. Figure 15.3 illustrates the structure of a system with a centralized updater.

If an optional node is installed, the software for it should exist in the bundle. It may be that there is no support for the new node in the current update bundle. In this case, the whole system must be updated to a newer bundle version that has support for the new

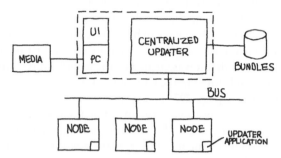

Figure 15.3: A system with a CENTRALIZED UPDATER. Updater, nodes and user interface PC are connected via the bus. Update bundles are stored by the CENTRALIZED UPDATER.

node before hardware can be activated. Note that in large set-ups it might be that not all hardware combinations are tested. There might therefore be issues with unusual combinations. On the other hand, different combinations are easier to test if all software components reside in one bundle. This usually means that various combinations are better handled by the bundle approach than in situations in which each software component is updated separately.

The CENTRALIZED UPDATER is in direct communication with each node being updated. A node should send status messages to the CENTRALIZED UPDATER whenever possible, to make progress visible and controllable. Such messages will indicate, for example, when a node enters update mode, when software upload is completed, when a memory block is written and when the update is complete. Based on these status messages, a simple retry mechanism can be implemented, for example for uploading functionality.

If the update of a node fails, the node's update application retries the update. The CENTRALIZED UPDATER is notified of such an occurrence. If the update cannot be completed successfully after a couple of retries, a decision must be made about whether the node can be updated or used at all. The maintenance engineer should be notified of the failure and informed about alternative solutions. There are at least three recourses: disable the failed node manually, get a new node that *can* be updated, or try to use another software bundle for the whole system. A different bundle might work in a system with many hardware versions and configurations with potentially incompatible software versions. If the update failed due to broken hardware, rollback is not possible, but the machine might still be operable to a limited degree if its control system implements LIMP HOME (page 185).

New hardware is typically delivered without software to ensure that it will be used with the correct software version. To activate a new node, a maintenance engineer has to run the system update when the node is added. If a node is taken from another machine as a spare part, it may contain software from a different bundle version than the current machine. If it cannot be updated to the same bundle version as the rest of the system, the maintenance engineer should disable the node manually. If the node has a version discrepancy with the bundle version, machine function may be undefined.

Malicious use and self-created software bundles are always a threat that should be prevented. This can be done by signing the bundles cryptographically. This is an important security precaution, especially if bundles can be delivered and installed by wireless. After the bundle has been copied to the system, its signature should first be verified, to ensure that the bundle is intact and that it was created by the manufacturer. Only after this may the bundle be processed and stored in the CENTRALIZED UPDATER.

START-UP NEGOTIATION (page 297) makes automatic node detection and handling possible. This enables the system to perform an automatic update on node insertion. If no suitable software exists, or if the node is malfunctioning, the updater can disable the node on the software level by telling it not to start any applications. There might also be dependencies between subsystems that are known to a start-up negotiator component. In this case it is best to first update those nodes on which others depend. This allows dependency issues to be discovered as soon as possible, and removes the need to roll back updates of the whole system if an update that includes dependencies fails.

If hardware failure is not acceptable, you can apply 1+1 REDUNDANCY (page 279), for example to duplicate a node's persistent memory, or even to duplicate the whole node. Update is then never applied to both redundant parts at the same time, as this might cause them to fail at the same time. Consequently a duplicated part that has not been touched and which works even if the update fails is always available. Redundancy can be visible to the centralized updater, or it can be an internal design for a hardware part that the centralized updater does not know about. In this case, the centralized updater sees only one device and the device itself takes care of the update. If duplicated memory is visible to the centralized updater, there should be some policy to decide responsibility for updating the second part of the duplicated hardware. It is also necessary to decide how to verify that the first part of the hardware is functional, whether testing is adequate, and whether the part can be used in production. In any case, maintenance personnel should always be informed of a failure, even when duplication exists.

If redundancy alone is not enough and high availability is required, a system can be designed such that its main application can be run while parts that are not executed are being updated. BUMPLESS UPDATE (page 310) achieves this.

The size of an update bundle can become large if nodes are updated using images of persistent memory data and there are many images in the bundle. The requirement for storage space might be significant if multiple bundles are stored in the CENTRALIZED UPDATER. In this case it might be sensible to have machine-specific bundles. COMPONENT-BASED CONFIGURATION (page 386) provides a way to differentiate the software for each machine type.

The whole update process can be carried out from a single point. This simplifies installation and updating of system software and reduces the probability of human error. Additionally, all software can be installed on the assembly line in a single operation.

If new hardware is available but there is no support for it in an older software bundle, the hardware cannot be put into use unless the software is updated for the whole system. After successful update, all system software becomes compatible.

Creating software bundles is hard work. It involves a lot of compatibility testing between different nodes and hardware versions. It might be cumbersome and expensive to test all possible combinations. On the other hand, potential compatibility issues are taken care of by the development team, rather than by maintenance personnel at software update.

If no automatic version-checking mechanism is implemented, attaching a node to a machine might result in software version discrepancy. Human interaction is required if a new node is taken from another machine. A new node should always be delivered without software. It is convenient for maintenance personnel if software is preinstalled on spare parts, but this can lead to version problems in the field. For this reason, it is better to make the update procedure as easy as possible and install correct versions in the field, as incorrect versions installed during manufacture can cause extended maintenance delays.

A software bundle might be large if it contains many images of persistent memory data. This might make it time-consuming to transfer to a machine, make it slow to update the machine, and limit how many bundles can be available on the machine at the same time. Additionally, its system bus throughput sets a limit on how quickly a machine can be updated.

Malicious use and self-created software bundles are a threat that should be prevented by signing the bundles. This is especially important if bundles can be delivered and installed wirelessly.

An underground mine loader requires an energy efficiency update. Its engine's fuel injection chart is optimized for low rotation speeds, and its hydraulics pistons are kept in continuous motion to avoid static friction. The update is delivered as a software bundle containing software for all possible nodes that can be attached to the loader. A maintenance engineer inserts a memory stick in the cabin PC's USB port. The system notices the inserted media, finds a software bundle file, verifies its checksum and signature, then copies it to the CENTRALIZED UPDATER's storage. The user interface notifies the maintenance engineer that a new system update is available.

The engineer displays a restricted maintenance menu and selects update of the machine software with the new software bundle. The CENTRALIZED UPDATER sends a command to all nodes to enter their update mode. Each node flags itself as being in update and reboots to activate its update application. When the update application is running on a node, it sends a notification to the CENTRALIZED UPDATER. The CENTRALIZED UPDATER sends software updates in 1 Mbyte blocks to those nodes that do not already have a software version that matches the corresponding bundled version. Each node that is being updated writes each block to its persistent memory, then sends a confirmation message to the CENTRALIZED UPDATER to receive a new block. When the whole update is written to memory, the node waits for further commands. When all nodes requiring software update have been updated, the CENTRALIZED UPDATER commands the nodes to enter their normal operating mode. Each node clears its 'under update' flag and reboots to start its main application. After the machine is operational, the maintenance engineer takes the machine for a test run to ensure that everything functions as expected.

15.3   Bumpless Update

The process that a control system is monitoring and controlling must not be interrupted. However, a control system software update causes a glitch in operation, as the update needs to be carried out when the controller is not in operating mode.

Therefore:

Divide program code into functional blocks that have defined entry points. Create a system that updates the program on a unit block by block, so that the block currently executing is not updated. When control leaves the block, it can be updated on the fly.

For the complete pattern, please see `www.wiley.com/go/controlsystemspatterns`.

CHAPTER

16

Human–Machine
Interface Patterns

*'I have always wished for my computer to be as easy to use as my telephone; my wish
has come true because I can no longer figure out how to use my telephone.'*

Bjarne Stroustrup

Sometimes a work machine is autonomous and doesn't have an operator. For example,
an elevator is an example of a machine whose user interface is minimal – a couple of simple buttons. However, a machine operator often has to have a more sophisticated way to
control the machine. This can be implemented with physical controls such as joysticks,
pedals, hand panels, dashboard buttons and so on. The control system may also need to
show information about the machine's status, task descriptions and so on, to make it user
friendly and to provide operator feedback. To save cabin space and build the machine
cost-effectively, meters and gauges are often implemented in software, using a graphical
user interface. HUMAN–MACHINE INTERFACE (page 313) describes how to implement

these so that the rest of the system is decoupled from the user interface and the controls have short response times.

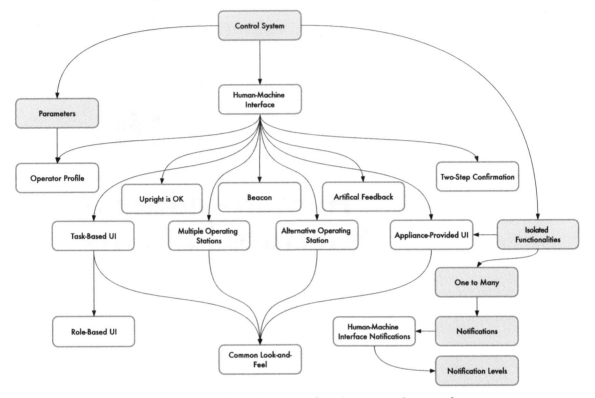

Figure 16.1: The sublanguage for a human–machine interface

Most of the patterns in this sublanguage (Figure 16.1) discuss how to implement an effective operator interface. UPRIGHT IS OK (page 324), BEACON (page 336), ARTIFICIAL FEEDBACK (page 317) and TWO-STEP CONFIRMATION (page 321) describe how to build the interface in a way that it is usable, understandable and easy to learn. Some of these aspects might be dictated by legislation. For example, it must be impossible to start a potentially hazardous operation accidentally, so TWO-STEP CONFIRMATION is required.

OPERATOR PROFILE (page 340) describes how to increase the operator's productivity and comfort by storing personalized settings in a single easily transferable file. This allows an operator to transport their own settings independent of the machine being controlled. MULTIPLE OPERATING STATIONS (page 335) and ALTERNATIVE OPERATING STATION (page 330) tackle the situation in which one operating station is not enough, for example because an operator cannot observe the whole of a process or task from the default operating station, or if it needs more than one operator.

A machine might have multiple user groups that need different services. For example, an operator only needs to control the machine, but a maintenance engineer might need to access diagnostics. ROLE-BASED UI (page 327) describes how to implement different user interfaces for different user groups. A machine might also have multiple use contexts, with the requirements for the user interface changing correspondingly. For example, a forest harvester operator needs different controls to drive the harvester on the road than when felling trees in the forest. The user interface should adapt to these varying operating contexts. TASK-BASED UI (page 326) describes how to tackle this problem.

Sometimes a task can depend on some optional accessory attached to the machine. The functions of agricultural machinery, for example, might vary greatly depending on the implements attached. APPLIANCE-PROVIDED UI (page 336) allows the user interface to be modified according the equipment installed.

Finally, COMMON LOOK-AND-FEEL (page 344) helps a developer to design user interfaces that cause less cognitive stress for an operator, as all user interfaces have a similar appearance and function in a consistent way. A COMMON LOOK-AND-FEEL also makes the HUMAN–MACHINE INTERFACE attractive, so that it offers the operator a great user experience.

16.1   Human–Machine Interface * *

...in a CONTROL SYSTEM (page 96) the operator needs to know the current status of the machine and information about the process to operate the machine efficiently. The operator uses physical controls such as joysticks, pedals, hand panels, dashboard buttons and so on to operate the machine. In some cases touch displays are used, as they require less wiring. To save cabin space and build the machine cost-effectively, some meters and gauges might be implemented in software using a graphical user interface. However, the physical controls should have short response times and high reliability, so that they are responsive in all situations. For example, braking should always have deterministic and minimal latency independent of CPU load. If status displays and graphical user interfaces (GUI) are required, a high-end node usually provides this (see SEPARATE REAL-TIME, page 237). This high-end node might not be designed to provide real-time functionality.

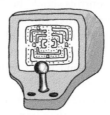

The control system should provide the machine operator with feedback and a way to operate the system.

There should be a way to show information about the system's status, task descriptions and so on, to make the machine user-friendly. If the machine can guide its operator about what to do next, or how the operator can improve the way they control the machine, productivity and efficiency can be increased.

The machine should remain operable even if the non-real-time level described in SEPARATE REAL-TIME (page 237) is malfunctioning. Graphical applications are usually run on a high-end level, so the graphical user interface normally resides on the non-real-time part. When the GUI is not available for the machine operator, the machine should remain operable, at least to some extent. Of course, in some machines, the absence of a graphical user interface may prevent use completely.

A single display showing gauges on its screen is usually cheaper than multiple physical gauges placed on the dashboard. One display also requires less wiring than separate physical gauges. Similarly, a single touch panel requires less wiring than several separate buttons.

There should be a way to provide fine-grained information about the system state. In many cases traditional gauges cannot show sufficiently detailed information. For example, in a car a dashboard light is often used to indicate a fault. However, this cannot show what the fault is by using an indicator light alone. When the CONTROL SYSTEM is used in the machine, more information on the fault is available and can be presented to the operator in a convenient way. Traditional gauges may also not be sufficiently accurate. There should be a way to present both the approximate magnitude of a value and the exact value.

Therefore:

Add a human-machine interface that supports ways to present information and controls to manipulate the machine. These are typically displays with GUIs, buzzers, joysticks, buttons and so on. The presentation of information and the controls of the machine must be decoupled, for example by using ONE TO MANY (page 131) communication and a message bus.

If SEPARATE REAL-TIME (page 237) has been applied, the natural place for the GUI is on the machine's high-end node. This high-end node usually has enough processing power to run the GUI. However, physical controls should be responsive even when the high-end node is not functioning. For example, after the machine is started using the ignition switch, the controls should be responsive in a couple of seconds even if the graphical user interface is not yet available. If the high-end node has broken down for some reason, the machine should be operable at least to some extent without it. Usually this is made possible by separating the GUI from the controls and connecting them using a bus. Another option would be to have the GUI running as a non-real-time task, whereas other control tasks would be real-time tasks running on the same controller or PC.

If a lot of messaging is required between different control units, it is advisable to create a separate HMI bus that is connected to the main bus of the machine via an HMI bus master (see ONE TO MANY, page 131). Once all control equipment (including the node running the GUI) is connected to the bus, they are then decoupled from each other. If a

Figure 16.2: The structure of a typical HUMAN–MACHINE INTERFACE on an architecture level when a separate HMI bus is used to connect different parts of the HMI

separate HMI bus is used, traffic on the main bus does not affect communication latency between the physical parts of the HMI and the GUI, and the load on the main bus is decreased. A bus of course always adds some latency to communication. Figure 16.2 illustrates the typical structure of this solution.

If the machine has MULTIPLE OPERATING STATIONS (page 335), use of a separate HMI bus for each operating station is a necessity, otherwise multiple controllers would have the same identity on the same bus. This would lead to a situation in which the node cannot be identified uniquely.

A graphical user interface is used to show machine status, for example oil pressure or RPM, as gauges. The user interface can also show NOTIFICATIONS (page 156) and other information about system state. A GUI can also show work plans, for example which blast holes should be drilled next by a mining drill rig, and production reports, such as how many trees have been felled. This kind of information increases operator productivity by showing them an optimal work order.

In process automation the user interface usually contains much information about the processes at hand, and it may be impossible to display all this information on one screen. A graphical user interface is therefore deployed in a control room and different screens used to display detailed information from different parts of the process. Figure 16.3 shows a typical setup.

Machine control must be implemented such that the machine can be controlled and the operator can even continue working if the graphical user interface is malfunctioning. In practice this means that the controls should be decoupled from the GUI. Controls are directly connected to the HMI bus, for example CAN joysticks, or are run as real-time tasks that read control values from analog joysticks and controls. In both cases, the graphical user interface is typically implemented as a non-real-time task. There is no benefit in implementing it as a real-time task, and it might be impossible anyway, due to limited processing power in the GUI PC. As information presented in the GUI originates from multiple sources, bus latencies might also make it impossible to present the information in real time. In addition, human operators have slow reaction times, making real-time updating pointless. To save hardware costs, the GUI is typically collocated with other non-real-time applications, so the load on the node hosting the GUI is not deterministic.

Figure 16.3: A control room with multiple graphical displays in a paper mill
Reproduced by permission of Metso Automation Oy

If the PC hosting the GUI malfunctions, its gauges cannot be displayed, and controlling the machine needs operator expertise, such as listening to the engine or manually supervising operations. Some functionality may become unavailable, but a mobile machine can still be driven. The most important gauges could be implemented in hardware (as CAN devices or analog gauges) so that they remain available when the GUI is not functioning.

Using a graphical user interface to show gauges can lead to significant cost reductions. As a GUI can support multiple views, gauges can be shown using different views on the same display. If hardware gauges were used, each would increase the cost of the machine. Cabin space is also saved, as one display is used instead of many hardware gauges.

If a machine has user groups, such as operator and maintenance personnel, you should consider providing a ROLE-BASED UI (page 327). If the machine can be used for multiple tasks, you might want to provide a TASK-BASED UI (page 326) for the operator. Different views in the GUI should have a COMMON LOOK-AND-FEEL (page 344) to make them easy to learn and use. The operator should be able to see at a glance that everything is functioning normally by using UPRIGHT IS OK (page 324) in the gauge design. Unintentional activation of functionalities can be prevented by using TWO-STEP CONFIRMATION (page 321). The user interface should provide feedback for the operator. Sometimes this is not naturally available – that is, the operator cannot see the results of actions immediately. If this is the case, you should implement ARTIFICIAL FEEDBACK (page 317). In many cases the operator must focus on the current task: the machine should use BEACON (page 336) to draw the operator's attention to any problem.

The operator can use the same settings easily on multiple machines by saving their user interface settings to an OPERATOR PROFILE (page 340). MULTIPLE OPERATING STATIONS

(page 335) and multiple HMIs might be required if the machine has multiple simultaneous operators. Sometimes the machine or some part of it, such as a cabin roof's support
pillars, may block the operator's view; you can consider adding an ALTERNATIVE OPER-
ATING STATION (page 330) to deal with this. If the machine uses NOTIFICATIONS (page
156) to indicate events, these can be shown in a HUMAN–MACHINE INTERFACE using the
mechanisms described in HMI NOTIFICATIONS (page 340).

An operator can steer a machine using controls such as joysticks, hand panels and so on,
and see machine status information such as RPM, speed and so on via the GUI. This offers an enhanced user experience and increases productivity. The GUI makes it possible
to show fine-grained information that traditional gauges could not present. For example,
information about fault situations can be shown on the display. In addition, work plans,
production reports and diagnostics can be shown, removing the need for paper plans.

As the GUI is implemented on a high-end node, it is possible to use common technologies in its implementation. Selecting commonly used technology improves its availability
later in the machine's lifecycle.

If the non-real-time part of the machine running the GUI malfunctions, the machine
can still be controlled using its control equipment, as this is decoupled from the GUI, for
example by using a bus. In the event of GUI malfunction, its extra benefits, such as presenting work plans, are lost.

An HMI makes the system more complex, and a machine might require an additional
bus in the cabin to ensure the availability of control functionality. Adding an additional
bus adds cost.

A pile-driver has controls such as joysticks and intelligent CAN devices connected directly to the HMI bus in the cabin. Control signals are bridged from this bus to the main bus
whenever controllers attached to the main bus need data that is produced on the HMI
bus. The HMI bus also has an attached PC. This receives control signals from the control
units via the HMI bus, and shows appropriate changes in its graphical user interface. The
PC runs Linux and the GUI is implemented with Qt to ensure portability. If the PC crashes or malfunctions, this does not disable the whole system, as the nodes responsible for
controlling the machine still receive control signals from the control equipment.

16.2   Artificial Feedback * *

ALSO KNOWN AS INSTANT FEEDBACK

…there is a distributed CONTROL SYSTEM (page 96) with a HUMAN–MACHINE INTER-
FACE (page 313). Some functionalities of the machine may be invisible to its operator and
have a significant execution time. For example, when a passenger calls an elevator, they

activate the system by pressing a call button. The elevator cabin takes some time to arrive at the target floor. While the operation is underway, the potential passenger cannot know which floor the cabin is on if there is no separate display for it. However, the passenger needs to know that the elevator call was received and that the elevator will arrive. A machine operator needs feedback that activation of a function was registered and will be run as soon as the machine is ready to do so. Some of a machine's functions might be such that the operator cannot see their effect even though they are carried out immediately. For example, if an operator is adjusting a pressure value, the result might not be visible, but it should be visualized somehow.

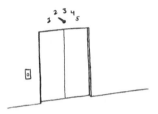

An operator needs to know whether activation of a function was successful, even when the results of activation are not immediately visible.

People are often impatient when interacting with machines and want instant feedback from their actions. Nielsen's principles for user interface design advise always giving user feedback (Molich & Nielsen, 1990). For example, a user expects something to happen immediately on pressing a button, but sometimes a function cannot be carried out immediately. In this case, the user needs confirmation of the action, otherwise they might think that their action was not registered, and repeat it.

Some functions generate natural feedback. For example, when starting a car, the driver turns the ignition key and gets feedback – the engine starts. However, sometimes feedback is not available. For example, a work machine operator might wear hearing protection, so might not be able to hear the engine. Even in this case the operator should be able to get feedback from the control system.

When the user activates a function, its feedback should be available until it has completed. This allows the user to be sure that the requested operation is being carried out.

Therefore:

Create a way to give instant feedback if activation of a function is successful. If no feedback is naturally available, use lights, sounds or some other method to inform the operator that activation of the function was registered.

In a work machine many functions do not take place immediately. For example, hydraulic pressure needs to be generated to move a boom, or a blade needs to reach a specific RPM before cutting can commence. However, the operator needs feedback instantly on pressing a button, otherwise may be left wondering if the machine registered the activation. They might even press the button again and the system cancel the requested operation, or activate it twice, causing confusion over whether the functionality was activated or not. If there is no natural feedback – something the operator hears, sees or senses – give artificial feedback. Figure 16.4 illustrates this approach.

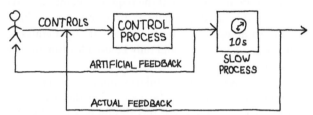

Figure 16.4: Sometimes feedback on the success of an action is delayed. In such cases, the designer should create a mechanism to provide fast ARTIFICIAL FEEDBACK to the user.

The most common way to provide artificial feedback is to use lights. For example, when cutting a tree with a feller buncher, the circular saw must reach a specific speed before the saw can be applied to the tree trunk. After the operator has activated the saw, a dashboard light therefore indicates that the machine is accelerating the saw. An alternative could be to use sound to acknowledge activation. However, using sound is problematic in noisy environments, as the operator might be using hearing protectors and be unable to heard feedback sounds. The sound should be unique, so that the operator can differentiate which action the feedback relates to, and that it is not an alarm. In general, sounds are used to draw an operator's attention away from the current task. See BEACON (page 336) for more details.

Deciding which sense to use for operator feedback is not always straightforward. For example, if the operator is trying to move a boom over the limits of its movement, it might be hard to determine how to give this kind of feedback efficiently. A HUMAN–MACHINE INTERFACE (HMI, page 313) could show an alert, but the operator has to remember to look at the screen. Alternatively, the boom-control joystick could vibrate to tell the operator that further movement is not possible, so that the operator knows instantly that the feedback is originating from the functionality controlled by the joystick. The HMI screen could present more detailed feedback as well, in the form of HMI NOTIFICATIONS (page 340).

Artificial feedback should be as tightly coupled to the functionality generating the feedback as possible. For example, in a drilling machine an indicator light in the drill activation button tells the operator whether automatic retraction of the drill is active. In the case of MULTIPLE OPERATING STATIONS (page 335) or ALTERNATIVE OPERATING STATION (page 330) feedback should be given on the screen where a function was activated. If there are multiple screens in a control room, feedback should also be given on the screen where the function was activated.

The length of feedback is important. A user should be given feedback for the duration of the function. For example, when calling an elevator, the call button's indicator light should remain lit until the cabin arrives at the floor from which it was requested. The user also wants to know how the function is progressing, so an elevator should show the floor where the cabin currently is. Generally, it is best practice to visualize that a machine is working on a requested function. For example, when an operator presses a button and processing the request takes a long time, the user interface can show some kind of animated process indicator to demonstrate that the request is being carried out.

Artificial feedback should be used sparingly, as an operator might be distracted by extraneous feedback. For example, if every button or key-press generates feedback, it soon gets annoying. Feedback mechanisms should only be used for functions whose result the operator cannot immediately see.

Sometimes key-press sounds might be useful to support a special user group with limited abilities. For example, if a machine can be operated by the visually-impaired, sounds could help in use of the machine. However, this should be treated as a special case and should be configurable and disabled by default.

Artificial feedback is used to show an operator that the control system is carrying out some function even though the operator cannot see or hear it. The operator should be notified when the operation has finished in case their attention is on something other than the activated function. You can use BEACON (page 336) or HMI NOTIFICATIONS (page 340) to draw the operator's attention when the function has completed.

After this pattern is applied, the operator is informed that the control system is carrying out a requested function even when there is no natural visual or aural feedback. This prevents the operator from unintentionally pressing the activation button multiple times, and makes the system more user-friendly.

Visual feedback for a function is provided on the display where the function can be selected. This makes it easier to notice any operator feedback the system is providing.

In some cases it might be hard to decide where feedback should be shown, for example if there is no display or warning light in the vicinity of the controls that activate a function. The designer must use sound or some other mean of feedback in this case. However, this is not an optimal solution, as the operator may not recognize the sound as feedback from a selected action, or, if wearing hearing protection, might not hear the sound.

When using lights to provide artificial feedback, it may be that a light is broken but the system is otherwise functioning normally. The operator now cannot get feedback as normal, so cannot be sure whether the system has failed completely, or only the signal light is dead. This will require further diagnosis.

A bulldozer driver is plowing snow in arctic conditions. The weather is cold; to make the working conditions comfortable, the driver activates the seat heater by pressing a button on the panel. Seat warming is not instant, as the heating element takes some time to warm up. So when the button is pressed, the indicator light in the button lights up to give feedback that the heater is activated. The driver does not need to wonder whether the button press was registered.

16.3   Two-Step Confirmation *

ALSO KNOWN AS DOUBLE CONFIRMATION

...a distributed CONTROL SYSTEM (page 96) with a HUMAN–MACHINE INTERFACE (page 313) has multiple functionalities. Some of the functionalities may require a long time to start, or take time to execute. Activation of such functionality may cause some machine resources to be unavailable for a time. The operator should therefore be particularly careful when activating them, and avoid unintentional activation. Sometimes inactivating some functionality in a control system may cause long-lasting consequences, so it should be ensured that the operator really wants to do so.

Unintentional (de)activation of a functionality that may have long-lasting consequences should be avoided, as it may prevent use of the machine.

Starting up or deactivating a functionality may take a long time, or the running time of the functionality may be long. If the functionality is activated unintentionally, it may take some time before the machine is ready for its next task, so accidental activation should be avoided. Sometimes an operator might want to test what happens when a specific button is pressed, but even in this case it may be safer for the operation not to be started immediately a control is activated in the GUI.

The activation process for a specific function does not need to be simple if it is not often used. In such a case, an operator is not likely to be irritated if the function requires multiple steps for activation, so the activation procedure can itself take time. For example, an emergency stop must take place immediately, but it's ok if activation of drilling in a drill rig takes five seconds, as this is small compared to a typical run time of 30 minutes or more.

Unintentional activation of functionality may affect a machine's environment. For example, if a mining drill rig is accidentally activated and starts drilling in the wrong position, it may create a badly-located blast hole. Even if drilling can be stopped, the half-drilled blast hole may make things harder if the blasting plans need to be revised.

Activation of functionality should not start unnoticed. An operator should always be aware that they have activated a function. If the operator is not aware that a function is in use, they cannot monitor its progress, or may try to initiate another, possibly conflicting action, such as driving the machine when the parking brake is on.

If the GUI reacts slowly to operator requests due to a heavy processing load, the operator might press a control button multiple times. This should not activate a function by itself, as this may have unexpected consequences.

Buttons whose function is to stop movement have hard real-time requirements and should not be implemented in a GUI, but rather as hardware buttons. This is stated in the European Machinery Directive (Machinery Directive, 2006). However, a hardware button's functionality may vary depending on the OPERATING MODES (page 175) selected.

Therefore:

Design the graphical user interface such that the operator needs to enable a function twice, changing the way in which this is achieved each time. This ensures that the operator must make a conscious decision to activate the function.

Normally a function is triggered by pressing a button on a hand panel. The function executed may vary depending on the operating mode. The operating mode should be selected from a GUI, so there is a two-step confirmation process for activating the function. Design the activation of long operations so that the operator needs to press two distinct buttons to activate the functionality. For example, the operator might need to select the function or operating mode from the GUI first, then activate the selected function using a physical button in the hand panel. The operator cannot therefore activate the function unintentionally.

Sometimes a function is not enabled immediately the operator presses a button to activate it. For example, it might take some time to generate the required hydraulic pressure. In such cases, this approach makes it possible to avoid double presses of the button while activation is commencing. For example, suppose the operator activates some function by pressing a button and the hydraulic pump starts to build up pressure. Once there is enough pressure for the required function, the operator can start using it by pressing another button. If there is no natural feedback from the initiation process and the operator must wait for the process to complete, you should provide ARTIFICIAL FEEDBACK (page 317) or use BEACON (page 336) to draw their attention when the operation is complete.

The operator should be guided to the button required to confirm an action. For example, once the operator has selected a function from the touch screen, the corresponding physical button on the hand panel could start to blink, to indicate that the operator is expected to press it. For further details, see BEACON and ARTIFICIAL FEEDBACK. Whatever guidance method is selected, it should be uniform for all actions (see COMMON LOOK-AND-FEEL, page 344).

Another advantage of double confirmation is that, if pressing the same button twice activates a function, malfunction of a button could accidentally activate the function. For example, a paper clip lost inside a keyboard and short-circuiting a key could generate key presses. This could cause accidental activation of some function. If two different keys are used, the probability of this is lessened. Another case is accidental activation of a function through inadvertent key presses. For example, an operator might be resting their arm on a hand panel and hit a button by accident. As long as confirmation of initiation of the corresponding function is required, no harm is done unless the second button is also pressed.

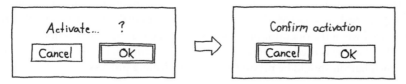

Figure 16.5: TWO-STEP CONFIRMATION can also be implemented as a pop-up

If this pattern is applied to other non-real-time functionality such as initiating diagnostics, the second activation (confirmation) might be implemented as a pop-up dialog. In this case, the default action of a pop-up should be *not* to activate the functionality (see Figure 16.5). In many user interfaces, a UI element such as a button is activated by pressing 'enter'. If confirmation is shown as a pop-up with the button confirming the action selected by default, an operator accidentally pressing the 'enter' key twice could activate the corresponding function. In this case the operator might not be able to read what the pop-up says before it disappears. Therefore the default option in the pop-up should be to cancel the function, or alternatively none of the pop-up's buttons should have focus initially.

This approach must not be used for functionalities that require immediate action, such as an emergency kill switch, which must be implemented with hardware (Machinery Directive, 2006). This approach should also be applied only to functions that take a long time to initiate or execute. Sometimes legislation may require a two-step confirmation for initiation. For example, in a hand-held powered tool, it might be mandatory to use two-step confirmation to ensure that the user has both hands on the tool when it is started. However, you should avoid overusing this approach, as it may decrease usability.

Unintentional activations or deactivations of a function can be avoided by two-step activation. The second step of this two-step activation uses different buttons or keys for user input than the first step. This ensures that the user is making a conscious choice when activating the function.

The user is informed about what they are about to do, so the function will not execute without their noticing it. Unintentional activation is avoided.

Designing a good user experience may be harder; double confirmation can be annoying, as it requires more intervention from an operator. You must design the interface carefully without overusing this pattern, as it decreases the fluency of work.

A two-step confirmation approach cannot be used for an emergency kill switch or similar functions, as in these cases response times have hard real-time requirements.

In a mining drill rig, the operator needs to activate drilling mode from the user interface when starting the drilling process, by pressing a corresponding button next to the screen. After drilling mode is selected, the button that activates drilling starts to blink. Drilling is only started when the operator presses this button, ensuring that it is not started unintentionally. Blinking is used to attract the operator's attention, to give feedback and to indicate which button should be pressed to start the drilling process.

16.4   Upright is OK *

…there is a machine CONTROL SYSTEM (page 96) with a HUMAN–MACHINE INTERFACE (page 313). The user interface is used to monitor several processes that are running simultaneously. These processes typically have measurable quantities, such as the RPM of a motor, that the operator should take into account when controlling the process, and which should stay stable during the process. Under normal operating conditions the operator is not concerned about the actual values of the quantities, but should be able to see at a glance that everything is functioning correctly. However, when something anomalous happens, the operator should be able to notice it and react quickly. NOTIFICATIONS (page 156) could be used to inform the operator about exceptional situations if the control system detects them. However, not all anomalous situations may be identified by the system, and so cannot be notified to the operator.

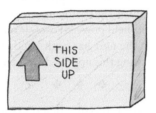

An operator is usually not interested in the details of the machine's status, but just needs a quick overview that everything is functioning normally.

There is a multitude of measured processes, and the operator must be able to see at a glance that everything is functioning normally. In this way, the operator does not need to concentrate on looking at gauges, but can focus on the work at hand.

In some countries it cannot be assumed that an operator can read or understand the (possibly foreign) language used in a graphical user interface. Reading also takes more time than a visual overview, and in fast-moving environments there might not be time to read exact information; the operator just needs to have a quick overview of the machine's status.

Interpretation of colors as indicators of danger may vary in different cultures. Red cannot always be assumed to denote an exceptional situation.

Traditional gauges are familiar to most users. In many cases the exact value of their measured variable is not interesting, but its magnitude is. For example, in a car it might not be a good idea to show RPM as a number, as this is harder to interpret than a traditional gauge that points to the RPM's approximate magnitude.

Therefore:

Use traditional gauges in the interface, even if the UI is implemented with graphical components. Use these gauges such that their needles are pointing upwards when their measured values are in their normal range. This makes it easy to get an overview that everything is functioning normally.

Figure 16.6: In a normal situation all gauges have their needles pointing upwards. Additional information about the measured quantities can be provided when necessary.

The gauge needles give essential information with a quick glance (see Figure 16.6). If the needle is pointing upwards, everything is functioning normally, and it is easy to spot when anything is out of normal working limits. No action is needed if all gauges point upwards. Any gauge needle that is pointing to the left is below normal operating level, and any needle that points right indicates that a value is running above normal conditions and may need attention. In some cultures, interpretation of needle positions (left and right) might differ. Needles should not be able to go full circle, as it might then be hard to interpret whether their value is within normal operating range.

An additional value can show the actual value of the measured quantity digitally. This can be ignored during normal operation, but it may help to see how quickly the variable is changing. For example, a driver may decide how quickly oil pressure is dropping and whether there is time to drive for repair, or whether immediate shut-down is necessary.

Even if an operator cannot read, it is easy to understand that everything is OK if a gauge needle is pointing upwards. Once a needle shifts from an upright position, the operator can call someone or carry out other remedial actions such as shutting down the machine. Colors are not needed to indicate that something is wrong, as NOTIFICATIONS (page 156) can show fault information. However, if the operator cannot read, information provided by NOTIFICATIONS may be useless, so it is good to have a visual way to show when something is going wrong. Colors are not very good for this, as different cultures may interpret them differently. In addition, an operator might be color-blind, so might find it hard or impossible to distinguish different colors.

An operator does not need to focus on gauges in normal situations, as a glance can indicate that everything is functioning normally. This enables the operator to focus on productive work. If there is an anomaly, it can be detected easily and the operator can start further investigation.

People who cannot read can use the machine safely, as they know that everything is OK when gauge needles are pointing upwards.

Traditional gauges are familiar to many people and are easy to read. It is easy to see the magnitude of the quantity just by a quick look. Accurate values would require an operator to interpret what the value means before taking action, slowing their response time. When using a traditional gauge, the operator does not need to interpret the meaning of a value, but can see the proportion of the quantity visually. It is easier to see that a needle is pointing to the middle than to interpret the meaning of a value. For example, 50 liters of diesel in the tank might not tell the operator much, but a needle in the middle of the scale shows immediately that half the diesel has been consumed.

It might be hard to present all monitored processes as traditional gauges. Sometimes the data produced by the process might be too complicated to present in this way. There may also be limited space on the display, preventing all gauges from fitting on one display at the same time.

This pattern can only be applied to consumables such as fuel to some extent. In a fuel level indicator the rightmost position is optimal and the leftmost the worst. In this case the semantics of the gauge is different from other gauges such as RPM.

❖ ❖ ❖

A mining drill rig's engine RPM, drill speed and oil pressure are shown as gauges in the user interface when in drilling mode. The operator focuses on boom position and drill penetration speed while drilling. Once in a while they glance at the gauges. As all gauge needles are in the upright position, the operator knows that the machine is functioning normally. Each gauge also indicates its normal operating range, overlapping the upright position on both sides.

16.5 Task-Based UI *

There are several tasks with different requirements for the user interface. If a single user interface view is used to cover all these diverse requirements, it results in low usability. On the other hand, several UI views are confusing if the current UI view does not correspond to the task the operator is actually carrying out.

Therefore:

Design an operating mode for each task. Create a separate UI view for each task, and change the active view automatically when the operator changes the operating mode.

For the complete pattern, please see www.wiley.com/go/controlsystemspatterns.

16.6   Role-Based UI * *

Also known as Own UI for Each Role

...a distributed CONTROL SYSTEM (page 96) has a lot of information available that needs to be shown in a HUMAN–MACHINE INTERFACE (page 313). For example, the statuses of the control system's various processes are shown, as well as information about possible faults. There may be PARAMETERS (page 380) that should be adjusted only by trained maintenance personnel or by assembly personnel on the production line. An operator only needs a subset of this information to control the machine. On the other hand, maintenance personnel may not be interested in some information that is presented during normal use. The operator must be able to see all elements related to control of the machine, whereas maintenance personnel or assembly personnel need other information.

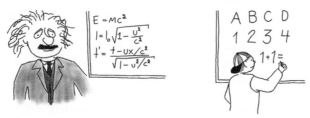

A machine's operator only needs such functionality in the UI that is required by their job description. All other functionality should be hidden from the UI to make the HMI more usable, and to prevent problems caused by unauthorized use of functionalities.

Users have different roles, for example machine operators and maintenance personnel. Each role should be made as easy and efficient as possible. Some functionalities should not be accessible by anyone without appropriate training.

The machine is easier to operate if only information that is relevant to the current user is shown on the display. For example, a drill rig operator needs information about the drilling process, but does not need to see the control system's error log. However, a maintenance engineer might find the error log useful when tracing a malfunction. As only relevant information is shown, a user can easily find information of interest from the display.

Maintenance or production-line personnel should have access to system parameters and be able to adjust them via the user interface. However, third-party maintenance personnel or the machine's operator should not have access to these parameters.

Access to specific information in the user interface should be limited. For example, an operator should not be able to do adjustments that could potentially damage the machine or void its warranty.

Therefore:

Create a separate user interface for each user group: operators, maintenance and production line personnel. Each group has different privileges that limit the available interface

views. User interface activation may require a dongle, password, or additional equipment.

First identify the different user roles. After identifying the roles, create a user interface for each role and decide how to change between roles. In many cases, the basic view – the operator's view – is the default and does not require any activation. Other roles' UIs can be activated typically via this UI, for example by entering a password. Some of the operator view's elements may then be hidden, and additional elements required by the activated role shown.

The operator's user interface can be the default when the machine is started. However, in some cases it might be advisable to identify the operator, for example if production information such as the number of trees cut is recorded separately for each operator. If OP-ERATOR PROFILE (page 340) is used, user identification can be used to restore operator-specific settings for the machine. The operator's user interface typically consists of the gauges, meters and controls required to operate the machine and to communicate with other systems, such as FLEET MANAGEMENT (page 372).

A maintenance engineer's user interface is activated separately, typically from the operator user interface, by entering a password. Other means of activation are possible, for example a dongle or external equipment attached to the machine. Once the user is identified, the UI corresponding to their job description is shown. This may mean that additional features are shown in navigation menus, or a completely different UI is shown. System parameters can be accessed and modified from the maintenance UI. The maintenance UI may provide more diagnostic information, for example fault logs. If the machine supports CONTROL SYSTEM OPTIONS (page 394), the different options can be enabled here. System self-diagnostics, FORCED INPUT VALUE (page 106) and SENSOR BYPASS (page 189) can only be used through the maintenance UI.

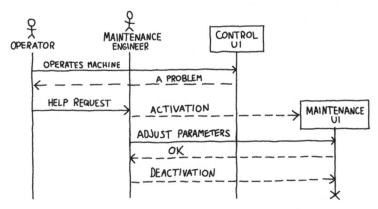

Figure 16.7: Sequence diagram showing adjustment of PARAMETERS when a ROLE-BASED UI is in use

Figure 16.7 shows a sequence diagram illustrating how an engineer can access a maintenance UI. The operator notices a malfunction and calls in the engineer to change a faulty part. The maintenance engineer activates the maintenance UI by entering a PIN code via the user interface. From this view the engineer can adjust parameters for new parts, for example sensor calibration values. Once the spare part is properly configured, the engineer deactivates the maintenance UI.

A user interface for production line personnel usually contains all the same functionalities as a maintenance UI, but offers extra functionality. Once a machine is assembled and tested in the factory, system parameters are set to factory default values and stored in persistent memory. The UI for production line personnel allows modification of these factory defaults, and setting parameters that cannot be changed afterwards. The UI may also allow modification of system configuration, such as the minimum set-up of controllers and sensors required to safely operate the system. Additionally, clean installation of control system software is usually only possible through this interface, although updates can typically be applied through a maintenance UI, or sometimes even through the operator's UI. The production line UI is usually enabled using equipment that is only available at the factory. A similar solution is also presented in LIMITED VIEW (Yoder & Barcalow, 2000).

The operator's user interface shows only information relevant for controlling the machine. The user experience is enhanced, as extraneous information is not shown. Similarly, other user roles have their own user interface designed specifically for their jobs.

The operator does not have access to information they are not supposed to modify: the same applies to maintenance personnel. This helps to control who can adjust the system and ensures that the operator cannot accidentally carry out operations that could void the machine's warranty.

New options can be enabled only by authorized maintenance personnel. Unauthorized 'cowboy' maintenance personnel cannot enable options or modify system parameters.

An additional identification mechanism for maintenance personnel and for the assembly team is required. This prevents use of third-party spare parts and service to some extent. On the other hand, the operator may not be able to carry out simple service tasks, as they cannot access the required information or GUI elements.

Additional functionalities required by roles other than the operator must be taken into account in the user interface design. It should be possible to integrate additional functionality into the user interface seamlessly, to make implementation fast. For example, user interface elements that are used by maintenance personnel to parameterize system parameters can be located in their own tab. Normally this tab is hidden, and only shown when the maintenance UI is activated. Implementing this kind of integration might require additional work and UI design.

A forest harvester has three different UIs. When the system is started, the operator user interface is shown as the default view. The operator can see the machine's status information from the UI and adjust parameters that affect work. For example, the operator can bind buttons to specific functions, for example sawing a log, feeding it and so on. The maintenance engineer has a dongle that they can plug into the machine. When the dongle is plugged in and identified, new user interface elements are shown in the UI. These allow the engineer to calibrate sensors or access system diagnostics. In the factory, the assembly team can connect a computer to the machine and install a new version of the control system software, or adjust factory default values for parameters.

16.7   Alternative Operating Station *

ALSO KNOWN AS ALTERNATIVE CONTROL METHOD

…in a CONTROL SYSTEM (page 96) with a HUMAN–MACHINE INTERFACE (page 313) the operator usually has an operating station with controls and a graphical user interface for operating the machine. The machine itself can be large, and the view from the operating station can be obstructed by pillars or moving parts such as a boom. Sometimes the operator needs a better view to carry out tasks properly. For example, if an implement is connected to the back of the machine and the cabin does not have a rear window or mirrors, the operator must get out of the cabin to get a better view.

The operator may not be able to observe all the details of a task from the default operating station, or the view from the operating station may blocked by parts of the machine itself.

Operating a machine might require precision control from the machine and the operator. For example, a drilling boom must be positioned carefully so that the hole will be drilled with the correct direction and orientation. It might be hard to see the exact angle and position of the boom from the cabin, and be easier to control the operation from a closer position. For example, when lowering the tail-gate of a truck, it may be hard to see from the cabin that there is nothing in the way. It is easier to move to the tail-gate and observe the situation from there.

Although modern work machine's cabins are designed for high visibility and comfort, obstacles such as supporting pillars might still block the operator's view. This is troublesome when the machine is operated where there is not much space and the machine cannot be positioned for better visibility. For example, in underground mines there is rarely much room to drive a machine to a different position to get a better view (see Figure 16.8, which shows a Sandvik underground mining drill rig type DL331-5C). The operator could leave the cabin and observe the situation, then come back to the cabin and steer the machine, and if necessary repeat this process. However, this would make the operator's work inefficient and physically exhausting if carried out over a long period.

Figure 16.8: The space in which a machine can maneuver in mines is always limited
Reproduced by permission of Sandvik Mining and Construction Oy

Safety is an important aspect. A machine operator needs to be sure that there is no-one in the working area of the machine, or will enter the area while the machine is working. In some cases, it is hard to see from the cabin that no-one is at risk if pillars or other machine parts create blind spots. Additionally, the machine operator should not be able to put themselves at risk by entering the working area when work is in progress.

Sometimes the operator also does mechanical work and their hands might get dirty, or they might be wearing workwear that prevents the use of sophisticated control equipment such as touch displays. This can limit the range of controls that the operator can use. Repeatedly washing their hands or removing protective gloves would soon become annoying.

Therefore:

Add an alternative operating station that provides the minimal controls for carrying out the task, located where the operator can better observe the work.

Design the alternative operating station so that it has only those controls required by the specific task for which it is intended, to make carrying out the task efficient through absence of extraneous controls. The controls can be specifically tailored for the task to be carried out using the alternative operating station, to allow the operator to wear suitable clothing while using this operating station. For example, the alternative operating station's controls could be operated while wearing gloves, while the main operating station would require removing gloves. When the alternative operating station is tailored for a specific task, it will probably not be used as a primary user interface, but only for the task for which it is intended. This gives some freedom in user interface design, for example when considering on which screen notifications should be shown.

You should also consider whether an additional display is needed for presenting information about the system's state, for example by using HMI NOTIFICATIONS (page 340). You also need to decide whether the alternative controls are fixed to the machine or whether they would be better located on a separate piece of equipment. The latter option could be implemented with a wireless controller, or by using a controller that can be attached with a separate cable when needed.

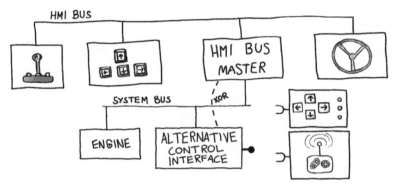

Figure 16.9: An HMI bus master selects which control method is in use

As Figure 16.9 shows, an HMI bus master can bridge between the HMI bus and the system bus to deliver data and control signals to the engine, transmission and so on via the system bus. An alternative operating station typically has its own controller on the system bus. When the alternative operating system is activated, the HMI bus master often stops bridging the control commands from the HMI bus. A handy way to implement this is to use OPERATING MODES (page 175). When the system is in a mode in which the alternative operating station is active, the HMI bus master must ignore command messages coming from the HMI bus. This excludes emergency stop, which should always remain functional, as mandated in the European Union's Machinery Directive, Section 1.2. (Machinery Directive, 2006). Transferring control to the alternative operating station must not cause unintentional movements. For example, another operator pressing a button while switchover is being carried out should not cause any action.

In some cases the HMI bus master could offer the interface for the alternative operating station. In this case the alternative control interface in Figure 16.9 is omitted and the HMI bus master offers the interface. The HMI bus master then selects which input is used: HMI bus commands, or commands coming from the alternative control interface. In this case it is also important that only one control method can be active at any one time.

The control method should be selected from the HMI in the cabin operating station, for example using a switch or button. This allows the control system to decide which safety mechanisms to use, for example to limit boom movements according to the control method in use. A different set of safety precautions should be applied when using the alternative operating station, for example to limit which functionalities can be used, as the operator is likely to be closer to implements when using the alternative operating station. If a forest harvester is operated using a remote control, for example, there is a risk that the operator could be struck by a log while maneuvering the boom.

If OPERATING MODES (page 175) has been applied, it is easy to implement a separate alternative operating mode for the machine. The control system's nodes can change their state to the corresponding mode when the alternative operating station in use. For example, nodes on the HMI bus can stop sending control messages when they enter an alternative control mode. The behavior of nodes on the system bus can change: for example, actuators can limit the range of movements. The operator activates the alternative control mode from a cabin switch, after which the alternative operating station can be used. Deactivation of the control method is carried out in a similar way. Other strategies for changing mode can also be used; for example, the control method could be switched to normal mode automatically when a cable connecting an alternative control unit is unplugged.

Alternative operating stations are typically used in mobile work machines. However, they can also be used in process automation systems: a monitoring station physically far from the actual process may make it impossible to see and control the process from the monitoring station, for example in fault situations. It might then be advisable to locate simple manual controls where they might be needed to sort out problems. In a paper mill, for example, paper flow might get interrupted by a fault, and the paper have to be re-fed through the machine manually before restarting automated flow. Controls for manual feed located next to the places where the paper might break can help with this. Emergency switches can also be placed at an alternative operating station. Figure 16.10 shows an example.

This pattern's solution is not suitable for implementing an emergency stop. This is usually implemented at the hardware level to make sure it remains functional even if there is a software fault. Hardware implementation also gives a faster response. Remember that the emergency stop should be functional from any operating station, even if an alternative operating station is in use.

VARIABLE MANAGER (page 201) helps to share data with an alternative operating station. If you use HMI NOTIFICATIONS (page 340) to show the operator information about events, you need to decide on which display the notification is shown – on the one that the operator is using is best. If an alternative operating station does not have its own display to inform the operator, you can apply BEACON (page 336) to draw the operator's attention to the machine's primary controls if a noteworthy event occurs.

If the alternative operating station is not fixed to the machine, the connection to the control unit may be lost. For example, a battery in a portable control unit can become depleted, or the cable connecting a hand-held unit may break. There should be some mechanism to detect these situations and allow the machine to enter a SAFE STATE (page 179) if connection to the alternative operating station is lost. This is also pointed out in

Figure 16.10: Even though a process is controlled from a control room, there may be a need for alternative operating stations placed nearer the machine itself

Reproduced by permission of Metso Automation Oy

Section 3.3.3 of the European Machinery Directive (Machinery Directive, 2006). If the control connection is lost, a separate emergency stop mechanism should be used to stop the machine. For example, if a system has a remote control unit, it can use a CAN module to send commands to the CAN bus. In addition, the control unit can employ a safety certified relay connected to the emergency stop circuit to check whether its connection is ok. This relay then stops the machine when necessary, avoiding emergency stop messages having to be delivered through the control unit's interface.

HEARTBEAT (page 120) can be used to monitor the health of the connection between the HMI bus master and an alternative operating station. When using a remote control unit as an alternative operating station, you should deploy security measures to prevent the system being controlled from an unauthorized operating station.

An operator can control the machine or work implement near the place where the actual work is done. The operator now has a good view of the work, as obstacles no longer block the view. However, the system should be designed so that the need to leave the main operating station is minimized.

An ALTERNATIVE OPERATING STATION also functions as a redundant station that can be used if the main operating station has broken down. This makes some control possible in fault situations, for example to move a forester's boom into the transportation position.

If mobile or hand-held, the connection to an alternative operating station may be more unreliable, and must be monitored. This may need additional resources, for example bus bandwidth, CPU time and so on.

As the operator is controlling the machine closer to the work, this potentially puts the operator in danger. Care must be taken while operating the machine from the alternative operating station to ensure that the operator cannot be endangered by moving parts.

An ALTERNATIVE OPERATING STATION increases development costs and might increase the cost of a machine. You can consider providing it as part of CONTROL SYSTEM OPTIONS (page 394), as the customer may not be willing to pay for extra control options.

Boreholes for ground-source heat pumps are usually drilled using low-end drilling machines. The machine may need to be driven to a drill site, perhaps even through narrow garden paths. The operator must avoid destroying vegetation or damaging garden sheds or other obstacles. The machine's cabin has poor visibility to the front, as its boom blocks the view, so driving the machine from the cabin makes damage more likely. The operator is therefore provided with a remote control unit. The operator enables the remote control unit by pressing a button on the HMI in the cabin. After this mode change, the machine responds to steering commands only from the remote control unit. The operator can now walk in front of the drilling machine and steer it with a better view. On the machine's software architecture level, the HMI bus master is set to an alternative control mode in which it ignores all the control messages coming from the HMI bus. The alternative operating station (the remote control) is used to receive control commands, which are then sent to the boom and drilling controllers. The HMI bus master sends status information to the remote control unit using the remote controller's interface, instead of bridging this information to the HMI bus and to actual devices.

16.8   Multiple Operating Stations *

The working environment may be such that several implements, such as booms, could be in use at the same time. Substantial cognitive stress may be imposed on the operator if they need to focus on controlling multiple implements simultaneously.

Therefore:

Add a new operating station for each task to be performed with the machine. These operating stations can be identical or specialized for a specific task. This allows several operators to control the machine at the same time.

For the complete pattern, please see www.wiley.com/go/controlsystemspatterns.

16.9 Appliance-Provided UI *

A multitude of optional equipment can be attached to a work machine. The optional equipment requires its own controls and displays, but there is not enough space in the cabin for all the additional controls.

Therefore:

Create a virtual terminal capable of presenting a user interface to the equipment's own HMI. Create a format for user interface templates and a way to present them on the virtual terminal. Each optional item of equipment then provides its own implementation of its user interface using the specified format. When equipment is attached to the machine, it sends its user interface presentation to the virtual terminal. The equipment can present information on the user interface view and receive control commands from the machine.

For the complete pattern, please see www.wiley.com/go/controlsystemspatterns.

16.10 Beacon *

...there is a CONTROL SYSTEM (page 96) with a HUMAN–MACHINE INTERFACE (page 313). The machine's operator must concentrate on the task at hand: cutting trees, driving the machine and so on. HMI NOTIFICATIONS (page 340) might have been applied to inform the operator about events occurring in the system. However, the operator may not notice notifications if their attention is focused elsewhere. Some events require immediate attention to avoid severe consequences. In a car, for example, if the control system notices a problem in the engine, the driver needs to stop the car immediately to prevent engine damage. Some HMI NOTIFICATIONS may merely be the machine informing the operator that a requested service is ready to be used. Sometimes these services need to be used immediately or the service becomes unavailable, for example ordering an elevator to a specific floor. If the passenger misses the elevator's arrival at their floor they must wait for the next one.

When a machine operator is concentrating on a task, important events might occur that need their attention. Such events should not pass unnoticed.

An operator should react to the events as soon as possible, otherwise their consequences may escalate. For example, if oil pressure drops too low, the operator must stop the machine immediately to avoid engine damage.

Some functions, such as self-diagnostics or serving an elevator call, might take time. The user or operator probably wants to do something else while the control system is executing the requested function. Once the function is complete, the control system should notify the user by drawing their attention to the event. If the user or operator misses the event, they might be unable to use the service offered by the machine. In the case of an elevator, its control system can continue to serve other passengers, so the user has to call the elevator again and wait for its arrival.

Even if event information is presented as HMI NOTIFICATIONS, these might pass unnoticed if the operator is not watching the screen and so does not see the notification. For example, a forwarder used to carry felled logs might have a rotating chair in its cabin. When the operator is loading logs onto a wagon they are facing backwards, and so are unable to see the screen displaying the notification.

There might be a need to show alarms or notifications on different displays, according to the direction in which the operator is facing or the operating station in use. In some systems there might be more than one display, placed so that they are visible only from a specific direction. In this case an operator might not notice warning lights if focused on some other display in the HMI. If the machine allows operations without an operator in the cabin, the operator might not notice a notification while monitoring the machine's operation away from the cabin. There should therefore be a way to draw the operator's attention when something noteworthy happens.

If feedback on control actions is always given using only one sense, for example vision, the operator may get used to this and lose attention due to sensory adaptation (Coon & Mitterrer, 2010). Multimodal feedback should be used, as using multiple senses is more powerful than using only one.

Therefore:

Draw an operator's attention to an important event by using sound effects, blinking or otherwise attention-getting indicator lights.

When an operator is using a machine they are focused on the task at hand. For example, a forest harvester operator felling logs is concentrating on controlling the boom and monitoring the log-feeding process. If the hydraulic pressure drops significantly this requires the operator's immediate attention. An HMI should therefore use blinking dashboard lights or alarms to catch the operator's attention when something important happens. Figure 16.11 illustrates this approach. In the figure, process A that the operator is monitoring also affects another process X. Once process X requires the operator's attention, some beacon such as an alarm sound is used to draw their attention to it.

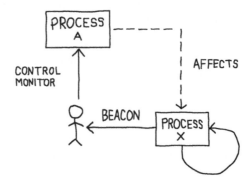

Figure 16.11: A beacon can be used to draw the operator's attention to a process that they are not actively monitoring

Flashing or blinking lights are the traditional way to catch an operator's attention. Sometimes user interface elements such as pop-ups or text fields can also blink to catch attention. Sounds are typically used for events requiring immediate action, because the event may compromise the safety of the operator, machine or its environment. Sounds also tend to be better than lights at catching an operator's attention. However, an operator may need to wear hearing protectors if the environment is noisy. In this case, whether sounds can be used to catch the operator's attention should be tested in practice, and possibly a combination of lights and sound effects used instead. Blinking lights are good for events that do not cause immediate danger if the operator does not react to them instantly. A third option for catching an operator's attention is to use touch and vibration. This can be used to give feedback through a joystick, for example if an operator tries to move some tool outside its normal limits. In some extreme cases the physical properties of a machine part are used to catch the operator's attention. For example, a bearing may contain a special material that starts to smell once the bearing is worn and needs to be replaced.

You should not use flashing lights that are too bright, as this may dazzle the operator, especially when working in dark environments such as mines or at night. However, an indicator light should still stand out from the normal control panel lights so that it catches the attention. The color of an indicator light is important, as a badly chosen color or too bright a light could affect an operator's night vision. The same indicator light color should be used for beacons indicating events of similar severity. For example, red could always be used to draw an operator's attention to faults. The control panel layout should be made such that indicators can be noticed easily. Blinking or flashing lights should be placed such that the light is at least within the operator's peripheral vision. The operator's mental model needs to be taken into account to help them associate the indicator light with the action causing the event: controls for functionality and their corresponding beacons should be placed near each other. However there are some exceptions to this. For example, if a machine allows operation without an operator in its cabin, the control system should still be able to draw the operator's attention to the machine. In this case lights need to be visible from outside the machine, or a buzzer that can be heard throughout the operating environment should be used.

If sounds are used to catch the operator's attention the direction of the sound is important. Humans tend to focus their attention on the source of a sound, so it should be near a display that is showing information about the event that has occurred. This draws the operator's focus to the information required to handle the situation. If the operator is not facing the display, for example felling logs and sitting backwards in the cabin, sound from the direction of the display is a good way to draw attention to the relevant display. In extreme circumstances the sound can be used to guide the operator to perform the correct control manoeuvre. In this case the volume of the sound needs to be loud enough for the operator to carry out the correct control manoeuvre instinctively.

The duration of an alarm sound is critical. It should not be too short, to give the operator time to recognize the sound's origin. This allows the operator time to find the source and see the notification on the screen. The corresponding notification should also be displayed for long enough. However the sound should not be too long, as this may stress the operator while taking remedial actions. If there is a continuous alarm while an operator is trying to work out its cause, this will distract the operator and may lead to rushed and consequently incorrect decisions.

If the machine has MULTIPLE OPERATING STATIONS (page 335) or an ALTERNATIVE OPERATING STATION (page 330), each station should probably have its own way to draw the operator's attention. In the case of multiple operating stations, you need to decide whether only the station causing the event should use BEACON to draw the operator's attention, or whether the event is such that all operators need to be alerted, and show information about it on all displays.

AUDIBLE ALARM (Yoder & Barcalow, 2000) describes similar solutions in a different domain, in which an audible alarm is used to catch developers' attention when a problem emerges in a system.

An operator is more likely to notice notifications, alarms, faults and so on, as their attention is drawn to the event using lights, sound or both. Sound can be used for events that require quicker operator response.

If beacons are overused, or used for events that are not important, the operator may get used to them or try to circumvent them. For example, if a buzzer sounds when the seat belt is not fastened and the operator's job requires them to leave the cabin often, the operator may try to fool the seat-belt sensor. If beacons are overused, operators may get used to them and no longer notice them.

If the operator trusts the beacon to draw their attention when something noteworthy happens and the beacon for some reason doesn't work, it may cause a situation in which the safety of the operator, machine or its environment is compromised. This might happen if the beacon is used rarely. It is therefore essential during maintenance to ensure that beacons are functioning, or use SELF-TESTS (page 106) to check this.

If a fault causes more than one notification, sound or error message it may create a stressful situation for the operator. You should therefore design the system such that a beacon indicates the root cause of a problem.

The use case of a beacon is to draw an operator's attention to something. However, in extreme environments it can be used in 'vice versa' fashion. A fighter jet's pilot wears headphones to monitor radio traffic and alarms. In a combat situation, an enemy may fire a missile at the jet. The jet's control system detects this and alerts the pilot by playing a loud sound from the direction in which the missile is approaching. Using this 3D sound image, the pilot instinctively performs the correct evasive manoeuvre to dodge the missile.

16.11 HMI Notifications

Many events occur in a system. Only some of the events are interesting to the operator. Some of these events may require an operator decision in order to continue operation.

Therefore:

Define a subset of notifications that are of interest to the operator. Create a HMI notification service to display these on the user interface. Some notifications are decisions that the system cannot resolve autonomously, and which therefore require an operator decision. The service should therefore be able to send a control command to the bus when the operator responds to a specific notification.

For the complete pattern, please see www.wiley.com/go/controlsystemspatterns.

16.12 Operator Profile * *

ALSO KNOWN AS FAVORITES

…there is a CONTROL SYSTEM (page 96) having a HUMAN–MACHINE INTERFACE (page 313) with a GUI where various settings can be adjusted using PARAMETERS (page 380). For example, the HMI might have configurable buttons whose function can be defined by the operator. The angle of the rear-view mirrors or the operator's chair might also be adjustable via the HMI. Each operator may have different preferences for these settings, as people's physical qualities differ. Operators may also have different user interface settings for the CONTROL SYSTEM, such as button layouts, language selections, graphical element positions and so on. For example, when controlling a boom with a joystick, different operators may prefer different control responses from the system. In addition, some operators may prefer to carry out some maneuvers by themselves rather than trust the automated sequences that the control system offers. A large work site may need multiple machines and operators just use the first available machine when starting a shift. There is then no dedicated machine for each operator, and any specific machine will not have an operator's preferred settings, just the previous operator's.

Personalized settings can increase the productivity and comfort of a machine operator. However, as multiple similar machines might be available but there is no dedicated machine for each operator, settings are likely to be changed by other operators. The operator's user experience and productivity can be increased if inconvenient readjustment of a machine's GUI settings and controls can be avoided when putting the machine to use.

Operators have different physical qualities: some are taller, some shorter, some weigh more, some are left-handed and so on. Because of this variation, an operator needs to be able to adjust settings such as the direction of mirrors, handedness of controls, font sizes on the screen and so on to use a machine safely and efficiently. Some settings might just be to fulfil different habits when using the machine. This adjustment process should be automated, otherwise the operator must readjust the settings each time they take over a fresh machine.

When there is a change of shift and a new operator starts using a machine, the adjustments should be carried out quickly to minimize the time required for switchover. This allows a new operator to start using the machine immediately without interruptions that impact productivity.

The HUMAN–MACHINE INTERFACE should support the operator's mental model of how to use the machine. To be able to work efficiently and comfortably the operator should be able to configure buttons and bind functions to them as desired. On a change of shift, however, a new operator starting to use the machine with the previous operator's settings will have to accommodate to them. This could create surprising or dangerous situations in the case of control bindings or joystick sensitivity. All machines should therefore work in a uniform way from the operator's viewpoint.

Adjusting settings each time a new operator takes over a machine is burdensome, so operators are not likely to do so. This can cause an operator to use a machine with suboptimal settings, such as mirrors adjusted wrongly. This may lead to dangerous situations and decrease the productivity of the operator. Thus settings should be automatically applied. When operating a machine is comfortable, the operator's productivity is likely to increase.

Different operators may have different preferences for what is shown on the graphical user interface. Extraneous user interface elements or information should be hidden in the user interface automatically. For example, guidance texts can be hidden by experienced operators, whereas a new operator might wish to have them displayed them in the UI.

Therefore:

Create a package containing all an operator's settings in a single easily transferable file. This file may be located on the control PC's hard disk, or it might be saved on removable media such as a memory stick. Provide an easy way to transfer the settings between machines and apply them.

An operator needs personalized settings to make the machine more usable. This personalized information forms the profile for the operator. Setting that make up a profile may include:

- Driving parameters, for example joystick sensitivity
- Parameters of specific functionalities, for example the response times of controls
- The list of installed third-party software with their corresponding settings
- GUI settings such as gauge types (digital or analog)
- Localization issues such as language selection, units

All personalized information should be packaged in a single easily portable file. This can be located on the control PC's hard disk or on removable media such as a memory stick. Once the operator has adjusted all machine settings to their liking, they can save the settings as their personal default. Typically this is carried out by selecting some sort of 'save settings' button in the GUI. At this point the settings might be stored locally on the machine and to removable media such as a memory stick. This allows the memory stick to function as an automatic backup of the operator's settings, and be loaded to another machine. There may be a dedicated slot in the dashboard to allow the operator to plug in their own memory stick when boarding the machine. Once the memory stick containing the operator profile is plugged in, the system should detect this automatically and ask the operator if the settings should be used. It may also make a local copy of the settings. If the memory stick is also used as an ignition key, the system can use the stored settings automatically when the machine is started. The control system should load the operator's settings and make adjustments accordingly. Listing 16.1 shows an excerpt from an example operator profile file.

```
Left_mirror_x_angle = -5;
Left_mirror_y_angle = 10;
…
UI_Selected_locale = fi_FI;
UI_show_tab_bar = true;
UI_background_color = black;
UI_text_color = grey;
```

Listing 16.1: Excerpt from an example operator profile file

In a control system with REMOTE ACCESS (page 361), the operator profile may even be fetched via wireless, for example using a 3G cellphone link. In this case there should be some kind of user authentication. Such authentication could be carried out using a personal USB stick-based ignition key, a more traditional username-password combination, or by PIN code authentication.

The operator profile may be stored for example as an XML or key-value pair file. If there is a need to update the operator profile file between control system software versions, it should also contain version information. The control system should handle the operator profile's conversion to a new software version. CONFIGURATION PARAMETER VERSIONS (page 385) addresses this problem.

CONTENT PERSONALIZATION introduces a similar mechanism for adaptive web applications (Koch & Rossi, 2002). When implementing an operator profile pattern, you need to remember that machines may differ, and that all settings are not applicable for all machines. If there are CONTROL SYSTEM OPTIONS (page 394) for example, some machines may have functionalities that other machines do not share, so that these features' settings are not applicable to all machines. Sometimes a machine might have spare parts that differ and have different properties. For example, the settings of an adjustable mirror may cause a different mirror angle when using a spare part. This might make the setting useless, or make some kind of compensation necessary. This makes development more complex.

The system is easier to use, as an operator can import their own settings from a memory stick or other media when taking over a machine. This means that the operator does not need to adjust settings each time they start to work with a new machine. Changing operator during a change of shift becomes smoother, as no extra time is needed to configure the machine for the new operator: the control system does that automatically.

An operator can transfer their personal settings from one machine to another using a memory stick or USB ignition key, or by authenticating to the machine and downloading the settings using REMOTE ACCESS.

An operator's settings are not lost if another operator or maintenance engineer makes changes to a machine's settings.

The machine's settings are stored in two places: in the control system's storage and on removable media. This creates an automatic backup mechanism for an operator's settings.

As the operator's settings are restored when the operator takes over a machine, button configurations are familiar to the operator and unexpected use situations can be avoided. For example, if a button was previously configured to have some other function than the new operator is used to, the function of the button will not surprise the operator, as their own configuration will be applied automatically.

Training and support becomes more challenging, as an operator might have personalized the GUI. If the operator asks for help from support personnel, they cannot know whether the operator has made adjustments to button configurations. When training and providing remote support, support personnel can no longer assume that a specific function is bound to a specific button.

Preserving operator profile settings between different control system versions might be hard as new features are developed and new GUI elements introduced. Additionally, compatibility with new hardware spare parts needs to be guaranteed.

A modern down-the-hole drill rig such as the Sandvik DI-550 shown in Figure 16.12 uses a memory stick as an ignition key: each operator in the quarry where the machine is used has their own personal key. When an operator plugs in their memory stick for the first time, the control system stores the rig's default settings on it. If the operator adjusts the cabin chair or changes the boom control parameters, the rig's control system saves these settings to the memory stick automatically. For example, if the operator selects a Cartesian model for boom control and binds functions to specific hand panel buttons, these settings are saved to their operator profile and memory stick. A quarry might employ multiple similar machines that operators have to use in their daily routine, not necessarily the same machine on every shift. When an operator uses their memory stick on a different machine, the control system restores their profile from the memory stick automatically. The rig then uses the operator's preferred settings, and its control system carries out the required adjustments automatically.

16.13 Common Look-and-Feel *

…there is a CONTROL SYSTEM (page 96) with a HUMAN–MACHINE INTERFACE (page 313). The machine has only a limited display for its HMI, as cabin space is limited. The cabin also has only a limited area from which the operator can see the screen or reach the controls. As the machine has many controls and indicators, all of them cannot fit in a single user interface view. Multiple user interface views are therefore needed to present the information to the operator. These views can also have different layouts. The operator may need to switch between views and remember readings and other information from

Figure 16.12: A modern down-the-hole drill rig offers a comfortable
and adjustable cabin for its operator

Reproduced by permission of Sandvik Mining and Construction

one view to another. Different views increase the operator's cognitive stress, as there is more to learn and remember when switching between them.

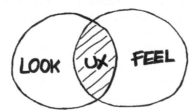

If the principles of user interface views an operator learns cannot be used throughout all views, operating the machine becomes inefficient and inconvenient.

Good usability increases efficiency, as an operator intuitively knows how to use the HUMAN–MACHINE INTERFACE. An operator should not have to wonder whether different terms, situations, or actions mean the same thing (Nielsen, 1994a). Inconsistent layouts and behavior in the HUMAN–MACHINE INTERFACE is likely to confuse the operator and decrease operability of the machine.

For rapid adoption of the CONTROL SYSTEM coupled with a short learning period, cognitive stress should be minimized. If an operator uses various models and types of machine from the same vendor, it should also be possible to use the principles learned on one machine in all of them.

The HUMAN–MACHINE INTERFACE should be attractive and offer the operator a great user experience, as this increases customer satisfaction and loyalty (Harvey, 2013). If a customer has a good experience with a product, they are more likely to buy a new machine from the same vendor. A good user experience is also likely to make operators recommend the machine to colleagues.

To create a brand, the machine manufacturer needs to make different machines and CONTROL SYSTEMS instantly recognizable. The machine operator and other stakeholders should be able to recognize that a machine is made by a specific manufacturer. This makes a brand better known.

Therefore:

Use unified layouts and coloring in all user interface views and notifications. UI elements and functionalities should be presented in the same way independent of the view.

Document interface guidelines that contain the rules for user interface design. The guideline document helps developers to design individual user interface views consistently. If there are multiple machines in a product family, the same guidelines must be applied to all machines, where appropriate, so that the layout and behavior of the user interface elements – a common look-and-feel – is the same in all machines. Optimally the same guidelines should be applied to all machines from the manufacturer wherever possible. This allows operators to learn how to use a new machine quickly if they already have experience with another machine in the same product family.

A user interface guideline document often describes visual design rules, including use of typefaces, icons, symbols and colors. Additionally, it can describe the layout styles for user interface views, and how elements should be placed within a view. In many cases, the guideline document also specifies how user input and output mechanisms work. If advanced UI elements with tactile feedback are used, the guidelines can advise what kind of behavior is recommended. For example, the guideline document could describe the simulated inertia draggable user interface elements should have, or how scrolling views should behave when they reach the limits of scrolling.

Base the user interface guideline document on a usability study carried out on machine operators – that is, the end users for the machine. For more information on how to design and carry out usability studies, see for example Chapter 6 of *Usability Engineering* (Nielsen, 1994b). You might need to create multiple guideline documents for different user groups, for example operators, maintenance personnel and assembly personnel. If this is the case, conduct multiple usability studies.

Figure 16.13 shows an example of a user interface view layout guideline. At the top of the view is a meter area, while the lower area is reserved for view-specific information and functionality. The left side of the view is reserved for buttons to change the OPERATING MODES (page 175) of the machine. This side bar and the status area at the bottom are common to all views. The status area is a dedicated area where notifications can be shown to the operator. The remainder of the view area is divided into two halves: the top half is reserved for showing gauges and meters dedicated to the selected functionality. The lower area is reserved for all other functionality-specific controls and information. The company name and logo is placed at the lower left of the view.

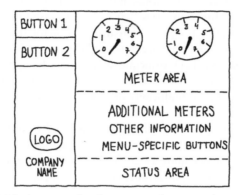

Figure 16.13: An example of a user interface view layout guideline

When designing a common look-and-feel, don't overdo it. If two functionalities are completely different, they really should be controlled in a unique way, and you should not try to unify them. Over-unifying control can result in inefficiency. In rare cases it can even be dangerous, for example if views are too similar and the operator cannot quickly distinguish the current functionality. However, you should still unify the use of colors, shapes, symbols and typefaces even if a common layout cannot be found.

The dynamic behavior of elements such as buttons, boxes and menus should function in a uniform way and be similarly located across user interface views. This is especially true for UI elements common to all views; for example, a 'back' button should appear in the same place in all views. If yellow is used for warning and red for error, for example, these colors should be used consistently across different screens, and these colors should not be used for other purposes. Similarly, if an exclamation mark is used to indicate an error, it should be used consistently in all screens where error information is shown.

This pattern is similar to VISUAL FRAMEWORK (Tidwell, 2011), although Tidwell's patterns are targeted at web designers.

COMMON LOOK-AND-FEEL makes the learning curve gentler. A machine operator can learn to use different control system views in a shorter time. If all machines from the same manufacturer have a HUMAN–MACHINE INTERFACE (page 313) that uses the same operating principles, the operator does not need to relearn the operating principles of each machine separately.

The pattern helps the operator to find functionalities that can be activated from the user interface. The functionalities appear in the same place in a layout independent of the view the operator is using. This makes the machine more operable and efficient, as the operator can find what they need with less effort.

COMMON LOOK-AND-FEEL makes machines from a specific manufacturer recognizable. Operators can know that a machine from a specific manufacturer can always be operated using the same principles.

Applying the pattern to colors and fonts in the user interface is straightforward. However, when applying it to functionalities that can be accessed through the GUI, it can sometimes be hard to find functionalities that are common for all user interface views. In addition, similar functionalities can have different behavior in different interface views.

The COMMON LOOK-AND-FEEL principle should only be applied to functionalities that really should be operated in the same way. If the approach is applied to all user interface elements regardless of their uniformity or lack of it, this may lead to inefficient control.

Creating comprehensive guidelines that can be applied to different products in the same product family can be a laborious and challenging task. In addition, conducting multiple usability studies may require a significant effort. Guideline documents also need to be updated from time to time when functionalities change.

COMMON LOOK-AND-FEEL is applied when designing the user interface of a forest harvester. The control system uses HMI NOTIFICATIONS (page 340) to show various NOTIFICATIONS (page 156) to the operator. COMMON LOOK-AND-FEEL is used to make these notifications uniform. All notify level notifications are styled with an exclamation mark on a green background, while warnings have an exclamation mark on a yellow background and fault notifications have a stop sign. This allows the operator to easily identify the types of HMI NOTIFICATIONS. The harvester also has different OPERATING MODES (page 175). Each of the modes has a corresponding user interface view. The operating mode and the corresponding UI view are selected by pressing a button next to the display. All these views have a similar layout. Meters are always shown in the top section of the view and textual information in the lower part. Various functionalities inherent to the operating mode are selected from a menu bar on the right of a view.

17

High-Level Services Patterns

'Information is just bits of data. Knowledge is putting them together. Wisdom is transcending them.'

Ram Dass

Nowadays a work machine seldom works alone – it is part of a larger ecosystem. Remote management systems require that a machine's control system can be accessed independently of the machine's physical location. As we discussed in *Openness for Third-Party Software* on page 60, it is common for at least part of a machine's software to be subcontracted, or even deployed, by companies other than the machine's manufacturer. All this requires support from the control system.

The sublanguage of high level services shown in Figure 17.1 is a collection of patterns adapting the control system to support various external systems. DIAGNOSTICS (page 350) collects information on the health of the system. Diagnostic information can be used to find out when a machine needs maintenance, so that proper maintenance can be planned in advance. BLACK BOX (page 355) refines this by storing important system events, so that it is possible to analyze the root cause of a failure afterwards even if the machine is in a non-working condition. THIRD-PARTY SANDBOX (page 355) provides an interface and tools for third-party application developers to implement extra functionality for the machine.

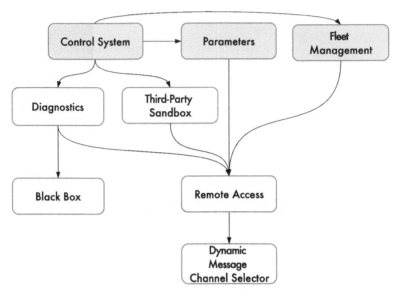

Figure 17.1: The sublanguage of patterns to provide high-level services such as accessing the control system remotely

Usually it is more efficient to access the information on the machine remotely than to transfer it using removable media such as memory sticks. REMOTE ACCESS (page 361) provides a solution for that. If several communication channels are available, REMOTE ACCESS can be further improved with DYNAMIC MESSAGE CHANNEL SELECTOR (page 365), which allows delivery of messages over the remote link using the optimal available channel. The pattern can also be used to limit traffic when only a costly communication channel is available.

17.1   Diagnostics *

...there is a CONTROL SYSTEM (page 96) that has hardware components that may malfunction or wear out. For this reason, the system requires maintenance. Spare parts and maintenance resources for the machine might be physically located far away from the machine. The machine may be in a location that is difficult to reach, and spare parts may not be immediately available at the nearest maintenance depot. In the worst case, maintenance personnel or even a developer with debugging tools may need to visit the machine, check out which parts are needed and revisit after the parts are available. Sometimes it may be time-consuming to find out which part needs to be replaced. All this wastes time, specialists to solve the problem may cost much more than local maintenance personnel, and the machine cannot be used while waiting for spares. To improve maintenance efficiency, information about which parts are wearing out should be known beforehand, so that preparations can be made and spare parts ordered in advance.

To avoid unplanned breaks in production, information on the health of the system is needed in order to plan proper maintenance.

Preventive maintenance is necessary to improve a machine's availability. This allows a machine to be called to a maintenance depot when it is not needed for work, so preventing disruptions to production. For example, a forest harvester could be maintained when it would need transportation from one stand to another in any case. Otherwise separate transportation from the stand to the maintenance depot and back to the stand again would be necessary, generating extra costs. In addition, if a replacement machine is needed, acquiring and transporting the machine to the work site needs to be planned in advance.

It is useful to know whether a machine can be serviced on site, or whether the machine must be transported to a maintenance depot. It is inefficient and time-consuming to send an engineer just to decide whether a replacement machine is needed. On the other hand, sending a replacement machine in vain is costly. Sometimes a machine might even be repaired without spare parts, for example by adjusting a proximity switch.

It is often possible to forecast the need for maintenance by monitoring specific properties of the process a machine is controlling, or the physical devices fitted to the machine. To achieve this, it is usually possible to add various sensors to measure the health of the machine. For example, the electrical conductivity of oil varies when the lubrication properties of the oil decreases as the machine used.

The behavior of various components during the lifecycle of a machine is not always known. A manufacturer's development team needs feedback, to deduce how a component wears out, or how its characteristics change when in use. This allows the machine's design to be changed for future models where necessary.

Usually it is better to change a component only when really required, not just to be on the safe side. Unnecessary maintenance wastes resources, causing extra cost, and is not environmentally friendly.

Therefore:

Add an on-board data collection component to the system, collecting information from sensors, messages from the bus and so on. In addition, create a diagnostic component to analyze this information and detect if a subsystem starts to operate poorly or erroneously. This analysis should be based on the known heuristics and value ranges. A deviation from these indicates the need for maintenance.

The data collection component should be attached to the machine so that it can collect the required information. If ONE TO MANY (page 131) has been applied, the diagnostic component is typically attached as a separate node and collects predefined message types. The data collection component often has a relatively small amount of processing power and storage space: the information collected is first stored to a small buffer, then transferred for analysis to a diagnostic component that is usually located off-board. This is implemented as a separate component, as it usually requires more processing power and storage space. If only limited storage space is available, the data collection component needs to transfer data for analysis more frequently. If this is not possible, for example if a connection is not available, data must be discarded or filtered. The design of the analysis component and its algorithms may require deep domain knowledge and dedicated experts, so it might be designed separately from the data-collection component. Based on the analysis it produces, the need for maintenance can be estimated, and maintenance scheduled when necessary.

The diagnostic data can be transferred to the analysis component using memory sticks or other removable media, but the update frequency could become long. If REMOTE ACCESS (page 361) has been applied, the data can be transferred more frequently, even in real time. DYNAMIC MESSAGE CHANNEL SELECTOR (page 365) should be used to limit the volume of transferred data, especially if a low-bandwidth communication channel such as GPRS or SMS is used. In some cases it may even be necessary to filter the data on board, so that only refined or relevant results are transmitted. However, if the diagnostic data is not complete, it will decrease its usefulness for further analysis.

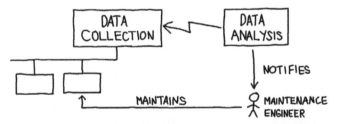

Figure 17.2: A data collection component attached to the bus uses REMOTE ACCESS to send collected data to be analyzed by the diagnostic component

Figure 17.2 illustrates the components and their relationship. The data collection node collects information from the bus and sends it for analysis via remote access. Based on this analysis, any component that is about to malfunction due to wear can be identified.

The analysis component running on the manufacturer's server can order maintenance for the machine automatically. The maintenance engineer gets information about the device that is about to malfunction, and can replace it with a spare part.

The diagnostic data gathered from the machine depends on the system and requirements set for diagnostics. There may be restrictions on what data it is possible to measure and collect. Typical data values include variables indicating the state of the engine and transmission, such as temperature values, oil pressures, fuel consumption and oil quality. COUNTERS (page 221) indicating variables such as hours of use, and production information can also be collected.

The data collection component usually collects the existing information from the system. Sometimes additional sensors may be installed to measure system health, as the sensors originally fitted may only be designed to support the machine's main functionality. If the system has a VARIABLE MANAGER (page 201) data can be retrieved from it. Collecting the data from a centralized VARIABLE MANAGER is an easy solution if the system has more than one message bus. However, in many cases this requires a software interface to the VARIABLE MANAGER instead of just listening to messages on the bus. Log files generated by NOTIFICATION LOGGING (page 166) can also be used as a source of diagnostic information. As a last resort the data collection component can use query-based communication to get its information. In this case you need to ensure that the diagnostic component does not disrupt other messaging on the bus.

For security and stability reasons, the diagnostic component is typically isolated from the rest of the system so that it can only read data values from the system, not control it. This prevents any malfunction in the diagnostic component from jeopardizing the system's functionality. This kind of isolation makes it easier to support different machine types with the same diagnostic component, especially if the machines use the same bus protocol. VARIABLE GUARD (page 208) and THIRD-PARTY SANDBOX (page 355) may help to implement the isolation of the diagnostic component. Information security must also be ensured. This usually means that diagnostic data should be encrypted to prevent unauthorized access.

To limit the volume of diagnostic information transmitted and/or to achieve better response time for diagnostics, an on-board diagnostic component can carry out basic analysis. If some data values are outside predefined limits, the diagnostic component can warn maintenance personnel or FLEET MANAGEMENT (page 372) about any potential risk of failure. HUMAN–MACHINE INTERFACE (page 313), BEACON (page 336) or HMI NOTIFICATIONS (page 340) can also be applied to display the result of on-board analysis to the operator. For example, if a machine's fuel consumption is higher than usual, the diagnostic component can warn the operator by means of a warning light, as excessive consumption may indicate a leak in the fuel system or the need for engine maintenance. The warning can also be transmitted for off-board analysis, so that maintenance personnel are aware of the problem.

One of the best-known implementation of DIAGNOSTICS in the computer domain is *self-monitoring, analysis and reporting technology*, or SMART (Stephen, 2006, Section 4.19). This monitors various reliability related values from computer hard disks, and reports possible deviations from predefined limits. SMART makes it possible to decrease the possibility of malfunction caused by mechanical wear and gradual degradation of storage surfaces. There are also existing standards for reporting collected diagnostic data, such as OBD-II (Birnbaum & Truglia, 2000), which is backed up by several SAE and ISO standards (SAE, 2003; ISO, 2011c). OPC unified architecture (Mahnke et al, 2009) can also be used to access a VARIABLE MANAGER, allowing maintenance personnel to collect information from the machine remotely without a separate data collection component.

Figure 17.3 shows a screenshot from a real off-board diagnostic application. The data for the application is collected by a dedicated component installed in machines. The diagnostic application allows machine usage to be visualized and production targets monitored.

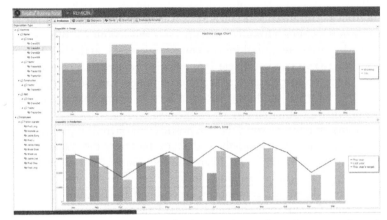

Figure 17.3: A diagnostics application displaying charts of production and machine use
Reproduced by permission of Remion Oy

❖   ❖   ❖

Diagnostic information can be used to find out when a machine needs maintenance. If wear can be identified, maintenance breaks can be planned in advance and replacement parts ordered. The frequency of transmission of diagnostics data should be high enough to allow maintenance personnel enough time to prepare.

Separate diagnostic and analysis components can profile how operators use a machine. This allows training to be focused on operators' areas of difficulty. If data is collected from multiple operators, analysis can show the most efficient way to operate the machine. Note that this kind of operator monitoring needs to be accepted by end users.

By inspecting the diagnostic data for a specific part just before it malfunctions and comparing it with diagnostic data originating from other machines, it is possible to extract fault patterns. A specific change in diagnostic data values might take place just before the part malfunctions. These fault patterns may help to deduce the rules and value ranges for the analysis component.

Malfunction in a data collection component or a diagnostic component may prevent a machine starting, even though they are optional for the machine's functionality. START-UP NEGOTIATION (page 297) can be resolve this.

A waste-shredding machine has a local DIAGNOSTICS application that gathers data such as engine oil pressure, the shredder's joint valve behavior, bearing temperatures, hydraulic pressure and information on machine use. The system has REMOTE ACCESS (page 361) on a cabin PC, which is connected to the manufacturer's network using a 3G GSM connection. The machine connects to the manufacturer's diagnostics server once a day if the connection is available, and sends its daily diagnostics data to the server for analysis. The analysis is carried out on the manufacturer's server, as this has more processing power and storage space than the machine's on-board cabin PC. The analysis compares the diagnostics data from the machine with that from other similar machines. If the analysis application detects differences in behavior patterns, or differences that exceed predefined thresholds, the analysis application calls the machine in for preventive maintenance.

17.2 Black Box

When a system malfunctions, the malfunction may prevent access to diagnostic data. It should be still possible to analyze the root cause of a failure afterwards even when the system is in a non-working condition.

Therefore:

Add a black box component to the system which keeps records of selected system events. The black box stores these events for a specific time for later inspection. Data in the black box component can be accessed with a separate tool even when the system is not functional.

For the complete pattern, please see www.wiley.com/go/controlsystemspatterns.

17.3 Third-Party Sandbox *

…there is a CONTROL SYSTEM (page 96) that implements SEPARATE REAL-TIME (page 237). The machine manufacturer has core competence in developing machine control systems, as they have a long history in hardware-based machine control. However, machine control alone is not enough, as more and more of the work needs to be automated with software. The amount of software in their machines is therefore growing. The manufacturer may not have enough resources to develop all the required software by themselves, or their development teams may lack competence in end-user application development. Some development therefore needs to be delegated to third parties. However, there are several types of third-party vendors, ranging from trusted subcontractors to open source communities and anything in between.

End users require more features from the system, so the manufacturer has to outsource development of applications that are not within their core competence. These applications cannot always be trusted not to compromise the operation of the system, either inadvertently or on purpose.

It is sometimes necessary for a machine control system provider to allow third-party vendors to implement their own software on the machine's control system. There can be many reasons why a machine control system provider should offer interfaces for other companies to access the system as a platform. Eklund and Bosch describe many benefits that companies can gain by opening up their systems (Eklund & Bosch, 2012). Openness may result in better software, as the control system manufacturer can focus on their core business and let third parties implement optional software that is more their domain of expertise. The open platform can then create a software ecosystem in which different companies with common interests can benefit from each other.

New innovations and ideas are more likely the more people develop their own software using the platform. As machine control systems have long lifecycles, opening up the control system as a platform may help the system adapt to unforeseen requirements and use cases. System lifecycle can be extended if an open system allows other parties to support the platform after the manufacturer has ceased to do so.

However, the level of trust varies between different types of third parties. Trust is usually defined by legally binding contracts between the machine manufacturer and the third parties. In some cases legal issues can be taken into account with licensing policies. Liability is a big aspect in trust, and affects how much control of a machine's functionality and data a third party should wield.

More revenue can be generated if time-to-market is shorter, as machines can be sold sooner. The core system is usually developed first, then more sophisticated features are integrated with this core later. Time-to-market itself is shortened if third parties can develop their features without being bound to the machine's release date. If features can be added at any time without extensive integration effort, is has a positive effect on applications that are not within the core competence of the machine manufacturer. In the case of a navigation application, for example, the machine development team does not need extensive knowledge of map formats, location deduction and so on if they just can provide GPS location information for third-party developers implementing a navigation application.

Openness must not override safety and security. Third-party software should not interfere with machine control-level applications or any other operator-level applications. Thus they are typically not mission-critical. Safety certifications usually demand that the core system, which is a safety-critical system, should be isolated to guarantee that no other software can interfere with it. Not all third parties can be trusted, so their applications should not affect safety or security in any way. Additionally, as the quality of a third-party application may be unknown, a crashing applications should not be able to affect the system in any way. Third-party software should not open or be able to use existing attack vectors for machine control-level systems. Safety assessment will be cheaper and easier if third-party software does not need to be taken into account. For example, a map application showing a work site is not safety-critical, so should not need to be safety certified.

Data security is also crucial. Third-party software cannot be allowed to access any sensitive information, such as an operator's personal information, business-critical data and so on, and may not alter control information in the core system, as this might compromise overall system safety. Even if the third party is trusted, it is easier to validate the core system's safety conformance if it can be guaranteed that third-party software cannot alter any safety related data or send unauthorized commands, even accidentally.

An in-house development team or trusted third-party developer can make programming errors or misinterpretations of the specifications. These human errors can cause applications to act in unpredictable ways. Even trusted applications therefore need additional safeguarding, as programming errors, hacking and physical malfunctions may cause applications to crash, send garbled information, or alter data they should not touch. In addition, in-house development may be carried out by several teams, so may also benefit from a degree of openness: clear responsibilities and good interfaces will help the teams to develop their subsystems independently.

Therefore:

Provide an interface and tools for third-party application developers. Third-party applications can use the machine's services only through this interface, so will not interfere with the machine's own applications. The interface provides common ways to access data and services.

Decide which kinds of third-party contractors and software providers the control system should support. Consider in-house development teams and open source developers as well as different companies. This defines the potential participants in your software ecosystem (Messerschmitt & Szyperski, 2003). Based on this, define an interface that provides all services these parties are allowed to use. The interface should include all services that won't compromise system security and safety. Examples of these functions could be drawing new windows on the HUMAN–MACHINE INTERFACE (page 313) screen, communication with other systems via REMOTE ACCESS (page 361) and reading specific sensor information from the system, for example GPS location data. The interface is usually implemented as a library or a Microsoft .NET component. After the implementation, the interface is documented and delivered to interested parties. The interface usually provides access only via the operator level provided by SEPARATE REAL-TIME (page 237), as this prevents third party applications from interfering with real-time control of the system. Even on the operator level, memory partitioning and other methods are usually needed, to prevent unauthorized access to other applications' memory space via memory pointers.

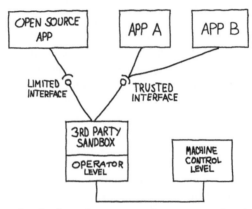

Figure 17.4: Different levels of trust between applications manifest themselves as multiple interfaces for third-party applications

If more control of services and data is desired, different groups of third-party vendors can be provided with different interfaces. For example, Figure 17.4 shows a limited interface for open source developers and a trusted interface for business partners. The interface provides access to the third-party sandbox, which in turn uses services from the operator level. The type of the interface used may depend on the level of trust, licenses and contracts. Another way to handle access issues is to provide an access control method to the interface. There are many ways to implement access control, for example by using credentials. Access control has to take safety and security issues into account, but it may also include new means to support the chosen business model. For example, in some cases an open source interface can be licensed so that it allows only development of further open source applications. In this way, any closed source application developer must either pay for a commercial license, or release the source code of the new application for anyone to use.

If third-party applications need to access multiple data sources, it is more convenient to give them access to variables in a VARIABLE MANAGER (page 201), but it is then advisable to limit access with a VARIABLE GUARD (page 208) that determines which of the third parties can read or write specific variables.

One way to implement a THIRD-PARTY SANDBOX is to provide a VIRTUAL RUNTIME ENVIRONMENT (page 272) that is specifically customized to provide services that a typical third-party application needs. If the manufacturer has a product line, the same VRE may be used for multiple similar products, increasing the number of viable targets for the third-party application. Sometimes a ready-made VRE can be used to provide the platform, cutting down development costs. The platform should also include some means for access control (see for example VARIABLE GUARD).

Updating a third-party sandbox can lead to a situation in which an installed third-party application ceases to work and also needs to be updated. A 'dependency hell' can be avoided by assigning version numbers to both third-party applications and the third-party sandbox itself. The third-party sandbox can then keep track of incompatibilities and prevent the use of deprecated applications. See (Donald, 2003) for more examples.

You must also consider the distribution and installation of third-party software. A memory stick can be used if distribution is limited and REMOTE ACCESS (page 361) is not available. If third-party applications are freely updateable, some means to enable this is also needed. If the machine has REMOTE ACCESS, this can be used to update the applications. In this case, a distribution infrastructure needs to be provided by the machine manufacturer. If the applications are run on a product platform, not all machines may have the same services available. Some safeguarding mechanism for installation is therefore needed to prevent unusable software being installed on the control system.

If in-house development teams have clearly isolated responsibilities and some of them are developing higher-level applications, these can also be installed on a third-party sandbox too. A FLEET MANAGEMENT (page 372) application is a typical example.

In some cases a third-party application may need sensor information that is not provided by the machine control system. The third-party provider may then choose to bundle any required sensors with the software; when the application is installed into the third-party sandbox, these additional sensors are also added to the system. There should therefore be a way to install such additional hardware on the operator's PC.

This pattern is similar to EXECUTION DOMAIN (Schumacher et al, 2005). EXECUTION DOMAIN creates an environment in which accessible resources and their access privileges are defined. THIRD-PARTY SANDBOX can be implemented in the automation domain with interoperability frameworks, for example, OPC/UA (Mahnke et al, 2009). OPC/UA provides several services for third-party integration, such as a standard interface to process data and access control methods. One practical way to implement a third-party sandbox with a real-time operating system is to use a technology called `jail` (jail, 2014), or some other operating system level virtualization mechanism such as `chroot` (chroot, 2014). These technologies allow a designer to allocate separate resources for user space applications so that they cannot interfere with each other.

After THIRD-PARTY SANDBOX has been applied, the control system can be extended with new applications developed by third parties. This makes the system extendable, and the development lead time can be shorter, as applications may be introduced after the product is launched. Third-party applications cannot inadvertently crash the whole system, and malicious attacks are more difficult, as the system does not provide direct access to sensitive functions and data. A deliberate attack cannot directly affect real-time control, and thus system safety is not easily compromised.

Opening up the platform makes new business models possible. This is seen most notably in cellphone platforms, where application stores allow the cellphone manufacturer to focus on the platform while most of the applications are provided by third parties.

The machine manufacturer must take other developers into account if they have to make modifications to the interface. It is not always clear what services must be included in the interface, so development is usually an incremental and iterative process. The manufacturer provides an initial version of the interface and third parties develop their software using this interface. If the interface does not provide all the required services, the third parties give feedback to the machine manufacturer, which in turn makes improvements to the interface. However, over-rapid changes to the interface may cause third-party applications to stop working. This will cause problems with end users, and may damage the reputation and business of the third-party vendor, and even cause them to abandon their support for the platform. Some kind of a roadmap is therefore required for future changes to the interface, so that third-party vendors have time to accommodate their code to a new version of the interface. Evolution of the interface is usually unavoidable as the platform develops and acquires new features: new features should also be available to third parties.

However, third-party software can still disturb the execution of the control system, for example by calling library functions excessively and loading the PC running the sandbox. Memory and storage space should not be depleted by a third-party application hogging them, for example due to a programming error. Some sort of access control with shortcut filtering is therefore needed. Memory resources and storage space can have quotas on them to prevent excessive allocation. The simplest way to implement these limitations could be, for example, to use the highest priorities (see CONCURRENT EXECUTION, page 229) for control applications and to reserve a static area in memory for them (see STATIC RESOURCE ALLOCATION, page 247). A WATCHDOG (page 101) can kill stalled third-party applications, and an EARLY WARNING (page 169) mechanism can warn an application if it consumes too many resources, or kill it if it does not release hoarded resources.

A railway company wishes to display up-to-date information about departures and arrivals. To make this information more accurate, they need speed and location information from the train control system. For liability reasons, the railway company should not have access to the train control system's services other than reading speed and position information, to allow it to display notifications such as announcements about delays, further connections, advertisements and so on. The train manufacturer therefore provides a library on the trains themselves, to give access to these services from the train's control system. The library is customized to provide only methods for performing the permitted operations. The track control software can call functions like `getVelocity()` via the third-party interface on the train. The interface then uses a VARIABLE MANAGER (page

201) and a CAN bus to fetch the actual data from the drive controller in the control system, and returns the value. The track control software can then use this information to calculate a train's estimated time of arrival.

17.4 Remote Access *

...there is a distributed CONTROL SYSTEM (page 96) that uses a HIGH-LEVEL PROTOCOL (page 137) communication between nodes. However, not all the data the nodes need to access may be stored locally to the machine. In the case of a drilling machine, for example, drilling plans are produced remotely in a mine control room, and the FLEET MANAGEMENT (page 372) application on the machine needs to access them. In addition, some third-party applications may need to access remote data sources: for example, navigation software may need to download map updates. Similarly, remote systems such as a remote diagnostics application might need to access data on the machine.

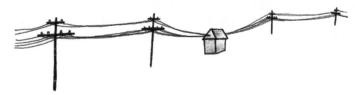

Services using the data that the machine collects are not necessarily on board the machine. Similarly, on-board applications may need data that is produced in a different location.

In a ubiquitous environment applications inherently need to communicate with other applications and systems. Applications need to exchange information in order to produce additional value. For example, if an application is meant to display drilling plans, it is not useful if it cannot access the newest plans created by an explosives expert in the mine control room. Work-planning applications are typically located remotely, so applications on board the machine need a way to retrieve data from them. On the other hand, applications at remote locations may use the data produced by the machine to produce additional value.

DIAGNOSTICS (page 350) data should be transferred to a maintenance system, so that maintenance personnel can analyze the data before a scheduled maintenance break and find out whether spare parts need to be ordered. However, the machine might be far away from the maintenance depot, so it is not feasible to transfer DIAGNOSTICS data with a memory stick or some other physical media. If there are many machines, or some of them are located remotely, data gathering is hard.

The machine's controllers may have limited processing power, making detailed on-board analysis of DIAGNOSTICS data impossible. A central repository can also store data relating to a longer period than could be stored on the machine, as the machine typically has limited storage space.

The control system software is likely to be updated during the lifecycle of the machine (see UPDATEABLE SOFTWARE, page 301). A new software version could offer higher productivity or improved features. However, updating each machine separately would be too laborious for maintenance personnel. If the update packages are delivered to the customers on memory sticks or other media, they might feel that support quality is low, as the machines are not updated by the manufacturer. Furthermore, the customer might have multiple machines, and it would be too laborious for them to distribute the updates.

If production plans change, a machine operator needs to be informed about changes as soon as possible, to avoid working on tasks that are no longer necessary. On the other hand, a production planning system or FLEET MANAGEMENT (page 372) might need to know about tasks carried out already, such as the cubic meters of wood sawn. If a machine breaks down, information about completed work could help a FLEET MANAGEMENT system to reallocate tasks to other machines. This kind of real-time planning and reporting needs frequent update cycles to work plans.

Sometimes the environment in which the machine is used is such that it would be more comfortable or safer for the operator to control the machine remotely. For example, explosive ordnance disposal is safer if done remotely.

Therefore:

Add an on-board remote connection gateway that enables communication between the machine and a remote party. The remote connection gateway transforms the messaging scheme used on the machine to suit local and remote parties' needs, and employs authentication.

In the simplest case a remote connection gateway is a node attached to the bus, bridging traffic to and from a remote location. For example, the gateway node reads CAN messages that are targeted to the node and sends the data to a remote location using TCP/IP. Incoming messages are converted to CAN messages and sent to the bus (Figure 17.5). COTS solutions exist for implementing this kind of remote connection gateway for many bus technologies. The remote connection can be seen as a special case of message bus and ONE TO MANY (page 131) communication.

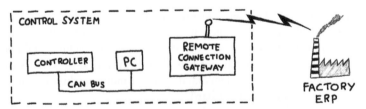

Figure 17.5: A remote connection gateway connected directly to a CAN bus

If SEPARATE REAL-TIME (page 237) has been applied, the system will be divided into a real-time machine control level and a non-real-time operator level. The operator level is typically implemented with a PC. If this is the case, the remote connection gateway has its natural location on this PC, as its operating system will offer ready-made facilities, such as a communication interface to manage communication with remote parties. If a communication interface exists, applications can use it in the operating system's normal way. As the remote connection gateway is located on the operator level, it cannot interfere with real-time machine control.

You should decide whether the machine's control system, when connected to remote parties, should act only as a client, or whether it needs to support incoming connections as well and act as a server. If this is the case, a service to take care of incoming connections is needed. Typically this server is deployed on the PC. This means that the server is also located on the operator level, and so also cannot interfere with real-time machine control. Sometimes this server can be an in-house application listening to a specific TCP/IP port, or sometimes a ready-made implementation such as Nginx (Nginx, 2013), lighttpd (Lighttpd, 2013) or even Apache web server (Apache, 2013). However, even in this case an application is needed to produce web pages from the data produced by the machine. If a file server is needed, you could use Cerberus (Cerberus, 2013) for example. A more useful out-of-the-box solution would be to use OPC/UA (Mahnke et al, 2009). This would allow direct access to process data through the server, and as OPC/UA is a standard, it would ensure compatibility with other systems. Ready-made open source implementations of OPC/UA servers are available, for example Open-OPC-UA-server (Opcua4j, 2013). Alternatively you could use DDS (OMG, 2007) to access process data on the machine.

A server creates an attack vector for hackers, so you should consider its deployment carefully: the server's software might have vulnerabilities that could be used to gain access to the machine. In addition, adding a server makes the machine vulnerable to DoS (denial of service) attacks, making it unavailable to its intended users. One common method of DoS attack is to saturate the target server with external communication requests so that it cannot respond to legitimate traffic, or responds so slowly that it is rendered useless. You should make sure that proper measures are taken to ensure the security of the system. You should also consider whether communication needs to be encrypted to prevent eavesdropping. If so, you might want to use a virtual private network (Mason, 2002), for example IPSec (Kent & Atkinson, 1998), OpenVPN (OpenVPN, 2013), or Secure Shell (IETF, 2005) to make the connection secure.

The remote connection gateway can be used to transfer DIAGNOSTICS (page 350) data from the machine to the manufacturer or a maintenance depot. Data can be transferred automatically without requiring the machine operator to do anything. The remote party might be a cloud service with enough capacity to process data from many machines. If data is transferred to an environment with potentially unlimited processing capabilities, more thorough analysis can be carried out. As data from multiple machines is gathered centrally, data from different machines can be compared to detect patterns and malfunctions. For example, oil pressure readings can follow a specific pattern in normal use. If a machine does not conform with this pattern, it can indicate a malfunction that needs to be inspected more closely. Over a longer period, data from different malfunctions can be gathered, leading to recognition of which kinds of malfunction cause specific changes in patterns of normal machine behavior.

The properties of a communication channel between the machine and remote party may vary depending on availability. For example, some channels may be costly and the data volume should be limited. DYNAMIC MESSAGE CHANNEL SELECTOR (page 365) describes how to choose an optimal communication channel for each situation.

A connection to a remote party may not be open continuously, perhaps for cost reasons. Sometimes a connection can be opened by sending an SMS message to the machine to command the machine to 'call home'. This would allow a manufacturer's research and development department to open up a connection when necessary. The limitation in this approach is that the machine must be powered on to enable the required hardware.

If VARIABLE MANAGER (page 201) has been applied to share system-wide information as variables, REMOTE ACCESS can be used to share this information with a remote location. If the machine is working as a part of a fleet, REMOTE ACCESS is a key component in coordination between multiple work machines. In this case, a SYSTEM ADAPTER (page 378) may need to be used to ensure compatibility with other, possibly legacy, systems. M2M COMMUNICATION (page 377) introduces peer-to-peer communication between work machines: in this case REMOTE ACCESS is used to communicate with other machines.

When implementing remote access to a work machine, you must consider the implications for functional safety. A systematic approach exists to assessing whether a given technological solution for remote access to control systems implies an unacceptable risk by jeopardizing the system's safety integrity level (Jaatun et al, 2008).

As information on the machine can be accessed remotely, data gathering for preventive maintenance, production management and so on is faster, as data can be transferred more frequently. Additionally, data transfer becomes independent of the machine's location, as the machine does not have to be accessed physically.

Software updates (see UPDATEABLE SOFTWARE, page 301) for the control system can be delivered over the air. This enables faster delivery of updates and decreases the updating effort for the machine's owner, as the updates do not need to be delivered using removable media. There are two options for updating the software: pull or push. Regardless of which approach is selected, the updates should be installed only when the machine's operator or maintenance engineer want to do so. Updating system software requires putting a machine into an update mode (see OPERATING MODES, page 175). As the remote connection gateway is the only access point to the machine, only this component needs to be updated if vulnerabilities are discovered. On the other hand, when new vulnerabilities are discovered, the software needs to be updated more urgently, to avoid the consequences of a possible attack. So REMOTE ACCESS increases the required update frequency.

If the customer thinks that a machine is malfunctioning, maintenance personnel can open a remote connection to the machine and try to diagnose the problem without physically visiting the machine. This might reduce costs, as maintenance personnel do not need to travel to the machine's location. On the other hand, if the malfunction can be diagnosed remotely and the need to transport it for maintenance determined, it would reduce costs. Additionally, if the system has PARAMETERS (page 380), the remote connection can be used to adjust these, so calibrating on-board devices becomes easier if maintenance personnel do not need to visit the machine to make adjustments.

Production reports and work orders can be transferred more frequently. This makes FLEET MANAGEMENT (page 372) more flexible.

The possibility of REMOTE ACCESS creates risk of unauthorized access to a machines' information. This might be a reason why you might not want to implement remote machine control using this approach. Denial-of-service attacks could also slow down the node on which a server is running. A remote connection gateway requires processing power (especially in a case of a server), so it might decrease the performance of the operator-level node.

As remote communication is isolated in one module, it is easy to limit its use, as communication is only possible for trusted applications. A remote connection gateway also makes remote operation of a machine possible.

A company manufacturing excavators discovers a serious software bug in one of their control system versions. Unfortunately they don't have records of machines and which software version they have. However, REMOTE ACCESS has been applied, and the excavators' control system has a server that can be connected to the factory when the machine is powered. The manufacturer implements a client application that connects to the work machine and checks the software version. If a machine's control system has the faulty software version, the manufacturer can send the software update package to the machine owner so that they can update it.

17.5   Dynamic Message Channel Selector *

...there is a distributed CONTROL SYSTEM (page 96) to which REMOTE ACCESS (page 361) has been applied to allow remote access to a machine's resources. The machine can support multiple channels of communication, implemented with technologies such as wireless LAN, satellite telephone or GPRS. As such machines are often mobile, they can be located at work sites around the globe, and various environmental factors can interfere with communication. For example, if a forest harvester works in a stand situated in the wilderness, there are probably no nearby terrestrial base transceiver stations. If a remote connection is needed, GPRS data cannot therefore be used, and only a costly satellite phone connection may be available. On the other hand, when the harvester is at the factory perimeter or at a maintenance depot, a wireless LAN may be available for high bandwidth data transfer. In another example, a mining drill rig is normally situated underground, where wireless LAN availability varies depending on location, as rock often blocks the signal. The location of a machine and available communication channels affect the bandwidth, communication costs, transfer rate and other attributes and constraints of the communication channel. This makes design of the communication scheme hard, as there are multiple trade-offs depending on the environment.

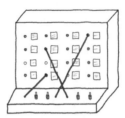

Multiple communication channels to access a machine may be available. Under differing circumstances some of these channels may not be available. The most suitable communication channel for the machine's circumstances should be used.

Many remote communication technologies are available, and it is relatively cheap to implement several of them on one machine. The implementation can be done with commercial off-the-shelf hardware, either as an additional chip on a controller or as a separate device that can be plugged directly into the message bus. It is reasonable to support multiple technologies, as wireless technologies have different kinds of communication properties and restrictions. For example, some of them provide communication that requires a dense base station infrastructure, but have high transfer rates, and so on.

The information stored on the machine has varying importance and urgency for a remote party. Information with high importance means that the remote party definitely needs to have access to the information. Conversely, low importance means that the remote party can manage without such information, which may only be needed for optimization purposes. A high urgency for information means that it is needed remotely soon after it is produced, otherwise it will be obsolete. Low urgency means that the information will be still relevant after a long period. The urgency factor is therefore a 'time-to-live' value for the information. For all information, communication quality should be optimized in terms of urgency and importance.

All information must be conveyed as messages that are sent via the chosen communication channel. As the information consists of varying amounts of data, some messages can be larger than others. However, the message size is not correlated with its importance or urgency. As a machine moves, the set of available messaging channels changes dynamically. There can be situations in which no communication channel is available.

Therefore:

Prioritize all communication channels based on their properties, such as cost. Add a selector component that changes the communication channel automatically if a higher priority channel is not available.

Organize communication channels according to the properties you want to optimize to achieve the best possible cost-effectiveness. Consider all communication properties, for example the security of the channel and possibility of eavesdropping, cost per sent amount of data, bandwidth, reliability, stability, latency and so on. Organize this information in a form of an array – Figure 17.6 shows an example. Some of the properties can be dynamic, as in the case of availability. The unit for a property can be, for example, an integer value from one to ten describing your view of the property for this channel. In Figure 17.6, for example, Iridium has low latency compared to wireless LAN, but a high cost per sent data unit. In addition to these channel properties, you should also take into account the nature of the data that has to be sent. Every item of data may have different requirements for urgency, importance, security and so on. The weighing of specific properties may also change depending on the operating context, such as the machine's OPERATING MODES (page 175). Now define a utility function that sets weights for different communication channel properties when given the required data properties and the operating context. The utility function uses these properties as a parameter.

	AVAILABLE	COST	STABILITY	SECURITY	LATENCY	BANDWIDTH	RELIABILITY
LAN	0	0	10	10	10	20	9
WLAN	0	1	5	5	7	10	3
3G	1	4	7	4	4	4	5
IRIDIUM	1	15	10	7	1	1	7

$$f_{UTILITY} \left(URGENCY, \; IMPORTANCE \; , \; PROPERTIES \, [\,] \right)$$

Figure 17.6: An example with four different wireless technologies with different properties

The utility function should return the most cost-effective channel for communication. It must take into account the availability of channels, as there might be no connectivity because of environmental factors such as terrain, location and so on. Figure 17.7 shows an example system. Wireless channels are organized so that a specific data item that has high urgency, importance, and reliability requirements will be sent using an Iridium satellite connection. The other option, 3G link, would be too slow and unreliable for this data.

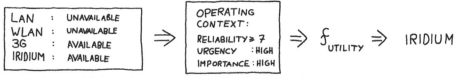

Figure 17.7: An example of a utility function, which takes the reliability, urgency and importance requirements for a specific data item as parameters

After the utility function is developed, add a selector component to the REMOTE ACCESS service that uses the utility function to select the best available channel. If there is no sensible option for sending the data, messages that have high importance but low urgency can be stored locally on machines, to be sent when the cost of transfer becomes feasible. High urgency data must be discarded if the delay before its transmission becomes too long. The component should also notify the application that tried to send the data if it is not currently possible.

One way to organize data transfer is to stop communication altogether for specific services if high bandwidth is not available. For example, if third-party software needs to be updated, it might be reasonable to block this if the communication channel is slow and/or too costly. Applications can be grouped, and communication allowed or denied for the whole group: Figure 17.8 shows an example of how different services could be grouped. When the availability of communication channels changes, the component selects the next suitable option from the list of available communication channels and adjusts the number of messages that can be sent through the selected channel.

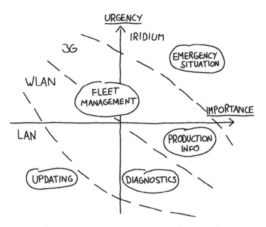

Figure 17.8: An example of weighting services according to their importance and urgency

The selector can also split non-urgent high-volume data into smaller chunks that are sent in the background if bandwidth needs to be allocated for more urgent messages. This takes more time, but the transfer does not hog all available bandwidth. In some cases, a digest of important information can be put into an SMS message for transmission to the remote party. Its delivery time becomes hard to predict, but at least some information gets through although there is no true wireless data connection available. A DYNAMIC MESSAGE CHANNEL SELECTOR can be used even if two similar channels are available, to maximize bandwidth. For example, if two radio channels are available to connect a machine to a remote party, they can both be used so long as this does not cost extra. This maximizes the volume of data that can be sent. If one channel becomes unavailable, data transfer is not disrupted, but just continues with lower bandwidth. The Internet Engineering Task Force has an experimental request for comments about multipath TCP extensions that could be useful here (Ford et al, 2013).

In some cases a DYNAMIC MESSAGE CHANNEL SELECTOR can also be used in local communications, for example if both Ethernet and CAN bus connections are available between two nodes. Ethernet might then be used to transfer large volumes of data such as diagnostics, while CAN is used for machine control. If the CAN bus is then severed, Ethernet could still be used to carry out some communication. However, this approach is limited to LIMP HOME (page 185) functionality, as there is no longer any determinism in communication. QOS CONTRACT (Loyall et al, 2002) presents a way to decouple quality of service measurement, adaptation and management from a functional application.

Messages over the remote link are delivered using the optimal channel. The solution may save communication costs, or provide the most reliable channel for data. It can also be used to make a machine switch to a more secure channel to prevent eavesdropping.

If several channels can be used in parallel, the availability of messaging and its bandwidth may be optimized. In some cases, messages can be sent in chunks, so that momentary unavailability of a channel won't disturb overall communication.

This solution makes the system more complex, and tracing bugs becomes harder. Selecting suboptimal parameters for the utility function may also cause unnecessary switching between two channels.

A rock crusher sends its production data to FLEET MANAGEMENT (page 372). Production information consists of rock type and volume, and diagnostics information about the velocity of the transfer conveyer belt, jaw speed and so on. The crusher's HUMAN–MACHINE INTERFACE (page 313) has a configurable setting that allows the operator to determine the properties of production information to be sent over a wireless link. The wireless link can be established as a wireless LAN or 3G GSM link, depending on the situation. The operator selects rock type and volume to have high importance but low urgency, because production information is essential for later stages of the processing chain, but it is possible to send the day's production information as a batch at the end of a shift. On the other hand, jaw and belt information has low importance but high urgency: such run-of-the-mill data is normally needed only to calculate the crusher's preventive maintenance needs, but if the belt or jaw jams the maintenance team has to be notified quickly.

As the crusher is usually located in an open-cast mine, it seldom has a wireless LAN connection with enough bandwidth to send all its data. If the crusher does not currently have wireless LAN access, it buffers production data for later transmission. Only critical messages, such machine incapacitation, are sent over the more costly 3G GSM link.

18

Fleet Management Patterns

*'I am one of billions. I am stardust gathered fleetingly into form. I will be ungathered.
The stardust will go on to be other things someday and I will be free.'*

Laini Taylor, 'Days of Blood & Starlight'

In a modern business environment the orchestration of multiple work machines is important, to optimize productivity and shorten lead times. 'Just-in-time' (JIT) delivery of a machine's output is crucial. JIT delivery means that no inventories of work build up, and later stages of a production chain do not need to wait for earlier stages to finish (Ohno, 1988; Liker, 2003). Fleet management and lean production is a large area and worthy of its own book. Here we present patterns that enable a single machine to be part of a fleet. The sublanguage of fleet management patterns shown in Figure 18.1 describes problems that arise when a machine must cooperate with other machines and the work is orchestrated by an external party such as an enterprise resource planning (ERP) system.

FLEET MANAGEMENT (page 372) shows how to minimize waiting times and inventories by enabling a machine to work as a part of a larger fleet. A fleet management application

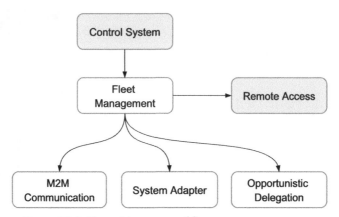

Figure 18.1: The sublanguage of fleet management patterns

is implemented on board, and is typically accessed via REMOTE ACCESS (page 361). M2M COMMUNICATION (page 377) refines this so that a machine can exchange information with other machines, to be able to collaborate autonomously. SYSTEM ADAPTER (page 378) describes how similar systems can be controlled in a unified way without knowing the details of machines in the fleet. Finally, OPPORTUNISTIC DELEGATION (page 377) shows how a task provided by a fleet management system can be delegated to a machine without first asking the machine's control system whether the machine can carry out the task. This approach is required when a fleet's status is constantly changing and it would take too long to ask whether the machine can do the task or not.

18.1   Fleet Management *

…a work machine has a CONTROL SYSTEM (page 96) that increases the machine's productivity. The efficiency of the production chain needs to be increased, so machines need to cooperate. For example, a forest harvester cuts trees and piles the logs on the stand in convenient places. If the forwarder does not know the exact location of these piles, the forwarder operator must search for them. This takes time and makes the work of the forwarder inefficient. Once the forwarder takes the logs to the nearest road, the logs wait there for further transportation. Long waiting times decrease the quality of the logs. Planning the work of later stages is difficult, as the time of completion of earlier stages is unknown. So production chain-level optimization is required as well as optimizing the efficiency of single machines with a CONTROL SYSTEM.

In a production chain work needs to be allocated to multiple machines. To minimize waiting times and inventories, the machines need to cooperate with those from other stages in the production chain.

Work plans and other information are typically managed by an enterprise resource planning (ERP) system. The ERP system is used to optimize workflow in the production chain. However, the ERP system also needs to access information from machines' control systems, but does not have the necessary facilities. In addition, the ERP system should be able to orchestrate the work itself.

Great business value gains are possible by optimizing the whole production chain, including multiple potentially different machines, rather than optimizing the work of a single machine. A single machine working more efficiently than others in the production chain, and thus producing inventory, is not an optimal situation in a lean business model. The control system therefore needs to be integrated with management of the whole production chain.

The production chain could be optimized based on information produced by a machine, such as location, maximum driving speed and so on. By using information produced by a machine, the ERP system can know production status and delivery times. This allows it to optimize work plans for the next stage in a production chain.

To carry out their tasks efficiently, a machine operator must have up-to-date work orders and plans. The control system should be able to display the work orders to allow convenient access to them. The operator also needs to provide production reports so that work progress can be monitored. Production reports should be produced by the control system automatically, so that the operator does not need to create them manually.

Therefore:

Implement a fleet management application and install it on board the machine. Within that application, create common interfaces and information models for all work machines, to manage them as a fleet. Production information, which conforms to the information model, can be transferred to and from the machine using the common interface. In this way the machine can exchange information and coordinate optimization of work with other machines via an ERP system.

The fleet management application can be implemented as a separate application in a THIRD-PARTY SANDBOX (page 355), or as an integral part of the CONTROL SYSTEM. This allows the fleet management application to access the required information about the machine, such as GPS location, current speed, fuel level and so on. A third option is to implement the fleet management application as a completely separate application having its own hardware. In this case, the fleet management application is likely not to be able to access the machine's information, as it is located for example on a cabin PC, but the fleet management system becomes easier to retrofit to legacy machines. In a retrofit solution, however, the machine operator often needs to input production information to the fleet management application manually.

The fleet management application has a connection to a fleet management server. The fleet management server can then have a further connection to an enterprise resource planning application (ERP). Alternatively, the fleet management server may be located in a control room. For example, in mines fleet management can be carried out manually by control room personnel, or automated by the system. The server is typically located in the vicinity of an ERP system to enable a fast connection. The fleet management server can receive work plan information from the ERP system and schedule planned tasks to machines in the production chain. The server sends information about these tasks to the machines, where the tasks are displayed for the operator using an on-board fleet management application.

Because a fleet may contain different kinds of machines from various manufacturers, common interfaces are needed to enable communication between the fleet management server and the machines. The interface can be designed using a suitable architecture approach such as REST (Fielding, 2001). In addition to common interfaces, a shared information model is needed. To establish that, you might use DOMAIN MODEL (Buschmann et al, 2007b), which describes a pattern approach for establishing a common language. DDS middleware also offers a mechanism to create a common information model (OMG, 2007). Figure 18.2 illustrates the basic principle of communication between the fleet management server and the machines. There are two interfaces: one for delivering work plans to the machines from the server, and a second interface for receiving production reports and machines' status information, such as location.

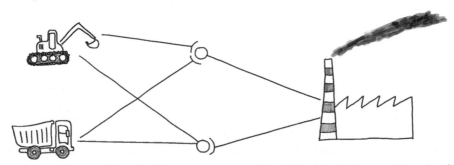

Figure 18.2: Two interfaces for fleet management: one to deliver work plans, and another for receiving production and status reports

Figure 18.3 illustrates an excerpt from a generic information model. In practice, the information model needs to be domain-specific. For example, in the forestry industry it

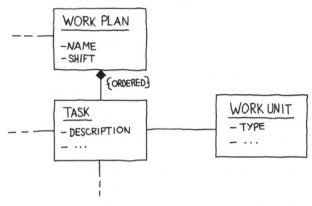

Figure 18.3: Excerpt from a generic information model

must contain information about tree types, length, quality and so on. The information model typically contains work plans, production reports and other necessary information to optimize the workflow. It may contain, for example, status information for machines, as well as environment-related concepts such as information about traffic jams or temporarily hazardous locations in the work environment.

The on-board fleet management application could be implemented using only removable media such as memory sticks, but it is very useful to apply REMOTE ACCESS (page 361) to enable remote access to machine data. Without this, the interaction between a machine and the fleet management server will be slow and cumbersome, as the information must be delivered manually. In some environments, such as a mine, where the fleet management server may be located close to machines, manual delivery of information at the beginning and the end of a shift is an option. However, in a typical work environment REMOTE ACCESS is a prerequisite for efficient fleet management.

Sometimes direct M2M COMMUNICATION (page 377) is required, so that machines can decide on the division of work or negotiate selected routes independently of the fleet management server. Communication with the fleet management server would be too slow to obtain such information, for example route negotiation. For more details on decentralized fleet management, see for example (Sørensen et al, 2010). If the fleet management system is used to give commands to machines, however, a different approach is required. In this case, the fleet management application's interface must be such that the fleet management server can communicate with machines independently of their type and capability. You might then consider applying SYSTEM ADAPTER (page 378) to implement such an interface. OPPORTUNISTIC DELEGATION (page 377) can be used to solve problems with dynamic work plan division amongst machines.

A machine operator can get up-to-date work plans from the fleet management application, and production reports can be sent automatically. In this way the whole fleet's work and the production chain can be optimized.

The fleet management system can provide value-adding services such as up-to-date production reports, GPS tracking of machines, and so on, as the information produced by machines can be used elsewhere.

To implement more sophisticated functionality, such as disabling a machine over the air, different interfaces are needed on top of fleet management. As machines in a fleet may offer different sets of functionalities, not all machines can implement all services. You might consider using SYSTEM ADAPTER to alleviate this problem.

To be effective, FLEET MANAGEMENT requires that all machines on a work site are connected to it. This requires the fleet management interface to be open and common for all fleet management applications. Designing such an interface might be challenging. Furthermore, retrofit solutions for legacy machines may be needed.

FLEET MANAGEMENT creates new error sources and attack vectors for a production chain. Erroneous or malicious work plans or production reports may cripple the whole chain. More focus on security issues is therefore needed in the control system and fleet management system design.

A harbor utilizes a fleet management system. The harbor's straddle carriers and container movers are part of the fleet management system. Ships bringing containers to the harbor are also handled as a part of the fleet, along with trucks transporting the containers from the harbor to customers. The harbor yard has a limited area, so only a limited number of containers can be stored in the harbor area ready for loading onto ships. Vice versa, containers from ships should spend only minimum time in the harbor yard. The harbor's ERP system needs to know the exact location of each container, so that it can optimize the ship loading process, or indicate where a container truck should go to pick up a specific container. The fleet management application's information model contains data on containers and work plans, for example the origin and destination of a container, schedules of ship movements, available straddle carriers and so on.

All straddle carriers in the harbor are equipped with a modern CONTROL SYSTEM (page 96) that has an integrated FLEET MANAGEMENT extension. Different straddle carriers have different capabilities, such as how high they can stack containers. The fleet management application gets the capability information from the control system and delivers an XML-formatted capabilities listing to the fleet management server. The work planner can use this information to allocate tasks to different machines. For example, if a container needs to be fetched from a high stack, this task would be assigned to a machine that is capable of it. The work plans are sent to the machine in XML format; once the container is moved, the completion of the task is notified to the harbor's ERP system via the fleet management server. Along with this notification, the new location of the container is delivered to the ERP system.

The fleet management system is used to optimize container traffic. Ship locations are tracked with GPS, and a geo-fencing feature is used. When a ship nears the harbor, the ERP system is notified that the ship is arriving with a given number of containers. The destinations and schedules of the containers are transferred to the ERP system. The effort and time required to unload the ship can be estimated accurately based on the number of containers, their destinations, previous experience, and the number of straddle carriers and container movers available. If not enough machine operators are available, they can be called in to work. The harbor master can also plan where to place the containers in the yard to make the unloading process smooth and make it easy to load the container trucks. The fleet management system sends work orders to straddle carriers and container movers, so that machine operators know which containers to pick up and where to move them. Ships may be loaded with containers from the harbor: the fleet management system alerts trucks to come to the harbor area for loading at suitable times. Some of the trucks might be loaded as soon as containers are unloaded from a ship, or at some later point when there is more time. Ships' unloading and loading times can be minimized, so that harbor's throughput is maximized and ship wait times are minimized.

18.2   M2M Communication

A number of machines work in the same fast-paced environment. Machines may need to share information with each other to ensure fluent operation or to warn other machines. A centralized communication mechanism would be too slow, or does not exist.

Therefore:

Allow peer-to-peer communication between machines by adding a client and server to each machine. Using this communication, a machine can send predefined messages that contain data such as their location and current environment information.

For the complete pattern, please see www.wiley.com/go/controlsystemspatterns.

18.3   Opportunistic Delegation

Fleet management needs to delegate dynamically emerging tasks for fleet members. The states of fleet members are constantly in flux. The fleet management application must determine the optimal fleet member to carry out a specific task, but while doing so the state of the fleet might change. Increasing the frequency of state updates from fleet members does not help, as the communication delay is too long.

Therefore:

Create a task delegator service for the fleet management system. This delegator allocates a task to a fleet member based on the best guess of the fleet member's state without separately querying whether it is able to do the task or not. If the fleet member can do the task, it takes ownership of the task and informs the delegator. If the fleet member cannot do the task, it notifies the delegator, which reallocates the task to another fleet member.

For the complete pattern, please see www.wiley.com/go/controlsystemspatterns.

18.4 System Adapter *

ALSO KNOWN AS DEVICE PROXY

A fleet consists of many kinds of machines from various vendors, carrying out several tasks. Customizing a fleet management system for each machine is expensive and time-consuming. From the fleet management's perspective, however, all machines could be managed in a similar way.

Therefore:

Create a system adapter that converts fleet management commands to a format that the system can use. In similar way, the adapter converts production data from machines to a format conforming to the fleet management application's information model. The system adapter becomes a client for the fleet management server, wrapping the actual system.

For the complete pattern, please see www.wiley.com/go/controlsystemspatterns.

CHAPTER

19

Patterns for System Configuration

'We seem to inhabit a universe made up of a small number of elements-particles-bits
that swirl in chaotic clouds, occasionally clustering together in geometrically logical
temporary configurations.'

Timothy Leary, 'Chaos & Cyber Culture'

Customers need different types of machines or machine variations, and product lines are typically used to support varying customer needs. During its lifecycle a machine might have multiple owners, and their needs may vary. This means that the machine's control system should be adaptable to different machines types and customer needs during its lifecycle.

During the machine's lifecycle its hardware components may be changed for various reasons. The replacement parts may have slightly different specifications, and so, for example in the case of a sensor, may produce slightly different measurements. Such differences need to be compensated for to guarantee proper functioning of the control system. The sublanguage of configuration patterns, shown in Figure 19.1, addresses these kinds

379

of customization and adjustment problems. The sublanguage helps to adapt the control system to varying customer needs and to cope with changes in the usage environment.

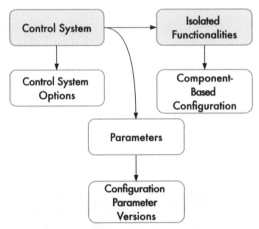

Figure 19.1: The sublanguage of system configuration patterns

CONTROL SYSTEM OPTIONS (page 394) shows how to provide solutions and optional accessories for each customer without creating a multitude of different control system software versions. PARAMETERS (page 380) tackles the long lifecycle of a machine. Physical parts age and wear out, and their behavior changes due to wear. In addition, the working environment may create a need for different behavior from the control system. The pattern suggests how to describe properties that are likely to change during a machine's lifecycle as configuration parameters. CONFIGURATION PARAMETER VERSIONS (page 385) refines PARAMETERS by adding parameter sets, so that when the control application is updated, the old parameter values that the operator might have adjusted are not overwritten. Finally, COMPONENT-BASED CONFIGURATION (page 386) refines ISOLATED FUNCTIONALITIES (page 110), separating software solutions (including firmware) from hardware solutions. Products can then be built by combining these isolated solutions using a configuration tool or configuration file. This gives flexibility when tailoring a product for a customer.

19.1 Parameters * *

...there is a CONTROL SYSTEM (page 96) with a HUMAN–MACHINE INTERFACE (page 313). Various sensors and actuators are used in the system. When the sensors and actuators age and wear through use, their properties change. Sensor values may drift and start to give less accurate measurements. Actuators may also start to react more slowly, require more power or need longer activation times to perform an operation. A machine may be used in various operating environments during its lifecycle. It might be used in an arctic environment, then sold to a second owner who uses it in a warmer climate. Because of such environmental changes, functionality needs to be tuned to better fit the environment. A machine may also have various operators with different preferences for its use. To enhance the user experience, operators may want to adjust the machine's preferences to suit their needs. When a machine is assembled, different hydraulic valves may act differently and require different currents to reach the same clearance. Similarly, angle sensors' zero points can depend on the angle at which they are installed. These differences in behavior need to be compensated for by the CONTROL SYSTEM and calibrated by assembly line personnel: compensation values cannot be hard-coded in the control program's code.

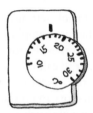

A machine must remain efficient during a long lifecycle regardless of the environment in which it is used. In addition, the different needs of various machine operators need to be addressed to guarantee the efficiency of work. This requires the control system to compensate for changing conditions.

Physical parts age and wear, and their behavior changes due to this. The control system should compensate for this change in order to maintain its performance.

Machine operators have different physical qualities or preferences, and the control system's UI designers may not be able to find a solution that will suit all operators. For example, some operators might be left-handed, or want a different joystick response. In both cases, the operator needs to adjust the control system to fit their needs.

Different countries' legislation require machines to function differently. For example, if a mining drill rig is used in Australia, opening the cabin door must stop all operation, whereas in other countries this is not required. Operators may prefer to be able to use a machine while the cabin door is open, if allowed. There is no sense in making different control system software versions for different countries, so there should be a way to specify this kind of behavior on the assembly line.

The environment may create a need for different behavior from the control system. In Finland, for example, conditions vary greatly between summer and winter, and the system needs to adapt to the changes caused by this. For example, the response of hydraulic steering may become very sluggish at low temperatures, because hydraulic oil becomes more viscous. This can happen even if the correct oils are used. This can be compensated for to some extent by adjusting the control system software.

During system testing there should be an easy way to adjust the control system's behavior, such as changing limit values for functions, or adjusting properties to known initial values. For example, if a development team is optimizing an automated sequence's behavior, it will make testing easier if limit values can be adjusted from the control system directly, without uploading new software to the machine.

During a machine's lifecycle some components might be replaced with other vendor's spare parts. For example, a sensor from a different vendor may produces slightly different measurement results. This difference should not affect control system functionality.

Therefore:

Describe properties that are likely to change during a machine's lifecycle as configuration parameters. Implement a user interface through which these parameters can be altered.

Configuration parameters are user-definable settings that control various aspects of a system's behavior. The machine's manufacturer supplies default values for all configuration parameters. An operator can then adjust these factory defaults depending on the circumstances in which the machine is used, or to calibrate system behavior. However, some parameters must not be adjustable by the operator, for example for safety reasons. The parameters are stored to persistent memory to prevent them being lost during power cycles. Often the parameters are stored in a file, such as an XML or .ini file on the cabin PC's hard disk. Each parameter also has a type, defining what kind of values the parameter represents.

When the operator adjusts parameters, they often affect system behavior immediately. However, some parameters might only be read during system start-up, so adjusting such parameters requires a system reboot. Some the parameters may also be alternatives, so that the operator can select which alternative is used. Adjusting parameters may also require the system to be put into a separate calibration mode (see OPERATING MODES (page 175) for details).

A separate user interface view for parameters should be added to system. From this UI the operator can see the parameters' current values and alter them when necessary. Adjustment of some parameters may need to be restricted to authorized maintenance or factory personnel. If this is the case, ROLE-BASED UI (page 327) offers an easy way to limit access to parameters for different user groups. In addition, an external tool might sometimes be used to set parameters. Parameters can also have limit values that define the range over which they can be adjusted. These limit values can also be described as parameters. Access to these limit values should be restricted to authorized personnel.

For the control system, access to parameter values needs to be fast, as many of them are used at the machine control level, which has real-time requirements (see SEPARATE REAL-TIME, page 237). To enable rapid access, parameter values need to be stored locally to the node where they are needed. Often the cabin PC has a backup copy of all parameters. Parameters can be accessed and altered using the HUMAN–MACHINE INTERFACE (page 313) on the cabin PC. When the parameter editing screen on the HMI is opened, the cabin PC fetches parameter values from the nodes to ensure that the displayed values are correct. When parameters are changed by the operator, their new values need to be transferred back to the respective node. Typically, parameter transfer is carried out immediately the parameters are input and accepted. The transfer mechanism can be seen as an instance of EARLY WORK (page 259). In most cases, machine control-related parameters cannot be set while a machine is in use; the machine needs to be stopped to adjust such parameters. VARIABLE MANAGER (page 201) offers an easy way to store and share the parameters with nodes.

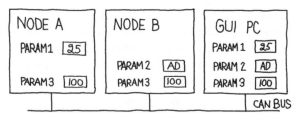

Figure 19.2: Each node stores parameters that are relevant for its functionality. Parameters are set centrally via a graphical user interface.

Figure 19.2 illustrates an example of parameter usage. All parameters are set through a GUI on the cabin PC. The PC stores a backup copy of all system parameters in an XML file. If there is a need to update a number of parameters, the backup parameter file can be overwritten and new values delivered to nodes.

If UPDATEABLE SOFTWARE (page 301) has been applied, parameters must be stored separately from applications, as updating the control system software should not change the parameter values set by the operator. Unfortunately, the update might introduce new parameters and these need to be made available. The new parameters can be added to the parameter file and factory default values applied to them. However, a situation in which the type of a parameter is changed during an update, for example from integer to double, is more problematic, as it means that all nodes need to have software that is compatible with the new version of the parameter, to avoid problems when the old application version uses integer instead of double and implicit type casts take place. Sometimes type casting between parameter types might be impossible. Note also that parameter groups may change between software versions. This is especially problematic if a parameter is moved from one group to another. To tackle such problems, see CONFIGURATION PARAMETER VERSIONS (page 385).

Parameters are typically set by the operator, but sometimes a control system may offer automation for finding optimal parameter values. In this case, the system usually has a separate automated calibration mode (see OPERATING MODES, page 175) that is used to gather data from the machine. The control system then tries to determine suitable values for parameters using this data. Automated calibration is implemented using a baseline of factory parameter defaults; the control system uses a utility function to adjust parameter values automatically to find optimum values. This kind of automatic calibration sequence increases machine usability and makes maintenance personnel's work easier, as after-service calibration is automated. However, automatically adjusted parameter values should never be used without confirmation from the operator or maintenance personnel.

As the same control system software may be used in different countries, there may be a need to show parameter values in different units from those used within the control system. You can use a VARIABLE VALUE TRANSLATOR (page 211) to convert the values. However, this presumes that VARIABLE MANAGER (page 201) is used. Sometimes there are functionalities in the machine that can be enabled or disabled when needed. PARAMETERS can be used to implement this functionality. PARAMETERS is also useful in implementing CONTROL SYSTEM OPTIONS (page 394).

If OPERATING MODES (page 175) has been applied, parameter sets can be formed. A parameter set is a group of parameter groups. When the operating mode is changed, a different parameter set can be used. For example, in LIMP HOME (page 185) mode a different parameter set could be used than in normal operation, for example to prevent the operator from driving the machine at full speed.

The control system behavior can be easily adjusted directly from the graphical user interface. Changes in the hardware setup can be compensated by altering parameters, and changes to the control system's code are not required. Adjustments made for the machine are not lost even when the software is updated.

Even in a simple control system, the number of parameters may grow surprisingly large, as there are many properties that could be adjusted. In addition, the number of parameters and the parameters' types may change between software versions. This means that either the whole control system needs to use the same software version, or new software versions need to support the parameter configuration of the old version. Otherwise, for example, if a sensor becomes unavailable and then fails, a new sensor model needs to be used. This new replacement sensor might have a newer software version and a different parameter set. The control system then needs to be updated to support the new sensor. However, some machines may still use the old sensor version. This means that the new control system software version needs to have support for both models of sensor. This increases the number of parameters that need to be stored in the parameter file. During a long machine lifecycle, the parameter count may become very large and managing them might become laborious.

Some parameters might be specific to a particular machine configuration or to a geographical zone. Selecting the correct set of parameter values during the control system software's build process might become challenging and usually requires separate tools for configuring the parameters. A lot of parameter groups might make parameter management even more challenging. Still, parameters make it possible to have a single control system software version for all machine variations; separate versions for all product variations are not needed.

A wine grape harvester uses a shaker mechanism to drop grapes onto a conveyor belt located inside the machine. This and many other functionalities need to be parameterized to ensure proper operation of the machine under various conditions and through its lifecycle. Listing 19.1 shows an excerpt of the parameter file for the machine.

```
#ShakerControl parameters
ShakerControl.shakerMaxAngle = 30;
ShakerControl.shakerMinAngle = 1;
ShakerControl.earlyWarningLimit = 50;

#ConveyorBeltSpeedUphill
ConveyorControl.beltSpeed = 1000;
ConveyorControl.maxDrivingSpeed = 15;

#ConveyorBeltSpeedDownhill
ConveyorControl.beltSpeed = 500;
ConveyorControl.maxDrivingSpeed= 5;

hullControl.defaultWineRowHeight = 1.2;
CabinPC.uiLanguageSelection = "it_IT";
```

Listing 19.1: Excerpt of the parameter file grape_harvester_vi.ini

The parameter file is a regular text file and contains name–value pairs. The left side defines the parameter name, and the right side the actual parameter value. Parameters are named using the following principle: each parameter starts with the name of the controller that uses the parameter, for example `ShakerControl`. The rest of the parameter name describes what the parameter adjusts; for example, `earlyWarningLimit` adjusts how many messages can be put in the buffer before an alarm is given (see EARLY WARNING, page 169). The behavior of the machine can now be adjusted easily by altering parameters. The parameter file of the wine grape harvester is stored on its cabin PC as a backup. The parameters can be adjusted from the PC's UI by navigating to a parameter configuration UI view. The harvester uses OPERATING MODES (page 175); navigating to the parameter view puts the system into parameter configuration mode, in which the machine is stopped and parameter values are fetched from the nodes so that they can be altered from the UI. When a value change is confirmed by the operator, the parameters are transferred to the respective nodes. The UI then leaves the parameter configuration view and the machine enters normal operating mode. Some of the parameters, such as `uiLanguageSelection`, also affect the cabin PC itself.

19.2   Configuration Parameter Versions

A control application update may change parameter values, introduce new parameters or change parameter types. During the update, the old parameter values should not be overwritten, as the operator might have adjusted them. However, it should be possible to overwrite the old parameter values when absolutely necessary, such as if their type changes.

Therefore:

Store the parameters separately from the application in the update bundle for each unit. Tag the parameter set for the unit with a version number that is distinct from the application version. The updated parameter set contains only new parameters or changed values for old parameters. This allows the old parameter values to be retained over the update.

For the complete pattern, please see www.wiley.com/go/controlsystemspatterns.

19.3 Component-Based Configuration *

***ALSO KNOWN AS* CONTROL SYSTEM VARIANCE, COMPONENT-BASED SETUP**

...there is a CONTROL SYSTEM (page 96) with ISOLATED FUNCTIONALITIES (page 110). Different customers have different needs: for example, some might want a tracked forest harvester instead of a wheeled one, depending on the terrain in which the machine is going to be used. A tracked model would require a different control application for the transmission controller than a wheeled model. However, from the manufacturer's point of view it is not profitable to create separate control system software versions for different products, as most of the functionalities are common to all machine models. Customization of software for each model or each customer has many downsides. During the lifecycle of a product range changes would need to be made to several products and customized variants of them. This is laborious and expensive. On the other hand, the manufactured quantity of machines is fairly small, so the benefits of mass-production cannot be gained easily.

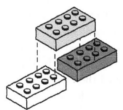

A single product design is not suitable for all customers, as their needs vary. The machine manufacturer cannot offer fully customized products, as modifying components for each customer is too laborious and would result in extensive software versioning. On the other hand, manufactured machine batches are too small to gain the benefits of mass-production.

ISOLATED FUNCTIONALITIES (page 110) describes a classic component model: application + firmware + hardware = component. When the pattern is applied, the system is built from these components. While this model is very popular, as it is easy to understand and makes it possible to use COTS components, it also has downsides. For example, if the system design requirements dictate dividing functionalities into several small entities, the number of components will increase. Furthermore, often only one control application is run on a single hardware component, thus increasing the number of nodes in the system. For example, a modern car designed with this approach might have over 100 nodes. This kind of system is error-prone, as it has many components that are potential sources of error. As there is a large number of components, there is also extensive wiring and a large number of connectors on the bus. These can break, and a single faulty device may take the whole system down. In addition, configuring a system with multiple nodes becomes more laborious when the number of nodes increases. From the software development point of view, the integration of components in such systems is a challenging task. Unfortunately, integration tasks are often carried out at a late stage of development, causing projects to miss deadlines when integration problems emerge. As the number of nodes in such a system is large, the system becomes expensive to build. A different kind of approach is needed.

Customer requirements for a work machine vary greatly, and thus one machine type does not fit all customers' needs. In addition, customers are not willing to pay extra for features they are not going to use, so different models of the machine are required to meet various demands. While products will have functionalities that are unique to a specific model, they still share many common functionalities. These use the same or similar hardware and software components. To avoid implementing the same functionality again and again, software components should be reusable in different models, preferably without any modifications. If modifications are implemented for different models, software versioning might become a problem when bug fixes or new features are developed, as the changes would have to be integrated and tested for each version separately.

To enable reuse software must not be tightly coupled with the hardware on which it runs, otherwise a hardware component would always require the corresponding software component. This is usually not possible. For example, a designer might want to reuse an application that employs messaging. However, in the new design, the capacity of the CAN bus might not be enough to support messaging, so an Ethernet-based bus would be required instead. However, the original hardware used in the old system may not have Ethernet ports. This prevents reuse of the software, as it is too dependent on the hardware. To avoid this, the software component should be decoupled from the hardware it uses.

A mass-production approach could be used to minimize unit price and allow more models of a machine. However, the work machine domain lies somewhere between mass-production, like cars, and highly customized projects like those in process automation. The number of machines manufactured can be small, for example a thousand. Production batches are too large to customize each machine to fit customer needs, but on the other hand customers often expect a close match to their needs, as the machines are costly.

Hardware components used in the system will vary during the lifecycle of the machine. The hardware, its drivers or its firmware may change. This means that hardware components may gain new parameters, have different behavior in fault situations, or even have a different bus communication rate. If the software is coupled with the hardware, it will require changes to support any new hardware introduced during its lifecycle. This would again cause software versioning problems.

Therefore:

Provide a way to design the system so that it consists of independent components. These components are either hardware or software components. All available components form a product platform component library. Components from the library can be used to build systems that satisfy varying customer needs. Create a description file for each software and hardware component describing its inputs and outputs. Also, create a unified way to describe the whole system using a configuration file. In this file, the desired software and hardware components are selected and the configuration parameters are set for the hardware setup of the system. The file also describes the connections between the software and hardware components. Finally, establish a tool chain to build the control system software based on the configuration file.

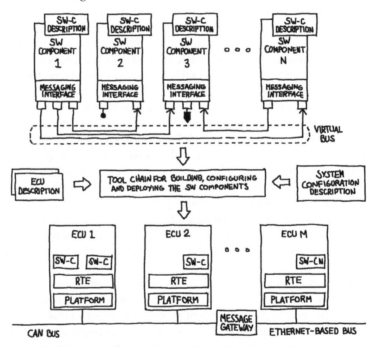

Figure 19.3: Component, ECU and system configuration descriptions are used as inputs for the tool chain that builds the control system from the product platform library components

Make the software components independent of the hardware used, for example by using the solutions described in HARDWARE ABSTRACTION LAYER (page 264), OPERATING SYSTEM ABSTRACTION (page 269) and VIRTUAL RUNTIME ENVIRONMENT (page 272). Create a configuration file for each control application in the system. The file should describe the inputs that the application requires and the outputs it will produce. This is known as the *signal interface* of the application. Use MESSAGING INTERFACE (page 143) to make the applications independent of the selected bus technology and protocols. The applications can then communicate through a virtual bus using the messaging interface and VARIABLE MANAGER (page 201).

The inputs and outputs of each application are described in the corresponding software component description file ('SW-C Description' in Figure 19.3). This file describes what kinds of signals the application needs – that is, the inputs and outputs of the application. Listing 19.2 shows an example excerpt from such a file. Input signals described in the file should have at least a name, type (for example unsigned 16-bit integer), unit and maximum update period. In addition, the file describes the maximum and minimum values for each signal. An application can monitor the health of its input producers based on the update period and limit information. If the maximum period is exceeded, there is probably some fault in the system. Similarly, if a value is out of range, it might indicate a malfunction in the information producer. Input signal definitions can optionally contain a human-readable description of the signal. Outputs are described in a similar way. Parameters for the application are also described in the SW-C file. Listing 19.2 includes a parameter for calibrating the zero point of boom extension. For a more detailed description of parameters, see PARAMETERS (page 380).

```xml
<?xml version="1.0" encoding="UTF-8">
<application name="boom_controller" />
 <inputs>
    <input-signal name="positionJoystickX" type="uint_16" unit=""
max_period="10ms" minimum_value="-32768"  maximum_value="32767">
   <description>Joystick deflection from zero X position</description>
 </input-signal>
    ...
 </input_signals>

 <outputs>
    <output-signal name="move_boom_left" type="uint_16"  unit="mA"
max_period="10ms">
   <description>Move boom left – PWM output value</description>
  </output-signal>
    ...
 </outputs>

 <parameters>
    <parameter name="boom_extension_zero_point" type="uint16" unit="mA" min="0"
max="2000" default_value="1000" />
    ...
 </parameters>
```

Listing 19.2: An excerpt from a software component description (SW-C) file

Create a build and configuration tool chain that takes the component description files as inputs. A tool should check that all the inputs required by the applications exist in the system. This means that, for each input, there must be at least one software component producing a corresponding output. The sensors used by the system therefore need to be described as software components. The build tool also takes ECU (electronic control units) descriptions – hardware component descriptions – and the system configuration description file, as inputs (see Figure 19.3). The contents of hardware description files depend on the system to be built. For example, the file can describe components' CANopen interfaces, or just the number of CAN ports.

The tool chain then maps the software inputs and outputs to the hardware components' input and output pins. Each software input should be mapped to some output of other components, either an actual hardware unit or a purely software one. This indicates that outputs should also be mapped to inputs. The tool configures the buses required for the signals that applications exchange. The signals are mapped to the actual messages exchanged on the bus. For example, in CANopen the signals described in component descriptions are mapped to PDOs, and PDO timing tests run. If the system consists of devices that are configured to use different bus technologies, the tool chain will configure multiple buses. It then uses a MESSAGE GATEWAY (page 148)) between the buses (see Figure 19.3).

To guide the configuration process, the tool chain also needs ECU descriptions as inputs. CANopen, for example, uses EDS files (Vector Informatik, 2011) to describe the hardware components. The tool chain also needs the desired system configuration as an input. This is typically described in a separate system configuration description file. Listing 19.3 shows an excerpt from such a system configuration file. To make the system design easier, the file could be produced using a visual tool in which the desired buses and hardware components can be selected. The visual tool would partially generate the file, and the final touches could then be added by editing the file manually.

All nodes present in the system are described in the configuration file, as shown in Listing 19.3. A name is given in the file for every node. The name is accompanied by the node type and whether the node is optional. A description of the node can also be given in plain text so that it can be displayed in the configuration tool if necessary. Applications that will run on the node are given within the node's description. The configuration tool then builds the software accordingly and may check that the timing and memory requirements of the applications are met when using the selected hardware. In some cases, the tool might even automatically select the cheapest possible hardware component that can be used based on the requirements. The configuration tool might also try to optimize the number of nodes by putting multiple applications on the same node if possible. This information can also be provided as a part of the configuration file.

The cycle time, SW-C description file, a unique identifier, name and path for the application binary, and start cycle is specified for each application. The cycle time tells the configurator tool how often an application needs to run to meet its timing requirements. Using this information, the configurator can check compliance with timing requirements if multiple applications are run on the same node. The application `id` field is an identifier that is used to identify the application uniquely. `app_binary_name` defines the path and binary file of the application for the configurator tool. The starting program cycle can be

```xml
<?xml version="1.0" encoding="UTF-8"?>
 <system_configuration_description machine_name="grape_harvester"
configuration_version="1.1" machine_serial_number="123BADBEEF>

<list_of_nodes>
  <node optional="false" name="boom_controller" description="node description"
node_type="machine_control_node">
 <applications>
        <application cycle_time="10ms"
swc_description_file="boom_control_app_description.xml" id="bc_app"
app_binary_name="bc_app"  start_cycle="1"/>
 <application cycle_time="30ms"
swc_description_file="boom_diagnostics_app_description.xml" id="bc_diag_app"
app_binary_name="bc_diag_app"  start_cycle="1"/>
 </applications>

    <node_id type="master" value="0x5" bus_key="CAN_bus1"/>
    <node_id type="slave" value="0x2" bus_key="CAN_bus2"/>

  ...
  <!-- Other node configuration here -->
  </node>
  <node optional="true"...

  </node>
</list_of_nodes>

<bus_list>
 <bus baudrate="500k" name="Boom bus" NMTMaster="boom_controller" id="CAN_bus1"
bus_type="CAN" protocol_type="canopen" />
 <bus baudrate="1M" name="Backbone bus" NMTMaster="cabin_pc"  id="CAN_bus2"
bus_type="CAN" protocol_type="canopen" />
</bus_list>

<hardware_components>
  <component id="PLC_2024"/>
  <component id="PLC_2038"/>
  <component id="EPM2"/>
  ...
</hardware_components>

<!-- See Control System Options pattern for more details ->
<control_system_options>
 <control_system_option name="winch"/>
 <control_system_option name="automatic_calibration"/>
 <control_system_option name="arctic_kit"/>
  ...
</control_system_options>

... <!--Other configurations -->

</system_configuration_description>
```

Listing 19.3: An excerpt from a system configuration description file describing nodes, applications, buses, hardware components and CONTROL SYSTEM OPTIONS specified with the last application parameter. This makes it possible to start execution of applications gradually.

Based on this application information, the configuration tool builds a statically scheduled control application for the selected hardware. Other information might be added to describe a node when needed. The description of a node also indicates to which buses the node will be attached. A single node can be attached to multiple nodes, as in Listing 19.3, if the hardware supports that. In the configuration, for example, node id and type (master, slave, etc.) can be given. Node id is the identifier that is used to address the node on the bus. However, these configurations might depend to some extent on the chosen bus technologies.

There is also a bus list specifying the system buses. Information specified depends on the selected bus technology, but usually baud rate, name, bus master, unique id, bus type and protocol are specified. Other additional information might be added when necessary. For a CANopen bus, for example, NMTMaster – the bus master – needs to be specified. However, for some bus technologies it is not necessary to define the bus master. Desired hardware components are also listed in the configuration file as a simple list. This instructs the configurator tool to use a specific set of hardware if multiple hardware components are available in the platform library. Available CONTROL SYSTEM OPTIONS (page 394) can also be described.

Based on the information in the system configuration description file, software component descriptions and ECU descriptions, the build tool can configure and compile the control system software (the lower part of Figure 19.3). The manufacturer stores the system configuration along with the machine's serial number for later use. This allows a new version of the control system software to be built for a specific machine if the platform and software components evolve or fixes are made to the code. The target machine can then be updated using UPDATEABLE SOFTWARE (page 301).

Additional calibration is required in the assembly phase, when the factory defaults for PARAMETERS (page 380) are adjusted for the current machine. If VARIABLE MANAGER (page 201) is used in the architecture design, it can be used to implement signal mapping between applications.

A component-based configuration approach for distributed real-time control system is also described by White and Smith (White & Schmidt, 2008). Larsson also discusses this topic in his dissertation (Larsson, 2000). Sometimes the term 'component-based configuration' is used to refer to dynamic configuration of a system (Rosa & Silva, 1997). However, the purpose of such patterns differ from the one described here.

Control system software can be built according to customer requirements without fear of extensive versioning. All control system versions use the same platform and component library. The system configuration dictates what kind of system will be built for a particular machine. However, the approach requires assembly line personnel to also support this approach, so the whole machine manufacturer's organization needs to support a component-based approach. Product management systems are needed to instruct assembly line personnel to build the machine using the desired hardware and to configure the software for the selected hardware.

A component-based approach is a cost-effective way to support varying customer requirements. It may also shorten the time to market of a new product, as a large portion of the components required in the new product's control system can be selected directly from the component library. Laborious manual configuration is also is automated by the tool chain.

Configuration of the system might become more complex. Many different parameters may need to be set when the system is configured. An application developer therefore has to know what needs to be described in the configuration file. However, good graphical tools will help developers to create configurations. The approach is also simpler than having all configurations within the code mass. Tools for checking that a configuration is valid may also be required.

The approach may limit the usage of COTS components. COTS components may have application and hardware bundled together. They can be used as a part of a system if a standardized bus interface is used to communicate with the component that has bundled software and hardware. However, if such hardware is used as a part of component-based system, problems might be encountered later. For example, the calibration values of any COTS components would need to be backed up on a cabin PC in case of failure. When a COTS part is replaced, its calibration values are restored from the cabin PC. If a COTS component does not support restoration of parameters over the bus, changes will be needed to the COTS component's software. The component vendor might not want to tailor their product for a single machine manufacturer. Even if the COTS vendor is willing to make the required changes, a control system software update might also be needed. In addition, any next generation of the COTS component would again require the same tailoring, and thus would be expensive. So when using a component-based approach, COTS use should be limited to software or hardware components that provide good decoupling of their hardware from their software.

A rock crusher manufacturer uses component-based configuration. All applications are implemented as separate components that can be run in a common Virtual Runtime Environment (page 272). All the manufacturer's machines are capable of this, as the Virtual Runtime Environment is implemented for all hardware components they support. Their sales staff are provided with a visual tool for creating system configurations. When sales staff negotiate with the customer, they add the desired features to the machine using the tool. The tool deduces from the features mix what kind of hardware is required to run the selected applications, and which buses are needed to meet the throughput requirements set by the applications. Once a machine is sold, the generated configuration, along with the list of selected hardware, is sent to the assembly-line personnel. After the hardware is installed during assembly, a separate tool is used to build the software for the specific machine. The machine's serial number and configuration are stored in the manufacturer's database. When a software update is needed, the serial number and configuration are used to build an updated version of the control system for the machine. If there is a need to change a hardware component when the machine is maintained, this is also updated in the manufacturer's database, so that the system configuration is kept up to date.

19.4 Control System Options *

…there is a CONTROL SYSTEM (page 96) in which sensors and controllers can be adjusted with PARAMETERS (page 380). Customers have different needs. Some might want more sophisticated features than others who are not willing to pay extra for features they don't need. A machine should be shipped with only the basic feature set, and the owner can then acquire more features if required. The machine may have multiple owners during its lifecycle. Even though the first owner did not need some feature, the second or third owners might. If the subsequent owners wants the feature, they should be able to acquire it. To make this approach viable from the control system software point of view, this kind of tailoring should have only minimal effect on the architecture.

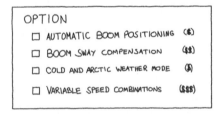

Customer needs vary greatly; for some the basic machine setup is enough, but some customers need additional features. Individual solutions should be provided for each customer at an affordable price without creating a plethora of different control system software versions.

The machine has features that are not required to carry out its basic task. Some of these extra features may add to the operator's comfort, or may be intended for specific environments. In the first case, a customer may not want to pay extra for comfort, and the decision should be left to the customer. In the second case, some customers may need them if the intended environment demands it, while others may not be willing to pay for such features.

Additional features should have a high rate of return on investment, so that customers will want them. Features should not be tailored for each customer separately, as this increases development cost and sale price.

New accessories and features may be launched after the deployment of the machine. The customer should be able to acquire and implement them easily. It should be easy for a customer to install and use accessories, to make such optional features more appealing.

Once a machine is sold to its second or subsequent owner, their needs may be different. For example, the second owner's operating environment might be different, causing a need for new features. To make the machine more appealing to its second owner, they should be able to buy new features from the manufacturer at the same time as buying the second-hand machine. Sometimes also the needs of the initial owner may change over time, creating a need for new features later in the machine's lifecycle.

Development of new features is easier when a system's basic functionality can be developed first and additional features added afterwards. This approach also allows agile and iterative development methods to be used more efficiently in control system development. It should also be possible to add new features without creating a new version of the software, to avoid version management challenges.

Branching of the code base to different versions should be avoided, as it makes merging bug fixes and changes back to the baseline code laborious and time-consuming. In addition, different versions would need to be tested separately. Therefore all control system code should be kept in one baseline version.

Therefore:

During development include in the control system all software components required by accessories. When a customer buys an optional accessory, the corresponding code block is enabled without having to install a different software version.

Include all the software for the control system in the installation package. This guarantees that each installation package contains software that is tested and known to work. If software required for an accessory were provided separately, it would require additional packaging and installation. Furthermore, it would be hard to ensure that the software was compatible with the machine's current software version. As all software for accessories is provided with the control system, there are no compatibility issues. If an accessory contains safety-critical software, it can be certified with the rest of the software in the bundle. The maintenance effort required also decreases, as all software package versions are compatible with all machines. In other words, the control system installation package can be installed regardless of the accessories that have been installed on a machine, as the installation package contains software for all accessories. If new features are developed and included in the software, a new update is released that also includes software for all possible accessories.

The control system always has the software for an accessory ready, and the option or accessory can be enabled from the machine's HUMAN–MACHINE INTERFACE (page 313). Different strategies for enabling an accessory can be used, depending on the situation. If the accessory contains new hardware, it is quite natural for the manufacturer's maintenance personnel to instal the new hardware and enable the option. If ROLE-BASED UI (page 327) has been applied, a maintenance engineer will have a different UI with extended usage rights. The maintenance engineer can then enable the option from the HMI by setting a parameter. If there is no ROLE-BASED UI, a code that must be entered in the HMI to activate the option can be used. If the option is purely a software option, for example an advanced control algorithm, the operator could enable it from the HMI by entering a code. Disabling accessories can be carried out in the same way, though usually this is not necessary.

Enabling new functionality could be automated; the control system could detect when a new accessory is installed and activate it. However, this is not advisable, as there should be some trained person present to check that the new functionality is working properly, and often hardware installation needs expertise and training. Automatic activation is therefore rarely used.

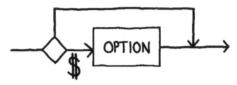

Figure 19.4: The principle of CONTROL SYSTEM OPTIONS: when the option is activated, the corresponding code block is executed

At the code level this approach means that a code block is selected dynamically: if the parameter for the option is enabled, the code block that controls the accessory is executed (see Figure 19.4). However, the parameter should not be the only variable used to control whether the code block is executed: the code itself should also check that the hardware required by the option is present. If the option has different versions of algorithms that can be activated using CONTROL SYSTEM OPTIONS, INTERCHANGEABLE ALGORITHM (page 193) can be used to make the algorithms interchangeable.

If different customer segments needing different feature sets can be identified, COMPONENT-BASED CONFIGURATION (page 386) should be used to create a product family. In this way the need for options decreases, but there will probably still be accessories that need to be sold as options.

The control system can now support additional features that the customer can buy separately from the machine. This makes it possible for the machine's subsequent owners to install new features after acquiring the machine. New features can be activated after the machine is delivered to the customer if the control system has UPDATEABLE SOFTWARE (page 301).

The solution presented in this pattern makes the system design more complex, as there is a need to check which features are enabled and which are not. This checking may also reduce performance to some extent, as the checks may contain queries to determine whether specific hardware is present.

If the number of control system options grows large, the software size increases significantly. The code might also becomes over-complex with different options. It might also be hard to see whether options are still valid and which can be removed from the code base.

Managing the code base and software versions becomes easier, as there is only one soft-ware version for all machines regardless of the accessories installed. CONTROL SYSTEM OPTIONS also makes it possible to create new business opportunities, as features can be licensed and activated for a specific period. For example, the machine's owner could ac-tivate some features for a limited time, and in this way save costs, as they don't need to buy them.

A machine's configuration management and documentation management over its life-cycle becomes more important, as support personnel may need to know which options have been enabled in a specific customer's machine. In addition, activated options should be persistent over software updates, so that the machine's owner can update the software without needing to reactivate any options.

Sometimes control system options share the same I/O pins or other resources, and thus are often mutually exclusive. This makes implementation and configuration of options more complex. On the other hand, it would be a waste of resources to add reserve I/O pins to the control system if options are not active simultaneously.

When the number of available options grows, it might be easier to divide the control system into two (or more) separate versions. However, deciding when it is better to im-plement two distinct versions is challenging.

A pile-driver's CONTROL SYSTEM (page 96) can position the boom to the right location and angle automatically. This can also be done manually by the operator. Automatic boom positioning is sold as a control system option. If the customer buys this option, a maintenance engineer installs two new sensors on the boom and connects them to the CAN bus. The engineer selects the operator's personalized user interface (see ROLE-BASED UI, page 327) and activates the automatic boom positioning functionality. The sys-tem performs SELF-TESTS (page 106) to check that the new hardware is present and work-ing as expected. If the self-checks pass, the operator can start using the new feature. On the code level, this means that new code blocks are run when PARAMETERS (page 380) have been changed. If the SELF-TESTS fail, the engineer needs to check that connections and wiring are correctly installed.

CHAPTER

20

Applying Patterns

'Few things are harder to put up with than the annoyance of a good example.'

Mark Twain

In this chapter we present a small example to show how an imaginary manufacturer could use some of our patterns to design a work machine. The idea is to show how the patterns work together, not to present a full-blown ready-made design. The resulting software architecture is for demonstration purposes and is not optimal to any degree.

A small engineering office, X-Machina, was called by one of their customers, a machine manufacturer. After negotiation, X-Machina agreed to develop a prototype for a new, next-generation loader. Even though X-Machina did not have previous experience of loaders, their design department produced the first hardware wireframe sketch in a couple of weeks. This sketch was accepted by the customer, and is shown in Figure 20.1. After these preparations, the project was launched with a hardware team and a system architect.

Figure 20.1: A wireframe sketch of the prototype loader

Reproduced by permission of Creanex Oy

Being a next generation model, the loader contained a plenty of new ideas, gathered in several brainstorming sessions. The participants of the workshops were various stakeholders, such as maintenance personnel, customer support and maintenance personnel, testers and end users. One of the most requested ideas was advanced full-scale automation. For example, previous bucket loaders had problems with bumpy or sloping terrain: the bucket contents could be spilled when a loader hit a bump or negotiated a steep slope, reducing the efficiency of soil moving.

Here are two examples of the requirements collected from the workshops:

■ When an operator drives the loader, the bucket should keep its position levelled automatically without intervention from the operator.

■ To improve service efficiency, the most common sources of malfunction should be able to indicate if they are about to fail.

From the beginning it was clear that this kind of automation would not be easy to design and implement. So the system architect used some time to research similar designs from the literature and existing solutions from the market. They also examined equivalent products from competitors. Ultimately, a colleague recommended a pattern language for designing such a system.

After reading a short introduction to patterns, the architect noticed that the first pattern, CONTROL SYSTEM (page 96) described exactly the same problem as the architect had:

The productivity of a work machine cannot be increased any further using traditional ways of building the machine – using hydraulics, electronics and mechanics. A new way to control the machine needs to be introduced to optimize the system functionality and to increase the number of automated functionalities. For the same reason, user experi-

*ence needs to be enhanced, and the system needs to connect to external information sys-
tems to make the machine an integral part of the whole production chain.*

Consequently, X-Machina hired a software architect to design the software part of the
system, while the system architect focussed on the hardware design and system integration. In addition, two software teams joined the development project.

Enthusiastically, the software architect immediately decided to use the pattern language approach to design the system. As a solution to the first problem, the pattern introduces a software control system to control the loader. In this way, sophisticated
automated functions can be implemented with software, which makes the life of the hardware team easier. The machine had a set of sensors to provide inputs to the control system. It also contained a set of actuators, such as valves and switches to control the
loader's functionality. Software was written to read these inputs and to control outputs.
The control application drives the outputs to specific value according to the inputs and
control algorithms implemented.

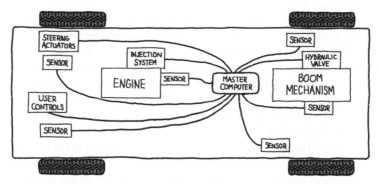

Figure 20.2: The system architecture of the loader after applying the first pattern of the
pattern language

The architecture of the resulting system now resembled Figure 20.2. A master computer executes the control application, which controls the engine and the boom mechanism
with their corresponding actuators, such a fuel injection system and several hydraulic
valves. The control application needs information from the system, which is gathered by
using several sensors. The sensors and the actuators are connected directly to the master
computer. Pedals and joysticks are used by the operator to operate the loader. Any changes in these controls are measured, and the information transmitted to the computer,
where application code transforms it into actuator movements.

The software architect had already learnt that, after applying a specific pattern, there
were several ways to improve the system design. The graph for the pattern language (see
the companion website at www.wiley.com/go/controlsystemspatterns) helped them to
determine the next potential patterns to look at. As the loader had high safety and robustness requirements, some fault-tolerance mechanisms, such as WATCHDOG (page
101), should be added to the control system. On the other hand, the traditional operator
controls – gauges and pedals – could be replaced with a graphical user interface by im-

plementing HUMAN–MACHINE INTERFACE (page 313). However, the software architect reasoned from Conway's Law (Conway, 1968) that the current monolithic architecture was far from optimal for development by several software teams. The modernization processes were therefore postponed and focus shifted to the architecture itself.

As several physical parts needed to be monitored or controlled, the amount of on-board wiring increased dramatically, as each sensor or actuator required its own wiring. In the workshops, the stakeholders from the assembly department especially asked that extensive wiring be avoided, to make assembly times shorter. Stakeholders from support also stated that extensive wiring had proved be error-prone in practice. In addition, the control system software formed a single point of failure, as would be run as a single application. So applying the next pattern, ISOLATED FUNCTIONALITIES (page 110), was very tempting, as it provides a 'divide and conquer'-based solution to the following problem:

As the control system evolves and gains new features, it becomes hard to maintain and understand its structure. In addition, the processing power of a single device running the software may be exceeded.

According to the solution of this pattern, the capabilities of the machine are matched with logical functional entities. These entities should be implemented as their own subsystems in order to isolate functionalities. This makes the system easier to manage and understand. Instead of directly controlling various hardware components with the master computer, there would be additional smaller computers – controllers – controlling the actuators. By applying this pattern, the second problem was also solved: once the functionalities were isolated, each team could work on a single functionality. So one team was assigned to implement controllers for the engine and boom, while the other focused on the master computer. This also increased safety, as a malfunction in the boom controller would not affect the functionality of the engine controller.

In the consequences section of the pattern, there was a hint to use a communication bus instead of traditional wiring:

Even though the system is distributed, adding new devices may be challenging. Adding a device requires new wiring, and may require changes to other controllers' code. ONE TO MANY *(page 131) describes situations in which there is a need to add, remove or change communicating parties during the lifecycle of the system.*

As the loader was only a prototype, it was certain that at least some new devices would be added to the system later. The communication bus was introduced in ONE TO MANY (page 131), so after applying these three patterns, the architecture of the system was far more understandable. For the bus implementation, CAN technology was selected, as it seemed to be a common technology in the industry. There were also a lot of CAN components on the market, so the technology selection seemed promising for potential growth. Figure 20.3 shows the improved version of the architecture.

Multiple problems can emerge when a bus topology is used in communication. The architect could tackle these issues with other patterns in the messaging sublanguage. However, it is usually more fruitful to also look at other sublanguages, rather than go straight to the details of one sublanguage at a time. The architect decided to focus on improving the operator interface of the machine first, so applied HUMAN–MACHINE INTERFACE

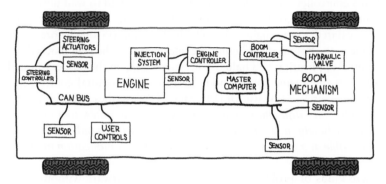

Figure 20.3: The system architecture after the architect has applied three patterns

(page 313). The resulting HMI consisted of physical control devices and a graphical user interface for the operator. For this purpose, a couple of Qt (Digia, 2013a) experts were hired. Unfortunately, none of the experts had previous experience of real-time systems. However, the software architect recollected Conway's Law: if multiple teams or subcontractors implement the control system software, the system probably needs to be divided into separate components (Conway, 1968) – the different teams would then have natural interfaces with each other. Because of this, the architect separated user interface design to its own team, also having dedicated hardware, a cabin PC, on the loader. This meant that the Qt designers did not have to worry about real-time issues. This separation was done by applying SEPARATE REAL-TIME (page 237):

There are always machine control functionalities in a system. To increase the productivity and operability of the machine, the system needs to offer high-level functionality such as a graphical user interface, Diagnostics and so on. The high-level functionalities' behavior may compromise the real-time requirements of machine control functionalities.

During development, the software teams worked iteratively in close cooperation with the hardware team: changes in the software required several changes to the hardware. As the hardware design progressed, components such as hydraulic cylinders for the bucket arms were selected. Selection of hardware also resulted in changes in the control application's code. Changes to the application code could have been minimized by applying patterns like HARDWARE ABSTRACTION LAYER (page 264) or VIRTUAL RUNTIME ENVIRONMENT (page 272), but as this was a prototype, the architect did not see value in investing in such solutions.

After weeks of hard work, the first operational prototype of the machine was delivered to the customer for evaluation. At first, the machine operated quite well and the customer was satisfied with the new automated functionalities. However, after days of hard testing, the engine just stopped, and required all control system hardware to be powered off before it could be restarted. A developer from X-Machina was immediately called to the test site to work out the source of the malfunction. After several debugging sessions, the developer found the root cause. In the design, communication was organized so that each controller sent its messages synchronously to all other nodes. If the bus was busy at the moment when a controller attempted to send a message, it had to wait until the bus was free. This wait period caused the control application to fail its real-time requirements. The situation escalated, as the engine controller had to wait too long before it could send a status message to the boom controller for the bucket arms. The wait blocked the execution of the control application and halted other messaging on the bus, crashing the control application on the engine control node. Deprived of essential control, the engine ceased to run. Fortunately, MESSAGE QUEUE (page 143) describes a similar problem:

Individual nodes have different messaging rates and cycle times, so a message cannot be processed immediately at the receiving end. On the other hand, sending a message might not be possible at a given moment, as some other communication might be taking place on the bus.

Because these kinds of problems can be solved with software without making any hardware changes, it would make development easier if the software could be changed regardless of the controller hardware. New versions of software could just be shipped to the customer and loaded to the controllers. So message queues were added to the software, and the test version of the loader software was improved by allowing software updates: UPDATEABLE SOFTWARE (page 301) was applied to the control system. To support the updates, the controllers had to be replaced with versions with rewritable flash memory chips.

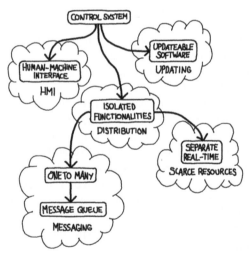

Figure 20.4: The patterns and pattern sublanguages applied for the prototype loader so far

The loader prototype was tested further and proved to function correctly. The patterns applied so far in the architecture of the loader's control system are shown in Figure 20.4 as a pattern graph. From now on, the architect could select which parts of the system might require further improvement, then follow the corresponding pattern sublanguage. For example, as the loader required a bucket balancing algorithm, INTERCHANGEABLE ALGORITHM (page 193) could be used to allow easy experimentation with different algorithm versions. The solution described in the pattern could be easily implemented on the boom controller to allow development of balancing algorithms.

The final architecture of the prototype loader is illustrated in Figure 20.5. The system now had a bus and controllers, including a master node, attached to it. The controllers used MESSAGE QUEUES (page 143) to allow asynchronous messaging. The cabin PC ran all the non-real-time applications in the system, while other nodes had real-time requirements. Controllers used actuators to steer and control the machine, and get control feedback and information about the environment from sensors. The cabin PC offered a graphical user interface for the operator to view system status. The cabin PC also acted as a master on the HMI sub-bus, to which all user controls such as joysticks and pedals were attached.

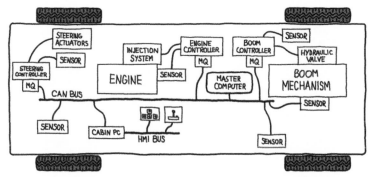

Figure 20.5: The final architecture of the prototype loader

This version was accepted as the basis for further development. The loader still did not fulfil all the requirements stakeholders had presented in the initial workshop. For example, it didn't offer bucket balancing, or information on components prone to malfunction. However, the system now had a functional basic control system, and plans ready for the bucket-balancing algorithms. The architect could continue the design and add REMOTE ACCESS (page 361) and DIAGNOSTICS (page 350) components to meet the malfunction analysis requirement.

After successful release of the next-generation loader, X-Machina wanted to be a part of the current trend for *service as a business*, so aimed to design its loader to support this trend. REMOTE ACCESS would open a possibility for remote DIAGNOSTICS. If maintenance breaks could be planned in advance, the customer could organize their workflow to avoid breaks in production when a machine was under maintenance. This was something the customer was willing to pay extra for, as it would optimize their revenue flow. X-Machina could also offer the machine as a service instead of selling it. Of course this would mean that X-Machina was responsible for machine availability, and so had to ensure that the customer could not do anything that would jeopardize availability. To achieve this, critical parts of the system should be accessible only by maintenance personnel. This could be achieved for example by limiting user interface access to some functionalities. This could be implemented by applying ROLE-BASED UI (page 327). REMOTE

ACCESS also enables several machines to work as a fleet, which increases the productivity of the whole fleet. In the future the customer may want fleet management applications: patterns from the fleet management sublanguage would help in the design.

Even though this example is a small one with imaginary participants, it should demonstrate how the design process can proceed when using a pattern language approach. The patterns are applied sequentially to solve problems as they arise. Simultaneously, the architecture will acquire its form bit by bit. While the patterns help in the design process, the optimal implementation is still required.

CHAPTER

21

Concluding Remarks

'I wanted a perfect ending. Now I've learned, the hard way, that some poems don't rhyme, and some stories don't have a clear beginning, middle, and end. Life is about not knowing, having to change, taking the moment and making the best of it, without knowing what's going to happen next. Delicious Ambiguity.'

Gilda Radner

In this book and on the companion website we present 80 patterns for the domain of work machines. The patterns form a pattern language that can be used to build software architectures for work machines in a generative way. How to combine the patterns when designing such a system has been demonstrated in an example. For some topics, the patterns presented here are just first inklings of other pattern languages. So we strongly encourage you, the reader, to familiarize yourself with other patterns and pattern languages as well.

A typical work machine designed today will probably still be in use in 2030. By then the world will have changed: some technologies common today will have vanished, and new ones taken their place. Nevertheless, the problems presented in our patterns will still exist, as they mostly emerge from the domain itself, not from the technologies used. A designer will therefore still need to answer all these questions one way or another. Of course, technological changes may make some of the problems less important in future, and some existing solutions or technologies listed in the pattern solutions will become outdated. Still, the solutions themselves will probably stand the test of time, as they do not rely on any specific technology, but rather on timeless ideas.

As the work environment changes and new requirements are set for machines, it will certainly spawn several *new* problems to solve. Some of the solutions to these problems will become so common that they can be documented as patterns. Patterns capture existing solutions, so it is not possible – or even wise – to try to provide solutions in this book for machines that will be designed in the 2030s. For this, we trust in the pattern community. We hope that you will join the movement and carry the torch forward by updating existing solutions and documenting new patterns for this pattern language if necessary.

We strongly encourage you to share these updates to the language with the rest of the community. Like any natural language, a pattern language will never be finished: it evolves all the time as people use it. The language will not stagnate as long as the world that the pattern language tries to describe is in constant change. And like any language, it can be declared dead if there are no speakers left. So take a good care of it!

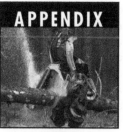

APPENDIX

A

Quality Attribute Table

Table A.1 summarizes the effect on different quality attributes of applying the patterns in this book. The patterns are presented in alphabetical order in the left-hand column. The consequences of applying the pattern on quality attributes and other properties are shown in the table as pluses and minuses. If a pattern has a positive consequence for a specific quality attribute, a plus sign is shown in the corresponding cell of the table. If the pattern has a negative consequence, a minus sign is shown in the cell. The magnitude of the influence is not presented. Sometimes a pattern might have both some positive and some negative consequences for a specific quality attribute. These are omitted from the table for clarity.

The quality attributes in the table are mainly taken from the ISO/IEC 9126 software engineering product quality standard (ISO, 2001). However, some of the quality attributes mentioned in the standard, such as *coexistence*, have so little meaning for control systems that they are omitted from the table to save space. The *understandability* and *learnability* sub-characteristics of *usability* are merged, as it is hard to distinguish between these two quality attributes in this domain.

There are also columns under the *Other* category in the table. We wanted to add this additional category, as sometimes the consequences of a pattern affect other properties of the system than are mentioned in ISO/IEC 9126. These properties are *safety, complexity, designability* and *cost effectiveness*. Safety is often a combination of several quality attributes, such as response time and fault tolerance. However, safety is such an important property of any work machine that we wanted to explicitly mark the patterns that affect the safety of the system. Complexity can also be seen as a combination of quality attributes under maintainability, but sometimes it is hard to define which ones. Thus we added it as a separate property. *Designability* means that when applying a pattern, the system design might become easier or harder after applying the pattern. The solution presented in the pattern might be hard to design, or the design might be more challenging after the pattern is applied – or easier. Finally, we added 'cost effectiveness' as some of the patterns might increase or decrease the manufacturing cost of a machine. Often this is an important property to consider when designing a machine control system.

Although the table might seem to be straightforward to read, we recommend care before jumping to any conclusion. The table has to be interpreted in the context of the pattern at hand. For example, when reading the pluses and minuses of FLEET MANAGEMENT (page 372), it should be interpreted as meaning that the pattern improves the cost effectiveness of the whole fleet and improves interoperability between machines. It doesn't improve interoperability on board a single machine. We therefore advise that the table is used as a quick reference to the consequences of a pattern, rather than as a tool to select a pattern to improve a specific quality attribute of the system being designed.

	FUNCTIONALITY				RELIABILITY					USABILITY			EFFICIENCY				MAINTAINABILITY							PORTABILITY			OTHER			
	SUITABILITY	ACCURACY	INTEROPERABILITY	SECURITY	MATURITY	FAULT TOLERANCE	PREDICTABILITY	AVAILABILITY	RECOVERABILITY	UNDERSTANDABILITY	OPERABILITY	ATTRACTIVENESS	RESPONSE TIME	THROUGHPUT	SCALABILITY	RESOURCE UTILIZATION	ANALYZABILITY	EXTENDABILITY	UPDATEABILITY	MODULARITY	CHANGEABILITY	STABILITY	TESTABILITY	ADAPTABILITY	REUSABILITY	INSTALLABILITY	SAFETY	COMPLEXITY	DESIGNABILITY	COST EFFECTIVENESS
1+1 Redundancy						+		+	+							−														−
Alternative Operating Station	+			−		+		+			+																−			
Appliance-Provided UI	+		+							−	+						−	+						−	+		−			
Artificial Feedback											+	+																		
Beacon										+	+																	−		
Black Box																	+							+				−		
Bootstrapper						+							−				+	+						+				+	+	

Table A.1   Quality attribute pattern table

	FUNCTIONALITY				RELIABILITY					USABILITY			EFFICIENCY				MAINTAINABILITY							PORTABILITY			OTHER			
	Suitability	Accuracy	Interoperability	Security	Maturity	Fault Tolerance	Predictability	Availability	Recoverability	Understandability	Operability	Attractiveness	Response Time	Throughput	Scalability	Resource Utilization	Analyzability	Extendability	Updateability	Modularity	Changeability	Stability	Testability	Adaptability	Reusability	Installability	Safety	Complexity	Designability	Cost Effectiveness
Bumpless Update								+											+									−		
Categorized Messages							−						+										−					+		
Centralized Updater																			+							+		−		
Common Look-and-Feel										+	+	+																	−	
Component-Based Configuration																		+		+	+		−	+				−		
Concurrent Execution													+		+		−	+					−					−		
Configuration Parameter Versions			+										−					+	+		+		−	+	+			−		
Control System	+	+	+					−			+	+					−	+	+	−								−		+
Control System Options	+							−									−	+					−					−		
Counters																	+		+									−		
Data Status				+	+				+								+						+				+			
Devil May Care					+								−									+						−		
Diagnostics				−			+	+						−			+						+							
Distributed Safety					+			−									−										+	−		
Dynamic Message Channel Selector				+			−	+								+	−											−	−	+
Early Warning								+								−	+						+				+			
Early Work					+								+			−												−		
Error Counter					+			+					−																−	
Fleet Management			+								+					−													−	+
Forced Input Value					+				+								+						+					−	−	
Global Time		+	+											−														−		
Half Tasks								+		−			−		+	+	−											−		+
Hardware Abstraction Layer													−			−	+	+		+	+			+	+			−		
Heartbeat					+	+								−			+						+				+	−		
High-Level Protocol	+		+		+								−	−	+		+	+			+					+		−		
HMI Notifications										+	+	−	+																	

Table A.1   Quality attribute pattern table (continued)

Pattern	FUNCTIONALITY				RELIABILITY					USABILITY			EFFICIENCY				MAINTAINABILITY							PORTABILITY			OTHER			
	Suitability	Accuracy	Interoperability	Security	Maturity	Fault Tolerance	Predictability	Availability	Recoverability	Understandability	Operability	Attractiveness	Response Time	Throughput	Scalability	Resource Utilization	Analyzability	Extendability	Updateability	Modularity	Changeability	Stability	Testability	Adaptability	Reusability	Installability	Safety	Complexity	Designability	Cost Effectiveness
Human–Machine Interface	+									+	+	+					+											−		
Interchangeable Algorithm											+		−					+			+	+			+			−		
Isolated Functionalities					+		+						−		+		−	+			+	+		+	+			−	−	
Limp Home					+	−	+	+																				−	−	
Locker Key													−	+	+	+				−										
M2M Communication			+	−									+															−		
Message Channel Multiplexing							+	+					+	−		−	+								+					
Message Gateway			+	+									−	−			+	+		+										
Message Queue													−			+									−					+
Messaging Interface													−					+			+			+	+				−	
Multiple Operating Stations	+							+		+																		−		−
Notification Levels							+						+	−			+											−		
Notification Logging													−			−	+							+						
Notifications					+									+	−						+									
One to Many			+											+	+	+		+			+			+				−		+
Operating Modes							+										+		+		+			+				−	−	
Operating System Abstraction													−			−								+	+			−		
Operator Profile										+	+									−									−	
Opportunistic Delegation								−					+	+			−							−						
Parameters		+																+			+			+					−	
Partial Results		−											−		+		−											−	−	+
Protocol Version Handshake			+				−						−				−	+	+		+		−		+			−		
Remote Access			+	−																+										
Role-Based UI	+			+						+	+																+		−	
Safe State													+														+		−	

Table A.1   Quality attribute pattern table (continued)

Pattern	SUITABILITY	ACCURACY	INTEROPERABILITY	SECURITY	MATURITY	FAULT TOLERANCE	PREDICTABILITY	AVAILABILITY	RECOVERABILITY	UNDERSTANDABILITY	OPERABILITY	ATTRACTIVENESS	RESPONSE TIME	THROUGHPUT	SCALABILITY	RESOURCE UTILIZATION	ANALYZABILITY	EXTENDABILITY	UPDATEABILITY	MODULARITY	CHANGEABILITY	STABILITY	TESTABILITY	ADAPTABILITY	REUSABILITY	INSTALLABILITY	SAFETY	COMPLEXITY	DESIGNABILITY	COST EFFECTIVENESS
Self-Tests									+								+										+	−		
Sensor Bypass						+		+	+	−																		−		
Separate Real-Time						+		+							+	+	+			+			+		+		+	−	−	
Snapshot									+								+						+					−		
Start-Up Negotiation			+			+		+					−					+			+		−			+		−		
Static Resource Allocation				+		+							+			−	−				−									
Static Scheduling		+				+											+	−			−		+					+	−	
System Adapter			+										−		+			+		+				+	+	+		−		
System Start-Up													−		+		+	+		+						+	+	−	−	
Task-Based UI	+									−	+																		−	
Third-Party Sandbox			+	−	−											−		+	−			+	+	+	+		+			
Two-Step Confirmation										+	−		−														+			
Unique Confirmation						+	+							−			+													
Updateable Software				+	−													+	+		+	−							−	
Upright is OK										+	+							−											−	
Variable Guard			+										−		−												+	−		
Variable Manager			+												+		+	+		+	+		+		+			−		
Variable Value Translator			+							+	+	+	−											+				−		
Vector Clock for Messages									+					−		−	+						+					−		
Virtual Runtime Environment				+									−		−									−	+	+	+	−		
Voting						+			+																			−		−
Watchdog						+		+															+					−		

Table A.1 Quality attribute pattern table (continued)

APPENDIX

B

Patlets

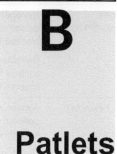

A *patlet* is a short summary of the problem and solution parts of a pattern. Patlets are often used as an aid to discovering patterns that helps to solve a particular problem. In this book we have used the patlet format in which the problem statement and the core of the solution are presented in full. We have not shortened these parts as, for example, is done in (Coplien & Harrison, 2004). We believe that this approach helps you to remember a pattern and understand what the pattern is about.

Table B.1 lists the patlets of all our patterns alphabetical order, to make it easy to check what each pattern is about from its name. This table can also be used as a quick reference to the patterns in our pattern language. In the table the page numbers of the patterns are also shown. If the table shows 'CW' instead of a page number, it means that the pattern can be found on the book's website at www.wiley.com/go/controlsystemspatterns.

PATTERN	PATLET	PAGE
1+1 REDUNDANCY	Some of a system's functionalities are mission-critical and so need be available at all times. However, it is possible for the hardware or software providing the functionality to fail or crash. Therefore: Duplicate any unit that controls a critical functionality. Assign one of the duplicates to active control of the functionality, and the other to be in hot standby mode. If the active unit fails, the hot standby unit takes over control of the functionality.	279
ALTERNATIVE OPERATING STATION	The operator may not be able to observe all the details of a task from the default operating station, or the view from the operating station may blocked by parts of the machine itself. Therefore: Add an alternative operating station that provides the minimal controls for carrying out the task, located where the operator can better observe the work.	330
APPLIANCE-PROVIDED UI	A multitude of optional equipment can be attached to a work machine. The optional equipment requires its own controls and displays, but there is not enough space in the cabin for all the additional controls. Therefore: Create a virtual terminal capable of presenting a user interface to the equipment's own HMI. Create a format for user interface templates and a way to present them on the virtual terminal. Each optional item of equipment then provides its own implementation of its user interface using the specified format. When equipment is attached to the machine, it sends its user interface presentation to the virtual terminal. The equipment can present information on the user interface view and receive control commands from the machine.	CW
ARTIFICIAL FEEDBACK	An operator needs to know whether activation of a function was successful, even when the results of activation are not immediately visible. Therefore: Create a way to give instant feedback if activation of a function is successful. If no feedback is naturally available, use lights, sounds or some other method to inform the operator that activation of the function was registered.	317
BEACON	When a machine operator is concentrating on a task, important events might occur that need their attention. Such events should not pass unnoticed. Therefore: Draw an operator's attention to an important event by using sound effects, blinking or otherwise attention-getting indicator lights.	336
BLACK BOX	When a system malfunctions, the malfunction may prevent access to diagnostic data. It should be still possible to analyze the root cause of a failure afterwards even when the system is in a non-working condition. Therefore: Add a black box component to the system which keeps records of selected system events. The black box stores these events for a specific time for later inspection. Data in the black box component can be accessed with a separate tool even when the system is not functional.	CW

Table B.1   Patlets of all patterns in the pattern language for distributed control systems

PATTERN	PATLET	PAGE
BOOTSTRAPPER	Before an application can be started the hardware should be in a defined state. Uninitialized hardware may cause unexpected behavior in the application.	288
	Therefore: Initialize the hardware during start-up so that the system is always in a consistent state. Where necessary, divide start-up into sequential stages, to overcome any resource limits and to implement separation of concerns (Hürsch & Videira-Lopes, 1995). Add a bootloader component with its own responsibilities for each stage.	
BUMPLESS UPDATE	The process that a control system is monitoring and controlling must not be interrupted. However, a control system software update causes a glitch in operation, as the update needs to be carried out when the controller is not in operating mode.	CW
	Therefore: Divide program code into functional blocks that have defined entry points. Create a system that updates the program on a unit block by block, so that the block currently executing is not updated. When control leaves the block, it can be updated on the fly.	
CATEGORIZED MESSAGES	As a message channel has limited throughput, not all messages will be delivered immediately. However, some messages relate to events, which may require immediate attention.	CW
	Therefore: Add a category to messages according to their importance. Importance can be based on type, sender or receiver, size and so on. Separate Message Queue (page 143)) are implemented for each category.	
CENTRALIZED UPDATER	Updating each node individually in a distributed system may cause a node's software to be incompatible with the rest of the system. This may result in an inoperable machine.	305
	Therefore: Deliver compatible software for all nodes bundled in a single package. Create a centralized updater component that distributes the software to nodes from the bundle. This updater component supervises the update process.	
COMMON LOOK-AND-FEEL	If the principles of user interface views an operator learns cannot be used throughout all views, operating the machine becomes inefficient and inconvenient.	344
	Therefore: Use unified layouts and coloring in all user interface views and notifications. UI elements and functionalities should be presented in the same way independent of the view.	

Table B.1 Patlets of all patterns in the pattern language for distributed control systems (continued)

PATTERN	PATLET	PAGE
COMPONENT-BASED CONFIGURATION	A single product design is not suitable for all customers, as their needs vary. The machine manufacturer cannot offer fully customized products, as modifying components for each customer is too laborious and would result in extensive software versioning. On the other hand, manufactured machine batches are too small to gain the benefits of mass-production.	386
	Therefore: Provide a way to design the system so that it consists of independent components. These components are either hardware or software components. All available components form a product platform component library. Components from the library can be used to build systems that satisfy varying customer needs. Create a description file for each software and hardware component describing its inputs and outputs. Also, create a unified way to describe the whole system using a configuration file. In this file, the desired software and hardware components are selected and the configuration parameters are set for the hardware setup of the system. The file also describes the connections between the software and hardware components. Finally, establish a tool chain to build the control system software based on the configuration file.	
CONCURRENT EXECUTION	When the number of operations in a system increases, a Super Loop architecture does not scale.	229
	Therefore: Collect operations that depend on each other into entities called tasks. Implement a ready queue for tasks that are ready to be executed. Implement a scheduler that takes the first task from the queue for execution. When the task has finished, it is returned to the queue if it needs to be executed again later. Alternating the execution of tasks creates a sense of concurrency.	
CONFIGURATION PARAMETER VERSIONS	A control application update may change parameter values, introduce new parameters or change parameter types. During the update, the old parameter values should not be overwritten, as the operator might have adjusted them. However, it should be possible to overwrite the old parameter values when absolutely necessary, such as if their type changes.	CW
	Therefore: Store the parameters separately from the application in the update bundle for each unit. Tag the parameter set for the unit with a version number that is distinct from the application version. The updated parameter set contains only new parameters or changed values for old parameters. This allows the old parameter values to be retained over the update.	

Table B.1   Patlets of all patterns in the pattern language for distributed control systems (continued)

PATTERN	PATLET	PAGE
CONTROL SYSTEM	The productivity of a work machine cannot be increased any further using traditional ways of building the machine – using hydraulics, electronics and mechanics. A new way to control the machine needs to be introduced to optimize the system functionality and to increase the number of automated functionalities. For the same reason, user experience needs to be enhanced, and the system needs to connect to external information systems to make the machine an integral part of the whole production chain.	96
	Therefore: Implement control system software that controls the machine and has interfaces to communicate with other machines and systems. The control system can automate many of the functionalities that were previously carried out manually by the machine operator. In addition, the control system can provide the operator with more fine-grained information about system state than could ever be provided without it. The control system also interacts with external information systems.	
CONTROL SYSTEM OPTIONS	Customer needs vary greatly; for some the basic machine setup is enough, but some customers need additional features. Individual solutions should be provided for each customer at an affordable price without creating a plethora of different control system software versions.	394
	Therefore: During development include in the control system all software components required by accessories. When a customer buys an optional accessory, the corresponding code block is enabled without having to install a different software version.	
COUNTERS	A system has events whose frequency of occurrence is interesting. These occurrences are countable quantities that may need to be stored persistently. One event may affect several countable quantities, some of which are global and some used only by a limited set of nodes. It is not always clear which node is responsible for storing the quantity.	CW
	Therefore: Create a service that provides counting functionality for different purposes. The service should offer different kind of counters, for example non-resetting usage counters, maintenance counters and resettable counters. The counters can count up or down, or can be driven by a timer.	
DATA STATUS	A data consumer cannot deduce its correctness based only on its contents. However, to function safely, the consumer must know whether the data is trustworthy and up to date, and does not originate from an inaccurate sensor.	217
	Therefore: Add status to each variable in the system as meta-information. Status information indicates the age and/or the state of the information (OK, 'INVALID', DERIVED_FAIL etc.). This allows a data consumer to see whether the data is fit to use for its purposes.	

Table B.1   Patlets of all patterns in the pattern language for distributed control systems (continued)

PATTERN	PATLET	PAGE
DEVIL MAY CARE	As the system is not yet ready to work normally due to start-up or mode changes, all kind of transient errors and faults can occur. However, these clear themselves after the system has stabilized, so any error recovery actions caused by transient errors would compromise system performance. Therefore: For transient phases, define a time interval in which the system may ignore predefined error situations. The system must reach a steady state before this period has elapsed. A steady state means that the system is ready for normal operation.	190
DIAGNOSTICS	To avoid unplanned breaks in production, information on the health of the system is needed in order to plan proper maintenance. Therefore: Add an on-board data collection component to the system, collecting information from sensors, messages from the bus and so on. In addition, create a diagnostic component to analyze this information and detect if a subsystem starts to operate poorly or erroneously. This analysis should be based on the known heuristics and value ranges. A deviation from these indicates the need for maintenance.	350
DISTRIBUTED SAFETY	A single malfunction affecting the behavior of a node may result in a serious incident. The consequences of the malfunction are unacceptable, but it is hard to eliminate sources of malfunctions. Therefore: Divide potentially harmful functionality into multiple nodes that communicate with each other. For each of these nodes, implement only a part of the potentially hazardous functionality, so that only cooperation can trigger the whole functionality.	116
DYNAMIC MESSAGE CHANNEL SELECTOR	Multiple communication channels to access a machine may be available. Under differing circumstances some of these channels may not be available. The most suitable communication channel for the machine's circumstances should be used. Therefore: Prioritize all communication channels based on their properties, such as cost. Add a selector component that changes the communication channel automatically if a higher priority channel is not available.	365
EARLY WARNING	In a control system, resources (for example CPU time, memory, oil and so on) can run out. The control system needs to start remedial actions to avoid hazardous consequences before resource availability reaches a critical level. A situation in which a resource is about to run out should be detected, as insufficient resources may crash the whole system or cause a hazard. For example, message buffer overflow could crash the system: it is too late to react to the situation once the resource has already become depleted. Therefore: Add an early warning mechanism that monitors the available level of a resource. Before the resource runs out, the mechanism warns concerned parties, such as the machine operator, so that remedial action can be taken.	169

Table B.1   Patlets of all patterns in the pattern language for distributed control systems (continued)

PATTERN	PATLET	PAGE
EARLY WORK	Because the system has strict real-time requirements, its response times must be predictable and fast. However, some operations may take a long time, or consume too much resources, for immediate response.	259
	Therefore: Prepare the task's execution beforehand by doing some of the task's work in advance. The preparations can be done at compile time or runtime, but before the main task is executed. Once the task has finished its preparations, it must free unnecessary resources so that they are available for the preparations of other tasks.	
ERROR COUNTER	Transient faults can occur in a system due to demanding conditions in the environment. These faults should not cause a machine to enter a Safe State (page 179), as they clear themselves after a short while. Substantial faults should be distinguished from transient faults.	CW
	Therefore: Create an error counter whose threshold can be set to specific value. The error counter is incremented every time a fault is reported. Once the threshold is met, an error is triggered. The counter is decremented or reset after a specific time has elapsed from the last fault report.	
FLEET MANAGEMENT	In a production chain work needs to be allocated to multiple machines. To minimize waiting times and inventories, the machines need to cooperate with those from other stages in the production chain.	372
	Therefore: Implement a fleet management application and install it on board the machine. Within that application, create common interfaces and information models for all work machines, to manage them as a fleet. Production information, which conforms to the information model, can be transferred to and from the machine using the common interface. In this way the machine can exchange information and coordinate optimization of work with other machines via an ERP system.	
FORCED INPUT VALUE	Functionality consists of a chain of units, their inputs and outputs. In a case of malfunction in specific functionality, it is hard to determine where the malfunction is by only monitoring the outputs of the chain. The malfunction can be in any of the control units or in the communication channel.	CW
	Therefore: Create a mechanism that can be used to force the control unit's input to a specific value. This forcing mechanism is added to each control unit, but is separated from the communication channel. This make it possible to check whether the output of the control unit receiving the forced input corresponds to the expected output. If the output is not correct, the control unit is malfunctioning, otherwise the communication channel is broken.	

Table B.1 Patlets of all patterns in the pattern language for distributed control systems (continued)

PATTERN	PATLET	PAGE
GLOBAL TIME	Different nodes in the system have their own internal clocks that can be set to the wrong time or which can drift and result in clock skew. However, all the nodes need to share common time in order to collaborate properly.	124
	Therefore: Use a single node's clock, for example a master unit's clock or external time source, such as a GPS or an atomic clock time signal, to provide global time and to synchronize clocks on all nodes. The external clock can also offer synchronization pulses to pace the collaboration of multiple nodes.	
HALF TASKS	To maintain determinism in response times, real-time tasks must be executed within a specific time window. However, intermittent tasks can occur that require immediate attention, such as device interrupts. These can interfere with the real-time requirements of an interrupted task.	254
	Therefore: Divide intermittent tasks into two parts. The first part acknowledges that the task is received and marks the fact that there is more work to do. The second part does the actual work while real-time tasks are not being executed.	
HARDWARE ABSTRACTION LAYER	Each vendor may have its own way of controlling hardware devices. If all the devices are controlled in a vendor-specific way, it makes the application code dependent on the selected hardware. To make applications portable, the hardware should be decoupled from the applications.	264
	Therefore: Create a hardware abstraction layer (HAL) between the application software and the hardware implementation of the control mechanisms of devices. In this layer, provide generic interfaces to access devices of a specific type in a uniform way. A HAL abstracts implementation details of the hardware behind these interfaces.	
HEARTBEAT	A node or a bus may malfunction silently. Any such malfunction should be detected in order to react to the situation.	120
	Therefore: Make a node send messages to another node at predetermined and regular intervals. The other node knows how long a message interval should be and waits for it. If the message does not arrive in time, remedial actions can be started.	
HIGH-LEVEL PROTOCOL	It is difficult to match a single messaging solution to all the communication requirements that can arise in a specific domain without tightly coupling communication with the selected technology.	137
	Therefore: Add a high-level protocol to decouple applications from low-level messaging. The payload of low-level messages should hold information that can be interpreted by a higher-level protocol. The high-level protocol forms a basis for additional services, such as acknowledgements, addressed messages and so on.	

Table B.1   Patlets of all patterns in the pattern language for distributed control systems (continued)

PATTERN	PATLET	PAGE
HMI NOTIFICATIONS	Many events occur in a system. Only some of the events are interesting to the operator. Some of these events may require an operator decision in order to continue operation.	CW
	Therefore: Define a subset of notifications that are of interest to the operator. Create a HMI notification service to display these on the user interface. Some notifications are decisions that the system cannot resolve autonomously, and which therefore require an operator decision. The service should therefore be able to send a control command to the bus when the operator responds to a specific notification.	
HUMAN–MACHINE INTERFACE	The control system should provide the machine operator with feedback and a way to operate the system.	313
	Therefore: Add a human-machine interface that supports ways to present information and controls to manipulate the machine. These are typically displays with GUIs, buzzers, joysticks, buttons and so on. The presentation of information and the controls of the machine must be decoupled, for example by using One to Many (page 131) communication and a message bus.	
INTERCHANGEABLE ALGORITHM	Different usage situations have different requirements for the control algorithm. It is hard to handle all situations just by parameterizing a single control algorithm.	193
	Therefore: Implement variants of the control algorithm as independent components. Add an algorithm selector component that provides the application with access to the control algorithm. When the control algorithm is called, the selector component determines which variation of the control algorithm should be used in the context of the call, and calls the selected implementation of the algorithm. The application uses the selector component instead of the actual algorithm.	
ISOLATED FUNCTIONALITIES	As the control system evolves and gains new features, it becomes hard to maintain and understand its structure. In addition, the processing power of a single device running the software may be exceeded.	110
	Therefore: Identify logically connected functionalities and compose these functionalities as manageable-sized entities. Implement each of these entities as their own subsystem in order to isolate functionalities.	
LIMP HOME	Even when part of the machine is malfunctioning, the machine should still be operable at least some to extent in order to make salvage operations possible and maintenance easier.	185
	Therefore: Divide sensors and actuators into groups according to their functionalities, such as drive train, boom operations and so on. Groups may overlap. A malfunctioning device only disables the groups it belongs to, and other groups remain operable.	

Table B.1 Patlets of all patterns in the pattern language for distributed control systems (continued)

PATTERN	PATLET	PAGE
LOCKER KEY	Copying large amounts of message data from one task to another takes time and requires resources. This may jeopardize the performance of the system. Therefore: Allocate shared memory for communicating tasks. Divide the memory into slots called lockers, which are identified with a key, such as a memory address. Store message data from a sending task to a locker and send a message containing only the locker key. The message receiver then uses the key to access the message data from the locker.	250
M2M COMMUNICATION	A number of machines work in the same fast-paced environment. Machines may need to share information with each other to ensure fluent operation or to warn other machines. A centralized communication mechanism would be too slow, or does not exist. Therefore: Allow peer-to-peer communication between machines by adding a client and server to each machine. Using this communication, a machine can send predefined messages that contain data such as their location and current environment information.	CW
MESSAGE CHANNEL MULTIPLEXING	To allow deterministic operation of a machine, it needs to be ensured that messages get delivered. A node may 'babble' to the bus and prevent other nodes from communicating. Therefore: Separate the communication channel from the physical bus by creating virtual channels. Virtual channels can be multiplexed onto one physical channel by dividing the channel into time slots. A virtual channel can also be divided over several physical buses.	CW
MESSAGE GATEWAY	Parts of a machine may have different communication needs, so various messaging channels are required. The parts need to cooperate as a whole, so the messaging channels should be connected. Therefore: Add a message gateway component to the system which routes message traffic between message channels. If needed, the component can filter messages according to specific criteria defined in the system configuration. In addition, the component translates messages from one protocol to another.	CW
MESSAGE QUEUE	Individual nodes have different messaging rates and cycle times, so a message cannot be processed immediately at the receiving end. On the other hand, sending a message might not be possible at a given moment, as some other communication might be taking place on the bus. Therefore: Spread message rate differences by making messaging asynchronous. Add queues to each node for receipt and transmission of messages. Implement mechanisms for putting messages in the queue and sending messages from the queue. The same mechanism can read messages from the bus, add them to the received messages queue, and notify the application about new messages.	143

Table B.1 Patlets of all patterns in the pattern language for distributed control systems (continued)

PATTERN	PATLET	PAGE
MESSAGING INTERFACE	A high-level protocol may change over time, or the same control system software may be used in different communication setups. This should not require changes to the implementation of applications.	CW
	Therefore: To make the application independent of the system bus technology and messaging protocol, construct a common application programming interface (API) to provide uniform messaging functionality. The API provides methods, for example for sending and receiving messages. Messages consist of data presented in the form of programming language structures.	
MULTIPLE OPERATING STATIONS	The working environment may be such that several implements, such as booms, could be in use at the same time. Substantial cognitive stress may be imposed on the operator if they need to focus on controlling multiple implements simultaneously.	CW
	Therefore: Add a new operating station for each task to be performed with the machine. These operating stations can be identical or specialized for a specific task. This allows several operators to control the machine at the same time.	
NOTIFICATION LEVELS	Different kinds of notifications should be grouped according to their severity in order to be able to determine their consequences in a deterministic way.	162
	Therefore: Add notification level information to notification data. Typical notification levels are notices, warnings and faults. The notification receiver has its own way of remedying the situation for each level. In addition, notification data is processed by dealing with the most urgent notifications first, to ensure short response times.	
NOTIFICATION LOGGING	To find out which transient faults have occurred and to analyze the root cause of a fault, there should be a way to find out which notifications have occurred in the system. It should be possible to view the notifications that occurred after the machine has been stopped.	166
	Therefore: Create a logging mechanism that logs notifications that occur in the system. Add timestamps, if necessary, and notification source to all logged notifications, allowing the order of notifications to be deduced.	
NOTIFICATIONS	The nodes have many kinds of status changes, for example a change of an operating mode, or a malfunction. Other nodes in the system need to react to or be aware of these status changes. However, it cannot be assumed that a single status message will get through.	156
	Therefore: Store event-related data in a ring buffer on the node producing the information. When an item is inserted into the ring buffer an event counter is incremented. Communicate this event counter value to the bus, so that other nodes interested in the status of the node can detect when new data is available in the ring buffer. They can then read the ring buffer contents using asynchronous communication.	

Table B.1   Patlets of all patterns in the pattern language for distributed control systems (continued)

PATTERN	PATLET	PAGE
ONE TO MANY	Every node has to know how to reach the recipients for information it produces, and this forms tight coupling between nodes. If communication requirements change, redesign of wiring or software on several nodes is necessary.	131
	Therefore: Build a network in which all nodes share the same communication medium. A bus network topology is normally used to connect nodes. Nodes send information as messages over this medium. All nodes can receive all messages from the network, and can see if there is anything relevant to them on the bus.	
OPERATING MODES	Different operating contexts create different requirements for the control system. These requirements are contradictory or not valid in all operating contexts. However, the control system is normally used in only one operating context at a time. During design time it is sufficient to focus on the subset of requirements that apply in a specific operating context.	175
	Therefore: Design the system so that it has multiple modes that correspond to specific operating contexts. While the system is in a mode, it only allows use of those functionalities that are relevant for the current operating context.	
OPERATING SYSTEM ABSTRACTION	The lifecycles of applications and the underlying operating system may differ. It should be possible to change the operating system with only minimal modifications to the application code.	269
	Therefore: Create an abstraction layer that implements all OS-dependent services. Use only this abstraction layer for OS services in application code.	
OPERATOR PROFILE	Personalized settings can increase the productivity and comfort of a machine operator. However, as multiple similar machines might be available but there is no dedicated machine for each operator, settings are likely to be changed by other operators. The operator's user experience and productivity can be increased if inconvenient readjustment of a machine's GUI settings and controls can be avoided when putting the machine to use.	340
	Therefore: Create a package containing all an operator's settings in a single easily transferable file. This file may be located on the control PC's hard disk, or it might be saved on removable media such as a memory stick. Provide an easy way to transfer the settings between machines and apply them.	

Table B.1   Patlets of all patterns in the pattern language for distributed control systems (continued)

PATTERN	PATLET	PAGE
OPPORTUNISTIC DELEGATION	Fleet management needs to delegate dynamically emerging tasks for fleet members. The states of fleet members are constantly in flux. The fleet management application must determine the optimal fleet member to carry out a specific task, but while doing so the state of the fleet might change. Increasing the frequency of state updates from fleet members does not help, as the communication delay is too long.	CW
	Therefore: Create a task delegator service for the fleet management system. This delegator allocates a task to a fleet member based on the best guess of the fleet member's state without separately querying whether it is able to do the task or not. If the fleet member can do the task, it takes ownership of the task and informs the delegator. If the fleet member cannot do the task, it notifies the delegator, which reallocates the task to another fleet member.	
PARAMETERS	A machine must remain efficient during a long lifecycle regardless of the environment in which it is used. In addition, the different needs of various machine operators need to be addressed to guarantee the efficiency of work. This requires the control system to compensate for changing conditions.	380
	Therefore: Describe properties that are likely to change during a machine's lifecycle as configuration parameters. Implement a user interface through which these parameters can be altered.	
PARTIAL RESULTS	Some real-time tasks need more time than the control loop's cycle time allows. However, the results of long real-time tasks are typically needed only every nth loop cycle.	243
	Therefore: Implement longer tasks so that an nth part of the task is executed in each loop cycle and the partial result is stored to memory. This allows new results from longer tasks to be ready every nth loop cycle.	
PROTOCOL VERSION HANDSHAKE	Nodes should use the latest version of a communication protocol, as it is probably the most efficient. However, a system may also have nodes that use older protocol versions, and there must be a way to communicate with them. The most efficient protocol common to all nodes should be determined.	CW
	Therefore: Design a handshake sequence common to all protocol versions. In the handshake, all nodes announce the highest protocol version they support during system start-up. Once nodes have announced their highest version, each node selects the highest common version for communication.	
REMOTE ACCESS	Services using the data that the machine collects are not necessarily on board the machine. Similarly, on-board applications may need data that is produced in a different location.	361
	Therefore: Add an on-board remote connection gateway that enables communication between the machine and a remote party. The remote connection gateway transforms the messaging scheme used on the machine to suit local and remote parties' needs, and employs authentication.	

Table B.1 Patlets of all patterns in the pattern language for distributed control systems (continued)

PATTERN	PATLET	PAGE
ROLE-BASED UI	A machine's operator only needs such functionality in the UI that is required by their job description. All other functionality should be hidden from the UI to make the HMI more usable, and to prevent problems caused by unauthorized use of functionalities. Therefore: Create a separate user interface for each user group: operators, maintenance and production line personnel. Each group has different privileges that limit the available interface views. User interface activation may require a dongle, password, or additional equipment.	327
SAFE STATE	When the control system tries to control a part of the machine that is malfunctioning, the machine may respond in an unpredictable way. Consequently, the machine may harm the operator, machine or surroundings. These kinds of situations should not take place. Therefore: Design a safe state that can be entered if the control system encounters a malfunction that cannot be handled autonomously. The safe state is such that it prevents the machine from causing harm. The safe state is device and functionality dependent and is not necessarily the same as the unpowered state.	179
SELF-TESTS	Rarely used functionalities, such as safety functions, may fail silently, as they are not actively used. It may be hard to detect these latent malfunctions. Therefore: For each device, design a test sequence consisting of inputs and their corresponding outputs. Run the test sequence periodically or once in a while, for example during every third system start-up. If the test sequence fails, it triggers a failure notification.	CW
SENSOR BYPASS	Some sensors are used in a system design merely to give small advantages in productivity or in the operator experience. When this kind of sensor malfunctions, it can cause suboptimal operation or stop the whole machine. Therefore: For each sensor of minor importance, implement a mechanism to replace the sensor's output value with a substitute value. The value can be a default, a user-defined value, a simulated value or the last known good value. In the event of a malfunction in the sensor, the substitute value can be used temporarily.	CW
SEPARATE REAL-TIME	*There are always machine control functionalities in a system. To increase the productivity and operability of the machine, the system needs to offer high-level functionality such as a graphical user interface, Diagnostics and so on. The high-level functionalities' behavior may compromise the real-time requirements of machine control functionalities.* Therefore: Divide the system into separate levels according to real-time requirements, for example into machine control and machine operator levels. Real-time functionalities are located on the machine control level, and non-real-time functionalities on the machine operator level. The levels cannot interfere with each other, as they use a message bus or other medium to communicate with each other.	237

Table B.1 Patlets of all patterns in the pattern language for distributed control systems (continued)

PATTERN	PATLET	PAGE
SNAPSHOT	The system-wide state is complex and changes all the time. Because of this, the operator or developer is usually not interested in system state as long as the machine functions normally. However, it is useful to examine the system-wide state at a specific moment later, to analyze and test the system after something of interest has occurred.	221
	Therefore: Implement a mechanism to save all state variables, along with the timestamp from the Variable Manager (page 201), as a snapshot. Create a toolset in the development environment to analyze and restore system-wide state from the snapshot, for further use.	
START-UP NEGOTIATION	A system's configuration may change between start-ups. Some devices are mandatory to ensure safe operation. In addition, optional devices might provide additional functionality. The available functionality is hard to determine from the current set of devices.	CW
	Therefore: Create a mechanism in which all nodes announce themselves by sending a message to the bus after starting up. In the message, a node declares its existence and announces its capabilities. Design a central node, a negotiator, that gathers this information and builds a list of the nodes that are present. Using this list, the negotiator determines the available functionality. A node is ignored if it does not declare its presence within a specific time.	
STATIC RESOURCE ALLOCATION	Real-time applications have to perform their operations within a given time to avoid severe failure, so the required resources must always be available.	247
	Therefore: Assign all the resources required for real-time applications at design time. When an application starts the actual resources, for example memory blocks, are reserved for it. This prevents execution time being affected by the nondeterministic timing of resource allocation.	
STATIC SCHEDULING	In a real-time environment, tasks should always be executed at a defined moment, to prevent system failure. However, scheduling can cause variance in the response times of applications, jeopardizing predictability.	234
	Therefore: Design scheduling with time slots of fixed length and divide the application into executable blocks. These may for example be functions or code blocks. The executable blocks are assigned to time slots at compile time.	
SYSTEM ADAPTER	A fleet consists of many kinds of machines from various vendors, carrying out several tasks. Customizing a fleet management system for each machine is expensive and time-consuming. From the fleet management's perspective, however, all machines could be managed in a similar way.	CW
	Therefore: Create a system adapter that converts fleet management commands to a format that the system can use. In similar way, the adapter converts production data from machines to a format conforming to the fleet management application's information model. The system adapter becomes a client for the fleet management server, wrapping the actual system.	

Table B.1 Patlets of all patterns in the pattern language for distributed control systems (continued)

PATTERN	PATLET	PAGE
SYSTEM START-UP	The nodes in a system have varied start-up times and their functionality may depend on other nodes. If one node depends on another node, it must not start its functionality before the other node is ready to allow correct operation. Therefore: Design the start-up order of devices based on their dependencies, boot-up times and resources requirements. Based on this order, divide nodes into master and slave nodes. A master nodes wait for its slave nodes before they start operating. When a slave node has started, it signals its master node. When all the slave nodes of a master node have started, the master node enters its normal operating mode.	293
TASK-BASED UI	There are several tasks with different requirements for the user interface. If a single user interface view is used to cover all these diverse requirements, it results in low usability. On the other hand, several UI views are confusing if the current UI view does not correspond to the task the operator is actually carrying out. Therefore: Design an operating mode for each task. Create a separate UI view for each task, and change the active view automatically when the operator changes the operating mode.	CW
THIRD-PARTY SANDBOX	End users require more features from the system, so the manufacturer has to outsource development of applications that are not within their core competence. These applications cannot always be trusted not to compromise the operation of the system, either inadvertently or on purpose. Therefore: Provide an interface and tools for third-party application developers. Third-party applications can use the machine's services only through this interface, so will not interfere with the machine's own applications. The interface provides common ways to access data and services.	355
TWO-STEP CONFIRMATION	Unintentional (de)activation of a functionality that may have long-lasting consequences should be avoided, as it may prevent use of the machine. Therefore: Design the graphical user interface such that the operator needs to enable a function twice, changing the way in which this is achieved each time. This ensures that the operator must make a conscious decision to activate the function.	321
UNIQUE CONFIRMATION	Messages in a distributed system may be delivered out of sequence. If all acknowledge messages are identical, the receiver has no means to determine which request was acknowledged. Therefore: For each request message, assign a unique identifier, which is represented in its own field. When the message is acknowledged, the response message contains the same unique identifier as the request. The requester keeps track of messages that are not yet acknowledged. In this way, the receiver of an acknowledgement always knows to which request the response applies, and can resend the request if necessary.	CW

Table B.1   Patlets of all patterns in the pattern language for distributed control systems (continued)

PATTERN	PATLET	PAGE
UPDATEABLE SOFTWARE	During a long lifecycle a system's requirements are likely to change for various reasons. The system should be adaptable to these changes to maintain its efficiency. Therefore: Place software on rewriteable persistent storage that is large enough for future needs. Use hardware that has enough capacity to accommodate additional future functionality. Implement an update mode to handle system update. Deliver new software over a wire and implement a separate updater application that updates the control application.	301
UPRIGHT IS OK	An operator is usually not interested in the details of the machine's status, but just needs a quick overview that everything is functioning normally. Therefore: Use traditional gauges in the interface, even if the UI is implemented with graphical components. Use these gauges such that their needles are pointing upwards when their measured values are in their normal range. This makes it easy to get an overview that everything is functioning normally.	324
VARIABLE GUARD	To allow third-party applications from untrusted parties to access the data produce by the control system, it must have control over what information each application can produce and consume. Therefore: Design a mechanism to guard the variables that checks whether an application is allowed to read variable values or submit their own changes to system state information. The mechanism is the only component that can directly access the Variable Manager.	208
VARIABLE MANAGER	Information exchange for collaboration is not within the responsibility of a local application, as the main purpose of the application on a specific node is to control some part of the machine. To facilitate efficient collaboration between nodes, however, the nodes need to share information. Therefore: For each node, add a component, Variable Manager, that stores the system information as variables and provides interfaces for reading and writing them. To make the information global, it is also sent to the bus whenever a variable is locally updated through the interface. Similarly, the Variable Manager updates the corresponding variables when it reads updated information from the bus.	201
VARIABLE VALUE TRANSLATOR	Different devices may use various measuring units internally, but they should also be able to use each other's information about the surrounding environment. Hard-coding of unit translations is not scalable, and the same translations may be needed throughout a system. Therefore: Add a converter service to the Variable Manager. The service includes interfaces to store and retrieve variables in suitable units regardless of the units the Variable Manager uses internally.	211

Table B.1   Patlets of all patterns in the pattern language for distributed control systems (continued)

PATTERN	PATLET	PAGE
VECTOR CLOCK FOR MESSAGES	In the case of failure the order of messages sent over the bus needs to be determined reliably to find out what caused the failure. However, the exact moment when a message was sent is not important.	149
	Therefore: Add a message counter to each node. This counter is increased whenever the node sends a message. Also add a vector clock to each node, which is used to timestamp all messages sent in the system. This vector clock consists of separate message counter values for all nodes, including the sending node's own counter. A node's vector clock is updated when a message containing a vector clock timestamp larger than receiving node's clock is received, or when the node's own message counter is increased.	
VIRTUAL RUNTIME ENVIRONMENT	Hardware is likely to change during a long product lifecycle, so applications need to be ported to run on new hardware. However, porting by recompiling the application is not always possible or desirable.	272
	Therefore: Virtualize the runtime environment by creating a hardware-independent execution platform for applications. The applications are compiled for the environment and executed in it. The runtime environment is ported to all the desired platforms.	
VOTING	A high level of correctness is required in a system with autonomous functions. Even though 1+1 Redundancy offers high availability, it does not ensure correctness of a single decision, as the master unit can give erroneous results.	282
	Therefore: Use redundant units to compute the control output independently, and add an additional unit, called a voter, to collect their output as votes. The voter determines the correct output based on the votes.	
WATCHDOG	To increase the safety of the whole system, malfunction of a node should be detected and recovery actions should be started automatically.	101
	Therefore: Add a watchdog component to put the node into a safe state if the application does not reset the watchdog within a given time limit.	

Table B.1 Patlets of all patterns in the pattern language for distributed control systems (continued)

Glossary

Actuator	A unit for moving or controlling a mechanism or system.
Bootstrapping	A technique in which one piece of software activates more complicated software during system start-up. See BOOTSTRAPPER (page 288) for more information.
Bucking (trees)	Bucking is the process of cutting a felled and delimbed tree into logs.
Bus	A communication medium that nodes can use to communicate with each other using messages. See also ONE TO MANY (page 131).
Capability	An action that a machine is capable of doing. One capability may require several functionalities for its operation. A capability can be for example moving the machine or drilling a hole.
Closed-control loop	A control system whose operation is based on input and feedback signal(s). It generates an output which often controls actuators.
Component	Encapsulation of a set of related functions or data. The term *component* may be used in the context of software or hardware components.
Control application	Software which realizes control loops for a specific functionality. A control application often has real-time requirements.
Control system	A software system handling the operations of the whole machine. It may communicate with other machines and systems for cooperation and information sharing.
Device	An actuator, controller or sensor which may be attached to a bus.

Distributed system	A set of physically separated nodes, which are interconnected to cooperate and control the machine as a whole.
Embedded system	A combination of hardware and software, which is usually designed for a dedicated function. It often has real-time computing constraints.
ERP	A set of applications that a company can use to manage business processes based on inputs from other information systems.
Fail-fast	A system or module that is designed to propagate any failure through its interfaces immediately. Fail-fast systems are usually designed to stop all operations at once.
Fleet	A set of machines in a production chain.
Feller buncher	A type of harvester used in logging. A motorized vehicle with an attachment that can gather several trees before felling them.
Forwarder	A forestry vehicle that carries felled logs from the stand to a roadside to await further transportation.
Functionality	A group of functions that carries out actions related to a common purpose, such as driving or boom control.
HMI (Human–machine interface)	A user interface where the operator can observe the machine's status and control machine operations using gauges, screens, indicators, joysticks, buttons, etc.
Geo-fencing	A virtual perimeter for a real world geographical area. This perimeter can be used to trigger functionalities within a fleet of machines; for example when a machine enters the area, other machines within it can be notified about the event.
Implement, work implement	A tool used to perform an action with a work machine. For example, one implement of a forest harvester is the harvester head, which does the tree felling, sawing, delimbing and so on.
Machine control level	The part of a control system which has real-time requirements. Control applications typically reside on this level. See SEPARATE REAL-TIME (page 237).
Message	A series of bytes in a specific format forms a message. A message has a sender and one or more intended receivers that have agreed on the format and semantics of the data conveyed by the message.

Node	An active electronic device that is attached to a bus that is capable of sending, receiving or forwarding information over a communications channel.
Normal operating mode	The mode in which a machine is available for work. See also OPERATING MODES (page 175).
Operator level	A high-level functionality without strict control-related real-time requirements. Such functionalities are for example GUI and diagnostic functions.
Optional equipment	Implements and other attachments that can be bought separately even years after a machine is initially purchased. For example, a winch could be added as optional equipment for a mining drill rig.
Parameter	A value that is related to adjusting the functionality of a system. Sometimes this can be used to activate new functionalities. See also PARAMETERS (page 380).
PDO	Process data objects (PDOs) are used in CANopen for broadcasting high-priority control and status information, such as the control voltage for a valve, or measured temperature.
PID controller	A proportional-integral-derivative controller calculates an error value as the difference between a measured process variable and a desired setpoint. The controller attempts to minimize the error by adjusting its outputs. It uses a proportional value to correct the current error and an integrated value to take past errors into account. The controller tries to predict future errors by using derived values.
PLC	A programmable logic controller is a general-purpose controller used to control processes or machine parts automatically.
Poka-yoke	A quality management concept that prevents human errors from occurring by designing a system such that incorrect parts cannot be assembled together, so that flaws and errors are easily identifiable. *Poka-yoke* is a Japanese term that is often translated as 'mistake-proofing'.
POST	Power-on self test: tests that verify hardware integrity automatically on application of power.
Process automation	Hardware and software used to control a process. For example, paper manufacturing can be highly automated by a process automation system.

Product	A single model of work machine.
Product family	A set of products that are derived from a common product platform. Also known as a *product line*.
Product platform	Common components of multiple products are combined as a product platform to make rapid product development possible.
Real-time	Real-time systems must respond within strict time constraints. In contrast, a non-real-time system may respond quickly, but cannot *guarantee* a response time.
RTOS	Real-Time Operating System, an operating system intended to run real-time applications.
SDO	Service data objects (SDOs) are used in peer-to-peer communication between two nodes. By using SDOs, object dictionary entries can be read and written. SDOs are used, for example, for configuring a node.
Sensor	A sensor is a device that measures a physical quantity. It converts the measurement into a signal that can be read by a controller.
Signal	A variable that is mapped to a specific message on the bus. See VARIABLE MANAGER (page 201) for more information.
State variables	State variables describe the state of a control system. For example, by accessing the system state variables it is possible to determine information such as operating mode, oil pressure and coolant temperature.
Straddle carrier	A heavy vehicle used in port terminals to move and stack containers.
Subsystem	A part of the system that usually provides a single functionality. This functionality could be, for example, controlling a boom.
System configuration	The current set of hardware and software components that are attached to a machine.
System state	The system state describes the current status of the whole work machine. The system state consists of the state variables of the system.
Task	A process or application that can be scheduled for execution and carries out one activity, usually by means of a single control loop. See also CONCURRENT EXECUTION (page 229) and STATIC SCHEDULING (page 234).

Timestamp   A timestamp uniquely identifies the moment when a specific event occurred. It usually contains date and time values.

Unit   A physical device. Unlike *node*, a *unit* is not necessarily attached to a bus.

References

3GPP, 2013	*3GPP Specification 22.042: Network Identity and Timezone.* http://www.3gpp.org/ftp/specs/html-INFO/22042.htm (accessed 8 June 2013)
3S-Smart Software, 2013	3S-Smart Software, 2013. *CODESYS – Industrial IEC 61131-3 PLC Programming.* http://www.codesys.com (accessed 1 Nov 2013)
Aarsten et al, 1996	Aarsten, A., Brugali, D. & Menga, G., 1996. Patterns for Three-Tier Client/Server Applications. *Proceedings of PLoP 1996.*
Agile Alliance, 2001	*Manifesto for Agile Software Development.* http://agilemanifesto.org (accessed 9 May 2012)
Alexander, 1975	Alexander, C., 1975. The Oregon Experiment. Center for Environmental Structure III. Oxford University Press, USA. ISBN 978-0195018240
Alexander, 1979	Alexander, C., 1979. *The Timeless Way of Building.* New York: Oxford University Press
Alexander et al, 1977	Alexander, C., Ishikawa, S. & Silverstein, M., 1977. *A Pattern Language: Towns, Buildings, Construction.* Oxford University Press
Alho & Mattila, 2013	Alho, P. & Mattila, J., 2013. Real-Time Service-Oriented Architectures: A Data-Centric Implementation for Distributed and Heterogeneous Robotic System. *In Proceedings of 4th IFIP TC 10 International Embedded Systems Symposium (IESS 2013),* pp. 262–271
Anderson & Romanski, 2011	Andersen, S. B. & Romanksi, G., 2011. Verification of Safety-Critical Software. *ACM Queue,* 9(8)
Armoush, 2010	Armoush, A., 2010. *Design Patterns for Safety-Critical Embedded Systems.* PhD thesis, RWTH Aachen University
Arnold, 2000	Arnold, D. N., 2000. *The Patriot Missile Failure.* http://www.ima.umn.edu/~arnold/disasters/patriot.html (accessed 8 Jun 2013)

Apache, 2013	The Apache Software Foundation, 2013. *The Apache HTTP Server Project.* http://httpd.apache.org/ (accessed 13 Jul 2013)
AUTOSAR, 2013	*AUTOSAR – AUTomotive Open System ARchitecture.* http://www.autosar.org/ (accessed 13 Jun 2013)
Avizienis, 1976	Avizienis, A., 1976. Fault-Tolerant Systems. *IEEE Transactions on Computers,* 25(12), pp. 1304–1312
Avizienis, 1985	Avizienis, A., 1985. The N-Version Approach to Fault-Tolerant Software. *IEEE Transactions on Software Engineering,* 11(12), pp. 1491–1501
Bachmann et al, 2007	Bachmann, F., Bass, L. & Nord, R., 2007. *Modifiability Tactics,* Pittsburgh: Carnegie-Mellon University, Software Engineering Institute (SEI)
Banker at al, 1993	Banker, R., Datar, S., Kemerer, C. & Zweig, D., 1993. Software Complexity and Maintenance Costs. *Communications of the ACM,* November, 36(11), pp. 81–94
Baskerville et al, 2011	Baskerville, R., Pries-Heje, J. & Madsen, S., 2011. Post-Agility: What follows a Decade of Agility. *Journal of Information and Software Technology,* 53(5), pp. 543–555
Bass et al, 2003	Bass, L., Clements, P. & Kazman, R., 2003. *Software Architecture in Practice.* 2nd edition, Addison-Wesley
Beckhoff, 2013	*EtherCAT Distributed Clocks.* http://infosys.beckhoff.com/english.php?content=./content/1033/ethercatsystem/html/bt_ethercat_dc_intro.htm&id= (accessed 20 Nov 2013)
Bengtsson et al, 2000	Bengtsson, P., Lassing, N., Bosch, J. & van Vliet, H., 2000. *Analyzing Software Architectures for Modifiability*
Berlin, 1953	Berlin, I., 1953. *The Hedgehog and the Fox: An Essay on Tolstoy's View of History.* Simon & Schuster
Birnbaum & Truglia, 2000	Birnbaum, R. & Truglia, J., 2000. *Getting to Know OBD II.* New York: A S T Training
Bosch, 2009	Bosch, J., 2009. From Software Product Lines to Software Ecosystems, *Proceedings of 13th Software Product Line Conference,* SPLC 2009
Burns, 1991	Burns, A., 1991. Scheduling Hard Real-Time Systems: A Review. *Software Engineering Journal,* 6(3), pp. 116–128
Buschmann at al, 1996	Buschmann, F., Meunier, R., Rohnert R., Sommerlad, P. & Stal, M., 1996. *Pattern-Oriented Software Architecture Volume 1: A System of Patterns.* John Wiley & Sons
Buschmann et al, 2007a	Buschmann, F., Henney, K. & Schmidt, D. C., 2007a. *Pattern-Oriented Software Architecture: On Patterns and Pattern Languages, Volume 5.* John Wiley & Sons
Buschmann et al, 2007b	Buschmann, F., Henney, K. & Schmidt, D. C., 2007. *Pattern-Oriented Software Architecture Volume 4: A Pattern Language for Distributed Computing.* John Wiley & Sons

Buschmann et al, 2012	Buschmann, F. Ameller, D.,Ayala, Claudia P., Cabot, J., Franch, X, 2012. Architecture Quality Revisited. *IEEE Software*, 29(4), pp. 22–24
CAN, 2000	CAN in Automation (CiA), 2000. *CiA 303–2: Representation of SI-Unites and Prefixes,* CAN in Automation
CAN, 2005	CAN in Automation, 2005. *CiA 415: CANopen Application Profile for Road Construction Machinery,* CiA
CAN, 2013a	CAN in Automation (CiA), 2013. *CANopen SYNC Protocol.* http://www.can-cia.org/index.php?id=206 (accessed 7 Jun 2013)
CAN, 2013b	CAN in Automation (CiA), 2013. *CiA 301 – CANopen Application Layer Specification.* http://www.can-cia.org/index.php?id=440 (accessed 14 Oct 2013)
CAN, 2013c	CAN in Automation (CiA), 2013. *Error Control Protocol.* http://www.can-cia.org/index.php?id=209 (accessed 20 Mar 2013)
Carlson et al, 1998	Carlson, A., Estepp, S. & Folwer, M., 1998. Temporal Patterns. In: *Proceedings of the 3rd European Conference on Pattern Languages of Programs.* Irsee, Germany
Cerberus, 2013	Cerberus LLC, 2013. *Cerberus FTP Server.* http://www.cerberusftp.com/ (accessed 11 Jul 2013)
Chrisman, 1998	Chrisman, N. R., Rethinking Levels of Measurement for Cartography. *Cartography and Geographic Information Science*, vol. 25, no. 4, October 1998, pp. 231–42(12)
chroot, 2014	FreeBSD man pages – CHROOT(8) FreeBSD System Manager's Manual http://www.freebsd.org/cgi/man.cgi?query=chroot&sektion=8&apropos=0&man path=FreeBSD+9.0-RELEASE+and+Ports (accessed 13 Jan 2014)
Chomsky, 1957	Chomsky, N., 1957. *Syntactic Structures.* 1st edition, Paris: Mouton & Co.
Cohen & Lefebvre, 2005	Cohen, H. & Lefebvre, C., 2005. *Handbook of Categorization in Cognitive Science.* Elsevier
Conway, 1968	Conway, M. E., 1968. How Do Committees Invent?. *Datamation,* 14(5), pp. 28–31
Coon & Mitterrer, 2010	Coon, D. & Mitterrer, J. O., 2010. *Psychology: A Journey.* 4th edition. Cengage Learning
Coplien, 2011	Coplien, J., 2011. *Truck Number pattern.* http://c2.com/cgi/wiki?TruckNumber (accessed 27 Nov 2013)
Coplien & Bjørnvig, 2010	Coplien, J. O. & Bjørnvig, G., 2010. *Lean Architecture: for Agile Software Development.* John Wiley & Sons
Coplien & Harrison, 2004	Coplien, J. O. & Harrison, N. B., 2004. *Organizational Patterns of Agile Software Development,* Upper Saddle River, NJ, USA: Prentice-Hall, Inc.
Corbet at al, 2005	Corbet, J., Rubini, A. & Kroah-Hartman, G., 2005. *Linux Device Drivers.* 3rd edition. O'Reilly

Coulouris et al, 2011	Coulouris, G., Dollimore, J., Kindberg, T. & Gordon, B., 2011. *Distributed Systems: Concepts and Design*. 5th edition. Addison-Wesley
Craig, 2006	Craig, I. D., *Virtual Machines*. Springer, 2006, ISBN 1-85233-969-1
Cristian, 1989	Cristian, F., 1989. Probabilistic Clock Synchronization. *Distributed Computing*, 3(3), pp. 146–158
Cunningham, 1992	Cunningham, W., 1992. *The WyCash Portfolio Management System*. Experience report, OOPSLA '92
Daniels, 1997	Daniels, F., 1997. The Reliable Hybrid Pattern A Generalized Software Fault Tolerant Design Pattern. In: *Proceedings of 4th Pattern Languages of Programs (PLoP) Conference*
Dawes et al, 2013	Dawes, B., Abrahams, D. & Rivera, R., 2013. *Boost C++ libraries*. http://www.boost.org/ (accessed 20 May 2013)
Davis & Burns, 2011	Davis, R. & Burns, A., 2011. A Survey of Hard Real-Time Scheduling for Multiprocessor Systems. *CM Computing Surveys (CSUR)*, 43(4)
de Mello, 1984	de Mello, A., 1984. *The Song of the Bird*. Reprint edition. Image
Deloitte, 2006	Deloitte, 2006. *The Service Revolution in Global Manufacturing Industries*. http://www.apec.org.au/docs/2011-11_training/deloitte2006.pdf (accessed 14 Nov 2013)
Denning, 1982	Denning, D. E., 1982. *Cryptography and Data Security*. Addison-Wesley
DENX, 2013	DENX Software Engineering, 2013. *Das U-Boot – the Universal Boot Loader*. http://www.denx.de/wiki/U-Boot (accessed 24 Nov 2013)
Dewey, 1876	Dewey, M., 1876. *A Classification and Subject Index, for Cataloguing and Arranging the Books and Pamphlets of a Library*
Digia, 2013a	Digia Plc, 2013. *Qt Project*. http://qt-project.org/ (accessed 31 Mar 2013)
Digia, 2013b	Digia Plc, 2013b. *Qt Internationalization*. http://qt-project.org/wiki/QtInternationalization (accessed 24 Nov 2013)
Dijkstra, 1965	Dijkstra, E. W., 1965. *Cooperating Sequential Processes*, Austin: E.W. Dijkstra Archive. Center for American History, University of Texas at Austin
Donald, 2003	Donald, J., 2003. *Improved Portability of Shared Libraries*, Princeton
Douglass, 2002	Douglass, B. P., 2002. *Real-Time Design Patterns: Robust Scalable Architecture for Real-Time Systems*. Addison-Wesley
Ebert & Jones, 2009	Ebert, C. & Jones, C., 2009. Embedded Software: Facts, Figures, and Future. *Computer*, 42(4), pp. 42–52
eCos, 2013	*RedBoot*. http://ecos.sourceware.org/redboot/ (accessed 23 Nov 2013)

Eklund & Bosch, 2012 — Eklund, U. & Bosch, J., 2012. Introducing Software Ecosystems for Mass-Produced Embedded Systems. Cambridge, USA, *Proceedings of Third International Conference on Software Business (ICSOB 2012)*

Eloranta et al, 2010 — Eloranta, V.-P., Koskinen, J., Leppänen, M. & Reijonen, V., 2010. *A Pattern Language for Distributed Machine Control Systems,* Tampere, ISBN 978-952-15-2319-9: Tampere University of Technology, Department of Software Systems, Report, vol. 9, p. 108

Eloranta et al, 2012 — Eloranta, V.-P., Hylli, O., Vepsäläinen, T. & Koskimies, K., 2012. TopDocs: Using Software Architecture Knowledge Base for Generating Topical Documents. In: *Proceedings of 10th Joint Working Conference on Software Architecture & 6th European Conference on Software Architecture*, pp. 191–195

Eloranta et al, 2013a — Eloranta, V.-P., Koskimies, K., Mikkonen, T. & Vuorinen, J., 2013. Scrum Anti-Patterns – An Empirical Study. *Proceedings of 20th Asian-Pacific Software Engineering Conference (APSEC 2013)*, Bangkok, Thailand. ISBN 978-0-4799-2144-7, pp. 503–51

Eloranta et al, 2013b — Eloranta, V.-P., Koskinen, J. & Leppänen, M., 2013. Key Success Factors in Control System Software Architecture. Nuremberg Germany, *Proceedings of 1st International Mobile Machine Control (MMC) Conference*. CAN CiA

Ensor, 1988 — Ensor, P., 1988. *The Functional Silo Syndrome*. AME Target 16

EventHelix, 2013a — EventHelix.com, 2013. *Protocol Layer Design Pattern*. http://www.eventhelix.com/realtimemantra/patterncatalog/protocol_layer.htm#.UoDU7nfXCB1 (accessed 09 Aug 2013)

EventHelix, 2013b — EventHelix.com, 2013. *Publish-Subscriber Design Patterns in Embedded Systems*. http://www.eventhelix.com/realtimemantra/patterns/publish_subscribe_patterns.htm#.UoCnzHfXCB0 (accessed 05 May 2013)

Felser & Sauter, 2002 — Felser, M. & Sauter, T., 2002. The Fieldbus War: History or Short Break Between Battles?. *4th IEEE International Workshop on Factory Communication Systems,* pp. 73–80

Fernandez, 2013 — Fernandez, E., 2013. *Security Patterns in Practice: Designing Secure Architectures Using Software Patterns*. John Wiley & Sons

Fielding, 2001 — Fielding, T., 2001. Representational State Transfer (REST), Chapter 5. In: *Architectural Styles and the Design of Network-Based Software Architectures*. California: University of California, pp. 76–106

FlexRay, 2005 — FlexRay Consortium, 2005. *Flexray Communications System – Protocol Specification Version 2.1 Revision A*. FlexRay Consortium

Foote & Yoder, 1997 — Foote, B. & Yoder, J., 1997. Big Ball of Mud. Monticello, Illinois, In: *Proceedings of Fourth Conference on Pattern Languages of Programs*

Foraker, 2013 — Foraker Labs, 2013. *Usability First – Usability Glossary*. http://www.usabilityfirst.com/glossary/mode-error/ (accessed 21 May 2013)

Ford et al, 2013   Ford, A., Raiciu, C., Handley, M. & Bonaventure, O., 2013. *Internet Engineering Task Force (IETF) Request for Comments: 6824 Category: Experimental – TCP Extensions for Multipath Operation with Multiple Addresses.* IETF

Gabriel, 2002   Gabriel, R. P., 2002. *Writer's Workshop and the Work of Making Things.* Boston, MA, USA: Addison-Wesley, Longman Publishing

Gamma et al, 1994   Gamma, E., Helm, R., Johnson, R. & Vlissides, J., 1994. *Design Patterns: Elements of Reusable Object-Oriented Software.* Addison-Wesley

Garlan & Shaw, 1994   Garlan, D. & Shaw, M., 1994. An Introduction to Software Architecture. In: V. Ambriola & G. Tortora, eds. *Advances in Software Engineering and Knowledge Engineering, Series on Software Engineering and Knowledge Engineering.* Singapore: World Scientific Publishing Company, pp. 1–39

Glass, 2001   Glass, R., 2001. Frequently Forgotten Fundamental Facts About Software Engineering. *IEEE Software,* 18(3), pp. 110–112

GLEG, 2013   *Agora Scada+ Exploit Pack.* http://gleg.net/agora_scada.shtml (accessed 20 Oct 2013)

Gleick, 1996   Gleick, J., 1996. *A Bug and a Crash: Sometimes a Bug is more than a Nuisance.* http://www.around.com/ariane.html (accessed 20 May 2013)

Global, 1998   Global Engineering Documents, 1998. *ANSI TIA/EIA-485-A Electrical Characteristics of Generators and Receivers for Use in Balanced Digital Multipoint Systems*

Glueck at al, 2007   Glueck, J., Koudal, P. & Vaessen, W., 2007. *The Service Revolution: Manufacturing's Missing Crown Jewel.* http://www.deloitte.com/view/en_US/us/Insights/Browse-by-Content-Type/deloitte-review/563a4d63e70fb110VgnVCM100000ba42f00aRCRD.htm (accessed 17 Jan 2014)

Goossens, 1999   Goossens, J., 1999. *Scheduling of Hard Real-Time Periodic Systems with Various Kinds of Deadline and Offset Constraints.* http://citeseerx.ist.psu.edu/viewdoc/download?doi=10.1.1.91.7330&rep=rep1&type=pdf: Université Libre de Bruxelles

Goswam, 2010   Goswam, U., 2010. *The Wiley-Blackwell Handbook of Childhood Cognitive Development.* 2nd edition. Wiley-Blackwell

Gusella & Zatti, 1987   Gusella, R. & Zatti, S., 1987. *The Accuracy of the Clock Synchronization Achieved by TEMPO in Berkeley UNIX 4.3BSD,* EECS Department, University of California, Berkeley

Hanmer, 2007   Hanmer, R., 2007. *Patterns for Fault Tolerant Software.* John Wiley & Sons

Hanmer, 2013   Hanmer, R., 2013. *Pattern-Oriented Software Architecture For Dummies.* John Wiley & Sons

Harrion et al, 2007   Harrison, N. B., Avgeriou, P. & Zdun, U., 2007. Using Patterns to Capture Architectural Decisions. *IEEE Software,* 24(4), pp. 38–45

Harrison, 1987	Harrison, R., 1987. Maintenance Giant Sleeps Undisturbed in Federal Data Centers. *Computerworld*, pp. 81–86
HART, 2013	HART Communication Foundation, 2013. *HART Protocol Specifications.* http://www.hartcomm.org/hcf/documents/documents_spec_list.html (accessed 25 Nov 2013)
Harvey, 2013	Harvey, A., 2013. *User Experience: What Is It and Why Should I Care?* http://usabilitygeek.com/user-experience/ (accessed 01 Aug 2013)
Hentrich et al, 2013	Hentrich, C., Zdun, U., Hlupic, V. & Dotsika, F., 2013. *An Approach for Supporting Pattern Mining and Validation through Grounded Theory and its Applications to Process-Driven SOA Patterns.* Presented in writer's workshop of EuroPLoP 2013
Herbsleb & Mockus, 2003	Herbsleb, J. & Mockus, A., 2003. An Empirical Study of Speed and Communication in Globally Distributed Software Development. *IEEE Software Engineering*, 29(6), pp. 481–494
Herzner et al, 2004	Herzner, W., Kubinger, W. & Gruber, M., 2004. Triple-T (Time-Triggered-Transmission) – A System of Patterns for Reliable Communication in Hard Real-Time Systems. In: *Proceedings of 9th European Conference on Pattern Languages of Programs (EuroPLoP 2004).* Irsee, Germany: Hillside Europe
Hillside Group, 2013	Hillside Group, 2013. *PLoP Conferences.* http://hillside.net/conferences/ (accessed 29 Oct 2013)
Hohpe & Woolf, 2003	Hohpe, G. & Woolf, B., 2003. *Enterprise Integration Patterns: Designing, Building, and Deploying Messaging Solutions.* Addison-Wesley Professional
Howard & LeBlanc, 2003	Howard, M. & LeBlanc, D., 2003. *Writing Secure Code.* 2nd edition. Microsoft Press
Hucko, 2013	Hucko, M., 2013. *Akkuleasing für Elektroautos: Ausgeliehen und Abgewürgt.* http://www.spiegel.de/auto/aktuell/elektroauto-renault-kann-aufladen-der-batterie-stoppen-a-930066.html (accessed 19 Nov 2013)
Hürsch & Videira-Lopes, 1995	Hürsch, W. L. & Videira-Lopes, C., 1995. *Separation of Concerns,* College of Computer Science Northeastern University
IEC, 2003a	IEC, 2003. *IEC 61158 Standard – Digital Data Communications for Measurement and Control – Fieldbus for Use in Industrial Control Systems: Part 2 Physical Layer Specification and Service Definition,* International Electrotechnical Commission
IEC, 2003b	IEC, 2003b. *IEC 61784-1 Standard: Digital Data Communications for Measurement and Control: Part 1 – Profile sets for Continuous and Discrete Manufacturing Relative to Fieldbus Use in Industrial Control Systems,* International Electrotechnical Commission
IEC, 2003c	*IEC 61511 standard: Functional Safety – Safety Instrumented Systems for the Process Industry Sector,* International Electrotechnical Commission
IEC, 2005a	IEC, 2005. *IEC/PAS 62407 (Ed 1.0), Real-Time Ethernet Control Automation Technology (EtherCAT),* International Electrotechnical Commission

IEC, 2005b	IEC, 2005. *ISO IEC 62061: Safety of Machinery – Functional Safety of Safety-Related Electrical, Electronic and Programmable Electronic Control Systems,* International Electrotechnical Commission
IEC, 2010a	IEC, 2010. *IEC 61508-3 Standard: Functional Safety of Electrical/Electronic/Programmable Electronic Safety-Related Systems Part 3,* International Electrotechnical Commission
IEC, 2010b	IEC, 2010. *IEC/TR 61491 – Electrical Equipment of Industrial Machines – Serial Data Link for Real-Time Communication Between Controls and Drives,* International Electrotechnical Commission
IEEE, 2008a	IEEE Standard, 2008. *802.3-2008 – IEEE Standard for Information Technology – Telecommunications and Information Exchange Between Systems – Local and Metropolitan Area Networks – Specific Requirements Part 3: Carrier Sense Multiple Access With Collision Detection (CSMA/CD).* IEEE
IEEE, 2008b	IEEE, 2008. *IEEE 1003.1-2008 – IEEE Standard for Information Technology – Portable Operating System Interface (POSIX(R)*
IETF, 2005	Network Working Group of the IETF, 2006. *The Secure Shell (SSH) Authentication Protocol,* IETF, RFC 4252
Immonen, 2013	Immonen, P., 2013. *Efficiency of a Diesel-Electric Mobile Working Machine.* Lappeeranta: Ph.D Thesis, Lappeenranta University of Technology
INMOS, 1988	INMOS Limited, 1988. *Occam 2 Reference Manual.* INMOS document number: 72-OCC-45-01. UK: Prentice Hall International
ISO, 1994	International ISO Standard, 1994. *ISO/IEC 7498-1:1994 Information technology – Open Systems Interconnection – Basic Reference Model: The Basic Model.* International Standardization Organization
ISO, 2001	International ISO standard, 2001. *ISO/IEC 9126-1:2001 Software Engineering – Product Quality – Part 1: Quality Model*
ISO, 2002	International ISO Standard, 2002. *Mark-II: ISO / IEC 20968:2002 Software Engineering – M1 II Function Point Analysis – Counting Practices Manual.* International Standardization Organization
ISO, 2003	International ISO Standard, 2003. *ISO 11898-2:2003 Road Vehicles – Controller Area Network (CAN) – Part 2: High-Speed Medium Access Unit.* International Standardization Organization
ISO, 2004	International ISO Standard, 2004. *ISO 11898-4: Road Vehicles – Controller Area Network (CAN): Part 4: Time-Triggered Communication.* International Standardization Organization
ISO, 2005	International ISO Standard, 2005. *NESMA: ISO / IEC 24570:2005 Software Engineering – NESMA Function Size Measurement Method Version 2.1 – Definitions and Counting Guidelines for the Application of Function Point Analysis.* International Standardization Organization

ISO, 2006 — International ISO Standard, 2006. *ISO 13849-1 Safety of Machinery – Safety-Related Parts of Control Systems – Part 1: General Principles for Design*. International Standardization Organization

ISO, 2008 — International ISO Standard, 2008. *FiSMA: ISO / IEC 29881:2008 Information Technology – Software and Systems Engineering – FiSMA 1.1 Functional Size Measurement Method*. International Standardization Organization

ISO, 2009 — International ISO Standard, 2009. *IFPUG: ISO/IEC 20926:2009 Software and Systems Engineering – Software Measurement – IFPUG Functional Size Measurement Method*. International Standardization Organization

ISO, 2011a — International ISO Standard, 2011a. *COSMIC: ISO/IEC 19761:2011 Software Engineering. A Functional Size Measurement Method*. International Standardization Organization

ISO, 2011b — International ISO Standard, 2011b. *ISO 26262-1 Road Vehicles – Functional Safety – Part 6: Product Development at the Software Level*. International Standardization Organization

ISO, 2011c — International ISO Standard, 2011. *ISO 15765-4:2011, Road vehicles – Diagnostic Communication over Controller Area Network (DoCAN) – Part 4: Requirements for Emissions-Related Systems*. International Standardization Organization

ISO, 2013 — International ISO Standard, 2013. *ISO/DIS 17987-6 Road vehicles – Local Interconnect Network (LIN) – Part 6: Protocol Conformance Test Specification*. International Standardization Organization

Ismail & Zainab, 2011 — Ismail, R. & Zainab, A. N., 2011. Information systems security in special and public libraries: an assessment of status. *Malaysian Journal of Library & Information Science,* 16(2), pp. 45–62

ITU-T, 1999 — ITU-T, International Telecommunication Union, 1999. *Formal Description Techniques (FDT) – Specification and Description Language (SDL)*. http://www.itu.int/ITU-T/studygroups/com10/languages/Z.100_1199.pdf (accessed 30 Mar 2013)

Jaatun et al, 2008 — Jaatun, M. G., Grøtan, T. & Line, M. B., 2008. Secure Safety: Secure Remote Access to Critical Safety Systems in Offshore Installations. In: C. Rong, M. G. Jaatun, F. E. Sandnes, L. T. Yang, eds. *Proceedings of 5th International Conference on Autonomic and Trusted Computing (ATC)*. Oslo, Norway: Springer, pp. 121–133

jail, 2014 — FreeBSD man pages – JAIL(2), FreeBSD System Calls Manual http://www.freebsd.org/cgi/man.cgi?query=jail&sektion=2&apropos=0&manpath =FreeBSD+9.2-RELEASE (accessed 13 Jan 2014)

JOC, 2012 — The Journal of Commerce, 2012. *The Joc Top 50 World Container Ports*. http://www.joc.com/sites/default/files/u48783/pdf/Top50-container-2012.pdf (accessed 05 Nov 2013)

Kazman & Bass, 1994 — Kazman, R. & Bass, L., 1994. *Toward Deriving Software Architectures From Quality Attributes*, Pittsburgh: Software Engineering Institute, Carnegie-Mellon University

Kazman et al, 2000   Kazman, R., Klein, M. & Clements, P., 2000. *ATAM: Method for Architecture Evaluation,* Carnegie-Mellon University / Software Engineering Institute

Kenji, 2001   Kenji, H., 2001. *Multi-Phase Startup, workshopped in MensorePLoP 2001.* http://objectclub.jp/technicaldoc/pattern/startup-2_3-e.doc (accessed 14 Oct 2013)

Kent & Atkinson, 1998   Kent, S. & Atkinson, R., 1998. *IP Encapsulating Security Payload (ESP),* IETF, RFC 2406

Kent & Cunningham, 1987   Kent, B. & Cunningham, W., 1987. *Using Pattern Languages for Object-Oriented Programs,* OOPSLA '87 Workshop on Specification and Design for Object-Oriented Programming

Kiczales, 1992   Kiczales, G., 1992. Towards a New Model of Abstraction in Software Engineering. In: *Proceedings of the IMSA'92 Workshop on Reflection and Meta-Level Architectures*

Kinney, & Wiruth, 1976   Kinney, G. F. & Wiruth, A., 1976. *Practical Risk Analysis for Safety Management,* California: Naval Weapons Center

Kircher & Jain, 2004   Kircher, M. & Jain, P., 2004. *Pattern-Oriented Software Architecture Volume 3.* John Wiley & Sons

Koch & Rossi, 2002   Koch, N. & Rossi, G., 2002. Patterns for Adaptive Web Applications. *Proceedings of 7th European Conference on Pattern Languages of Programs (EuroPLoP 2002)*

Kone, 2013   Kone Inc., 2013. *Kone EcoSpace.* http://cdn.kone.com/www.kone.us/Images/kone-ecospace-elevator.pdf?v=2 (accessed 01 Nov 2013)

Kopetz, 1997   Kopetz, H., 1997. *Real-Time Systems: Design Principles for Distributed Embedded Applications.* Norwell, MA: Kluwer Academic Publishers

Kopetz & Ochsenreiter, 1987   Kopetz, H. & Ochsenreiter, W., 1987. Clock Synchronization in Distributed Real-Time Systems. *IEEE Transactions on Computers, 36*(8), pp. 933–940

Kruchten, 2009   Kruchten, P., 2009. Documentation of Software Architecture from a Knowledge Management Perspective – Design Representation. In: M. Ali Babar, T. Dingsøyr, P. Lago & H. Vliet, eds. *Software Architecture Knowledge Management – Theory and Practice.* Springer Berlin Heidelberg, pp. 39–57

Krueger, 2002   Krueger, C. W., 2002. Variation Management for Software Production Lines. In: *Software Product Lines.* Springer Berlin Heidelberg, pp. 37–48

Kushner, 2013   Kushner, D., 2013. *The Real Story of Stuxnet, IEEE Spectrum.* http://spectrum.ieee.org/telecom/security/the-real-story-of-stuxnet (accessed 19 Oct 2013)

Lahtinen & Leppänen, 2002   Lahtinen, S. & Leppänen, M., 2002. *Testing Embedded Software in Workstation Environment,* Master of Science Thesis, Tampere University of Technology

Lamport et al, 1982   Lamport, L., Shostak, R. & Pease, M., 1982. The Byzantine Generals Problem. *Transactions on Programming Languages and Systems, 4*(3), pp. 382–401

Lampson & Redell, 1980	Lampson, B. W. & Redell, D. D., 1980. Experience with Processes and Monitors in Mesa. *Communications ACM,* 23(2), pp. 105–117
Larsson, 2000	Larsson, M., 2000. *Applying Configuration Management,* Uppsala, Sweden: IT Licentiate thesis 2000-007 MRTC Report 00/24
Lassing at al, 2002	Lassing, N., Bengtsson, P., van Vliet, H. & Bosch, J., 2002. Experiences with ALMA: Architecture-Level Modifiability Analysis – Architecture Analysis Experiences. *Journal of Systems and Computing,* 61(1), pp. 47–57
Leppänen, 2013	Leppänen, M., 2013. Patterns for Messaging in Distributed Machine Control Systems. Tampere, Finland, In: *Proceedings of VikingPLoP 2013 – A Nordic PLoP Conference*
Leppänen et al, 2009	Leppänen, M., Koskinen, J. & Mikkonen, T., 2009. Discovering a Pattern Language for Embedded Machine Control Systems Using Architecture Evaluation Methods. Tampere, Finland, In: *Proceedings of SPLST 2009 Conference*
Lientz & Swanson, 1980	Lientz, B. & Swanson, E., 1980. *Software Maintenance Management.* Addison-Wesley
Lighttpd, 2013	*Lighttpd – Fly Light.* http://www.lighttpd.net/ (accessed 13 Jul 2013)
Liker, 2003	Liker, J., 2003. *The Toyota Way: 14 Management Principles from the World's Greatest Manufacturer.* 1st edition. McGraw-Hill
Loyall et al, 2002	Loyall, J. P. Rubel, P., Schantz, R., Atighetchi, M., Zinky, J., 2002. Emerging Patterns in Adaptive, Distributed Real-Time, Embedded Middleware. In: *Proceedings of the 7th European Conference on Pattern Languages of Programs.* Irsee, Germany
Löhr et al, 2010	Löhr, H., Sadeghi, A.-R. & Winandy, M., 2010. Patterns for Secure Boot and Secure Storage in Computer Systems. IEEE, In: *Proceedings of Availability, Reliability, and Security (ARES '10)*
Machinery Directive, 2006	*Directive 2006/42/EC of the European Parliament and of the Council on Machinery, and Amending Directive 95/16/EC.* http://eurlex.europa.eu/LexUriServ/LexUriServ.do?uri=OJ:L:2006:157:0024:0086:EN:PDF (accessed 13 Mar 2013)
Mahnke et al, 2009	Mahnke, W., Leitner, S.-H. & Damm, M., 2009. *OPC Unified Architecture.* Springer
Mann, 2002	Mann, C. C., 2002. Homeland Insecurity. *The Atlantic Webzine*
Masmano et al, 2008	Masmano, M., Ripoll, I., Balbastre, P. & Crespo, A., 2008. A Constant-Time Dynamic Storage Allocator for Real-Time Systems. *Real-Time Systems,* 40(2), pp. 149–179
Mason, 2002	Mason, A. G., 2002. *Cisco Secure Virtual Private Network.* Cisco Press
MathWorks, 2013	MathWorks, 2013. *Simulink – Simulation and Model-Based Design.* http://www.mathworks.se/products/simulink/ (accessed 14 Nov 2013)
Mattson et al, 2004	Mattson, T., Sanders, B. & Massinqill, B., 2004. *Patterns for Parallel Programming.* Pearson Education International

McCabe, 1976	McCabe, T., 1976. A Complexity Measure. *IEEE Transactions on Software Engineering,* 2(4), pp. 308–320
McCollum, 1996	McCollum, C. M., 1996. *Type Laundering as a Software Design Pattern for Creating Hardware Abstraction Layers in C++.* Master Thesis, University of Victoria
McConnell, 2004	McConnell, S., 2004. *Code Complete: A Practical Handbook of Software Construction.* 2nd edition. Microsoft Press
McMillan, 2010	McMillan, R., 2010. *Computer World, Siemens: Stuxnet Worm Hit Industrial Systems.* http://www.computerworld.com/s/article/9185419/Siemens_Stuxnet_worm_hit_ind ustrial_systems?taxonomyId=142&pageNumber=1 (accessed 20 Oct 2013)
Messerschmitt & Szyperski, 2003	Messerschmitt, D. G. & Szyperski, C., 2003. *Software Ecosystem: Understanding an Indispensable Technology and Industry.* Cambridge, MA, USA: MIT Press
Micrium, 2013	Micrium, 2013. *µC / OS-II Overview Micrium.* http://micrium.com/rtos/ucosii/overview (accessed 24 Nov 2013)
Mike2.0, 2013	Mike2.0, 2013. *The Open Source Standard for Information Management – Big Data Definition.* http://mike2.openmethodology.org/wiki/Big_Data_Definition (accessed 01 Nov 2013)
Mills, 1989	Mills, D. L., 1989. *Internet Time Synchronization: The Network Time Protocol,* Delaware: DARPA Network Working Group
Mills, 1991	Mills, D. L., 1991. Internet Time Synchronization: the Network Time Protocol. *IEEE Transactions on Communications,* 39(10), pp. 1482–1493
Milos & Billar, 2013	Milos, V. & Billar, A., 2013. *Safety Issues in Human-Robot Interactions.* Karlsruhe, Germany
Mira, 2013	Mira Ltd, 2013. *MISRA – The Motor Industry Software Reliability Association.* http://www.misra.org.uk/ (accessed 09 Sep 2013)
Modbus, 2012	Modbus Organization, 2012. *Modbus Application Protocol Specification v1.1b3.* http://www.modbus.org/docs/Modbus_Application_Protocol_V1_1b3.pdf (accessed 25 Nov 2013)
Molich & Nielsen, 1990	Molich, R. & Nielsen, J., 1990. Improving a Human-Computer Dialogue. *Communications of the ACM,* 33(3), pp. 338–348
Mollison & Anderson, 2011	Mollison, M. & Anderson, J., 2011. Virtual Real-Time Scheduling, Porto, Portugal, In: *Proceedings of 7th Annual Workshop on Operating Systems Platforms for Embedded Real-Time Applications*
Moore, 1965	Moore, G. E., 1965. *Cramming More Components onto Integrated Circuits,* Electronics Magazine
Moore, 2005	Moore, G. A., 2005. *Dealing with Darwin: How Great Companies Innovate at Every Phase of Their Evolution.* Portfolio Trade

Murphy, 2013   Murphy, S., 2013. *Oklahoma Jury: Toyota Liable in Acceleration Crash*.
http://news.yahoo.com/okla-jury-toyota-liable-acceleration-crash-222731708.html
(accessed 28 Jan 2014)

Nelson, 1990   Nelson, V., 1990. Fault-Tolerant Computing: Fundamental Concepts.
Computer, 23(7), pp. 19–25

New Holland, 2013   New Holland Agriculture, 2013. *Clean Energy.*
http://www.thecleanenergyleader.com/en/faq.html (accessed 1 Nov 2013)

Nginx, 2013   *Nginx.* http://nginx.org/ (accessed 8 Aug 2013)

Nielsen, 1994a   Nielsen, J., 1994. Heuristic Evaluation. In: J. Nielsen & R. L. Mack, eds.
Usability Inspection Methods. New York, NY: John Wiley & Sons

Nielsen, 1994b   Nielsen, J., 1994. *Usability Engineering.* Academic Press

Nilsen & Gao, 1995   Nilsen, K. D. & Gao, H., 1995. The Real-Time Behavior of Dynamic Memory
Management in C++. *Proceedings of the 1st IEEE Real-Time Technology and
Applications Symposium (RTAS'95),* pp. 142–153

Noble & Weir, 2001   Noble, J. & Weir, C., 2001. *Small Memory Software: Patterns for Systems with
Limited Memory.* Boston, Ma, USA: Addison-Wesley Longman Publishing Co.

Ohno, 1988   Ohno, T., 1988. *Toyota Production System: Beyond Large-Scale Production.*
Cambridge, MA: Productivity Press

OMG, 2007   OMG DDS, 2007. *Data Distribution Service (DDS), Version 1.2.*
http://www.omg.org/spec/DDS/1.2 (accessed 4 Mar 2013)

OMG, 2011   *Object Management Group, Unified Modelling Language (UML) v 2.4.1.*
http://www.omg.org/spec/UML/2.4.1/ (accessed 30 May 2013)

Opcua4j, 2013   *Open-Opc-Ua-Server – Open source Implementation of an Opc Ua Server in Java.*
https://code.google.com/p/open-opc-ua-server/ (accessed 9 Jul 2013)

OpenVPN, 2013   OpenVPN Technologies, Inc., 2013. *OpenVPN – OpenSource VPN.*
http://openvpn.net/ (accessed 20 Jul 2013)

OPL, 2010   OPL Working Group, 2010. *A Pattern Language for Parallel Programming, v 2.0.*
http://parlab.eecs.berkeley.edu/wiki/patterns/patterns (accessed 15 Jul 2013)

Ortega-Arjona, 2010   Ortega-Arjona, J. L., 2010. *Patterns for Parallel Software Design.* John Wiley & Sons,
ISBN: 978-0-470-69734-4

OR-OSHA, 2009   *Oregon Occupational Safety and Health Division (OR-OSHA), Division 2 (29 Cfr
1910), General Occupational Safety & Health Rules Subdivision O: Machinery and
Machine Guarding.* http://www.cbs.state.or.us/osha/pdf/rules/division_2/div2_o.pdf
(accessed 20 Nov 2013)

Paulson, 2006   Paulson, L. D., 2006. Services Science: A New Field for Today's Economy.
IEEE Computer, 39(8), pp. 18–21

PCD, 2013   PCD Community, 2013. *Process Control Daemon (PCD).*
http://sourceforge.net/projects/pcd/ (accessed 14 Oct 2013)

Peng & Dömer, 2012   Peng, H. & Dömer, R., 2012. *Towards A Unified Hardware Abstraction Layer Architecture for Embedded Systems,* California: Center for Embedded Computer Systems, Technical Report 12–14

Pirsig, 1974   Pirsig, R., 1974. *Zen and the Art of Motorcycle Maintenance: An Inquiry into Values.* William Morrow & Company

Pohl et al, 2005   Pohl, K., Böckle, G. & Van Der Linden, F., 2005. *Software Product Line Engineering: Foundations, Principles, and Techniques.* Springer

Pont, 2001   Pont, M. J., 2001. *Patterns for Time-Triggered Embedded Systems: Building Reliable Applications with the 8051 Family of Microcontrollers.* Addison-Wesley

Portland, 2003   Portland Pattern Repository, 2003. *Canonical Form.*
http://c2.com/cgi/wiki?CanonicalForm (accessed 19 Sep 2013)

Portland, 2007   Portland Pattern Community, 2007. *Circular Buffer.*
http://c2.com/cgi/wiki?CircularBuffer (accessed 14 Mar 2013)

Portland, 2011   Portland Pattern Repository, 2011. *Alexandrian Form.*
http://c2.com/cgi/wiki?AlexandrianForm (accessed 19 Sep 2013)

Pradalier et al, 2005   Pradalier, C., Hermosillo, J., Koike, C., Braillon, C., Bessière, P. & Laugier, C., 2005. The Cycab: A Car-Like Robot Navigating Autonomously and Safely among Pedestrians. *Robotics and Autonomous Systems,* Osa/vuosikerta 50, pp. 51–67

Preschern et al, 2013   Preschern, C., Kajtazovic, N. & Kreiner, C., 2013. Catalog of Safety Tactics in the Light of the IEC 61508 Safety Lifecycle. *Proceedings of VikingPLoP 2013,* pp. 79–95

Prismtech, 2013   *OpenSplice DDS – Data Distribution Service Use Cases.*
http://www.prismtech.com/opensplice/industry-solutions/use-cases
(accessed 23 Sep 2013)

Pärssinen & Turunen, 2000   Pärssinen, J. & Turunen, M., 2000. Patterns for Protocol System Architecture. In: *Proceedings of 5th European Conference on Pattern Languages of Programs (EuroPLoP 2000).* Irsee, Germany: Hillside Europe

Randell, 1987   Randell, B., 1987. Design Fault Tolerance. In: A. Avizienis, H. Kopetz & J. Laprie, eds. *The Evolution of Fault-Tolerant Computing.* Vienna: Springer-Verlag, pp. 251–270

Rauhamäki & Kuikka, 2013   Rauhamäki, J. & Kuikka, S., 2013. Patterns for Control System Safety. To appear in: *Proceedings of 18th European Conference on Pattern Languages of Programs (EuroPLoP 2013).* Irsee, Germany

Rauhamäki at al, 2012a   Rauhamäki, J., Vepsäläinen, T. & Kuikka, S., 2012. Functional Safety System Patterns. In: *Proceedings of VikingPLoP 2012,* Saariselkä, Finland, Tampere University of Technology

Rauhamäki et al, 2012b   Rauhamäki, J., Vepsäläinen, T. & Kuikka, S., 2012b. Architectural Patterns for Functional Safety. In: V. Eloranta, J. Koskinen & M. Leppänen, eds. *Proceedings of VikingPLoP 2012*. Tampere, Finland: Tampere University of Technology, pp. 48–68

Raymond, 1999   Raymond, E., 1999. The Cathedral and the Bazaar. *Knowledge, Technology & Policy,* 12(3), pp. 23–49

Raynal & Singhal, 1996   Raynal, M. & Singhal, M., 1996. Logical time: Capturing Causality in Distributed Systems. *IEEE Computer,* 29(2), pp. 49–56

RCC, 2004   *IRIG Standard 200-04: IRIG Serial Time Code Formats,* Timing Committee Telecommunications, Timing Group and Range Commanders Council

Real Time Eng., 2013   Real Time Engineers Ltd., 2013. *FreeRTOS – Market Leading RTOS for Embedded Systems with Internet of Things Extension.* http://www.freertos.org (accessed 24 Nov 2013)

Real Time Inn., 2011   Real-Time Innovations, 2011. *Design Pattern: One to Many.* http://www.rti.com/docs/One_To_Many_Use_Case.pdf (accessed 10 Sep 2013)

Red Hat, 2013   *Red Hat Enterprise MRG.* http://www.redhat.com/products/mrg/ (accessed 18 Jun 2013)

Reeves, 1997   Reeves, G. E., 1997. *What Really Happened on Mars?* http://research.microsoft.com/en-us/um/people/mbj/Mars_Pathfinder/Authoritative _Account.html (accessed 5 Jun 2013)

Ricard, 1987   Ricard, L., 1987. GM's Just-in-Time Operating Philosophy. In: Y. Shetty & V. Buehler, eds. *Quality, Productivity and Innovation.* New York: Elsevier Science Publishing, pp. 315–329

Ries, 2011   Ries, E., 2011. *The Lean Startup: How Today's Entrepreneurs Use Continuous Innovation to Create Radically Successful Businesses.* Crown Publishing

Riley, 1986   Riley, P. H., 1986. *Failsafe Electronic Control Systems.* USA, U.S. Pat. No. 4718229

Rockwell, 2011   Rockwell Automation, 2011. *Safebook 4 – Safety Related Control Systems for Machinery.* http://www.cedes-sa.com/de/assets/File/PDF/safebook/SAFEBK_RM002B_EN_P.pd f (accessed 20 Oct 2013)

Rosa & Silva, 1997   Rosa, F. A. & Silva, A. R., 1997. Component Configurer: A Design Pattern for Component-Based Configuration. *Proceedings of EuroPLoP 1997*

Royce, 1970   Managing the Development of Large Software Systems. *Proceedings of IEEE WESCON,* 26(8)

Rubel, 1995   Rubel, B., 1995. Patterns for Generating a Layered Architecture. In: J. Coplien & D. Schmidt, eds., *Pattern Languages of Program Design (PLOPD) 1.* Reading, Massachusetts: Addison-Wesley, pp. 119–128

SAE, 2003	SAE International, 2003. *On-Board Diagnostics for Light and Medium Duty Vehicles Standards Manual*. Pennsylvania
SAE, 2013	SAE International, 2013. *Serial Control and Communications Heavy Duty Vehicle Network – Top Level Document, J1939 Standard,* SAE International
Saha, 2012	Saha, H., 2012. Improving Development Efficiency and Quality of Distributed IEC 61131-3 Applications with CANopen System Design. In: *Proceedings of 13th International CAN Conference (iCC)*. CAN in Automation, pp. 15–21
Saha, 2013	Saha, H., 2013. SI-Unit and Scaling Management in CANopen. *CANopen Newsletter*, 13 March, pp. 30–35
Samek, 2008	Samek, M., 2008. *Practical UML Statecharts in C/C++: Event-Driven Programming for Embedded Systems*. 2nd edition. CRC Press
Saridakis, 2002	Saridakis, T., 2002. *A System of Patterns for Fault Tolerance*. Irsee, Germany, In: *Proceedings of Seventh European Conference on Pattern Languages of Programs*, EuroPLoP 2002
Schmidt, 1999	Schmidt, D. C., 1999. *Why Software Reuse has Failed and How to Make It Work for You*. http://www.cse.wustl.edu/~schmidt/reuse-lessons.html (accessed 23 Nov 2013)
Schumacher et al, 2005	Schumacher, M., Fernandez-Buglioni, E., Hybertson, D., Buschmann, B. & Sommerlad, P., 2005. *Security Patterns: Integrating Security and Systems Engineering*. John Wiley & Sons
Schwaber, 1995	Schwaber, K., 1995. *Scrum Development Process*. ACM, pp. 117–134
Schütz, 2006	Schütz, D., 2006. Boot Loader pattern. In: *Proceedings of 11th European Conference on Pattern Languages of Programs (EuroPLoP 2006)*
Schütz, 2009	Schütz, D., 2009. Variability Reverse Engineering. *Proceedings of 14th European Conference on Pattern Languages of Programs (EuroPLoP'09)*
Schütz, 2010	Schütz, D., 2010. Transition to Product Line Engineering. *Proceedings of the 15th European Conference on Pattern Languages of Programs (EuroPLoP'10)*, pp. 19:1–19:4
Schütz, 2011	Schütz, D., 2011. Product Line Engineering – The Big Picture. *Proceedings of 16th European Conference on Pattern Languages of Programs (EuroPLoP'09)*
Scott & Kazman, 2009	Scott, J. & Kazman, R., 2009. *Realizing and Refining Architectural Tactics: Availability,* Pittsburgh: Carnegie-Mellon University, Software Engineering Institute
Scrum, 2013	Scrum Pattern Community, 2013. *ScrumPLoP*. http://www.scrumplop.org/ (accessed 27 Nov 2013)
SDL, 2013	*Simple DirectMedia Layer – Homepage*. http://www.libsdl.org/ (accessed 1 Apr 2013)
SecurityFocus, 2010	SecurityFocus, 2010. *Bugtraq Security Forums*. http://www.securityfocus.com/archive (accessed 20 Oct 2013)

Shingo, 1986 — Shingo, S., 1986. *Zero Quality Control: Source Inspection and the Poka-Yoke System*. Portland, Oregon. Productivity Press

Shirey, 2007 — Shirey, R., 2007. *RFC 4949, Internet Security Glossary, Version 2*. http://tools.ietf.org/html/rfc4949 (accessed 5 Nov 2013)

Shore, 2004 — Shore, J., 2004. Fail fast [software debugging. *IEEE Software*, 21(5), pp. 21–25

Sink, 2013 — Sink, P., 2013. *Eight Popular Open Architecture Fieldbuses and Industrial Ethernet: A Guide to the Pros and Cons for Users and OEMs*. http://www.ien.com/article/eight-popular-open/562 (accessed 26 Nov 2013)

Sjoberg et al, 2013 — Sjoberg, D., Yamashita, A., Anda, B. C. D., Mockus, A. & Dyba, T., 2013. Quantifying the Effect of Code Smells on Maintenance Effort. *IEEE Transactions on Software Engineering*, 39(8), pp. 1144–1156

Smith & Nair, 2005 — Smith. J., & Nair, R., 2005. *Virtual Machines: Versatile Platforms for Systems and Processes*, (The Morgan Kaufmann Series in Computer Architecture and Design). Morgan Kaufmann Publishers Inc., San Francisco, CA, USA

Smith & Simpson, 2004 — Smith, D. & Simpson, K., 2004. *Functional Safety. A Straightforward Guide to Applying IEC 61508 and Related Standards*. 2nd edition. Butterworth-Heinemann

Snir at al, 1995 — Snir, M., Otto, S., Huss-Lederman, S., Walker, D. & Dongarra, J., 1995. *MPI: The Complete Reference*. MA, USA: MIT Press Cambridge

Snowden & Boone, 2007 — Snowden, D. & Boone, M., 2007. A Leader's Framework for Decision Making. *Harvard Business Review*, pp. 69–76

SQLite, 2013 — SQLite community, 2013. *SQLite*. http://www.sqlite.org/ (accessed 3 Mar 2013)

Stalling, 2008 — Stalling, W., 2008. *Operating Systems: Internals and Design Principles*. 6th edition. Pearson Education International

Stephen, 2006 — Stephen, C. E., 2006. *American National Standard – Information Technology – AT Attachment 8 – ATA/ATAPI Command Set (ATA8-ACS)*. http://www.t13.org/Documents/UploadedDocuments/docs2006/D1699r3f-ATA8-ACS.pdf (accessed 28 Oct 2013)

Stephenson et al, 1999 — Stephenson, A. G., Mulville, D. R., Bauer, F. H., Dukeman, G. A., Norvig, P., LaPiana, L. S., Rutledge, P. J., Folta, D. & Sackheim, R., 1999. *Mars Climate Orbiter Mishap Investigation Board Phase*, NASA

Stevens, 1946 — Stevens, S. S., 1946. On the Theory of Scales of Measurement. *Journal of Science*, vol. 103, issue 2684, pp. 677–680

Stevens et al, 1974 — Stevens, W., Myers, G. & Constantine, L., 1974. Structured Design. *IBM Systems Journal*, 13(2), pp. 115–139

Stouffer, 2005 — Stouffer, K., 2005. NIST Industrial Control System Security Activities. Chicago, IL, *Proceedings of the ISA Expo*

Szabo, 2004 — Szabo, N., 2004. *Patterns of Integrity – Separation of Duties*. http://szabo.best.vwh.net/separationofduties.html (accessed 18 Jul 2013)

Sørensen et al, 2010   Sørensen, C., Fountas, S., Nash, E., Pesonen, L., Bochtis, D., Pedersen, S. M., Basso, B. & Blackmore, S. B., 2010. Conceptual model of a future farm management information system. *Computers and Electronics in Agriculture*, 72(1), pp. 37–47

Tidwell, 2011   Tidwell, J., 2011. *Designing Interfaces – Patterns for Effective Interaction Design.* 2nd edition. O'Reilly Media

Tiilikainen & Manner, 2013   Tiilikainen, S. & Manner, J., 2013. *Suomen automaatioverkkojen haavoittuvuus (Vulnerability level of Finnish automation networks)*, Aalto University. https://research.comnet.aalto.fi/public/Aalto-Shodan-Raportti-julkinen.pdf (accessed 20 Oct 2013)

Tracz, 1988   Tracz, W., 1988. Software Reuse Myths. *ACM SIGSOFT Software Engineering Notes,* 13(1), pp. 17–21

Upright, 2013   UpRight Community, 2013. *Upright – Making Distributed Systems Up (available) and Right (correct).* http://code.google.com/p/upright/ (accessed 7 Nov 2013)

USAF, 2013   *Air Force Instruction 91-104 – Nuclear Surety Tamper Control and Detection Programs,* Department of the Air Force

van Heesch et al, 2014   van Heesch, U., Eloranta, V., Avgeriou, P. & Koskimies, K. H. N., 2014. DCAR – Decision-Centric Architecture Reviews. To appear in: *IEEE Software*

Van Gurp et al, 2011   Van Gurp, J., Bosch, J. & Svahnberg, M., 2001. On the Notion of Variability in Software Product Lines. *Proceedings of Working IEEE/IFIP Conference on Software Architecture*

Webber & Gomaa, 2004   Webber, D. L. & Gomaa, H., 2004. Modeling variability in software product lines with the variation point model. *Science of Computer Programming,* 53(3), pp. 305–331

Webel & Fliege, 2004   Webel, C. & Fliege, I., 2004. *SDL Design Patterns and Components Watchdog and Heartbeat,* Kaiserslautern, Germany: Computer Science Department, University of Kaiserslautern

Webster, 2013   Webster, G., 2013. *NASA'S Mars Curiosity Debuts Autonomous Navigation.* http://www.jpl.nasa.gov/news/news.php?release=2013-259 (accessed 18 Oct 2013)

Vector Informatik, 2011   *EDS files for CANopen devices.* http://canopen-solutions.com/canopen_eds_en.html (accessed 24 Nov 2013)

Vector Informatik, 2013   *CANalyzer.* http://vector.com/vi_canalyzer_en.html (accessed 25 Nov 2013)

Weigmann & Kilian, 2004   Weigmann, J. & Kilian, G., 2004. *Decentralization with PROFIBUS DP/DPV1: Architecture and Fundamentals, Configuration and Use with SIMATIC S7.* 2nd edition. Publicis

Weiss & Noori, 2013   Weiss, M. & Noori, N., 2013. Enabling Contributions in Open Source Projects. Irsee, Germany, In: *Proceedings of 18th European Conference on Pattern Languages of Programs (EuroPLoP 2013)*

VersionOne, 2013   *7th Annual State of Agile Survey.,* VersionOne

Viitala et al, 2013	Viitala, J., Eloranta, V.-P. & Koskinen, J., 2013. *Personal Communications and Lecture at Software Architecture Course.* Tampere University of Technology
Vuori at al, 2011	Vuori, M., Virtanen, H., Koskinen, J. & Katara, M., 2011. *Safety Process Patterns in the Context of IEC 61508-3,* Tampere: Tampere University of Technology, http://URN.fi/URN:NBN:fi:tty-2011061414701
White & Schmidt, 2008	White, J. & Schmidt, D. C., 2008. Automated Configuration of Component-Based Distributed Real-Time and Embedded Systems from Feature Models. Seoul, Korea, *Proceedings of the 17th World Congress The International Federation of Automatic Control*
Wolf et al, 2004	Wolf, M., Weimerskirch, A. & Paar, C., 2004. Security in Automotive Bus Systems. *Proceedings of the Workshop on Embedded Security in Cars (escar)'04*
Xenomai, 2012	*Xenomai: Real-Time Framework for Linux.* http://www.xenomai.org/ (accessed 18 Jun 2013)
Xiong, 2006	Xiong, M. Parsons, J., Edmondson, J., Nguyen. H. & Schmidt, D. C., 2006. *Evaluating the Performance of Publish/Subscribe Platforms for Information Management in Distributed Real-Time and Embedded Systems*
Xun et al, 2010	Xun, L., Ortiz, P. J., Browne, J., Franklin, D., Oliver, J. Y., Geyer, R., Zhou, Y. & Chong, F. T., 2010. *Smartphone Evolution and Reuse: Establishing a More Sustainable Model.* IEEE, pp. 476–484
Yoder & Barcalow, 2000	Yoder, J. & Barcalow, J., 2000. Architectural Patterns for Enabling Application Security. In: N. Harrison, B. Foote & H. Rohnert, eds., *Pattern Languages of Program Design 4.* Reading, MA: Addison-Wesley, pp. 301–336

Index of Patterns

Entries in small capitals refer to citations of patterns described in this book.
Entries in sentence case refer to external citations of patterns.
The page numbers of pattern descriptions are in bold.

Index

Printed and bound by CPI Group (UK) Ltd, Croydon, CR0 4YY

27/10/2024

14580379-0003